Personal Property

Commentary and Materials

R. G. HAMMOND

Auckland

Oxford University Press

Oxford   New York   Melbourne

Oxford University Press

Oxford University Press, Walton Street, Oxford OX 2 6DP

OXFORD NEW YORK TORONTO
DELHI BOMBAY CALCUTTA MADRAS KARACHI
PETALING JAYA SINGAPORE HONG KONG TOKYO
NAIROBI DAR ES SALAAM CAPE TOWN
MELBOURNE AUCKLAND
and associated companies in
BERLIN and IBADAN

Oxford is a trade mark of Oxford University Press

First published 1990
Revised edition published 1992
© R. G. Hammond 1990, 1992

PO3\26

ISBN 0 19 558244 6
(First edition ISBN 0 19 558217 9)

Cover designed by Chris O'Brien
Photoset in Bembo by Wright & Carman
and printed in Hong Kong
Published by Oxford University Press
1A Matai Road, Greenlane, Auckland 5, New Zealand

Contents

Appendices

Preface

This book was born of desperation. In 1988 I arrived back at my Alma Mater in New Zealand after some years teaching and research in North American universities. The then Dean of Law at the University of Auckland, Dr Brookfield, did not act as a former Dean of Law at Yale is said to have acted with respect to the late Grant Gilmore. Upon presenting himself as the new Assistant Professor of Law, Gilmore was told; 'You will teach Sales.' Gilmore has recorded his response as being, 'I said, "Yes Sir!" Thus did I become a commercial lawyer.' Dr Brookfield was too gentle a person to ever allocate courses in that manner. He did however tell me that Auckland had a compulsory new Property course occupying a full year. As the new Professor of Commercial Law I thought it appropriate that I should agree to take on the Personal Property section of this new course. Also I agreed to provide something of an introduction to the broader concepts of property, possession, the justifications for a private property regime, and so on.

On investigation I found that things had not altered all that much from my undergraduate days. New Zealand has had a tradition of excellent writing on real property. Several of my former teachers and colleagues at Auckland had, over the years, kept that tradition firmly alive. These persons included the late Professor Peter Sim, Professor George Hinde, Dr Don McMorland, and Professor Brookfield himself. But the standard reference on Personal Property—that by the late Professor Hamish Gray of Canterbury—is still only in its fifth (1968) edition! And there was still nothing in print on the broader contextual or policy dimensions of property.

Nor was there likely to be in the foreseeable future. Property law is still largely the subject of two distinct phenomena in New Zealand. First, it is subject to apartheid. That is, it is taught in various ways and in various courses in New Zealand law schools. But doubtless for reasons which seem good and sufficient to individual teachers and the various law schools there have been only the beginnings of attempts to evolve integrated courses on Property. Secondly, one does not get the impression from the existing published materials how dynamic the modern law of property is. Whilst it is certainly true that Property has not been immune (and ought not to be) from quite distinct rules which can and should be the subject of rigorous doctrinal study, it is also true that many of the most acute contemporary public policy dilemmas are being fought out under the Property rubric. Does one have a property right in one's body parts? Who 'owns' the airwaves? How should entertainers' claims to exploit their personality be expressed? As a property interest? In short, what legal meaning does Property have today, and for the foreseeable future? What are the implications, both legal and social, of such an understanding as we now have of the rubric?

In the end, as so many other law teachers before me have done in this, as in other subjects, I bent the knee to the insistent demands of necessity and the very real needs of my students for a basic resource book.

The materials in this book are designed to occupy approximately one half of a full year Property course. In Part One I have dealt with the concept of property and the justifications for the institution. I have included material designed to take students into some of the newer claims to proprietary rights. Part Two is (in New Zealand terms) more traditional and deals with fundamental legal concerns and concepts like ownership and possession, transfer of personal property interests, gifts, bailments, remedies for interference with personal property and so on. Part Three is an introduction to registration systems for interests in personalty. I have had the difficulty with it that the government's intentions with respect to personal property security legislation can, at the time of writing, only be described — at best — as murky. I have accordingly kept the material fairly general and 'adaptable'.

I have contemplated that in the other half of the year (or in the second semester as the case may be) real property would be dealt with. Students in that area will have access to the works of the authors I have already mentioned. It would be a good thing if some other law teacher could be tempted or cajoled into preparing a set of cases and materials on real property as a companion volume to this one.

The book makes no particular claim to intellectual rearrangement of the law. There must be a twofold objective to any general Property course. To study property is to study socio-economic relations, history, and reform. Within that context, there is a constant tension between the difficult objectives of promoting stability and accommodating change. The second objective is to study a particular and fundamental area of the law. Students find property law difficult because it has a long history, and a complicated structure. In coming to terms with it students have to be prepared to grapple with legal method and legal reasoning. They must read raw materials, not just texts, and be required to confront fundamental questions of law *and* policy.

Hence the book is not a reference book in the normal sense of that term. It is more like a source book. The material in it is designed to be read closely before class. If it is found to be useful in assisting students to get to grips with the fundamental legal issues relating to property, as well as something of the past and the present of one of the central institutions in our society, and the implications of that institution, I shall be well satisfied. I shall be even more satisfied if students are encouraged to enlarge their critical awareness of this institution through their study of these materials.

A book like this owes many debts. I was privileged to take my property courses at Auckland from an unusual combination of persons: Nadja Tollemache (now the New Zealand Ombudsman), Professor Stefan Riesenfeld (who was visiting Auckland from Berkeley), Professor Douglas Whalen and Professor George Hinde. Mr Robert Megarry QC (as he then was) also visited Auckland and lectured with both a flourish and deep learning. Subsequently in North America I learned much, both about classroom teaching and the subject, from Professor John Cribbet, my Dean and colleague at the University of Illinois (and subsequently President of that University). Professor Cribbett was also President of the Association of American Law Schools and had produced both standard casebooks and treatises on property law in the United States. In Canada the casebooks of the late Bora Laskin (then a member of the University of Toronto Faculty of Law but subsequently Chief Justice of Canada) were as fearsome as any in the common law world for their difficulty, and notorious on that account. But they repaid the effort one had to put into them. Finally, as Director of the Institute of Law Research and Reform at the University of Alberta, I was privileged to have on my staff Professor Allison Dunham (Professor Emeritus at the University of Chicago Law School, one of the most distinguished American property scholars and a former compatriot of Karl Llewellyn on the United States Uniform Commercial Code). Both he and Professor Tom Mapp, another of my colleagues at the Institute, exhibited an unremitting rigour which enhanced a number of the Institute's reports in the property area. Their constant insistence that one return always to first principle is a salutary reminder to student and teacher alike.

Preface to the Revised Edition

It has become necessary to reprint this work. This is not a new edition. However, the practical necessities of a reprint have made it possible to add, in the Appendix, the decision of the Supreme Court of California in *Moore*, the decision of the Privy Council in the *Elders* case, and to include some material relating to the controversy surrounding the death of Billy T James. I have also taken the opportunity, where space has permitted, to add further references to recent works. In particular, since this book was published there have appeared the important works on property rights by Professors Waldron and Munzer. These are of real significance to the ongoing debate over the justification(s) for private property rights.

I would have liked to have added material relating to chattels on hire purchase, or otherwise secured, which (allegedly) become fixtures. Such cases often have added complications such as Romalpa clauses. For teaching purposes, this is a very useful line of authorities, as well as being of considerable practical significance in the current economic climate. However, the development of this line of material will have to await a new edition. A useful starting point for persons who may wish to do so for teaching purposes, is David Coopers' recent article, Retaining Title to Fixtures in (1991) 6 Auckland University Law Review 477.

As some reviewers have noted, this book was an ambitious undertaking. However, having had the benefit of using the material for three years, with an enthusiastic response from students, I am satisfied that it is a useful source book for a foundation-type property course. It of course assumes that students will advance to other courses in commercial law and secured transactions. That is in fact the pattern at the Auckland University Law School, where this set of materials took shape.

Acknowledgements

A book of this kind necessarily borrows heavily from other published works. I have sought permission from all sources of such material, and the references are given in the text. I make specific reference hereunder to the authors, publishers and journals who have generously given permission to reproduce in this text works already in print.

Cohen, *Dialogue on Private Property*. Reprinted by permission of Rutgers Law Review from (1954) 9 Rutgers Law Rev. 357.

Dickens, *The Control of Living Body Materials*. Reprinted by permission of the author and the University of Toronto Press from (1967) 27 UTLJ 180.

Dickens, *Control of Excised Tissues Pending Implantation*. Reprinted by permission of the author and publisher from (1990) Vol. 7 No. 1 Transplantation/Implantation Today 36.

Harris, *The Concept of Possession in English Law*. Reprinted by permission of the author and Oxford University Press from *Oxford Essays in Jurisprudence* (1961) (A G Guest ed.).

Honore, *Ownership*. Reprinted by permission of the author and Oxford University Press from *Oxford Essays in Jurisprudence* (1961) (A G Guest ed.).

Law Commission, *A Personal Property Securities Act for New Zealand*. Various extracts from Report No 8 (1989) under that title.

Law Commission, *Reform of Personal Property Security Law*. Various extracts from Preliminary Paper No 6 (1988) under that title.

Mathews, *Whose Body? People as Property*. Reprinted by permission of Sweet & Maxwell from (1983) 36 Current Legal Problems 193.

Reich, *The New Property*. Reprinted by permission of The Yale Law Journal Company and Fred B Rothman & Company from (1964) 73 Yale L.J. 733.

Reisenfeld, *The Quagmire of Chattels Security in New Zealand*. Reprinted by permission of the Legal Research Foundation from Occasional Paper No 4, The Legal Research Foundation (1970).

Smith, *Stealing the Body and its Parts*. Reprinted by permission of the author and Sweet & Maxwell from [1976] Crim L.R. 622.

Tay & Kamenka, *Some Theses on Property*. Reprinted by permission of the authors and the University of New South Wales Law Journal from (1988) 11 UNSWLJ 1.

The New Zealand Council of Law Reporting. Cases from the New Zealand Law Reports.

I also examined a number of published works and unpublished sets of teaching materials when selecting material for this work. In particular I acknowledge my indebtedness to the various editions of Casner and Leach, *Cases and Text on Property* (Little, Brown & Co.); Donahue Kauper and Martin, *Property* (West); Dukeminier and Krier, *Property* (Little, Brown & Co.); Cribbet Fritz and Johnston, *Property: Cases & Materials* (Foundation Press); Sackville and Neave, *Property Law* (Butterworths); and unpublished sets of teaching materials from Dalhousie University Law School; Osgoode Hall Law School; and the Faculty of Law, University of Alberta.

A Note to Students

This book contains cases, legislation, academic writing and some commentary by me. It is designed to be read, *carefully, before class*. The materials have been selected because they, in one way or another, raise fundamental matters and questions suitable for both classroom discussion and private study and reflection.

New Zealand law students do not always understand the purpose of this approach to teaching. Some resentment at having to prepare *before* class, and awkwardness at 'exposing' one's thinking in class is sometimes apparent. This is unfortunate. The material will have to be read, if only for examination purposes. It is easier to sort out one's understanding as one goes along, rather than in the hurried atmosphere of finals. And professionally, lawyers' thinking is always subject to rigorous scrutiny. The sooner a professional attitude is developed to that, the better.

But there is much more to it than that. A distinguished American law school not so long ago carried out a most interesting experiment. It collated previous teaching evaluations, and then interviewed the same students five and ten years *after* they had graduated. At the time they were in law school students tended to rate highly teachers who gave clear and concise notes. A decade later most of these former students had changed their minds. The teachers who had made the most important contributions to them personally, and to their professional careers, were said to be those who had forced them to think—hard—about fundamental questions of law, policy and values. Anything less is an abdication of the reasons for having a *University* degree in law. And it short-changes students. There are no simple, straightforward answers, no 'rules' to be learnt, and mechanically applied. There is only the constant effort required to understand.

Finally, be careful of the reuse of the materials in this text as an *official* source (as in moots or the like). These are *edited* materials. In some cases portions of text, or footnotes or references have been edited out. If you intend to use the work for that sort of purpose you *must* check the original authority.

Part 1

Part 1

1

The Concept of Property

Legal conceptions and lay conceptions of property do not coincide. If the mythical 'person in the street' were to be asked, 'what is property?' the respondent would almost certainly suggest that property has something to do with *tangible* objects. That is, land or their car or their family dog. If pressed further, such a person might say that property can also encompass some *intangible* things, such as money owed for services performed (a debt) or the goodwill of a business. And if you were to ask, 'What is the principal consequence of saying that something is property?' such a person would probably assert that the statement 'It is mine' comprehends the exclusion of others from that thing. What is mine is not yours.

Most lawyers trained in the common law tradition, if you asked them the question, 'What is property?' would probably say something like this: 'By characterizing a person's interest as "proprietary" we lawyers are indicating the existence of certain rights in relation to something, which may be tangible or intangible, which must be respected by all other persons.'

The common lawyer's assertion that property is about *relationships* rather than about *objects* is of fundamental importance to a study of the legal character and incidents of property. The materials in this chapter have been selected for three reasons. First, to enable you to grapple with that assertion. Secondly, they have also been chosen as an introduction to the complex nature of the relationships between persons and society with respect to the conceptualized thing in respect of which property is asserted, and the difficulties which arise in determining the boundaries and incidents of a property right. Thirdly, lawyers talk of personal obligations and proprietary obligations. What distinguishes the two? This is a deceptively simple question which causes a good deal of difficulty both in theory and in practice.

International News Service v *Associated Press*

United States Supreme Court
248 US 215 (1918)

[The parties were competitors in the gathering and distribution of news and its publication for profit in newspapers throughout The United States. The Associated Press gathered news from all over the world and distributed news reports daily to its 950 member newspapers for publication. Each member agreed to use the reports only in its own newspaper and to make no other use of the reports. This service cost about $3,500,000 annually to maintain. The Associated Press, in this action, claimed an injunction, *inter alia*, to restrain the defendant from copying news reports from bulletin boards and from early editions of its members' newspapers in the Eastern States and selling these reports, either bodily or after re-writing, to the defendant's customers. The defendant was telegraphing the reports to its customers in the Western States, the three hour time differential allowing sufficient time to incorporate the reports in their newspapers in those states. The Associated Press did not copyright its news reports because there was insufficient time to file all reports. The District Court declined to issue a preliminary injunction, but on appeal the Circuit Court of Appeals directed the issue of an injunction restraining the bodily taking of the words or substance of the complainant's news until its commercial value as news had passed away. The defendant appealed to the Supreme Court.]

MR. JUSTICE PITNEY delivered the opinion of the majority of the court.

*   *   *

In considering the general question of property in news matter, it is necessary to recognize its dual character, distinguishing between the substance of the information and the particular form or collocation of words in which the writer has communicated it.

No doubt news articles often possess a literary quality, and are the subject of literary property at the common law; nor do we question that such an article, as a literary production, is the subject of copyright by the terms of the act as it now stands. * * *

But the news element — the information respecting current events contained in the literary production — is not the creation of the writer, but is a report of matters that ordinarily are publici juris; it is the history of the day. It is not to be supposed that the framers of the Constitution, when they empowered Congress "to promote the progress of science and useful arts by securing for limited times to authors and inventors the exclusive right to their respective writings and discoveries" (Const. art. 1, § 8, par. 8), intended to confer upon one who might happen to be the first to report a historic event the exclusive right for any period to spread the knowledge of it.

We need spend no time, however, upon the general question of property in news matter at common law, or the application of the copyright act, since it seems to us the case must turn upon the question of unfair competition in business. And, in our opinion, this does not depend upon any general right of property analogous to the common-law right of the proprietor of an unpublished work to prevent its publication without his consent; nor is it foreclosed by showing that the benefits of the copyright act have been waived. We are dealing here not with restrictions upon publication but with the very facilities and processes of publication. The peculiar value of news is in the spreading of it while it is fresh; and it is evident that a valuable property interest in the news, as news, cannot be maintained by keeping it secret. Besides, except for matters improperly disclosed, or published in breach of trust or confidence, or in violation of law, none of which is involved in this branch of the case, the news of current events may be regarded as common property. What we are concerned with is the business of making it known to the world, in which both parties to the present suit are engaged. That business consists in maintaining a prompt, sure, steady, and reliable service designed to place the daily events of the world at the breakfast table of the millions at a price that, while of trifling moment to each reader, is sufficient in the aggregate to afford compensation for the cost of gathering and distributing it, with the added profit so necessary as an incentive to effective action in the commercial world. The service thus performed for newspaper readers is not only innocent but extremely useful in itself, and indubitably constitutes a legitimate business. The parties are competitors in this field; and, on fundamental principles, applicable here as elsewhere, when the rights or privileges of the one are liable to conflict with those of the other, each party is under a duty so to conduct its own business as not unnecessarily or unfairly to injure that of the other. * * *

Obviously, the question of what is unfair competition in business must be determined with particular reference to the character and circumstances of the business. The question here is not so much the rights of either party as against the public but their rights as between themselves. See Morison v. Moat, 9 Hare, 241, 258. And, although we may and do assume that neither party has any remaining property interest as against the public in uncopyrighted news matter after the moment of its first publication, it by no means follows that there is no remaining property interest in it as between themselves. For, to both of them alike, news matter, however little susceptible of ownership or dominion in the absolute sense, is stock in trade, to be gathered at the cost of enterprise, organization, skill, labor, and money, and to be distributed and sold to those who will pay money for it, as for any other merchandise. Regarding the news, therefore, as but the material out of which both parties are seeking to make profits at the same time and in the same field, we hardly can fail to recognize that for this purpose, and as between them, it must be regarded as quasi property, irrespective of the rights of either as against the public.

* * *

The question, whether one who has gathered general information or news at pains and expense for the purpose of subsequent publication through the press has such an interest in its publication as may be protected from interference, has been raised many times, although never, perhaps, in the precise form in which it is now presented.

Board of Trade v. Christie Grain & Stock Co., 198 U.S. 236, 250, 25 S.Ct. 637, 49 L.Ed. 1031, related to the distribution of quotations of prices on dealings upon a board of trade, which were collected by plaintiff and communicated on confidential terms to numerous persons under a contract not to make them public. This court held that, apart from certain special objections that were overruled, plaintiff's collection of quotations was entitled to the protection of the law; that, like a trade secret, plaintiff might keep to itself the work done at its expense, and did not lose its right by communicating the result to persons, even if many, in confidential relations to itself, under a contract not to make it public; and that strangers should be restrained from getting at the knowledge by inducing a breach of trust.

In National Tel. News Co. v. Western Union Tel. Co., 119 Fed. 294, 56

C.C.A. 198, 60 L.R.A. 805, the Circuit Court of Appeals for the Seventh Circuit dealt with news matter gathered and transmitted by a telegraph company, and consisting merely of a notation of current events having but a transient value due to quick transmission and distribution; and, while declaring that this was not copyrightable although printed on a tape by tickers in the offices of the recipients, and that it was a commercial not a literary product, nevertheless held that the business of gathering and communicating the news—the service of purveying it—was a legitimate business, meeting a distinctive commercial want and adding to the facilities of the business world, and partaking of the nature of property in a sense that entitled it to the protection of a court of equity against piracy.

Other cases are cited, but none that we deem it necessary to mention.

Not only do the acquisition and transmission of news require elaborate organization and a large expenditure of money, skill, and effort; not only has it an exchange value to the gatherer, dependent chiefly upon its novelty and freshness, the regularity of the service, its reputed reliability and thoroughness, and its adaptability to the public needs; but also, as is evident, the news has an exchange value to one who can misappropriate it.

The peculiar features of the case arise from the fact that, while novelty and freshness form so important an element in the success of the business, the very processes of distribution and publication necessarily occupy a good deal of time. Complainant's service, as well as defendant's, is a daily service to daily newspapers; most of the foreign news reaches this country at the Atlantic seaboard, principally at the city of New York, and because of this, and of time differentials, due to the earth's rotation, the distribution of news matter throughout the country is principally from east to west; and, since in speed the telegraph and telephone easily outstrip the rotation of the earth, it is a simple matter for defendant to take complainant's news from bulletins or early editions of complainant's members in the eastern cities and at the mere cost of telegraphic transmission cause it to be published in western papers issued at least as early as those served by complainant. Besides this, and irrespective of time differentials, irregularities in telegraphic transmission on different lines, and the normal consumption of time in printing and distributing the newspaper, result in permitting printed news to be placed in the hands of defendant's readers sometimes simultaneously with the service of competing Associated Press papers, occasionally even earlier.

Defendant insists that when, with the sanction and approval of complainant, and as the result of the use of its news for the very purpose for which it is distributed, a portion of complainant's members communicate it to the general public by posting it upon bulletin boards so that all may read, or by issuing it to newspapers and distributing it indiscriminately, complainant no longer has the right to control the use to be made of it; that when it thus reaches the light of day it becomes the common possession of all to whom it is accessible; and that any purchaser of a newspaper has the right to communicate the intelligence which it contains to anybody and for any purpose, even for the purpose of selling it for profit to newspapers published for profit in competition with complainant's members.

The fault in the reasoning lies in applying as a test the right of the complainant as against the public, instead of considering the rights of complainant and defendant, competitors in business, as between themselves. The right of the purchaser of a single newspaper to spread knowledge of its contents gratuitously, for any legitimate purpose not unreasonably interfering with complainant's right to make merchandise of it, may be admitted; but to transmit that news for commercial use, in competition with complainant—which is what defendant has done and seeks to justify—is a very different matter. In doing this defendant, by its very act, admits that it is taking material that has been acquired by complainant as the result of organization and the expenditure of labor, skill and money, and which is salable by complainant for money, and that defendant in appropriating it and selling it as its own is endeavoring to reap where is has not sown, and by disposing of it to newspapers that are competitors of complainant's members is appropriating to itself the harvest of those who have sown. Stripped of all disguises, the process amounts to an unauthorized interference, with the normal operation of complainant's legitimate business precisely at the point where the profit is to be reaped, in order to divert a material portion of the profit from those who have earned it to those who have not; with special advantage to defendant in the competition because of the fact that it is not burdened with any part of the expense of gathering the news. The transaction speaks for itself, and a court of equity ought not to hesitate long in characterizing it as unfair competition in business.

The underlying principle is much the same as that which lies at the base of the equitable theory of consideration in the law of trusts—that he who has fairly paid the price should have the beneficial use of the property. Pom.Eq.Jur. § 981. It is no answer to say that complainant spends its money for that which is too fugitive or evanescent to be the subject of property. That might, and for the purposes of the discussion we are assuming that it would, furnish an answer in a common-law controversy. But in a court of equity, where the question is one of unfair competition, if that which complainant has acquired fairly at substantial cost may be sold fairly at substantial profit, a competitor, who is misappropriating it for the purpose of disposing of it to his own profit and to the disadvantage of the complainant cannot be heard to say that it is too fugitive or evanescent to be regarded as property. It has all the attributes of property necessary for determining that a misappropriation of it by a competitor is unfair competition because contrary to good conscience.

The contention that the news is abandoned to the public for all purposes when published in the first newspaper is untenable. Abandonment is a question of intent, and the entire organization of the Associated Press negatives such a purpose. The cost of the service would be prohibitive if the reward were to be so limited. No single newspaper, no small group of newspapers, could sustain the expenditure. Indeed, it is one of the most obvious results of defendant's theory that, by permitting indiscriminate publication by anybody and everybody for purposes of profit in competition with the newsgatherer, it would render publication profitless, or so little profitable as in effect to cut off the service by rendering the cost prohibitive in comparison with the return. The practical needs and requirements of the business are reflected in complainant's by-laws which have been referred to. Their effect is that publication by each member must be deemed not by any means an abandonment of the news to the world for any and all purposes, but a publication for limited purposes; for the benefit of the readers of the bulletin or the newspaper as such; not for the purpose of making merchandise of it as news, with the result of depriving complainant's other members of their reasonable opportunity to obtain just returns for their expenditures.

It is to be observed that the view we adopt does not result in giving to complainant the right to monopolize either the gathering or the distribution of the news, or, without complying with the copyright act, to prevent the reproduction of its news articles, but only postpones participation by complainant's competitor in the processes of distribution and reproduction of news that it has not gathered, and only to the extent necessary to prevent that competitor from reaping the fruits of complainant's efforts and expenditure, to the partial exclusion of complainant, and in violation of the principle that underlies the maxim "sic utere tuo," etc.

It is said that the elements of unfair competition are lacking because there is no attempt by defendant to palm off its goods as those of the complainant, characteristic of the most familiar, if not the most typical, cases of unfair competition. Howe Scale Co. v. Wyckoff, Seamans, etc., 198 U.S. 118, 140, 25 S.Ct. 609, 49 L.Ed. 972. But we cannot concede that the right to equitable relief is confined to that class of cases. In the present case the fraud upon complainant's rights is more direct and obvious. Regarding news matter as the mere material from which these two competing parties are endeavoring to make money, and treating it, therefore, as quasi property for the purposes of their business because they are both selling it as such, defendant's conduct differs from the ordinary case of unfair competition in trade principally in this that, instead of selling its own goods as those of complainant, it substitutes misappropriation in the place of misrepresentation, and sells complainant's goods as its own.

Besides the misappropriation, there are elements of imitation, of false pretense, in defendant's practices. The device of rewriting complainant's news articles, frequently resorted to, carries its own comment. The habitual failure to give credit to complainant for that which is taken is significant. Indeed, the entire system of appropriating complainant's news and transmitting it as a commercial product to defendant's clients and patrons amounts to a false representation to them and to their newspaper readers that the news transmitted is the result of defendant's own investigation in the field. But these elements, although accentuating the wrong, are not the essence of it. It is something more than the advantage of celebrity of which complainant is being deprived.

The doctrine of unclean hands is invoked as a bar to relief; it being insisted that defendant's practices against which complainant seeks an injunction are not different from the practice attributed to complainant, of utilizing defendant's news published by its subscribers. At this point it becomes necessary to consider a distinction ∗ ∗ ∗ between two kinds of use that may be made by one news agency of news taken from the bulletin and newspapers of the other. The first is the bodily appropriation of a statement of fact or a news article, with or without rewriting, but without independent investigation or other expense. ∗ ∗ ∗ This practice complainant denies having pursued and the denial was sustained by the finding of the District Court. It is not contended by defendant that the finding can be set aside, upon the proofs as they now stand. The other use is to take the news of a rival agency as a "tip" to be investigated, and if verified by independent investigation the news thus gathered is sold. This practice complainant admits that it has pursued and still is willing that defendant shall employ.

∗   ∗   ∗

As to securing "tips" from a competing news agency, the District Court (240) Fed. 991, 995), while not sanctioning the practice, found that both parties had adopted it in accordance with common business usage, in the belief that their conduct was technically lawful, and hence did not find in it any sufficient ground for attributing unclean hands to complainant. The Circuit Court of Appeals (245 Fed. 247, 157 C.C.A. 436) found that the tip habit, though discouraged by complainant, was "incurably journalistic," and that there was "no difficulty in discriminating between the utilization of tips and bodily appropriation of another's labor in accumulating and stating information."

We are inclined to think a distinction may be drawn between the utilization of tips and the bodily appropriation of news matter, either in its original form or after rewriting and without independent investigation and verification: whatever may appear at the final hearing, the proofs as they now stand recognize such a distinction; both parties avowedly recognize the practice of taking tips, and neither party alleges it to be unlawful or to amount to unfair competition in business. In a line of English cases a somewhat analogous practice has been held not to amount to an infringement of the copyright of a directory or other book containing compiled information. * * *

There is some criticism of the injunction that was directed by the District Court upon the going down of the mandate from the Circuit Court of Appeals. In brief, it restrains any taking or gainfully using of the complainant's news, either bodily or in substance from bulletins issued by the complainant or any of its members, or from editions of their newspapers, *until its commercial value as news to the complainant and all of its members has passed away.*" The part complained of is the clause we have italicized; but if this be indefinite, it is no more so than the criticism. Perhaps it would be better that the terms of the injunction be made specific, and so framed as to confine the restraint to an extent consistent with the reasonable protection of complainant's newspapers, each in its own area and for a specified time after its publication, against the competitive use of pirated news by defendant's customers. But the case presents practical difficulties; and we have not the materials, either in the way of a definite suggestion of amendment, or in the way of proofs, upon which to frame the specific injunction; hence, while not expressing approval of the form adopted by the District Court, we decline to modify it at this preliminary stage of the case, and will leave that court to deal with the matter upon appropriate application made to it for the purpose.

The decree of the Circuit Court of Appeals will be

Affirmed.

MR. JUSTICE CLARKE took no part in the consideration or decision of this case.

MR. JUSTICE HOLMES , dissenting.

When an uncopyrighted combination of words is published there is no general right to forbid other people repeating them — in other words there is no property in the combination or in the thoughts or facts that the words express. Property, a creation of law, does not arise from value, although exchangeable — a matter of fact. Many exchangeable values may be destroyed intentionally without compensation. Property depends upon exclusion by law from interference, and a person is not excluded from using any combination of words merely because some one has used it before, even if it took labor and genius to make it. If a given person is to be prohibited from making the use of words that his neighbors are free to make some other ground must be found. One such ground is vaguely expressed in the phrase unfair trade. This means that the words are repeated by a competitor in business in such a way as to convey a misrepresentation that materially injures the person who first used them, by appropriating credit of some kind which the first user has earned. The ordinary case is a representation by device, appearance, or other indirection that the defendant's goods come from the plaintiff. But the only reason why it is actionable to make such a representation is that it tends to give the defendant an advantage in his competition with the plaintiff and that it is thought undesirable that an advantage should be gained in that way. Apart from that the defendant may use such unpatented devices and uncopyrighted combinations of words as he likes. The ordinary case, I say, is palming off the defendant's product as the plaintiff's, but the same evil may follow from the opposite falsehood—from saying whether in words or by implication that the plaintiff's product is the defendant's, and that, it seems to me, is what has happened here.

Fresh news is got only by enterprise and expense. To produce such news as it is produced by the defendant represents by implication that it has been acquired by the defendant's enterprise and at its expense. When it comes from one of the great news collecting agencies like the Associated Press, the source generally is indicated, plainly importing that credit; and that such a representation is implied may be inferred with some confidence from the unwillingness of the defendant to give the credit and tell the truth. If the plaintiff produces the news at the same time that the defendant does, the defendant's presentation impliedly denies to the plaintiff the credit of collecting the facts and assumes that credit to the defendant. If the plaintiff is later in Western cities it naturally will be supposed to have obtained its information from the defendant. The falsehood is a little more subtle, the injury a little more indirect, than in ordinary cases of unfair trade, but I think that the principle that condemns the one condemns the other. It is a question of how strong an infusion of fraud is necessary to turn a flavour into a poison. The dose seems to me strong enough here to need a remedy from the law. But as, in my view, the only ground of complaint that can be recognized without legislation is the implied misstatement, it can be corrected by stating the truth; and a suitable acknowledgement of the source is all that the plaintiff can require. I think that within the limits recognized by the decision of the Court the defendant should be enjoined from publishing news obtained from the Associated Press for [x] hours after publication by the plaintiff unless it gives express credit to the Associated Press; the number of hours and the form of acknowledgement to be settled by the District Court.

Mr. Justice McKenna concurs in this opinion.

Mr. Justice Brandeis, dissenting.

*   *   *

No question of statutory copyright is involved. The sole question for our consideration is this: Was the International News Service properly enjoined from using, or causing to be used gainfully, news of which it acquired knowledge by lawful means (namely, by reading publicly posted bulletins or papers purchased by it in the open market) merely because the news had been originally gathered by the Associated Press and continued to be of value to some of its members, or because it did not reveal the source from which it was acquired?

The "ticker" cases, the cases concerning literary and artistic compositions, and cases of unfair competition were relied upon in support of the injunction. But it is admitted that none of those cases affords a complete analogy with that before us. The question presented for decision is new, and it is important.

News is a report of recent occurrences. The business of the news agency is to gather systematically knowledge of such occurrences of interest and to distribute reports thereof. The Associated Press contended that knowledge so acquired is property, because it costs money and labor to produce and because it has value for which those who have it not are ready to pay; that it remains property and is entitled to protection as long as it has commercial value as news; and that to protect it effectively the defendant must be enjoined from making, or causing to be made, any gainful use of it while it retains such value. An essential element of individual property is the legal right to exclude others from enjoying it. If the property is private, the right of exclusion may be absolute; if the property is affected with a public interest, the right of exclusion is qualified. But the fact that a product of the mind has cost its producer money and labor, and has a value for which others are willing to pay, is not sufficient to ensure to it this legal attribute of property. The general rule of law is, that the noblest of human productions—knowledge, truths ascertained, conceptions, and ideas—become, after voluntary communication to others, free as the air to common use. Upon these incorporeal productions the attribute of property is continued after such communication only in certain classes of cases where public policy has seemed to demand it. These exceptions are confined to productions which, in some degree, involve creation, invention, or discovery. But by no means all such are endowed with this attribute of property. The creations which are recognized as property by the common law are literary, dramatic, musical, and other artistic creations; and these have also protection under the copyright statutes. The inventions and discoveries upon which this attribute of property is conferred only by statute, are the few comprised within the patent law. There are also many other cases in which courts interfere to prevent curtailment of plaintiff's enjoyment of incorporeal productions; and in which the right to relief is often called a property right, but is such only in a special sense. In those cases, the plaintiff has no absolute right to the protection of his production; he has merely the qualified right to be protected as against the defendant's acts, because of the special relation in which the latter stands or the wrongful method or means employed in acquiring the knowledge or the manner in which it is used. Protection of this character is afforded where the suit is based upon breach of contract or of trust or upon unfair competition.

The knowledge for which protection is sought in the case at bar is not of a kind upon which the law has heretofore conferred the attributes of property; nor is the manner of its acquisition or use nor the purpose to which it is applied, such as has heretofore been recognized as entitling a plaintiff to relief.

First. Plaintiff's principal reliance was upon the "ticker" cases; but they do not support its contention. The leading cases on this subject rest the grant of relief, not upon the existence of a general property right in news, but upon the breach of a contract or trust concerning the use of news communicated; and that element is lacking here.＊＊＊

Second. Plaintiff also relied upon the cases which hold that the common law right of the producer to prohibit copying is not lost by the private circulation of a literary composition, the delivery of a lecture, the exhibition of a painting, or the performance of a dramatic or musical composition. These cases rest upon the ground that the common law recognizes such productions as property which, despite restricted communication, continues until there is a dedication to the public under the copyright statutes or otherwise. But they are inapplicable for two reasons: (1) At common law, as under the copyright acts, intellectual productions are entitled to such protection only if there is underneath something evincing the mind of a creator or originator, however modest the requirements. The mere record of isolated happenings, whether in words or by photographs not involving artistic skill, are denied such protection. (2) At common law, as under the copyright acts, the element in intellectual productions which secures such protection, is not the knowledge, truths, ideas, or emotions which the composition expresses, but the form or sequence in which they are expressed; that is, "some new collocation of visible or audible points—of lines, colors, sounds, or words." * * *

Third. If news be treated as possessing the characteristics not of a trade secret, but of literary property, then the earliest issue of a paper of general circulation or the earliest public posting of a bulletin which embodies such news would, under the established rules governing literary property, operate as a publication, and all property in the news would then cease. Resisting this conclusion, plaintiff relied upon the cases which hold that uncopyrighted intellectual and artistic property survives private circulation or a restricted publication; and it contended that in each issue of each paper, a restriction is to be implied, that the news shall not be used gainfully in competition with the Associated Press or any of its members. There is no basis for such an implication. But it is, also, well settled that where the publication is in fact a general one—even express words of restriction upon use are inoperative. In other words, a general publication is effective to dedicate literary property to the public, regardless of the actual intent of its owner. * * *

Fourth. Plaintiff further contended that defendant's practice constitutes unfair competition, because there is "appropriation without cost to itself of values created by" the plaintiff; and it is upon this ground that the decision of this court appears to be based. To appropriate and use for profit, knowledge and ideas produced by other men, without making compensation or even acknowledgement, may be inconsistent with a finer sense of propriety; but, with the exceptions indicated above, the law has heretofore sanctioned the practice. Thus it was held that one may ordinarily make and sell anything in any form, may copy with exactness that which another has produced, or may otherwise use his ideas without his consent and without the payment of compensation, and yet not inflict a legal injury; and that ordinarily one is at perfect liberty to find out, if he can by lawful means, trade secrets of another, however valuable, and then use the knowledge so acquired gainfully, although it cost the original owner much in effort and in money to collect or produce. Such taking and gainful use of a product of another which, for reasons of public policy, the law has refused to endow with the attributes of property, does not become unlawful because the product happens to have been taken from a rival and is used in competition with him. The unfairness in competition which hitherto has been recognized by the law as a basis for relief, lay in the manner or means of conducting the business; and the manner or means held legally unfair, involves either fraud or force or the doing of acts otherwise prohibited by law. In the "passing off" cases (the typical and most common case of unfair competition), the wrong consists in fraudulently representing by word or act that defendant's goods are those of plaintiff. See Hanover Milling Co. v. Metcalf, 240 U.S. 403, 412-413, 36 S.Ct. 357, 60 L.Ed. 713. In the other cases, the diversion of trade was effected through physical or moral coercion, or by inducing breaches of contract or of trust or by enticing away employees. In some others, called cases of simulated competition, relief was granted because defendant's purpose was unlawful; namely, not competition but deliberate and wanton destruction of plaintiff's business.

*   *   *

It is also suggested that the fact that defendant does not refer to the Associated Press as the source of the news may furnish a basis for relief. But the defendant and its subscribers, unlike members of the Associated Press, were under no contractual obligation to disclose the source of the news; and there is no rule of law requiring acknowledgement to be made where uncopyrighted matter is reproduced. * * *

Fifth. The great development of agencies now furnishing country-wide distribution of news, the vastness of our territory, and improvements in the means of transmitting intelligence, have made it possible for a news agency or newspapers to obtain, without paying compensation, the fruit of another's efforts and to use news so obtained gainfully in competition with the original collector. The injustice of such action is obvious. But to give relief against it would involve more than the application of existing rules of law to new facts. It would require the making of a new rule in analogy to existing ones. The unwritten law possesses capacity for growth; and has often satisfied new demands for justice by invoking analogies or by expanding a rule or principle. This process has been in the main wisely applied and should not be discontinued. Where the problem is relatively simple, as it is apt to be when private interests only are involved, it generally proves adequate. But with the increasing complexity of society, the public interest tends to become omnipresent; and the problems presented by new demands for justice cease to be simple. Then the creation or recognition by courts of a new private right may work serious injury to the general public, unless the boundaries of the right are definitely established and wisely guarded. In order to reconcile the new private right with the public interest, it may be necessary to prescribe limitations and rules for its enjoyment; and also to provide administrative machinery for enforcing the rules. It is largely for this reason that, in the effort to meet the many new demands for justice incident to a rapidly changing civilization, resort to legislation has latterly been had with increasing frequency.

The rule for which the plaintiff contends would effect an important extension of property rights and a corresponding curtailment of the free use of knowledge and of ideas; and the facts of this case admonish us of the danger involved in recognizing such a property right in news, without imposing upon news-gatherers corresponding obligations. * * *

A Legislature, urged to enact a law by which one news agency or newspaper may prevent appropriation of the fruits of its labors by another, would consider such facts and possibilities and others which appropriate inquiry might disclose. Legislators might conclude that it was impossible to put an end to the obvious injustice involved in such appropriation of news, without opening the door to other evils, greater than that sought to be remedied.* * *

Or legislators dealing with the subject might conclude, that the right to news values should be protected to the extent of permitting recovery of damages for any unauthorized use, but that protection by injunction should be denied, just as courts of equity ordinarily refuse (perhaps in the interest of free speech) to restrain actionable libels, and for other reasons decline to protect by injunction mere political rights; and as Congress has prohibited courts from enjoining the illegal assessment or collection of federal taxes. If a Legislature concluded to recognize property in published news to the extent of permitting recovery at law, it might, with a view to making the remedy more certain and adequate, provide a fixed measure of damages, as in the case of copyright infringement.

Or again, a Legislature might conclude that it was unwise to recognize even so limited a property right in published news as that above indicated; but that a news agency should, on some conditions, be given full protection of its business; and to that end a remedy by injunction as well as one for damages should be granted, where news collected by it is gainfully used without permission. If a Legislature concluded (as at least one court has held, New York and Chicago Grain and Stock Exchange v. Board of Trade, 127 Ill. 153, 19 N.E. 855, 2 L.R.A. 411, 11 Am.St.Rep. 107) that under certain circumstances news-gathering is a business affected with a public interest; it might declare that, in such cases, news should be protected against appropriation, only if the gatherer assumed the obligation of supplying it at reasonable rates and without discrimination, to all papers which applied therefor. If legislators reached that conclusion, they would probably go further, and prescribe the conditions under which and the extent to which the protection should be afforded; and they might also provide the administrative machinery necessary for insuring to the public, the press, and the news agencies, full enjoyment of the rights so conferred.

Courts are ill-equipped to make the investigations which should precede a determination of the limitations which should be set upon any property right in news or of the circumstances under which news gathered by a private agency should be deemed affected with a public interest. Courts would be powerless to prescribe the detailed regulations essential to full enjoyment of the rights conferred or to introduce the machinery required for enforcement of such regulations. Considerations such as these should lead us to decline to establish a new rule of law in the effort to redress a newly disclosed wrong, although the propriety of some remedy appears to be clear.

Notes and Questions

1. It may appear to you that INS were outright pirates and were attempting to appropriate the result of AP's reportage in a quite inappropriate manner. There is a background to the case. In 1916 the British Government banned INS, which was owned by the Hearst organization, from using Official Press Bureau facilities

for the transmission of news from that country. Hearst correspondents had claimed in despatches to America that the British Navy had admitted an 'overwhelming defeat' by the German Navy at the Battle of Jutland, which was the major naval battle of the First World War. At that time censorship of war news emanating from Britain was in force. The Home Secretary indicated in the British House of Commons that no such news account had been passed by the Censor. This alleged 'garbling' of the news was cited as the justification for the ban relating to the Hearst organization. The *New York American* (a Hearst-owned newspaper) then published a statement by INS which then read (*inter alia*):

> the English censors have been threatening for many months to deny the [INS organisation] the privilege of the mails and cables because [INS] did not print the kind of news that the English desire to have printed in this country . . . it is the intention of [INS] to continue printing the news, all the news, and nothing but the news. [*New York Times*, October 11, 1916 at 11 column 4 as cited in Kitch, *Legal Regulation of the Competitive Process* (1972) 24.]

Given this denial of access, was the Hearst organisation justified in adopting the course which it did?

2. What does INS decide?

3. Review again the judgment of Mr Justice Brandeis. This is one of the most famous dissents in American law. Do you agree with his views on the relative institutional competence of courts and legislatures to deal with the creation of property rights?

4. It is doubtful if a common law tort of unfair competition exists in New Zealand. In a series of cases concerning wines a decade ago it appeared that such a tort was emerging in the United Kingdom. Cross J in *Vine Products Ltd* v *McKenzie* [1969] RPC 1 at 23 spoke of the law beginning to go 'beyond the well trodden paths of passing off into the unmapped area of "unfair trading" or "unlawful competition" '. And in the Supreme Court of Canada, Estey J said recently:

> The role played by the tort of passing off in the Common Law has undoubtedly expanded to take into account the changing commercial realities in the present day community. The simple wrong of selling one's goods deceitfully as those of another is not now the core of the action. It is the protection of the community from the consequential damage of unfair competition or unfair trading. [*Seiko Time Canada* v *Consumers Distributing Co* (1984) 29 CCLT 296, 312.]

However, in Australia the High Court in *Moorgate Tobacco Ltd* v *Philip Morris* (1984) 56 ALR 193 was extremely critical of the notion of a tortious right of action against unfair competition and the decision in INS. It said at 214:

> The rejection of a general action for 'unfair competition' involves no more than a recognition of the fact that the existence of such an action is inconsistent with the established limits of the traditional and statutory causes of action which are available to a trader in respect of damage caused or threatened by a competitor. Those limits, which define the boundary between the area of legal or equitable restraint and protection and the area of untramelled competition, increasingly reflect what the

responsible Parliament or Parliaments have determined to be the appropriate balance between competing claims and policies. Neither legal principle nor social utility requires or warrants the obliteration of that boundary by the importation of high-sounding generalisations, for judicial indulgence of idiosyncratic notions of what is fair in the market place.

And in *Warnick* v *Townend & Sons* [1979] AC 731, the House of Lords also appear to have rejected such a notion. For the law in New Zealand see A F Grant, Unfair Competition in New Zealand [1985] NZLJ 242. See also Terry, Unfair Competition and Misappropriation of a Competitor's Trade Values [1988] 51 MLR 296. Should a New Zealand court follow the decision of the High Court? And, if there is no tortious right does that strengthen the claim of plaintiffs to proprietary protection? Why?

5. In New Zealand the Fair Trading Act 1980, section 9, provides: 'No person shall, in trade, engage in conduct that is misleading or deceptive or is likely to mislead or deceive'. Could INS's actions be brought within this provision? In *Taylors Textiles Services Auckland Ltd* v *Taylor Brothers Ltd* [1988] 2 NZLR 1 Cooke P suggested that proceedings under the Fair Trading Act are likely to largely replace passing off actions. Would such a development affect your views?

6. What are the real consequences of saying that something is to be protected as a proprietary right as compared with protection under the law of torts, or as compared with protection of news under a statutory provision such as the Fair Trading Act? And what are the relative strengths and weaknesses of the different causes of action viewed from the perspective of (a) the plaintiff and (b) the defendant and (c) society?

7. In *BBC Enterprises* v *Hi-Tech Xtravision (The Times*, 28 November 1989) Scott J held that since no one had property rights in the waves in the ether produced by wireless telegraphic transmission, the BBC could not prevent members of the public in mainland Europe from receiving programmes by means of a decoder supplied by a person other than the BBC under section 298 of the Copyright Designs and Patents Act 1988 (UK). The prohibitions imposed by that Act did not apply outside the UK. Therefore the BBC had 'to rely on some private right that would be infringed by the unauthorized reception of its European broadcasts. No civil right of that nature was known to the general law and none was created by the 1988 Act', which had been 'ineptly' drafted. Does the INS approach have anything to commend it in a case of that kind? And does this suggest a residual role in the law for the misappropriation doctrine? If there is room for such a doctrine, what does one mean by misappropriation? Does it presuppose the taking of a property interest? [Now reported in (1991) 20 IPR 368].

Victoria Park Racing and Recreation Ground Co v Taylor

High Court of Australia
(1937) 58 CLR 479

[The plaintiff owned a racecourse. Descriptions of races taking place on the racecourse were broadcast contemporaneously without the plaintiff's permission from a platform erected on land adjoining the racecourse. There were three defendants: one was

Mr. Taylor, the owner of the adjoining land who had erected the platform there so that the racecourse and the notice board could be plainly observed; the second was Mr. Angles, who stood on the platform and commented on the races by telephone, announcing the winner in each race; the third defendant was the Commonwealth Broadcasting Corporation which broadcast the commentaries of Mr. Angles. The plaintiff wanted to prevent the defendants from carrying on their activities because fewer people attended the races and paid admission as a result of the live broadcast of events on the racecourse.

The plaintiff appealed to the High Court of Australia from a decision of Nicholas, J. in the Supreme Court of New South Wales which refused the plaintiff's request for an injunction. In the High Court the appeal was dismissed by Latham, CJ, Dixon and McTiernan, JJ (Rich and Evatt, JJ, dissenting).]

LATHAM, CJ

*   *   *

I am unable to see that any right of the plaintiff has been violated or any wrong done to him. Any person is entitled to look over the plaintiff's fences and to see what goes on in the plaintiff's land. If the plaintiff desires to prevent this, the plaintiff can erect a higher fence. Further, if the plaintiff desires to prevent its notice boards being seen by people from outside the enclosure, it can place them in such a position that they are not visible to such people. At sports grounds and other places of entertainment it is the lawful, natural and common practice to put up fences and other structures to prevent people who are not prepared to pay for admission from getting the benefit of the entertainment. In my opinion, the law cannot by an injunction in effect erect fences which the plaintiff is not prepared to provide. The defendant does no wrong to the plaintiff by looking at what takes place on the plaintiff's land. Further, he does no wrong to the plaintiff by describing to other persons, to as wide an audience as he can obtain, what takes place on the plaintiff's ground. The court has not been referred to any principle of law which prevents any man from describing anything which he sees anywhere if he does not make defamatory statements, infringe the law as to offensive language, & c., break a contract, or wrongully reveal confidential information. The defendants did not infringe the law in any of these respects.

It has been argued that by the expenditure of money the plaintiff has created a spectacle and that it therefore has what is described as a quasi-property in the spectacle which the law will protect. The vagueness of this proposition is apparent upon its face. What it really means is that there is some principle (apart from contract or confidential relationship) which prevents people in some circumstances from opening their eyes and seeing something and then describing what they see. The court has not been referred to any authority in English law which supports the general contention that if a person chooses to organize an entertainment or to do anything else which other persons are able to see he has a right to obtain from a court an order that they shall not describe to anybody what they see. If the claim depends upon interference with a proprietary right it is difficult to see how it can be material to consider whether the interference is large or small — whether the description is communicated to many persons by broadcasting or by a newspaper report, or only to a few persons in conversation or correspondence.

Further, as I have already said, the mere fact that damage results to a plaintiff from such a description cannot be relied upon as a cause of action.

I find difficulty in attaching any precise meaning to the phrase "property in a spectacle." A "spectacle" cannot be "owned" in any ordinary sense of that word. Even if there were any legal principle which prevented one person from gaining an advantage for himself or causing damage to another by describing a spectacle produced by that other person, the rights of the latter person could be described as property only in a metaphorical sense. Any appropriateness in the metaphor would depend upon the existence of the legal principle. The principle cannot itself be based upon such a metaphor.

RICH J. A man has no absolute right "within the ambit of his own land" to act as he pleases. His right is qualified and such of his acts as invade his neighbour's property are lawful only in so far as they are reasonable having regard to his own circumstances and those of his neighbour (*Law Quarterly Review*, vol. 52, p. 460; vol. 53, p. 3). The plaintiff's case must, I am prepared to concede, rest on what is called nuisance. But it must not be overlooked that this means no more than that he must complain of some impairment of the rights flowing from occupation and ownership of land. One of the prime purposes of occupation of land is the pursuit of profitable enterprises for which the exclusion of others is necessary either totally or except upon conditions which may include payment. In the present case in virtue of its occupation and ownership the plaintiff carries on the business of admitting to the land for payment patrons of racing. There it entertains them by a spectacle, by a competition in the comparative merits of racehorses, and it attempts by all reasonable means to give to those whom it admits the exclusive right of witnessing the spectacle, the competition and of using the collated information in betting while that is possible on its various events. This use of its rights as occupier is usual, reasonable and profitable. So much no one can dispute. If it be true that an adjacent owner has an unqualified and absolute right to overlook an ocupier whatever may be the enterprise he is carrying on and to make any profitable use to which what he sees can be put, whether in his capacity of adjacent owner or otherwise, then to that extent the right of the occupier carrying on the enterprise must be modified and treated in law as less extensive and ample than perhaps is usually understood. But can the adjacent owner by virtue of his occupation and ownership use his land in such an unusual way as the erection of a platform involves, bring mechanical appliances into connection with that use, i.e., the microphone and land line to the studio, and then by combining regularity of observation with dissemination for gain of the information so obtained give the potential patrons a mental picture of the spectacle, an account of the competition between the horses and of the collated information needed for betting, for all of which they would otherwise have recourse to the racecourse and pay? To admit that the adjacent owner may overlook does not answer this question affirmatively.

There can be no right to extend the normal use of his land by the adjoining owner indefinitely. He may within limits make fires, create smoke and use vibratory machinery. He may consume all the water he finds on his land, but he has no absolute right to dirty it. Defendants' rights are related to plaintiff's rights and each owner's rights may be limited by the rights of the other. *Sic utere tuo* is not the premise in a syllogism but does indicate the fact that *damnum* may spring from *injuria* even though the defendant can say: "I am an owner." All the nuisance cases, including in that category *Rylands* v. *Fletcher*, are mere illustrations of a very general principle "that law grows and . . . though the principles of law remain unchanged, yet (and it is one of the advantages of the common law) their application is to be changed with the changing circumstances of the times. Some persons may call this retrogression, I call it progression of human opinion" (*R.* v. *Ramsay and Foote*). I adapt Lord *Macmillan's* words and say: "the categories of 'nuisance' are not closed" (*Donoghue* v. *Stevenson*). Nuisance is not trespass on the case and physical or material interference is not necessary. The "vibration" cases and the "besetting and eavesdropping" cases are certainly against such a contention. What appears to me to be the real point in this case is that the right of view or observation from adjacent land has never been held to be an absolute and complete right of property incident to the occupation of that land and exercisable at all hazards notwithstanding its destructive effect upon the enjoyment of the land overlooked. In the absence of any authority to the contrary I hold that there is a limit to this right of overlooking and that the limit must be found in an attempt to reconcile the right of free prospect from one piece of land with the right of profitable enjoyment of another.

Indeed the prospects of television make our present decision a very important one, and I venture to think that the advance of that art may force the courts to recognize that protection against the complete exposure of the doings of the individual may be a right indispensable to the enjoyment of life. For these reasons I am of opinion that the plaintiff's grievance, although of an unprecedented character, falls within the settled principles upon which the action for nuisance depends. Holding this opinion it is unnecessary for me to discuss the question of copyright raised in the case.

I think that the appeal should be allowed.

DIXON J. The foundation of the plaintiff company's case is no doubt the fact that persons who otherwise would attend race meetings stay away because they listen to the broadcast made by the defendant Angles from the tower overlooking the course. Beginning with the damage thus suffered and with the repetition that may be expected, the plaintiff company says that, unless a justification for causing it exists, the defendants or some of them must be liable, inasmuch as it is their unauthorized acts that inflict the loss. It is said that to look for a definite category or form of action into which to fit the plaintiff's complaint is to reverse the proper order of thought in the present stage of the law's development. In such a case it is for the defendants to point to the ground upon which the law allows them so to interfere with the normal course of the plaintiff's business as to cause damage.

There is, in my opinion, little to be gained by inquiring whether in English law the foundation of a delictual liability is unjustifiable damage or breach of specific duty. The law of tort has fallen into great confusion, but, in the main, what acts and omissions result in responsibility and what do not are matters defined by long-established rules of law from which judges ought not wittingly to depart and no light is shed upon a given case by large generalizations about them. We know that, if upon such facts as the present the plaintiff could recover at common law, his cause of action must have its source in an action upon the case and that in such an action, speaking generally, damage was the gist of the action. There is, perhaps, nothing wrong either historically or analytically in regarding an action for damage suffered by words, by deceit or by negligence as founded upon the damage and treating the unjustifiable conduct of the defendant who caused it as matter of inducement. But, whether his conduct be so described or be called more simply a wrongful act or omission, it remains true that it must answer a known description, or, in other words, respond to the tests or criteria laid down by established principle.

The plaintiff's counsel relied in the first instance upon an action on the case in the nature of nuisance. The premises of the plaintiff are occupied by it for the purpose of a racecourse. They have the natural advantage of not being overlooked by any surrounding heights or raised ground. They have been furnished with all the equipment of a racecourse and so enclosed as to prevent any unauthorized ingress or, unless by some such exceptional devices as the defendants have adopted, any unauthorized view of the spectacle. The plaintiff can thus exclude the public who do not pay and can exclude them not only from presence at, but also from knowledge of, the proceedings upon the course. It is upon the ability to do this that the profitable character of the enterprise ultimately depends. The position of and the improvements to the land thus fit it for a racecourse and give its occupation a particular value. The defendants then proceed by an unusual use of their premises to deprive the plaintiff's land of this value, to strip it of its exclusiveness. By the tower placed where the race will be fully visible and equipped with microphone and line, they enable Angles to see the spectacle and convey its substance by broadcast. The effect is, the plaintiff says just as if they supplied the plaintiff's customers with elevated vantage points round the course from which they could witness all that otherwise would attract them and induce them to pay the price of admission to the course. The feature in which the plaintiff finds the wrong of nuisance is the impairment or deprivation of the advantages possessed by the plaintiff's land as a racecourse by means of a non-natural and unusual use of the defendants' land.

This treatment of the case will not, I think, hold water. It may be conceded that inferferences of a physical nature, as by fumes, smell and noise, are not the only means of committing a private nuisance. But the essence of the wrong is the detraction from the occupier's enjoyment of the natural rights belonging to, or in the case of easements, of the acquired rights annexed to, the occupation of land. The law fixes those rights. Diversion of custom from a business carried on upon the land may be brought about by noise, fumes, obstruction of the frontage or any other interference with the enjoyment of recognized rights arising from the occupation of property and, if so, it forms a legitimate head of damage recoverable for the wrong; but it is not the wrong itself. The existence or the use of a microphone upon neighbouring land is, of course, no nuisance. If one, who could not see the spectacle, took upon himself to broadcast a fictitious account of the races he might conceivably render himself liable in a form of action in which his falsehood played a part, but he would commit no nuisance. It is the obtaining a view of the premises which is the foundation of the allegation. But English law is, rightly or wrongly, clear that the natural rights of an occupier do not include freedom from the view and inspection of neighbouring occupiers or of other persons who enable themselves to overlook the premises. An occupier of land is at liberty to exclude his neighbour's view by any physical means he can adopt. But while it is no wrongful act on his part to block the prospect from adjacent land, it is no wrongful act on the part of any person on such land to avail himself of what prospect exists or can be obtained. Not only is it lawful on the part of those occupying premises in the vicinity to overlook the land from any natural vantage point, but artificial erections may be made which destroy the privacy existing under natural conditions. In *Chandler* v. *Thompson Le Blanc* J. said that, although an action for opening a window to disturb the plaintiff's privacy was to be read of in the books, he had never known such an action maintained, and when he was in the common pleas he had heard it laid down by *Eyre* L.C.J. that such an action did not lie and that the only remedy was to build on the adjoining land opposite to the offensive window. After that date there is, I think, no trace in the authorities of any doctrine to the contrary. In *Johnson* v. *Wyatt Turner* L.J. said: "That the windows of the house may be overlooked, and its comparative privacy destroyed, and its value thus diminished by the proposed erection ∗ ∗ ∗ are matters with which, as I apprehend, we have nothing to do," that is, they afforded no ground for an injunction. This principle formed one of the subsidiary reasons upon which the decision of the House of Lords was based in *Tapling* v. *Jones*. Lord *Chelmsford* said: — "the owner of a house has a right at all times ∗ ∗ ∗ to open as many windows in his own house as he pleases. By the exercise of the right he may materially interfere with the comfort and enjoyment of his neighbour; but of this species of injury the law takes no cognizance. It leaves everyone to his self-defence against an annoyance of this description; and the only remedy in the power of the adjoining owner is to build on his own ground, and so to shut out the offensive windows".

When this principle is applied to the plaintiff's case it means, I think, that the essential element upon which it depends is lacking. So far as freedom from view or inspection is a natural or acquired physical characteristic of the site, giving it value for the purpose of the business or pursuit which the plaintiff conducts, it is a characteristic which is not a legally protected interest. It is not a natural right for breach of which a legal remedy is given, either by an action in the nature of nuisance or otherwise. The fact is that the substance of the plaintiff's complaint goes to interference, not with its enjoyment of the land, but with the profitable conduct of its business. If English law had followed the course of development that has recently taken place in the United States, the "broadcasting rights" in respect of the races might have been protected as part of the quasi-property created by the enterprise, organization and labour of the plaintiff in establishing and equipping a racecourse and doing all that is necessary to conduct race meetings. But courts of equity have not in British jurisdictions thrown the protection of an injunction around all the intangible elements of value, that is, value in exchange, which may flow from the exercise by an individual of his powers or resources whether in the organization of a business or undertaking or the use of ingenuity, knowledge, skill or labour. This is sufficiently evidenced by the history of the law of copyright and by the fact that the exclusive right to invention, trade marks, designs, trade name and reputation are dealt with in English law as special heads of protected interests and not under a wide generalization.

In dissenting from a judgment of the Supreme Court of the United States by which the organized collection of news by a news service was held to give it in equity a quasi-property protected against appropriation by rival news agencies, *Brandeis* J. gave reasons which substantially represent the English view and he supported his opinion by a citation of much English authority (*International News Service* v. *Associated Press*). His judgment appears to me to contain an adequate answer both upon principle and authority to the suggestion that the defendants are misappropriating or abstracting something which the plaintiff has created and alone is entitled to turn to value. Briefly, the answer is that it is not because the individual has by his efforts put himself in a position to obtain value for what he can give that his right to give it becomes protected by law and so assumes the exclusiveness of property, but because the intangible or incorporeal right he claims falls within a recognized category to which legal or equitable protection attaches.

In my opinion, the right to exclude the defendants from broadcasting a description of the occurrences they can see upon the plaintiff's land is not given by law. It is not an interest falling within any category which is protected at law or in equity. I have had the advantage of reading the judgment of *Rich* J., but I am unable to regard the considerations which are there set out as justifying what I consider amounts not simply to a new application of settled principle but to the introduction into the law of new doctrine.

EVATT, J.:

Here the plaintiff contends that the defendants are guilty of the tort of nuisance. It cannot point at once to a decisive precedent in its favour, but the statements of general principle in *Donoghue* v. *Stevenson* are equally applicable to the tort of nuisance. A definition of the tort of nuisance was attempted by Sir *Frederick Pollock*, who said: —

> "Private nuisance is the using or authorizing the use of one's property, or of anything under one's control, so as to injuriously affect an owner or occupier of property — (a) by diminishing the value of that property; (b) by continuously interfering with his power of control or enjoyment of that property; (c) by causing material disturbance or annoyance to him in his use or occupation of that property. What amounts to material disturbance or annoyance is a question of fact to be decided with regard to the character of the neighbourhood, the ordinary habits of life and reasonable expectations of persons there dwelling, and other relevant circumstances" (*Indian Civil Wrongs Bill*, c. VII., sec. 55).

At an earlier date, *Pollock* C.B. had indicated the danger of too rigid a definition of nuisance. He said: — "I do not think that the nuisance for which an action will lie is capable of any legal definition which will be applicable to all cases and useful in deciding them. The question so entirely depends on the surrounding circumstances — the place where, the time when, the alleged nuisance, what, the mode of committing it, how, and the duration of it, whether temporary or permanent" (*Bamford* v. *Turnley*).

In the present case, the plaintiff relies upon all the surrounding circumstances. Its use and occupation of land is interfered with, its business profits are lessened, and the value of the land is diminished or jeopardized by the conduct of the defendants. The defendants' operations are conducted to the plaintiff's detriment, not casually but systematically, not temporarily but indefinitely; they use a suburban bungalow in an unreasonable and grotesque manner, and do so in the course of a gainful pursuit which strikes at the plaintiff's profitable use of its land, precisely at the point where the profit must be earned, viz., the entrance gates. Many analogies to the defendants' operations have been suggested, but few of them are applicable. The newspaper which is published a considerable time after a race has been run competes only with other newspapers, and can have little or no effect upon the profitable employment of the plaintiff's land. A photographer overlooking the course and subsequently publishing a photograph in a newspaper or elsewhere does not injure the plaintiff. Individuals who observe the racing from their own homes or those of their friends could not interfere with the plaintiff's beneficial use of its course. On the other hand, the defendants' operations are fairly comparable with those who, by the employment of moving picture films, television and broadcasting would convey to the public generally (i) from a point of vantage specially constructed; (ii) simultaneously with the actual running of the races, (iii) visual, verbal or audible representations of each and every portion of the races. If such a plan of campaign were pursued, it would result in what has been proved here, viz., actual pecuniary loss to the occupier of the racecourse and a depreciation in the value of his land, at least so long as the conduct is continued. In principle, such a plan may be regarded as equivalent to the erection by a landowner of a special stand outside a cricket ground for the sole purpose of enabling the public to witness the cricket match at an admission price which is lower than that charged to the public bodies who own the ground, and, at great expense, organize the game.

In concluding that, in such cases, no actionable nuisance would be created, the defendants insist that the law of England does not recognize any general right of privacy. That is true, but it carries the defendants no further, because it is not merely an interference with privacy which is here relied upon, and it is not the law that every interference with privacy must be lawful. The defendants also say that the law of England does not forbid one person to overlook the property of another. That also is true in the sense that the fact that one individual possesses the means of watching, and sometimes watches what goes on on his neighbours' land, does not make the former's action unlawful. But it is equally erroneous to assume that under no circumstances can systematic watching amount to a civil wrong, for an analysis of the cases of *J. Lyons & Sons* v. *Wilkins* and *Ward Locke & Co. (Ltd.)* v. *Operative Printers' Assistants' Society* indicates that, under some circumstances, the common law regards "watching and besetting" as a private nuisance, although no trespass to land has been committed.

In the United States, in the case of *International News Service* v. *Associated Press*, Brandeis J. regarded the "*Our Dogs*" *Case* as illustrating a principle that "news" is not property in the strict sense, and that a person who creates an event or spectacle does not thereby entitle himself to the exclusive right of first publishing the "news" or photograph of the event or spectacle. But it is an extreme application of the English cases to say that because *some* overlooking is permissible, all overlooking is necessarily lawful. In my opinion, the decision in the *International News Service Case* evidences an appreciation of the function of law under modern conditions, and I believe that the judgments of the majority and of *Holmes* J. commend themselves as expositions of principles which are *not* alien to English law.

If I may borrow some phrases from the majority decision, I would say that in the present case it is indisputable that the defendant broadcasting company has "endeavoured to reap where it has not sown," and that it has enabled all its listeners to appropriate to themselves "the harvest of those who have sown." Here, too, the interference with the plaintiff's profitable use of its land takes place "precisely at the point where the profit is to be reaped, in order to divert a material portion of the profit from those who have earned it to those who have not". For here, not only does the broadcasting company make its own business profits from its broadcasts of the plaintiff's races; it does so, in part at least, by conveying to its patrons and listeners the benefit of being present at the racecourse without payment. Indeed, its expert announcer seems to be incapable of remembering the fact that he is not on the plaintiff's course nor broadcasting with its permission, for, over and over again, he suggests that his broadcast is coming from within the course. The fact that here, as in the *International News Service Case*, the conduct of the defendants cannot be regarded as honest should not be overlooked if the statement of Lord *Esher* is still true that "any proposition the result of which would be to show that the common law of England is wholly unreasonable and unjust, cannot be part of the common law of England" (quoted in *Donoghue* v. *Stevenson*).

The fact that there is no previous English decision which is comparable to the present does not tell against the plaintiff because not only is simultaneous broadcasting or television quite new, but, so far as I know, no one has, as yet, constructed high grandstands outside recognized sports grounds for the purpose of viewing the sports and of enriching themselves at the expense of the occupier.

[McTernan, J. delivered a judgment agreeing with the Chief Justice and Dixon, J.]

Appeal dismissed.

Notes and Questions

1. How would you characterize the differences in approach between the judgments of Chief Justice Latham, Dixon J, Rich J and Evatt J?

2. Is this a property case at all?

3. Why did the High Court reject the plaintiff's claim? Because there was no economic value to the activity? As a matter of social policy? Or because there were problems of legal enforceability of rights in a spectacle? And why does Latham CJ have difficulty in attaching any precise meaning to the phrase 'property in a spectacle'?

4. In his *Principles of the Civil Code*, Jeremy Bentham made this assertion: 'Property and law are born together, and die together. Before laws were made there was no property; take away laws, and property ceases.' What does Bentham mean? And is *Victoria Park* an illustration of his assertion?

5. In New Zealand it is possible under sections 123-125 of the Property Law Act 1953 (RS Vol 22) to create easements of light and air, to, for instance protect a view. Is there a difference between protecting a view and protecting a spectacle?

Dialogue on Private Property

Felix Cohen
(1954) 9 Rutgers L Rev 357

*   *   *

Does Private Property Exist?

Now, let us see if we can get a clearer notion of the kind of facts that we are dealing with when we talk about property. We have all agreed that there is such a thing as private property in the United States, but suppose we run into a sceptic who refuses to accept our agreement. What evidence, Mr. Black, can you produce to show that private property really exists?

B. Well, here is a book that is my property. You can see it, feel it, weigh it. What better proof could there be of the existence of private property?

C. I can see the shape and color of the book very well, but I don't see its propertiness. What sort of evidence can you put forward to show that the book is your property?

B. Well, I paid for it.

C. Did you pay for your last haircut?

B. Yes.

C. And did you pay for last year's tuition, and last month's board, and your last railroad trip?

B. Yes.

C. But these things are not your property just because you paid for them, are they?

B. No, I suppose not, but now you are talking about past events and I am talking about a material object, a book, that I bought and paid for, which is something quite different from last year's tuition, or last night's dinner.

C. You could cite in support of that distinction, the definition of property given by Aigler, Bigelow and Powell:

> Human beings . . . have various needs and desires. Many of these relate to external objects with which they are in some way associated. . . . The law of property may be looked at as an attempt upon the part of the state, acting through its courts and administrative officers, to give a systematized recognition of and protection of these attitudes and desires on the part of individuals towards things.

B. Yes, I think that clarifies our idea of property.

C. But is the copyright to a song a material, external object?

B. No. I suppose not.

C. And what about a mortgage or a patent on a chemical process or a future interest? These things can be property without being material objects, can't they?

B. Yes, I suppose they can.

C. Then what makes something property may be something intangible, invisible, unweighable, without shape or color?

B. I suppose that may be true in some cases, at least with respect to certain forms of intangible property.

C. Well, let's take the simplest case of tangible property, a piece of real estate, an acre of land on the outskirts of New Haven that you, let us assume, own in fee simple absolute. Would you say that the soil and the rock and the trees are tangible?

B. Yes, they certainly are.

C. But if you cut down the trees and sell them for firewood, the real property is still there on the outskirts of New Haven?

B. Yes.

C. And if you cut the sod and sell that, and dig up the top soil and sand and gravel and rock and sell that, the real property is still there on the outskirts of New Haven and you still have your fee simple absolute?

B. Yes.

C. Then a fee simple absolute is a sector of space in time and no more tangible than a song or a patent?

B. I see no way of avoiding that conclusion.

C. But you are not happy with this conclusion?

B. No, your questions seem to make property vanish into empty space.

C. Perhaps that is because you are assuming that reality always has a position in space. It seems to me that you and Aigler, Bigelow and Powell, are all prisoners of common sense, which is usually the metaphysics of 500 years back. In this case the current common sense is the metaphysical doctrine of Duns Scotus, William of Occam, and other 14th and 15th century scholastics who held that all reality is tangible and exists in space. That idea runs through a great deal of common law doctrine. Take, for example, the ceremony of *livery of seizin,* by which in transferring a possessory estate in land you actually pick up a piece of the sod and soil and hand to the grantee; or take the old common law rule that a mortgage consists of a piece of paper, and if this piece of paper is destroyed, the mortgage disappears. Why should we assume that all reality exists in space? Do our differences of opinion exist in space? Why not recognize that spacial existence is only one of many realms of reality and that in dealing with the law we cannot limit ourselves entirely to the realm of spacial or physical existence?

Property as Social Relations

Can we all agree at this point that essentially this institution of private property that we are trying to identify in outline is not a collection of physical objects, but rather a set of relationships—like our conversation or our differences of opinion? If we can agree on this, at least tentatively, perhaps we can go on to the narrower question, what sort of relationship exactly is this property? Is it a relationship of a man to a thing, or is it a relationship among men? Mr. Delaney, does Hegel have any light to throw on this issue?

D. Hegel seems to think that property involves the relationship of a man to a thing. He says:

A person must translate his freedom into an external sphere, in order that he may achieve his ideal existence.

And then he says:

A person has the right to direct his will upon any object, as his real and positive end. The object thus becomes his. As it has no end in itself, it receives its meaning and soul from his will. Mankind has the absolute right of appropriation over all things.

C. Is that pretty close to Blackstone's definition of property?

D. Yes, Blackstone refers to property as the "sole and despotic dominion which one man claims and exercises over the external things of the world, in total exclusion of the right of any other individual in the universe."
And Blackstone also says:

> In the beginning of the world, we are informed by Holy Writ, the all-bountiful Creator gave to man "dominion over all the earth; and over the fish of the sea, and over the fowl of the air, and over every living thing that moveth on the earth." This is the only true and solid foundation of man's dominion over external things, whatever airy metaphysical notions may have been stated by fanciful writers upon this subject.

C. And under that view, would you say that Adam, when no other individuals existed, had a property right over all the earth?

D. I think Hegel and Blackstone would have to say that, but I would have some doubts since we have seen that property may not involve external objects at all.

C. Well, now in the world we live in, could you point to any examples of property in Blackstone's sense of "sole and despotic dominion . . . over the external things of the world, in total exclusion of the right of any other individual in the universe?"

D. No, I don't think I could.

C. What does Von Jhering mean when he says, in the passage quoted by Ely (at p. 13 of the *Readings*) that an absolute right of property would result in the dissolution of society?

D. I suppose he means that society could not exist without laws of taxation, eminent domain, public nuisances, etc., and if any property owner could really do anything he pleased with his own property, the rights of all his neighbors would be undermined.

C. Exactly. In fact, private property as we know it is always subject to limitations based on the rights of other individuals in the universe. These limitations make up a large part of the law of taxation, the law of eminent domain, the law of nuisance, the obligations of property owners to use due care in the maintenance and operation of their property, and so on. Property in the Blackstonian sense doesn't actually exist either in communist or in capitalist countries. At any rate, the physical relationship of man to thing that Blackstone and Hegel are talking about is not what distinguishes the privately owned steel plant in the United States from the government plant in Soviet Russia, is it?

D. No, I suppose not.

C. Can we agree then that this institution of property that we are trying to understand may or may not involve external physical objects, but always does involve relations between people. Unless there is some dissent to that proposition, I suggest that we consider this as our fourth tentative conclusion with respect to the nature of property. Property, at least the kind of institution that we are talking about when we distinguish between a capitalist and communist country, is basically a set of relations among men, which may or may not involve external physical objects. Would you dissent from that conclusion, Mrs. Evans?

E. Well, calling property a set of relations among men is such a vague generality that I'd hardly dare dissent from it.

Property and Wealth

C. Of course you're right, and yet a generality that is true may be more useful than a more specific idea like Blackstone's that is false. But can we make our conception of property more specific without excluding any of the rights we recognize as property rights? Have you any suggestions, Mrs. Evans, to help us clarify this set of relations that we call property? Do you see any point in the suggestion of Hamilton that property is essentially an economic concept?

E. Yes, it seems to me that when we are talking about property we are really talking about economic goods or wealth.

C. Mrs. Evans, I have here some personal papers that are of no possible value to anyone else in the world. If somebody took these papers from me and I brought suit to have them returned, do you think the court would require the return of these papers?

E. Yes, I suppose it would.

C. Would you then say that these papers are my property even though they have no economic value?

E. Yes, I would.

C. Or let us suppose that I have an inalienable life estate in a piece of land for which I have no possible use. Economically, the land is a burden rather than an advantage to me. Still, if somebody trespassed on it I could get at least a nominal judgment. Would you call that estate my private property?

E. Yes, I suppose we would have to call it private property.

C. Then there is such a thing as valueless property, and economic value is not essential to the existence of legal property?

E. Yes, I suppose we would have to accept that conclusion.

C. What about the other side of Hamilton's equation between wealth and property? Could there be wealth that did not consist of private property? Suppose I discover a new form of exercise that increases the life-span of diabetics. Would that discovery add to the wealth of mankind?

E. Yes, I suppose it would, if put to use.

C. And to the extent that I were willing to communicate that discovery to individuals and charge them for the teaching, the discovery would be of value to me, would it not?

E. Yes, I suppose it would.

C. And yet this bit of knowledge which I could not prevent anyone else from using or discovering would not be property, would it?

E. No, I suppose not.

C. Then it seems to me we have come to the conclusion that not only is there valueless property, but there is also propertyless value.

E. I see no way of avoiding that conclusion.

C. Would you agree that air is extremely valuable to all of us?

E. Yes, of course.

C. Why then is there no property in air?

E. I suppose because there is no scarcity.

C. Suppose there were no scarcity of any material objects.

E. I suppose then there would be no property in material objects.

C. Would you say then that private property is a function of privation?

E. Yes, I suppose it is, in the sense that if there is no possibility of privation there cannot be private property.

C. And would you also say that wealth is a function of plenty?

E. Yes, if we think of wealth broadly as covering the whole field of human goods, or utilities, or enjoyments.

C. Then, wealth and property are in some ways opposites rather than identical?

E. I am not sure what that means, practically.

C. Doesn't it mean, practically, that if we could create a situation in which no man lacked for bread, bread would cease to be an object of property; and if conversely, we could create artificial scarcities in air or sunshine, and then relax these scarcites for a consideration, air and sunshine might become objects of property? Or, more generally, a society might increase the sum of its goods and enjoyments by eliminating one scarcity after another and thus reducing the effective scope of private property.

E. Yes. I suppose that is so. At least, I don't see how one can maintain that private property is identical with goods or wealth.

C. Well, that seems to leave us with a further point of general agreement. Property may exist without value; value may exist without property; private property as a function of privation may even have an inverse relation to wealth; in short, property is not wealth. But what is it? We are still not beyond the vague generality that property is a set of social relations among human beings.

The Case of the Montana Mule

C. Mr. F., there's a big cottonwood tree at the southeast corner of Wright Hagerty's ranch, about 30 miles north of Browning, Montana, and under that tree this morning a mule was born. Who owns the mule?

F. I don't know.

C. Do you own the mule?

F. No.

C. How do you know you don't own the mule? You just said you didn't know who owns the mule. Might it not be you?

F. Well, I suppose that it is possible that I might own a mule I never saw, but I don't think I do.

C. You don't plan to declare this mule on your personal property tax returns?

F. No.

C. Why not, if you really don't know whether you own it? Or do you know?

F. Well, I never had any relation to any mules in Montana.

C. Suppose you did have a relation to this mule. Suppose it turns out that the mule's father was your jackass. Would that make you the owner of the mule?

F. I don't think it would.

C. Suppose you owned the land on which the mule was born. Would that make you the owner of the mule?

F. No.

C. Suppose you owned a piece of unfenced prairie in Montana and the mule's mother during her pregnancy ate some of your grass. Would that make you the owner of the mule?

F. No, I don't think it would.

C. Well, then you seem to know more about the ownership of this Montana mule than you admitted a few moments ago. Now tell us who really owns the mule.

F. I suppose the owner of the mare owns the mule.

C. Exactly. But tell us how you come to that conclusion.

F. Well, I think that is the law of Montana.

C. Yes, and of all other states and countries, as far as I know. For example, the Laws of Manu, which are supposed to be the oldest legal code in the world, declare:

50. Should a bull beget a hundred calves on cows not owned by his master, those calves belong solely to the proprietors of the cows; and the strength of the bull was wasted. (Institutes of Hindu Law or the Ordinances of Manu [translated and edited by S. G. Grady, c. 10].)

Now how does it happen, do you suppose, that the law of Montana in the twentieth century A.D. corresponds to the law of India of 4000 years or so ago? Is this an example of what Aristotle calls natural justice, which is everywhere the same, as distinguished from conventional justice which varies from place to place and from time to time?

F. Well, it does seem to be in accordance with the laws of nature that the progeny of the mother belong to the owner of the mother.

C. Wouldn't it be just as much in accordance with the laws of nature to say that the progeny of the father belong to the owner of the father?

F. I suppose that might be so, as a matter of simple biology, but as a practical matter it might be pretty hard to determine just which jackass was the mule's father.

C. Then, as a practical matter we are dealing with something more than biology. We are dealing with the human need for certainty in property distribution. If you plant seed in your neighbor's field the biological connection between your seed and the resulting plants is perfectly natural, but under the laws of Montana and all other states the crop belongs to the landowner. And the Laws of Manu say the same thing:

49. They, who have no property in the field, but having grain in their possession, sow it in soil owned by another, can receive no advantage whatever from the corn, which may be produced. (Institutes of Hindu Law or the Ordinances of Manu [translated and edited by S. G. Grady, c. 10].)

Would you say here that as a matter of certainty it is generally easier to say who owns a field than to say who owned the seeds that were planted in it?

F. Yes, as a general rule I think that would be the case.

C. Then whether we call our rule of property in livestock an example of natural law or not, its naturalness has some relation to the social need for certainty, which seems to exist in 48 different states and 48 different centuries. Do you think that property law reflects some such human demand for certainty?

F. I think it does in the cases we have been discussing.

C. Couldn't we have some other equally certain and definite rule, say that the mule belongs to the owner of the land where it was born.

F. It might be a hard thing to do to locate the mule's birth-place, but the young mule will show us its own mother when it's hungry.

C. Suppose we decided that the mule should belong to the first roper. Wouldn't that be a simple and definite rule?

F. Yes, but it wouldn't be fair to the owner of the mare who was responsible for its care during pregnancy if a perfect stranger could come along and pick up the offspring.

C. Now, you are assuming that something more than certainty is involved in rules of property law, and that somehow such rules have something to do with ideas of fairness, and you could make out a good case for that proposition in this case. But suppose you are trying to explain this to a cowboy who has just roped this mule and doesn't see the fairness of this rule that makes it the property of the mare owner. Are there any more objective standards that you could point to in support of this rule? What would be the economic consequences of a rule that made the mule the property of the first roper instead of the mare-owner?

F. I think that livestock owners wouldn't be so likely to breed their mares or cows if anybody else could come along and take title to the offspring.

C. You think then that the rule that the owner of the mare owns the mule contributes to economic productivity?

F. Yes.

C. But tell me, is there any reason to suppose that the owner of the mare will be able to raise the mule more economically than, say, the first roper or the owner of the ground on which the mule was born?

F. Well, so long as the mule depends upon its mother's milk, it will be less expensive to raise it if the owner of the mother owns the offspring. And presumably the owner of the mother has physical control over his animals, and no extra effort is involved in his controlling the offspring as long as they are dependent upon their mother.

C. So, in effect, the rule we are talking about takes advantage of the natural dependency of the offspring on the mother animal. By enlisting the force of habit or inertia, this rule economizes on the human efforts that might otherwise be expended in establishing control over the new animal. The owner of the mare has achieved the object of all military strategy—he has gotten there "fustest with the mostest." We don't need to pay a troop of Texas Rangers to seize the mule and deliver it to the owner of the jackass father who may be many miles away. But why should we have a simple definite rule in all these cases? Wouldn't it be better to have a more flexible standard so that we might consider in each case what the owner of the mare contributed, what the owner of the jackass contributed, what was contributed by the grass owner who paid for the mare's dinners, and then on the basis of all the facts we might reach a result that would do justice to all the circumstances of each individual case?

F. The trouble with that is that the expense of holding such investigations might exceed the value of the mule.

C. And would it be easier or harder to borrow from the bank to run a livestock business if the owner of a mare or a cow didn't know in advance that it would own the offspring?

F. If I were a banker I'd certainly hesitate to make a livestock loan to a herd owner without such a simple definite rule.

C. Could we sum up this situation, then, by saying that this particular rule of property law that the owner of the mare owns the offspring has appealed to many different societies across hundreds of generations because this rule contributes to the economy by attaching a reward to planned production; is simple, certain, and economical to administer; fits in with existing human and animal habits and forces; and appeals to the sense of fairness of human beings in many places and generations?

F. I think that summarizes the relevant factors.

C. And would you expect that similar social considerations might lead to the development of other rules of property law, and that where these various considerations of productivity, certainty, enforceability, and fairness point in divergent directions instead of converging on a single solution, we might find more controversial problems of private ownership?

F. That would seem to be a reasonable reference.

Ownership, Use and Sale

C. Suppose we pass, then, to a slightly more difficult problem. Mrs. Farnsworth, do you own any songs?

F. No.

C. How do you know that you don't own any songs? What does it mean to say that somebody owns a song?

F. Well, I suppose it means that the owner has a right to sing the song himself, and has a right to charge others for the privilege of singing the song, or at least for making commercial use of the song.

C. You and I have the right to sing "Auld Lang Syne" without paying anyone for the privilege, don't we?

F. Yes. I suppose so.

C. Then, the right to sing can exist even where there is no property right?

F. Yes.

C. Can a corporation sing?

F. No. I don't suppose so.

C. But a corporation can own the copyright to a song, can't it?

F. Yes.

C. Then ownership can exist without the possibility of the owner's enjoying or using what he owns.

F. Yes, I suppose so.

C. Then the criterion of use as a mark of ownership breaks down at both ends. We can have use without ownership and ownership without use. What about the other half of your criterion, the possibility of charging others for the use of something. Suppose you secure a lease on an apartment with the condition that you can't assign the lease, can't sublease the apartment, can't have pets or babies on the premises and can't take in boarders. Might you not still have a property interest even though you couldn't sell it?

F. Yes, I suppose there is such a thing as non-saleable property.

C. And what about the other side of that equation. Is it possible that you can buy or sell what is not property at all, services, for example?

F. Yes, I suppose I have to retreat from the position that the right to sell is a distinctive characteristic of private property.

C. But wait, now, before you retreat too far. When you say that an owner can charge somebody else for the use of what he owns you mean, don't you, that he can charge somebody else if that person is willing to pay?

F. Yes, of course that is understood.

C. But I could charge you for walking across Brooklyn Bridge if you were willing to pay for it and that would not be proof that I had a property right in Brooklyn Bridge, would it?

F. No, but in that case I could walk across Brooklyn Bridge without paying you, and in the case of the song, if you owned the song, you could exclude me from the use of the song unless I made the payment.

Exclusion and Exclusiveness

C. Well, then, we are really talking about a right of exclusion, aren't we? What you are really saying is that ownership is a particular kind of legal relation in which the owner has a right to exclude the non-owner from something or other. That is really the point that Ely and Morris Cohen both make, isn't it?

F. Yes, I think that is where they find a difference between property and other rights.

C. Do you agree, then, with Ely's statement: "By property we mean an exclusive right to control an economic good"?

F. Yes, I think that is a fair statement, except that what is controlled may be an economic evil rather than a good, or even a worthless thing, as we agreed a while ago.

C. Suppose I have acquired a non-exclusive easement to cross a piece of land. That might be a very valuable right to me, might it not, if that were the only way of reaching my house from the public streets?

F. Yes.

C. But by definition this would not be exclusive and would not be property in Ely's sense.

F. No, I suppose not.

C. And if I own a beach in common with 600 other people, I would not have an exclusive right to control the beach, would I?

F. No.

C. But aren't these non-exclusive rights property in the fundamental sense that I can exclude third parties from certain types of interference with my activities?

F. Yes, I suppose even a non-exclusive right of way wouldn't amount to anything if you couldn't exclude others from fencing off the right of way.

C. Can we agree, then, that the essential factor that we are reaching for here is the power to exclude, whether that power is exclusive or shared with others?

F. Yes, I think that is an essential factor. There may be others.

C. Is there any dissent from that proposition? If not, let us put this down as one more point of agreement in our analysis of the meaning of private property. Private property may or may not involve a right to use something oneself. It may or may not involve a right to sell, but whatever else it involves, it must at least involve a right to exclude others from doing something.

Now, Mr. Galub, if you agree that a property right always involves a power to exclude, would you also agree that a power to exclude always involves a property right?

G. No, not necessarily.

C. The Yale football team might have the power to exclude the Princeton team from the goal line, but that would not make a goal line Yale property, would it?

G. No, I think we would have to agree more precisely on just what we mean by a power to exclude.

Property and Law

C. Does Bentham offer any help in clarifying this idea of power?

G. Yes, I think he does. He draws a distinction between physical power and the power that is derived from government. He says:

> Property and law are born together, and die together. Before laws were made there was no property; take away laws, and property ceases.

C. Then can you say that the kind of power to exclude that is essential to the institution of property is the power that exists when we can count upon agencies of the state to help us to exclude others from some activity?

G. Yes, I think that would help to clarify the idea of property.

C. Would you say, then, that there is no property without sovereignty and that property relationships always involve government, — in other words, that property is a function of government or sovereignty?

G. Yes, that is what Morris R. Cohen, Ely, Hamilton, and Bentham all say, and I think they are right as far as they go.

C. Could you conceive of a government without property?

G. Yes, I suppose you might have a purely communistic state with no private property.

C. Suppose you had not a communistic state but a state governed by the Mad Duchess of Alice in Wonderland. Suppose you never could tell whether she would dispose of any problem by the command "off with his head", or some other command. Would you then be able to count on the support of the state in excluding third parties from the use of a patent or anything else.

G. No, by hypothesis, you have made private property impossible.

C. In other words, the existence of private property presupposes not only sovereignty but some predictable course of sovereign action, so that the so-called property owner can count on state help in certain situations?

G. Yes, I suppose that is part of what Bentham means when he says that property involves established expectations of being able to derive certain advantages from what one possesses, that expectation based on physical strength is very tenuous, because others can gang up and take away the goods of the strong man, but "a strong and permanent expectation can result only from law."

C. Well, now, if we can agree that in order to have private property we must be able to count on governmental help in excluding others from certain activities, that tells us something important about property. But we still don't have a definition of property unless we can say that wherever there is a power to exclude others with governmental help of some activity there we have private property. Would such a statement be correct in your opinion?

G. I am not sure.

C. Suppose I live on a street where commercial vehicles are not permitted. If I see a truck coming down the street I can call a policeman and get the aid of the state in excluding the truck from the street. Does that mean that I have a property right in the street?

G. No, you might have a right to call upon the aid of the state in stopping all kinds of criminal activities, but that would not give you a property right in those activities.

C. Exactly. But if I could not only stop a truck from using the street in front of my house and secure the help of the state in enforcing that prohibition, but could also, on my own responsibility, grant permission to somebody to drive a truck on the street and charge him for the privilege and have the assistance of the state in enforcing such decisions, then would you say that I had a property right in the use of the street?

G. Yes, I think you would. That would be the kind of property that the owner of a toll road would have.

C. Private property, then presupposes a realm of private freedom. Without freedom to bar one man from a certain activity and to allow another man to engage in that activity we would have no property. If all activities were permitted or prohibited by general laws there would be no private property. Does that make sense to you, Mr. Galub?

G. Yes, I suppose we could say that the existence of private property represents in some ways a middle ground between the absence of government and the complete determination of human activities by government. I suppose that is really what Morris Cohen is driving at in the article on "Property and Sovereignty" when he talks about private property as a delegation of sovereign power in certain limited areas. In those areas the government doesn't make a final decision but agrees to back up whatever decision the so-called owner of property makes.

C. Very clearly put, I think. Now suppose we put together all the conclusions we have been able to agree upon so far in our discussion: Private property is a relationship among human beings such that the so-called owner can exclude others from certain activities or permit others to engage in those activities and in either case secure the assistance of the law in carrying out his decision. Would that be a sound definition of private property?

G. I'm not sure what it means to say that a definition is sound or not.

C. Good. The same word may mean different things to different people. Therefore, asking whether a definition is true or false is a meaningless question. But we can ask whether a definition is useful or useless. And that may depend upon whether the definition can be used in a self-consistent manner and whether it can help to clarify the problems with which we want to deal. Now, with that explanantion what do you think of our definition of private property?

G. Well, I'd rather postpone any judgment as to the utility of a definition until we see how it is to be used and what help it may give us. But at least I don't see any self-contradiction in this definition.

C. Would you go further and say that a definition which distinguishes between private property and other legal relationships is more useful than a definition like that of the A.L.I. which applies in effect to all legal relations, and is also more useful than the Blackstonian definition which applies to nothing at all in the real world?

G. Yes.

C. And would you say that our definition of private property in so far as it includes copyrights and patents and fee simples and is not limited to external objects is more useful than the definitions of Hegel, Aigler, Bigelow, and Powell in terms of external objects?

G. Agreed.

C. Do you find any ambiguities in our definition that might be cleared up by a more precise use of language?

G. I'm not sure.

Property and Contract

C. Isn't there a basic ambiguity in our use of the word "exclusion"? May that not cover two quite different things, a right against the world and a right against a specific individual based perhaps upon his own agreement? Suppose I am operating a string of 50 laundry machines in Washington, and I enter into a contract with you by which I sell you the machines and agree that I will stay out of the laundry business in Washington during the next ten years. Do you see any important difference between the rights that you would acquire over the machines and the rights that you would acquire with respect to my entering the laundry business?

G. I suppose that one important difference would be that so far as your entering the laundry business is concerned, I have a right to exclude you, but that right applies only to the person who made the contract, whereas with respect to the machines themselves, my right to exclude applies to the whole world.

C. Exactly. And while both these rights are derived from contract and might be called contractual rights, we may find it useful to distinguish those rights that apply only against the contracting party and those rights that apply against the world at large and call rights of the latter kind property rights. I don't say that this strict definition of property is universally followed, but I think generally we will find it more useful than any broader definition of property.

Now, at this point, it may be useful to summarize our analysis of property in terms of a simple label. Suppose we say, that is property to which the following label can be attached:

To the world:

> Keep off X unless you have my permission, which I may grant or withhold.
>   Signed: Private citizen
>   Endorsed: The state

Let me offer the caution that such a label does not remove the penumbra of ambiguity that attaches to every word that we use in any definition. As William

James says, "The word 'and' trails along after every sentence." No definition can be more precise than the subject permits. Aristotle remarks that it is a mark of immaturity to expect the same degree of precision in human affairs as in mathematics. All of the terms of our definition shade off imperceptibly into other things. Private citizen: consider how many imperceptible shadings there are in the range from private citizen through corporate official, public utility employee, and government corporation and the state itself. Or consider the shadings between the state and various other types of organization. Consider the initial words, "To the world", and the large middle ground between a direction to the whole world and a direction to a specific individual.

Any definition of property, to be useful, must reflect the fact that property merges by imperceptible degrees into government, contract, force, and value.

Questions

1. What, in Cohen's analysis, is property?
2. Is there any relationship between Cohen's views on property and the assertion of Jeremy Bentham, *supra*?

Some Basic Distinctions

Lawyers do not generally talk about property in the abstract. Perhaps the most important distinctions our law has made have been those between real property (land) and personal property (things other than land), between ownership and possession, and between legal and equitable interests. It is critical for the whole of your legal studies that you develop a proper appreciation of the meaning and consequences of these classifications. You should also, as a matter of critical awareness, ask yourself whether these distinctions make sense in theory and whether they are useful or functional in contemporary circumstances. These distinctions are dealt with in detail in Part II.

Statutory Definitions of Property

There are a number of statutes in New Zealand that refer to 'property'. Perhaps the most important are the following:

1. Property Law Act 1952 (RS Vol 22), section 2. 'Property includes real and personal property, and any estate or interest in any property real or personal, and any debt, and any thing in action, and any other right or interest.'
2. The Crimes Act 1961 (RS Vol 1), section 2 repeats that definition for the purposes of that statute. In section 217 of the Crimes Act, things capable of being stolen are defined as:

> Every inanimate thing whatsoever, and every thing growing out of the earth, which is the property of any person, and either is or may be made movable, is capable of being stolen as soon as it becomes movable, although it is made movable in order to steal it.

Under section 218 electricity can be stolen, and section 219 defines animals capable of being stolen.

Questions

1. Should the definition of property be the same for criminal and civil law? What about income tax legislation, or capital gains tax? Or any other piece of legislation?

2. Look at the concluding words of the Property Law Act definition. Are they intended to widen the definition beyond real or personal property? What, if anything, do they add? Do they mean for instance, that in the BBC case, *supra*, intercepting a signal off the air without consent might amount to a criminal offence of unlawful interference with the property of another person? What if the BBC signal were to be electronically jammed?

3. How does one go about interpreting the word 'property' in a statute where it is not defined?

A Judical Definition of Property

In *National Provincial Bank* v *Ainsworth* [1965] AC 1175, 1247 Lord Wilberforce suggested that 'before a right or an interest can be admitted into the category of property, or a right affecting property, it must be definable, identifiable by third parties, and have some degree of permanence or stability'.

Notes and Questions

1. This is very much a common law perspective—it sees property in terms of rights relating to (usually) tangible subject matter, rather than looking to the *res* itself. See further on this viewpoint, Holdsworth, *A History of English Law*, Vol 3, 318-360.

2. Are there other criteria you would add to those suggested by Lord Wilberforce? Would you disagree with, or wish to modify, any of His Lordship's criteria?

3. In, Property in Thin Air (1991) 50 CLJ 252 Professor Gray gives us a trenchant analysis of *Victoria Park Raceway*. He suggests that 'Proudhon got it all wrong. Property is not theft—it is fraud. Few other legal notions operate such gross or systematic deception' (page 252). He also claims (page 306) that '"property" terminology is merely talk without substance—a filling of empty space with empty words . . . in the end the "property" notion, in all its conceptual fragility, is but a shadow of the individual and collective human response to a world of limited resources and attenuated altruism.' How much force do you think there is in this line of argument?

2

Justifications for Property

How private property regimes come about, how they manifest themselves in various societies, and the justifications for these regimes are questions of central importance to any society. Not surprisingly these questions have attracted a wealth of literature from a variety of perspectives. Political science, political economy, sociology, anthropology, economics, history and philosophy have all contributed.

A university education in law should encourage an appreciation of the principal lines of justifications for private property regimes and of critiques by leading thinkers. The perspective offered by the various schools of thought have been and continue to be reflected in case law. They also influence policy makers and legislators. The materials in this chapter are designed to acquaint students with the various schools. Students should also endeavour to identify their influence in the material in subsequent chapters.

Sovereignty or Occupation Theory

One of the oldest justifications for private property rights is simply that of being there first. This notion 'is a venerable and persistent one', L Becker, *Property Rights, Philosophic Foundations* (1977) 25. But be careful. The question here is, when does first possession make one a 'true' owner? In the law relating to 'finders', as we shall see presently, possession can create rights against all but true owners.

The argument that first possession, first capture or first occupancy can make one a true owner dates back to continental writers in the Middle Ages. Hugo Grotius and later Pufendorf suggested that the earth's material things were originally held in common. Because people want those material things (and hence a scarcity value arises) the institution—as they termed it—of private property was needed to preserve peace and order. The division of property would take place according to agreements. These may be explicit or they may be implied by occupation. Occupation was an important—perhaps a primary—mode of acquisition. Although governments modified rules of acquisition, governments had to recognize the property rights of citizens. See Schlatter, *Private Property: The History of an Idea* (1951) 130-1.

Commentaries

Sir William Blackstone
Vol II. paras 2-5, 14-15, (1765-1769)

In the beginning of the world, we are informed by holy writ, the all-bountiful Creator gave to man "dominion over all the earth, and over the fish of the sea, and over the fowl of the air, and over every living thing that moveth upon the earth." This is the only true and solid foundation of man's dominion over external things, whatever airy metaphysical notions may have been started by fanciful writers upon this subject. The earth, therefore, and all things therein, are the general property of all mankind, exclusive of other beings, from the immediate gift of the Creator. And, while the earth continued bare of inhabitants, it is reasonable to suppose that all was in common among them, and that every one took from the public stock to his own use such things as his immediate necessities required.

* * *

* * * Not that this communication of goods seems ever to have been applicable, even in the earliest stages, to aught but the *substance* of the thing; nor could it be extended to the *use* of it. For, by the law of nature and reason, he, who first began to use it, acquired therein a kind of transient property, that lasted so long as he was using it, and no longer: or, to speak with greater precision, the *right* of possession continued for the same time only that the *act* of possession lasted. Thus the ground was in common, and no part of it was the permanent property of any man in particular; yet whoever was in the occupation of any determined spot of it, for rest, for shade, or the like, acquired for the time a sort of ownership, from which it would have been unjust, and contrary to the law of nature, to have driven him by force: but the instant that he quitted the use or occupation of it, another might seize it, without injustice. * * *

But when mankind increased in number, craft, and ambition, it became necessary to entertain conceptions of more permanent dominions; and to appropriate to individuals not the immediate *use* only, but the very *substance* of the thing to be used. Otherwise innumerable tumults must have arisen, and the good order of the world be continually broken and disturbed, while a variety of persons were striving who should get the first occupation of the same thing, or disputing which of them had actually gained it. As human life also grew more and more refined, abundance of conveniences were devised to render it more easy, commodious, and agreeable; as, habitations for shelter and safety, and raiment for warmth and decency. But no man would be at the trouble to provide either, so long as he had only an usufructuary property in them, which was to cease the instant that he quitted possession; if, as soon as he walked out of his tent, or pulled off his garments, the next stranger who came by would have a right to inhabit the one, and to wear the other. In the case of habitations in particular, it was natural to observe, that even the brute creation, to whom every thing else was in common, maintained a kind of permanent property in their dwellings, especially for the protection of their young; that the birds of the air had nests, and the beasts of the field had caverns, the invasion of which they esteemed a very flagrant injustice, and would sacrifice their lives to preserve them. Hence a property was soon established in every man's house and home-stall: which seem to have been originally mere temporary huts or movable cabins, suited to the design of Providence for more speedily peopling the earth, and suited to the wandering life of their owners, before any extensive property in the soil or ground was established. And there can be no doubt, but that movables of every kind became sooner appropriated than the permanent substantial soil: partly because they were more susceptible of a long occupancy, which might be continued for months together without any sensible interruption, and at length by usage ripen into an established right; but principally because few of them could be fit for use, till improved and ameliorated by the bodily labor of the occupant, which bodily labor, bestowed upon any subject which before lay in common to all men, is universally allowed to give the fairest and most reasonable title to an exclusive property therein. * * *

But, after all, there are some few things, which notwithstanding the general introduction and continuance of property, must still unavoidably remain in common; being such wherein nothing but an usufructuary property is capable of being had; and therefore they still belong to the first occupant, during the time he holds possession of them, and no longer. Such (among others) are the elements of light, air, and water; which a man may occupy by means of his windows, his gardens, his mills, and other conveniences: such also are the generality of those animals which are said to be *feræ naturæ*, or of a wild and untamable disposition; which any man may seize upon and keep for his own use and pleasure. All these things, so long as they remain in possession, every man has a right to enjoy without disturbance; but if once they escape from his custody, or he voluntarily abandons the use of them, they return to the common stock, and any man else has an equal right to seize and enjoy them afterwards.

Again: there are other things in which a permanent property *may* subsist, not only as to the temporary use, but also the solid substance; and which yet would be frequently found without a proprietor, had not the wisdom of the law provided a remedy to obviate this inconvenience. Such are forests and other waste grounds, which were omitted to be appropriated in the general distribution of lands; such also are wrecks, estrays, and that species of wild animals which the arbitrary constitutions of positive law have distinguished from the rest by the well-known appellation of game. With regard to these and some others, as disturbances and quarrels would frequently arise among individuals, contending about the acquisition of this species of property by first occupancy, the law has therefore wisely cut up the root of dissension, by vesting the things themselves in the sovereign of the state: or else in his representatives appointed and authorized by him, being usually the lords of manors. And thus the legislature of England has universally promoted the grand ends of civil society, the peace and security of individuals, by steadily pursuing that wise and orderly maxim, of assigning to every thing capable of ownership a legal and determinate owner.

Note

Blackstone has been praised and condemned. For the former see Milsom, The Nature of Blackstone's Achievement (1981) 1 Ox J Legal Studies 1; for the latter, Kennedy, The Structure of Blackstone's Commentaries (1979) 28 Buffalo L Rev 209.

Pierson v *Post*

Supreme Court of New York
3 Caines 175 (1805)

This was an action of trespass on the case commenced in a justice's court, by the present defendant against the now plaintiff.

The declaration stated that Post, being in possession of certain dogs and hounds under his command, did, "upon a certain wild and uninhabited, unpossessed and waste land, called the beach, find and start one of those noxious beasts called a fox," and whilst there hunting, chasing and pursuing the same with his dogs and hounds, and when in view thereof, Pierson, well knowing the fox was so hunted and pursued, did, in the sight of Post, to prevent his catching the same, kill and carry it off. A verdict having been rendered for the plaintiff below, the defendant there sued out a *certiorari*, and now assigned for error, that the declaration and the matters therein contained were not sufficient in law to maintain an action. * * *

TOMPKINS, J., delivered the opinion of the court. This cause comes before us on a return to a *certiorari* directed to one of the justices of Queens county.

The question submitted by the counsel in this cause for our determination is, whether Lodowick Post, by the pursuit with his hounds in the manner alleged in his declaration, acquired such a right to, or property in, the fox, as will sustain an action against Pierson for killing and taking him away?

The cause was argued with much ability by the counsel on both sides, and presents for our decision a novel and nice question. It is admitted that a fox is an animal *feræ naturæ*, and that property in such animals is acquired by occupancy only. These admissions narrow the discussion to the simple question of what acts amount to occupancy, applied to acquiring right to wild animals?

If we have recourse to the ancient writers upon general principles of law, the judgment below is obviously erroneous. Justinian's Institutes, lib. 2, tit. 1, s. 13, and Fleta, lib. 3, c. 2, p. 175, adopt the principle, that pursuit alone vests no property or right in the huntsman; and that even pursuit, accompanied with wounding, is equally ineffectual for that purpose, unless the animal be actually taken. The same principle is recognised by Bracton, lib. 2, c. 1, p. 8.

Puffendorf, lib. 4, c. 6, s. 2, and 10, defines occupancy of beasts *feræ naturæ*, to be the actual corporal possession of them, and Bynkershoek is cited as coinciding in this definition. It is indeed with hesitation that Puffendorf affirms that a wild beast mortally wounded, or greatly maimed, cannot be fairly intercepted by another, whilst the pursuit of the person inflicting the wound continues. The foregoing authorities are decisive to show that mere pursuit gave Post no legal right to the fox, but that he became the property of Pierson, who intercepted and killed him.

It therefore only remains to inquire whether there are any contrary principles, or authorities, to be found in other books, which ought to induce a different decision. Most of the cases which have occurred in England, relating to property in wild animals, have either been discussed and decided upon the principles of their positive statute regulations, or have arisen between the huntsman and the owner of the land upon which beasts *feræ naturæ* have been apprehended; the former claiming them by title of occupancy, and the latter *ratione soli*. Little satisfactory aid can, therefore, be derived from the English reporters.

Barbeyrac, in his notes on Puffendorf, does not accede to the definition of occupancy by the latter, but, on the contrary, affirms, that actual bodily seizure is not, in all cases, necessary to constitute possession of wild animals. He does not, however *describe* the acts which, according to his ideas, will amount to an appropriation of such animals to private use, so as to exclude the claims of all other persons, by title of occupancy, to the same animals; and he is far from averring that pursuit alone is sufficient for that purpose. To a certain extent, and as far as Barbeyrac appears to me to go, his objections to Puffendorf's definition of occupancy are reasonable and correct. That is to say, that actual bodily seizure is not indispensable to acquire right to, or possession of, wild beasts; but that, on the contrary, the mortal wounding of such beasts, by one not abandoning his pursuit, may, with the utmost propriety, be deemed possession of him; since, thereby, the pursuer manifests an unequivocal intention of appropriating the animal to his individual use, has deprived him of his natural liberty, and brought him within his certain control. So also, encompassing and securing such animals with nets and toils, or otherwise intercepting them in such a manner as to deprive them of their natural liberty, and render escape impossible, may justly be deemed to give possession of them to those persons who, by their industry and labour, have used such means of apprehending them. Barbeyrac seems to have adopted, and had in view of his notes, the more accurate opinion of Grotius, with respect to occupancy. * * * The case now under consideration is one of mere pursuit, and presents no circumstances or acts which can bring it within the definition of occupancy by Puffendorf, or Grotius, or the ideas of Barbeyrac upon that subject.

* * *

We are the more readily inclined to confine possession or occupancy of beasts *feræ naturæ*, within the limits prescribed by the learned authors above cited, for the sake of certainty, and preserving peace and order in society. If the first seeing, starting, or pursuing such animals, without having so wounded, circumvented or ensnared them, so as to deprive them of their natural liberty, and subject them to the control of their pursuer, should afford the basis of actions against others for intercepting and killing them, it would prove a fertile source of quarrels and litigation.

However uncourteous or unkind the conduct of Pierson towards Post, in this instance, may have been, yet his act was productive of no injury or damage for which a legal remedy can be applied. We are of opinion the judgment below was erroneous, and ought to be reversed.

LIVINGSTONE, J. My opinion differs from that of the court. Of six exceptions, taken to the proceedings below, all are abandoned except the third, which reduces the controversy to a single question.

Whether a person who, with his own hounds, starts and hunts a fox on waste and uninhabited ground, and is on the point of seizing his prey, acquires such an interest in the animal, as to have a right of action against another, who in view of the huntsman and his dogs in full pursuit, and with knowledge of the chase, shall kill and carry him away?

This is a knotty point, and should have been submitted to the arbitration of sportsmen, without poring over Justinian, Fleta, Bracton, Puffendorf, Locke, Barbeyrac, or Blackstone, all of whom have been cited: they would have had no difficulty in coming to a prompt and correct conclusion. In a court thus constituted, the skin and carcass of poor *reynard* would have been properly disposed of, and a precedent set, interfering with no usage or custom which the experience of ages has sanctioned, and which must be so well known to every votary of Diana. But the parties have referred the question to our judgment, and we must dispose of it as well as we can, from the partial lights we possess, leaving to a higher tribunal, the correction of any mistake which we may be so unfortunate as to make. By the pleadings it is admitted that a fox is a "wild and noxious beast". Both parties have regarded him, as the law of nations does a pirate, "*hostem humani generis*," and although "*de mortuis nil nisi bonum,* " be a maxim of our profession, the memory of the deceased has not been spared. His depredations on farmers and on barn yards have not been forgotten; and to put him to death wherever found, is allowed to be meritorious, and of public benefit. Hence it follows, that our decision should have in view the greatest possible encouragement to the destruction of an animal, so cunning and ruthless in his career. But who would keep a pack of hounds; or what gentleman, at the sound of the horn, and at peep of day, would mount his steed, and for hours together, "*sub jove frigido*," or a vertical sun, pursue the windings of this wily quadruped, if, just as night came on, and his stratagems and strength were nearly exhausted, a saucy intruder, who had not shared in the honours or labours of the chase, were permitted to come in at the death, and bear away in triumph the object of pursuit? Whatever Justinian may have thought of the matter, it must be recollected that his code was compiled many hundred years ago, and it would be very hard indeed, at the distance of so many centuries, not to have a right to establish a rule for ourselves. In his day, we read of no order of men who made it a business, in the language of the declaration in this cause, "with hounds and dogs to find, start, pursue, hunt, and chase," these animals, and that, too, without any other motive that the preservation of Roman poultry; if this diversion had been then in fashion, the lawyers who composed his institutes, would have taken care not to pass it by, without suitable encouragement. If any thing, therefore, in the digests or pandects shall appear to militate against the defendant in error, who, on this occasion, was the foxhunter, we have only to say *tempora mutantur*; and if men themselves change with the times, why should not laws also undergo an alteration?

It may be expected, however, by the learned counsel, that more particular notice be taken of their authorities. I have examined them all, and feel great difficulty in determining, whether to acquire dominion over a thing, before in common, it be sufficient that we barely see it, or know where it is, or wish for it, or make a declaration of our will respecting it; or whether, in the case of wild beasts, setting a trap, or lying in wait, or starting, or pursuing, be enough; or if an actual wounding, or killing, or bodily tact and occupation be necessary. Writers on general law, who have favoured us with their speculations on these points, differ on them all; but, great as is the diversity of sentiment among them, some conclusion must be adopted on the question immediately before us. After mature deliberation, I embrace that of Barbeyrac, as the most rational, and least liable to objection. If at liberty, we might imitate the courtesy of a certain emperor, who, to avoid giving offence to the advocates of any of these different doctrines, adopted a middle course, and by ingenious distinctions, rendered it difficult to say (as often happens after a fierce and angry contest) to whom the palm of victory belonged. He ordained, that if a beast be followed with *large dogs and hounds*, he shall belong to the hunter, not to the chance occupant; and in like manner, if he be killed or wounded with a lance or sword; but if chased with *beagles only*, then he passed to the captor, not to the first pursuer. If slain with a dart, a sling, or a bow, he fell to the hunter, if still in chase, and not to him who might afterwards find and seize him.

Now, as we are without any municipal regulations of our own, and the pursuit here, for aught that appears on the case, being with dogs and hounds of *imperial stature*, we are at liberty to adopt one of the provisions just cited, which comports also with the learned conclusion of Barbeyrac, that property in animals *feræ naturæ* may be acquired without bodily touch or manucaption, provided the pursuer be within reach, or have *reasonable* prospect (which certainly existed here) of taking, what he has *thus* discovered an intention of converting to his own use.

When we reflect also that the interest of our husbandmen, the most useful of men in any community, will be advanced by the destruction of a beast so pernicious and incorrigible, we cannot greatly err, in saying, that a pursuit like the present, through waste and unoccupied lands, and which must inevitably and speedily have terminated in corporal possession, or bodily *seisin*, confers such a right to the object of it, as to make any one a wrongdoer, who shall interfere and shoulder the spoil. The justice's judgment ought, therefore, in my opinion, to be affirmed.

Judgment of reversal.

Notes and Questions

1. How would you characterize the style of reasoning of the majority judges as compared with that of Judge Livingstone?

2. The majority seem to have been concerned with certainty and peace and order. Does the majority judgment advance those goals? And what are the benefits and disadvantages of certainty rules with respect to land and personal property?

3. Assume X has netted some rainbow trout in a Taupo tributary. He transports them (alive) to Taumarunui and puts them into a wire enclosure he has built in a stream on his farm. Y opens the door and lets them escape into the stream. What is the result? Does it matter whether the netting was illegal or not?

4. An example of the capture rule working at its most extreme — the so called 'walls of death' or driftnetting, as practised by some countries is found in the Pacific. Each driftnet is a free-floating plastic net of up to sixty-four kilometres long and fifteen feet deep. This leads to overcapture. New Zealand scientists say the South Pacific albacore tuna will be wiped out in 2-5 years. One 175 vessel fleet in the North Pacific killed more than 14,000 porpoises and 750,000 sea-birds in one season. In Micronesia one dolphin was killed for every nine tuna caught. What does this suggest to you about the rule as formulated by the majority? And about the nature of legal inquiries in general?

5. The occupancy theory has come under attack from anthropologists as a description of the origin of property. See Lowie, Incorporeal Property in Primitive Society (1928) 37 Yale LJ 551. Whatever the historical or anthropological origins of private property, does it provide an adequate theory in today's more complex world? See M Cohen, *Law and the Social Order* (1933) 49-51.

6. How far is the notion of occupancy a moral basis which is reflected in the law's apparent willingness to protect possession?

7. The question of 'occupancy' has also engaged the attention of novelists. In *Moby Dick* a whale is harpooned but then gets away. It is wounded by the first harpooning. This may or may not slow it down. It is harpooned again by a second crew, who claim it as their own. Whose whale is it?

8. Some writers continue to defend first occupancy as a justification for property rights. See Epstein, Possession as the Real Root of Title (1979) 13 Georgia L Rev 1221. See also Rose, Possession as the Origin of Property (1985) 52 U Chi L Rev 73.

9. It is easy today to forget how critically important rights to game and wild animals were in earlier ages. Indeed for centuries these were a matter of fundamental social and legal importance. Jerome Hall notes that in Anglo-Saxon times,

> cattle were by far the most important of the possessions. Horses and oxen were the means of transportation and communication. Horses were essential for the conduct of war. Oxen drew the ploughs. . . . Food, transportation and communication, war, tillage, all depended, therefore upon these lesser creatures. It is not surprising, then, to find that cattle were used as the common medium of exchange, and that they represented the commodity of greatest value. . . . The paramount importance of movable property, and especially of cattle, as the foundation-image upon which the rules [of theft] were constructed, is apparent. Thus one primary rule was the result of the distinction between *feræ naturæ* and goods in possession (cattle). [*Theft, Law and Society* (2nd ed, 1935) 82].

10. On the English gaming laws and their relationship with the criminal law see Hay, *Albion's Fatal Tree* (1977). See also Lund, Early American Wildlife Law (1976) 51 NYU L Rev 703.

11. In New Zealand the hunting and ownership of certain wild animals is now controlled by statute. See the Wild Animal Control Act 1977. This statute replaced the Noxious Animals Act of 1956. 'Wild animals' means any deer (including wapiti and moose), chamois, thar, wallaby, opossum, pigs 'living in a wild state' (section 2) and goats (see section 20). Under section 9 of the Act, 'all wild animals shall be the property of the Crown.' However the Crown is not liable for damage done by any wild animal. The presence of any wild animal on any land 'confers no right of ownership of the wild animal or its carcass on the owner or occupier of the land' save as is permitted by the Act. Hunting of these animals requires permission in terms of the Act. Liberation of these wild animals is also controlled. The Wildlife Act 1953 (RS Vol 7) has extensive provisions relating to 'wildlife' other than the above animals. Under that Act, 'wildlife' means 'any animal that is living in a wild state' (see section 2). Certain wildlife are declared to be game; some are partially protected, and some are fully protected. Provision is made for wildlife sanctuaries, refuges and management reserves. The Act also regulates Acclimatisation Societies. 'Possession' in section 2A is defined as follows:

> any animal or thing shall be in the possession of any person when that person has, alone or jointly or in association with any other person, possession of or control over the animal or thing, or possession of or control over any vessel, vehicle, container, package, or place in or on which the animal or thing is.

At the time of writing the Minister of Conservation has announced that there is to be a review of this legislation.

Labour Theory

The occupancy theory reflects patterns of thought which are both primitive and medieval. The seventeenth and eighteenth centuries witnessed a prolonged period of struggle between a feudal conception of society and the emergence of a capitalistic society marked more closely by individual rights. Fundamental changes took place in the way men thought about property. The word 'men' is used deliberately. This reconsideration was made by men and I am not aware of contemporary published works by women on the subject.

One scholar of this period noted:

> Born with a body, it is in the natural order of things that a man should have property rights over it; to deny him these would make him a slave. From this fundamental premise the social philosophers of the eighteenth century Enlightenment argued the case for the recognition of private property as existing by natural right. Their thoughts were variations on earlier themes, running back to the schoolmen of Christendom and beyond to the thinkers of the ancient classical world.
>
> The changes of the eighteenth century were a bridge between the capitalism of the modern Western world and the field and fief economies of the past. Men were seeking pathways to freedom from religious intolerance and from the suzerainty of landed wealth. To contemporaries of every age the world appears new; and to the men of the eighteenth century especially, novelty and change came apace. The age of science was following the age of reason; political and religious emancipation were in the air; the foreshadowing of inventions and industrial development alerted the curious; and the cry of the dispossessed disturbed the land. The issues of the day, the right place of property not least amongst them, were faced and discussed. We who live in a world far more cramped and congested than the expansive habitat of the eighteenth century and the wider laterals of earlier ages are paradoxical, for with us the place of property is not a central and serious theme of debate, but rather the subject of unreflective assumptions. [Denman, *The Place of Property* (1978) 1].

The most influential thinker of this new persuasion was John Locke. See Merino, *Natural Justice and Private Property* (1922) 27-31.

Two Treatises on Civil Government

John Locke
Book II, Paras 25-51 (1690)

* * * I shall endeavour to show how men might come to have a property in several parts of that which God gave to mankind in common, and that without any express compact of all the commoners. * * *

27. Though the earth and all inferior creatures be common to all men, yet every man has a "property" in his own "person." This nobody has any right to but himself. The "labour" of his body and the "work" of his hands, we may say,

are properly his. Whatsoever, then, he removes out of the state that Nature hath provided and left it in, he hath mixed his labour with it, and joined to it something that is his own, and thereby makes it his property. It being by him removed from the common state Nature placed it in, it hath by this labour something annexed to it that excludes the common right of other men. For this "labour" being the unquestionable property of the labourer, no man but he can have a right to what that is once joined to, at least where there is enough, and as good left in common for others.

28. He that is nourished by the acorns he picked up under an oak, or the apples he gathered from the trees in the wood, has certainly appropriated them to himself. Nobody can deny but the nourishment is his. I ask, then, when did they begin to be his? when he digested? or when he ate? or when he boiled? or when he brought them home? or when he picked them up? And it is plain, if the first gathering made them not his, nothing else could. That labour put a distinction between them and common. That added something to them more than Nature, the common mother of all, had done, and so they became his private right. And will any one say he had no right to those acorns or apples he thus appropriated because he had not the consent of all mankind to make them his? Was it a robbery thus to assume to himself what belonged to all in common? If such a consent as that was necessary, man had starved, notwithstanding the plenty God had given him. We see in commons, which remain so by compact, that it is the taking any part of what is common, and removing it out of the state Nature leaves it in, which begins the property, without which the common is of no use. And the taking of this or that part does not depend on the express consent of all the commoners. Thus, the grass my horse has bit, the turfs my servant has cut, and the ore I have digged in any place, where I have a right to them in common with others, become my property without the assignation or consent of anybody. The labour that was mine, removing them out of that common state they were in, hath fixed my property in them. * * *

30. Thus this law of reason makes the deer that Indian's who hath killed it; it is allowed to be his goods who hath bestowed his labour upon it, though, before, it was the common right of every one. . . . And even amongst us, the hare that any one is hunting is thought his who pursues her during the chase. For being a beast that is still looked upon as common, and no man's private possession, whoever has employed so much labour about any of that kind as to find and pursue her has thereby removed her from the state of Nature wherein she was common, and hath began a property.

31. It will, perhaps, be objected to this, that if gathering the acorns or other fruits of the earth, &c., makes a right to them, then any one may engross as much as he will. To which I answer, Not so. The same law of Nature that does by this means give us property, does also bound that property too. "God has given us all things richly" (1 Tim. vi 12). Is the voice of reason confirmed by inspiration? But how far has He given it us—"to enjoy?" As much as any one can make use of to any advantage of life before it spoils, so much he may by his labour fix a property in. Whatever is beyond this is more than his share, and belongs to others. Nothing was made by God for man to spoil or destroy. And thus considering the plenty of natural provisions there was a long time in the world, and the few

splendours and to how small a part of that provision the industry of one man could extend itself and engross it to the prejudice of others, especially keeping within the bounds set by reason of what might serve for his use, there could be then little room for quarrels or contentions about property so established.

32. But the chief matter of property being now not the fruits of the earth and the beasts that subsist on it, but the earth itself, as that which takes in and carries with it all the rest; I think it is plain that property in that too is acquired as the former. As much land as a man tills, plants, improves, cultivates, and can use the product of, so much is his property. He by his labour does, as it were, enclose it from the common. ***

33. Nor was this appropriation of any parcel of land, by improving it, any prejudice to any other man, since there was still enough and as good left, and more than the yet unprovided could use. So that, in effect, there was never the less left for others because of his enclosure for himself. ***

34. God gave the world to men in common, but since He gave it them for their benefit and the greatest conveniences of life they were capable to draw from it, it cannot be supposed he meant it should always remain common and uncultivated. He gave it to the use of the industrious and rational (and labour was to be his title to it); not to the fancy or covetousness of the quarrelsome and contentious. He that had as good left for his improvement as was already taken up needed not complain, ought not to meddle with what was already improved by another's labour; if he did it is plain he desired the benefit of another's pains, which he had no right to, and not the ground which God had given him, in common with others, to labour on, and whereof there was as good left as that already possessed; and more than he knew what to do with, or his industry could reach to.

35. It is true, in land that is common in England or any other country, where there are plenty of people under government who have money and commerce, no one can enclose or appropriate any part without the consent of all his fellow-commoners; because this is left common by compact—*i.e.*, by the law of the land, which is not to be violated. And, though it be common in respect of some men, it is not so to all mankind, but is the joint propriety of this country, or this parish. Besides, the remainder, after such enclosure, would not be as good to the rest of the commoners as the whole was, when they could all make use of the whole; whereas in the beginning and first peopling of the great common of the world it was quite otherwise. The law man was under was rather for appropriating. God commanded, and his wants forced him to labour. That was his property, which could not be taken from him wherever he had fixed it. And hence subduing or cultivating the earth and having dominion, we see, are joined together. The one gave title to the other. So that God, by commanding to subdue, gave authority so far to appropriate. And the condition of human life, which requires labour and materials to work on, necessarily introduce private possessions.

36. The measure of property Nature, well set, by the extent of men's labour and the conveniency of life. No man's labour could subdue or appropriate all, nor could his enjoyment consume more than a small part; so that it was impossible for any man, this way, to entrench upon the right of another or acquire to himself a property, to the prejudice of his neighbour, who would still have room for as

good and as large a possession (after the other had taken out his) as before it was appropriated. * * * [T]he same rule of propriety—viz., that every man should have as much as he could make use of, would hold still in the world, without straitening anybody, since there is land enough in the world to suffice double the inhabitants, had not the invention of money, and the tacit agreement of men to put a value on it, introduced (by consent) larger possessions and a right to them; which, how it has done, I shall by-and-by show more at large.

37. This is certain, that in the beginning, before the desire of having more than men needed had altered the intrinsic value of things, which depends only on their usefulness to the life of man, or had agreed that a little piece of yellow metal, which would keep without wasting or decay, should be worth a great piece of flesh or a whole heap of corn, though men had a right to appropriate by their labour, each one to himself, as much of the things of Nature as he could use, yet this could not be much, nor to the prejudice of others, where the same plenty was still left, to those who would use the same industry.

Before the appropriation of land, he who gathered as much of the wild fruit, killed, caught, or tamed as many of the beasts as he could—he that so employed his pains about any of the spontaneous products of Nature as any way to alter them from the state nature put them in, by placing any of his labour on them, did thereby acquire a propriety in them; but if they perished in his possession without their due use—if the fruits rotted or the venison putrefied before he could spend it, he offended against the common law of Nature, and was liable to be punished: he invaded his neighbour's share, for he had no right farther than his use called for any of them, and they might serve to afford him conveniences of life.

38. The same measures governed the possession of land, too. Whatsoever he tilled and reaped, laid up and made use of before it spoiled, that was his peculiar right; whatsoever he enclosed, and could feed and make use of, the cattle and product was also his. But if either the grass or his enclosure rotted on the ground, or the fruit of his planting perished without gathering and laying up, this part of the earth, notwithstanding his enclosure, was still to be looked on as waste, and might be the possession of any other. * * *

39. And thus, without supposing any private dominion and property in Adam over all the world, exclusive of all other men, which can no way be proved, nor any one's property be made out from it, but supposing the world, given as it was to the children of men in common, we see how labour could make men distinct titles to several parcels of it for their private uses, wherein there could be no doubt of right, no room for quarrel.

40. Nor is it so strange as, perhaps before consideration, it may appear, that the property of labour should be able to overbalance the community of land, for it is labour indeed that puts the difference of value on everything. * * * I think it will be but a very modest computation to say, that of the products of the earth useful to the life of man, nine-tenths are the effects of labour. Nay, if we will rightly estimate things as they come to our use, and cast up the several expenses about them—what in them is purely owing to nature and what to labour—we shall find that in most of them ninety-nine hundredths are wholly to be put on the account of labour.

41. There cannot be a clearer demonstration of anything than several nations

of the Americans are of this, who are rich in land and poor in all the comforts of life; whom Nature, having furnished as liberally as any other people with the materials of plenty—*i.e.*, a fruitful soil, apt to produce in abundance what might serve for food, raiment, and delight; yet, for want of improving it by labour, have not one hundredth part of the conveniences we enjoy, and a king of a large and fruitful territory there feeds, lodges, and is clad worse than a day labourer in England. * * *

45. Thus labour, in the beginning, gave a right of property, wherever any one was pleased to employ it, upon what was common, which remained a long while, the far greater part, contented themselves with what unassisted Nature offered to their necessities; and though afterwards, in some parts of the world, where the increase of people and stock, with the use of money, had made land scarce, and so of some value, the several communities settled the bounds of their distinct territories, and by laws, within themselves, regulated the properties of the private men of their society, and so, by compact and agreement, settled the property which labour and industry began. And the leagues that have been made between several states and kingdoms, either expressly or tacitly disowning all claim and right to the land in the other's possession, have, by common consent, given up their pretences to their natural common right, which originally they had to those countries; and so have, by positive agreement, settled a property amongst themselves, in distinct parts of the world; yet there are still great tracts of ground to be found, which the inhabitants thereof, not having joined with the rest of mankind in the consent of the use of their common money, lie waste, and are more than the people who dwell on it, do, or can make use of, and so still lie in common; though this can scarce happen amongst that part of mankind that have consented to the use of money.

46. The greatest part of things really useful to the life of man, and such as the necessity of subsisting made the first commoners of the world look after—as it doth the Americans now—are generally things of short duration, such as—if they are not consumed by use—will decay and perish of themselves. Gold, silver, and diamonds are things that fancy or agreement hath put the value on, more than real use and the necessary support of life. Now of those good things which Nature hath provided in common, every one hath a right (as hath been said) to as much as he could use, and had a property in all he could effect with his labour; all that his industry could extend to, to alter from the state Nature had put it in, was his. He that gathered a hundred bushels of acorns or apples had thereby a property in them; they were his goods as soon as gathered. He was only to look that he used them before they spoiled, else he took more than his share, and robbed others. And, indeed, it was a foolish thing, as well as dishonest, to hoard up more than he could make use of. If he gave away a part to anybody else, so that it perished not uselessly in his possession, these he also made use of. And if he also bartered away plums that would have rotted in a week, for nuts that would last good for his eating a whole year, he did no injury; he wasted not the common stock; destroyed no part of the portion of goods that belonged to others, so long as nothing perished uselessly in his hands. Again, if he would give his nuts for a piece of metal, pleased with its colour, or exchange his sheep for shells, or wool for a sparkling pebble or a diamond, and keep those by him all his life, he invaded

not the right of others; he might heap up as much of these durable things as he pleased; the exceeding of the bounds of his just property not lying in the largeness of his possession, but the perishing of anything uselessly in it.

47. And thus came in the use of money; some lasting thing that men might keep without spoiling, and that, by mutual consent, men would take in exchange for the truly useful but perishable supports of life.

48. And as different degrees of industry were apt to give men possessions in different proportions, so this invention of money gave them the opportunity to continue and enlarge them. * * * Where there is not something both lasting and scarce, and so valuable to be hoarded up, there men will not be apt to enlarge their possessions of land, were it never so rich, never so free for them to take. For I ask, what would a man value ten thousand or an hundred thousand acres of excellent land, ready cultivated and well stocked, too, with cattle, in the middle of the inland parts of America, where he had no hopes of commerce with other parts of the world, to draw money to him by the sale of the product? It would not be worth the enclosing, and we should see him give up again to the wild common of Nature whatever was more than would supply the conveniences of life, to be had there for him and his family.

49. Thus, in the beginning, all the world was America, and more so than that is now; for no such thing as money was anywhere known. Find out something that hath the use and value of money amongst his neighbours, you shall see the same man will begin presently to enlarge his possessions.

50. But since gold and silver, being little useful to the life of man, in proportion to food, raiment, and carriage, has its value only from the consent of men—whereof labour yet makes in great part the measure—it is plain that the consent of men have agreed to a disproportionate and unequal possession of the earth—I mean out of the bounds of society and compact; for in governments the laws regulate it; they having, by consent, found out and agreed in a way how a man may, rightfully and without injury, possess more than he himself can make use of by receiving gold and silver, which may continue long in a man's possession without decaying for the overplus, and agreeing those metals should have a value.

51. And thus, I think, it is very easy to conceive, without any difficulty, how labour could at first begin a title of property in the common things of Nature, and how the spending it upon our uses bounded it; so that there could then be no reason of quarrelling about title, nor any doubt about the largeness of possession it gave. Right and conveniency went together. For as a man had a right to all he could employ his labour upon, so he had no temptation to labour for more than he could make use of. This left no room for controversy about the title, nor for encroachment on the right of others. What portion a man carved to himself was easily seen; and it was useless, as well as dishonest, to carve himself too much, or take more than he needed.

Notes

1. Locke's labour theory became the basis of the classic liberal theory of property which is still espoused by many persons today. It shows itself in arguments about intellectual property rights and in arguments by proponents of doctrines of unfair

competition or reaping what one has not sown. A person who has created something through his or her own wit, intelligence or labour will routinely, in the western tradition, argue 'it is mine' on this account alone. The theory attracts the support of entrepreneurs and 'rugged individualists'. The strongest attacks on Lockean theory have come from those who believe that social obligations should be imposed by government in the name of some 'greater' social good. See Hamilton, Property — According to Locke (1932) 41 Yale LJ 864. See also MacPherson, *The Political Theory of Possessive Individualism* (1962) 214-15.

2. For an interesting attempt to square both occupancy theory with labour theory see the judgment of Yates, J in *Millar v Taylor*, (1796) 4 Burr. 2303; 98 ER 201. See also Hammond, *The Law and Ideas* (Legal Research Foundation, 1989).

3. Tully, *A Discourse on Property: John Locke and His Adversaries* (1980) gives a full account of the historical origins of Locke's theory and emphasizes its natural law foundations. See also Nozick, *Anarchy, State and Utopia* (1974) 174-78.

Utilitarianism

By the nineteenth century the tension between the individual and the growing activities of the state was well apparent. The notion that the state itself conferred property rights and could perform 'adjustments' in the name of the 'best interests of all' was taking hold. Moreover,

> by the late eighteenth century property was increasingly becoming subsumed to contract, that is . . . taking on the qualities and functions of capital; and . . . this function reinforced rather than negated the flexible 'instrumental' character of property as an institution. [Property thereby] facilitated the complex holding, use or rights in property in an even more subtle form than hitherto. [Rubin & Sugarman, *Law Economy and Society* (1984) 42.]

The principal English utilitarian was Jeremy Bentham. Extracts from his best known work follow.

Principles of the Civil Code

Jeremy Bentham
Chapters 7-12 (first published in French in 1802, and in English in 1830).

Chapter VII: Of Security

We come now to the principle object of law, — the care of security. That inestimable good, the distinctive index of civilization, is entirely the work of law. Without law there is no security; and, consequently, no abundance, and not even a certainty of subsistence; and the only equality which can exist in such a state of things is an equality of misery.

To form a just idea of the benefits of law, it is only necessary to consider the condition of savages. They strive incessantly against famine; which sometimes cuts off entire tribes. Rivalry for subsistence produces among them the most cruel wars;

and, like beasts of prey, men pursue men, as a means of sustenance. The fear of this terrible calamity silences the softer sentiments of nature; pity unites with insensibility in putting to death the old men who can hunt no longer.

Let us now examine what passes at those terrible epochs when civilized society returns almost to the savage state; that is, during war, when the laws on which security depends are in part suspended. Every instant of its duration is fertile in calamities; at every step which it prints upon the earth, at every movement which it makes, the existing mass of riches, the fund of abundance and of subsistence, decreases and disappears. The cottage is ravaged as well as the palace; and how often the rage, the caprice even of a moment, delivers up to destruction the slow produce of the labours of an age!

Law alone has done that which all the natural sentiments united have not the power to do. Law alone is able to create a fixed and durable possession which merits the name of property. Law alone can accustom men to bow their heads under the yoke of foresight, hard at first to bear, but afterwards light and agreeable. Nothing but law can encourage men to labours superfluous for the present, and which can be enjoyed only in the future. Economy has as many enemies as there are dissipators—men who wish to enjoy without giving themselves the trouble of producing. Labour is too painful for idleness; it is too slow for impatience. Fraud and injustice secretly conspire to appropriate its fruits. Insolence and audacity think to ravish them by open force. Thus security is assailed on every side—ever threatened, never tranquil, it exists in the midst of alarms. The legislator needs a vigilance always sustained, a power always in action, to defend it against this crowd of indefatigable enemies.

Law does not say to man, *Labour, and I will reward you;* but it says: *Labour, and I will assure to you the enjoyment of the fruits of your labor—that natural and sufficient recompense which without me you cannot preserve; I will insure it by arresting the hand which may seek to ravish it from you.* If industry creates, it is law which preserves; if at the first moment we owe all to labour, at the second moment, and at every other, we are indebted for everything to law.

To form a precise idea of the extent to which ought to be given to the principle of security, we must consider that man is not like the animals, limited to the present, whether as respects suffering or enjoyment; but that he is susceptible of pains and pleasures by anticipation; and that it is not enough to secure him from actual loss, but it is necessary also to guarantee him, as far as possible, against future loss. It is necessary to prolong the idea of his security through all the perspective which his imagination is capable of measuring.

This presentiment, which has so marked an influence upon the fate of man, is called *expectation*. It is hence that we have the power of forming a general plan of conduct; it is hence that the successive instants which compose the duration of life are not like isolated and independent points, but become continuous parts of a whole. *Expectation* is a chain which unites our present existence to our future existence, and which passes beyond us to the generation which is to follow. The sensibility of man extends through all the links of this chain.

The principle of security extends to the maintenance of all these expectations; it requires that events, so far as they depend upon laws, should conform to the expectations which law itself has created.

Every attack upon this sentiment produces a distinct and special evil, which may be called a *pain of disappointment*.

It is a proof of great confusion in the ideas of lawyers, that they have never given any particular attention to a sentiment which exercises so powerful an influence upon human life. The word *expectation* is scarcely found in their vocabulary. Scarce a single argument founded upon that principle appears in their writings. They have followed it, without doubt, in many respects; but they have followed it by instinct rather than by reason. If they had known its extreme importance they would not have failed to *name* it and to mark it, instead of leaving it unnoticed in the crowd.

Chapter VIII: Of Property

The better to understand the advantages of law, let us endeavour to form a clear idea of *property*. We shall see that there is no such thing as natural property, and that it is entirely the work of law.

Property is nothing but a basis of expectation; the expectation of deriving certain advantages from a thing which we are said to possess, in consequence of the relation in which we stand towards it.

There is no image, no painting, no visible trait, which can express the relation that constitutes property. It is not material, is is metaphysical; it is a mere conception of the mind.

To have a thing in our hands, to keep it, to make it, to sell it, to work it up into something else, to use it—none of these physical circumstances, nor all united, convey the idea of property. A piece of stuff which is actually in the Indies may belong to me, while the dress I wear may not. The aliment which is incorporated into my very body may belong to another, to whom I am bound to account for it.

The idea of property consists in an established expectation; in the persuasion of being able to draw such or such an advantage from the thing possessed, according to the nature of the case. Now this expectation, this persuasion, can only be the work of law. I cannot count upon the enjoyment of that which I regard as mine, except through the promise of the law which guarantees it to me. It is law alone which permits me to forget my natural weakness. It is only through the protection of law that I am able to inclose a field, and to give myself up to its cultivation with the sure though distant hope of harvest.

But it may be asked, What is it that serves as a basis to law, upon which to begin operations, when it adopts objects which, under the name of property, it promises to protect? Have not men, in the primitive state, a *natural* expectation of enjoying certain things—an expectation drawn from sources anterior to law?

Yes. There have been from the beginning, and there always will be, circumstances in which a man may secure himself, by his own means, in the enjoyment of certain things. But the catalogue of these cases is very limited. The savage who has killed a deer may hope to keep it for himself, so long as his cave is undiscovered; so long as he watches to defend it, and is stronger than his rivals; but that is all. How miserable and precarious is such a possession! If we suppose the least agreement among savages to respect the acquisitions of each other, we see the introduction of a principle to which no name can be given but that of law. A feeble and momentary expectation may result from time to time from circumstances purely physical; but a strong and permanent expectation can result only from law. That which, in the natural state, was an almost invisible thread, in the social state becomes a cable.

Property and law are born together, and die together. Before laws were made there was no property; take away laws, and property ceases.

As regards property, security consists in receiving no check, no shock, no derangement to the expectation founded on the laws, of enjoying such and such a portion of good. The legislator owes the greatest respect to this expectation which he has himself produced. When he does not contradict it, he does what is essential to the happiness of society; when he disturbs it, he always produces a proportionate sum of evil.

Chapter IX: Answer to an Objection

But perhaps the laws of property are good for those who have property, and oppressive to those who have none. The poor man, perhaps, is more miserable than he would be without laws.

The laws, in creating property, have created riches only in relation to poverty. Poverty is not the work of the laws; it is the primitive condition of the human race. The man who subsists only from day to day is precisely the man of nature—the savage. The poor man, in civilized society, obtains nothing, I admit, except by painful labour; but, in the natural state, can he obtain anything except by the sweat of his brow? Has not the chase its fatigues, fishing its dangers, and war its uncertainties? And if man seems to love this adventurous life; if he has an instinct warm for this kind of perils; if the savage enjoys with delight an idleness so dearly bought;—must we thence conclude that he is happier than our cultivators? No. Their labour is more uniform, but their reward is more sure; the woman's lot is far more agreeable; childhood and old age have more resources; the species multiplies in a proportion a thousand times greater,—and that alone suffices to show on which side is the superiority of happiness. Thus the laws, in creating riches, are the benefactors of those who remain in the poverty of nature. All participate more or less in the pleasures, the advantages, and the resources of civilized society. The industry and the labour of the poor place them among the candidates of fortune. And have they not the pleasures of acquisition? Does not hope mix with their labours? Is the security which the law gives of no importance to them? Those who look down from above upon the inferior ranks see all objects smaller; but towards the base of the pyramid it is the summit which in turn is lost. Comparisons are never dreamed of; the wish of what seems impossible does not torment. So that, in fact, all things considered, the protection of the laws may contribute as much to the happiness of the cottage as to the security of the palace.

It is astonishing that a writer so judicious as Beccaria has interposed, in a work dictated by the soundest philosophy, a doubt subversive of social order. *The right of property*, he says, *is a terrible right, which perhaps is not necessary.* Tyrannical and sanguinary laws have been founded upon that right; it has been frightfully abused; but the right itself presents only ideas of pleasure, abundance, and security. It is that right which has vanquished the natural aversion to labour; which has given to man the empire of the earth; which has brought to an end the migratory life of nations; which has produced the love of country and a regard for posterity. Men universally desire to enjoy speedily — to enjoy without labour. It is that desire which is terrible; since it arms all who have not against all who have. The law which restrains that desire is the noblest triumph of humanity over itself.

Chapter X: Analysis of the Evils which Result from Attacks upon Property

We have already seen that subsistence depends upon the laws which assure to the labourer the produce of his labour. But it is desirable more exactly to analyze the evils which result from violations of property. They may be reduced for four heads.

1st. *Evil of Non-Possession.* — If the acquisition of a portion of wealth is a good, it follows that the non-possession of it is an evil, though only a negative evil. Thus, although men in the condition of primitive poverty may not have specially felt the want of a good which they knew not, yet it is clear that they have lost all the happiness which might have resulted from its possession, and of which we have the enjoyment. The loss of a portion of good, though we knew nothing of it, is still a loss. Are you doing me no harm when, by false representations, you deter my friend from conferring upon me a favour which I did not expect? In what consists the harm? In the negative evil which results from not possessing that which, but for your falsehoods, I should have had.

2nd. *Pain of Losing.* — Everything which I possess, or to which I have a title, I consider in my own mind as destined always to belong to me. I make it the basis of my expectations, and of the hopes of those dependent upon me: and I form my plan of life accordingly. Every part of my property may have, in my estimation, besides its intrinsic value, a value of affection — as an inheritance from my ancestors, as the reward of my own labour, or as the future dependence of my children. Everything about it represents to my eye that part of myself which I have put into it — those cares, that industry, that economy which denied itself present pleasures to make provision for the future. Thus our property becomes a part of our being, and cannot be torn from us without rendering us to the quick.

3rd. *Fear of Losing.* — To regret for what we have lost is joined inquietude as to what we possess, and even as to what we may acquire. For the greater part of the object which compose subsistence and abundance being perishable matters, future acquisitions are a necessary supplement to present possessions. When insecurity reaches a certain point, the fear of losing prevents us from enjoying what we possess already. The care of preserving condemns us to a thousand sad and painful precautions, which yet are always liable to fail of their end. Treasures are hidden or conveyed away. Enjoyment becomes sombre, furtive, and solitary. It fears to show itself, lest cupidity should be informed of a chance to plunder.

4th. *Deadening of Industry.* — When I despair of making myself sure of the produce of my labour, I only seek to exist from day to day. I am unwilling to give myself cares which will only be profitable to my enemies. Besides, the will to labour is not enough; means are wanting. While waiting to reap, in the meantime I must live. A single loss may deprive me of the capacity of action, without having quenched the spirit of industry, or without having paralyzed my will. Thus the three first evils affect the passive faculties of the individual, while the fourth extends to his active faculties, and more or less benumbs them.

It appears from this analysis that the two first evils do not go beyond the individual injured; while the two latter spread through society, and occupy an indefinite space. An attack upon the property of an individual excites alarm among other proprietors. This sentiment spreads from neighbour to neighbour, till at last the contagion possesses the entire body of the state.＊ ＊ ＊

Chapter XI: Opposition Between Security and Equality

In consulting the grand principle of security, what ought the legislator to decree respecting the mass of property already existing?

He ought to maintain the distribution as it is actually established. It is this which, under the name of *justice*, is regarded as his first duty. This is a general and simple rule, which applies itself to all states; and which adapts itself to all places, even those of the most opposite character. There is nothing more different than the state of property in America, in England, in Hungary, and in Russia. Generally, in the first of these countries, the cultivator is a proprietor; in the second, a tenant; in the third, attached to the glebe; in the fourth, a slave. However, the supreme principle of security commands the preservation of all these distributions, though their nature is so different, and though they do not produce the same sum of happiness.How make another distribution without taking away from each that which he has? And how despoil any without attacking the security of all? When your new repartition is disarranged—that is to say, the day after its establishment— how avoid making a second? Why not correct it in the same way? And in the meantime, what becomes of security? Where is happiness? Where is industry?

When security and equality are in conflict, it will not do to hesitate a moment. Equality must yield. The first is the foundation of life; subsistence, abundance, happiness, everything depends upon it. Equality produces only a certain portion of good. Besides, whatever we may do, it will never be perfect; it may exist a day; but the revolutions of the morrow will overturn it. The establishment of perfect equality is a chimera; all we can do is to diminish inequality.

If violent causes, such as a revolution of government, a division, or a conquest, should bring about an overturn of property, it would be a great calamity; but it would be transitory; it would diminish; it would repair itself in time. Industry is a vigorous plant which resists many amputations, and through which a nutritious sap begins to circulate with the first rays of returning summer. But if property should be overturned with the direct intention of establishing an equality of possessions,the evil would be irreparable. No more security, no more industry, no more abundance! Society would return to the savage state whence it emerged. ＊ ＊ ＊

Chapter XII: Means of Uniting Security and Equality

Is it necessary that between these two rivals, *Security* and *Equality*, there should be an opposition, an eternal war? To a certain point they are incompatible; but with a little patience and address they may, in a great measure, be reconciled.

The only mediator between these contrary interests is time. Do you wish to follow the counsels of equality without contravening those of security?—await the natural epoch which puts an end to hopes and fears, the epoch of death.

When property by the death of the proprietor ceases to have an owner, the law can interfere in its distribution, either by limiting in certain respects the testamentary power, in order to prevent too great an accumulation of wealth in the hands of an individual; or by regulating the succession in favour of equality in cases where the deceased has left no consort, nor relation in the direct line, and has made no will. The question then relates to new acquirers who have formed no expectations; and equality may do what is best for all without disappointing any. At present I only indicate the principle: the development of it may be seen in the second book.

When the question is to correct a kind of civil inequality, such as slavery, it is necessary to pay the same attention to the right of property; to submit it to a slow operation, and to advance towards the subordinate object without sacrificing the principal object. Men who are rendered free by these gradations, will be much more capable of being so than if you had taught them to tread justice under foot, for the sake of introducing a new social order. ∗ ∗ ∗

Notes and Questions

1. Bentham's successor was John Stuart Mill. He argued, along utilitarian lines, that social institutions should be assessed by the degree to which they could be expected to contribute to public happiness or well-being. And, in his *Principles of Political Economy* (1848) he defended an extensive system of private property. For instance, he strongly advocated the rights to own land and inherit property but he was amongst the early writers to insist that when, for some reason or other, the state appropriates property, it must pay compensation.

2. Present day law and economics analysis emphasizes economic efficiency as the most appropriate vehicle for distribution of property rights. See Posner, *Economic Analysis of Law* (2nd ed, 1977) 34-9, suggesting three criteria for an 'efficient system of property rights': universality, exclusivity and transferability. Demsetz, Toward a Theory of Property Rights 57 Am. Econ Rev 347-357 (Pap & Proc 1967), begins a classic article with the sentence, 'In the world of Robinson Crusoe property rights play no role.' What do you make of that statement? What are its implications?

3. In the same article Demsetz also discusses the concept of 'externalities', which is central to present day law and economics analysis.

> Externalities exist whenever some person, say X, makes a decision about how to use resources without taking full account of the full effects of the decision. X ignores some of the effects — some of the costs or benefits that would result from a particular activity, for example — because they fall on others. They are "external" to X, hence the label *externalities*. As a consequence of externalities, resources tend to be "misallocated", which is to say used in one way when another way would make society as a whole better off. [Dukeminier & Krier, *Property* (1981) 53].

Can you think of property transactions which give rise to problems of externalities?

Marxist Approaches to Property

By the nineteenth century, as the effects of industrial capitalism became apparent, strong opposition to the 'received wisdom', to use J. K. Galbraith's phrase, with respect to strong systems of individual property rights began to emerge. By far the strongest opponent of the perceived evils of capitalism was Marx. He was outraged by individuals being reduced to commodities and strongly argued that that reduction was driven by the property relations of capitalism.

Manifesto of the Communist Party

Marx and Engels, 1902.

* * * The theoretical conclusions of the Communists are in no way based on ideas or principles that have been invented, or discovered, by this or that would-be universal reformer.

They merely express, in general terms, actual relations springing from an existing class struggle, from a historical movement going on under our very eyes. The abolition of existing property relations is not at all a distinctive feature of Communism.

All property relations in the past have continually been subject to historical change consequent upon the change in historical conditions.

The French Revolution, for example, abolished feudal property in favor of bourgeois property.

The distinguishing feature of Communism is not the abolition of property generally, but the abolition of bourgeois property. But modern bourgeois private property is the final and most complete expression of the system of producing and appropriating products, that is based on class antagonism, on the exploitation of the many by the few.

In this sense, the theory of the Communists may be summed up in the single sentence: Abolition of private property.

We Communists have been reproached with the desire of abolishing the right of personally acquiring property as the fruit of a man's own labor, which property is alleged to be the ground work of all personal freedom, activity and independence.

Hard-worn, self-acquired, self-earned property! Do you mean the property of the petty artisan and of the small peasant, a form of property that preceded the bourgeois form? There is no need to abolish that; the development of industry has to a great extent already destroyed it, and is still destroying it daily.

Or do you mean modern bourgeois private property?

But does wage-labor create any property for the laborer? Not a bit. It creates capital, i.e., that kind of property which exploits wage-labor, and which cannot increase except upon condition of getting a new supply of wage-labor for fresh exploitation. Property, in its present form, is based on the antagonism of capital and wage-labor. Let us examine both sides of this antagonism.

To be a capitalist, is to have not only a purely personal, but a social status in production. Capital is a collective product, and only by the united action of many members, nay, in the last resort, only by the united action of all members of society, can it be set in motion.

Capital is therefore not a personal, it is a social power.

When, therefore, capital is converted into common property, into the property of all members of society, personal property is not thereby transformed into social property. It is only the social character of the property that is changed. It loses its class-character.

Let us now take wage-labor.

The average price of wage-labor is the minimum wage, i.e., that quantum of the means of subsistence, which is absolutely requisite to keep the laborer in bare existence as a laborer. What, therefore, the wage-laborer appropriates by means of his labor, merely suffices to prolong and reproduce a bare existence. We by no means intend to abolish this personal appropriation of the products of labor, an appropriation that is made for the maintenance and reproduction of human life, and that leaves no surplus where with to command the labor of others. All that we want to do away with is the miserable character of this appropriation, under which the laborer lives merely to increase capital, and is allowed to live only in so far as the interest of the ruling class requires it.

In bourgeois society, living labor is but a means to increase accumulated labor. In Communist society, accumulated labor is but a means to widen, to enrich, to promote the existence of the laborer.

In bourgeois society, therefore, the past dominates the present; in communist society, the present dominates the past. In bourgeois society capital is independent and has individuality, while the living person is dependent and has no individuality.

And the abolition of this state of things is called by the bourgeois, abolition of individuality and freedom! And rightly so. The abolition of bourgeois individuality, bourgeois independence, and bourgeois freedom is undoubtedly aimed at.

By freedom is meant, under the present bourgeois conditions of production, free trade, free selling and buying.

But if selling and buying disappears, free selling and buying disappears also. This talk about free selling and buying, and all the other "brave words" of our bourgeoisie about freedom in general, have a meaning, if any, only in contrast with restricted selling and buying, with the fettered traders of the Middle Ages, but have no meaning when opposed to the Communistic abolition of buying and selling, of the bourgeois conditions of production, and of the bourgeoisie itself.

You are horrified at our intending to do away with private property. But in your existing society, private property is already done away with for nine-tenths of the population; its existence for the few is solely due to its non-existence in the hands of those nine-tenths. You reproach us, therefore, with intending to do away with a form of property, the necessary condition for whose existence is, the non-existence of any property for the immense majority of society.

In one word, you reproach us with intending to do away with your property. Precisely so; that is just what we intend.

From the moment when labor can no longer be converted into capital, money, or rent, into a social power capable of being monopolized, i.e., from the moment when individual property can no longer be transformed into bourgeois property, into capital, from that moment, you say, individuality vanishes.

You must, therefore, confess that by "individual" you mean no other person than the bourgeois, than the middle-class owner of property. This person must, indeed, be swept out of the way, and made impossible.

Communism deprives no man of the power to appropriate the products of society:

all that it does is to deprive him of the power to subjugate the labor of others by means of such appropriation.

It has been objected, that upon the abolition of private property all work will cease, and universal laziness will overtake us.

According to this, bourgeois society ought long ago to have gone to the dogs through sheer idleness; for those of its members who work, acquire nothing, and those who acquire anything, do not work. The whole of this objection is but another expression of the tautology: that there can no longer be any wage-labor when there is no longer any capital.

All objections urged against the Communistic mode of producing and appropriating material products, have, in the same way, been urged against the Communistic modes of producing and appropriating intellectual products. Just as, to the bourgeois, the disappearance of class property is the disappearance of production itself, so the disappearance of class culture is to him identical with the disappearance of all culture.

That culture, the loss of which he laments, is, for the enormous majority, a mere training to act as a machine.

But don't wrangle with us so long as you apply, to our intended abolition of bourgeois property, the standard of your bourgeois notions of freedom, culture, law, etc. Your very ideas are but the outgrowth of the conditions of your bourgeois production and bourgeois property, just as your jurisprudence is but the will of your class made into a law for all, a will, whose essential character and direction are determined by the economic conditions of existence of your class.

The selfish misconception that induces you to transform into eternal laws of nature and of reason, the social forms springing from your present mode of production and form of property—historical relations that rise and disappear in the progress of production—this misconception you share with every ruling class that has preceded you. What you see clearly in the case of ancient property, what you admit in the case of feudal property, you are of course forbidden to admit in the case of your own bourgeois form of property. * * *

We have seen above, that the first step in the revolution by the working class, is to raise the proletariat to the position of ruling class, to win the battle of democracy.

The proletariat will use its political supremacy, to wrest, by degrees, all capital from the bourgeoisie, to centralize all instruments of production in the hands of the State, i.e., of the proletariat organized as the ruling class; and to increase the total of productive forces as rapidly as possible.

Of course, in the beginning, this cannot be effected except by means of despotic inroads on the rights of property, and on the conditions of bourgeois production; by means of measures, therefore, which appear economically insufficient and untenable, but which, in the course of the movement, outstrip themselves, necessitate further inroads upon the old social order, and are unavoidable as a means of entirely revolutionizing the mode of production.

These measures will of course be different in different countries.

Nevertheless in the most advanced countries the following will be pretty generally applicable:

1. Abolition of property in land and application of all rents of land to public purposes.

2. A heavy progressive or graduated income tax.

3. Abolition of all right of inheritance.

4. Confiscation of the property of all emigrants and rebels.

5. Centralization of credit in the hands of the state, by means of a national bank with State capital and an exclusive monopoly.

6. Centralization of the means of communication and transport in the hands of the State.

7. Extension of factories and instruments of production owned by the State; the bringing into cultivation of waste lands, and the improvement of the soil generally in accordance with a common plan.

8. Equal liability of all to labor. Establishment of industrial armies, especially for agriculture.

9. Combination of agriculture with manufacturing industries: gradual abolition of the distinction between town and country, by a more equable distribution of population over the country.

10. Free education for all children in public schools. Abolition of children's factory labor in its present form. Combination of education with industrial production, etc., etc.

When, in the course of development, class distinctions have disappeared, and all production has been concentrated in the hands of a vast association of the whole nation, the public power will lose its political character. Political power, properly so called, is merely the organized power of one class for oppressing another. If the proletariat during its contest with the bourgeoisie is compelled, by the force of circumstances, to organize itself as a class, if, by means of a revolution, it makes itself the ruling class, and, as such, sweeps away by force the old conditions of production, then it will, along with these conditions, have swept away the conditions for the existence of class antagonisms, and of classes generally, and will thereby have abolished its own supremacy as a class.

In place of the old bourgeois society, with its classes and class antagonisms, we shall have an association, in which the free development of each is the condition for the free development of all. * * *

The Communists disdain to conceal their views and aims. They openly declare that their ends can be attained only by the forcible overthrow of all existing social conditions. Let the ruling classes tremble at a Communistic revolution. The proletarians have nothing to lose but their chains. They have a world to win.

Working men of all countries, unite!

Notes and Questions

1. In the Soviet Union, even before the recent reform movement, some rights of private property were recognized. Most tangible items of personal property and certain rights in dwelling places were recognized, but private property that gave 'power' was not. Private production of capital and consumer goods was not recognized. See generally, Maggs, The Security of Individually-Owned Property Under Soviet Law (1961) Duke LJ 525. See also Berle, Property, Production and Revolution (1965) 65 Col. L Rev 1.

2. Is a Marxist conception of property rights inconsistent with the basic premise that there must be a right to exclude for property to exist?

Property in the Welfare State

By the twentieth century, and particularly after the New Deal legislation of the 1930s in the United States and the welfare state measures enacted in the countries of the British Commonwealth, many persons had become entitled in some form or another to various kinds of benefit of the State. This raised two important questions with respect to the concept of property. Should such benefits be considered to be 'property rights' in and of themselves? And, did property in the welfare state have an important role to play in regulating the relationship between individuals and the State?

The case of *Flemming* v *Nestor* in the United States Supreme Court concerning the deprivation of a pension benefit provoked an important essay on property relations in the welfare state by (then) Yale Law Professor Charles Reich.

Flemming v Nestor

United State Supreme Court
363 US 603 (1960)

Mr. Justice Harlan delivered the opinion of the Court.

From a decision of the District Court for the District of Columbia holding § 202 (n) of the Social Security Act (68 Stat. 1083, as amended, 42 U.S.C. § 402 (n)) unconstitutional, the Secretary of Health, Education, and Welfare takes this direct appeal pursuant to 28 U.S.C. § 1252. The challenged section provides for the termination of old-age, survivor, and disability insurance benefits payable to, or in certain cases in respect of, an alien individual who after September 1, 1954 (the date of enactment of the section), is deported under § 241(a) of the Immigration and Nationality Act (8 U.S.C. § 1251 (a)) on any one of certain grounds specified in § 202 (n).

Appellee, an alien, immigrated to this country from Bulgaria in 1913, and became eligible for old-age benefits in November 1955. In July 1956 he was deported pursuant to § 241(a)(6)(C)(i) of the Immigration and Nationality Act for having been a member of the Communist Party from 1933 to 1939. This being one of the benefit-termination deportation grounds specified in § 202(n), appellee's benefits were terminated soon thereafter, and notice of the termination was given to his wife, who had remained in this country * * *

We think that the District Court erred in holding that § 202(n) deprived appellee of an "accrued property right." 169 F. Supp., at 934. Appellee's right to Social Security benefits cannot properly be considered to have been of that order. * * *

The Social Security system may be accurately described as a form of social insurance, enacted pursuant to Congress' power to "spend money in aid of the 'general welfare,' " *Helvering* v. *Davis, supra,* at 640, whereby persons gainfully employed, and those who employ them, are taxed to permit the payment of benefits to the retired and disabled, and their dependents. Plainly the expectation is that many members of the present productive work force will in turn become beneficiaries rather than supporters of the program. But each worker's benefits, though flowing from the contributions he made to the national economy while actively employed, are not dependent on the degree to which he was called upon to support the system by taxation. It is apparent that the noncontractual interest of an employee covered by the Act cannot be soundly analogized to that of the holder of an annuity, whose right to benefits is bottomed on his contractual premium payments. * * *

We must conclude that a person covered by the Act has not such a right in benefit payments as would make every defeasance of "accrued" interests violative of the Due Process Clause of the Fifth Amendment.

This is not to say, however, that Congress may exercise its power to modify the statutory scheme free of all constitutional restraint. The interest of a covered employee under the Act is of sufficient substance to fall within the protection from arbitrary governmental action afforded by the Due Process Clause. * * *

[The Due Process Clause arises out of the Fifth Amendment of the U.S. Constitution. It provides that "* * * [N]o person shall * * * be deprived of life, liberty or property without due process of law; nor shall private property be taken for public use without just compensation." After some analysis of the due process point Harlan concluded as follows.]

We need go no further to find support for our conclusion that this provision of the Act cannot be condemned as so lacking in rational justification as to offend due process.

The New Property

C Reich
(1964) 73 Yale L J 733.

The New Feudalism

The characteristics of the public interest state are varied, but there is an underlying philosophy that unites them. This is the doctrine that the wealth that flows from government is held by its recipients conditionally, subject to confiscation in the interests of the paramount state. This philosophy is epitomized in the most important of all judicial decisions concerning government largess, the case of *Flemming v. Nestor.* * * *

The implications of *Flemming v. Nestor* are profound. No form of government largess is more personal or individual than an old age pension. No form is more clearly earned by the recipient, who, together with his employer, contributes to the Social Security fund during the years of his employment. No form is more obviously a compulsory substitute for private property; the tax on wage earner and employer might readily have gone to higher pay and higher savings instead. No form is more relied on, and more often thought of as property. No form is more vital to the independence and dignity of the individual. Yet under the philosophy of Congress and the Court, a man or woman, after a lifetime of work, has no rights which may not be taken away to serve some public policy. The

Court makes no effort to balance the interests at stake. The public policy that justifies cutting off benefits need not even be an important one or a wise one—so long as it is not utterly irrational, the Court will not interfere. In any clash between individual rights and public policy, the latter is automatically held to be superior.

The philosophy of *Flemming v. Nestor*, * * * resembles the philosophy of feudal tenure. Wealth is not "owned" or "vested" in the holders. Instead, it is held conditionally, the conditions being ones which seek to ensure the fulfillment of obligations imposed by the state. Just as the feudal system linked lord and vassal through a system of mutual dependence, obligation, and loyalty, so government largess binds man to the state. And, it may be added, loyalty or fealty to the state is often one of the essential conditions of modern tenure. In the many decisions taking away government largess for refusal to sign loyalty oaths, belonging to "subversive" organizations, or other similar grounds, there is more than a suggestion of the condition of fealty demanded in older times.

The comparison to the general outlines of the feudal system may best be seen by recapitulating some of the chief features of government largess. (1) Increasingly we turn over wealth and rights to government, which reallocates and redistributes them in the many forms of largess; (2) there is a merging of public and private, in which lines of private ownership are blurred; (3) the administration of the system has given rise to special laws and special tribunals, outside the ordinary structure of government; (4) the right to possess and use government largess is bound up with the recipient's legal status; status is both the basis for receiving largess and a consequence of receiving it; hence the new wealth is not readily transferable; (5) individuals hold the wealth conditionally rather than absolutely; the conditions are usually obligations owed to the government or to the public, and may include the obligation of loyalty to the government; the obligations may be changed or increased at the will of the state; (6) for breach of condition the wealth may be forfeited or escheated back to the government; (7) the sovereign power is shared with large private interests; (8) the object of the whole system is to enforce "the public interest"—the interest of the state or society or the lord paramount—by means of the distribution and use of wealth in such a way as to create and maintain dependence. * * *

The public interest state is not with us yet. But we are left with large questions. If the day comes when most private ownership is supplanted by government largess, how then will governmental power over individuals be contained? * * * What will happen to the Constitution and particularly the Bill of Rights, if their limits may be bypassed by purchase, and if people lack an independent base from which to assert their individuality and claim their rights? Without the security of the person which individual wealth provides and which largess fails to provide, what, indeed, will we become?

The public interest state, as visualized above, represents in one sense the triumph of society over private property. This triumph is the end point of a great and necessary movement for reform. But somehow the result is different from what the reformers wanted. Somehow the idealistic concept of the public interest has summoned up a doctrine monstrous and oppressive. It is time to take another look at private property, and at the "public interest" philosophy that dominates its modern substitute, the largess of government.

Property and Liberty

Property is a legal institution the essence of which is the creation and protection of certain private rights in wealth of any kind. The institution performs many different functions. One of these functions is to draw a boundary between public and private power. Property draws a circle around the activities of each private individual or organization. Within that circle, the owner has a greater degree of freedom than without. Outside, he must justify or explain his actions, and show his authority. Within, he is master, and the state must explain and justify any interference. It is as if property shifted the burden of proof; outside, the individual has the burden; inside, the burden is on government to demonstrate that something the owner wishes to do should not be done.

Thus, property performs the function of maintaining independence, dignity and pluralism in society by creating zones within which the majority has to yield to the owner. Whim, caprice, irrationality and "antisocial" activities are given the protection of law; the owner may do what all or most of his neighbors decry. The Bill of Rights also serves this function, but while the Bill of Rights comes into play only at extraordinary moments of conflict or crisis, property affords day-to-day protection in the ordinary affairs of life. Indeed, in the final analysis the Bill of Rights depends upon the existence of private property. Political rights presuppose that individuals and private groups have the will and the means to act independently. But so long as individuals are motivated largely by self-interest, their well-being must first be independent. Civil liberties must have a basis in property, or bills of rights will not preserve them.

Property is not a natural right but a deliberate construction by society. If such an institution did not exist, it would be necessary to create it, in order to have the kind of society we wish. The majority cannot be expected, on specific issues, to yield its power to a minority. Only if the minority's will is established as a general principle can it keep the majority at bay in a given instance. Like the Bill of Rights, property represents a general, long range protection of individual and private interests, created by the majority for the ultimate good of all.

Today, however, it is widely thought that property and liberty are separable things; that there may, in fact, be conflicts between "property rights" and "personal rights." Why has this view been accepted? The explanation is found at least partly in the transformations which have taken place in property.

During the industrial revolution, when property was liberated from feudal restraints, philosophers hailed property as the basis of liberty, and argued that it must be free from the demands of government or society. But as private property grew, so did abuses resulting from its use. In a crowded world, a man's use of his property increasingly affected his neighbor, and one man's exercise of a right might seriously impair the rights of others. Property became power over others; the farm landowner, the city landlord, and the working man's boss were able to oppress their tenants or employees. Great aggregations of property resulted in private control of entire industries and basic services capable of affecting a whole area or even a nation. At the same time, much private property lost its individuality and in effect became socialized. Multiple ownership of corporations helped to separate personality from property, and property from power. When the corporations began to stop competing, to merge, agree, and make mutual plans, they became private governments. Finally, they sought the aid and partnership of the state, and thus by their own volition became part of public government.

These changes led to a movement for reform, which sought to limit arbitrary private power and protect the common man. Property rights were considered more the enemy than the friend of liberty. The reformers argued that property must be separated from personality. * * *

The struggle between abuse and reform made it easy to forget the basic importance of individual private property. The defense of private property was almost entirely a defense of its abuses — an attempt to defend not individual property but arbitrary private power over other human beings. Since this defense was cloaked in a defense of private property, it was natural for the reformers to attack too broadly. Walter Lippmann saw this in 1934:

> But the issue between the giant corporation and the public should not be allowed to obscure the truth that the only dependable foundation of personal liberty is the economic security of private property.

> *   *   *

> For we must not expect to find in ordinary men the stuff of martyrs, and we must, therefore, secure their freedom by their normal motives. There is no surer way to give men the courage to be free than to insure them a competence upon which they can rely.

The reform took away some of the power of the corporations and transferred it to government. In this transfer there was much good, for power was made responsive to the majority rather than to the arbitrary and selfish few. But the reform did not restore the individual to his domain. What the corporation had taken from him, the reform simply handed on to government. And government carried further the powers formerly exercised by the corporation. Government as an employer, or as a dispenser of wealth, has used the theory that it was handing out gratuities to claim a managerial power as great as that which the capitalists claimed. Moreover, the corporations allied themselves with, or actually took over, part of government's system of power. Today it is the combined power of government and the corporations that presses against the individual.

From the individual's point of view, it is not any particular kind of power, but all kinds of power, that are to be feared. This is the lesson of the public interest state. The mere fact that power is derived from the majority does not necessarily make it less oppressive. Liberty is more than the right to do what the majority wants, or to do what is "reasonable". Liberty is the right to defy the majority, and to do what is unreasonable. The great error of the public interest state is that it assumes an identity between the public interest and the interest of the majority. * * *

Largess and the Public Interest

The fact that the reform tended to make much private wealth subject to "the public interest" has great significance, but it does not adequately explain the dependent position of the individual and the weakening of civil liberties in the public interest state. The reformers intended to enhance the values of democracy and liberty; their basic concern was the preservation of a free society. But after they established the primacy of "the public interest," what meaning was given to that phrase? In particular, what values does it embody as it has been employed to regulate government largess?

Reduced to simplest terms, "the public interest" has usually meant this: government largess may be denied or taken away if this will serve some legitimate public policy. The policy may be one directly related to the largess itself, or it may be some collateral objective of government. A contract may be denied if this will promote fair labor standards. A television license may be refused if this will promote the policies of the antitrust laws. * * * A liquor license may be revoked to promote civil rights. A franchise for a barber's college may not be given out if it will hurt the local economy, nor a taxi franchise if it will seriously injure the earning capacity of other taxis.

Most of these objectives are laudable, and all are within the power of government. The great difficulty is that they are simplistic. Concentration on a single policy or value obscures other values that may be at stake. Some of these competing values are other public policies; for example, the policy of the best possible television service to the public may compete with observance of the antitrust laws. The legislature is the natural arbiter of such conflicts. But the conflicts may also be more fundamental. In the regulation of government largess, achievement of specific policy goals may undermine the independence of the individual. Where such conflicts exist, a simplistic notion of the public interest may unwittingly destroy some values.

* * *

From Largess to Right

Eventually those forms of largess which are closely linked to status must be deemed to be held as of right. Like property, such largess could be governed by a system of regulation plus civil or criminal sanctions, rather than a system based upon denial, suspension and revocation. As things now stand, violations lead to for-feitures — outright confiscation of wealth and status. But there is surely no need for these drastic results. Confiscation, if used at all, should be the ultimate, not the most common and convenient penalty. The presumption should be that the professional man will keep his license, and the welfare recipient his pension. These interests should be "vested." If revocation is necessary, not by reason of the fault of the individual holder, but by reason of overriding demands of public policy, perhaps payment of just compensation would be appropriate. The individual should not bear the entire loss for a remedy primarily intended to benefit the community. * * *

At the very least, it is time to reconsider the theories under which new forms of wealth are regulated, and by which governmental power over them is measured. It is time to recognize that "the public interest" is all too often a reassuring platitude that covers up sharp clashes of conflicting values, and hides fundamental choices. It is time to see that the "privilege" or "gratuity" concept, as applied to wealth dispensed by government, is not much different from the absolute right of ownership that private capital once invoked to justify arbitrary power over employees and the public.

Above all, the time has come for us to remember what the framers of the Constitution knew so well—that "a power over a man's subsistence amounts to a power over his will." We cannot safely entrust our livelihoods and our rights to the discretion of authorities, examiners, boards of control, character committees, regents, or license commissioners. We cannot permit any official or agency to pretend to sole knowledge of the public good. We cannot put the independence of any man—＊＊＊ wholly in the power of other men.

If the individual is to survive in a collective society, he must have protection against its ruthless pressures. There must be sanctuaries or enclaves where no majority can reach. To shelter the solitary human spirit does not merely make possible the fulfillment of individuals; it also gives society the power to change, to grow, and to regenerate, and hence to endure. These were the objects which property sought to achieve, and can no longer achieve. The challenge of the future will be to construct, for the society that is coming, institutions and laws to carry on this work. Just as the Homestead Act was a deliberate effort to foster individual values at an earlier time, so we must try to build an economic basis for liberty today—a Homestead Act for rootless twentieth century man. We must create a new property.

Notes and Questions

1. Does this case offend your sense of justice? Why? What was the result in the lives of the plaintiff and his wife?

2. Reich appears to be arguing that property is essential to the freedom of the individual in the modern welfare state. How does property achieve this freedom?

3. Apply Bentham's views to *Flemming*. What would be the result?

4. An American property casebook, Donaghue, Kauper & Martin, *Property* asks this question, at 162, 'Did Fleming lose his case because he had no property, or did he have no property because he lost?' What is your response to that question?

5. Almost one in every three adults (29 per cent) requires a cash handout from the government to survive in New Zealand today. These 750,449 people receive unemployment benefits, the domestic purposes benefit, invalid benefits, sickness benefits, widow's benefits or national superannuation. In 1980, about 20 per cent of the population received benefits of this kind. These figures do not include recipients of government superannuation. See *New Zealand Herald*, 6 December 1989, section 3 page 1, quoting a National Bank study. The various statutes contain rights of appeal or review.

6. The New Zealand Bill of Rights introduced into Parliament in 1989 provides in part 2 for certain civil and political rights. Clauses 12-17 cover such matters as freedom of thought, expression, association, peaceful assembly and movement. If freedom of property is as important as Reich argues, should the right to property receive 'constitutional' protection? Would you agree with Neumann, The Concept of Political Freedom (1953) 53 Columbia Law Review 901, 926, who suggests:

"Most of the continental civil rights catalogues make a clear distinction between property and other civil rights, the protection of the latter being far more stringent than that of the former. One very simple consideration will make clear the instrumentalist role of property: all constitutions permit the condemnation of private property with adequate compensation. Yet no civilised constitution could possibly permit the State to do away with a person's life or liberty for public purposes even with more than adequate compensation. The value of political freedom is absolute: that of property is merely relative to it. Thus the tasks of political theory concerned with man's freedom are to analyse whether property fulfils its function as an efficient instrument of freedom, and to discover what institutional changes are necessary to maximise its effectiveness."

7. The Canadian Bill of Rights (S.C. 1960 c. 44) — on which the New Zealand Bill draws heavily — *did* include as a fundamental right 'enjoyment of property and the right not to be deprived thereof except by due process of law . . .'. Why would the legislators not have included such a provision in New Zealand?

8. Reich's analysis suggests that our conception of wealth has changed — and will continue to change. Where once the most important possessions were tangible objects — land and cows — today things like one's job and pension are increasingly recognized as forms of wealth. On the problems this poses for legal ordering and property, see Simmonds, The Changing Face of Private Law: Doctrinal Categories and the Regulatory State (1982) 2 Legal Studies 257; Cribbet, Concepts in Transition: The Search for a New Definition of Property (1986) U Illinois L Rev 1; Williams, Liberty and Power: The Problem of Government Benefits (1983) 12 J Legal Studies 3.

9. How far does the notion of 'New Property' rest upon a concept of public trust held by nominees, for example investment institutions and employers, for deserving beneficiaries? For an argument that it does, see Yanncone, Property and Stewardship — Private Property plus Social Interest equals Social Property (1928) 23 S Dak L Rev 71.

Property and Personhood

There is a relatively fine line between personhood and property. Hegel in *The Philosophy of Right* (trans T. Knox, Oxford University Press, London 1821/1952) endeavoured to get to grips with this relationship from a philosopher's point of view. He suggested that as the general will found corporate expression in the State, so a person's personality found expression in that person's possessions. A denial of private property could cramp and fetter human personality by blocking the freedom of will to have and to hold, to give and share. A recent article which builds on Hegel in contemporary circumstances is that by Margaret Radin, Property in Personhood (1982) 34 Stanford L Rev 957. Her argument is that 'to achieve proper self-development — to be a *person* — an individual needs some control over resources in the external environment. The necessary assurances of control take the form of property rights.' (957). She also suggests that 'the personhood perspective is often implicit in the connections that courts and commentators find between property and privacy or between property and liberty.'

Notes and Questions

1. Radin's assertion can be tested against *Foster* v *Mountford & Rigby Ltd* (1976)

14 ALR 71. A scientist learned aboriginal tribal secrets, and he proposed to publish a book containing these secrets. An application for an injunction is made to prevent publication. On what theory should a Court proceed? That there is a breach of confidence involved? (equity); that there is a breach of privacy? (tort) or that the secrets were property? Does it matter? What are the consequences of these different approaches?

2. This conception of property should not be confused with feminist legal theory. Feminist theory currently holds that male-derived legal theory produces a morality of rights — an 'illegitimate' heirarchy — whereas women are said to be more concerned with a web of connection. (See Karst's brilliant essay, Woman's Constitution (1984) Duke L J 447). Radin's conception is one for every person. However Radin does suggest that there is 'in Hegel's theory a foundation for the communitarian claim that each community is an organic entity in which private property ownership does not make sense.' (*id.* 976).

3. Karl Renner has suggested that property leads inevitably to 'micro' organizations similar to the state: 'power over matter begets personal power'. See *The Institutions of Private Law and Their Social Function* (1949) 107. According to such a view property is a political relationship between persons. How far do you subscribe to that view?

4. Mary Ann Glendon in *The New Family and the New Property* (1981) canvasses the changing balance of family, work and government and the significance of New Property rights. Her work also emphasizes a changed conception of personhood in this context.

5. For a challenging and different analysis of property problems in general, see Calabresi and Melamed, Property Rules, Liability Rules, and Inalienability: One View of the Cathedral (1972) 85 Harv L Rev 1089. Their approach involves a quite different way of looking at things. An entitlement is protected by a property rule if B can get it from A only by paying whatever price A sets as a willing seller. Likewise if A can obtain an injunction to prevent B's interference. The entitlement is protected by a liability rule if B can obtain it from A by paying some extrinsically determined price (which includes the 'market' price) even if A is not a willing seller, or if A can obtain only damages on account of B's interference. Their use of language and classifications are quite unorthodox. But, what do you think of the approach? Can you think of applications of it?

Final Questions

One writer has said:

> The historical theory of property is not a theory of stasis. It allows of change, expects change, but not the climacteric of revolution. Change in the course of nature measures its own time. By that chronology there is judged what at any given time is the just form of property for a people within a society. Neither Marx nor Mill nor any other radical or revolutionary can with impunity force the pace of change in nature. [Denman, *supra*].

Do you agree? And, what is the just form of property for New Zealand society today?

Further Reading

1. For excellent recent essays on legal theory and contemporary property law see Cotterell, The Law of Property and Legal Theory in Twining (ed) *Legal Theory and Common Law* (1986) 81-98; and Vandevelde, The New Property of the Nineteenth Century: The Development of the Modern Concept of Property (1980) 29 Buffalo Law Review 325.

2. For personhood perspectives, see also Salter, Justifying Private Property Rights: A Message from Hegel's Jurisprudential Writings (1987) 7 Legal Studies 245; Trasler, The Psychology of Ownership and Possession in Hollowell, *Property and Social Relations* (1982) 32.

3. Two major new monographs on property are Waldron, *The Right to Private Property* (1988) and Munzer, *A Theory of Property (1990)*. See also the review essays of Waldron by Paul, Can Rights Move Left? in (1990) 88 Michigan Law Review 1622, and Pottage, Property: Reappropriating Hegel (1990) 53 Modern Law Review 259.

4. For the problems of private property in relation to written constitutions see Nedelsky, *Private Property and the Limits of American Constitutionalism* (1991).

5. For natural law perspectives on justifications of property see Buckley, *Natural Law and the Theory of Property: Grotius to Hume* (1991).

6. For an argument that there is a common law of property which 'exhibits an internal unity worthy of moral respect' see Brudner, The Unity of Property Law (1991) 4 The Canadian Journal of Law and Jurisprudence 3.

7. Professor Reich was invited to revisit his thesis in, The New Property After 25 Years (1990) 24 University of San Francisco Law Review 223. According to (1991) 100 Yale Law Journal at 1462, Reich's article is the most widely cited article ever published by the Yale Law Journal. Why do you think that might be? Reich continues to assert that 'only by preserving an individual sector can we control our destiny.' See his, The Individual Sector (1991) 100 Yale Law Journal 1409.

3

Social Restrictions on the Alienation
of Personal Property

The general principle of the law is that a person may use his or her property in any lawful manner. That is, I may decide to plant wheat or corn on my property and the choice is mine. Or, I may use my axe to break up concrete in my driveway and render the axe quite useless for any other purpose. Again, the choice is mine.

The common law jurisdictions know no concept of *dominium*, or absolute title, whether with respect to goods or land. The fee simple is held of the Crown in the case of land. And restraints have, in the public interest, been placed upon the manner in which a person may use his or her land. The most obvious example in contemporary society involves land use restrictions imposed by town planning legislation. I may be the registered proprietor of a parcel of land in the centre of Auckland but that alone does not give me the right to build a steel foundry upon it. To proceed with such an enterprise I would have to obtain (unless the land was zoned for that purpose) appropriate planning permission, and in all probability a number of other permissions to draw water, to emit noxious fumes and so on. Indeed, in the case of land a great many uses of land require permissions or consents or waivers of one kind or another.

Personal property has been relatively unconstrained by the law as to its usage and alienation. Of course, if I negligently drive my motor vehicle into your motor vehicle I may have to pay you damages. And if I employ my axe to bludgeon you to death I commit a crime. But on the whole the restrictions on the *usage* of personal property have been much less than in the case of land.

This chapter is designed to do two things. First, to reinforce the notion that the existence, and the ambit of proprietary rights—including those with respect to personal property—are socially conditioned. Nothing flows inexorably from the existence or intrinsic character of a particular object. No item of property is above the law, and as Bentham put it, cannot exist without the law. Secondly, to explore in depth two subject areas where social concern has arisen over asserted personal property rights: the sale of preserved Māori heads, and the export of cultural property.

The Case of Māori Heads

Some Māori tattooed or mokoed their faces. A practice developed in the nineteenth century whereby mokoed, preserved Māori heads (moko mōkai) were bought and traded by whalers who visited New Zealand.

When, last century, Maori people realized they could purchase a musket for two Maori heads, instead of having to labour hard to clean a tonne of flax for a musket, a boom started in the sale of tattooed heads. At the peak of the Maori head trading, a head could be bought for £2 in George Street, Sydney until this traffic in human heads was declared illegal by the then Governor of New South Wales, Governor Darling, on 16 April 1831. This ruling did not completely stop the trade in Maori heads, but it did slow down. More than one musket-hungry chief offered for sale Maori heads with good tattoos, to the customers' specific orders. They invited the visiting whale ship captains to place their order and when the ship returned a few months later, the Maori would have the head of one of their slaves suitably tattooed and perfectly preserved and dried to order. Many a poor slave suffered a horrible fate of being mokoed only to be murdered for his head. 'A good looking slave might be elaborately tattooed', wrote Major General Robley, 'so that when required his head might pass as that of a distinguished rangatira'. When the traffic became general, natives ceased to preserve the heads of their friends, in case they should fall into the hands of others and be sold. [*Sunday Star*, 15 May 1988, A13].

A New Zealand government early this century rejected an offer from overseas to buy back thirty-five tattooed Māori heads for £1000 and a number of heads found their way into museums overseas.

In 1988 an English woman, Mrs Weller-Poley, put a preserved head up for auction in the United Kingdom. According to the *New Zealand Herald*, Saturday, 16 July 1988, section 1 p 2, 'the head had come into her possession through her husband's family, but she did not know more than that.' Survival International, a United Nations accredited organization, which works for the rights of 'threatened tribal peoples' throughout the world, intervened on behalf of Māori. It advised Bonhams, the English auctioneers, that the proposed auction showed 'contemptible lack of respect for the Maori people' (*New Zealand Herald* 14 May 1988 section 1, 16). Bonham's had estimated that the head would auction for approximately £17,000. Mrs Weller-Poley did not withdraw the head from auction. Christies, another English auction house, did however cancel the sale of a collection of human heads from the Amazon Basin, Papua New Guinea and Peru because of the controversy. *The Times* of London joined in the controversy when Bernard Levin wrote an article under the headline 'Foul Deeds of Desecration' in which he argued that selling preserved heads would be the same as auctioneering lampshades made from the skin of Jews exterminated by Hitler. (*New Zealand Herald*, Wednesday, 8 June 1988, section 1, 10) Still Mrs Weller-Poley did not withdraw the head from auction or make any offer to return it to New Zealand.

It was decided to institute legal proceedings to endeavour to halt the sale of the head. In the result, the Maori Council, supported financially by the New Zealand Government, began legal proceedings with the aim of securing an injunction stopping the sale of the head which Mrs Weller-Poley claimed to be her personal property. In the event, Sir Graham Latimer, the Chairman of the New Zealand Maori Council and the rangatira (chief) of the deceased's probable iwi (Ngapuhi), made an application for letters of administration of the estate and the effects of the deceased.

Mr Justice Greig granted the application. (HC Wellington P580/88, 19 May 1989; and see Brookfield, Note, (1989) New Zealand Recent Law Rev 217-18).

His Honour said the grant was made for the limited purpose of enabling legal proceedings to go ahead, to give the deceased a proper burial according to Māori law and custom and to prevent any further indignity being placed upon him.

Following the proceedings, Mrs Weller-Poley agreed to stay the auction. A settlement was reached whereby she received a carved greenstone mere in return for the preserved head. (*New Zealand Herald*, Saturday 16 July 1988, section 1, 2).

Notes and Questions

1. There does not appear to be legislation in either New Zealand or England to prevent such a sale taking place. Counsel for the New Zealand Maori Council had to rely on law relating to the rights, indeed the duties, of executors, that is persons lawfully appointed to act for the estate of deceased persons who have not left a will, to see to the burial of the deceased according to law (which seems to include Māori customary law in pre-colonial days?). In this particular case that tactic produced a sufficient period of time to allow a settlement to be successfully negotiated.

2. But why should a Court, faced with an application for an injunction to prevent a sale on the foregoing facts, not simply have enjoined, that is, made an order preventing the sale, on the grounds that public policy so required? Restrictions on the right of use and disposal of land are commonplace. And if ever there was a case of appalling insensitivity of the grossest kind with respect to alleged 'personal property' this was it. Indeed, why should a preserved human head not be *res nullius*? What problems would such an approach raise?

3. As a matter of existing law, there were very serious problems in the way of the plaintiff New Zealand Maori Council. In the first place an injunction is normally only granted in aid of a right known to the law, although there is some authority for the proposition that even an arguable right may sustain an injunction. (See *Paton* v *Trustees of PBAS* [1978] 2 All ER 987). Here the argument would presumably have to be that somebody could be prevented from selling an item of personal property, a human head, that was 'theirs'. In short, the Court would have had to be prepared to say, on such an application, that it was prepared to create a right of interference in the sale of an item of personal property on the grounds of public policy, in this case that of an affront to cultural sensitivities and human dignity. Public policy, as it is so often said, is an unruly horse. Would you have allowed such a claim? On what basis? And how would you deal with the fact that the application for an injunction was being made in England to prevent a sale in that jurisdiction?

Cultural Property in General

Any movable object can be or can become a 'cultural object'. In some cultures, with the passage of time a stone can become an object of immense value. One authority has defined cultural objects as 'including works of art, archaeological, historical and ethnological objects (but not limited to them) and which are generally considered as being the material evidence of a certain stage of civilisation'. (Professor Lalieve, A General View of the Law Relating to Cultural Property (March 1988)

International Legal Practitioner 18.) Increasingly governments world wide have begun to enact legislation designed to prevent the sale or removal from a given jurisdiction of matters of that character.

Not everyone is entirely happy with these restrictions. Professor John Merryman, at the First Geneva Conference on the International Trade and Works of Art said:

> A licit international trade in art, while allowing works to go where they are most valued and most likely to be cared for, can advance the international interest. National restrictions on the free movement of art, on the contrary, threaten the international interest . . . the traffic will go on and become illegal (with the risk of destruction and loss of cultural information). Excessively retentive national laws are contrary to the international interests and cultural preservation, integrity and distribution-access. An expanded, licit, international trade in art is more likely to advance the general interest in the 'cultural heritage of all mankind' ". [Cited in Lalieve, *supra*]

The dispute between nationalist or ethnic groups and internationalists illustrates the complex nature of these questions and the need for the careful balancing of interests that modern personal property legislation requires.

As to Oceania, 'the small island states of the Pacific, as well as New Zealand and Australia, were relatively late in the field of the protection of the cultural heritage.' (O'Keefe & Prott, *Law and the Cultural Heritage* vol 1 (1984) 68; and see the Review thereof by Philip Wright in (1985) 5 Auckland Univ L Rev 261.) New Zealand has the Historic Places Act 1980, which governs the use of archaeological sites, historic areas, historic buildings and historic places. Like other Pacific states, New Zealand tried to preserve indigenous relics by controlling their export. A Maori Antiquities Act 1901 and a subsequent 1908 Act both related to export control, as did the Historical Articles Act 1962, which repealed the 1908 Act. That Act was replaced by the present Antiquities Act 1975.

Antiquities Act 1975

2. **Interpretation**—In this Act, unless the context otherwise requires,—
    "Antiquity" means—
    (a) Any chattel of any kind whatsoever, not being a chattel to which any of paragraphs (b) to (h) of this definition applies, which—
        (i) Is of national, historical, scientific, or artistic importance; and
        (ii) Relates to the European discovery, settlement, or development of New Zealand; and
    (iii) Is, or appears to be, more than 60 years old:
    (b) Any artifact:
    (c) Any book, diary, letter, document, paper, record, or other written matter (whether in manuscript or printed form), photographic negative or print, film, printed reproduction of any picture, or sound recording—
        (i) Which relates to New Zealand and is of national, historical, scientific, artistic, or literary importance; and
        (ii) Which is more than 60 years old; and
    (iii) Of which, in the case of a book first printed and published in

New Zealand, no copy is in the custody of the National Library
of New Zealand:

(d) Any work of art which relates to New Zealand, is more than
60 years old, and is of national, historical, or artistic value of importance:

(e) Any type specimen of any animal, plant, or mineral existing or
formerly existing in New Zealand:

(f) Any meteorite or part of a meteorite recovered in New Zealand:

(g) Any bones, feathers, or other parts or the eggs of the moa or
other species of animals, birds, reptiles, or amphibians native to New
Zealand which are generally believed to be extinct:

(h) Any ship, boat, or aircraft, or any part of any ship, boat, or
aircraft, or any equipment, cargo, or article belonging to any ship,
boat, or aircraft in any case where that ship, boat, or aircraft has been,
or appears to have been, a wreck in New Zealand, or within the
territorial waters of New Zealand, for more than 60 years and that
ship, boat, aircraft, equipment, cargo, or article, as the case may be,
is of national, historical, scientific, or artistic value or importance:

"Artifact" means any chattel, carving, object, or thing which relates to the
history, art, culture, traditions, or economy of the Maori or other pre-
European inhabitants of New Zealand and which was or appears to have
been manufactured or modified in New Zealand by any such inhabitant,
or brought to New Zealand by an ancestor of any such inhabitant, or
used by any such inhabitant, prior to 1902:

"Book" means any collection of printed sheets of paper or other material,
and includes every part or division of a book and every pamphlet, magazine,
periodical, sheet of letterpress, sheet of music, map, plan, chart, art print,
or table separately published:

"Collector" means any person or body (whether incorporated or
unincorporated), other than a licensed auctioneer, a licensed secondhand
dealer, or a public museum, possessing one or more artifacts:

"Found", in relation to any artifact, means discovered or obtained in
circumstances which do not indicate with reasonable certainty the lawful
ownership of the artifact and which suggest that the artifact was last in
the lawful possession of a person who at the time of finding is no longer
alive; and "finding" and "finds" have corresponding meanings:

"Work of art" means—

(a) Any painting in oil or watercolours or any other painting
medium, framed or unframed, on any material:

(b) Any ink, pencil, or charcoal drawing or pastel or any drawing
using any other graphic medium, framed or unframed, on any material:

(c) Any hand engraved or hand etched block, plate, or other
material and any hand printed impression, framed or unframed, thereof:

(d) Any hand drawn lithographic stone or other material and any
hand printed impression, framed or unframed, thereof:

(e) Any sculpture, including casting, in any material whether in
the round, in relief, or in intaglio.

"Replica of an artifact" means an accurate copy of a specific individual artifact:

5. Restrictions on export of antiquities—(1) It shall not be lawful after the commencement of this Act for any person to remove or attempt to remove any antiquity from New Zealand otherwise than pursuant to the authority and in conformity with the terms and conditions of a written certificate of permission given by the Secretary under this Act:

Provided that the Secretary may from time to time, by notice in the *Gazette*, exempt any class or classes of antiquities from the provisions of this section where he is satisfied that—

(a) Sufficient examples of that class or those classes are held in public ownership in New Zealand; and

(b) It would not be contrary to the public interest to exempt that class or those classes.

(2) Every person who, without reasonable excuse, contravenes any provision of this section or of the terms and conditions of a written certificate of permission given pursuant to subsection (1) of this section commits an offence, and shall be liable on summary conviction to a fine not exceeeding $1,000.

(3) Nothing in this section shall apply to any antiquity lawfully taken and ordinarily kept outside New Zealand but temporarily within New Zealand.

6. Application for permission—(1) Every application for permission to remove an antiquity from New Zealand shall be in the form provided by the Secretary.

(2) The Secretary, in considering any application under this section, shall, in respect of the antiquity sought to be removed, have regard to:

(a) Its historical, archaeological, scientific, cultural, literary, artistic, or other special national or local importance; and

(b) Its spiritual or emotional association with the people of New Zealand or any group or section thereof; and

(c) Its rarity; and

(d) The extent to which similar articles are held in public ownership in New Zealand; and

(e) The probable effect of its removal on historical or scientific study or research in New Zealand; and

(f) Any other matters which appear to him to be relevant.

(3) After having regard to the matters referred to in subsection (2) of this section and after making such inquiries and investigations and seeking such expert opinion as he thinks fit, the Secretary may grant his permission, either unconditionally or subject to such terms and conditions as may be imposed by him in writing, for the removal of the antiquity from New Zealand:

Provided that the Secretary shall refuse to grant his permission unless he is satisfied that the removal of the antiquity—

(a) Would not be to the substantial detriment of historical or scientific study or research in New Zealand; and

(b) Would not be contrary to the public interest.

7. Certificate of permission—Where permission is granted by the Secretary for the removal of any antiquity from New Zealand, a certificate shall be issued to the applicant under the hand of the Secretary.

Cf. 1962, No. 37, s. 7

8. Conditions imposed by Secretary—(1) Without prejudice to the generality of the authority given under this Act to impose terms and conditions, the Secretary may, when granting permission to remove any antiquity from New Zealand, impose conditions —

    (a) Requiring the owner to permit the antiquity to be copied by photography, cast, or otherwise in such manner, in such numbers, and by such person, as the Secretary may direct:

    (b) Requiring the owner of the antiquity to deliver it to such person as the Secretary may direct for the purpose of being packed and dispatched from New Zealand, at the cost and risk of the owner, to the address specified by the owner:

    (c) Requiring the antiquity to be returned to New Zealand no later than the date of the expiry of a period specified in the certificate of permission to remove the antiquity from New Zealand.

(2) Every copy made pursuant to paragraph (a) of subsection (1) of this section shall, subject to the provisions of the Copyright Act 1962, be the property of the Crown and shall be kept in safe custody in accordance with the directions of the Secretary.

11. Establishing the ownership and custody of artifacts — (1) Any artifact found anywhere in New Zealand or within the territorial waters of New Zealand after the commencement of this Act is hereby declared as deemed to be prima facie the property of the Crown:

Provided that where any artifact has been recovered from the grave of any person or persons whose identity is known the matter shall be referred to the Maori Land Court to determine who is the proper person or who are the proper persons to hold custody of the artifact.

(2) Notwithstanding the provisions of subsection (1) of this section, if actual or traditional ownership, rightful possession, or custody of any artifact referred to in that subsection is subsequently claimed, the Minister or any person who may have any right, title, estate, or interest in any such artifact may apply to the Maori Land Court to exercise any part of its jurisdiction under section 12 of this Act:

Provided that no right, title, estate, or interest in any such artifact shall exist or be deemed to exist solely by virtue of ownership of the land from which the artifact was found or recovered.

(3) Every person who, after the commencement of this Act, finds any artifact anywhere in New Zealand or within the territorial waters of New Zealand shall, within 28 days of finding the artifact, notify either the Secretary or the nearest public museum, which shall notify the Secretary, of the finding of the artifact:

Provided that in the case of any artifact found during the course of any archaeological investigation authorised by the New Zealand Historic Places Trust under section 9H of the Historic Places Act 1954, the notification shall be made within 28 days of the completion of the field work undertaken in connection with the investigation.

(4) Upon receipt of a notification in accordance with subsection (3) of this section, the Secretary shall take such action as he deems appropriate to provide for the examination of the artifact, its recording and its custody, either by the finder or otherwise, and on such conditions as the Secretary deems fit.

(5) Every person who finds any artifact, knowing or having reasonable cause to suspect that it is an artifact, and contravenes subsection (3) of this section commits an offence, and shall be liable on summary conviction to a fine not exceeding $500.

12. Maori Land Court's jurisdiction over artifacts — (1) The Maori Land Court shall have jurisdiction in respect to any artifact to which section 11 of this Act applies —

(a) To determine for the purposes of any proceeding or upon application by the Minister or by any person authorised to apply under subsection (2) of the said section 11 whether or not the subject-matter of the proceeding or application is an artifact:

(b) To hear and determine as between any persons applying under subsection (2) of the said section 11 any claim, whether at law or in equity, to the actual or traditional ownership, rightful possession, or custody of any artifact, or to any right, title, estate, or interest therein:

(c) In the case of any artifact recovered from a grave to determine, if possible, the proper person or persons to hold custody of the artifact:

(d) To make an order prohibiting any person from dealing with or doing any injury to any artifact which is the subject-matter of any application to the Court, or of any application to the Chief Judge in respect of the exercise of any jurisdiction specially conferred on him by the Maori Affairs Act 1953 or otherwise, if in any case the application has not been finally disposed of by the Court or the Chief Judge or the Appellate Court, as the case may be:

(e) To vest in any person or persons as trustee or trustees any artifact for safekeeping and preservation:

(f) To enforce the obligations of the trust (whether by way of an order or otherwise) against any person or persons appointed by the Court as trustee or trustees:

(g) To appoint a new trustee or trustees for any artifact held in trust, under the same conditions as laid down in section 443 of the Maori Affairs Act 1953.

(2) The Maori Land Court shall have jurisdiction to make an order prohibiting any offering for sale, or parting with possession, of any artifact (whether or not an artifact to which section 11 of this Act applies) by any person if that artifact is in the power or possession of that person by way of gift according to Maori custom and usage.

(3) The provisions of section 30(1)(f) of the Maori Affairs Act 1953 shall apply in respect of any matter in respect of which the Maori Land Court has jurisdiction under subsection (1) or subsection (2) of this section.

13. Disposal of artifacts — (1) It shall not be lawful after the commencement of this Act for any person to sell or otherwise dispose of any artifact, knowing or having reasonable cause to suspect that it is an artifact, otherwise than to a registered collector or to a public museum or through the offices of a licensed auctioneer or a licensed secondhand dealer:

Provided that this subsection shall not apply to any disposition by any person to a relative of that person, whether by way of gift *inter vivos*, or pursuant to a testamentary disposition, or under the intestacy of that person, or by survivorship on the death of that person.

(2) Notwithstanding anything in subsection (1) of this section, no person or institution entrusted with the custody of any artifact in accordance with the terms of subsection (4) of section 11 of this Act may dispose of that artifact other than at the direction of the Secretary.

(3) Without limiting in any way his powers under subsection (2) of this section, the Secretary may, on application and subject to such conditions as he considers necessary, authorise approved institutions to employ destructive analytical techniques to specified artifacts or to specified classes of artifacts.

(4) Every person, other than a registered collector, who contravenes the provisions of this section commits an offence, and shall be liable on summary conviction to a fine not exceeding $1,000.

(5) On the conviction of any person of an offence against this section in respect of the disposition of any artifact, the Court may, if it thinks fit, declare the artifact to be forfeit to the Crown.

(6) Where any artifact is forfeited to the Crown pursuant to this section, it shall be delivered to the Minister and retained in safe custody according to his directions.

18. Replica of artifact—(1) Any person who manufactures for sale a replica of any artifact shall be required to identify it clearly and permanently as such.

(2) Every person who, without reasonable cause, fails to comply with the provisions of subsection (1) of this section commits an offence, and shall be liable on summary conviction to a fine not exceeding $500.

Notes and Questions

1. It will be observed that the statute sets up a bipartite scheme. On the one hand it again attempts to regulate the export of antiquities from New Zealand without the permission of the Secretary for Internal Affairs. Māori artefacts, on the other hand, under section 11 are declared to be 'prima facie' the property of the Crown. Jurisdiction over such artefacts is given to the Maori Land Court. The Act also provides for registration of collections of artefacts.

2. Does this scheme go far enough? Does it go too far? How do you reconcile the statutory scheme, which purports to preserve New Zealand's cultural heritage, with the interests of the wider advancement of knowledge and international concerns to which Professor Merryman adverted (*supra*)?

3. It has become common, particularly in universities, to endeavour to assemble substantial research collections. Such collections add prestige to a university and attract graduate students as well as preserving documents. For instance, the University of Illinois has the best collection of Milton's works, private papers and papers relating to Milton, of any university in the world. Somebody wishing to undertake research on Milton must travel to that source. North American universities in particular have specialized in particular persons or subjects and accumulate material relating to them. Is this a good thing or a bad thing? Should we be concerned about the 'loss' of New Zealand paintings overseas?

4. As the case of *Attorney General of New Zealand* v *Ortiz* [1962] 3 WLR 570 (Court of Appeal); [1983] 2 All ER 93 (House of Lords) illustrates, enforcement of legislation of this kind, if the particular item is successfully exported, is difficult.

5. Difficult conflict of laws questions can also arise as to the determination of title to stolen goods. See *Winkworth* v *Christie, Manson & Woods Ltd* [1980] 1 All E R 1121.

6. See generally, Morris, Legal and Ethical Issues in the Trade in Cultural Property (1990) NZLJ 40. She suggests that three interests are at stake in cultural property cases. First, *preservation* (why?). Second, *integrity* (the notion that certain types of works have cultural meaning only if retained in their context). Third, *accessibility* (the term may mean several things, including intergenerational accessibility so as to be able to hand down cultural identity).

7. The Department of Internal Affairs has released an Issues Paper as a preliminary step towards the introduction of a new Protection of Movable Cultural Property Bill. The Paper suggests that there are three concerns with the present New Zealand legislation. First, that the Act is difficult to enforce. (Why?) Second, that 'the legislation dealing with taonga Maori needs to take greater account of the Treaty of Waitangi'. Third, after *Ortiz* there has been 'a growing interest in New Zealand being able to accede to the 1970 UNESCO Convention [on the means of dealing with cultural property].'

The proposed legislation would contain three central features. First, under the existing act, 'newly found' Māori items made or modified prior to 1902 are declared to be prima facie the property of the Crown. The proposed legislation would ensure that Māori items remain the property of Māori in accordance with the Treaty of Waitangi. Second, the Bill would set up a Cultural Heritage Control List specifying categories of objects which may not be exported without a permit from the Secretary for Internal Affairs. Third, all those trading in taonga tukuiho would need to be licensed by the Secretary of Internal Affairs. (Taonga tukuiho has been defined as 'any movable object created by or modified by the Maori or by their descendants or any other person; (a) which is of cultural, spiritual, historical, aesthetic, or heritage significance and value to the Maori; and (b) which has been handed down a descent line of not less than two generations; or, is not less than 50 years old').

8. For a thoroughly engrossing account of the controversy over the Elgin marbles see Merryman, Thinking about the Elgin Marbles (1984-85) 83 Michigan Law Rev 1881. See also, Bator, An Essay on the International Trade in Art (1981-82) 34 Stanford Law Rev 275, and Kenety, Who Owns the Past? The Need for Legal Reform and Reciprocity in the International Art Trade (1990) 23 Cornell International Law Journal 1.

9. For the problems of indigenous peoples and cultural property see Clements, Misconceptions of Culture: Native Peoples and Cultural Property under Canadian Law (1991) 49 Univ of Toronto Faculty of Law Rev 1.

4

Emerging Property Rights

The materials in this chapter cover four subject areas where claims to new kinds of proprietary rights have been made in recent years. The materials are included for three reasons.

First, it is obvious that the law changes from time to time. How and why it does so, and the relative importance of changes in society, the economy and politics, and the intellectual forces acting on the law are matters of some debate. The conventional wisdom is that property law changes, and has changed, more slowly than many other areas of the law. This, it is said, reflects the necessity for property law to be more 'certain' than other areas of the law. This argument *may* be true in relation to land and chattels. But, in recent years there have been a number of claims for an enlarged conception of property. These assertions of 'extended concepts of property' afford an opportunity to review changes in the legal subject matter which the law has had to address, and may also reflect changes in the way in which we think about law in general and property law in particular.

Secondly, in some of the new subject areas, the claims are based on statutory provisions which use the word 'property' without further elaboration. Lawyers and judges then have to define the term. How are they to do so? What techniques do they employ? How successful have contemporary legal systems been in confronting this problem?

Thirdly, these new kinds of claims raise problems for lawyers in the definition of legal concepts and the intellectual arrangement of the law. They pose problems as to the consequences thereof: for example, limitation periods and precise remedies. In many ways these claims to new kinds of property are testing the limits of the traditional categorizations of the law and are also deserving of study on that account.

The four areas we shall consider here are: property rights to information; property rights to one's own personality; property rights to human body parts; and property rights in a degree or professional training as matrimonial property.

Property Rights to Information

Over the last quarter of a century the notion that advanced countries are now information societies or post-industrial societies has increasingly gained currency in both academic and popular literature. There is talk of communications revolutions or a third wave in civilization. Behind the various phrases used lies the notion that the production and distribution of information is an economic activity of very considerable value. The notion is that Western societies have proceeded through agrarian revolutions and industrial revolutions and are now encountering a third kind of revolution. The argument is not that each wave has succeeded the last, because agriculture and industry are still important. Rather the new information sector is like adding an additional layer to an already complex societal sponge cake. Some studies indicate that more than fifty per cent of gross national product and more than fifty per cent of the entire work force are now devoted to the production and dissemination of information and that there has been a concomitant growth in the service sector.

According to Herbert S Dordick: 'New Zealand ranks high on the world ladder of information societies. In 1976 [it] came second only to the United States among the Pacific Basin countries in the number of information workers in the work force.' (*Information Technology and Economic Growth in New Zealand* (1987), 16; and see generally, Lyon, *The Information Society* (1988)).

Undoubtedly because of the value of much information *per se* or in accumulated terms, or because of the competitive edge it can give in the market place, individuals and businesses have become more aware of the need to protect what they, in lay terms, describe as their 'proprietary' information.

Traditionally the common law refused to regard information as property. Thus, in *Boardman* v *Phipps* [1967] 2 A.C. 46, the House of Lords, by a majority, said that information could not form the subject matter of a trust. And in *Oxford* v *Moss* [1979] Crim Law Rev 119 (QB) it was held that the misappropriation of an examination paper by a student could lead to a charge of stealing the paper itself, but not the information contained therein. Against that background, consider the following case.

Stewart v The Queen

Supreme Court of Canada
[1988] 1 SCR 963; 50 DLR (4th) 1.

[A Union was wishing to organize the formation of a new labour bargaining unit involving approximately 600 employees of a hotel in Toronto. It was unable to obtain the names, addresses and telephone numbers of the employees because of the hotel policy that such information be treated as confidential. This hotel also barred Union representatives from the premises. Stewart was hired to obtain the names and addresses of these 600 employees. He offered a security guard at the hotel a fee to obtain this information. This security guard, at all relevant times, had not been authorized by any of the appropriate people, nor did he have any consent or right whatsoever to access the personnel files, payroll printouts or any hotel record whatsoever for names, addresses or telephone numbers of employees. He knew that the hotel had refused to divulge any such information to the Union, its representatives and agents. This case did not involve an attempt to obtain a physical object. It was agreed by the Crown and the appellant that no tangible object, such as a list containing the information sought, would have been taken had the scheme been carried out. The security guard reported the offer to his security chief and the police. As a result, a telephone conversation involving Stewart was recorded and Stewart was charged with (amongst other things) counselling theft.

The trial judge held that information *per se* cannot be the subject matter of a charge of theft; the Ontario Court of Appeal by a two to one majority reversed him. The case proceeded to the Supreme Court of Canada. The extract below is taken from the unanimous judgment of that Court, delivered by LAMER J.].

*   *   *

Theft

Section 283(1) of the *Criminal Code* reads as follows:

> 283(1) Every one commits theft who fraudulently and without colour of right takes, or fraudulently and without colour of right converts to his use or to the use of another person, anything whether animate or inanimate, with intent,
>> (a) to deprive, temporarily or absolutely, the owner of it or a person who has a special property or interest in it, of the thing or of his property or interest in it,
>> (b) to pledge it or deposit it as security,
>> (c) to part with it under a condition with respect to its return that the person who parts with it may be unable to perform, or
>> (d) to deal with it in such a manner that it cannot be restored in the condition in which it was at the time it was taken or converted.

In order to be convicted of theft, one has to take or convert "anything whether animate or inanimate" with the requisite intent as described in paras. (a) to (d). To determine whether confidential information can be the object of theft, the meaning of "anything" must be ascertained. The word "anything" is very comprehensive and is not in itself restricted in any way. As such it could include both tangible things and intangibles. Appellant contends that the offence of theft contemplates only physical objects. Under Canadian law as it now stands, however, "anything" has been held to encompass certain choses in action, which are intangibles. In *R. v. Scallen, supra,* the accused was convicted on a charge of theft of credit in a financial institution. The British Columbia Court of Appeal held that bank credit was included in "anything" under s. 283(1) (at p. 473):

> I see no reason to construe "anything" in s. 283(1) with stress on "thing", and I think the word should be construed in its broad sense and to mean exactly what it says, that theft can be committed of "anything" that was property. That would include a bank credit in a bank account—which any normal person having one would describe by saying that "he had money in the bank". I think it would be difficult to convince him otherwise, even if in strict domestic law all he had was the right to draw money from the bank in cash, by banknotes, by cheque or by transfers elsewhere.

The reasoning in *Scallen*, with which I am in agreement, was followed in *R. v. Hardy* (1980), 57 C.C.C. (2d) 73, 25 B.C.L.R. 362 (B.C.C.A.). Since certain choses in action can be the subject of theft, what must be decided for the purpose of this appeal is whether intangibles other than choses in action are to be included in the word "anything".

In *R. v. Offley* (1986), 28 C.C.C. (3d) 1, 11 C.P.R. (3d) 231, 70 A.R. 365, the Alberta Court of Appeal was of the view that information, even when qualified as confidential, is not "anything" within the meaning of s. 283(1), because it is intrinsically incapable of being an inanimate thing. In that case, the accused offered money to a police officer to run for him security checks on job applicants through the Canadian Police Information Centre, knowing that this information was available only to law enforcement agencies. As in the case before us, he was charged with counselling theft of information. The court disagreed with the majority decision of the Ontario Court of Appeal in the case at bar and acquitted the accused.

We are here dealing not with the theft of a list or any other tangible object containing confidential information, but with the theft of confidential information *per se*, a pure intangible. As mentioned earlier, the assumption that no tangible object would have been taken was part of the agreed statement of facts, and the case was argued throughout on that basis. The word "anything" is not in itself a bar to including any intangible, whatever its nature. However, its meaning must be determined within the context of s. 283 of the *Code*. Indeed, while sexual intercourse was found to be included in "anything" within the meaning of the extortion provision (*R. v. Bird*, [1970] 3 C.C.C. 340, 71 W.W.R. 256, 9 C.R.N.S. 1 (B.C.C.A.)), it does not necessarily follow that the same must be found under our law of theft.

In my view, the wording of s. 283 restricts the meaning of "anything" in two ways. First, whether tangible or intangible, "anything" must be of a nature such that it can be the subject of a proprietary right. Secondly, the property must be capable of being taken or converted in a manner that results in the deprivation of the victim.

With respect to the first restriction, the courts below have decided the case on the assumption that "anything" has to be property. While appellant's counsel takes issue with the relevancy of this qualification, I am of the view that such qualification is proper. In my opinion, it is clear that to be the object of theft, "anything" must be property in the sense that to be stolen, it has to belong in some way to someone. For instance, no conviction for theft would arise out of a taking or converting of the air that we breathe, because air is not property.

It can be argued—as Professor Weinrib does in "Information and Property" (1988), 38 U.T.L.J. 117—that confidential information is property for the purposes of civil law. Indeed, it possesses many of the characteristics of other forms of property: for example, a trade secret, which is a particular kind of confidential information, can be sold, licensed or bequeathed, it can be the subject of a trust or passed to a trustee in bankruptcy. In the commercial field, there are reasons to grant some form of protection to the possessor of confidential information: it is the product of labour, skill and expenditure, and its unauthorized use would undermine productive efforts which ought to be encouraged. As the term "property" is simply a reference to the cluster of rights assigned to the owner, this protection could be given in the form of proprietary rights. The cases demonstrate that English and Canadian civil law protect confidential information. However, the legal basis for doing so has not been clearly established by the courts. Some cases have treated confidential information as property, and thus have entitled the owner to exclude others from the use thereof: *Aas v. Benham*, [1891] 2 Ch. 244 (C.A.) *Exchange Telegraph Co. Ltd. v. Gregory & Co.*, [1896] 1 Q.B. 147 (C.A.); *Exchange Telegraph*

Co., Ltd. v. Central News, Ltd., [1897] 2 Ch. 48; *Exchange Telegraph Co. v. Howard* (1906), 22 T.L.R. 375 (Ch. Div.). On the other hand, the courts have recognized certain rights with respect to confidential information in the guise of an equitable obligation of good faith: *Peter Pan Manufacturing Corp. v. Corsets Silhouette, Ltd.,* [1963] 3 All E.R. 402 (Ch. Div.); *Saltman Engineering Co., Ltd. v. Campbell Engineering Co., Ltd.,* [1963] 3 All E.R. 413n (C.A.); *Argyll v. Argyll,* [1965] 2 W.L.R. 790 (Ch. Div.); *Pre-Cam Exploration & Development Ltd. v. McTavish* (1966), 57 D.L.R. (2d) 557, 50 C.P.R. 299, [1966] S.C.R. 551; *Seager v. Copydex, Ltd.,* [1967] 2 All E.R. 415 (C.A.); *Boardman v. Phipps* [1967] 2 A.C. 46 (H.L.); *Fraser v. Evans,* [1968] 3 W.L.R. 1172 (C.A.).

It appears that the protection afforded to confidential information in most civil cases arises more from an obligation of good faith or a fiduciary relationship than from a proprietary interest. No Canadian court has so far conclusively decided that confidential information is property, with all the civil consequences that such a finding would entail. The case-law is therefore of little assistance to us in the present case.

It is possible that, with time, confidential information will come to be considered as property in the civil law or even be granted special legal protection by statutory enactment. Even if confidential information were to be considered as property under civil law, it does not, however, automatically follow that it qualifies as property for the purposes of criminal law. Conversely, the fact that something is not property under civil law is likewise not conclusive for the purpose of criminal law. Whether or not confidential information is property under the *Criminal Code* should be decided in the perspective of the criminal law.

In *Oxford v. Moss* (1978), 68 Cr. App. R. 183, the Divisional Court had to decide whether confidential information was "intangible property" for the purposes of the *Theft Act, 1968*. A student was accused of stealing an examination paper that he hoped to return without being detected. After considering a number of civil authorities dealing with the subject of confidential information, Smith J. wrote (at pp. 185-6):

> Those are cases concerned with what is described as the duty to be of good faith. They are clear illustrations of the proposition that, if a person obtains information which is given to him in confidence and then sets out to take an unfair advantage of it, the courts will restrain him by way of an order of injunction or will condemn him in damages if an injunction is found to be inappropriate. It seems to me, speaking for my part, that they are of little assistance in the present situation in which we have to consider whether there is property in the information which is capable of being the subject of a charge of theft. In my judgment, it is clear that the answer to that question must be no.

In civil law, the characterization of something as property triggers a series of legal consequences. That characterization has the same effect under the criminal law, although the consequences are somewhat different. If confidential information is considered as property for the purposes of the theft section, other sections of the *Criminal Code* relating to offences against property may also apply: ss. 27 (use of force to prevent commission of offence), 38 (defence of movable property), 39 (defence with claim of right), 302 (robbery), 312 (possession of property obtained by crime), 350 (disposal of property to defraud creditors), 616 (restitution of property), 653 (compensation for loss of property), and 654 (compensation to *bona fide* purchasers). For example, let us assume a person obtains confidential information by the commission of a crime, such as theft if it were possible. If, after having memorized the information, that person is incapable of erasing it from his memory, he could, one might argue, be charged with an offence under s. 312 of the *Criminal Code* for each day that he is unable to forget the information.

Furthermore, the qualification of confidential information as property must be done in each case by examining the purposes and context of the civil and criminal law. It is understandable that one who possesses valuable information would want to protect it from unauthorized use and reproduction. In civil litigation, this protection can be afforded by the courts because they simply have to balance the interests of the parties involved. However, criminal law is designed to prevent wrongs against society as a whole. From a social point of view, whether confidential information should be protected requires a weighing of interests much broader than those of the parties involved. As opposed to the alleged owner of the information, society's best advantage may well be to favour the free flow of information and greater accessibility by all. Would society be willing to prosecute the person who discloses to the public a cure for cancer, although its discoverer wanted to keep it confidential?

The criminalization of certain types of conduct should not be done lightly. If the unauthorized appropriation of confidential information becomes a criminal offence, there would be far-reaching consequences that the courts are not in a position to contemplate. For instance, the existence of such an offence would have serious implications with respect to the mobility of labour. In "Theft of Information" (1984), 100 L.Q. Rev. 252, Hammond points out (at p. 260) the problem that would follow:

> [W]hat is significant for present purposes about the traditional civil law formulations with respect to such [employee] covenants is that, notwithstanding their difficulties of application, they do allow a balance to be struck in particular cases between the various interests at stake. The criminal law on the other hand allocates responsibility in black and white terms. There is either an offence or there is not. Every employee who leaves a position in Canada now faces criminal sanctions if he misjudges a line which judges have had enormous difficulty in drawing in civil law cases.

This indirect restriction on the mobility of labour is only one of the many undesirable consequences that could result from a hasty extension of criminal provisions by qualifying confidential information as property.

Moreover, because of the inherent nature of information, treating confidential information as property *simpliciter* for the purposes of the law of theft would create a host of practical problems. For instance, what is the precise definition of "confidential information"? Is confidentiality based on the alleged owner's intent or on some objective criteria? At what point does information cease to be confidential and would it therefore fall outside the scope of the criminal law? Should only confidential information be protected under the criminal law, or any type of information deemed to be of some commercial value? I am of the view that, given recent technological developments, confidential information, and in some instances, information of a commercial value, is in need of some protection through our criminal law. Be that as it may, in my opinion, the extent to which this should be done and the manner in which it should be done are best left to be determined by Parliament rather than by the courts.

Indeed, the realm of information must be approached in a comprehensive way, taking into account the competing interests in the free flow of information and in one's right to confidentiality or again, one's economic interests in certain kinds of information. The choices to be made rest upon political judgments that, in my view, are matters of legislative action and not of judicial decision. Illustrative of this is the complexity of the schemes suggested to legislatures and Parliaments by the various reform agencies in this country, the United Kingdom and the United States: *e.g.* Institute of Law Research and Reform, *Trade Secrets*, Report No. 46, July, 1986.

For these reasons, I am of the opinion that, as a matter of policy, confidential information should not be property for the purposes of s. 283 of the *Code*. To the extent that protection is warranted for confidential information, it should be granted through legislative enactment and not through judicial extension of the concept of property or of the scope of the theft provision under the *Criminal Code*.

Although this conclusion is sufficient to dispose of the appeal on the charge of counselling theft, I will also consider the second restriction to the scope of the word "anything", that is, that property must be capable of being taken or converted in a manner that results in the deprivation of the victim. Tangible things present no difficulty in this regard, as it is easy to conceive how they can be both taken and converted. On the other hand, pure intangibles, as they have no physical existence, can obviously only be converted, not taken. The "taking" of an intangible could only occur where such intangible is embodied in a tangible object, for example, a cheque, a share certificate or a list containing information. However, that would not result in the taking of the intangible *per se*, but rather of the physical object evidencing it.

The question is thus whether confidential information is of a nature such that it can be taken or converted. In my opinion, except in very rare and highly unusual circumstances, it is not. As we have seen, information *per se* cannot be the subject of a taking. As for conversion, it is defined as an act of interference with a chattel inconsistent with the right of another, whereby that other is deprived of the use and possession of it. Confidential information is not of a nature such that it can be converted because if one appropriates confidential information without taking a physical object, for example, by memorizing or copying the information or by intercepting a private conversation, the alleged owner is not deprived of the use or possession thereof. Since there is no deprivation, there can be no conversion. The only thing that the victim would be deprived of is the confidentiality of the information. In my opinion, confidentiality cannot be the subject of theft because it does not fall within the meaning of "anything" as defined above.

It is no doubt possible to imagine far-fetched situations where the victim would actually be deprived of confidential information; for instance, to give but one example, if an outsider elicits from an employee of the company, who is the only employee to hold a secret formula, not only that confidential information but also the undertaking to keep it secret from his employer. In these circumstances, assuming that confidential information is property, the element of deprivation would be met. However, we must recognize that these factual situations are somewhat fanciful and will seldom occur. It would be odd indeed that these rare situations be covered by the law of theft, while the vast majority of cases concerning the appropriation of confidential information would remain beyond the reach of our theft section. I am thus of the view that as a matter of policy, it is best to exclude altogether confidential information from the realm of theft.

In the case at bar, the majority of the Court of Appeal held that if Hart had taken the information requested, the hotel would not have been deprived of the information, but of its character of confidentiality. As a result, the court was of the opinion that Hart would have had the intent set out in s. 283(1)(*d*, that is, dealing with the information in such a manner that it could not be restored in its original, confidential, condition. With respect, the Court of Appeal did not properly consider the *actus reus* required for committing the offence, that is, a taking or a conversion. As I said, one cannot be deprived of confidentiality, because one cannot own confidentiality. One enjoys it. Therefore, appellant should not have been convicted on the sole basis that he might have had the intent set out in s. 283(1)(*d*) since the commission of the *actus reus* was not and could not be established.

Before this court, respondent also argued that appellant intended to deprive the hotel of the special property or interest which it had in the list, contrary to s. 283(1)(*a*). Respondent contended that this special property or interest is what gave the list its value, namely, its confidentiality, and thus that the absence of intent to deprive of the use of the information is irrelevant. I cannot agree with this suggestion. The "special property or interest" in s. 283(1)(*a*) refers to a proprietary possessory right in the thing stolen. This section contemplates, for example, the case of the owner of an object who, having pawned it, steals it back from the pawnbroker. Theft would then be committed because the pawnbroker has a special property or interest in the object, even against the owner. Although confidentiality might give some value to the information, it does not confer a special property or interest in it to anyone. Since confidential information is not property, it follows that one cannot have a proprietary possessory right in something that is not property. Furthermore, as I have said above, establishing that an offender has the intent required is not sufficient proof of guilt if the *actus reus* has not been committed.

As an additional ground for finding guilt, Cory J.A. held that even if information *per se* is not property, there still remains a right of property in confidential information which is now protected by the provisions of the *Copyright Act*. As copyright is, in his view, property, it falls within the scope of s. 283(1) and can therefore be the object of theft. The employer's list in the case at bar is indeed a "literary work" as defined in s. 2 of the Act, and thus the subject of copyright under s. 3 thereof. Does that mean, however, that the unauthorized reproduction of copyrighted information amounts to theft?

Copyright is defined as the exclusive right to produce or reproduce a work in its material form (s. 3). A mere copier of documents, be they confidential or not, does not acquire the copyright nor deprive its owner of any part thereof. No matter how many copies are made of a work, the copyright owner still possesses the sole right to reproduce or authorize the reproduction of his work. Such copying constitutes an infringement of the copyright under s. 17 of the Act, but it cannot in any way be theft under the criminal law. While one can, in certain circumstances, steal a chose in action, the rights provided in the *Copyright Act* cannot be taken or converted as their owner would never suffer deprivation. Therefore, whether or not copyright is property, it cannot, in my opinion, be the object of theft under s. 283(1) of the *Code*.

To summarize in a schematic way: "anything" is not restricted to tangibles, but includes intangibles. To be the subject of theft it must, however:

1. be property of some sort;
2. be property capable of being:
   (a) taken—therefore intangibles are excluded; or
   (b) converted—and may be an intangible;
   (c) taken or converted in a way that deprives the owner of his proprietary interest in some way.

Confidential information should not be, for policy reasons, considered as property by the courts for the purposes of the law of theft. In any event, were it considered such, it is not capable of being taken as only tangibles can be taken. It cannot be converted, not because it is intangible, but because, save very exceptional far-fetched circumstances, the owner would never be deprived of it.

For all these reasons, I am of the opinion that confidential information does not come within the meaning of the word "anything" of s. 283(1) of the *Criminal Code*.

Notes and Questions

1. The decision in *Stewart* is a novel one in the British Commonwealth and provoked much controversy before and after the decision. This author suggested in several articles that the Court of Appeal decision in *Stewart* and certain other developments like it represented an improper extension of proprietary concepts. I said that *Stewart* was inconsistent with earlier authority, amounted to unwelcome judicial activism; that courts were not the sort of place to be making those kinds of extensions either to the criminal law or to proprietary concepts, and that the case would lead to undesirable consequences. (See Hammond, Theft of Information (1984) 100 LQR 252; Electronic Crime in Canadian Courts (1986) 6 Oxford J Legal Studies 145; The Misappropriation of Commercial Information in the Computer Age (1986) 64 Can. Bar Review 342. For comment after the decision of the Supreme Court by me see *R v Stewart*: The Final Judgment? (1989) 11 Supreme Court Law Review 421). The best reasoned reply to my views is that of Weinrib in Information and Property (1988) 38 UTLJ 117 (arguing that the Court of Appeal decision in *Stewart* is a natural and desirable application of the concept of property, and of the protection that follows from that categorization).

2. In 1981 I suggested:

The most striking characteristic of information is that it does not fit easily with extended concepts of property. First, sole ownership is vastly complicated in the case of information. The act of theft is often impossible to detect and difficult to prove. A piece of information can be 'owned' by two people at the same time without any denial of the conventional benefits of ownership. Second, some kinds of information can be infinitely multiplied at low cost. Third, information generally does not depreciate with use and some kinds of information of a theoretical character actually inflate in value with usage. Fourth, unused information is, in general, of no use but the moment information is used it reveals both its existence and content and may actually enter what is conventionally referred to as the public domain. Fifth, the creation of information is routinely a joint activity and the apportionment of creativity is then rendered extraordinarily difficult. Sixth, the creation of technology and information is tending to move on shorter frequencies: commercial advantage is inextricably intertwined with innovation. Longer frequency functional vehicles such as the statutory monopolies, are becoming increasingly inappropriate for this pronounced shift in commercial time frames. Seventh, the volume of available information has reached overwhelming proportions . . . [but] the disabilities of the individual in relation to the sum of knowledge become progressively more severe as the sum increases. Eight, in economic terms, public goods are separated from private goods by a principle of exclusion. Although that principle can still apply to information it is routinely invoked only at considerable cost. [Quantum Physics, Econometric Models and Property Rights to Information (1981) 27 McGill LJ 47, 54]

Are there other characteristics of information that would make its characterization as property difficult? Impossible?

3. Professor Weirib says that: 'The taking of confidential information is just as real a taking as the theft of tangibles. It should also attract criminal sanctions, and for the same reasons.' (150). Do you agree?

4. How else might confidential information be protected? One can, of course, insert a restraint of trade clause in a contract, subject to the usual rules about such clauses, viz. that they be reasonable both in the public interest and as between the parties (*Nordenfelt* v *Maxim Nordenfelt Guns and Ammunition Co.* [1894] AC 535) and the adjustment powers of New Zealand courts under the Illegal Contracts Act 1970. In the law of torts there are the various economic torts such as passing off, and, if it exists in New Zealand, unfair competition. And equity has long recognized a doctrine of breach of confidence. Under that doctrine a person who discloses information imparted to him or her in confidence, in circumstances which import an obligation of confidence, and without just cause or excuse, can be restrained and in some circumstances may be liable for damages. See, for the latest illustration in New Zealand, the Spy Catcher litigation (*Attorney General for the UK* v *Wellington Newspapers* [1988] 1 NZLR 129 and 180). In the British Commonwealth it has been generally thought that an action in breach of confidence involves a purely personal right. Because of this the Australian High Court in *Moorgate, supra,* held that the rights of a party entitled to the confidence are not assignable and not proprietary in character. (See Hammond, Breach of Confidence: Assignability of Rights (1986) 2 IPJ 247). Does such a holding make sense?

5. The border line between proprietary rights and rights protected by a breach of confidence can be difficult to define. Consider again the case of *Foster* v *Mountford & Rigby Ltd.* (1976-7) 14 ALR 71. It will be recalled that in that case an academic researcher wrote a book containing revelations of Australian aboriginal cultural

and religious secret ceremonies disclosed in confidence to Mountford some twenty-five years before. The book was prefaced by a caveat that where aboriginals were concerned the contents should be used only after consultation with local male religious leaders. The local aboriginal council (an unincorporated body) sought, on behalf of the aboriginal people concerned, an injunction prohibiting publication of the book within the Northern Territories.

How would you present such an argument? That the tribe had property in its secrets? Or, that there was an obligation enforceable in equity not to reveal the secrets? And, if we are to say that somebody had a property right to the tribal secrets, who would that somebody be, and on what basis would the claim rest? What would the consequences of a claim sounding in property be? What would the consequences of a claim sounding in equity be? Could the claim be mounted on more than one basis? What would the consequences of that be?

6. The argument that information *per se* does not amount to property does not mean that particular kinds of information could not, and should not, receive proprietary protection. For instance, in its report to the Minister of Justice on Insider Trading in 1987 the New Zealand Securities Commission recommended that in various ways certain kinds of confidential corporate information should be treated as being proprietary in character. And in Report No 46 (1986), *Trade Secrets*, to the Federal and Provincial Governments in Canada, the Institute of Law Research and Reform in Canada recommended that the misappropriation of trade secrets should give rise to a civil action and also amount to a criminal offence. On the other hand, in 1973 the Torts and General Law Reform Committee of New Zealand recommended that judicial protection of confidential business information should be left to the judiciary. More recently, in the United Kingdom, the Law Commission in *Breach of Confidence* (Law Com No 110 (1981)) recommended a statutory scheme of protection.

Why do you think there is such a marked diversity of opinion between academic commentators, judges and law reform bodies on these issues? Assume that you are counsel to the Justice Department or the Law Commission in Wellington. Would you recommend that the civil law and the criminal law be aligned as to what might be taken to be confidential information? Why? What kinds of actions or penalties would you wish to see enacted in New Zealand today? What remedies would you provide in civil actions?

7. Why do we protect secrets at all? See Bok, *Secrets: On the Ethics of Concealment and Revelation* (1984).

Property in Personality and Image

Just as there have been attempts to turn information into a commodity and describe it as a proprietary interest, so there have been attempts recently in some jurisdictions to turn personality and image into a commodity. The question here is seemingly simple but very complex from a legal point of view. Does Paul Holmes have a sufficiently distinct image or personality that copying it (even outside copyright law) infringes a proprietary right? Can a member of the All Blacks or Allison Roe claim to protect something distinctive about themselves? Cases in the entertainment law area have become particularly important in an age when entertainment industries are amongst the fastest growing service industries in the world. The material that follows is merely designed to raise the issues.

Krouse v *Chrysler Canada Ltd*

Ontario Court of Appeal
(1974) 1 OR (2d) 225; 40 DLR (3d) 15

Krouse was a professional gridiron (football) player for the Hamilton Tiger Cats in Canada. A photograph of him taken in the course of a game was used on a promotional device known as the *Plymouth Pro Football Spotter* which was distributed by Chrysler during the Canadian football season. This picture was used without Krouse's permission and without payment of any endorsement fee. Krouse claimed damages under the heading of an invasion of privacy but it was also suggested that Chrysler had appropriated his identity for commercial purposes without his consent or compensation, thereby impairing his ability to gain endorsements with other automobile manufacturers. In the Supreme Court of Ontario ((1972) 25 DLR (3d) 49) Haines J awarded Krouse $1000 in damages. His Lordship questioned whether there was a property right in the indicia of one's identity, image or personality. He said:

> Was this wrongful appropriation a taking of a property right of Krouse's? . . . His picture for advertising purposes has real value as advertisers fell it enhances saleability and it is common practice to pay for endorsements and the like. One would think that the wrongful appropriation of that which in the business world has commercial value and is traded daily must *ipso facto* involve a property right which the Courts protect. Property being an open-ended concept to protect the possession and use of that which has measureable commercial value, logic seems to impel such results.

The matter was appealed to the Ontario Court of Appeal. There the decision was reversed. The Court of Appeal thought that Chrysler was merely seeking to gain a trade advantage by associating itself with football, which is a popular sport. The picture was not a deliberate association with any particular team or player and could not fairly be regarded as an endorsement by Krouse of Chrysler products. But Estey J did say: '[The] common law does contemplate a concept in the law of torts which may be broadly classified as an appropriation of one's personality'.

Zacchini v *Scripts-Howard Broadcasting Co.*

United States Supreme Court
433 U.S. 562 (1977).

[Zacchini developed a spectacle in which he acted as a 'human cannon ball'. He was shot from a cannon into a net some two hundred feet away. This act took some fifteen seconds and was video taped in its entirety at a county fair in Ohio by a reporter for the defendant broadcasting company. The event was televised later the same day. The case eventually reached the Supreme Court of the United States where Mr Justice White described Zacchini's property interest, and the rationale for its existence, at pages 573-78 in the following terms.]

* * *The differences between these two torts are important. First, the State's interests in providing a cause of action in each instance are different. "The interest protected" in permitting recovery for placing the plaintiff in a false light "is clearly that of reputation, with the same overtones of mental distress as in defamation." Prosser, supra, 48 Calif L Rev, at 400. By contrast, the State's interest in permitting a "right of publicity" is in protecting the proprietary interest of the individual in his act in part to encourage such entertainment. As we later note, the State's interest is closely analogous to the goals of patent and copyright law, focusing on the right of the individual to reap the reward of his endeavors and having little to do with protecting feelings or reputation. Second, the two torts differ in the degree to which they intrude on dissemination of information to the public. In "false light" cases the only way to protect the interests involved is to attempt to minimize publication of the damaging matter, while in "right of publicity" cases the only question is who gets to do the publishing. An entertainer such as petitioner usually has no objection to the widespread publication of his act as long as he gets the commercial benefit of such publication. Indeed, in the present case petitioner did not seek to enjoin the broadcast of his act; he simply [**433 US 574**] sought compensation for the broadcast in the form of damages.

Nor does it appear that our later cases, such as Rosenbloom v Metromedia, Inc. 403 US 29, 29 L Ed 2d 296, 91 S Ct 1811 (1971); Gertz v Robert Welch, Inc. 418 US 323, 41 L Ed 2d 789, 94 S Ct 2997 (1974); and Time, Inc. v Firestone, 424 US 448, 47 L Ed 2d 154, 96 S Ct 958 (1976), require or furnish substantial support for the Ohio court's privilege ruling. These cases, like New York Times, emphasize the protection extended to the press by the First Amendment in defamation cases, particularly when suit is brought by a public official or a public figure. None of them involve an alleged appropriation by the press of a right of publicity existing under state law.

[**2b**] Moreover, Time, Inc. v Hill, New York Times, Metromedia, Gertz, and Firestone all involved the reporting of events; in none of them was there an attempt to broadcast or publish an entire act for which the performer ordinarily gets paid. It is evident, and there is no claim here to the contrary, that petitioner's state-law right of publicity would not serve to prevent respondent from reporting the newsworthy facts about petitioner's act. Wherever the line in particular situations is to be drawn between media reports that are protected and [**433 US 575**] those that are not, we are quite sure that the First and Fourteenth Amendments do not immunize the media when they broadcast a performer's entire act without his consent. The Constitution no more prevents a State from requiring respondent to compensate petitioner for broadcasting his act on television than it would privilege respondent to film and broadcast a copyrighted dramatic work without liability to the copyright owner, Copyrights Act, 90 Stat 2541 (1976); cf. Kalem Co. v Harper Bros. 222 US 55, 56 L Ed 92, 32 S Ct 20 (1911); Manners v Morosco, 252 US 317, 64 L Ed 590, 40 S Ct 335 (1920), or to film and broadcast a prize fight, Ettore v Philco Television Broadcasting Corp. 229 F2d 481 (CA3), cert denied, 351 US 926, 100 L Ed 1456, 76 S Ct 783 (1956); or a baseball game,

Pittsburgh Athletic Co. v KQV Broadcasting Co. 24 F Supp 490 (WD Pa 1938), where the promoters or the participants had other plans for publicizing the event. There are ample reasons for reaching this conclusion.

The broadcast of a film of petitioner's entire act poses a substantial threat to the economic value of that performance. As the Ohio court recognized, this act is the product of petitioner's own talents and energy, the end result of much time, effort, and expense. Much of its economic value lies in the "right of exclusive control over the publicity given to his performance"; if the public can see the act free on television, it will be less willing to pay to see it at the fair. The [433 US 576] effect of a public broadcast of the performance is similar to preventing petitioner from charging an admission fee. "The rationale for [protecting the right of publicity] is the straightforward one of preventing unjust enrichment by the theft of good will. No social purpose is served by having the defendant get free some aspect of the plaintiff that would have market value and for which he would normally pay." Kalven, Privacy in Tort Law—Were Warren and Brandeis Wrong?, 31 Law & Contemp Prob 326, 331 (1966). Moreover, the broadcast of petitioner's entire performance, unlike the unauthorized use of another's name for purposes of trade or the incidental use of a name or picture by the press, goes to the heart of petitioner's ability to earn a living as an entertainer. Thus, in this case, Ohio has recognized what may be the strongest case for a "right of publicity"—involving, not the appropriation of an entertainer's reputation to enhance the attractiveness of a commercial product, but the appropriation of the very activity by which the entertainer acquired his reputation in the first place.

[8, 9] Of course, Ohio's decision to protect petitioner's right of publicity here rests on more than a desire to compensate the performer for the time and effort invested in his act; the protection provides an economic incentive for him to make the investment required to produce a performance of interest to the public. This same consideration underlies the patent and copyright laws long enforced by this Court. As the Court stated in Mazer v Stein, 347 US 201, 219, 98 L Ed 630, 74 S Ct 460 (1954):

> "The economic philosophy behind the clause empowering Congress to grant patents and copyrights is the conviction that encouragement of individual effort by personal gain is the best way to advance public welfare through the talents of authors and inventors in 'Science and useful Arts.' Sacrificial days devoted to such creative activities deserve rewards commensurate with the services rendered."

[433 US 577] These laws perhaps regard the "reward to the owner [as] a secondary consideration," United States v Paramount Pictures, 334 US 131, 158, 92 L Ed 1260, 68 S Ct 915 (1948), but they were "intended definitely to grant valuable, enforceable rights" in order to afford greater encouragement to the production of works of benefit to the public. Washingtonian Publishing Co. v Pearson, 306 US 30, 36, 83 L Ed 470, 59 S Ct 397 (1939). The Constitution does not prevent Ohio from making a similar choice here in deciding to protect the entertainer's incentive in order to encourage the production of this type of work. Cf. Goldstein v California, 412 US 546, 37 L Ed 2d 163, 93 S Ct 2303 (1973); Kewanee Oil Co. v Bicron Corp. 416 US 470, 40 L Ed 2d 315, 94 S Ct 1879, 69 Ohio Ops 2d 235 (1974). [433 US 578]

[10, 11] There is no doubt that entertainment, as well as news, enjoys First Amendment protection. It is also true that entertainment itself can be important news. Time, Inc. v Hill. But it is important to note that neither the public nor respondent will be deprived of the benefit of petitioner's performance as long as his commercial stake in his act is appropriately recognized. Petitioner does not seek to enjoin the broadcast of his performance; he simply wants to be paid for it. Nor do we think that a state-law damages remedy against respondent would represent a species of liability without fault contrary to the letter or spirit of Gertz v Robert Welch, Inc. 418 US 323, 41 L Ed 2d 789, 94 S Ct 2997 (1974). Respondent knew exactly that petitioner objected to televising his act, but nevertheless displayed the entire film.

[12] We conclude that although the State of Ohio may as a [433 US 579] matter of its own law privilege the press in the circumstances of this case, the First and Fourteenth Amendments do not require it to do so.

Reversed.

Notes and Questions

1. Do cases like *Krouse* and *Zacchini* overrule or go beyond *Victoria Park* by recognizing that one can have property rights in a spectacle? If so, what is the basis of these kinds of property claims?

2. Do these kinds of claims amount to *true* property claims? If so, is property in personality and image obtainable by contract or transmissible by will? If the answer to these questions is in the affirmative, are we not talking about true property interests?

Further Reading

1. For commentary on a right of publicity see Frazer, Appropriation of Personality—A New Tort? (1983) 99 LQR 281 and Howell, The Common Law Appropriation of Personality Tort (1986) 2 IPJ 149.

2. For US case law on the effect of such an interest being created, see the following cases concerning the estates of Laurel and Hardy, Elvis Presley and Bella Lugosi. *Price v Hal Roach Studio* 400 F Supp. 836 (1975); *Factors etc. Box Car Enterprises v Pro Art Inc* 579 F(2d) 215 (1978); *Lugosi v Universal Pictures* 603 P (2d) 425 (1979). See also Terrell and Smith, Publicity, Liberty, and Intellectual Property: A Conceptual and Economic Analysis of the Inheritability Issue (1985) 34 Emory L J 1.

Property in Human Body Parts

In an earlier chapter we noted the difficulties raised by the Māori heads case. In this section we look more generally at the problem of human body parts. We live in an age in which it has become increasingly possible to transfer human organs from one person to another. The most publicized instances have probably been the heart transplants, but other organ transplants are routinely performed.

How is the law to deal with this situation? Should an individual be able to sell one of his or her kidneys to another person? Or, after a person is 'dead', by whatever definition of death is adopted, should that person's legal representatives be able to sell a part of that person's body, such as the corneas, to somebody else?

Some of the older philosophical writers emphasized that people have property in their own bodies. You will recall that Locke thought that somehow *all* other property was a derivative of bodily property: ". . . every man has a property in his own person; this nobody has the right to but himself", (*Of Civil Government*). But courts have been reluctant to characterize the human body and its parts as the subject matter of property. In reading the following materials consider the reasons for this reluctance, whether those reasons are well-founded in today's circumstances, and the kinds of problems that the public, lawyers, the courts and legislators face in erecting a legal regime to deal with this subject matter.

The Common Law

The common law position was that a person does *not* 'own' his or her body. Hence, a dead body could not be stolen. But those persons responsible for the estate of a deceased person had the right and the duty to see to proper burial according to law (*R v Sharpe* (1857) D & B 160; 169 ER 959). Under the Cemeteries Act 1908 a person may in their lifetime direct (in writing) that their body is to be cremated, but their executors are not bound to carry out this direction.

The rights of a person to their own living tissue or organs are more complicated and controversial.

Stealing the Body and its Parts

A T H Smith
[1976] Crim L R 622

The incidental disclosure in *Welsh* that a man was convicted of theft for pouring down the sink a urine sample that he had given in compliance with section 9 of the Road Traffic Act 1972 raises questions about the treatment of the human body, its parts and its products as the proper subject-matter of theft.

A person commits theft by appropriating property belonging to another (Theft Act 1968, s. 1 (1)). What counts as "property" for this purpose is not defined by the Act, this being a matter for the law generally. There was a rule at common law, the origins of which are obscure, that there could be no property in the human body for the purpose of the law of larceny, and it is generally supposed that the same rule applies to theft. That a man does now "own" his body is perhaps an intelligible proposition. Interference with the body is the invasion of a personal right, not a proprietary right.

The judges permitted the logic of this rule to survive the death of the person in question. A man's body, not being his property, was not part of his estate passing to his personal representatives on his death. The corpse was no more a subject of property than the living body. East reports what seems to be the first case directly in point. Trover was brought against a *Dr. Handyside* (1749) for the recovery of the bodies of Siamese twins, and it was held by Willis C.J. that no action would lie "as no person had any property in corpses." How the Doctor came by this *lusus naturae*, who sought possession of them and why, is not disclosed. Nor is any explanation given for the rule. But jurists and judges transposed the rule into the criminal law. Readers of *The Tale of Two Cities* will remember the activities of Jerry Cruncher, who was known in polite circles as a "resurrectionist" but more prosaically as a "body snatcher". He dug up corpses after burial and disposed of them secretly for the purposes of dissection. He was not a thief, because the judges took the view that a corpse was *res nullius*; but such conduct was held to be a common law misdemeanour.

Authority for this view was rather scanty. Blackstone asserted that "stealing the corpse itself, which has no owner (though a matter of great indecency), is no felony, unless some of the grave-clothes be stolen with it." No judicial authority for this is cited, the reader being referred to a previous statement where *Haynes's Case* is mentioned but not discussed. That was a case in which William Haynes dug up four bodies, removed the shrouds and replaced them. He was convicted of stealing the shrouds. It was resolved by all the judges at Serjeant's Inn in Fleet Street that *inter alia*, "the dead body is not capable of any property." It is clear from the context in which the remark is uttered that the judges meant that the corpse could not own property because it was like earth.

Despite these murky origins, the rule that there could be no property in a corpse assumed in this country the proportions of an unalterable truth. Not so in either America or Canada. Nor is the peculiar view of corpses taken by the criminal law wholeheartedly accepted by the civil law. The executor (or other person having possession of the corpse) has "property" in it for the purpose of proprietary remedies, at least to the extent that the law recognises, as incidental to the duty to dispose of the body, rights to the possession of the body until it is disposed of.

How far the no-property rule extends even in the criminal law is a matter of conjecture. After a period of time, a body may acquire attributes that differentiate it from a corpse awaiting burial, especially where work has been expended on it by reducing it to a skeleton or mummifying it. Nor does there seem to be authority dealing with severed parts of the body or its products, although magistrates have held it to be theft to cut another's hair against his (more commonly perhaps her) will. Since the person taking from a live human being will invariably be guilty of some form of assault, the addition of a charge of theft in such circumstances would seem to be rather pointless. In any case, it would seem logically to follow from the no-property rule that severed parts of the body are not the proper subject-matter of theft, but in the absence of authority the point is approachable in terms of principle.

Nobody acquainted with modern jurisprudence would quarrel with the opening words of *Crossley Vaines on Personal Property* that "property is a word of different meanings" (p.3). It may be used to mean different things in different contexts, and the courts are free to (and should) examine the policy behind the rule in which the word appears. There are two principal reasons why the no-property rule should be confined within narrow limits. As a purely legal matter, it is anomalous. Even if it is true that the corpse is *res nullius* at the moment of death, there is no reason why it should not become property by *occupatio*. If the civil law recognises and protects rights to possession, there is no reason why the criminal law should not do likewise. Similar arguments apply to parts of the body which, like the corpse itself, might lose their character as such, as when human hair is manufactured into wigs. But irrespective of whether this ever happens, there are in purely practical terms strong grounds for refusing to extend the no-property rule to the parts and products of the human body. As a result of advances in medical science, many parts of the body have a usefulness unimaginable to our forbears. Use can now be made of the eyes, bones and skin and, provided they can be utilised with sufficient speed to prevent anoxic damage, the heart, liver and kidneys. Although the point might rarely arise in practice, it would seem absurd that these valuable objects (for they are when severed nothing more) should continue to be treated as *res nullius*. There is no reason why blood, eye or sperm banks should be denied the protection of the criminal law. Nor should it matter that the limb is eventually useless or that, like the urine sample in *Welsh*, the thing taken is of little commercial value. The value rule is not reproduced in the Act, and since the Act makes no special provision excluding parts of the body, it is submitted that they fall under the general rule relating to the theft of property.

Perhaps the strongest argument against a reappraisal of the no-property rule at this stage is that the medical profession is in practice the group most likely to fall foul of it. It has recently been held that it is an offence under section 1(4) of the Human Tissue Act 1961, punishable by unlimited fine or imprisonment, for a person other than a full registered medical practitioner to remove part of a dead body. It could be argued that this provides ample protection against unauthorised tampering with therapeutically useful corpses without at the same time jeopardising the medical profession. Indeed doctors might be forgiven for thinking that the law has already proved itself hopelessly slow in responding to urgent medical problems. That a fresh obstacle should be raised at this stage is but a further example of an unnecessarily legalistic and obstructive approach.

In reply, the following points could be made. It is precisely the advance in medical knowledge, which has added a new dimension to the usefulness of the deceased human body, that necessitates a fresh look at the law. A rule premised on medical knowledge not much more advanced than that of Harvey scarcely commands much respect. As has been pointed out, the rule is in any case an anomaly of uncertain ambit, and although a prosecution for theft is unlikely, it cannot be ruled out altogether. It is in just such emotively charged areas that a private prosecution is an ever present possibility. As it is, it is uncertain whether the doctor who proceeds otherwise than in accordance with the provisions of the Human Tissue Act commits an offence. Contradictory views have been expressed. And there is, in any case, argument about the scope of the provisions of that Act, section 1(2) of which provides that "the person lawfully in possession of" a body may authorise its use for therapeutic purposes. Whether this enables hospital authorities to grant permission has been questioned. Certainly, it would seem that once the executors have demanded the body, there is a strong case for saying that the hospital is no longer in possession and cannot authorise use of the body even though this may override the expressed wishes of the deceased.

For several years, the law in this area has been under review. Most legislative proposals have been aimed at making body organs more readily available. If these proposals should ever materialise, the opportunities for misunderstandings are increased. It is suggested that we would be unwise to proceed without some consideration of the impact that this might have on the law of theft.

Hunter v Hunter

(1930) 65 OLR 586

An aged man had been a devout Protestant all his life. His wife was a devout Roman Catholic. During his last illness he said he wished to be buried where his wife would be buried. This was taken to mean a Roman Catholic cemetery. He was baptized by a Catholic priest, and received into the Roman Catholic Church on the 30th April. Two weeks later he died. There was some conflict over his mental condition during his last illness. One of his sons was named as executor in the deceased's last will, which was admitted to probate. There was a contest between members of his family as to where he should be buried. It was held that the executor son had the right to the body for burial purposes, even against the widow, and an injunction was granted preventing other members of the family from interfering in the burial.

The Control of Living Body Materials

B Dickens
(1967) 27 UTLJ 142, 180-3.

A philosophical approach to the origination from a living body of independently tangible material or of fluids capable of isolation may be to consider them *res nullius*, that is, corporeal items in the legal ownership of nobody. They might be reduced into possession by the first person to obtain physical control who intends to exercise contol over them, in accordance with a test of classical jurisprudence. Thus prescription of possession from which ownership may be inferred would by definition afford the human source no prior interest. In a sophisticated legal system where personal property rights are highly developed, the list of items constituting *res nullius* is short. The concepts of property and ownership has tended to be pragmatic, evolving in response to economic or spiritual recognition of objects as having values; 'property' described a valuable right or interest in a thing, moreover, rather than the thing itself. * * *

No theoretical limit can be set to how far the law may go in recognizing new property interests. Materials as abstract as gas may be possessed or stolen, as may electricity, and vibration has been treated as an 'object' in trespass and possibly nuisance law. * * *

The characterization of separated body materials as *res nullius* might serve the interests of neither the human source nor others. To suggest that material immediately passes into the absolute ownership of the hospital or physician undertaking or supervising its removal and intending to appropriate it might defeat the source's justifiable interest in its use or disposition and the purpose of its specific donation, for instance for diagnosis, transplantation, or a particular research project. It may be inadequate regarding even body wastes, of which a person will normally relieve himself as speedily and conveniently as possible compatible with social delicacy, expecting and hoping never to hear of it again. Sanitary regulations and the general law of nuisance required one in charge of premises or land on which such waste is discharged adequately to dispose of it, and his claim that it is *res nullius* and that he has not reduced it into his possession will carry little weight; liability is attached, however, as an incident of land tenure rather than of control of the materials per se.

Recognizing waste materials as *res nullius*, capable of exclusive legal control by a person first possessing them, clearly will not serve the interests of the human source. Similarly, recognition as *res nullius* of materials such as a limb, or digit severed from the human source in an accident or in an assault may be inconsistent with his interests in its preservation for prompt surgical rejoining to his body. His claim to it should not be impaired by the chance of the item falling upon another's land or being retrieved and retained by stranger not implicated in causing the loss. A better approach, therefore, may be to consider the human source as having an incohate right of property in materials issuing from his body, which right he might expressly or by implication abandon to another, or similarly make prevail over a contending claim.

This may well accord to the sentimental reaction to the origination of body material in its separate state. The right is better considered incohate than fully constituted, since the material may never in fact come under the sources notional or physical control. He may be unconscious, for instance, when it is separated, and it may be deemed abandoned, perhaps to hospitals, very soon after it is first isolated. Traditional jurisprudential tests of, for instance, intention, possession, and control as affecting ownership may more easily be preserved by considering the initial interest of the source prima facie a superior right to that of any other person but a right only in prospect.

Whose Body? People as Property

P Matthews
(1983) 36 Current Legal Problems 193.

We have attempted to examine the reasons and authorities for the view that human tissue and products cannot be the subject of property. A major stumbling block has been to decide what we should understand by "property" at all, and to what extent definitions of property in one context should apply in any other. Whilst it does seem difficult to conceive of buried corpses as in any realistic way "property" (unless it can be seen as part of the realty), the difficulty is less acute in the case of unburied corpses or cremated remains, and, particularly in cases where burial is not intended, it does seem hard to say that no-one should have any rights in such material amounting to property, at least to the extent of giving it the protection of the theft and criminal damage legislation.

Finally, where parts and products of living people are concerned, the question is even less tainted by morbid or sentimental considerations, and it is submitted that there is no justification for holding the "no-property" rule to apply here. If a flourishing "spare-part" market should arise, then it is up to Parliament to regulate it, rather than to leave the matter to the inconsequential dicta of judges and commentators who lived in times when medicine was so undeveloped as to rest virtually on a par with sorcery and alchemy. But so far as the general rule regarding property in human tissue is concerned, then given the dearth of binding authority in England, the persuasive value of the view of judges in other jurisdictions, and the pragmatic common law adaptability we prize so highly, surely it is possible to bring up to date this long-neglected corner of our law, without waiting for Parliament to act?

The Human Tissue Act

In New Zealand The Human Tissue Act 1964 (RS vol 16, 169) contains provisions relating to post-mortem examinations, the practice of anatomy, and the removal of human tissue for therapeutic purposes and for purposes of medical education and research.

Under section 3 thereof, if any person, either in writing at any time or orally in the presence of two or more witnesses during that person's last illness, has expressed a request that their body or any specified part of their body may be used after their death for therapeutic purpoes or for purposes of medical education or research, the person lawfully in possession of the body after death may, unless such person has reason to believe that the request was subsequently withdrawn, authorize the removal from the body of any part or, as the case may be, the specified part, for use in accordance with the request.

Without limiting that provision a person lawfully in possession of the body of a deceased person may authorize the removal of any part from the body for use for therapeutic purposes if, 'having made such reasonable inquiry as may be practicable' that person has no reason to believe (a) that the deceased person had expressed an objection to his or her body being so dealt with after death, and had not withdrawn it; or (b) that the surviving spouse or any surviving relatives of the deceased person objects to the body being so dealt with.

Under section 7 of the same statute the Governor-General in Council may from time to time authorize the establishment of schools of anatomy. It is not lawful for any person to perform an anatomical examination or to receive or have in their possession any body for an anatomical examination at any place other than a school of anatomy.

Any post-mortem or anatomical examination for the removal of any part of a body pursuant to this Act is required to be done (pursuant to section 11 of the Act) "in a manner that avoids unnecessary mutilation of the body which is being examined or from which such removal is being effected, and the removal [shall be conducted] in an orderly, quiet and decent manner".

The statute is dated, and does not make provision, as do many human tissue statutes in other parts of the British Commonwealth, for *inter vivos* gifts for transplantations. For instance, under the Alberta Human Tissue Gift Act (RSA

1980 c12 s 3) any adult person who is mentally competent to consent and is able to make a free and informed decision may in a writing signed by him consent to the removal forthwith from his body of the tissues specified in the consent and the implantation of those tissues in the body of another living person. A consent given under that section is 'full authority for any physician' to make any examination necessary and 'to remove forthwith that tissue from the body of the person who gave the consent'.

Notes and Questions

1. A gives a kidney to B. A then finds that her remaining kidney is failing. Assuming it to be medically possible, should A be able to reclaim 'her' kidney? Should these kinds of problems be left to development by the judiciary? Should they be legislated for? What sorts of principles should inform such legislation? What sorts of drafting problems would you foresee in preparing legislation of that kind?

2. In a case currently pending in California (*Moore* v *Regents of the University of California*, Los Angeles Superior Court No C 513 755) the following occurred. Mr Moore was diagnosed as having a rare cancer, and his diseased spleen was surgically removed. After the operation, Mr Moore's doctor and a university colleague experimented with cells from the spleen and developed a cell line that proved extremely valuable both therapeutically and for research. The cell line was patented and sold to biotechnology firms. Mr Moore has sued the researchers, the University and several biotechnology firms, alleging proprietary and other claims. The case is noted by Allan in (1986) 6 California Lawyer, 22. Mr Allan notes:

> Is a patient entitled to any profits from biomedical products that were developed from the patient's own flesh and blood. The answer may hinge on whether traditional property rights adhere to a patient's pound of flesh as it is researched, metamorphosed and marketed by others.

How would you resolve such a claim? See Appendix.

3. In Human Tissue Research: Who Owns the Results? (1987) 14 J of College and University Law 260, Allen Wagner suggests that 'transfer of a thing transfers all its incidents, unless expressly reserved. . . . In contrast, an abandonment places the property in the state of naure and makes it available to a subsequent taker's claim by occupancy.' (271). What do you say to his propositions?

4. What are the relevant public policy considerations in this sort of case? Should there be a property interest in unknown advantages? Should there be a property interest in natural processes? (This has much troubled Courts dealing with patent cases. Why?) Would an implied reservation inhibit the research process?

5. Late in 1989 the British General Medical Council's professional conduct committee began hearing a case against three doctors accused of taking part or acquiescing 'in the sale of human organs'. The case related to the transfer of kidneys from four Turkish nationals to certain recipients. The four were paid 'thousands of dollars' for their kidneys. But one woman in India who sold one of her kidneys received 'just the price of an alarm clock and battery'. Apart from any questions

as to the legality of the organ transplants, Mr Roger Henderson QC, told the tribunal that it appeared that the unhealthy rich in wealthy countries were preying on poor third world countries for organs.

Matrimonial Property—Property in a Degree

In most jurisdictions in the last twenty years legislatures have instituted new matrimonial property regimes designed to overcome certain restrictions on married women owning property; to declare that some or all of the assets of a marriage are matrimonial property and to better ensure a fair and equitable division of matrimonial property upon the dissolution of marriage. The New Zealand scheme— first enacted in 1963—follows quite closely upon North American developments (particularly those of Ontario) in providing for matrimonial property and non-matrimonial property. The broad presumption with respect to matrimonial property is that such property is to be divided equally on the dissolution of marriage. Some regimes, often called community property regimes, go further and treat all assets of the spouses as being subject to equal or some specified division.

Questions have arisen from time to time under these new statutory regimes as to what is 'property'? One issue which has proved troublesome in North America, and will ultimately raise its head in New Zealand, is the question of whether a degree (and particularly a professional qualification) can be considered to be property for the purposes of legislation of this kind.

Woodworth v Woodworth

Court of Appeals
337 NW (2d) 332

T. M. Burns, Presiding Judge.

On January 6, 1982, the parties' divorce was finalized. Both parties appeal as of right.

The parties were married on June 27, 1970, after plaintiff had graduated from Central Michigan University with a bachelor's degree in secondary education and defendant had graduated from Lansing Community College with an associates degree. They then moved to Jonesville, where plaintiff worked as a teacher and coach for the high school and defendant worked as a nursery school teacher in Hillsdale. In the Fall of 1973, they sold their house, quit their jobs, and moved to Detroit, where plaintiff attended Wayne State Law School. Three years later, they moved to Lansing where plaintiff took and passed the bar exam and accepted a job as a research attorney with the Court of Appeals. Plaintiff is now a partner in a Lansing law firm.

For all intents and purposes, the marriage ended on August 25, 1980, when the parties separated. The following summarizes each party's earnings during the marriage:

YEAR	PLAINTIFF		DEFENDANT	
1970	$ 2,591	Jonesville HS teacher/coach	$ 1,422	Nursery School Tech.
			$2 549	Grant Company (clerk)
1971	$ 7,989	Teacher	$ 4,236	Teacher
	$ 410	St. Anthony Ch. (instructor)	$ 280	St. Anthony Ch. (instructor)
1972	$ 9,691	Teacher	$ 2,525	Teacher
1973	$ 6,557	Teacher	986	Bank Teller
1974	$ 2,483	Legal Aid (student lawyer)	$ 6,572	Bank Teller
1975	$ 2,588	Legal Aid (student lawyer)	$ 1,050	Bank Teller
			$ 8,191	Dept/Social Services (case worker)
1976	$ 6,342	Court of Appeals (attorney)	$10,276	Dept/Social Services (case worker)
1977	$12,493	Court of Appeals (attorney)	$ 1,586	Dept/Social Services (case worker)
	$ 5,595	Asst. Pros. Atty.		
1978	$21,085	Asst. Pros. Atty.	$-0-	
1979	$27,247	Asst. Pros. Atty.	$-0-	
1980	$ 2,057	Asst. Pros. Atty.	$-0-	
	$30,000	Private Practice		

The basic issue in this case is whether or not plaintiff's law degree is marital property subject to distribution. The trial court held that it was, valued it at $20,000 and awarded this amount to defendant in payments of $2,000 over ten years. Plaintiff contends that his law degree is not such a marital asset. We disagree.

The facts reveal that plaintiff's law degree was the end product of a concerted family effort. Both parties planned their family life around the effort to attain plaintiff's degree. Toward this end, the family divided the daily tasks encountered in living. While the law degree did not preempt all other facets of their lives, it did become the main focus and goal of their activities. Plaintiff left his job in Jonesville and the family relocated to Detroit so that plaintiff could attend law school. In Detroit, defendant sought and obtained full time employment to support the family.

[1] We conclude, therefore, that plaintiff's law degree was the result of mutual sacrifice and effort by both plaintiff and defendant. While plaintiff studied and attended classes, defendant carried her share of the burden as well as sharing vicariously in the stress of the experience known as the "paper chase".

We believe that fairness dictates that the spouse who did not earn an advanced degree be compensated whenever the advanced degree is the product of such concerted family investment. The degree holder has expended great effort to obtain the degree not only for him—or herself, but also to benefit the family as a whole. The other spouse has shared in this effort and contributed in other ways as well, not merely as a gift to the student spouse nor merely to share individually in the benefits but to help the marital unit as a whole.

This conclusion finds support in *Vaclav v. Vaclav*, 96 Mich.App. 584, 293 N.W.2d 613 (1980), and *Moss v. Moss*, 80 Mich.App. 693, 264, N.W.2d 97 (1978), *Iv.*

den. 402 Mich. 946 (1978), which held that an advanced degree is an asset which could be considered in a property settlement. In addition, other jurisdictions have allowed the spouse who did not earn an advanced degree to recover: *In re Marriage of Lundberg*, 107 Wis.2d 1, 318 N.W.2d 918 (1982); *O'Brien v. O'Brien*, 114 Misc.2d 233, 452 N.Y.S.2d 801 (1982); *DeLa Rosa v. DeLa Rosa*, 309 N.W.2d 755 (Minn. 1981); *Hubbard v. Hubbard*, 603 P.2d 747 (Okl. 1979); *In re Marriage of Horstmann*, 263 N.W.2d 885 (Iowa 1978); *Daniels v. Daniels*, 90 Ohio. L.Abs. 161, 20 Ohio Ops.2d 458, 185 N.E.2d 773 (Ohio App. 1961).

We are aware that numerous other cases have held that an advanced degree is not a marital asset and may be considered only (if at all) in determining alimony: *In re Marriage of Sullivan*, 134 Cal.App.3d 634, 184 Cal.Rptr 796 (1982); *Lesman v. Lesman*, 88 App.Div.2d 153, 452, N.Y.S.2d 935 (1982); *Mahoney v. Mahoney*, 182 N.J.Super. 598, 442 A.2d 1062 (1982); *Wisner v. Wisner*, 129 Ariz. 333, 631 P.2d 115 (Ariz. App. 1971); *In re Marriage of Goldstein*, 97 Ill.App.3d 1023, 53 Ill.Dec. 397, 423 N.E.2d 1201 (1981); *In re Marriage of McManama*, 399 N.E.2d 371 (Ind. 1980); *Frausto v. Frausto*, 611 S.W.2d 656 (Tex.Civ.App. 1980); *Graham v. Graham*, 194 Colo. 429, 574 P.2d 75 (1978); *Nastrom v. Nastrom*, 262 N.W.2d 487 (N.D. 1978); *Muckleroy v. Muckleroy*, 84 N.M. 14, 498 P.2d 1357 (1972); *Todd v. Todd*, 272 Cal.App.2d 786, 78 Ca.Rptr. 131 (1969).

However, we reject the reasons given in these cases to support their conclusions. The cases first contend that an advanced degree is simply not "property":

> "An educational degree, such as an M.B.A., is simply not encompassed by the broad views of the concept of 'property'. It does not have an exchange value or any objective transferable value on an open market. It is personal to the holder. It terminates on death of the holder and is not inheritable. It cannot be assigned, sold, transferred, conveyed, or pledged. An advanced degree is a cumulative product of many years of previous education, combined with diligence and hard work. It may not be acquired by the mere expenditure of money. It is simply an intellectual achievement that may potentially assist in the future acquisition of property. In our view, it has none of the attributes of property in the usual sense of that term." *Graham, supra*, 194 Colo. 432, 574 P.2d 75.

Yet whether or not an advanced degree can physically or metaphysically be defined as "property" is beside the point. Courts must instead focus on the most equitable solution to dissolving the marriage and dividing among the respective parties what they have.

> "[T]he student spouse will walk away with a degree and the support spouse will depart with little more than the knowledge that he or she has substantially contributed toward the attainment of that degree." Comment, *The Interest of the Community in a Professional Education*, 10 Cal. West L. Rev. 590 (1974).

In *DeLa Rosa, supra*, 309 N.W.2d 758, the Minnesota Supreme Court added:

> "[O]ne spouse has foregone the immediate enjoyment of earned income to enable the other to pursue an advanced education on a full-time basis. Typically, this sacrifice is made with the expectation that the parties will enjoy a higher standard of living in the future."

Where, as in this case, the family goal of obtaining the law degree was the purpose of the substantial contribution and sacrifice, both the degree holder and his or her spouse are entitled to share in the fruits of the degree. The trial judge recognized as much:

> "Here the plaintiff quit his job and entered law school. The defendant secured employment so plaintiff could become a professional with far greater earning capacity than he had, which would benefit him and their children. To permit this, upon divorce, to benefit only the party who secured the professional degree is unconscionable."

The next argument is that a marriage is not a commercial enterprise and that neither spouse's expectations are necessarily going to be met after the divorce:

> "I do not believe that a spouse who works and contributes to the education of the other spouse during marriage normally does so in the expectation of compensation." *Sullivan, supra*, 184 Cal.Rptr. 801 (Kaufman, P.J., concurring).

Furthermore:

> "They do not nor do they expect to pay each other for their respective contributions in any commercial sense. Rather, they work together, in both income and nonincome producing ways, in their joint, mutual and individual interests.
>
> "The termination of the marriage represents, if nothing else, the disappointment of expectations, financial and nonfinancial, which were hoped to be achieved by and during the continuation of the relationship. It does not, however, in our view, represent a commercial investment loss. Recompense for the disappointed expectations resulting from the failure of the marital entity to survive cannot, therefore, be made to the spouses on a strictly commercial basis which, after the fact, seeks to assign monetary values to the contributions consensually made by each of the spouses during the marriage.

*   *   *

> "If the plan fails by reason of the termination of the marriage, we do not regard the supporting spouse's consequent loss of expectation by itself as any more compensable or demanding of solicitude than the loss of expectations of any other spouse who, in the hope and anticipation of the endurance of the relationship in its commitments, has invested a portion of his or her life, youth, energy and labor in a failed marriage." *Mahoney, supra*, 182 N.J.Super. 612-614, 442 A.2d 1062.

We agree that a marriage is not intrinsically a commercial enterprise. Instead, it is a relationship sanctioned by law governed at its essence by fidelity and troth. Neither partner usually expects to be compensated for his or her efforts. But that consideration does not end the discussion. We are not presently concerned with how best to characterize a marriage while it endures. Instead, we are concerned with how best to distribute between the parties what they have once the marriage has for all intents and purposes dissolved. In other words:

> "To allow a student spouse * * * to leave a marriage with all the benefit of additional education and a professional license without compensation to the spouse who bore

much of the burdens incident to procurring these would be unfair ∗ ∗ ∗" *O'Brien,* *supra*, 452 N.Y.S.2d 805.

Furthermore, we also agree that divorce courts cannot recompense expectations. However, we are not talking about an expectation here. Defendant is not asking us to compensate for a failed expectation that her husband would become a wealthy lawyer and subsequently support her for the rest of her life. Instead, she is merely seeking her share of the fruits of a degree which she helped him earn. We fail to see the difference between compensating her for a degree which she helped him earn and compensating her for a house in his name which her earnings helped him buy.

The third argument against including an advanced degree as marital property is that its valuation is too speculative. In *Lesman, supra*, 452 N.Y.S.2d 938-939, the Court stated:

> "Gross inequities may result from predicating distribution awards upon the speculative expectation of enhanced future earnings, since distributive awards, unlike maintenance, once fixed may not be modified to meet future realities. It is almost impossible to predict what amount of enhanced earnings, if any, will result from a professional education. The degree of financial success attained by those holding a professional degree varies greatly. Some, even, may earn less from their professional practices than they could have earned from non-professional work. Moreover, others, due to choice or factors beyond their control, may never practice their professions."

Michigan has already recognized that:

> "Interests which are contingent upon the happening of an event which may or may not occur are not distributable. The party seeking to include the interest in the marital estate bears the burden of proving a reasonable ascertainable value; if the burden is not met, the interest should not be considered an asset subject to distribution." *Miller v. Miller*, 83 Mich.App. 672, 677, 269 N.W.2d 264 (1978).

However, future earnings due to an advanced degree are not "too speculative". While a degree holder spouse might change professions, earn less than projected at trial, or even die, courts have proved adept at measuring future earnings in such contexts as personal injury, wrongful death, and workers' compensation actions. In fact, pain and suffering, professional goodwill and mental distress, within these general legal issues, have similar valuation "problems". *Graham, supra* 194 Colo. 434, 574 P.2d 75 (Carrigan, J., dissenting); *Inman, supra*; Moore, *Should a Professional Degree Be Considered a Marital Asset Upon Divorce?*, 15 Akron L. Rev. 543, 547 (1982) We, therefore, do not believe that the *Miller* contingency caveat applies to future earnings.

The last argument is that these matters are best considered when awarding alimony rather than when distributing property. See *Mahoney, supra*, 182 N.J.Super. 612-614, 442 A.2d 1062. A trial judge is given wide discretion in awarding alimony. *Westrate v. Westrate*, 50 Mich.App. 673, 213 N.W.2d 860 (1973), *Iv. den.* 391 Mich. 812 (1974). However, alimony is basically for the other spouse's support. *Kavanagh v. Kavanagh*, 30 Mich.App. 636, 186 N.W.2d 870 (1971), *Iv. den.* 384 Mich.

843 (1971). The considerations for whether or not a spouse is entitled to support are different than for dividing the marital property. *McLain v. McLain*, 108 Mich.App. 166, 310 N.W.2d 316 (1981), listed eleven factors that the trial judge is to consider in determining whether or not to award alimony. Some of these deal with the parties' financial condition and their ability to support themselves. If the spouse has already supported the other spouse through graduate school, he or she is quite possibly already presently capable of supporting him or herself. Furthermore, M.C.L.A. § 552.13; M.S.A. § 25.93 gives the trial court discretion to end alimony if the spouse receiving it remarries. We do not believe that the trial judge should be allowed to deprive the spouse who does not have an advanced degree of the fruits of the marriage and award it all to the other spouse merely because he or she has remarried. Such a situation would necessarily cause that spouse to think twice about remarrying. Se *O'Brien, supra; Hubbard, supra.*

Having determined that the defendant is entitled to compensation in this case, we must next determine how she is to be compensated. Two basic methods have been proposed—a percentage share of the present value of the future earnings attributable to the degree or restitution.

The Courts in *Inman, supra, Horstmann, supra,* and *DeLa Rosa, supra,* limited the recovery to restitution for any money given to the student spouse to earn the degree. While this solution may be equitable in some circumstances, we do not believe that restitution is an adequate remedy in this case. Limiting the recovery to restitution "would provide [the supporting spouse] no realization of [his or] her expectation of economic benefit from the career for which the education laid the foundation". Pinnell, *Divorce After Professional School: Education and Future Earning Capacity May Be Marital Property*, 44 Mo.L.Rev. 329, 335 (1979). Clearly, in this case, the degree was a family investment, rather than a gift or a benefit to the degree holder alone. Treating the degree as such a gift would unjustly enrich the degree holder to the extent that the degree's value exceeds its cost. Loper, *Horstmann v. Horstmann: Present Right to Practice a Profession as Marital Property*, 56 Den.L.J. 677, 689 (1979). We note that this case does not involve the situation where both parties simultaneously earned substantially similar advanced degrees during the marriage. In such a situation, equity suggests that the parties have already amply compensated each other. .

[2] The trial court in this case valued plaintiff's law degree at $20,000 and ruled that plaintiff must pay defendant $2,000 per year for ten years. We are unable to determine how this value was reached and, therefore, remand to the trial court to permit that court to revalue the degree in light of the following factors: the length of the marriage after the degree was obtained, the sources and extent of financial support given plaintiff during his years in law school, and the overall division of the parties' marital property. In determining the degree's present value, the trial court should estimate what the person holding the degree is likely to make in that particular job market and subtract from that what he or she would probably have earned without the degree. *Recompense for Financing Spouse's Education: Legal Protection for the Marital Investor in Human Capital*, 28 Kan.L.Rev. 379, 382-384 (1980). The ultimate objective in a property distribution is to be fair. *Darwish v. Darwish*, 100 Mich. App. 758, 300 N.W.2d 399 (1980). Both parties may present new evidence on these matters and the degree's valuation.

One of the tragedies of this divorce, as in so many others, is that what used to be financially adequate is no longer enough. As the trial court aptly stated: "The table-cloths * * * will not cover both tables." We, therefore, note that the trial court has discretion to order that the payments be made on an installment basis as was done in *Moss, supra,* and *O'Brien, supra.* If the trial court should order such a payment schedule, the trial court should also consider the possibility of insuring these payments by a life insurance policy on plaintiff's life benefitting defendant. * * *

Notes and Questions

1. The relevant provision in the New Zealand legislation is section 8 of the Matrimonial Property Act 1976, which *inter alia* catches 'all property acquired by either the husband or the wife after the marriage.' (Section 8(e)). 'Property' is defined in the same terms as in the Property Law Act 1952.

2. How is a Court to approach a statutory provision like this, in the absence of authority? One possible answer is to say that the question is one of pure statutory construction. That is, the words of the statute are to be considered in themselves and in their context of the Act. The purpose of the Act has always to be clearly kept most in mind. That said, difficult questions still arise. Why? Legislators may themselves have deliberately, or inadvertently, 'fudged' the question. That is, the word or phrase may have been left open deliberately as an expression to be filled in and developed judicially by the courts. In such circumstances, courts may well wish to have regard to decisions in cognate areas, although they are of persuasive authority only. In the end courts have to be guided by their own construction of the statute in a broad purposive sense and by considerations of both legal and social principle. Do you think the expression 'property' was deliberately left open in this statute? How could you find out? Would your research be relevant? Admissible?

3. Alternatively, should a Court adopt common law or equitable notions of property or a broader or narrower concept?

4. How would you decide *Woodworth* in New Zealand today, assuming the absence of any binding authority?

5. In *Whithead* v *Burrell* (1983) 47 BCLR 211 (SC) a property claim to a professional degree was denied. In Ontario in *Re Corless* (1987) 34 DLR (4th) 594 it was held that the right to practice law is a property right, but since it cannot be exchanged *per se* it has no value.

6. If a professional degree *is* property, should the concept also be extended to increased earning capacity arising from a trade training or even acquired skills, where the acquisition of those skills have resulted in assistance whether direct or indirect, by a spouse? And what of the situation of *de facto* partners?

7. For a good note on the US heartbalm statutes, see Note, Heartbalm Statutes and Deceit Actions (1985) 83 Michigan Law Review 1770.

Extended Property and Legal Theory

The difficulties which cases of the kind discussed in this chapter raise for legal theory fall broadly into two categories. First, the cases in this chapter (and there are other areas which could have been considered) raise very serious problems for the traditional doctrinal classifications of the law. It has often been observed that law is a relatively low-level intellectual endeavour. Lawyers create classifications and whether something comes within that classification or not has traditionally determined whether there is a cause of action and what kind of relief is then available.

In the last decade a considerable blurring of the traditional substantive classifications of the law has taken place. This has discomforted formalists who see the preservation of the doctrinal categories of the law as extremely important and has delighted nihilists and instrumentalists. Instrumentalists tend to be more overtly policy oriented, and think of 'property' as being no more than a label to be attached to achieve a desired end. Is that what is happening in these new areas of case law? Is this a good thing or a bad thing?

The second broad issue raised by these new areas of case law and legislation is with respect to the concept of property itself. As should by now be apparent, absolutist concepts of property have gradually given way (rightly or wrongly) to a more instrumental concept of property. From this point the picture becomes considerably more difficult to analyse and more diffused. Instrumental ends involve choices, but the desired ends are not always carefully articulated by judges and legislators. Personal, moral and cultural aims are often mixed up with distributional ones. As one writer put it, 'sexual, and racial equality, the right to control one's body, the right to a safe and clean environment rank alongside the question of who owns what.' (Edgeworth, Post Property?: a Post Modern Conception of Private Property (1988) 11 UNSWLJ 87, 115). Edgeworth ends with a clarion call: "The politics of *becoming* are precisely the post-modernist's call: to create new vocabularies in order to create new selves, new identities, new communities in the face of economic orders controlled by multinational corporations under the banner of private property or state socialist systems extolling a bureaucratised public ownership." Can courts achieve those objectives? For that matter, can legislatures?

Finally, a number of very well-qualified commentators have pointed to the grossly over-simplified way in which we tend to think of property today. The following essay was written as an introduction, but also forms an appropriate conclusion against which you may care to test the material you have read so far.

Some Theses on Property

Tay & Kamenka
(1988) 11 UNSWLJ 1

I. The Concept of Property

1. *Property is that which is owned.* Ownership is the *prima facie* ultimate power and right to use, control, enjoy and exclude others. It is a relationship both to the item owned and to other people. There is no ownership where it is impossible, in logic or in fact, to reduce something to possession and control. What Marxists and others have seen as the ever-increasing reduction of the world and everything in it to private property rests on the constant extension of the possibility of ownership as a result of scientific, technological and economic capacity to use.

2. *States extend their possessions in the same way as individuals; so do tribes and communities.* The treasures of the earth and of the seabed, land, air and water, and

even heavenly bodies, are now susceptible of ownership in a way and on a scale not known in most of human history. Socialist and Marxist-socialist states exercise their claims to sovereignty and the ownership it involves in ways and by means which are in no manner different from those pursued by states that recognise as central to their social systems the possibility of both 'private' and 'public' ownership of the means of production, distribution and exchange. They do so in relation to other countries and in relation to their own citizens. Their interest in ownership and control is the same as anybody else's: the exploitation of a resource for defence, for production, for wealth, or prestige. These are *infra*-jural facts—a useful reminder that the world is not simply the product of ideology or of law.

3. *The distinction between private ownership and public ownership is not central or even important for a general theory of ownership, or for a discussion of many of its social effects.* Nor is it central to a general theory of law or to the overcoming of so-called economic 'contradictions', of the fact that resources have to be allocated between alternative uses without meeting all possible demands or treating everyone equally.

4. *All ownership, and therefore all property, is in an important sense private or privatising.* It divides those who have the power and the right to exclude from, to control and dispose of a particular item of property from those who do not, who have no privileged connection with it. In that respect, 'public' ownership is the same ownership as 'private', individual or corporation ownership; state ownership the same as community ownership; clan ownership the same as that of persons. 'Private' does not mean individual, just as 'owner' does not and need not mean a single person or even a human being at all. In Ancient Sumeria, the temple and the associated workshops belonged to the god of the temple, in whose name and on whose behalf the temple manager—the *ensi*—issued commands that did not simply reflect the manager's will. To say *anyone* may use, control or dispose of without let or hindrance is to say this is not, or this is no longer, owned. A 'common' is a true common if and only if anyone has access for any purpose at any time and no one is excluded. Historically, that has not been the meaning of 'a common'.

5. In discussing the core meaning of the concept of ownership or of property, *it is not useful to import differences between types of owners or changes in some of the social functions and importance of property into the core concept of ownership itself.* We should not convert material differences into logical or conceptual differences, confuse a legal concept with its role and effects, whether in society or the law. The meaning of a concept is not simply its use; something about it determines how and where it can be used.

6. *In all societies, there are things that are owned, that constitute property that is in our sense private, and things that are not.* Communist constitutions protect personal property. Many Utopian constitutions, like monastic orders, professed not to, but protected state or community property. Even in comparatively undifferentiated societies with no ranks or classes and no, or little, agricultural use of land, there will be sacred things, symbols of authority, objects used in ritual, wives and other personal possessions for which some people are owners or custodians and from which some or all others are excluded. Nothing indicates the role of property in such societies more clearly than the social importance of the formalised exchange of gifts in such societies. Concepts of ownership may be very weakly developed, unimportant in the wider context of conceptions of the inherently sacred and

powerful, or of the claims of the tribe or group, but they exist. For the tribal infant 'promised in marriage', they are very important indeed. Some things—such as air or water or even land—may be seen by particular societies as physically or morally incapable of being owned, as more powerful than human beings. The same or other items may be specifically excluded from ownership by custom or law.

7. *There are no natural eternal necessities in the matter of the scope of ownership, though the physical capacity to control may vary over time as a result of both technological and political change.* The territorial claims of countries can contract and expand, advances in science and technology producing some striking expansions. A cadaver may be incapable of being owned for non-material reasons—until it becomes a source of valuable products: soap for the Nazis, organs for those needing a transplant. Then decent societies and lawyers cogitate, while the Hitlers and the Himmlers simply cut the Gordian Knot.

8. *There are and there have been no enduring social owners or rulers whose power over their property is logically absolute.* The sixteenth-century Ottoman Sulton Suleiman (The Magnificent,The Educator, the pattern for Max Weber's conception of sultanism as arbitrary personal power to rule) was subject to the laws of Islam. He had to recognise, for instance, quite different forms of tenure for conquered lands, for traditional Muslim lands, for Mecca and Medina, for Muslims and for infidels. His claim to ownership of land conquered from infidels was based on Islamic law. In China, a renewed attempt to introduce state distribution and control of land on different terms for different purposes was inaugurated by the Northern Wei from 485A.D. and applied more universally under the Sui and the Tang; it became inoperable because the landholdings of officials and of Buddhist monasteries retained their independence. In England after the Conquest, the King had ultimate ownership of all land; in European monarchies the sovereign had not but could be subject as Holy Roman Emperor or Prince to the Court in Vienna in respect of complaints by subject or prince. Neither the crown nor its power was indivisible. Further, the power ascribed to ownership, like all other social power, is distributed along a continuum which ranges in principle from utter impotence to absolute irresistability, but in fact rarely reaches either end. Nor are the most common forms of interference with ownership necessarily based on competing claims to ownership; people are deprived of their lands and possessions for specific reasons— rebellion, felony, the requirements of war or *raison d'état*. They may be forced, as a matter of social policy, to recognise the claims of heirs and dependants, of wider social concerns, of the King, the Church and of the Social Plan.

9. *In law and social life, ownership is a burden as well as a privilege, a responsibility as well as an advantage.* The need to make someone ultimately responsible for the care and control of property and for harm that flows from it is the reason that the concept of property has not been excised from any modern socialist or Marxist-socialist legal system. State and 'collective' property and delegated operational management remain central to economies that reject—or rejected until recently— 'private' property in the means of production, distribution and exchange. 'Collective' ownership does not mean ownership by all the people. Ownership will continue to remain central to some aspects of social control, as it remained in the utopian fantasies of the past and in Babeuf's and Saint-Simon's projects for the future. There it was concealed under such phrases as 'the social fund' that constitutes

the material wealth of a society and the administrators who will decide on its allocation. To make property a public function — the favourite slogan of the socialist Saint-Simonians gathered around *Le Globe* — is not to abolish the concept or to universalise effective power and control. It is to shift the practical focus from ownership to authorised administrative control.

10. *The rights and powers conferred by ownership are not and never have been indefeasible or unlimited, in law or in administrative reality.* The respect accorded to the right of the property owner including even the state can change, and has changed, dramatically. So can and do the respect and importance ascribed to different types of property and to different types of property owners. Neither the concept of property nor the social and legal importance of that concept in the abstract need be affected by that.

The distinction between the kinds of items owned and the different uses they are put to is crucial in considering the controls and limitations that may properly be put upon ownership rights. Such distinctions have been made throughout history and continue to be made as differences between the character and economic uses of property multiply. There are limitations, too, on the scale of ownership in certain areas, on concentration of ownership, on ownership in politically or socially sensitive areas.

11. *Ownership, even in its core meaning, is not a logical simple.* Its various components — for ownership is a bundle of rights and powers — are differentiable both as rights and as realities. They can and do come apart. There are degrees of enjoyment, of capacity to use, of control, of power to alienate. Formal ownership and actual control can and do part company, especially conspicuously in modern times as they did in feudal times. Further, the sort of rights that owners and others claim and exercise need not always be derived from or justified by the concept of ownership, though the Common Law did, for a long period, feel most comfortable with those rights against property — such as easements — which were themselves attached to property. There are traditional rights to use temporarily or at will sacred sites, to gather fruits of the field or wood from the forest, to cross boundaries in search of pasture, to have peaceful enjoyment, *etc.* Not the abstract rights of ownership but new economic uses, population pressures, conquest, *etc.* provide the motive power that most frequently creates or destroys such rights. Socially, ownership is not the be-all and end-all of human relationships to things or persons that can be owned. Slaves, in Rome and elsewhere, commanded Caesar's household and the free or freed men who served in it. Paradoxically, slavery was a legal concept but not an economic one. Similarly, there are grades and graduations between property and the *res nullius* — not all relationships to land or objects can be forced into one of these two pigeonholes. Law has more than one principle and more than one set of classifications. We do no service to law or to humanity in the long run by seeking to vindicate rights we seek or approve of by attaching them to the nearest sacred cow — whether it be property, or the right over one's body, or privacy or the freedom of speech. Constitutions can come and go; rights are not all derivable from one right. Lists of rights are not, by their nature, finite or uncriticisable. Advocacy is not the same as thinking about law or society. Property is not and never has been the foundation of all rights, of all social power, or of all social evils. It has been a significant bulwark against political, governmental

and religious power, not by standing in principle opposed to them but by fragmenting or helping to fragment and balance competing claims of King, baron, church and corporations, of state and citizens, of bureaucracies and those whom they administer. For ownership, as we have said, privatises—though only within limits. Exploitation can be based on proprietorial power; the worst forms of exploitation known to history were not. Neither were the theory of so-called bourgeois democracy, or of nineteenth-century liberalism, confined to the defence of property or derived from it. A history of modern Europe that reduces Protestantism, the Enlightenment and the French Revolution to the defence of 'bourgeois' private property and the free market is bad history and worse social theory.

II. Changes in the Nature and Power of Ownership

1. The concepts of ownership and possession tempt us, as they tempted Blackstone, to begin with the primary model of a relationship between a human owner or possessor and a corporeal thing that is owned or possessed. English law, unlike Roman law, recognised early the ownership or possession of incorporeal hereditaments and even of rights not necessarily connected with land, *e.g.* a chose in action. The advantages and disadvantages of following the English course cannnot be elucidated by inspecting the core concept of ownership: to follow one course or another is not to make a mistake about the meaning of ownership. It is to construct a legal system along one of several possible lines. It is only in relation to the implications for the systematic development of law, or at least for a branch of law, that one can decide whether people should simply have rights or own them—be, as they once were, seised of them. The contemporary interest in treating welfare rights, pension rights *etc.* as forms of property, or as deserving the protection given to property rights, derives partly from a specifically American constitutional guarantee; but it also reflects the attempt to confer on dependants the dignity of ownership and on claimants its security.

2. No one can look at legal or economic history over the last few centuries without recognising the extent to which tangible, material possession and control have given way to indicia of title and of power to control, to buy, to hold and sustain. In part, such powers are conferred by law and not simply recognised by it. In a predominantly agricultural society, the household and the land worked by it—the property—were not only the focus of everyday economic activity, but to a considerable extent the base and organising principle of social duties and relationships, of the order of labour, of social welfare, *etc.* Of course, this was never the whole story. There were duties to King or prince, to the church, to the (external) Law. Nevertheless, for much of the population, property—tangible, material property—or holding and the relations that sprang from it seemed the centre and basis of their lives that would continue to be the centre and basis of their children's lives.

3. The commercialisation of society, or of significant parts of it, did not begin with the sixteenth and seventeenth-century development of a conscious European urban bourgeoisie. Contracts and exchange, the registration of deeds and covenants, were well-known to the Mesopotamians and the Egyptians two thousand years before Christ. The private law of the Romans was the law first of a great commercial

city full of strangers and then of a great commercial empire full of nations. The basic principles, procedures and forms of so-called bourgeois law may have been used but they were certainly not created by the bourgeoisie. Neither were the power and independence of money, as Octavian-Augustus was well aware while using his privy purse — the revenues of Egypt — against the Senate.

4. A host of modern developments from the eighteenth century onward have nevertheless fatally undermined, in many areas, the paradigm of ownership as direct possession and control of a tangible material thing allegedly fused with one's own labour or a concretisation of individual will. We are now more conscious than ever that ownership consists of a bundle of rights and powers, none of which are absolute in practice and any one of which can be separated or dealt with individually. Professor A. M. Honoré, in his essay on Ownership in the first (1961) *Oxford Essays in Jurisprudence*, saw 'full' (or the 'liberal' concept of) ownership as involving eleven elements or legal incidents: the right to possess — *i.e.*, to exclusive physical control, literally or metaphorically; the right to use; the right to manage; the right to the income; the right to the capital — *i.e.* the power to alienate, consume, waste, modify or destroy; the right to security; the power to transmit, to devise or bequeath; the absence of a term to one's ownership rights; responsibility for harmful use; liability to execution; and that there will be rules governing the reversion of lapsed ownership rights. These elements of full legal ownership, Professor Honoré argued, are found in all 'mature' legal systems, though each of them is susceptible of varying definitions that affect emphasis and practical consequences. But in all such systems, the practical separability of these elements is also recognised. In England, the eighteenth-century movement toward creating certainty and security of title, accompanied by a most sophisticated recognition of simultaneous variety of interests in a single piece of land, facilitated their mortgageability and made possible much of the economic leap forward in the latter part of that century. The commercial share did even more to separate, physically, interests in property from actual physical contact with it or awareness of it; it assumed an incorporeal life of its own. Money and investments produced interest, dividends; at the same time, in relation to material property — to factories, mines, banks — they fragmented ownership, even more so as pension funds, trusts and holding companies came to own more and more shares. Finance capitalism, as the Marxists call it, was not based on or suited to the paradigm of the mill owner directly exercising authority over his mill and the workers employed in it.

At the same time, as Karl Renner stressed at the beginning of the century, more and more 'private' property depended economically on its public functions. The bank and the railway station invite all and sundry to enter; so do the department store and the petrol pump proprietor. The distinction between private property and public property, between the bank and the post office, the toll road and the ordinary road becomes more and more blurred, while the owners — whoever they may be — become increasingly invisible. When they do appear, they appear in the guise and through the authority of managers or of financial manipulators. Further, as the state takes on more and more active economic roles, private enterprise of any significant size becomes more and more dependent on state backing and support.

The scale of property has become so vast, as we have written elsewhere, the sources from which it draws its wealth so multifarious and pervasive and its social effects and ramifications so great, that modern men and women are having increasing difficulty thinking of property as private, as the concretisation of an individual will reifying itself in land or objects, as a walled-in area into which others may not enter. There is, in other words, a shift of attention from the property whose paradigm is the household, the fenced-in or marked-off piece of land, the specific bales that make up a cargo or consignment, to the corporation, the hospital, the defence establishment, the transport or power utility whose 'property' spreads throughout the society and whose existence is dependent upon subsidies, state protection, public provision of facilities, *etc.* In these circumstances, a view of society and a view of property as a collection of isolated and isolatable windowless monads that come into collision only externally and as a departure from the norm become untenable. Much property becomes social in the sense that its base and its effects can no longer be contained within the framework of the traditional picture. The major sphere of social life passes from the private to the public, not merely in the sense that more and more activity is state activity, but in the sense that more and more 'private' property becomes public in its scale and its effect, in the sense that the oil company is felt to be as 'public' as the state electricity utility, the private hospital and the private school, with their growing need for massive state subsidies, as public as the municipal hospital and the state school. In these areas, respect for the sanctity of private property and the right of the 'owner' to do as he or she wills, have gone.

The shift in public attention and social preponderance has been from a quasi-individualistic, quasi-*Gemeinschaft* concept of property typified in its *Gemeinschaft* aspects by the household as the locus of rights and duties and in it individualistic aspects by property directly used and/or consumed, through a *Gesellschaft* concept typified by the commercial share as an *indicium* of title and power to alienate without let or hindrance, to a bureaucratic-administrative concept of operational management linked with the growing scale of complexity of production, ever-increasing social interdependence and the consequent growth in power and scope of state activity. The development or the problems this poses can not be dealt with adequately by simply contrasting social property with private property and pleading for a return to a feudal sense of public obligation and accountability or by extending the concept of private property to include new, non-proprietorial claims to use and benefit based on a politically-recognised social status by saying that property was long seen as a right to a revenue. It was always more than that for anyone but the placement and the stockjobbers who were treated with contempt. The concept of property, the way in which it is legally defined and the extent to which it is legally, socially and politically protected, raise immediately the most fundamental problems of political philosophy and social life.

This, then, accounts for the sharply declining significance ascribed by people at large to the distinction between private and public ownership. Radicals, indeed, have increasingly shifted, in the West, from attacks on ownership as such to demands for participation and public supervision, in both private and public sectors. They form hit teams rather than colleges of administrators. Leaders of communist countries, on the other hand, increasingly extol the advantages of private enterprise, participation in profit and responsiveness to market demands. The debate between left and right can no longer plausibly counterpose public purposes and private profit and it no longer centres on ownership or on the concept of property. As Lawrence

Becker puts it in his excellent book *Property Rights: Philosophic Foundations* (1977) at page 3:

> The riskiness of writing about property has largely disappeared. The problem now is whether there is any longer any point in doing so. The main lines of argument for the general justification of property have long since been laid down; the vulnerable areas in those justifications have been identified; alternatives to private ownership have been proposed; weaknesses in this proposal have been explored. It seems unlikely that any new discussion could make a significant contribution to theory. And it seems even less likely that it could have significant practical consequences. The changes in property rights which have occurred in the last six or seven decades—and those which will doubtless occur in the next six or seven—are startling, to say the least. But they have not—nor are they likely to begin to—come about as the result of a clear and comprehensive new theory of property. The modern industrial state is so complex, its basic institutions so entrenched and interdependent, that basic changes come about more by the accidental confluence of particular interests than by design. The action guidance moral philosophy might provide thus seems a bit beside the point.

So one might add are the traditional individualist justifications of property as containing the owner's labour, being a reification of his will, *etc*. The defence of private property lies not in its origin but in its pluralist social consequences and in the nature of that which seeks totally to replace it.

The loss of interest in the question of ownership as the primary social question is linked with a steady diminution in the power of ownership. *Laissez-faire* capitalism, never as pervasive in a reality as its critics often claim, is dead. Owners today are constrained—whether sufficiently or not—in virtually everything they do by interventionist state legislation and regulation, by publicity and special interest watchdog groups, by the increasing sophistication and assertiveness of their employees and their customers who have ready access to publicity. There are great and important differences in respect of these matters between some areas of enterprise and economic life and others; the difference between private and public ownership, of a hospital, a factory or an airline, is not significant once adequate restraints are imposed on all operations and operators within an industry. Nor can the right to intervene, protest, participate be treated at all plausibly as a rival property right. Property increasingly functions in society and in law as one of many possibly competing and conflicting rights. So far as the liberty of the citizen is concerned and the citizen's power to affect and control his/her life, the abolition of non-public ownership in means of production, distribution and exchange has led to no significant liberation or overcoming of alienation; on the contrary.

Social critics are right in seeing that the nature and social function of property in important areas of property holding have undergone the kind of changes described by Karl Renner and later by Berle and Means and in a very simplified version by C. B. Macpherson. This has both undermined socialism and in some ways strengthened it by undermining respect for the private as much as it has undermined, more recently, respect for state or public ownership. Other factors, however, have worked in a contrary direction. Enormous increases in purchasing power by the mass of the population, in home- and car-ownership, in the spread of consumer durables have universalised, or at least greatly expanded, personal property and the ordinary person's interest in seeing it safeguarded. If it was ever true that the workers had nothing to lose but their chains, that they were a propertyless class and therefore capable of ushering in the society without property, it is certainly not true now.

Modern, post-industrial society in the West, as Daniel Bell has argued, has lost the coherent dominant ideology that appeared to characterise the Victorian age with its elevation of the rights and duties of the property-holder. There is now, in the West, a sharp 'contradiction' between an economic ideology based on efficiency and the 'rational' use of resources, a political ideology that increasingly elevates equality and a culture that puts more and more weight on self-expression, instant gratification and moral relativism. Both confusion and the disgust expressed in violence are the result, though much increased tolerance and a greater appreciation of the possibility of balancing competing and conflicting outlooks and concerns is another.

At the general level of social and legal ideology, much the same must be recognised of the rights of and to property. As the creation of objects becomes less arduous and the cost of labour continues to rise, the value placed on human life has risen sharply in relation to that placed on property—though it has not done so in those countries where labour is cheap and the standard of living is low. In our own society, though, one has to recognise the importance of property as part of reasonable living conditions and standards. It is, on the positive side, a guarantee for the individual of space to develop capacities and live as he or she wishes to and as a basis for the enterprise, responsibility and involvement that a society needs in its economic activities, in encouraging production and in sheeting home responsibility for harm. Simply to pass over in silence the right to property that was incorporated in the Universal Declaration of Human Rights and then drop it in subsequent UN Covenants is preposterous. At the same time, property rights, like many other rights, are defeasible. In specific social contexts, they can and do compete and conflict with other rights, they can bear savagely on those who do not own or control. They are no longer and never should have been trumps in the game of life. Deciding when and how and to what extent, they should be limited, interfered with, modified, supervised and controlled, by law, by regulation, by administrative discretion, is a matter that requires care and consideration, rather than trumpet blasts and emotive advocacy. It is, in short, a moral question, for which no handbook provides simple and timeless answers. In so far as it is also a legal question, the trend—here as in relation to other fundamental legal concepts—is increasingly practical, fragmenting, geared to particular problems or areas. Property for the purposes of the Family Law Court parts company from property for the purposes of probate or trust. Today more than ever, we focus on consequences, on remedies, rather than conceptual foundations and theoretical coherence. In law, as in ideology, we have gone beyond the simple-minded stage of being for or against property.

Questions

1. If Kamenka and Tay are correct in saying that there is a plurality of meanings of property in contemporary society, (Is this what they are saying? Are they correct?)

what are the implications of that for legal theory? It is all very well to speak of a 'pluralistic' general and legal environment. If the thesis is correct, are collisions between these various meanings recognized? Inevitable? Reconcilable?

Further Reading

1. Cotterell, The Law of Property and Legal Theory in Twining, *Legal Theory and Common Law* (1986), 81 and Hammond, *The Law and Ideas* (1989), have both recently called for a reappraisal of the concept of property in contemporary circumstances.

2. See also Kent, Property Power and Authority (1975) 41 Brooklyn L Rev 541 and Bowles & Ginters, *Democracy and Capitalism: Property, Community and the Contradictions of Modern Social Thought* (1986).

Part 2

5

Ownership, Title and Possession

Within the broad ambit of property law, lawyers have developed a technical classification which is due more to historical evolution than anything else. Although the classifications lawyers use in their everyday work would, in all probability, not be adopted if we were erecting a new system from the ground up, as matters stand they are deeply entrenched in our law. It is of the utmost importance that students gain a clear understanding of these concepts. Failure to do so will mean that in many courses elsewhere in their study of law, and in subsequent professional life, they will have great difficulty understanding other important matters.

Real Property and Personal Property

These terms date back at least as far as the *Institutes of Justinian*. After the Bible this was the most important textbook in medieval European universities. The *Institutes* were divided into four parts: Persons, Things, Obligations, and Actions. According to the distinguished English legal historian, Professor F. W. Maitland, the distinction between Persons and Things was appropriated by medieval English lawyers to distinguish two different kinds of remedies. Real remedies were those under which a successful plaintiff recovered the thing itself. Personal remedies were restricted to *the value of the thing itself*. By the thirteenth century there were developed remedies for the recovery of land. But movables could not be recovered through a 'real' action. Maitland suggested that this was because most chattels were perishable. And it was easy enough to assess the value of something movable. Moreover, or so the theory went, if the plaintiff gets the value of an ox, he gets something as good as an ox. (1932, 368). Maitland thought this was the 'much to be regretted' origin of 'all our talk' about real and personal property. An action comes to be a 'real' action if possession of land can be had via the agency of a court. It is 'personal' if a plaintiff gets damages. In time, therefore, lawyers came to distinguish between realty and personalty.

This in turn had very important consequences for the development of property law in general. Chattels—or movable property—were dealt with, in the event of disputes, through litigation. Realty, on the other hand, came to be dealt with through increasingly sophisticated systems of conveyancing. Personal property law, in other words, historically has been remedial in character; real property has been conveyancing-oriented. Later in this book you will encounter some material on registration systems for security interests in personal property. It may be that with the evolution of enhanced systems of registration of interests in personal property rights, the absurd dichotomy which Maitland identified will begin to fade away into the mists of history. And the emphasis on a bipolar approach to litigation — that is, towards first identifying the right infringed, and then the most appropriate remedy — which has been encouraged by the New Zealand Court of Appeal since at least *Day* v *Mead* [1987] 2 NZLR 443, may also influence the breakdown of the historically fundamental distinction between realty and personalty.

Personal Property

As a further subdivision, lawyers generally divide personal property into tangible movables (which include goods and money) and intangible movables, which are usually called *choses in action*. This latter term is difficult. Originally it meant a debt. The basic notion is that if X owes Y $1000 and Y has refused or neglected to pay, X has to sue for that sum. On the other hand, the subject matter of a *chose in possession* (say, a tractor) is something the relevant party can use there and then. Gradually, however, the term *chose in action* became extended to cover all other intangible forms of personal property. Hence it now includes things like copyrights, patents, shares and so on. The distinction today is however increasingly between tangible and intangible personal property.

Ownership

This term is one of the most difficult concepts in our legal system. One thing at least is quite clear. Our law does not recognize ownership in the same absolute sense as Roman law did. Roman law recognized a concept of *dominium* upon which all the civil law systems have modelled their treatment of ownership. This was to be distinguished from possession.

Whoever was entitled to a thing (of whatever kind) could claim it from anyone else who had control by an action called *vindicatio*. The claimant offered to prove that the thing was his and the proceedings did not even name a defendant. The 'owner' was the person who claimed a thing by this action. Possession, on the other hand, was really a matter of fact. Roman law did, however, give some protection to possessors (irrespective of the ultimate legal entitlement) and possession could, in some circumstances, mature into ownership.

In the final form which *dominium* took in the *Corpus Juris* it was as close to absolute ownership as any legal system has ever come. An 'owner' had a nearly absolute title. That is, there was an almost absolute right to dispose of the thing owned. There were

> very few restrictions of a public law character. [The incumbrances on ownership] were kept down to the lowest possible number, and where they existed they were carefully distinguished from the *dominium* over the thing, which was regarded as retaining its character of a general undifferentiated right over the thing capable of resuming its original plenitude by the mere disappearance of the incumbrance [Lawson and Rudden, *The Law of Property* (2nd ed) 114].

The concept of ownership in the common law legal systems is less clear-cut.

A distinction between ownership and possession is fundamental. And clearly an 'owner' has something better than a 'mere possessor'. But how much more? One way of looking at it, is that a possessor has some *specific rights*. If I lend you my book for one week, you may use it (with an appropriate degree of care, of which more later) during that time. You may not sell it. It is not yours to sell. The owner, on the other hand, has something more general, the largest collection of rights in that book after all other lawful restrictions have been taken into account. Another way of describing ownership in our legal system is to describe *the incidents which attach to it*, as Professor Honoré does in the extract later in this chapter.

Legal and Equitable Ownership

Legal title, in the case of chattels, involves undivided ownership, although there can be ownership in common. And it is possible to have a trust of, for instance, a valuable painting, and hence there can be both legal and equitable ownership of that chattel. Equitable title to goods (or land) does involve divided ownership. If I declare that I hold painting X for my daughter Y on her attaining her majority, legal title is in me (the settlor) and beneficial ownership is in Y. Our relationship is then that of trustee and beneficiary. It is possible, in other words, to have legal and equitable interests in both realty and personalty.

Interest and Title

There are terms which also cause much confusion. In a Torrens system of title to land, the term title has a specific technical, meaning. It means the actual Certificate of Title issued to the owner of the fee simple, describing, and indeed creating, the interest therein set out. Thus when a New Zealand lawyer says that X has title to a piece of land (Y) he or she is usually making a quite technical assertion about ownership under that system. 'Title' is a convenient shorthand way of condensing a number of things. Of course, it is also possible that Z might have a possessory title of some kind. And it is possible for quite complicated interests to exist in land at the same time, whilst still leaving X with 'title.' For instance A may have rights to extract metal from B's land. In the case of goods, there can only be 'two independent legal titles in goods at any one time . . . the best title and a possessory title' (Goode, *Commercial Law* (1982), 53).

In the result, lawyers draw a distinction between an interest (the right or accumulation of rights to the particular 'asset') and a title (the strength of that right or rights against others).

Haslem v Lockwood

Supreme Court of Errors, Connecticut
37 Conn. 500 (1871)

Trover, for a quantity of manure; brought before a justice of the peace and appealed by the defendant to the Court of Common Pleas for the county of Fairfield, and tried in that court, on the general issue closed to the court, before BREWSTER, J.

On the trial it was proved that the plaintiff employed two men to gather into heaps, on the evening of April 6th, 1869, some maure that lay scattered along the side of a public highway, for several rods, in the borough of Stamford, intending to remove the same to his own land the next evening. The men began to scrape the manure into heaps at six o'clock in the evening, and after gathering eighteen heaps, or about six cart-loads, left the same at eight o'clock in the evening in the street. The heaps consisted chiefly of manure made by horses hitched to the railing of the public park in, and belonging to, the borough of Stamford, and was all gathered between the center of the highway and the park; the rest of the heaps consisting of dirt, straw and the ordinary scrapings of highways. The defendant on the next morning, seeing the heaps, endeavored without success to ascertain who had made them, and inquired of the warden of the borough if he had given permission to any one to remove them, and ascertained from him that he had not. He thereupon, before noon on that day, removed the heaps and also the rest of the manure scattered along the side of the highway adjacent to the park, to his own land.

The plaintiff and defendant both claimed to have received authority from the warden to remove the manure before the 6th of April, but in fact neither had any legal authority from the warden, or from any officer of the borough or of the town. The borough of Stamford was the sole adjoining proprietor of the land on which the manure lay scattered before it was gathered by the plaintiff. No notice was left on the heaps or near by, by the plaintiff or his workmen, to indicate who had gathered them, nor had the plaintiff or his workmen any actual possession of the heaps after eight o'clock in the evening on the 6th of April.

Neither the plaintiff while gathering, nor the defendant while removing the heaps, was interfered with or opposed by any one. The removal of the manure and scrapings was calculated to improve the appearance and health of the borough. The six loads were worth one dollar per load. The plaintiff, on ascertaining that the defendant had removed the manure, demanded payment for the same, which the defendant refused. Neither the plaintiff nor defendant owned any land adjacent to the place where the manure lay. The highway was kept in repair by the town of Stamford.

On the above facts the plaintiff claimed, and prayed the court to rule, that the manure was personal property which had been abandoned by its owners and became by such abandonment the property of the first person who should take possession of the same, which the plaintiff had done by gathering it into heaps, and that it was not and never had been a part of the real estate of the borough or of any one else who might be regarded as owning the fee of the soil. He further claimed that if it was a part of the real estate, it was taken without committing a trespass, and with the tacit consent of the owners of such real estate, and that thereby it became his personal property of which he was lawfully possessed, and at least that he had acquired such an interest in it as would enable him to hold it against any person except the owner of the land or some person claiming under the owner.

The defendant claimed, upon the above facts, that the manure being dropped upon and spread out over the surface of the earth was a part of the real estate, and belonged to the owner of the fee, subject to the public easement; that the fee was either in the borough of Stamford or the town of Stamford, or in the parties who owned the lands adjacent; that therefore the scraping up of the manure, mixed with the soil, if real estate, did not change its nature to that of personal estate, unless it was removed, whether the plaintiff had the consent of the owner of the fee or not; and that, unless the heaps became personal property, the plaintiff could not maintain his action. The defendant further claimed, as matter of law, that if the manure was always personal estate, or became personal estate after being scraped up into heaps, the plaintiff, by leaving it from eight o'clock in the evening until noon the next day, abandoned all right of possession which he might have had, and could not, therefore, maintain his action.

The court ruled adversely to the claims of the plaintiff and held that on the facts proved the plaintiff had not made out a sufficient interest in, or right of possession to, the subject matter in dispute, to authorize a recovery in the suit, and rendered judgment for the defendant.

The plaintiff moved for a new trial for error in this ruling of the court.

Curtis and Hoyt [Counsel for the plaintiff-appellant], in support of the motion.

1. The manure in question was personal property abandoned by its owners.**

2. It never became a part of the real estate on which it was abandoned.**

3. It being personal property abandoned by its owners, and lying upon the highway, and neither the owners of the fee nor the proper authorities of the town and borough having by any act of theirs shown any intention to appropriate the same, it became lawful for the plaintiff to gather it up and remove it from the highway, providing he did not commit a trespass, and removed it without objection from the owners of the land.** And no trespass was in fact committted. No person interfered with the plaintiff or made any objection. This court cannot presume a trespass to have been committed.**

4. But if the manure had become a part of the real estate, yet when it was gathered into heaps by the plaintiff it was severed from the realty and became personal estate.** And being gathered without molestation from any person owning or claiming to own the land, it is to be considered as having been taken by the tacit consent of such owner.**

5. The plaintiff therefore acquired not only a valid legal possession, but a title by occupancy, and by having expended labor and money upon the property. Such a title is a good legal title against every person but the true owner.

6. If the plaintiff had a legal title then he had the constructive possession. If he had legal possession, and only left the property for a short time intending to return and take it away, then he might maintain an action against a wrong doer for taking it away.** The leaving of property for a short time, intending to return, does not constitute an abandonment. The property is still to be considered as in the possession of the plaintiff.

Olmstead [Counsel for the defendant-respondent], contra.

1. The manure mixed with the dirt and ordinary scrapings of the highway, being spread out over the surface of the highway, was a part of the *real estate*, and belonged to the owner of the fee, subject to the public easement.**

2. The scraping up of the manure and dirt into piles, if the same was a part of the real estate, did not change its nature to that of *personal property*, unless there was a severance of it from the realty by removal, (which there was not), whether the plaintiff had the consent of the owner of the fee or not, which consent it is conceded the plaintiff did not have.

3. Unless the scraping up of the heaps made their substance *personal property*, the plaintiff could not maintain his action either for trespass or trespass on the case.

4. In trespass *de bonis asportatis*, or trover, the plaintiff must have had the *actual possession*, or a right to the immediate possession, in order to recover.**

5. If the manure was always personal estate, it being spread upon the surface of the earth, it was in possession of the owner of the fee, who was not the plaintiff.** The scraping of it into heaps, unless it was removed, would not change the *possession* from the owner of the fee to the plaintiff. The plaintiff therefore never had the *possession*.

6. If the heaps were personal property the plaintiff never had any right in the property, but only *mere possession*, if anything, which he abandoned by leaving the same upon the public highway from 8 o'clock in the evening until 12 o'clock the next day, without leaving any notice on or about the property, or any one to exercise control over the same in his behalf.**

PARK, Judge. We think the manure scattered upon the ground, under the circumstances of this case, was personal property. The cases referred to by the defendant to show that it was real estate are not in point. The principle of those cases is, that manure made in the usual course of husbandry upon a farm is so attached to and connected with the realty that, in the absence of any express stipulation to the contrary, it becomes appurtenant to it. The principle was established for the benefit of agriculture. It found its origin in the fact that it is essential to the successful cultivation of a farm that the manure, produced from the droppings of cattle and swine fed upon the products of the farm, and composted with earth and vegetable matter taken from the land, should be used to supply the drain made upon the soil in the production of crops, which otherwise would become impoverished and barren; and in the fact that manure so produced is generally regarded by farmers in this country as part of the realty and has been so treated by landlords and tenants from time immemorial.**

But this principle does not apply to the droppings of animals driven by travelers upon the highway. The highway is not used, and cannot be used, for the purpose of agriculture. The manure is of no benefit whatsoever to it, but on the contrary is a detriment; and in cities and large villages it becomes a nuisance, and is removed by public officers at public expense. The finding in this case is, "that the removal of the manure and scraping was calculated to improve the appearance and health of the borough." It is therefore evident that the cases relied upon by the defendant have no application to the case.

But it is said that if the manure was personal property, it was in the possession of the owner of the fee, and the scraping it into heaps by the plaintiff did not change the possession, but it continued as before, and that therefore the plaintiff cannot recover, for he neither had the possession nor the right to the immediate possession.

The manure originally belonged to the travelers whose animals dropped it, but it being worthless to them was immediately abandoned; and whether it then became the property of the borough of Stamford which owned the fee of the land on which the manure lay, it is unnecessary to determine; for, if it did, the case finds that the removal of the filth would be an improvement to the borough, and no objection was made by any one to the use that the plaintiff attempted to make of it. Considering the character of such accumulations upon highways in cities and villages, and the light in which they are everywhere regarded as closely settled communities, we cannot believe that the borough in this instance would have had any objection to the act of the plaintiff removing a nuisance that affected the public health and the appearance of the streets. At all events, we think the facts of the case show a sufficient right in the plaintiff to the immediate possession of the property as against a mere wrong doer.

The defendant appears before the court in no enviable light. He does not pretend that he had a right to the manure, even when scattered upon the highway, superior to that of the plaintiff but after the plaintiff had changed its original condition and greatly enhanced its value by his labor, he seized and appropriated to his own use the fruits of the plaintiff's outlay, and now seeks immunity from responsibility on the ground that the plaintiff was a wrong doer as well as himself. The conduct of the defendant is in keeping with his claim, and neither commends itself to the favorable consideration of the court. The plaintiff had the peaceable and quiet possession of the property; and we deem this sufficient until the borough of Stamford shall make complaint.

It is further claimed that if the plaintiff had a right to the property by virtue of occupancy, he lost the right when he ceased to retain the actual possession of the manure after scraping it into heaps.

We do not question the general doctrine, that where the right by occupancy exists, it exists no longer than the party retains the actual possession of the property, or till he appropriates it to his own use by removing it to some other place. If he leaves the property at the place where it was discovered, and does nothing whatsoever to enhance its value or change its nature, his right by occupancy is unquestionably gone. But the question is, if a party finds property comparatively worthless, as the plaintiff found the property in question, owing to its scattered condition upon the highway, and greatly increases its value by his labor and expense, does he lose his right if he leaves it a reasonable time to procure the means to take it away, when such means are necessary for its removal?

Suppose a teamster with a load of grain, while traveling the highway, discovers a rent in one of his bags, and finds that his grain is scattered upon the road for the distance of a mile. He considers the labor of collecting his corn of more value than the property itself, and he therefore abandons it, and pursues his way. *A* afterwards finds the grain in this condition and gathers it kernel by kernel into heaps by the side of the road, and leaves it a reasonable time to procure the means necessary for its removal. While he is gone for his bag, *B* discovers the grain thus conveniently collected in heaps and appropriates it to his own use. Has *A* any remedy? If he has not, the law in this instance is open to just reproach. We think under such circumstances *A* would have a reasonable time to remove the property, and during such reasonable time his right to it would be protected. If this is so, then the principle applies to the case under consideration.

A reasonable time for the removal of this manure had not elapsed when the defendant seized and converted it to his own use. The statute regulating the rights of parties in the gathering of sea-weed, give the party who heaps it upon a public beach twenty-four hours in which to remove it, and that length of time for the removal of the property we think would not be unreasonable in most cases like the present one.

We therefore advise the Court of Common Pleas to grant a new trial. In this opinion the other judges concurred.

Ownership

Professor A M Honoré
Oxford Essays in Jurisprudence (1961) (A G Guest ed.).

Ownership is one of the characteristic institutions of human society. A people to whom ownership was unknown, or who accorded it a minor place in their arrangements, who meant by *meum* and *tuum* no more than 'what I (or you) presently hold' would live in a world that is not our world. Yet to see why their world would be different, and to assess the plausibility of vaguely conceived schemes to replace 'ownership' by 'public administration', or of vaguely stated claims that the importance of ownership has declined or its character changed in the twentieth century, we need first to have a clear idea of what ownership is.

I propose, therefore, to begin by giving an account of the standard incidents of ownership: *i.e.* those legal rights, duties and other incidents which apply, in the ordinary case, to the person who has the greatest interest in a thing admitted by a mature legal system. To do so will be to analyse the concept of ownership, by which I mean the 'liberal' concept of 'full' individual ownership, rather than any more restricted notion to which the same label may be attached in certain contexts * * *

If ownership is provisionally defined as the *greatest possible interest in a thing which a mature system of law recognizes*, then it follows that, since all mature systems admit the existence of 'interests' in 'things', all mature systems have, in a sense, a concept of ownership. Indeed, even primitive systems, like that of the Trobriand islanders, have rules by which certain persons, such as the 'owners' of canoes, have greater interests in certain things than anyone else.

For mature legal systems it is possible to make a larger claim. In them certain important legal incidents are found, which are common to different systems. If it were not so, 'He owns that umbrella', said in a purely English context, would mean something different from 'He owns that umbrella', preferred as a translation of 'Ce parapluie est à lui'. Yet, as we know, they mean the same. There is indeed, a substantial similarity in the position of one who 'owns' an umbrella in England, France, Russia, China, and any other modern country one may care to mention. Everywhere the 'owner' can, in the simple uncomplicated case, in which no other person has an interest in the thing, use it, stop others using it, lend it, sell it or leave it by will. Nowhere may he use it to poke his neighbour in the ribs or to knock over his vase. Ownership, *dominium, propriété, Eigentum* and similar words stand not merely for the greatest interest in things in particular systems but for a type of interest with common features transcending particular systems. It must surely be important to know what these common features are?

*   *   *

I now list what appear to be the standard incidents of ownership. They may be regarded as necessary ingredients in the notion of ownership, in the sense that, if a system did not admit them, and did not provide for them to be united in a single person, we would conclude that it did not know the liberal concept of ownership, though it might still have a modified version of ownership, either of a primitive or sophisticated sort. But the listed incidents are not individually necessary, though they may be together sufficient, conditions for the person of inherence to be designated 'owner' of a particular thing in a given system. As we have seen, the use of 'owner' will extend to cases in which not all the listed incidents are present.

Ownership comprises the right to possess, the right to use, the right to manage, the right to the income of the thing, the right to the capital, the right to security, the rights or incidents of transmissibility and absence of term, the prohibition of harmful use, liability to execution, and the incident of residuarity: this makes eleven leading incidents. Obviously, there are alternative ways of classifying the incidents; moreover, it is fashionable to speak of ownership as if it were just a bundle of rights, in which case at least two items in the list would have to be omitted.

No doubt the concentration in the same person of the right (liberty) of using as one wishes, the right to exclude others, the power of alienating and an immunity from expropriation is a cardinal feature of the institution. Yet it would be a distortion — and one of which the eighteenth century, with its over-emphasis on subjective rights, was patently guilty — to speak as if this concentration of patiently garnered rights was the only legally or socially important characteristic of the owner's position. The present analysis, by emphasizing that the owner is subject to characteristic prohibitions and limitations, and that ownership comprises at least one important incident independent of the owner's choice, is an attempt to redress the balance.

(1) The Right to Possess

The right to possess, *viz.* to have exclusive physical control of a thing, or to have such control as the nature of the thing admits, is the foundation on which the whole superstructure of ownership rests. It may be divided into two aspects, the right (claim) to be put in exclusive control of a thing and the right to remain in control, *viz.* the claim that others should not without permission, interfere. Unless a legal system provides some rules and procedures for attaining these ends it cannot be said to protect ownership.

It is of the essence of the right to possess that it is *in rem* in the sense of availing against persons generally. This does not, of course, mean that an owner is necessarily entitled to exclude everyone from his property. We happily speak of the ownership of land, yet a largish number of officials have the right of entering on private land without the owner's consent, for some limited period and purpose. On the other hand, a general licence so to enter on the 'property' of others would put an end to the institution of landowning as we now know it.

The protection of the right to possess (still using 'possess' in the convenient, though over-simple, sense of 'have exclusive physical control') should be sharply marked off from the protection of mere present possession. To exclude others from what one presently holds is an instinct found in babies and even, as Holmes points out, in animals, of which the seal gives a striking example. To sustain this instinct by legal rules is to protect possession but not, as such, to protect the right to possess and so not to protect ownership. If dispossession without the possessor's consent is, in general, forbidden, the possessor is given a right *in rem*, valid against persons generally, what he has lost or had taken from him, and to obtain from them what is due to him but not yet handed over. * * *

To have worked out the notion of 'having a right to' as distinct from merely 'having', or if that is too subjective a way of putting it, of rules allocating things to people as opposed to rules merely forbidding forcible taking was a major intellectual achievement. Without it society would have been impossible. Yet the distinction is apt to be overlooked by English lawyers, who are accustomed to the rule that every adverse possession is a root of title, *i.e.* gives rise to a right to possess, or at least that '*de facto* possession is *prima facie* evidence of seisin in fee and right to possession'.

The owner, then, has characteristically a battery of remedies in order to obtain, keep and, if necessary, get back the thing owned. Remedies such as the actions for ejectment and wrongful detention and the *vindicatio* are designed to enable the plaintiff either to obtain or to get back a thing, or at least to put some pressure on the defendant to hand it over. Others, such as the actions for trespass to land and goods, the Roman possessory interdicts and their modern counterparts are primarily directed towards enabling a present possessor to keep possession. Few of the remedies mentioned are confined to the owner; most of them are available also to persons with a right to possess falling short of ownership, and some to mere possessors. Conversely, there will be cases in which they are not available to the owner, for instance because he has voluntarily parted with possession for a temporary purpose, as by hiring the thing out. The availability of such remedies is clearly not a necessary and sufficient condition of owning a thing; what is necessary, in order that there may be ownership of things at all, is that such remedies shall be available to the owner in the usual case in which no other person has a right to exclude him from the thing.

(2) The Right to Use

The present incident and the next two overlap. On a wide interpretation of 'use', management and income fall within use. On a narrow interpretation, 'use' refers to the owner's personal use and enjoyment of the thing owned. On this interpretation it excludes management and income.

The right (liberty) to use at one's discretion has rightly been recognized as a cardinal feature of ownership, and the fact that, as we shall see, certain limitations on use also fall within the standard incidents of ownership does not detract from its importance, since the standard limitations are, in general, rather precisely defined, while the permissible types of use constitute an open list.

(3) The Right to Manage

The right to manage is the right to decide how and by whom the thing owned shall be used. This right depends, legally, on a cluster of powers, chiefly powers of licensing acts which would otherwise be unlawful and powers of contracting: the power to admit others to one's land, to permit others to use one's things, to define the limits of such permission, and to contract effectively in regard to the use (in the literal sense) and exploitation of the thing owned. An owner may not merely sit in his own deck chair but may validly license others to sit in it, lend it, impose conditions on the borrower, direct how it is to be painted or cleaned, contract for it to be mended in a particular way. This is the sphere of management in relation to a simple object like a deck chair. When we consider more complex cases, like the ownership of a business, the complex of powers which make up the right to manage seems still more prominent. The power to direct how resources are to be used and exploited is one of the cardinal types of economic and political power; the owner's legal powers of management are one, but only one possible basis for it. Many observers have drawn attention to the growth of managerial power divorced from legal ownership; in such cases it may be that we should speak of split ownership or redefine our notion of the thing owned. This does not affect the fact that the right to manage is an important element in the notion of ownership; indeed, the fact that we feel doubts in these cases whether the 'legal owner' *really* owns is a testimony to its importance. * * *

(4) The Right to the Income

To use or occupy a thing may be regarded as the simplest way of deriving an income from it, of enjoying it. It is, for instance, expressly contemplated by the English income tax legislation that the rent-free use or occupation of a house is a form of income, and only the inconvenience of assessing and collecting the tax presumably prevents the extension of this principle to movables.

Income in the more ordinary sense (fruits, rents, profits) may be thought of as a surrogate of use, a benefit derived from forgoing personal use of a thing and allowing others to use it for rewards; as a reward for work done in exploiting the thing; or as the brute product of a thing, made by nature or by other persons. Obviously the line to be drawn between the earned and unearned income from a thing cannot be firmly drawn. * * *

(5) The Right to the Capital

The right to the capital consists in the power to alienate the thing and the liberty to consume, waste or destroy the whole or part of it: clearly it has an important economic aspect. The latter liberty need not be regarded as unrestricted; but a general provision requiring things to be conserved in the public interest, so far as not consumed by use in the ordinary way, would perhaps be inconsistent with the liberal idea of ownership. * * *

An owner normally has both the power of disposition and the power of transferring title. Disposition on death is not permitted in many primitive societies but seems to form an essential element in the mature notion of ownership. The tenacity of the right of testation once it has been recognized is shown by the Soviet experience. The earliest writers were hostile to inheritance, but gradually Soviet law has come to admit that citizens may dispose freely of their 'personal property' on death, subject to limits not unlike those known elsewhere.

(6) The Right to Security

An important aspect of the owner's position is that he should be able to look forward to remaining owner indefinitely if he so chooses and he remains solvent.

His right to do so may be called the right to security. Legally, this is in effect an immunity from expropriation, based on rules which provide that, apart from bankruptcy and execution for debt, the transmission of ownership is consensual.

However, a general right to security, availing against others, is consistent with the existence of a power to expropriate or divest in the state or public authorities. From the point of view of security of property, it is important that when expropriation takes place, adequate compensation should be paid; but a general power to expropriate subject to paying compensation would be fatal to the institution of ownership as we know it. Holmes' paradox, that where specific restitution of goods is not a normal remedy, expropriation and wrongful conversion are equivalent, obscures the vital distinction between acts which a legal system permits as rightful and those which it reprobates as wrongful: but if wrongful conversion were general and went unchecked, ownership as we know it would disappear, though damages were regularly paid.

In some systems, as (*semble*) English law, a private individual may destroy another's property without compensation when this is necessary in order to protect his own person or property from a greater danger. Such a rule is consistent with security of property only because of its exceptional character. Again, the state's (or local authority's) power of expropriation is usually limited to certain classes of thing and certain limited purposes. A general power to expropriate any property for any purpose would be inconsistent with the institution of ownership. If, under such a system, compensation were regularly paid, we might say either that ownership was not recognized in that system, or that money alone could be owned, 'money' here meaning a strictly fungible claim on the resources of the community. As we shall see, 'ownership' of such claims in not identical with the ownership of material objects and simple claims.

[7] The Incident of Transmissibility

It is often said that one of the main characteristics of the owner's interest is its 'duration'. In England, at least, the doctrine of estates made lawyers familiar with the notion of the 'duration' of an interest and Maitland, in a luminous metaphor, spoke of estates as 'projected upon the plane of time'.

Yet this notion is by no means as simple as it seems. What is called 'unlimited' duration (*perpétuité*) comprises at least two elements (i) that the interest can be transmitted to the holder's successors and so on *ad infinitum*. (The fact that in medieval land law all interests were considered 'temporary' is one reason why the terminology of ownership failed to take root, with consequences which have endured long after the cause has disappeared); (ii) that it is not certain to determine at a future date. These two elements may be called 'transmissibility' and 'absence of term' respectively. We are here concerned with the former.

No one, as Austin points out, can enjoy a thing after he is dead (except vicariously) so that, in a sense, no interest can outlast death. But an interest which is transmissible to the holder's successors (persons designated by or closely related to the holder who obtains the property after him) is more valuable than one which stops with his death. This is so both because on alienation the alienee or, if transmissibility is generally recognized, the alienee's successors, are thereby enabled to enjoy the thing after the alienor's death so that a better price can be obtained for the thing, and because, even if alienation were not recognized, the present holder would by the very fact of transmissibility be dispensed *pro tanto* from making provision for his intestate heirs. Hence, for example, the moment when the tenant in fee acquired a heritable (though not yet fully alienable) right was a crucial moment in the evolution of the fee simple. Heritability by the state would not, of course, amount to transmissibility in the present sense: it is assumed that the transmission is in some sense *advantageous* to the transmitter.

Transmissibility can, of course, be admitted, yet stop short at the first, second or third generation of transmittees. The owner's interest is characterized by *indefinite* transmissability, no limit being placed on the possible number of transmissions, though the nature of the thing may well limit the actual number.

In deference to the conventional view that the exercise of a right must depend on the choice of the holder, I have refrained from calling transmissiblity a right. It is, however, clearly something in which the holder has an economic interest, and it may be that the notion of a right requires revision in order to take account of incidents not depending on the holder's choice which are nevertheless of value to him.

(8) The Incident of Absence of Term

This is the second part of what is vaguely called 'duration.' The rules of a legal system usually seem to provide for determinate, indeterminate and determinable interests. The first are certain to determine at a future date or on the occurrence of a future event which is certain to occur. In this class come leases for however long a term, copyrights, etc. Indeterminate interests are those, such as ownership and easements, to which no term is set. Should the holder live for ever, he would, in the ordinary way, be able to continue in the enjoyment of them for ever. Since humans beings are mortal, he will in practice only be able to enjoy them for a limited period, after which the fate of his interest depends on its transmissibility. Again, since human beings are mortal, interests for life, whether of the holder or another, must be regarded as determinate. The notion of an indeterminate interest, in the full sense, therefore requires the notion of transmissibility, but if the latter were not recognized, there would still be value to the holder in the fact that his interest was not due to determine on a fixed date or on the occurrence of some contingency, like a general election, which is certain to occur sooner or later. * * *

(9) The Prohibition of Harmful Use

An owner's liberty to use and manage the thing owned as he chooses is in mature systems of law, as in primitive systems, subject to the condition that uses harmful to other members of society are forbidden. There may, indeed, be much dispute over what is to count as 'harm' and to what extent give and take demands that minor inconvenience between neighbours shall be tolerated. Nevertheless, at least for material objects, one can always point to abuses which a legal system will not allow.

I may use my car freely but not in order to run my neighbour down, or to demolish his gate, or even to go on his land if he protests; nor may I drive uninsured. I may build on my land as I choose, but not in such a way that my building collapses on my neighbour's land. I may let off fireworks on Guy Fawkes night, but not in such a way as to set fire to my neighbour's house. These and similar limitations on the use of things are so familiar and so obviously essential to the existence of an orderly community that they are not often thought of as incidents of ownership; yet, without them 'ownership' would be a destructive force.

(10) Liability to Execution

Of a somewhat similar character is the liability of the owner's interest to be taken away from him for debt, either by execution of a judgment debt or on insolvency. Without such a general liability the growth of credit would be impeded and ownership would, again, be an instrument by which the owner could defraud his creditors. This incident, therefore, which may be called *executability*, seems to constitute one of the standard ingredients of the liberal area of ownership. * * *

(11) Residuary Character

A legal system might recognize interests in things less than ownership and might have a rule that on the determination of such interests, the rights in question lapsed and could be exercised by no one, or by the first person to exercise them after their lapse. There might be leases and easements; yet, on their extinction, no one would be entitled to exercise rights similar to those of the former lessee or of the holder of the easement. This would be unlike any system known to us and I think we should be driven to say that in such a system the institution of ownership did not extend to any thing in which limited interests existed. In such things there would, paradoxically, be interests less than ownership but no ownership.

This fantasy is intended to bring out the point that it is characteristic of ownership that an owner has a residuary right in the thing owned. In practice, legal systems have rules providing that on the lapse of an interest rights, including liberties, analogous to the rights formerly vested in the holder of the interest, vest in or are exercisable by someone else, who may be said to acquire the 'corresponding rights.' Of course, the 'corresponding rights' are not the same rights as were formerly vested in the holder of the interest. The easement holder had a right to exclude the owner; now the owner has a right to exclude the easement holder. The latter right is not identical with, but corresponds to, the former.

It is true that corresponding rights do not always arise when an interest is determined. Sometimes, when ownership is abandoned, no corresponding right vests in another; the thing is simply *res derelicta*. Sometimes, on the other hand, when ownership is abandoned, a new ownership vests in the state, as is the case in South Africa when land has been abandoned.

It seems, however, a safe generalization that, whenever an interest less than ownership terminates, legal systems always provide for corresponding rights to vest in another. When easements terminate, the 'owner' can exercise the corresponding rights, and when bailments terminate, the same is true. It looks as if we have found a simple explanation of the usage we are investigating, but this turns out to be but another deceptive short cut. For it is not a sufficient condition of *A*'s being the owner of a thing that, on the determination of *B*'s interests in it, corresponding rights vest in or are exercisable by *A*. On the determination of a sub-lease, the rights in question become exercisable by the lessee, not by the 'owner' of the property.

Can we then say that the 'owner' is the ultimate residuary? When the sub-lessee's interest determines the lessee acquires the corresponding rights; but when the lessee's right determines the 'owner' acquires these rights. Hence the 'owner' appears to be identified as the ultimate residuary. The difficulty is that the series may be continued, for on the determination of the 'owners' interest the state may acquire the corresponding rights; is the state's interest ownership or a mere expectancy?

A warning is here necessary. We are approaching the troubled waters of split ownership. Puzzles about the location of ownership are often generated by the fact that an ultimate residuary right is not coupled with present alienability or with the other standard incidents we have listed. ✽ ✽ ✽

We are of course here concerned not with the puzzles of split ownership but with simple cases in which the existence of *B*'s lesser interest in a thing is clearly consistent with *A*'s owning it. To explain the usage in such cases it is helpful to point out that it is a necessary but not sufficient condition of *A*'s being owner that, either immediately or ultimately, the extinction of other interests would enure for his benefit. In the end, it turns out that residuarity is merely one of the standard incidents of ownership, important no doubt, but not entitled to any special status. ✽ ✽ ✽

Bateman TV Ltd v *Bateman*

[1971] NZLR 453 (CA)
(Judgments of NORTH P and RICHMOND J, who concurred, are omitted).

The facts as taken from the judgment of Turner J were as follows:

On 14 April 1967 the respondent Thomas entered into a written conditional purchase agreement with Croydon Motors Ltd whereby that company conditionally agreed to sell and he conditionally agreed to purchase a new Daimler Sovereign motor car registered number DU 7490. On 24 April, ten days later, the respondent Bateman entered into a similar agreement in writing with the same vendor as to a second new Daimler Sovereign motor car. The purchase price of the Daimler cars was £3,156 in the first case and £3,147 in the second. In each case the purchaser was given credit for a sum of £2,000 for a traded in used Daimler car, and also for a small cash deposit—£150 15s. 8d in the first case and £174 8s 8d in the second. The respective purchasers agreed to pay the balances, amounting in each case to approximately £1,000, with the charges made in respect thereof, by eleven monthly instalments of approximately £90 each. Title to the cars was not to pass until all the moneys had been paid. In due course all the moneys were paid, and title accordingly passed to the purchasers named in the agreements.

The two agreements were put in in evidence in the Court below before Macarthur J. It was not suggested before him, or before us, that they were "shams", or that they were intended by the parties thereto to take effect *inter se* otherwise than according to their tenor. What was contended was that though the agreements were intended to take effect and took effect according to their tenor, the respective purchasers took the cars as trustees for the company of which they were the sole shareholders and directors. The transactions which the agreements evidenced were not quite usual, and the unusual features which are most relevant in the dispute before us are:

1 At the time of entering into the agreements the purchasers were the directors, and the only directors, and were also the only shareholders, of Bateman Television Ltd, now in liquidation, whose liquidator is the appellant in these proceedings.

2 The "trade-in" valued at £2,000, which was given by each purchaser as a deposit, was in each case a Daimler car which was at the time of giving it the property of Bateman Television Ltd, and in which at that time neither purchaser had any legal or equitable interests whatever.

3 The eleven subsequent instalments of purchase money paid to discharge each purchaser's liability were all paid by the cheques of an associated company—Bateman TV Hire Ltd—a company having the same shareholders and directors as Bateman Television Ltd, and now, like it, being wound up by the Court. Bateman TV Hire Ltd showed the cheques so paid in its books as advances to Bateman Television Ltd, and the entries corresponded with similar entries in the books of Bateman Television Ltd.

In these circumstances Macarthur J was asked to determine the question, who was the true owner of the cars? He was invited to determine this question on an originating application made to the Supreme Court at Christchurch on 24 July 1969 by the provisional liquidator of the company. At the time of making the application the provisional liquidator had possession of the cars pursuant to an order of the Court made in this regard pursuant to the provisions of s 252 of the Companies Act 1955 on 23 December 1968. He had quite properly formed the opinion that the cars would depreciate if kept unused; and in view of the fact that a decision of this Court as to the validity of the order winding up the company was the subject of a current appeal to the Judicial Committee of the Privy Council, he thought that it might be some time before the conclusion of the litigation enabled him to deal with them. He therefore made application to the Supreme Court under s 241 for directions; and it was upon this application that both parties agreed before Macarthur J that he should determine the true ownership of the cars. It very soon occurred to the learned Judge that the particular proceeding before him was not one well adapted to the determination of such a question, for it was proposed that he should decide the matter on the affidavits containing little detail, as to which it was proposed to cross-examine only one of the deponents—Mr Currie, the former secretary of the company. It must have been apparent that highly controversial questions of fact must soon emerge, for the resolution of which the procedure in a formally constituted action would be more appropriate. Nevertheless the liquidator, for reasons which at this stage of the matter do not very clearly appear, elected to have the question of ownership determined on the proceedings as they stood before Macarthur J: and after some preliminary demur the learned Judge agreed to defer to the insistence of the parties and to decide the matter as he had been asked to do.

For the liquidator it was contended that the whole of the purchase price having been paid from the company's funds and assets, it would amount to a fraud on the company's creditors if the directors were found entitled to the vehicles, the company being left with no more than unsecured claims against the directors personally. For the respondents it was argued that the transactions which I have described were intended to take effect according to their tenor, and that this being the intention of the parties they must so take effect; that the directors of a company were admittedly in a fiduciary relationship to the company as to certain matters; but that this company had not been defrauded, nor had any breach of fiduciary duty been proved. It was denied that the respondents had any duty in law to the creditors of the company; and it was contended, finally, that the company had acquiesced in or ratified whatever had been done.

Macarthur J held for the respondents.

TURNER J. [After setting out the facts, ante, 455]. Macarthur J disallowed the appellant's contention that the directors at the time of purchasing the vehicles purchased them in trust for the company. He cited *Lewin on Trusts*, 16th ed 130:

> "No trust will result unless the person advances the money in the character of a purchaser. Thus, where property is purchased with borrowed money and without any declaration of trust in favour of the lender, no resulting trust will be presumed in favour of the lender —

See *Aveling v Knipe* (1815) 19 Ves 441; *Re Cooke* (1857) 6 Ir Ch R 430", and after quoting *Underhill on Trusts*, 11th ed 185, much to the same effect, he said:

> "In my opinion Mr Patterson's submission must be accepted. I do not think that the evidence establishes that either the Television Company or the Hire Company paid the consideration moneys in the character of a purchaser. The records made in the cheque book and cash book of the Television Company in relation to the purchases from Croydon Motors in April 1967 are inconclusive. There is nothing in those records to show whether the payments in respect of the two motor cars were made on behalf of the company or whether they were made on behalf of the directors. And the original entries which were made in the journal and the ledger were not made until several months later, that is to say in August 1968, when Mr Currie was writing up the books. There is no evidence of any resolution of the company or of the directors in regard to the matter. No doubt the transactions in relation to the two Daimler cars in dispute should have been recorded in much clearer form. But the position now is that the onus rests on the provisional liquidator of the Television Company to establish his claim to the two motor vehicles and in my opinion the evidence is insufficient to discharge that onus."

I agree with the learned Judge in the Court below that the agreements between the two directors and Croydon Motors Ltd were effective as between the parties thereto to vest the legal title to the two cars severally in the two respondents immediately upon the last instalment of purchase money being paid to the vendor (or more correctly to the vendor's assignee of the conditional purchase agreements); and this notwithstanding that the whole of the consideration given had been found either by the company or by its associated company Bateman TV Hire Ltd. The only question remaining is whether, this fact notwithstanding, the directors, having at law the property in the cars, held them in trust for the company.

It is no doubt true that, as is observed by the editors of *Lewin* in the passage cited above, no trust in favour of the company will result from the transactions, which I have described unless the company advanced the moneys "in the character of a purchaser". It is perfectly clear, for instance, at least as the evidence appears in this proceeding, that Bateman TV Hire Ltd could not have contended that because it found the instalments the cars became its property in equity. The reason is because on the evidence it could not be contended that Bateman TV Hire Ltd paid these instalments "in the character of a purchaser". It paid them, as is perfectly clear from the evidence of Mr Currie—and indeed this is not in dispute—as the banker of the Bateman group of companies, treating them as advances to Bateman Television Ltd and debiting them to that company as a loan in its books. The result of this is that in equity, as well as at law, Bateman TV Hire Ltd is deemed to have lent the moneys to Bateman Television Ltd and as between these two companies and the directors of both of them the instalments of purchase money on the cars must be deemed to have been paid by Bateman Television Ltd, albeit with moneys advanced to it by way of loan by Bateman TV Hire Ltd.

Macarthur J asked himself the question whether Bateman Television Ltd, in paying the instalments, had advanced these moneys in the character of a purchaser of the cars, and he decided as a matter of fact that it had not. We were asked by counsel for the appellant to re-examine this finding.

The finding is not one of primary fact. It is not one which depends in any way on credibility. Macarthur J simply decided that the evidence which had been placed before the Court was insufficient to support the conclusion that the company had advanced the moneys "in the character of a purchaser"—and the evidence which he examined was affidavit evidence in which only the testimony of Mr Currie was subjected to the test of cross-examination. Clearly this was a case in which this Court is entitled to reassess the effect in law of the evidence, and, if it thinks it right to come to a conclusion different from that at which the trial Judge arrived to revise that conclusion.

In the judgment appealed from Macarthur J in coming to his conclusion on fact, expressly assumed that the onus of proof on the question before him rested on the liquidator. In one sense of the words "onus of proof" there can be no doubt that the trial Judge was right in this assumption. On pleadings—if they can be called such—ill-adapted for the purpose, and certainly inadequately indicating where the onus was submitted by them to be, two parties asked the learned Judge to decide which of them was the owner of two motor cars. Those cars had been purchased by the respondents, and the written contracts for their purchase indicated that the title to them had passed from the vendors to the respondents. Before the order of the Court of 23 December 1968 (which must in these proceedings be taken as determining no question of title) the cars were in the possession of the respondents. For the purposes of these proceedings, therefore, the respondents must be taken as beginning with both title and possession in their favour. In these circumstances it can hardly be doubted that an onus rested upon the liquidator to show an equitable title in the cars the legal title of which was admittedly in the respondents. But although this was the way in which the matter began before Macarthur J, it seems to me that as soon as the liquidator had shown that all the funds and property passing as consideration for the purchases were funds and property of the company, he had done all that was necessary to raise a presumption in his favour. At this point, while the onus of establishing his cause of action still remained "at the end of the day"—as it must always remain on a claimant—upon the liquidator, the evidentiary burden necessary to move that onus had been for the moment discharged.

The Venture [1908] P 218 was a case in which two brothers had purchased a yacht in the name of one of them. The other (the plaintiff) had provided a substantial part of the purchase price. The first brother, in whose name the yacht was put, died. A claim by the surviving brother against the executors of the dead one for a declaration tht the yacht was held partly in trust for him was upheld in the Court of Appeal, Farwell LJ saying in delivering the judgment of the Court at p 229:

> "In my opinion a great deal of time and money has been wasted in discussing a point which really does not arise, or which need not have arisen. It would have been amply sufficient to call Mr Percy Stone (the surviving brother), and when he had once proved — as in my judgment the report of the Registrar shews that he did — that he found £550, part of the purchase-money, the ordinary rule applies. That rule is stated by Eyre CB in *Dyer v Dyer* (1788) 2 Cox Eq 92; 30 ER 42 as follows: 'The clear result of all the cases, without single exception, is, that the trust of a legal estate, whether freehold, copyhold or leasehold; whether taken in the names of the purchaser and others, jointly, or in the names of others without that of the purchaser; whether in one name or several, whether jointly or successive, results to the man who advances the purchase-money; and it goes on a strict analogy to the rule of the common law, that, where a feoffment is made without consideration, the use results to the feoffer.' Since trusts and equities are now recognised, and may be enforced under the Merchant Shipping Acts, this principle extends to ships, although under the old Registry Acts it did not.
>
> "It follows that when it is once proved that Percy Stone advanced £550 of the £1,050 purchase-money for this yacht he thereupon became entitled to fifty-five 105ths. That being the presumption, it was of course, open to the other side to displace that presumption, but, it was no incumbent upon Percy Stone to prove more than that. It was for the other side to displace that presumption if they could, but they offered no evidence at all. I regret that there should have been this reference. It seems to have done no good.
>
> "The result is that, in our opinion, the order ought to be discharged, and there ought to be an order for the payment of fifty-five 105ths of the proceeds to the appellant."

The Venture was unfortunately not cited to Macarthur J in argument in the Court below. If he had had the opportunity of considering it, he might well have adopted a different approach to the question which he had to decide. Having had the advantage in this Court of hearing counsel's submissions upon it, I accept it as directly in point. The result of counsel's omission to make the same submissions in the Court below was that the learned trial Judge misdirected himself on the onus of proof. I think that he should have directed himself that the whole of the consideration for these purchases having moved from the company, a presumption arose from that fact of a resulting trust in the company's favour — *Dyer v Dyer* (supra) and *The Venture* (supra). He should then have inquired whether in this particular case circumstances were proved by which the presumption of resulting trust should be regarded as rebutted — *Standing v Bowring* (1885) 31 Ch D 282 per Cotton LJ at p 287; *The Venture* in the passage which I have cited at length above. And the result of such an inquiry must have been that there was no satisfactory evidence in this case or any circumstances by which the presumption of resulting trust could be rebutted; and indeed, on the contrary, that such circumstances as were proved supported that presumption.

Cases of resulting trusts arising from sets of facts like those in this case seem to me to fall into three distinct classes. First there is the case in which A purchases a property with his own funds, putting it in the name of B. This was the position in *Re Scottish Equitable Life Assurance Society* [1902] 1 Ch 282. Such cases are typified by Joyce J in the *Scottish Equitable Life* case at p 286 as:

"It comes really to this: a purchase by one in the name of another with no other circumstances at all proved."

In these cases a presumption of resulting trust at once arises; but the case before us is not one of these.

The second class of cases is that in which A, using funds provided by B, purchases, *in the absence of B*, a property, putting it in his own name. Here, if the evidence is such that B, can be said to have advanced the moneys to A *in the character of a purchaser*, there will be a resulting trust; *aliter*, if the moneys appear to have been advanced by him to A in the character of a lender. This is the case of which the editor of *Lewin* is so careful to speak, and it is illustrated by *Re Cooke* (1857) 6 Ir Ch R 430. But the case before us is not this case; for, as I shall presently remark, in the case before us the party who found the moneys—the company— was present at the transactions of purchase with full knowledge of what was being done.

There is a third class of case, perhaps the most common of all, where both parties take part in the purchase, the funds or part of them being found by one and the title being taken in the name of the other. On these facts without more being proved a presumption arises that the advance was made "in the character of a purchaser", though the evidence may show that this was not so, and that the advance was a loan, or partly a loan. So in *Aveling v Knipe* (1815) 19 Ves Jun 441; 34 ER 580—one of the cases cited in *Lewin*—two brothers purchased in their joint names, but the consideration moneys were found by one only of them. The other brother subsequently paid to his co-purchaser half of the purchase price. One brother then died, and the question was, whether the property had been held by them jointly or whether there was at the date of the transaction a resulting trust in favour of him alone who had provided the required funds. It was held that the evidence established that half of the moneys had been advanced by way of loan. In *Diwell v Farnes* [1959] 1 WLR 624; [1959] 2 All ER 379, however, the decision was to the opposite effect, on different facts; there the presumption of resulting trust was not rebutted. *The Venture* (supra), on which I have relied, forms one of this class of case. There, too, the moneys had been found in the character of a purchaser, and a resulting trust arose accordingly. The case before us on this appeal falls into this class also, and for the reasons which I will now give I have easily been brought to the conclusion that the moneys and property which the company furnished in this case were furnished "in the character of a purchaser".

It is true that in the meagre affidavit of two paragraphs—one each—in which the respondents placed before the Court the only testimony which they thought fit to give of the transaction now under question, each said separately that he had "purchased . . . in his own name and on his own behalf" the car which came into his possession. But whether he purchased so as to acquire the equitable estate is not a simple question of fact, but is largely, if not entirely, one of law, to be determined not by the purchaser, but by the Court on an examination of the acts and declarations of the parties in the transaction.

If the acts and declarations of the parties in those purchases are examined, what inference is possible from the proved facts, more likely than that the company furnished the used cars "in the character of purchaser" of the new ones? That the company had *given, gratis*, to the directors, its valuable assets, to be their own, to enable them to purchase with them cars which should be solely theirs, has only to be suggested to be rejected. That must be thought a priori in the highest degree improbable, and it becomes all the more so when it is observed that there is not one word of evidence to support such an inference. It is impossible, too, to regard the transaction as one in which the old cars were merely *lent* to the directors, and thus to bring the case within (say) *Aveling v Knipe*; for the cars must be regarded as having been handed over to the directors by the company on terms enabling them to pass the *title* of them to Croydon Motors. No question of the *loan* of them therefore can possibly arise. And it is impossible to regard the directors as having *bought* the cars from the company, on terms constituting the company their unsecured creditors for the total amounts of the purchase moneys. The entries in the books which the secretary made in September 1968 (eighteen months later) did indeed *then* deal with the matter as if they had been—at that later date—sold to the directors by the company; but there is no word in the evidence to suggest that anyone thought of this idea in April 1967, or indeed until September 1968, with the liquidation of the company imminent. I cannot think of any other possible version of the transaction as between the company and its directors which it is possible to suggest; and of all these obviously the most probable, and by far the most probable, must be that the company put in the cars "in the character of a purchaser". The result must be that Macarthur J should have held that no circumstance was proved to rebut the presumption of resulting trust.

I regard the case before us as one comparable in all respects to *The Venture*. It is certainly not a case in which the purchase was carried out by the purchasers in the absence of the party advancing the consideration. The company knew all about the transactions of purchase, and must be regarded as present, at least by one of its directors, at each of the transactions. It is impossible too, on the evidence, to separate the two transactions, regarding them as unconnected with each other. They must be thought of as two collateral connected transactions, both of which took place with the full knowledge, and indeed the co-operation, of the company. This is therefore a case like *The Venture* where both parties were present together at the transaction of purchase, one finding the consideration, and the title going into the name of the other. In such a case where no satisfactory evidence is produced to rebut it, a presumption will arise to a resulting trust in favour of him who finds the consideration.

Moreover it has been well said that the strength of the initial presumption of a resulting trust may be different in different types of case. Thus in *Fowkes v Pascoe* (1875) LR 10 Ch 343 Mellish LJ said at p 352:

"Now, the presumption must, beyond all question, bear very different weight in different cases. In some cases it would be very strong indeed. If, for instance, a man invested a sum of stock in the name of himself and his solicitor, the inference would be very strong indeed that it was intended solely for the purpose of a trust, and the Court would require very strong evidence on the part of the solicitor to prove that it was intended as a gift: and certainly his own evidence would not be sufficient. On the other hand, a man may make an investment of stock in the name of himself and some person, although not a child or wife, yet in such a position to him as to make it extremely probable that the investment was intended as a gift. In such a case, although the rule of law, if there was no evidence at all, would compel the Court to say that the presumption of trust must prevail, even if the court might not believe that the fact was in accordance with the presumption, yet, if there is evidence to rebut the presumption, then, in my opinion, the Court must go into the actual facts. And if we are to go into the actual facts, and look at the circumstances of this investment, it appears to me utterly impossible, as the Lord Justice has said, to come to any other conclusion than that the first investment was made for the purpose of gift and not for the purpose of trust. It was either for the purpose of trust or else for the purpose of gift; and therefore any evidence which shews it was not for the purpose of trust is evidence to shew that it was for the purpose of gift."

If the learned Lord Justice's words are applied to the case now before us, must it not be remembered that the matter starts with two directors bringing to their transaction two valuable cars to which they themselves had no title, the cars being owned by a company to which, by virtue of their position as its directors, they already owed a fiduciary duty? It seems to me that Mellish LJ's illustration of a purchase in the name of a solicitor is one very much in point in the present case, and the circumstances which I have just recalled must in themselves initially incline the Court against an inference destructive of a resulting trust in favour of the company.

If, then, as I have for myself concluded must have been the case, these cars, though purchased in the name of the directors, were held by them in trust for the company, did anything subsequently occur to alter that position? Nothing was submitted in this regard before us, except the conversation between the directors and the secretary in the month of September 1968, and the resulting entries in the company's records which were then made. It will be recalled that the last cash instalments of purchase money had been paid in June 1968. As at that stage no record of the transactions had apparently as yet been made in the company's books. As at 31 March 1967 these books had of course shown the old cars as assets of the company. The transactions wherein the new cars were purchased had not then yet been entered into. In August 1968 the secretary was writing up the books of the company as at 31 March 1968, and there arose in his mind the question as to how the transactions of April and May 1967 should be recorded. He then made entries showing the two new cars as the property of the company.

This of course by itself could not bring the Court to find the cars to be the property of the company: for at best it amounts to a self-serving statement upon which the company cannot rest its case for the ownership of the cars. But two comments may legitimately be made. The first is that the entry certainly does no harm to the company's case: the entry which the secretary made in August is entirely consistent with the proposition, if it can be independently established, that the cars were at that time held by directors in trust for the company. The second comment is that the secretary has sworn that the directors were consulted before the entry was made. He does not remember the details of the conversation, but when called to give evidence orally before Macarthur J he said:

> "Were those initial entries made on instructions? It is difficult to recall. The cars were bought in April 1967. I would say that the question of treatment of these cars would have been discussed with the directors. It is difficult to recall what decisions were made I would I can (sic) clearly recall being instructed by the directors to transfer these cars into their own names subsequent to this original journal entry. I can only say in respect of the original entry that the matter would have been discussed".

The directors gave no evidence before Macarthur J; nor do they allude to this matter in the affidavit which they filed. It must therefore appear on uncontradicted evidence that the entries of August 1968 were made with their knowledge and approval.

In September other entries were made. It will be as well to transcribe the evidence — very small in volume — which describes how this was done. The matter is referred to in only one of the affidvaits filed — that of the secretary. In his affidavit the secretary said:

> "Ownership: To record the purchase of the motor vehicles I made a journal entry in August 1968 when the accounts for the year ended 31 March 1968 were being finalised charging the motor vehicles to the motor vehicle accounts of the Company. At the time of the purchase, namely April 1967, and at the time the journal entry was made in August 1968, the directors' current accounts were in debit. Subsequently, in September 1968, acting on the instructions of the directors, a journal entry was made which removed the motor vehicles from the motor vehicle account and transferred them to the accounts of the directors which were still in debit. This was the position of the motor vehicles as at the date the Company was placed in provisional liquidation, namely 10 October 1968."

Mr Currie was cross-examined on this evidence. He was first questioned as to the entries made in August, showing the vehicles as the property of the company. His cross-examination then proceeded:

> "What is the next entry? One page 21 there is an entry debiting the directors. That is Messrs Bateman and Thomas? Yes. And crediting the Motor Vehicle A/c. For the full purchase price of the two vehicles. You debited Bateman and Thomas with the full price of the two vehicles? Yes. When did you write the entry? That would be approximately September 1968. Were those entries which you refer to the entry regarding the motor vehicle A/c and the entry regarding Bateman and Thomas made in the course of writing up the books for year ending 31 March 1968? Yes. Was there any entry as between Bateman TV Hire Ltd whose cheques they were and Bateman TV Ltd? Yes. What happened to that entry? There are two entries on page 19 of the journal the first entry debits Croydon Finance and credits Bateman TV Hire Ltd with the amount of $2,527 being the amount of the instalments paid to the finance company by Bateman TV Hire Ltd and the second entry is a debit to Croydon Motors Ltd crediting Bateman TV Hire Ltd for an amount of $651.44 being the deposit paid by Bateman TV Hire Ltd."

Re-examined by Mr Williamson he testified, in the short passage which I have already extracted as to the instructions which he had been given by the directors to transfer the cars into their own names.

What emerges is reasonably clear. In August the books of the company, written up by the secretary as at 31 March 1968, showed the cars as the property of the company. The secretary had thus written up the books after discussion with the directors. In September the company was in imminent danger of being wound up by its creditors. (Actually a petition was presented on 30 September, a provisional liquidator was appointed on 10 October, and a winding up order made on 12 December.) The directors instructed the secretary to make entries in the books so as to record the vehicles as theirs, and to show them as owing to the company as an unsecured debt the amounts of the purchase prices; and he made those entries as instructed.

Was this enough to terminate the trust on which these directors held the cars for the company? I think not. Perhaps if the company in formal meeting had passed a resolution, duly recorded at the time, and had then executed an agreement in due form purporting to sell the cars to the directors at specified prices on specified credit terms, and the directors had in turn bound themselves by signing promissory notes or other securities evidencing their obligations to pay accordingly, I might by the production of such cogent evidence have been brought to the conclusion that it had indeed effectively sold its interest in the cars, even though such an act would undoubtedly have amounted to a moral fraud upon its creditors. Had these things been done with bell book and candle, the creditors would have had to rely upon such statutory remedies as might have been available to them. But I am not willing to recognise the meagre evidence put forward of a mere informal conversation, the details of which the secretary cannot now remember, unsupported by any testimony given by either director, as sufficient to bring the Court to a conclusion that the company did indeed effectively discharge the directors from the trust upon which they had until then held the cars, or to enable them to set up a defence never pleaded and certainly unsupported by any evidence from them — that of sale by the company in September 1968.

Macarthur J did not make any finding on the effect of the conversation of September 1968. If it is to be held effective as a sale of the equitable interest in the cars by company to directors, such a conclusion must be one of fact, or mixed fact and law to be made in this Court. I decline to make it on the vague and unsatisfactory evidence produced.

My attention has been drawn, by another member of the Court, to the decision of Finlay J in *Bobbie Pins Ltd v Robertson* [1950] NZLR 301, one of the last cases in which my brother North appeared when at the Bar. There Finlay J decided, to quote the last paragraph of the headnote, that:

> "A company is bound by a transaction, intra vires and honest though irregular, which has the assent of all the corporators, as it is competent for the corporators, if they are unanimous, to waive all formalities. It is immaterial whether that assent is given at different times or simultaneously."

That decision was given in a case in which (a) the authority of all the corporators to what was done was clearly and satisfactorily proved, (b) all formalities were satisfactorily shown to have been waived (c) the transaction was one which was intra vires of the corporation and (d) (perhaps the most important of all) it was an honest transaction. I do not apply it in this case, partly because all or most of the special considerations which appealed to Finlay J are only too lacking here.

For these reasons, I am of opinion that the decision to which Macarthur J came in the Court below was wrong, and that he should have answered the question put to him in favour of the liquidator, holding that the property in the cars was in the company. I would consequently allow the appeal.

Notes and Questions

1. Analyse the kind of interests each of the various parties in *Bateman* had.

2. For an interesting Australian case on the goods, realty, and personalty problem see *Stokman* v *Mills* [1966] 1 NSWR 612 (CA). In 1955 the vendors sold a heap of slate on their property. The slate heap had been on the land since an earlier owner of a quarrying enterprise ceased business in 1931. It covered two acres, and was over fifty feet high in some places. The heap was the only known source of slate in NSW for the Canberra building industry. How should a Court deal with the heap of slate? Is it realty, personalty, or even 'goods' for sale purposes? Why does that matter? And can 'property' change character in the course of a transaction?

3. Is the traditional classification of property rights satisfactory today?

4. Are these factors relevant to that question?

(i) In matters of succession in New Zealand there is no distinction in the rules for realty and personalty, although some legal draftsmen still talk about 'devising' real property and 'bequeathing' personalty.

(ii) Some statutes still draw distinctions and talk of corporeal and incorporeal property.

5. Cohen, in his article (Dialogue, chapter 1, *supra*) seems to suggest that the interests of all owners do *not* differ from each other today. His objection is that today there are not inherent differences between the principles which should govern real property and personal property. Goode, *Commercial Law* (1982), 52 on the other hand suggests there *are* real differences in kind which (*semble?*) should be preserved.

> . . . Land is governed primarily by property law concepts, goods and choses in action by commercial law concepts; land law is concerned essentially with status, commercial law with obligations. But . . . many rules of property law apply equally well to land and chattels.

Is Goode's statement universally true? For instance, Air New Zealand some years ago ordered 747-400s for its fleet. Is it true to say of such a case that 'an ox is an ox is an ox'? And Air New Zealand surely also has a 'status' interest in that aeroplane?

6. Associate-Professor Bernard Brown has noted the importance of 'popular legal symbolism of ownership and possession' in relation to property and changes in

property law. When somebody talks, for instance, about 'his' car, even though it is subject to a hire-purchase agreement, this 'must be important to the gradual evolution of our law about conversion and the position of the *bona fide* buyer from a non-owner.' (Popular Legal Symbolism and Criminal Law Reform [1979] 3 Crim L J 133, 135). See also his, *Shibboleths of Law* (1987), and Stone, The Reification of Legal Concepts: Muschinski v Dodds (1986) 9 UNSWLJ 63. Do you agree?

7. For further reading see Goode, *Commercial Law* (1982), Chap. 2 'Basic Concepts of Personal Property', and Lawson and Rudden, *The Law of Property* (2nd ed), Chap. II, 'The Classification of Things'. For Roman Law, see Lawson and Rudden, 114 'Ownership' and Stein, *Legal Institutions* (1984), 144.

Possession

Possession, like ownership, is a very difficult term, and the way lawyers use the term does not necessarily correspond with lay understandings of it.

Some preliminary points should be made here. First, it is vital to appreciate the force of possession in the common law tradition. Our law of remedies in many ways turns on possession rather than ownership. Secondly, possession in many circumstances *does* amount to a form of title, as we shall see in the 'finders' cases (*infra*). Thirdly, in general, 'possession is indivisible. Like ownership it can only be held and transferred entire' (Goode, *Id*. 61). Fourthly, viewed in spatial terms, once acquired, possession continues until the asset passes into the possession of another or abandonment takes place. Fifthly, a study of possession is invaluable because it demonstrates how, in the common law tradition, title is a *relative* thing, whereas in the civil law tradition it is not. There title and ownership are not distinguished.

In the result, when looking at personal property, lawyers are interested in the relative quality of a given title. This is not an abstract inquiry, but is something to be judged by reference to its beginnings in time relative to that of others. Further, the word 'possession' now occurs in a number of legal contexts. It is possible that for the purpose of particular statutory provisions, 'possession' may have a particular meaning. (Consider, for instance, 'possession' of stolen goods in criminal law).

Some of the most useful cases with which to gain an appreciation of the relativity of possession and title are the so called 'finders cases'.

Armory v *Delamirie*

Kings Bench, 1722
1 Strange 505

The plaintiff being a chimney sweeper's boy found a jewel and carried it to the defendant's shop (who was a goldsmith) to know what it was, and delivered it into the hands of the apprentice, who under pretence of weighing it, took out the stones, and calling to the master to let him know it came to three halfpence, the master offered the boy the money, who refused to take it, and insisted to have the thing again; whereupon the apprentice delivered him back the socket without the stones. And now in trover against the master these points were ruled:

1. That the finder of a jewel, though he does not by such finding acquire an absolute property or ownership, yet he has such a property as will enable him to keep it against all but the rightful owner, and consequently may maintain trover.

2. That the action well lay against the master, who gives a credit to his apprentice, and is answerable for his neglect.

3. As to the value of the jewel several of the trade were examined to prove what jewel of the finest water that would fit the socket would be worth; and the Chief Justice (Pratt) directed the jury, that unless the defendant did produce the jewel, and shew it not be of the finest water, they should presume the strongest against him, and make the value of the best jewels the measure of their damages: which they accordingly did.

Hannah v Peel

[1945] K B 509

Action tried by Birkett, J.

On December 13, 1938, the freehold of Gwernhaylod House, Overton-on-Dee, Shropshire, was conveyed to the defendant, Major Hugh Edward Ethelston Peel, who from that time to the end of 1940 never himself occupied the house and it remained unoccupied until October 5, 1939, when it was requisitioned, but after some months was released from requisition. Thereafter it remained unoccupied until July 18, 1940, when it was again requisitioned, the defendant being compensated by a payment at the rate of 250*l*. a year. In August, 1940, the plaintiff, Duncan Hannah, a lance-corporal, serving in a battery of the Royal Artillery, was stationed at the house and on the 21st of that month, when in a bedroom, used as a sick-bay, he was adjusting the black-out curtains when his hand touched something on the top of a window-frame, loose in a crevice, which he thought was a piece of dirt or plaster. The plaintiff grasped it and dropped it on the outside window ledge. On the following morning he saw that it was a brooch covered with cobwebs and dirt. Later, he took it with him when he went home on leave and his wife having told him it might be of value, at the end of October, 1940, he informed his commanding officer of his find and, on his advice, handed it over to the police, receiving a receipt for it. In August, 1942, the owner not having been found the police handed the brooch to the defendant, who sold it on October, 1942, for 66*l*., to Messrs. Spink & Sons, Ltd., of London, who resold it in the following month for 88*l*. There was no evidence that the defendant had any knowledge of the existence of the brooch before it was found by the plaintiff. The defendant had offered the plaintiff a reward for the brooch, but the plaintiff refused to accept this and maintained throughout his right to the possession of the brooch as against all persons other than the owner, who was unknown. By a letter, dated October 5, 1942, the plaintiff's solicitors demanded the return of the brooch from the defendant, but it was not returned and on October 21, 1943, the plaintiff issued his writ claiming the return of the brooch, or its value, and damages for its detention. By his defence, the defendant claimed the brooch on the ground that he was the owner of Gwernhaylod House and in possession thereof. ∗ ∗ ∗

BIRKETT, J. There is no issue of fact in this case between the parties. As to the issue in law, the rival claims of the parties can be stated in this way: The plaintiff says: "I claim the brooch as its finder and I have a good title against all the world, save only the true owner." The defendant says: "My claim is superior to yours inasmuch as I am the freeholder. The brooch was found on my property, although I was never in occupation, and my title, therefore, ousts yours and in the absence of the true owner I am entitled to the brooch or its value." Unhappily the law on this issue is in a very uncertain state and there is need of an authoritative decision of a higher court. Obviously if it could be said with certainty that this is the law, that the finder of a lost article, wherever found, has a good title against all the world save the true owner, then, of course, all my difficulties would be resolved; or again, if it could be said with equal certainty that this is the law, that the possessor of land is entitled as against the finder to all chattels found on the land, again my difficulties would be resolved. But, unfortunately, the authorities give some support to each of these conflicting propositions. * * *

The case of Bridges v. Hawkesworth, 21 L.J. (Q.B.) 75, 15 Jur. 1079, was * * * an appeal against a decision of the county court judge at Westminster. The facts appear to have been that in the year 1847 the plaintiff, who was a commercial traveller, called on a firm named Byfield & Hawkesworth on business, as he was in the habit of doing, and as he was leaving the shop he picked up a small parcel which was lying on the floor. He immediately showed it to the shopman, and opened it in his presence, when it was found to consist of a quantity of Bank of England notes, to the amount of 65*l*. The defendant, who was a partner in the firm of Byfield & Hawkesworth, was then called, and the plaintiff told him he had found the notes, and asked the defendant to keep them until the owner appeared to claim them. Then various advertisements were put in the papers asking for the owner, but the true owner was never found. No person having appeared to claim them, and three years having elapsed since they were found, the plaintiff applied to the defendant to have the notes returned to him, and offered to pay the expenses of the advertisements, and to give an indemnity. The defendant refused to deliver them up to the plaintiff, and an action was brought in the county court of Westminster in consequence of that refusal. The county court judge decided that the defendant, the shopkeeper, was entitled to the custody of the notes as against the plaintiff, and gave judgment for the defendant. Thereupon the appeal was brought which came before the court composed by Patteson, J., and Wightman, J. Patteson, J., said:

> "The notes which are the subject of this action were incidentally dropped, by mere accident, in the shop of the defendant, by the owner of them. The facts do not warrant the supposition that they had been deposited there intentionally, nor has the case been put at all upon that ground. The plaintiff found them on the floor, they being manifestly lost by someone. The general right of the finder to any article which has been lost, as against all the world, except the true owner, was established in the case of Armory v. Delamirie, 1 Str. 505, which has never been disputed. This right would clearly have accrued to the plaintiff had the notes been picked up by him outside the shop of the defendant and if he once had the right, the case finds that he did not intend, by delivering the notes to the defendant, to waive the title (if any) which he had to them, but they were handed to the defendant merely for the purpose of delivering them to the owner should he appear."

Then a little later:

"The case, therefore, resolves itself into the single point on which it appears that the learned judge decided it, namely, whether the circumstance of the notes being found inside the defendant's shop gives him, the defendant, the right to have them as against the plaintiff, who found them."

After discussing the cases, and the argument, the learned judge said:

"If the discovery had never been communicated to the defendant, could the real owner have had any cause of action against him because they were found in his house? Certainly not. The notes never were in the custody of the defendant, nor within the protection of his house, before they were found, as they would have been had they been intentionally deposited there; and the defendant has come under no responsibility, except from the communication made to him by the plaintiff, the finder, and the steps taken by way of advertisement. ∗ ∗ ∗ We find, therefore, no circumstances in this case to take it out of the general rule of law, that the finder of a lost article is entitled to it as against all persons except the real owner, and we think that that rule must prevail, and that the learned judge was mistaken in holding that the place in which they were found makes any legal difference. Our judgment, therefore, is that the plaintiff is entitled to these notes as against the defendant."

It is to be observed that in Bridges v. Hawkesworth, which has been the subject of immense disputation, neither counsel put forward any argument on the fact that the notes were found in a shop. Counsel for the appellant assumed throughout that the position was the same as if the parcel had been found in a private house, and the learned judge spoke of "the protection of his" (the shopkeeper's) "house." The case for the appellant was that the shopkeeper never knew of the notes. Again, what is curious is that there was no suggestion that the place where the notes were found was in any way material; indeed, the judge in giving the judgment of the court expressly repudiates this and said in terms "The learned judge was mistaken in holding that the place in which they were found makes any legal difference." It is, therefore, a little remarkable that in South Staffordshire Water Co. v. Sharman, [1896] 2 Q.B. 47, Lord Russell of Killowen, C.J., said:

"The case of Bridges v. Hawkesworth stands by itself, and on special grounds; and on those grounds it seems to me that the decision in that case was right. Someone had accidentally dropped a bundle of banknotes in a public shop. The shopkeeper did not know they had been dropped, and did not in any sense exercise control over them. The shop was open to the public, and they were invited to come there."

That might be a matter of some doubt. Customers were invited there, but whether the public at large was, might be open to some question. Lord Russell continued:

"A customer picked up the notes and gave them to the shopkeper in order that he might advertise them. The owner of the notes was not found, and the finder then sought to recover them from the shopkeeper. It was held that he was entitled to do so, the ground of the decision being, as was pointed out by Patteson, J., that the notes, being dropped in the public part of the shop, were never in the custody of the shopkeeper, or within the protection of his house."

Patteson, J., never made any reference to the public part of the shop and, indeed, went out of his way to say that the learned county court judge was wrong in holding that the place where they were found made any legal difference.

Bridges v. Hawkesworth has been the subject of considerable comment by text-book writers and, amongst others, by Mr. Justice Oliver Wendell Holmes, Sir Frederick Pollock and Sir John Salmond. All three agree that the case was rightly decided, but they differ as to the grounds on which it was decided and put forward grounds, none of which, so far as I can discover, were ever advanced by the judges who decided the case. Mr. Justice Oliver Wendell Holmes wrote, in The Common Law (1881) at p. 222:

> "Common law judges and civilians would agree that the finder got possession first and so could keep it as against the shopkeeper. For the shopkeeper, not knowing of the thing, could not have the intent to appropriate it, and, having invited the public to his shop, he could not have the intent to exclude them from it."

So he introduces the matter of two intents which are not referred to by the judges who heard the case. Sir Frederick Pollock, whilst he agreed with Mr. Justice Holmes that Bridges v. Hawkesworth was properly decided, wrote, in Possession in the Common Law (Pollock and Wright) at p. 39:

> "In such a case as Bridges v. Hawkesworth where a parcel of banknotes was dropped on the floor in the part of a shop frequented by customers, it is impossible to say that the shopkeeper has any possession in fact. He does not expect objects of that kind to be on the floor of his shop, and some customer is more likely than the shopkeeper or his servant to see and take them up if they do come there."

He emphasizes the lack of de facto control on the part of the shopkeeper. Sir John Salmond wrote, in Jurisprudence (9th ed.) 382:

> "In Bridges v. Hawkesworth a parcel of banknotes was dropped on the floor of the defendant's shop, where they were found by the plaintiff, a customer. It was held that the plaintiff had a good title to them as against the defendant. For the plaintiff, and not the defendant, was the first to acquire possession of them. The defendant had not the necessary animus, for he did not know of their existence."

Professor Goodhart, in our own day, in his work Essays in Jurisprudence and the Common Law (1931) has put forward a further view that perhaps Bridges v. Hawkesworth was wrongly decided. It is clear from the decision in Bridges v. Hawkesworth that an occupier of land does not in all cases possess an unattached thing on his land even though the true owner has lost possession.

With regard to South Staffordshire Water Co. v. Sharman, [1862] 2 Q.B. 44, the first two lines of the headnote are: "The possessor of land is generally entitled, as against the finder, to chattels found on the land." I am not sure that this is accurate. The facts were that the defendant Sharman, while cleaning out, under the orders of the plaintiffs, the South Staffordshire Water Company, a pool of water on their land, found two rings embedded in the mud at the bottom of the pool. He declined to deliver them to the plaintiffs, but failed to discover the real owner. In an action brought by the company against Sharman in detinue it was held that the company was entitled to the rings. Lord Russell of Killowen, C.J., said:

"The plaintiffs are the freeholders of the locus in quo, and as such they have the right to forbid anybody coming on their land or in any way interfering with it. They had the right to say that their pool should be cleaned out in any way that they thought fit, and to direct what should be done with anything found in the pool in the course of such cleaning out. It is no doubt right, as the counsel for the defendant contended, to say that the plaintiffs must show that they had actual control over the locus in quo and the things in it; but under the circumstances, can it be said that the Minster Pool and whatever might be in that pool were not under the control of the plaintiffs? In my opinion they were. * * * The principle on which this case must be decided, and the distinction which must be drawn between this case and that of Bridges v. Hawkesworth, is to be found in a passage in Pollock and Wright's Essay on Possession in the Common Law, p. 41: 'The possession of land carries with it in general, by our law, possession of everything which is attached to or under that land, and, in the absence of a better title elsewhere, the right to possess it also.' "

And it makes no difference that the possessor is not aware of the thing's existence.

* * *

Then Lord Russell cited the passage which I read earlier in this judgment and continued: "It is somewhat strange" — I venture to echo those words —

"that there is no more direct authority on the question; but the general principle seems to me to be that where a person has possession of house or land, with a manifest intention to exercise control over it and the things which may be upon or in it, then, if something is found on that land, whether by an employee of the owner or by a stranger, the presumption is that the possession of that thing is in the owner of the locus in quo."

It is to be observed that Lord Russell there is extending the meaning of the passage he had cited from Pollock and Wright's essay on Possession in the Common Law, where the learned authors say that the possession of "land carries with it possession of everything which is attached to or under that land." Then Lord Russell adds possession of everything which may be on or in that land. South Staffordshire Water Co. v Sharman, which was relied on by counsel for the defendant, has also been the subject of some discussion. It has been said that it establishes that if a man finds a thing as the servant or agent of another, he finds it not for himself, but for that other, and indeed that seems to afford a sufficient explanation of the case. The rings found at the bottom of the pool were not in the possession of the company, but it seems that though Sharman was the first to obtain possession of them, he obtained them for his employers and could claim no title for himself.

The only other case to which I need refer is Elwes v. Brigg Gas Co., 33 Ch. D. 562, in which land had been demised to a gas company for ninety-nine years with a reservation to the lessor of all mines and minerals. A pre-historic boat embedded in the soil was discovered by the lessees when they were digging to make a gasholder. It was held that the boat, whether regarded as a mineral or as part of the soil in which it was embedded when discovered, or as a chattel, did not pass to the lessees by the demise, but was the property of the lessor though he was ignorant of its existence at the time of granting the lease. Chitty, J., said:

> "The first question which does actually arise in this case is whether the boat belonged to the plaintiff at the time of the granting of the lease. I hold that it did, whether it ought to be regarded as a mineral, or as part of the soil within the maxim above cited, or as a chattel. If it was a mineral or part of the soil in the sense above indicated, then it clearly belonged to the owners of the inheritance as part of the inheritance itself. But if it ought to be regarded as a chattel, I hold the property in the chattel was vested in the plaintiff, for the following reasons."

Then he gave the reasons, and continued:

> "The plaintiff then being thus in possession of the chattel, it follows that the property in the chattel was vested in him. Obviously the right of the original owner could not be established; it had for centuries been lost or barred, even supposing that the property had not been abandoned when the boat was first left on the spot where it was found. The plaintiff, then, had a lawful possession, good against all the world, and therefore the property in the boat. In my opinion it makes no difference, in these circumstances, that the plaintiff was not aware of the existence of the boat."

A review of these judgments shows that the authorities are in an unsatisfactory state. * * *

It is fairly clear from the authorities that a man possesses everything which is attached to or under his land. Secondly, it would appear to be the law from the authorities I have cited, and particularly from Bridges v. Hawkesworth, that a man does not necessarily possess a thing which is lying unattached on the surface of his land even though the thing is not possessed by someone else. A difficulty, however, arises * * * because the rule which governs things an occupier possesses as against those which he does not, has never been very clearly formulated in our law. He may possess everything on the land from which he intends to exclude others, if Mr. Justice Holmes is right; or he may possess those things of which he has a de facto control, if Sir Frederick Pollock is right.

There is no doubt that in this case the brooch was lost in the ordinary meaning of that term, and I should imagine it had been lost for a very considerable time. Indeed, from this correspondence it appears that at one time the predecessors in title of the defendant were considering making some claim. But the moment the plaintiff discovered that the brooch might be of some value, he took the advice of his commanding officer and handed it to the police. His conduct was commendable and meritorious. The defendant was never physically in possession of these premises at any time. It is clear that the brooch was never his, in the ordinary acceptation of the term, in that he had the prior possession. He had no knowledge of it, until it was brought to his notice by the finder. A discussion of the merits does not seem to help, but it is clear on the facts that the brooch was "lost" in the ordinary meaning of that word and it was "found" by the plaintiff in the ordinary meaning of that word, that its true owner has never been found, that the defendant was the owner of the premises and had his notice drawn to this matter by the plaintiff, who found the brooch. In those circumstances I propose to follow the decision in Bridges v. Hawkesworth, and to give judgment in this case for the plaintiff for 66*l*.

Judgment for plaintiff.

Parker v British Airways Board

[1982] 2 W L R 503 (CA)

APPEAL from the Brentford County Court.

On November 15, 1978, while the plaintiff, Alan George Parker, was waiting as a passenger in the executive lounge at terminal one of London Heathrow Airport he found a gentleman's gold bracelet lying on the floor. The bracelet had been lost by its rightful owner. The plaintiff delivered the bracelet to an employee of the defendants, British Airways Board, together with particulars of the plaintiff's name and address and orally requested that in the event of the bracelet not being claimed by the rightful owner it should be returned to the plaintiff. The bracelet was never claimed. But despite the plaintiff's requests for its return to him, the defendants sold it on June 17, 1979.

The plaintiff issued proceedings in the county court alleging that he suffered loss and damage, namely, £850, being the value of the bracelet and sought the return of the bracelet or its value and damages for the defendants' wrongful interference therewith; and alternatively, damages for conversion and interest.

The defendants alleged in their defence that the executive lounge could be entered by visitors only at the express invitation of the defendants and then only provided that they were in possession of the appropriate documentation. It was not a part of the terminal to which the public nor even the passengers had access as of right. At all material times the defendants owned and occupied and controlled the executive lounge where the bracelet was found and therefore, they acquired a better title to it than did the plaintiff. They counterclaimed for a declaration that they acquired a better title to the bracelet than the plaintiff.

Mr. Derek Holden, sitting as a deputy circuit judge, decided on November 5, 1980, that the defendants had wrongfully interfered with the gold bracelet and were liable to the plaintiff for its value together with interest.

By a notice of appeal dated November 20, 1980, the defendants appealed on the grounds, inter alia, that the judge erred in law in holding that the plaintiff had a better title than did the defendants to the bracelet, and in rejecting the submissions put forward by the defendants, namely, (1) where an occupier of premises had de facto control and he intended to actively possess or prevent others (other than the true owner) from possessing chattels, which might be lost on premises, then he acquired a better title to those chattels than the finder; (2) the plaintiff was not a true finder because at the time of the loss the occupier possessed the chattels as against the then unascertained owner.

DONALDSON L.J. delivered the first judgment. On November 15, 1978, the plaintiff, Alan George Parker, had a date with fate—and perhaps with legal immortality. He found himself in the international executive lounge at terminal one, Heathrow Airport. And that was not all that he found. He also found a gold bracelet lying on the floor.

We know very little about the plaintiff, and it would be nice to know more. He was lawfully in the lounge and, as events showed, he was an honest man. Clearly he had not forgotten the schoolboy maxim "Finders keepers." But, equally clearly, he was well aware of the adult qualification "unless the true owner claims the article." He had had to clear customs and security to reach the lounge. He was almost certainly an outgoing passenger because the defendants, British Airways Board, as lessees of the lounge from the British Airports Authority and its occupiers, limit its use to passengers who hold first class tickets or boarding passes or who are member of their Executive Club, which is a passengers' "club". Perhaps the plaintiff's flight had just been called and he was pressed for time. Perhaps the only officials in sight were employees of the defendants. Whatever the reason, he gave the bracelet to an anonymous official of the defendants instead of to the police. He also gave the official a note of his name and address and asked for the bracelet to be returned to him if it was not claimed by the owner. The official handed the bracelet to the lost property department of the defendants.

Thus far the story is unremarkable. The plaintiff, the defendants' official and the defendants themselves had all acted as one would have hoped and expected them to act. Thereafter matters took what, to the plaintiff, was an unexpected turn. Although the owner never claimed the bracelet, the defendants did not return it to the plaintiff. Instead they sold it and kept the proceeds which amounted to £850. The plaintiff discovered what had happened and was more than a little annoyed. I can understand his annoyance. He sued the defendants in the Brentford County Court and was awarded £850 as damages and £50 as interest. The defendants now appeal.

It is astonishing that there should be any doubt as to who is right. But there is. Indeed, it seems that the academics have been debating this problem for years. In 1971 the Law Reform Committee reported that it was by no means clear who had the better claim to lost property when the protagonists were the finder and the occupier of the premises where the property was found. Whatever else may be in doubt, the committee was abundantly right in this conclusion. The committee recommended legislative action but, as is not uncommon, nothing has been done. The rights of the parties thus depend upon the common law.

As a matter of legal theory, the common law has a ready made solution for every problem and it is only for the judges, as legal technicians, to find it. The reality is somewhat different. Take the present case. The conflicting rights of finder and occupier have indeed been considered by various courts in the past. But under the rules of English jurisprudence, none of their decisions binds this court. We therefore had both the right and the duty to extend and adapt the common law in the light of established principles and the current needs of the community. This is not to say that we start with a clean sheet. In doing so, we should draw from the experience of the past as revealed by the previous decisions of the courts. In this connection we have been greatly assisted both by the arguments of counsel, and in particular those of Mr. Desch upon whom the main burden fell, and by the admirable judgment of the deputy judge in the county court.

Neither the plaintiff nor the defendants lay any claim to the bracelet either as owner of it or as one who derives title from that owner. The plaintiff's claim is founded upon the ancient common law rule that the act of finding a chattel which has been lost and taking control of it gives the finder rights with respect to that chattel. The defendants' claim has a different basis. They cannot and do not claim to have found the bracelet when it was handed to them by the plaintiff. At that stage it was no longer lost and they received and accepted the bracelet from the plaintiff on terms that it would be returned to him if the owner could not be found. They must and do claim on the basis that they had rights in relation to the bracelet immediately *before* the plaintiff found it and that these rights are superior to the plaintiff's. The defendants' claim is based upon the proposition that at common law an occupier of land has such rights over all lost chattels which are on that land, whether or not the occupier knows of their existence.

The common law right asserted by Mr. Parker has been recognised for centuries. In its simplest form it was asserted by the chimney sweep's boy who, in 1722, found a jewel and offered it to a jeweller for sale. The jeweller refused either to pay a price acceptable to the boy or to return it and the boy sued the jeweller for its value: *Armory* v. *Delamirie* (1722) 1 Stra. 505. Pratt C.J. ruled:

> "That the finder of a jewel, though he does not by such finding acquire an absolute property or ownership, yet he has such a property as will enable him to keep it against all but the rightful owner, and consequently may maintain trover."

In that case the jeweller clearly had no rights in relation to the jewel immediately before the boy found it and any rights which he acquired when he received it from the boy stemmed from the boy himself. The jeweller could only have succeeded if the fact of finding and taking control of the jewel conferred no rights upon the boy. The court would then have been faced with two claimants, neither of which had any legal right, but one had de facto possession. The rule as stated by Pratt C.J. must be right as a general proposition, for otherwise lost property would be subject to a free-for-all in which the physically weakest would go to the wall.

Pratt C.J.'s ruling is, however, only a general proposition which requires definition. Thus one who "finds" a lost chattel in the sense of becoming aware of its presence, but who does no more, is not a "finder" for this purpose and does not, as such, acquire any rights.

Some qualification has also to be made in the case of the trespassing finder. The person vis à vis whom he is a trespasser has a better title. The fundamental basis of this is clearly public policy. Wrongdoers should not benefit from their wrongdoing. This requirement would be met if the trespassing finder acquired no rights. That would, however, produce the free-for-all situation to which I have already referred, in that anyone could take the article from the trespassing finder. Accordingly, the common law has been obliged to give rights to someone else, the owner ex hypothesi being unknown. The obvious candidate is the occupier of the property upon which the finder was trespassing.

Curiously enough, it is difficult to find any case in which the rule is stated in this simple form, but I have no doubt that this is the law. It is reflected in the judgment of Chitty J in *Elwes* v. *Brigg Gas Co.* (1886) 33 Ch.D. 562, 568, although the chattel concerned was beneath the surface of the soil and so subject to different considerations. It is also reflected in the judgment of Lord Goddard C.J.

in *Hibbert* v. *McKiernan* [1948] 2 K.B. 142, 149. That was a criminal case concerning the theft of "lost" golf balls on the private land of a club. The only issue was whether for the purposes of the criminal law property in the golf balls could be laid in someone other than the alleged thief. The indictment named the members of the club, who were occupiers of the land, as having property in the balls, and it is clear that at the time when the balls were taken the members were very clearly asserting such a right, even to the extent of mounting a police patrol to warn off trespassers seeking to harvest lost balls.

It was in this context that we were also referred to the opinion of the Judicial Committee in *Glenwood Lumber Co. Ltd.* v. *Phillips* [1904] A.C. 405 and in particular to remarks by Lord Davey, at p. 410. However, there the occupier knew of the presence of the logs on the land and had a claim to them as owner as well as occupier. Furthermore, it was not a finding case, for the logs were never lost.

One might have expected there to be decisions clearly qualifying the general rule where the circumstances are that someone finds a chattel and thereupon forms the dishonest intention of keeping it regardless of the rights of the true owner or of anyone else. But that is not the case. There could be a number of reasons. Dishonest finders will often be trespassers. They are unlikely to risk invoking the law, particularly against another subsequent dishonest taker, and a subsequent honest taker is likely to have a superior title: see, for example, *Buckley* v. *Gross* (1863) 3 B. & S. 566. However, he probably has some title, albeit a frail one because of the need to avoid a free-for-all. This seems to be the law in Ontario, Canada: *Bird* v. *Fort Frances* [1949] 2 D.L.R. 791.

In the interests of clearing the ground and identifying the problem, let me now turn to another situation in respect of which the law is reasonably clear. This is that of chattels which are attached to realty (land or buildings) when they are found. If the finder is not a wrongdoer, he may have some rights, but the occupier of the land or building will have a better title. The rationale of this rule is probably either that the chattel is to be treated as an integral part of the realty as against all but the true owner and so incapable of being lost or that the "finder" has to do something to the realty in order to get at or detach the chattel and, if he is not thereby to become a trespasser, will have to justify his actions by reference to some form of licence from the occupier. In all likely circumstances that licence will give the occupier a superior right to that of the finder.

Authority for this view of the law is to be found in *South Staffordshire Water Co.* v. *Sharman* [1896] 2 Q.B. 44 where the defendant was employed by the occupier of land to remove mud from the bottom of a pond. He found two gold rings embedded in the mud. The plaintiff occupier was held to be entitled to the rings. Dicta of Lord Russell of Killowen C.J., with whom Wills J. agreed, not only support the law as I have stated it, but go further and may support the defendants' contention that an occupier of a building has a claim to articles found *in* that building as opposed to being found attached to or forming part of it. However, it is more convenient to consider these dicta hereafter. *Elwes* v. *Brigg Gas Co.*, 33 Ch.D. 562, to which we were also referred in this context, concerned a prehistoric boat embedded in land. But I think that, when analysed, the issue really turned upon rival claims by the plaintiff, to be the true owner in the sense of being the tenant for life of the realty, of the minerals in the land and of the boat if it was a chattel and by the defendants as lessees rather than as finders.

Again, in the interest of clearing the ground, I should like to dispose briefly of some of the other cases to which we were quite rightly referred and to do so upon the grounds that, when analysed, they do not really bear upon the instant problem. Thus, *In re Cohen, decd.; National Provincial Bank Ltd.* v. *Katz* [1953] Ch. 88 concerned money hidden in a flat formerly occupied by a husband and wife who had died. The issue was whether the money belonged to the estate of the husband or to that of the wife. The money has been hidden and not lost and this was not a finding case at all. In *Johnson* v. *Pickering* [1907] 2 K.B. 437 the issue was whether the sheriff on behalf of a judgment creditor had a claim to money which the judgment debtor took to his house at a time when the sheriff had taken walking possession of that house, albeit the sheriff had been unaware of the arrival of the money. This again is not a finding case. In *Moffatt* v. *Kazana* [1969] 2 Q.B. 152 the claimant established a title derived from that of the true owner. This does not help. Finally, there is *Hannah* v. *Peel* [1945] K.B. 509. This was indeed a finding case, but the claimant was the non-occupying owner of the house in which the brooch was found. The occupier was the Crown, which made no claim either as occupier or as employer of the finder. It was held that the non-occupying owner had no right to the brooch and that therefore the finder's claim prevailed. What the position would have been if the Crown had made a claim was not considered.

I must now return to the respective claims of the plaintiff and the defendants. Mr. Brown, for the plaintiff, relies heavily upon the decision of Patteson J. and Wightman J., sitting in banc in *Bridges* v. *Hawkesworth* (1851) 21 L.J. Q.B. 75; 15 Jur. 1079. It was an appeal from the county court by case stated. The relevant facts, as found, were as follows. Mr. Bridges was a commercial traveller and in the course of his business he called upon the defendant at his shop. As he was leaving the shop, he picked up a small parcel which was lying on the floor, showed it to the shopman and, upon opening it in his presence, found that it contained £65 in notes. Mr. Hawkesworth was called and Mr. Bridges asked him to keep the notes until the owner claimed them. Mr. Hawkesworth advertised for the true owner, but no claimant came forward. Three years later Mr. Bridges asked for the money and offered to indemnify Mr. Hawkesworth in respect of the expenses which he had incurred in advertising for the owner. Mr. Hawkesworth refused to pay over the money and Mr. Bridges sued for it. The county court judge dismissed his claim and he appealed.

Patteson J. gave the judgment of the court. The decision is sufficiently important, and the judgment sufficiently short and difficult to find, for me to feel justified in reproducing it in full. In so doing, I take the text of the report in the *Jurist*, 15 Jur. 1079, 1082 but refer to the *Law Journal* version, 21 L.J. Q.B. 75, 77-78, in square brackets where they differ. It reads:

"The notes which are the subject of this action were incidentally ['evidently'] dropped by mere accident, in the shop of the defendant, by the owner of them. The facts do not warrant the supposition that they had been deposited there intentionally, nor has the case been put at all upon that ground. The plaintiff found them on the floor, they being manifestly lost by some one. The general right of the finder to any article which has been lost, as against all the world, except the true owner, was established in * * * *Armory* v. *Delamirie*, 1 Stra. 505, which has never been disputed. This right would clearly have accrued to the plaintiff had the notes been picked up by him outside the shop of the defendant; and if he once had the right, the case finds that he did not intend, by delivering the notes to the defendant, to waive the title (if any) which he had to them, but they were handed to the defendant merely for the purpose of delivering them to the owner, should he appear. Nothing that was done afterwards has altered the state of things; the advertisements inserted ['indeed'] in the newspaper, referring to the defendant, had the same object; the plaintiff has tendered the expense of those advertisements to the defendant, and offered him an indemnity against any claim to be made by the real owner, and has demanded the notes. The case, therefore, resolves itself into the single point on which it appears that the learned judge decided it, namely, whether the circumstance of the notes being found inside [word emphasised in *Law Journal*] the defendant's shop gives him, the defendant, the right to have them as against the plaintiff, who found them. There is no authority in our law to be found directly in point. Perhaps the nearest case is that of *Merry* v. *Green* (1841) 7 M. & W. 623, but it differs in many respects from the present. We were referred, in the course of the argument, to the learned work of Von Savigny, edited by Perry C.J.; but even this work, full as it is of subtle distinctions and nice reasonings, does not afford a solution of the present question. It was well asked, on the argument, if the defendant has the right, *when* did it accrue to him? If at all, it must have been antecedent to the finding by the plaintiff, for that finding could not give the defendant any right. If the notes had been accidently kicked into the shop ['the street' in *Law Journal*, which must be right], and there found by someone passing by, could it be contended that the defendant was entitled to them from the mere fact of their being originally dropped in his shop? If the discovery had never ['not'] been communicated to the defendant, could the real owner have had any cause of action against him because they were found in his house? Certainly not. The notes never were in the custody of the defendant, nor within the protection of his house, before they were found, as they would have been had they been intentionally deposited there; and the defendant has come under no responsibility, except from the communication made to him by the plaintiff, the finder, and the steps taken by way of advertisement. These steps were really taken by the defendant as the agent of the plaintiff, and he has been offered an indemnity, the sufficiency of which is not disputed. We find, therefore, no circumstances in this case to take it out of the general rule of law, that the finder of a lost article is entitled to it as against all persons except the real owner, and we think that that rule must prevail, and that the learned judge was mistaken in holding that the place in which they were found makes any legal difference. Our judgment, therefore, is, that the plaintiff is entitled to these notes as against the defendant; that the judgment of the court below must be reversed, and judgment given for the plaintiff for £50."

The ratio of this decision seems to me to be solely that the unknown presence of the notes on the premises occupied by Mr. Hawkesworth could not without more, give him any rights or impose any duty upon him in relation to the notes.

Mr. Desch for the defendants, submits that *Bridges* v. *Hawkesworth*, 15 Jur. 1079, can be distinguished and he referred us to the judgment of Lord Russell of Killowen C.J., with which Wills J. agreed, in *South Staffordshire Water Co.* v. *Sharman* [1896] 2 Q.B. 44. *Sharman's* case itself is readily distinguishable, either upon the ground that the rings were in the mud and thus part of the realty or upon the ground that the finders were employed by the plaintiff to remove the mud and had a clear right to direct how the mud and anything in it should be disposed of, or upon both grounds. However, Lord Russell of Killowen C.J. in distinguishing *Bridges* v. *Hawkesworth* expressed views which, in Mr. Desch's submission, point to the defendants having a superior claim to that of the plaintiff on the facts of the instant case. Lord Russell of Killowen C.J. said, at p. 46:

"The principle on which this case must be decided, and the distinction which must be drawn between this case and that of *Bridges* v. *Hawkesworth*, is to be found in a passage in *Pollock and Wright, Possession in the Common Law*, p. 41: 'the possession of land carries with it in general, by our law, possession of everything which is attached to or under that land, and, in the absence of a better title elsewhere, the right to possess it also. And it makes no difference that the possessor is not aware of the thing's existence * * * It is free to anyone who requires a specific intention as part of a de facto possession to treat this as a positive rule of law. But it seems preferable to say that the legal possession rests on a real de facto possession, constituted by the occupier's general power and intent to exclude unauthorised interference.' That is the ground on which I prefer to base my judgment. There is a broad distinction between this case and those cited from *Blackstone's Commentaries*. Those were cases in which a thing was cast into a public place or into the sea—into a place, in fact, of which it could not be said that anyone had a real de facto possession, or a general power and intent to exclude unauthorised interference * * * *Bridges* v. *Hawkeswoth* stands by itself, and on special grounds; and on those grounds it seems to me that the decision in that case was right. Someone had accidentally dropped a bundle of banknotes in a public shop. The shopkeeper did not know they had been dropped, and did not in any sense exercise control over them. The shop was open to the public, and they were invited to come there. A customer picked up the notes and gave them to the shopkeeper in order that he might advertise them. The owner of the notes was not found, and the finder then sought to recover them from the shopkeeper. It was held that he was entitled to do so, the ground of the decision being, as was pointed out by Patteson J., that the notes, being dropped in the public part of the shop, were never in the custody of the shopkeeper, or 'within the protection of his house.' It is somewhat strange that there is no more direct authority on the question; but the general principle seems to me to be that where a person has possession of house or land, with a manifest intention to exercise control over it and the things which may be upon or in it, then, if something is found on that land, whether by an employee of the owner or by a stranger, the presumption is that the possession of that thing is in the owner of the locus in quo."

For my part, I can find no trace in the report of *Bridges* v. *Hawkesworth*, 21 L.J. Q.B. 75, of any reliance by Patteson, J. upon the fact that the notes were found in what may be described as the public part of the shop. He could, and I think would, have said that if the notes had been accidentally dropped in the *private* part unbeknownst to Mr. Hawkesworth and had later been accidentally kicked into the street, Mr. Hawkesworth would have had no duty to the true owner and no rights superior to that of the finder.

However, I would accept Lord Russell of Killowen C.J.'s statement of the general principle in *South Staffordshire Water Co.* v. *Sharman* [1896] 2 Q.B. 4, 46–47, provided that the occupier's intention to exercise control over anything which might be on the premises was manifest. But it is impossible to go further and to hold that the mere right of an occupier to exercise such control is sufficient to give him rights in relation to lost property on his premises without overruling *Bridges* v. *Hawkesworth*, 21 L.J. Q.B. 75. Mr. Hawkesworth undoubtedly had a right to exercise such control, but his defence failed.

South Staffordshire Water Co. v. *Sharman* was followed and applied by McNair J. in *City of London Corporation* v. *Appleyard* [1963] 1 W.L.R. 982. There workmen demolishing a building found money in a safe which was recessed in one of the walls. The lease from the corporation to the building owners preserved the corporation's right to any article of value found upon any remains of former buildings and the workmen were employed by contractors working for the building owners. McNair J. upheld the corporation's claim. The workmen claimed as finders, but it is clear law that a servant or agent who finds in the course of his employment or agency is obliged to account to his employer or principal. The contractor similarly was bound to account to the building owner and the building owner, who was the occupier, was contractually bound to account to the corporation. The principal interest of the decision lies in the comment of McNair J., at p. 987, that he did not understand Lord Russell of Killowen C.J. as intending to qualify or extend the principle stated in *Pollock and Wright, Possession in the Common Law* (1888), p. 41, that possession of land carries with it possession of everything which is *attached to or under* that land when the Chief Justice restated the principle [1896] 2 Q.B. 44, 47:

> "* * * where a person has possession of house or land, with a manifest intention to exercise control over it and the things which may be *upon or in* it, then, if something is found *on* that land, whether by an employee of the owner or by a stranger, the presumption is that the possession of that thing is in the *owner* of the locus in quo." (My emphasis).

We were also referred to two Canadian authorities. In *Grafstein* v. *Holme and Freeman* (1958) 12 D.L.R. (2d) 727, the Ontario Court of Appeal considered the competing claims of Mr. Grafstein, the owner-occupier of a dry goods store, and Mr. Holme and Mr. Freeman, his employees. Mr. Holme found a locked box in premises which Mr. Grafstein had acquired as an extension to his store. He showed it unopened to Mr. Grafstein and was told to put it on a shelf and leave it there. Two years later Mr. Holme and Mr. Freeman decided to open the box and found that it contained Canadian $38,000 in notes. The court treated the moment of finding the money as that at which the box was opened, rather than when the box was found. It held that Mr. Grafstein had a superior claim because he took possession and control of the box and of its unknown contents when its existence was first brought to his attention. LeBel J.A. took a different view of Lord Russell of Killowen C.J.'s judgment in *South Staffordshire Water Co.* v. *Sharman* [1896] 2 Q.B. 44 from that of McNair J. in *City of London Corporation* v. *Appleyard* [1963] 1 W.L.R. 982. He considered that Lord Russell of Killowen C.J. intended to extend the statement of principle in *Pollock and Wright, Possession in the Common Law* to include things upon land or in a house. He commented, 12 D.L.R. (2d) 727, 734:

"∗ ∗ ∗ I do not think that anyone could seriously quarrel with the principle as extended by Lord Russell in that way so long as it is established in evidence as a basis for the presumption that the occupier has in fact the 'possession of house or land, with a manifest intention to exercise control over it [i.e., the land or the house] and the things which may be upon or in it ∗ ∗ ∗ ' I say this because I think there must be a natural presumption of possession in favour of the person in occupation—a presumption which hardly needs a legal decision for its authority."

The court did not decide the issues upon the basis that Messrs. Holme and Freeman were the employees of Mr. Grafstein acting within the scope of their employment, and LeBel J.A. indicated that in his view a claim by Mr. Grafstein based upon that relationship might well have failed.

The second Canadian decision is that of the Manitoba Court of Appeal in *Kowal* v. *Ellis* (1977) 76 D.L.R. (3d) 546. The plaintiff was driving across the defendant's land when he saw an abandoned pump on that land. Some question arose as to whether he was a trespasser, but the court held that at the time when he took possession of the pump he had the defendant's permission to go on the land. The judgment of the court was delivered by O'Sullivan J.A. and, so far as is material, was in the following terms, at pp. 548-549:

"The plaintiff, when he took possession of the pump, acquired a special property in it arising out of his relationship to the unknown owner. The relationship was one of bailment and, like any other bailee, the plaintiff has become entitled to sue in trover or, as here, in detinue anyone who has interfered with his right of possession, save only the true owner or someone claiming through or on behalf of the true owner. This is in accord with what was decided by Patteson J., in *Bridges* v. *Hawkesworth*, 21 L.J. Q.B. 75, 78: 'We find, therefore, no circumstances in this case to take it out of the general rule of law, that the finder of a lost article is entitled to it as against all parties except the real owner, and we think that that rule must prevail. ∗ ∗ ∗ ' *Bridges* v. *Hawkesworth*, was followed by Birkett J. in *Hannah* v. *Peel* [1945] K.B. 509. It follows that the plaintiff is entitled to possession of the pump, unless the defendant asserts and proves a title to the pump superior to that of the plaintiff. Such a superior title may arise independently of the original owner of the pump if the original owner has dealt with it in such a way as to enable the landowner to assert a claim as owner of the chattel, or it may arise by reason of the landowner having himself already become the bailee of the chattel on behalf of the true owner. In *Elwes* v. *Brigg Gas Co.*, 33 Ch.D. 562, the landowner succeeded against the finder of a boat because the landowner proved that it was the owner of the boat, which had become embedded in the soil. In that case, Chitty J. said, at p. 568: 'The first question which does actually arise in this case is whether the boat belonged to the plaintiff [landowner] ∗ ∗ ∗ I hold that it did ∗ ∗ ∗ ' Naturally, a bailee by finding must surrender possession to the true owner of the chattel and, once it was held that the landowner owned the boat, the case was closed. A similar result was effected in *Hibbert* v. *McKiernan* [1948] 2 K.B. 142. Once there was a finding that the golf balls belonged to the members of the golf course, it followed that the finder had no right of possession as against the true owners of the balls. One can imagine cases where a chattel is abandoned by its first land owner and may then become the property of someone else, perhaps a landowner who exercises control and dominion over it. In such a case, the landowner would assert a claim against the finder, not by virtue of his right as owner of land, but by virtue of his right as owner of the chattel. In the case before us, however, the defendant asserts no such right of ownership. The pump in question appears to have been cached rather than abandoned. So this is a case where the defendant does not even assert that he is the owner of the chattel in question; that being so, the defendant can succeed only by showing that he himself was in possession of the pump at the time of the finding in such a way that he, the defendant, had already constituted himself a bailee for the true owner. I know there have been weighty opinions expressed in favour of the proposition that the possessor of land possesses all that is on the land, and there is a sense in which that may be so, but to oust the claim of a bailee by finding it is not enough to establish some kind of metaphysical possession. What must be shown is that the landowner claimant, who has not acquired ownership of a chattel, is a prior bailee of the chattel with all the rights, but also with all the obligations, of a bailee. I am sure that no one would be more surprised than the defendant if, prior to the finding by the plaintiff, the true owner had come along and asserted that the defendant landowner owed him any duty either to take care of the pump or to seek out the owner of it. The reality is that the defendant, not even being aware of the existence of the pump, owed no duty with respect to it to its true owner. He was not a bailee of the pump and consequently has no claim to possession which can prevail over the special property which the plaintiff has by virtue of his having become a bailee by finding."

One of the great merits of the common law is that it is usually sufficiently flexible to take account of the changing needs of a continually changing society. Accordingly, Mr. Desch rightly directed our attention to the need to have common law rules which will facilitate rather than hinder the ascertainment of the true owner of a lost chattel and a reunion between the two. In his submission the law should confer rights upon the occupier of the land where a lost chattel was found which were superior to those of the finder, since the loser is more likely to make inquiries at the place of loss. I see the force of this submission. However, I think that it is also true that if this were the rule and finders had no prospect of any reward, they would be tempted to pass by without taking any action or to become concealed keepers of articles which they found. Furthermore, if a finder is under a duty to take reasonable steps to reunite the true owner with his lost property, this will usually involve an obligation to inform the occupier of the land of the fact that the article has been found and where it is to be kept.

In a dispute of this nature there are two quite separate problems. The first is to determine the general principles or rules of law which are applicable. The second, which is often the more troublesome, is to apply those principles or rules to the factual situation. I propose to confront those two problems separately.

Rights and obligations of the finder

1. The finder of a chattel acquires no rights over it unless (a) it has been abandoned or lost and (b) he takes it into his care and control.

2. The finder of a chattel acquires very limited rights over it if he takes it into his care and control with dishonest intent or in the course of trespassing.

3. Subject to the foregoing and to point 4 below, a finder of a chattel, whilst not acquiring any absolute property or ownership in the chattel, acquires a right to keep it against all but the true owner or those in a position to claim through the true owner or one who can assert a prior right to keep the chattel which was subsisting at the time when the finder took the chattel into his care and control.

4. Unless otherwise agreed, any servant or agent who finds a chattel in the course of his employment or agency and not wholly incidentally or collaterally thereto and who takes it into his care and control does so on behalf of his employer or principal who acquires a finder's rights to the exclusion of those of the actual finder.

5. A person having a finder's rights has an obligation to take such measures as in all the circumstances are reasonable to acquaint the true owner of the finding and present whereabouts of the chattel and to care for it meanwhile.

Rights and liabilities of an occupier

1. An occupier of land has rights superior to those of a finder over chattels in or attached to that land and an occupier of a building has similar rights in respect of chattels attached to that building, whether in either case the occupier is aware of the presence of the chattel.

2. An occupier of a building has rights superior to those of a finder over chattels upon or in, but not attached to, that building if, but only if, before the chattel is found, he has manifested an intention to exercise control over the building and the things which may be upon it or in it.

3. An occupier who manifests an intention to exercise control over a building and the things which may be upon or in it so as to acquire rights superior to those of a finder is under an obligation to take such measures as in all the circumstances are reasonable to ensure that lost chattels are found and, upon their being found, whether by him or by a third party, to acquaint the true owner of the finding and to care for the chattels meanwhile. The manifestation of intention may be express or implied from the circumstances including, in particular, the circumstance that the occupier manifestly accepts or is obliged by law to accept liability for chattels lost upon his "premises," e.g. an innkeeper or carrier's liability.

4. An "occupier" of a chattel, e.g. a ship, motor car, caravan or aircraft, is to be treated as if he were the occupier of a building for the purposes of the foregoing rules.

Application to the instant case

The plaintiff was not a trespasser in the executive lounge and, in taking the bracelet into his care and control, he was acting with obvious honesty. Prima facie, therefore, he had a full finder's rights and obligations. He in fact discharged those obligations by handing the bracelet to an official of the defendants' although he could equally have done so by handing the bracelet to the police or in other ways such as informing the police of the find and himself caring for the bracelet.

The plaintiff's prima facie entitlement to a finder's rights was not displaced in favour of an employer or principal. There is no evidence that he was in the executive lounge in the course of any employment or agency and, if he was, the finding of the bracelet was quite clearly collateral thereto. The position would have been otherwise in the case of most or perhaps all the defendants' employees.

The defendants, for their part, cannot assert any title to the bracelet based upon the rights of an occupier over chattels attached to a building. The bracelet was lying loose on the floor. Their claim must, on my view of the law, be based upon a manifest intention to exercise control over the lounge and all things which might be in it. The evidence is that they claimed the right to decide who should and who should not be permitted to enter and use the lounge, but their control was in general exercised upon the basis of classes or categories of user and the availability of the lounge in the light of the need to clean and maintain it. I do not doubt that they also claimed the right to exclude individual undesirables, such as drunks, and specific types of chattels such as guns and bombs. But this control has no real relevance to a manifest intention to assert custody and control over lost articles. There was no evidence that they searched for such articles regularly or at all.

Evidence was given of staff instructions which govern the action to be taken by employees of the defendants if they found lost articles or lost chattels were handed to them. But these instructions were not published to users of the lounge and in any event I think that they were intended to do no more than instruct the staff on how they were to act in the course of their employment.

It was suggested in argument that in some circumstances the intention of the occupier to assert control over articles lost on his premises speaks for itself. I think that this is right. If a bank manager saw fit to show me round a vault containing safe deposits and I found a gold bracelet on the floor, I should have no doubt that the bank had a better title than I, and the reason is the manifest intention to exercise a very high degree of control. At the other extreme is the park to which the public has unrestricted access during daylight hours. During those hours there is no manifest intention to exercise any such control. In between these extremes are the forecourts of petrol filling stations, unfenced front gardens of private houses, and public parts of shops and supermarkets as part of an almost infinite variety of land, premises and circumstances.

This lounge is in the middle band and in my judgment, on the evidence available, there was no sufficient manifestation of any intention to exercise control over lost property before it was found such as would give the defendants a right superior to that of the plaintiff or indeed any right over the bracelet. As the true owner has never come forward, it is a case of "finders keepers."

I would therefore dismiss the appeal.

[EVERLEIGH, L. J., and Sir DAVID CAIRNS delivered concurring judgments]

The Concept of Possession in English Law

D R Harris, in *Oxford Lectures on Jurisprudence* (A G Guest ed. 1961).

The concept of Possession has always had a strong fascination for lawyers. Many writers have attempted to analyse the concept whether in Roman law, in a modern system, such as German law, or in English law. It is not the intention of the present writer to review in detail any previous theories of possession, but rather to suggest a new approach to the concept so far as English law is concerned. English judges have been rightly suspicious of a uniform rigid 'theory' of possession in the common law: for instance, Earl Jowitt has said '—in truth, the English law has never worked out a completely logical and exhaustive definition of "possession".'

It is the thesis of this essay that the English decisions preclude us from laying down any conditions, such as physical control or a certain kind of intention, as absolutely essential for a judicial ruling that a man possesses something. A theory which postulates physical control and intention of one kind or another as the basic ingredients of possession must include artificial glosses or fictions to cover the actual English decisions; we find the ideas of 'constructive' physical control or of 'constructive' intention to act as owner, propounded to make the theories fit the cases. The writer has attempted to read the cases with an open mind in order to discover those factors which have weighed with English judges in reaching a conclusion that a man is entitled to the benefit of a rule of law expressed in terms of possession, *e.g.* 'Because *A* was in possession of this ring when *B* took it, *A* can recover £50 damages from *B* for trespass.'

Professor Hart has show us that it is impossible to *define* a legal concept, and that the task of legal writers should be rather to *describe* the use of a word like 'possession', in the particular legal rules in which it occurs. 'Possession' in the legal sense has no meaning at all apart from the rule of law in which it is used as a tool of legal thought. In the imaginary judgment just quoted, 'Because *A* was in possession . . .', the word 'possession' is really a piece of legal shorthand, which, in an abbreviated form, states a legal conclusion based on the application of law to particular facts.

We should therefore study the way in which the word 'possession' is used in English rules of law; we cannot study the legal concept of possession in the abstract, for the word has no legal meaning apart from the context of these particular rules. We should look at such rules as the following, which are merely a selection of 'possessory' rules in English law:

(1)   The plaintiff in an action of trespass to goods must, have been in *possession* at the time of the interference alleged against the defendant.

(2)   The plaintiff in an action for conversion of goods must, at the time of the conversion, have either been in *actual possession* of them, or been *entitled to the immediate possession* of them.

(3)   As soon as the vendor of land has let the purchaser into *possession* under an oral contract, there is an act of part performance which renders it too late for either party to repudiate the contract on the ground that there is no memorandum or note in writing as required by section 40(1) of the Law of Property Act, 1925.

(4)   Where an owner of land is entitled to possession, the twelve-year period of limitation under the Limitation Act, 1939, runs against him from the moment *adverse possession* is taken by another.

(5)   ' "Delivery" means voluntary transfer of *possession* from one person to another.' (Section 62 of the Sale of Goods Act, 1893).

(6)   'Where a mercantile agent is, with the consent of the owner, in *possession* of goods, any sale, pledge or other disposition of the goods, made by him when acting in the ordinary course of business of a mercantile agent, shall . . . be . . . valid . . .' (Section 2(1) of the Factors Act, 1889.)

(7)   'A bailee . . . receives *possession* of a thing from another . . . upon an undertaking with the other person . . . to keep and return . . . to him the specific thing . . .'

(8)   'The expression "owner" [in the statutory definition of larceny] includes any part owner, or person having *possession* or control of, or a special property in, anything capable of being stolen.' (Section 1(2)(iii) of the Larceny Act, 1916).

(9)   A taking, for the purposes of larceny, 'consists in acquisition of *possession* without the consent of the previous possessor to part with the *possession*'.

These rules, all employing the word 'possession', deal with such different situations that it is not in the least surprising that English judges have not adopted any consistent approach to the meaning of possession. They have used 'possession' in the various rules of law as a functional and relative concept, which gives them some discretion in applying an abstract rule to a concrete set of facts. When a plaintiff has claimed the benefit of a rule expressly based on possession of a chattel at a certain time, the judge has tended subconsciously to ask himself a question like this: 'Do the facts show that before or at the relevant time the plaintiff had entered into a sufficiently close relationship with the chattel that he ought to be given the benefit of this particular rule against this particular defendant?'

In marginal cases, the judge clearly has a discretion to decide the issue of possession one way or the other, according to his own appraisal of the relative merits of the parties' cases, and of the social purpose of the rule in question. But this is not to say that the judge's decision depends on his own whim, for the courts are evolving a list of factors which must be considered when deciding whether the plaintiff's relationship to the chattel amounts to possession.

The following lists of factors which may be relevant to a conclusion that a man 'possesses' a chattel is based on a reading of many cases. No single factor in the list will necessarily be decisive on the issue of 'possession', for that is a legal conclusion based on the cumulative effect of those factors which the court holds operative in the circumstances. The judge will weigh up the relevant factors in order to decide whether on balance they come down in favour of the plaintiff or against him. This approach should not be unfamiliar to English lawyers: other concepts, such as what is 'a judicial or quasi-judicial decision' as distinguished from 'a purely administrative decision' in administrative law, or the concept of what is 'reasonable in all the circumstances' in the law of torts, are in frequent use in our courts, though they are not based on any rigid criteria.

Nor is the following list of factors exhaustive. There is no reason why the judges should not in the future be faced with additional factors which ought to be considered on the issue of 'possession'; the judicial view of justice or of the policy behind a particular 'possessory' rule may well change, and demand that weight should be given to new factors in certain circumstances. This essay, following the list of factors, will attempt to examine some decisions by using this approach.

I. Factors Relevant to Possession

The following is a list of factors which have been held relevant to a conclusion that the plaintiff has acquired 'possession' of a chattel for the purposes of a particular rule of law.

Three preliminary observations on this introductory sentence are necessary. First, the 'the plaintiff' is merely illustrative of the person invoking, or subject to, a possessory rule; according to the circumstances, of course, he may be the defendant, the accused or a third party, such as a mercantile agent. Secondly, this essay deals mainly with possession of chattels, though it is submitted that possession of land in English law may be approached in the same way with a similar list of factors.

Thirdly, this sentence, in using the words 'acquired possession' adopts the view of Holmes and Kocourek that the law is concerned only with the acquisition and loss of possession, and not its retention. There is no need to ask what is necessary to 'retain' possession, since once the plaintiff is held to have acquired possession, he continues to be entitled in law to the benefit of the possessory rule, until he 'loses' possession, *e.g.* when he abandons the chattel, or a stranger acquires possession of it. There is no need to think of possession as a continuing physical relationship between a man and an object, or as depending on a continuing, conscious intention. Once the facts which justify the application of the possessory rule arise in the first place, they need not necessarily continue to exist in the same form, degree or intensity. The court will continue to apply the word 'possession' to the plaintiff's relationship with the object until the law recognizes that changed facts operate to divest the plaintiff of his possessory right.

It is true that judges often speak as if the facts necessary for possession must continue; they ask, for instance in trespass cases, 'Was the plaintiff in possession at the time of the defendant's interference?' rather than 'Had the plaintiff acquired possession before the defendant's interference and had nothing occurred to divest that possession?' But it is submitted that the latter question is the vital one. Where it is not clear how or when the plaintiff first acquired possession, an inquiry into the facts relevant to the plaintiff's possession at the time of the defendant's interference may justify an inference of lawful acquisition.

Factors (1) and (2): Physical Control

(1)   The degree of physical control over the chattel which the plaintiff actually exercises, or is immediately able to exercise. The plaintiff's degree of physical control should not be considered in isolation, but in relation to the greatest degree of physical control which it is possible for the particular plaintiff to exercise over the particular chattel. Thus the limited physical control of a child or an epileptic may be properly recognized, as is the limited control possible over a very large chattel or a wreck at the bottom of the sea. The plaintiff's physical control must also be compared with that of the defendant or anyone else. (Factor 2).

(2)   The degree of physical control over the chattel actually or potentially exercised by any other person, whether the defendant or a stranger. Obviously, factor (1) must be weighed against factor (2). A limited degree of physical control exercised by the plaintiff may suffice for the acquisition of possession in the absence of opposition from others, but if other persons are at the same moment attempting to seize or hold the chattel, the plaintiff's control over it must be greater and more exclusive, unless a further factor is applicable, *e.g.* the lawfulness of the plaintiff's attempt to gain control. For if the parties were each asserting a similar degree of control over the object, the courts will award possession to whichever of the contending parties had a relatively better right to possess than the other. A high degree of physical control is necessary for the original acquisition of possession and ownership of something not possessed or owned by anyone: *occupatio* of a *res nullius* in Roman law. Decisions on the capture of fish and of wild animals show that possession is acquired only when the thing cannot escape of its own power; the net

must have closed completely around the fish; close pursuit, short of actual capture, of a wild animal is likewise insufficient.

Factors (3)—(6): Knowledge and Intention

(3)   The plaintiff's knowledge of (*a*) the existence of the chattel, and (*b*) its major attributes or qualities, and (*c*) its location at the relevant time.

(4)   The plaintiff's intention in regard to the chattel. Such intention, of course, must be based on his knowledge (Factor (3)).

It is impossible to draw the conclusion from the reported cases that English judges have regarded only one kind of intention as relevant to possession. Sometimes they have referred to the plaintiff's intention to act as owner of the chattel, at other times to his intention to exclude other persons from it. The weight to be given to the plaintiff's knowledge and intention depends on whether the defendant or any stranger also had such knowledge and intention. (Factors (5) and (6)). If the plaintiff is the only person who knows of the chattel and its location, and the only one who intends to exercise control over it, his claim to be in a unique relationship with it will be greatly strengthened.

(5)   The knowledge of the defendant, or of any stranger to the dispute, of the existence of the chattel, its attributes and location (as in Factor (3)).

(6)   The intention of the defendant, or of any stranger, in regard to the chattel (as in Factor (4)). Under this head, the court may also consider the intention of a previous possessor of the chattel to deliver possession or exclusive control over it to the plaintiff, by way of sale, gift, bailment or otherwise.

Factors (5) and (6) are important in order to assess the weight to be given to factors (3) and (4). If both the parties to the dispute knew of the existence and location of the chattel, the crucial factor maybe the intent of only one of them to exercise control over it or to exclude others from it; if both parties had knowledge and also a similar intention in regard to it (or if neither party had knowledge or intention) other factors will decide the issue, *e.g.* the relative degrees of physical control exercised by the parties, or the fact that one was the occupier of the premises where the chattel lay.

In civil cases, especially those concerning delivery or bailment of chattels, the intention of the parties is often decisive in the acquisition of possession. Where a possessor deliberately intends to transfer possession to another person there is sometimes no transfer of physical control over the chattel, sometimes a very limited transfer of control. There is some authority that goods under lock and key may be delivered to another person by delivering the key, partly as a 'symbol' of possession, and partly, as Pollock argues, as 'such a transfer of control in fact as the nature of the case admits'. The delivery of a key, considered in the abstract, is neutral in regard to the possession of what is locked up; it is the intention of the parties to the transaction which determines whether possession of the premises or goods locked up is to pass to the recipient of the key.

In *Ashby* v. *Tolhurst*, the intention of the parties was all-important. The question was whether there had been a bailment (involving delivery of possession to the bailee) when the plaintiff left his car in the defendant's car park for a nominal fee. The Court of Appeal decided that there was no intention to deliver possession to the defendants. It was merely a licence whereby the defendant granted the plaintiff permission to leave his car on the defendant's land; the plaintiff therefore still possessed it even while it stood on another's land.

Factor (7): The Possession of Premises

The legal relationship of the plaintiff (compared with that of the defendant) to the premises where the chattel is lying at the relevant time: the plaintiff may be the occupier, or the owner and occupier; or he may be merely a licensee or trespasser. Similarly, the defendant may fall into any one of these categories. This factor may be vital when the preceding factors give no clear answer to the issue of possession. For instance, in order to protect occupiers against trespassers, the courts are likely to hold that an occupier possesses chattels lying thereon despite his ignorance of them. If the occupier of premises claims possession of chattels lying thereon, the courts have sometimes considered relevant the intention of the occupier to exclude other persons from his premises and so from any chattels which may happen to be there. In many cases, of course, this factor is not relevant *e.g.* because no one occupies the place where the chattel lies, or because the occupier is not a party to the dispute and makes no claim to the chattel; the other factors in the list will then govern the question of possession.

A factor similar to the occupation of land is the possession of a vehicle or other container, such as a bureau, in which a chattel is lying. The possessor of the vehicle or container may be held to possess the chattel even when he does not know of it.

Factor (8): Other Legal Relationships or Special Rules of Law Applicable to the Facts

The facts may bring into operation an overall legal relationship between the parties to the dispute, or between one of them and a third party, which governs the question of possession by virtue of a special rule as to which person in that relationship enjoys possession. The most notable instance is the rule that, at least as against his master, a servant, who in the course of his service receives chattels from his master, has mere custody of them and not possession, for the master still enjoys possession through his servant. Such a rule generally awards possession to one person in the relationship irrespective of the preceding factors of physical control, knowledge, intention or occupation of premises. The law directs peremptorily that persons in a certain category may or may not enjoy the benefit of possessory rules.

The law governing the relationship of bailor and bailee, principal and mercantile agent under the Factors Act 1889, and buyer and seller, are other cases where special rules covering possession and its legal consequences have been developed. Similarly there is a special rule that a guest using the chattels or his host, such as his furniture and cutlery, has custody not possession; the host continues to possess his chattels though his guest may have complete physical control over them at the moment. Likewise a shopkeeper retains possession of goods which he permits a customer to handle and inspect.

These special rules have resulted from particular historical or economic conditions, and reflect a particular policy of the law in the given circumstances, which can only be implemented by superimposing a precise rule on the usual factors determining possession.

Factor (9): The Policy Behind the Rule

The last factor is the judge's concept of the social purpose of the particular rule of law relied on by the plaintiff. Especially in cases where the judge is left undecided by the preceding factors, he will, whether consciously or unconsciously, ask himself a question to this effect: 'Will a conclusion that the plaintiff was in possession of the chattel at the relevant time tend to carry out the social purpose of this rule of law in the particular circumstances of the case?' The determining factor, when the other factors appear to be evenly balanced, may often be the assumed purpose of the rule in question; the judge can hardly attempt to examine the physical or psychological facts apart from the legal rule, and apart from his foreknowledge of the result in the case before him if he decides for the plaintiff on the issue of possession.

The reported decisions on larceny provide an outstanding illustration of the importance of this factor, and these will be considered in some detail later in this essay.

A cursory examination of the selected possessory rules quoted above will reveal the quite different topics they cover; naturally the policies behind the different rules must vary, and this justifies the courts in giving varying weight to the different factors relevant to possession according to the particular rule in question. The lack of consistency in the English decisions on possession is quite defensible on this ground. Emphasis on a particular factor may assist the court in carrying out the purpose of one possessory rule, whereas a similar emphasis on the same factor would hinder the achievement of the purpose of another rule.

It is not suggested that any English judge has yet, in a reported decision, consciously worked through a list of factors such as the one just tabulated. This list is an attempt to elucidate a process of judicial reasoning which has apparently been mainly subconscious in the past. This process of weighing various factors has been kept in bounds by another subconscious approach to possession problems through an 'ideal' concept of possession. The judges seem to have had at the back of their minds a perfect pattern in which the possessor has complete, exclusive and unchallenged physical control over the object, full knowledge of its existence, attributes and location, and a manifest intention to 'act as its owner' and to exclude all other persons from it. But in the practical world, however, the judges realize that justice and expediency compel constant modification of the ideal pattern, as is cogently illustrated by the authorities to be analysed in this essay. The plaintiff may have a very limited degree of physical control over the object; or he may have no intention in regard to an object of whose existence he is unaware, though he does exercise control over the place where the object is lying; or he may have a clear intention to exclude other people from the object, though he has no physical control at the moment.

The judges seem sub-consciously to be asking themselves whether the facts before them are sufficiently analogous to the perfect pattern of possession for the plaintiff to be given the particular remedy he desires. It is during this process that the various factors outlined in the list above are weighed against each other. The approach of the judges appears to be essentially functional and empirical, since they are prepared to allow further departures from this ideal concept of possession for the purposes of some rules of law than for others. The fact that a particular rule of law is based on 'possession' permits a judge to exercise some discretion to achieve justice on the merits of the actual case before him, when he decides whether or not to accord 'possession' to the facts.

Notes, Questions and Problems

1. What is the rule in *Armory* v *Delamirie*?

2. Now suppose A loses a watch she had earlier found and that it is subsequently found by B. A sues B for the return of the watch. Who wins?

3. The cause of action in *Armory* was in trover. As you have learned in Torts, that is a common law action for money damages on account of the defendant's conversion to his or her own use of a chattel owned or possessed by the plaintiff. Assuming the court finds for the plaintiff, what is really happening in such an action?

4. What is the measure of damages in a case like *Armory*? The value of the chattel at the time of conversion? The value of the interest? (What does *that* mean?) Which, if any measure did the court adopt? Is that a sound measure?

5. A owns Blackacre. There is natural gas beneath it. He exhausts that gas. He then pumps natural gas which he acquires elsewhere into the space below Blackacre for storage purposes. This gas then escapes (underground) into the adjoining land of B. B withdraws that gas for profit. A sues B. What cause of action would you plead? What result? How would you calculate the damages, assuming liability exists? See *Hammond* v *Kentucky Natural Gas Co.* 75 S.W. 2d 204 (1934). Assume, for the purposes of this question, that there are no relevant statutory provisions.

6. The Police Act 1958 (R.S.17) provides (s. 58) that where a member of the Police is in possession of 'any property of any kind' . . . and 'it is doubtful whether a person claiming the property, or which of any two or more persons so claiming is in possession thereof . . .' a District Court Judge '. . . may make an order for the delivery of the property to any person . . . appearing to be the owner thereof, or entitled to the possession thereof, or, if the owner or person entitled to possession cannot be ascertained, may make such order with respect to possession of the property as he thinks fit.' Section 58(3) provides that if an action is commenced 'against any member of the Police or the Crown [for recovery of the property or its value] after such an order is made, the order may be raised in bar of the action.' But, 'no order or delivery shall affect the right of any persons entitled by law to possession of the property to recover the same.'

A leaves her purse, containing $500 in cash, in a restaurant owned by B. C, a waitress, hands it to B, the owner of the restaurant, at the close of business, saying she found it under Table X. B hands the purse to Constable D. (1) C makes an application to the District Court, as the 'finder', for both the purse and the money. B also claims same. What would be the result? (2) A sues the Police, saying, that if they had looked inside the purse, they could have located her address quite easily. What result? (3) A sues whoever the judge awarded the purse to for the return of both it and $500. What result?

7. Section 59 of the Police Act 1958 provides that 'any goods and chattels which have come into the possession of any member of the Police and which are unclaimed

after being held for not less than three months shall be sold by public auction.'
A notice of the sale must have been published three times 'in some newspaper
circulating in the district in which the sale is to be held.'

A's bicycle is stolen. Six months later the Police recover a quantity of stolen
goods, but do not identify A's bicycle. It is auctioned under this section. B buys
the bicycle at auction. A sues B for the return of the bicycle or its value. What
would be the result? What if the auction was advertised only twice? Would the
result be different?

8. For further readings on possession see, Tay, Possession and the Modern Law
of Finding (1964) 4 Sydney L Rev 383 and The Concept of Possession in the
Common Law: Foundations for a New Approach (1964) 4 Melb L Rev 476; Harris,
Comment (1964) 4 Melb L Rev 498.

Nemo dat quod non habet

Title to land in New Zealand is now, happily, a relatively settled matter under
the Land Transfer Act. In general, the person entitled to dispose of the land is
the person on the register for the time being.

Title to tangible and intangible goods—personal property—is a rather more
complex matter. The Latin tag *nemo dat quod non habet* means: 'no one gives what
he does not have.' You cannot transfer—whether by way of gift, sale, or by way
of succession on your death—better rights than you have yourself. In principle
therefore, if B steals A's car, and sells it to C, A is entitled to assert his rights
to that car. And in some circumstances he can assert rights to the products or
proceeds of the asset.

There are now a good many statutory exceptions to the *nemo dat* rule (for instance
under the Sale of Goods Act 1908) and where they exist, it is largely as a matter
of commercial convenience.

Hence the common law did not espouse the position taken up in some other
legal systems that anyone who, in good faith, buys and takes possession obtains
a good title even though the possessor from whom it was obtained was not the
owner. A rule expressed that way would protect commerce against ownership.
If effect, the common law preferred to protect title, but with exceptions designed
to overcome the worst excesses of such a rule.

The exceptions, and the rule, are considered in detail in courses on commercial
law, but by way of general indication only here, have evolved with time. In medieval
times there was an exception in favour of a market overt. This was an 'open market'
where goods could be bought direct from producers. The exception protected buyers
in such a market, and increased the popularity of such a market. There is no market
overt in New Zealand. In the nineteenth century a practice of mercantile agents
grew up. These were agents who sold for others. Nineteenth century statutes
protected persons who bought in good faith through such agents. This protection
in turn was extended, under the Sale of Goods Acts, to protect a purchaser from
a merchant who had sold X to another person, but yet remained in possession
of X. In the twentieth century some financing legislation contains exceptions to
the *nemo dat* rule.

In the result, our law has reached something of a pragmatic compromise with respect to title to goods between the concerns of ownership and the concerns of commerce. As Lord Denning put it in *Bishopsgate Motor Finance Corp Ltd* v *Transport Brakes Ltd* [1949] 1 K B 322 at 366:

> In the development of our law, two principles have striven for mastery. The first is for the protection of property: no one can give a better title than he himself possesses. The second is the protection of commercial transactions. The person who takes in good faith and for value without notice should get a good title. The first principle has held sway for some time, but it has been modified by the common law itself and by statute to meet the needs of our own times.

Notes

1. On title to goods and chattels in New Zealand see Garrow and Gray, *Law of Personal Property in New Zealand* (5th ed), chapter 2.

2. Historically, *nemo dat* came from Roman law, and reflected the power of ownership in that system. French law (Article 2279 of the Civil Code) goes the other way: 'En fait de meibles la possession vaut title.' A bona fide buyer who takes possession *gets* title. An attempt was made in Article 9 of the United States Commercial Code to balance the conflicting interests at stake.

Jus tertii

This is another formidable sounding Latin tag. The problem arises this way. Defendant B admits that his title to goods X is 'weaker' than plaintiff A's. But can he defeat a claim by A by saying that there is, out there somewhere, a shadowy C who has an earlier and better title than A? If A succeeds in his action and now has X in his possession, A loses as against C if proceedings are brought by C, and C's title is established. But can B say that, as A could not retain X as against C, so A cannot recover from him?

In general, the answer the common law gave is, 'no.' If a plaintiff is in actual possession and the defendant interferes with that possession, it is not enough to show there exists a third person with superior property rights. The defendant must show that the interference was committted with the authority of that third person.

This *jus tertii* rule has been much criticized. Salmond and Heuston, *Torts* (19th ed) 123 said of it: 'There was something unjust and indeed absurd, about a legal system which refused to listen to a defendant's incontrovertible proof that the plaintiff had no title to the goods whose value he nevertheless claimed from the defendant.' And see the 18th Report of the Law Reform Committee (Cmnd 4774 (1971)), paras 51-78. Subsequently Section 8 of the Torts (Interference With Goods) Act 1977 (UK) abolished the rule in England. The common law still applies in New Zealand.

Notes

1. For two good articles see Atiyah, A Re-Examination of the Jus Tertii in Conversion (1955) 18 MLR 97; Jolly, The Jus Tertii and the Third Man (1955) 18 MLR 371.

2. As to remedies for interference with goods in New Zealand, these are still the classical tort remedies of trespass to goods, trover (conversion) and detinue. A bailor has the obligations described in the cases in Chapter 6, (*infra.*).

3. In *Tamworth Industries Limited* v *Attorney General* (Eichelbaum CJ, Wellington, A 458/85; 15/6/1991) the Police had acted on a search warrant and had found money associated with a cache of cannabis on property owned by Tamworth. A director of that company (D) was acquitted of possession of cannabis for supply. The High Court rejected Tamworth's claim (in conversion) founded on the Police having paid the money into the Consolidated Fund following on D's trial. The Chief Justice held that the policy behind the principal in *Parker* is that without those rules, rights to lost property would be subject to a 'free for all' in which victory would go to those sufficiently strong or devious, and that reuniting property with owner is more likely if the rights of the occupier have primacy, but if they weigh too heavily against finders this will encourage dishonesty. Here, the presence of derelict buildings with ready access to the public gave rise to no inference of exertion of control by the occupier. The Chief Justice also held (obiter) that the fact that the money was tainted by connection with crime would not have prevented Tamworth obtaining its ownership. The Chief Justice discussed the authorities on this point. He came to the conclusion (reluctantly) that the dissent of Wiley J in *Collis* [1990] 2 NZLR 287 is to be preferred to the decision of the majority in that case. The decision also contains observations on the operation of the Police Act 1958 in these kinds of cases.

6

Bailment

Bailments are among the most commonplace of transactions. Every person routinely entrusts personal property to the custody of some other person. Bailment is closely intertwined with the law of carriage, accommodation, and repairs to goods, and in the various common law jurisdictions there are several statutes which modify common law obligations. Hence an understanding of the law relating to bailment is important to all lawyers, but particularly those who practise in the transport and insurance fields, where claims routinely occur. Yet bailments are difficult to classify in the law. Elements of property, contract and tort overlap.

A Typical Problem

Assume A goes to restaurant X. She is wearing a valuable fur coat. She leaves it with hostess B, who puts it in the cloakroom behind the reception desk. Sometime during the evening, it is stolen. The restaurant is owned by C. The problem suggests these basic issues. Is the relationship between A and C (or B) governed by contract, tort, property, or perhaps all three? Does the doctrinal classification matter? What, if any, duty of care do B or C have to A? What is the standard of any duty of care owed? Does the fact the the 'deposit' may be gratuitous or for value of some kind affect the position arising between the parties? What, if any, effect do warning notices of one kind or another—perhaps purporting to exclude liability altogether—have on the transaction?

The Juridical Nature of Bailment

This problem also hints at the hybrid nature of the transaction. The fur coat is *delivered* to C (or B). At that point there is a separation of ownership (which is in A), and possession, which has to be in either B or C. Which is it? Does it matter? The word bailment in fact comes from the French verb bailler, meaning 'to deliver'. However the relationship between the parties is generally created by contract. Hence it will be affected by the terms of that contract. But it is enforcable through tort remedies. Why?

The Subject Matter of Bailments

As a general principle, bailment applies only to chattels. It does not apply to land or to intangible property, such as goodwill. Why would the law adopt this stance?

Creation of Bailments

Professor Palmer, in a standard treatise (*Bailments*, 1979), suggested that there are six possible theories as to the 'essential formative elements in bailments' (*Id.* 11). A bailment requires: (1) a delivery of possession; (2) a contract giving rise to possession; (3) consensus or agreement giving rise to possession; (4) a voluntary possession; (5) a knowing but not voluntary possession; (6) possession and no more.

It will be noted that each of these theories requires possession as an essential ingredient. However the degree of mental knowledge and physical activity varies under each theory. Palmer suggests that the better view is that 'duties arise under a bailment in two principal ways: by implication of law, as a result of the possessory relationship, or by virtue of an agreement between the parties.' (*Id.* 52). What are the consequences, in law, of such a conceptualization?

Some Cases on the Nature of and Duties Arising Under Bailment

Coggs v Bernard

(1703) 2 Ld. Raym. 909; 92 ER 107

In this famous case, Holt CJ suggested a sixfold division of bailments adopted from Roman law.

1. Gratuitious bailment of chattels for the use of the bailee. This is a straight 'loan', without more.
2. Bailment of chattels for reward. This is a hire or rent.
3. Deposit of chattels with a bailee for safe custody, with or without payment.
4. Pledge of chattels as security for money advanced.
5. Gratuitous bailment of chattels for something to be done to them.
6. Bailment of chattels for reward for something to be done to them.

Motor Mart v Webb

[1958] NZLR 784

TURNER J: It would be a mistake to conclude that the transaction of bailment is one which has refused and still refuses to undergo the evolution and adaptation which the common law imposes upon every legal institution; and although the bailments known to Roman Law were sufficient for Lord Holt in 1703, I decline to assume that, under the pressure and stresses of modern legal necessity, some new mutation may not have burst into flower, of a quality to startle the author of the Institutes were he privileged to behold it.

[In this case a hire purchase transaction was held to give rise to a bailment].

Houghland v Low (Luxury Coaches)

[1962] 1 QB 694

The following statement of facts is taken from the judgment of Ormerod L.J.: The plaintiff, Mrs. Beatrice Winnie Houghland, and her husband, who had since died, old age pensioners, arranged to go on a trip to Jersey, which was organised under the aegis of a body called the Good Companions Club, through a travel agency known as Carefree Travel. The party returned from Jersey to Southampton on September 21, 1960, to journey to Hoylake, Cheshire, where the plaintiff lived, in one of the defendants' motor coaches. When the party boarded the coach at Southampton after their baggage had been examined by the Customs Authorities, the suitcases of all the members of the party were loaded into the boot of the coach, which was locked by the driver. The coach then started on its journey. It stopped at Oxford, where the driver needed to take a water-can out of the boot, he unlocked the boot for that purpose, but immediately relocked it. The boot then remained locked until the coach arrived at Ternhill, Shropshire, where the party stopped for tea. For some reason the coach engine would not start again after tea, and the driver telephoned to the defendant's office and spoke to the managing director, asking for a relief coach. There was a delay of some three hours, but eventually a relief coach arrived, driven by the managing director. During this delay the original coach stood unattended in the dark at Ternhill. On the arrival of the relief coach, the managing director went off to have tea whilst the driver of the first coach superintended the loading of the party's luggage into the relief coach. The unloading of the luggage from the first coach and its transfer to the relief coach was carried out by the passengers themselves without any supervision. The reloading of the luggage into the boot of the relief coach was supervised by the driver of the first coach, who was experienced in stowing luggage. When, so far as the driver was aware, the whole of the luggage had been stowed in the relief coach, the boot was locked, and the relief coach proceeded to Hoylake. The only time that the boot of the relief coach was unlocked was when, as the coach was nearing Hoylake, various members of the party finally left it: on those occasions the driver unlocked the boot, took out whatever luggage they asked for, and relocked the boot. The coach eventually arrived at Hoylake but the plaintiff and her husband could not find their suitcase, and careful inquiry failed to locate it.

The plaintiff sued the defendants in detinue for "delivery up" of the said suitcase and the contents thereof or £82 10s. 11d. for "their value". Alternatively, she sued them in negligence for damages in a sum not exceeding £100. The judge found that the defendants were bailees of the suitcase, and that the bailment was a gratuitous bailment. The judge also found that it was probably at Ternhill that the suitcase was either taken or lost, and he awarded the plaintiff £82 10s. 11d. The defendants appealed.

ORMEROD L.J. stated the facts and continued: The judge, according to the note that we have of his judgment — indeed, we have two notes, each taken by counsel in the case — found in the first place that the driver of the coach was a bailee of the suitcase, and that the bailment was a gratuitous bailment. I am not sure that there is any evidence for the latter finding; and indeed, I might well, I think, have come to a different conclusion. But Mr. McNeill, on behalf of the plaintiff, was given an opportunity of filing a notice asking for that particular finding to be set aside, but found it unnecessary to avail himself of the opportunity.

The judge then found that it was probably at Ternhill that the suitcase was either taken or lost, and in the circumstances he decided that the defendants were liable to pay the plaintiff £82 10s. 11d.

The objection made to the judgment, as I understand it, is that, as this was a gratuitious bailment, the high degree of negligence required, otherwise called gross negligence in some of the cases, has not been established; that the judge made no finding of negligence, and that, in the circumstances, the judgment should not stand. I am bound to say that I am not sure what is meant by the term "gross negligence" which has been in use for a long time in cases of this kind. There is no doubt, of course, that it is a phraase which has been commonly used in cases of this sort since the time of *Coggs* v. *Bernard*, when the distinction was made in a judgment of Lord Holt C.J. which has been frequently referred to and cited; but as we know from the judgment of Lord Chelmsford in *Giblin* v.*McMullen*, that it was said, after referring to the use of the term "gross negligence" over a long period: "At last, Lord Cranworth (then Baron Rolfe) in the case of *Wilson* v *Brett*, objected to it, saying that he 'could see no difference between negligence and gross negligence;' that it was the same thing, with the addition of a vituperative 'epithet.' And this critical observation has been since approved of by other eminent judges."

For my part, I have always found some difficulty in understanding just what was "gross negligence," because it appears to me that the standard of care required in a case of bailment, or any other type of case, is the standard demanded by the circumstances of that particular case. It seems to me that to try and put a bailment, for instance, into a watertight compartment — such as gratuitous bailment on the one hand, and bailment for reward on the other — is to overlook the fact that there might well be an infinite variety of cases, which might come into one or the other category. The question that we have to consider in a case of this kind, if it is necessary to consider negligence, is whether in the circumstances of this particular case a sufficient standard of care has been observed by the defendants or their servants.

First, I think, I should deal with the question of detinue. It has been admitted by Mr. Somerset Jones on behalf of the defendants that this is a case where a prima facie case has been established by the plaintiff. If that be so, I find it difficult to appreciate that there can be any grounds for appeal. Mr. Somerset Jones has endeavoured to establish, and he has done it by reference to authority, that to found a prima facie case is not sufficient — that there must, in addition, be affirmative evidence before the plaintiff can succeed. I am bound to say that is a doctrine which rather surprises me. If a prima facie case is once established, it is something which may be rebutted easily, but it can only be rebutted by evidence, and that is not present in this case; and therefore, the prima facie case having been established still remains.

Supposing that the claim is one in detinue, then it would appear that once the bailment has been established, and once the failure of the bailee to hand over the articles in question has been proved, there is a prima facie case, and the plaintiff is entitled to recover, unless the defendant can establish to the satisfaction of the court a defence; and that, I think, is very clear from the words used by Bankes L.J. in *Coldman* v. *Hill* in a passage that appears to me to be important in this case:

> "I think the law still is that if a bailee is sued in detinue only, it is a good answer for him to say that the goods were stolen without any default on his part, as the general bailment laid in the declaration pledges the plaintiff to the proof of nothing except that the goods were in the defendant's hands and were wrongfully detained."

So far, so good, but it is, of course, in those circumstances for the defendants to establish affirmatively, not only that the goods were stolen, but that they were stolen without default on their part; in other words, that there was no negligence on their part in the care which they took of the goods.

Applying that principle here, Mr. Somerset Jones has been at pains to point out that the judge has made no finding that these goods were in fact stolen. The only view that the judge has expressed on the point is: "It is impossible to say what happened to this suitcase when it was lost on its journey," and with that I am bound to agree. It was put on the coach at Southampton, and it was not, in the boot of the relief coach when it arrived at Hoylake. The judge has come to the conclusion that, on the probabilities, and again I agree with him, something happened to that suitcase when the transfer took place at Ternhill, or when the coach was delayed for some considerable period of time there. There seems to be no doubt that for something like three hours in the darkness that coach remained there unattended.

In these circumstances, I find it difficult to appreciate what substance there is in the complaint made by Mr. Somerset Jones that in this case the judge, in treating this as a case of detinue, was in error. But let us suppose for a moment that the issue here is an issue in negligence: then he admits, and I think properly admits, that there is a prima facie case against the defendants derived from the fact that the suitcase was found by the judge to have been put on the coach at Southampton, and was not on the second coach when it arrived at its destination at Hoylake. In those circumstances, it is for the defendants to adduce evidence which will rebut a presumption of negligence.

But the case goes further than that. The evidence is that when the first coach was at Ternhill, and when the relief coach arrived driven by the managing director of the defendants, and while he went for his tea, the luggage was transferred from the first coach to the relief coach, and this was done by being supervised at the relief coach end without any supervision of any kind at the first coach end; and anything might have happened to a suitcase being transferred from one coach to the other. The defendants had their managing director there, and it was not unreasonable to expect that he and the driver between them might have supervised the transfer of this luggage from one coach to another. That did not happen; the transfer took place in the manner described. There was no supervision of the baggage being taken from the first coach. The driver of the coach said that he trusted the passengers, and it may be he was justified in doing that. It may well be that the passengers were honest; but in the darkness of the night, who is to know that some suitcase was not stolen by someone who had nothing at all to do with that particular trip?

In the circumstances, I fail to see where the judge went wrong, and I would dismiss this appeal.

WILLMER L.J. I agree, and there is not much that I wish to add. In my judgment, this appeal fails on the facts. In saying that I do not think that it makes any difference whether the case is put in detinue, or whether it is treated as an action on the case for negligence. Whichever be the correct approach, it has been admitted in argument that the plaintiff, by proving the delivery of the suitcase at Southampton and its non-return on the arrival of the coach at Hoylake, made out a prima facie case. That prima facie case stands unless and until it is rebutted. The burden was on the defendants to adduce evidence in rebuttal. They could discharge that burden by proving what in fact did happen to the suitcase, and by showing that what did happen happened without any default on their part. They certainly did not succeed in doing that, for the judge was left in the position that he simply did not know what did happen to the suitcase.

Alternatively, the defendants could discharge the burden upon them by showing that, although they could not put their finger on what actually did happen to the suitcase, nevertheless, whatever did occur occurred notwithstanding all reasonable care having been exercised by them throughout the whole of the journey. Clearly the judge was not satisfied that they had proved the exercise of any such degree of care throughout the whole of the journey. On the evidence, particularly having regard to his preference for the plaintiff's evidence as against that called for the defendants, it was plainly open to him to come to that conclusion. All we know is that, in relation to the stop at Ternhill, this coach was apparently standing deserted in the middle of the night for a period of three hours. When the relief coach arrived, and the time came to transfer the luggage, this was done apparently with only the one member of the defendants' staff supervising the reloading on the second coach, and with no supervision at all over the discharge of the luggage from the first coach. In those circumstances, it is only too clear that the defendants entirely failed to show that throughout the period, when they had this suitcase in their custody, they exercised reasonable care.

I, therefore, agree that this appeal must fail.

Walker v *Watson*

[1974] 2 NZLR 175

MAHON J. This is an appeal from a judgment of the Magistrate's Court at Auckland wherein the respondent recovered from the appellant $1575.04 in respect of damage caused to his motorcar which at the time of the occurrence of the damage had been in the custody of the appellant.

The evidence disclosed that the respondent, a young man of 27, owned an MG sports car valued at about $3,000. On the weekend of 19-20 May 1972 the respondent travelled in his car to Hastings in the company of the appellant and another girl, both of whom are in their early twenties. The respondent had been previously disqualified from driving and his car was driven at the weekend by one or other of the two girls. On the afternoon of Sunday, 21 May, the respondent and the appellant and the other girl, whose name was Elizabeth Laery, returned to Auckland in the respondent's car. Before leaving on the journey to Auckland the two girls had a few drinks and at an early stage of the trip back to Auckland they stopped at a hotel and bought 12 quart bottles of beer. Either on that occasion or at an earlier time they had also acquired two bottles of sparkling wine. On the journey back to Auckland the appellant drove the car. The respondent did not drink during the journey but as they drove along the appellant and Miss Laery were drinking from the bottles which they had bought and by the time they reached their destination in Auckland the two girls had drunk the 12 quarts of beer. Apart from the two bottles of sparkling wine which were also in the vehicle, the girls drank three gallons of bottled beer between them. As the car was being driven by the appellant along the motorway approaching Auckland it swerved on more than one occasion and the respondent was compelled to grasp the steering wheel on those occasions in order to bring the vehicle back to a relatively straight course.

The journey ended at the residence of the appellant in Remuera Road, and he and the two girls entered the house and found therein a young man who was staying there as a guest of the respondent and who was passing the time by drinking red wine. The evidence of the respondent did not disclose whether the appellant and her girlfriend drank any of the red wine. At this stage the time was about 9.30 pm. The two girls decided they would spend the night at the respondent's house. One of them, the appellant, already held her parents' consent to this course, but Miss Laery did not, and she felt herself obliged to telephone her parents and advise them of her intentions. Miss Laery's parents lodged a strong objection to their daughter spending the night at the respondent's house and on the telephone an argument developed in which the appellant also took part. The telephone discussion terminated with either the appellant or Miss Laery flinging the telephone to the ground in a fit of petulance and breaking it. The girls then decided to go off to conduct a personal confrontation with Miss Laery's parents. They advised the respondent that they would need his car for that purpose.

The respondent had previously lent his car to one or both of the two girls. He had at that time been disqualified from driving for a period of some weeks and on different occasions the girls had not only borrowed his car but had used the vehicle to pick him up from hotels at his request. They had had the car in their possession throughout each of the two nights which preceded the journey to Hastings. When the respondent was asked to lend his sports car to the appellant and Miss Laery on this occasion he would therefore have been following an accepted course of procedure if he had merely handed over the keys. But on this occasion he initially refused to do so. It was only in consequence of repeated and truculent demands by the two girls that he finally surrendered the keys and his evidence was that he lent the car specifically to the appellant as he did not consider Miss Laery fit to drive. According to the evidence of the respondent, he only intended the girls to drive to the home of Miss Laery's parents and he expected them to come back with the car. After the departure of the appellant and Miss Laery the respondent and his guest sat up for a while talking and then retired for the night.

The narrative must now be taken up at a different point. Some time after 11 pm, when the car had been in the custody of the two young ladies for about two hours, a complaint was received by the Newmarket police. This was to the effect that an MG sports car bearing the registration number of the respondent's car was travelling through the night along the streets of Auckland in charge of two young ladies who were said to be drinking out of champagne bottles. A patrol car was despatched from the Newmarket Police Station in an endeavour to locate this vehicle and its occupants, but before the car could be located it left the road in Tamaki Drive and careered into a stone wall. The appellant and Miss Laery were taken to the nearest hospital. The police had some difficulty in ascertaining who had been driving as this was a matter which each of the young ladies was unable to recall. At about 5 am a blood sample was taken from the appellant and this disclosed a blood-alcohol content of 285 milligrammes. Seeing that the accident occurred more than four hours earlier, it seemed inevitable that at the time of the accident the appellant had been maintaining a blood-alcohol level of well over 300 milligrammes.

In the light of the circumstances just described, the respondent brought proceedings in the Magistrate's Court to recover the cost of repairs to his car. He sued both the appellant and Miss Laery. Mr Bryers, counsel for the respondent, correctly foresaw that the defence of volenti non fit injuria might be raised against the respondent, and in the alternative the further defence of contributory negligence. In an attempt to preclude such a result he drew the statement of claim not in tort but in contract. The statement of claim alleged that on the relevant date the respondent bailed the motorcar to the appellant and/or Miss Laery, and that in breach of the terms of bailment the bailees failed to take reasonable care of the chattel entrusted to their custody.

Upon the hearing of the action in the Magistrate's Court the appellant and Miss Laery did not give evidence. The only evidence was that of the respondent and of the police officer from Newmarket who had been looking for the sports car and who arrived at the scene of the accident just after it had occurred. The certificate of the appellant's blood-alcohol analysis was put in by consent. The respondent's evidence was along the general lines which I have already indicated. At the conclusion of the respondent's case it was argued by counsel for each of the defendants that the defence of volenti non fit injuria, though not applicable to claims in contract generally, was nevertheless available in an action based upon a contract of bailment. However, the learned Magistrate rejected this view. He held that the claim was for breach of contract and that the defences of volenti and contributory negligence were accordingly not available.

Counsel for the appellant protested in his submissions on appeal, as he had also done before the learned Magistrate, at being deprived of a meritorious and perhaps conclusive defence by reason of the form of pleading which had been adopted by the respondent's advisers but in my opinion it is clear enough that the constraint considered to have been imposed by these procedural fetters was more apparent than real. Some classes of bailment are derived from a completed contract between bailor and bailee. This, however, is a case of gratuitious bailment. There was no element of contract present. No consideration moved from the appellant when she took possession of the car with the consent of the respondent. The only duties which arose in consequence of the bailment were the ordinary duties which the law imposes as incidents of that special relationship. There were no contractual terms super-added. The appellant assumed the ordinary duty of a bailee to take care of the chattel entrusted to her custody. Any action for breach of that duty lay in tort, not in contract. In *Paton on Bailment* the learned author expresses the matter in decisive terms. He says, at p 40:

> "It is now recognised that gratuitous bailment, by its very definition, has nothing to do with the law of contract at all."

In *Morris v C W Martin & Sons Ltd* [1966] 1 QB 716; [1965] 2 All ER 725 (CA) a question arose as to the liability of sub-bailees. It was held that they were liable to the original bailor for breach of the duty of care. The following passage appears in the judgment of Diplock LJ (as he then was):

> "The legal relationship of bailor and bailee of a chattel can exist independently of any contract, for the legal concept of bailment as creating a relationship which gives rise to duties owed by a bailee to a bailor is derived from Roman law and is older in our common law than the legal concept of parol contract as giving rise to legal duties owed by one party to the other party thereto. The nature of those legal duties, in particular as to the degree of care which the bailee is bound to exercise in the custody of the goods and as to his duty to re-deliver them, varies according to the circumstances in which and purposes for which the goods are delivered to the bailee" (ibid, 731; 734).

Then there is a later case also concerned with the liability of sub-bailees, which is *Gilchrist Watt & Sanderson Pty Ltd v York Products Pty Ltd* [1970] 1 WLR 1262; [1970] 3 All ER 825 (PC). In this case the Judicial Committee adopted and applied the decision in *Morris v C W Martin & Sons Ltd* (supra). The advice of the Board was delivered by Lord Pearson. He said:

> "Both on principle and on old as well as recent authority it is clear that, although there was no contract or attornment between the plaintiffs and the defendants, the defendants by voluntarily taking possession of the plaintiffs' goods in the circumstances assumed an obligation to take due care of them and are liable to the plaintiffs for their failure to do so . . . ." (ibid, 1270; 832)

It follows that in the present case the true cause of action was negligence. The fact that the claim is pleaded as breach of contract does not affect the situation. In *Turner v Stallibrass* [1898] 1 QB 56 it was held that an action founded on the common law liability of a bailee was an action founded on tort within the meaning of a section of the County Courts Act which made different provisions for costs depending on whether the claim was brought in contract or in tort. The plaintiff had sued for negligent performance for a contract of agistment. The Court of Appeal held that although the pleadings were drawn in contract the real cause of action was the breach by the defendant of his common law duty as bailee. Lord Justice Rigby said, in the course of his judgment:

> "The question whether an action falls within one class or the other depends on the facts of the case, not on the form in which the action is brought. It has long ago been settled that the form of the pleadings is for this purpose immaterial" (ibid, 59).

In the present case the statement of claim alleged a failure to take reasonable care of the motorcar in breach of what were described as "contractual terms of the bailment" but, as I have said, there can be no doubt that the true cause of action was in negligence. It therefore followed, in my opinion, that counsel for the appellant was correct when he contended in the Court below that the defence of volenti was open on this claim founded on breach of the duty of care owed by a bailee.

The learned Magistrate did not determine the defence of volenti because he held it was not available. The factual foundation for the defence was the collection of circumstances surrounding the bailment and in order to consider the question of volenti it is necessary to determine what the factual circumstances were. I have considered whether I should not send the case back to the Magistrate's Court for determination of this factual issue but I have come to the conclusion that such a course is unnecessary. The matter I think resolves itself into a question of legitimate inference from established facts. I have already described the narrative of events which led up to the respondent lending the car to the appellant. The appellant and Miss Laery had drunk between them three gallons of bottled beer during the journey to Auckland. It was not clearly shown whether they joined the respondent's guest in his wine-drinking following their arrival at the respondent's house, but the respondent did not distinctly say in his evidence that the two girls had nothing to drink after their arrival and it has to be remembered that they were recovering from a long and tiring journey in which a very large quantity of liquor had already been consumed. To accept that the two girls neither demanded nor accepted some further refreshment at the respondent's premises seems almost to require an act of faith. The onus lay upon the appellant in the Court below to establish on the balance of probabilities that she was unfit to drive when the car was entrusted to her care, and in my view the facts clearly established this proposition. The two girls were accustomed to taking the respondent's car away for the night and his initial persistent refusal to lend the car on this occasion, coupled with the admitted facts as to the previous consumption of liquor by the appellant and her friend, and their intransigent behaviour at his house, are in my view conclusive against the self-serving assertion of the respondent that he thought the appellant was fit to drive. The respondent therefore lent his car to a girl who was, to his knowledge, incapable through liquor of driving it safely. She later drove the car off the road into a wall when she was, without question, very drunk. No doubt she and her companion obtained other liquor after they took possession of the vehicle but I must infer that this was a not unnatural consequence of their alcoholic condition when they drove away from the respondent's house. The question left for determination is whether, on these facts, the appellant owed any duty of care to the respondent during the period of hours following her resumption of possession of the car, or alternatively, whether the respondent voluntarily and knowingly assumed the risk of breach of that duty on the part of the appellant, taking his chance of damage from a known risk.

The extent of the application of the maxim volenti non fit injuria was recently considered in New Zealand by the Court of Appeal in *Morrison v Union Steam Ship Co of New Zealand Ltd* [1964] NZLR 468. The consent of the plaintiff to assume the risk may be implied from his conduct but it was pointed out by Turner J in the case just cited that there must be some antecedent transaction between the plaintiff and defendant from which the plaintiff's assent may be clearly inferred. It is not sufficient to show by inference that the plaintiff merely encountered a recognised risk and consented to a possible consequence of injury or damage. The plaintiff must also be shown to have consented to run that risk in the sense of agreeing that he and not the negligent defendant would bear the resultant loss. In the present case the respondent entered freely and voluntarily into a transaction with the appellant which presented obvious danager to the respondent's property, and having regard to the past relationship between the parties and in particular to the events which had occurred earlier in the day the respondent must be assumed, in my opinion, to have accepted the presently existing risk of damage to his car by negligent driving, and to have impliedly undertaken to bear any loss or damage himself. It was submitted by Mr Bryers for the respondent that the terms of bailment envisaged only a journey by the appellant to Miss Laery's home and then back to the respondent's home, but I do not think the evidence supports that view of the matter. The two girls were in the habit of taking the car away for the night and the respondent and his friend retired for the night after the departure of the girls. There was no suggestion that they wait up for the girls to return. In my opinion the risk which was assumed by the respondent extended to all the activities of the appellant in handling the car throughout the remainder of the night.

It may be, as was suggested in *Insurance Commissioner v Joyce* (1948) 77 CLR 39 that in these circumstances the correct legal answer is that no duty of care existed at all but, as Dixon J said, the distinction between that concept and the different concept of assumption of risk is of little consequence in most cases. For the reasons which I have given I am of the opinion that under all the circumstances of the case the respondent, in handing over his car to a girl who was unfit to drive, voluntarily assumed not only the physical but also the legal risk of any damage which might be caused by the negligent driving of the appellant. Accordingly the respondent was precluded from recovering damages in his action.

In the Court below Mr Williams contended in the alternative that the respondent was prevented by the rule of public policy from succeeding in his action. He submitted that the respondent was particeps criminis to an offence of drunken driving committed by the appellant in breach of the Transport Act 1962, and while accepting that this defence was not available in the ordinary action of negligence, nevertheless contended that it was available in the case of bailment involving use of the bailed chattel in a manner proscribed by the criminal law. This submission was rejected by the learned Magistrate and although I express no concluded opinion on the matter I think there was considerable force in that argument also.

The appeal is accordingly allowed and the case remitted to the Magistrate's Court for the entry of judgment for the appellant with costs and disbursements in that Court according to scale. Miss Laery was held not liable in the Magistrate's Court on the ground that the car was lent not to her but to the appellant and Miss Laery was not a party to this appeal.

Appeal allowed.

Conway v Cockram Motors

[1986] 1 NZLR 382

HARDIE BOYS J. This is a plaintiff's appeal against a District Court judgment in an action founded on an alleged breach of the defendant's obligations as a bailee. The facts are not in dispute. The appellant left his BMW car, valued at $55,000 with the respondent, a licensed motor vehicle dealer, for sale on his behalf. The respondent placed the vehicle in its showroom and left it there for the night, unlocked, with the ignition keys on the sun visor. This is a normal, almost universal practice, to enable prompt removal in the event of fire. There was no burglar alarm, and no security guards visited the premises. The showrooom is on the corner of Colombo Street and Moorhouse Avenue, and was well lit by both lights on the premises and adjacent street lighting. At about 11 pm an intruder entered the premises by smashing a window in the door of the workshop, which is at the rear of the premises, and which leads into the showroom. He attempted without success to open the doors leading from the showroom to the yard outside. These doors were padlocked on the inside and it seems although he was able to remove the padlocks he could still not open the doors, which are bi-folding and difficult to manage. Then, having found the keys of the appellant's car, he started it up and drove it through the closed doors and through a stout steel safety chain stretched across the driveway from the yard to the street. The showroom doors were smashed, and a steel pipe set in the ground to secure one end of the safety chain was shorn off. The car was later recovered, but as a result of its impact with the doors and the chain it was damaged to the extent of $6704.63. The appellant sued the respondent for this sum.

It was accepted in both the District Court and this Court that the obligations of a gratuitous bailee and of a bailee for reward are so nearly identical that it is unnecessary to determine into which class the respondent fell: see *Port Swettenham Authority v T W Wu & Co (M) Sdn Bhd* [1978] 3 All ER 337, 339, per Lord Salmon delivering the judgment of the Privy Council. The bailee's obligation is to take all reasonable and proper care, an obligation which Hutchison J in *Barton Ginger & Co Ltd v Wellington Harbour Board* [1951] NZLR 673, 676 spelled out as "the exercise of the care and diligence which a careful and vigilant man would exercise in the custody of his own chattel of the like character and in the like circumstances". This statement was adopted by Turner J in *Petersen v Papakura Motor Sales Ltd* [1957] NZLR 495, 497. But the onus is not on the bailor to prove a breach of the obligation. He need prove only loss or damage. Then, in the *Port Swettenham Authority* case at p 340 in Lord Salmon's words, "the onus is always on the bailee, whether he be a bailee for reward or a gratuitious bailee, to prove that the loss of any goods bailed to him was not caused by any fault of his". He may discharge that onus in two ways. First, he may show that he was not at fault, that the damage "took place notwithstanding that [he] had taken all reasonable precautions to guard against the danger": *Brook's Wharf and Bull Wharf Ltd v Goodman Brothers* [1937] 1 KB 534, 539 per Lord Wright MR. He may also discharge it by showing that although he did not take proper precautions, the loss would have occurred even had he done so. Whilst these principles are now well established, it is not entirely clear what standard of proof the bailee has to meet in respect of the second ground of defence, lack of causation. The uncertainty arises from the judgments of the Court of Appeal in England in *British Road Services Ltd v Arthur V Crutchley & Co Ltd* [1968] 1 All ER 811. At first instance, Cairns J held that it is sufficient for the bailee to prove that its breach of duty probably did not cause the loss: see [1967] 2 All ER 785, 791. In the Court of Appeal Lord Pearson decided the case on the basis that it was "not unlikely, indeed . . . probable" that the loss would not have occurred if further precautions had been taken: [1968] 1 All ER 811, 820. Sachs LJ thought, without deciding, that the test might be more stringent, requiring proof that there was no reasonable chance that the loss would not have occurred.

In arguing this appeal, Mr Hall seemed to have adopted the second of these tests, for he said that a bailee's liability is virtually absolute. I do not think the cases go that far, but the view I take of the case does not require me to resolve the point. Moreover on the way the appeal was argued, the point does not even arise for the appellant's case was simply that the keys ought not to have been left in the car. Had they not been left there, it is of course highly unlikely that the car would have been taken. Mr Hall advanced other allegations of negligence, namely the absence of a burglar alarm and of a security guard patrol, but he saw those as background matters, enabling him to submit that the respondent was at fault in leaving the keys in the car when there was no alarm and no patrol.

The District Court Judge took the view that it was reasonable for the keys to have been left where they were, as a precaution in case of fire, and that therefore there was no breach on the respondent's part. He referred to a concession made by counsel — counsel of eminence then and of much greater eminence since — in *Petersen v Papakura Motor Sales Ltd* and discussed by Turner J in his judgment at p 497. It was a rather similar case, in that it involved the theft of an unlocked motorcar from a dealer's showroom. The key had been left in the ignition, as a precaution in the event of a fire. The thief was able to open the showroom door from the inside. The pleadings had alleged negligence in leaving the car unlocked with the key in the ignition, but counsel had abandoned that allegation after the reason for this had been explained. Turner J seems to have accepted this as a proper course, commenting only that this factor remained as a circumstance to be taken into account in considering what other precautions ought to have been observed.

Mr Hall referred me to the decision of the High Court of Australia in *Pitt Son & Badgery Ltd v Proulefco SA* (1984) 58 ALJR 246, which involved only a question of fact, but which is of value for present purposes in what was said by Gibbs CJ (with whose judgment the rest of the Court concurred) about the bailee's duty. The bailee had a wool store which was damaged by a fire lit by an intruder who had got in through a hole in the fence. The bailee was held to have been negligent in not providing a secure fence, and the damage to have been the direct result of that failure. In response to a submission that arson was a rare, perhaps unknown, occurrence in wool stores and it was therefore not unreasonable to fail to guard against it, Gibbs CJ said (p 247):

"However, the duty of the appellant was not simply to guard against arson. It was to take reasonable care to keep the wool safe, and therefore to prevent damage from any sort of intruders, whether thieves, vandals or the unexpected arsonist."

If the present case is approached in the light of the overall duty of the respondent, then I think the Judge's conclusion about the keys is shown to be correct. The respondent's duty was to guard against fire as well as against theft, and therefore it was entirely proper as a safeguard against fire for the normal practice to be followed and for the keys to be left on the sun visor. Had they not been, and had there been a fire, the respondent would plainly have been at fault in not following standard practice.

This being the common practice, it is quite likely that a criminal would know of it. And so it appears to me that the real question in the case is whether the respondent has established that it took proper care to keep the car safe from an intruder with that knowledge. The showroom contained vehicles with a total value of about three-quarters of a million dollars, and plainly visible to passers-by. The workshop door was set well back from the Colombo Street frontage. It was clearly easy enough to gain entry. Anyone who did gain entry had ready access to the appellant's car, which was a high-powered and attractive temptation. Was the respondent then entitled to rely on the doors and the safety chain as sufficient to prevent theft, without taking the further precaution of an alarm or a patrol?

The usefulness of a patrol was not explored, and I do not think the case can turn upon that. It appears from the evidence that there are at least two kinds of alarm, one which produces a loud sound, the other which is soundless but activates a signal at the police station. The former would surely have been an immediate deterrent to any intruder in well-lit premises such as these. It might well have dissuaded this particular intruder from his attempts to open the showroom door, and from breaking out when the attention of any passer-by would have been drawn to the premises. The latter might well have brought the police to the premises before he had left.

Considerations such as these show that the distinction between fault and causation in these cases where the onus is on the bailee, is imprecise. They are probably relevant to both points. First, though, it is necessary to decide whether the respondent has shown that it was not incumbent on it to provide an alarm system. In my opinion, it has not done so. In reality, there was little impediment to an intruder removing a vehicle from the showroom. I do not think it can reasonably be assumed that once he had got that far, the safety chain would be a barrier that he would not attempt to pass through. Thus appropriate measures to prevent such eventualities were called for, and there were none. The fact that the respondent had recently been acquired by new shareholders is beside the point. The point, as I see it, is that the respondent has not shown that it took the necessary degree of care.

Having reached this conclusion it is necessary to consider whether, had an alarm system been installed, the damage would in any event have occurred. Whatever the correct standard of proof, the respondent has not satisfied me that it would have occurred. Indeed I think it highly likely, for the reasons already given, that it would not.

Therefore, although I agree with the District Court Judge's reasoning, I consider that he reached the wrong conclusion. The appeal is accordingly allowed, the judgment entered for the respondent (defendant) in the lower Court is set aside and I order the judgment be entered for the appellant (plaintiff in that Court) for the agreed sum of $6704.63 together with interest thereon at 11% from the date the proceedings were issued, 29 May 1984, and costs and disbursements in accordance with scale or as fixed by the Registrar of that Court. I allow the appellant $200 costs on the appeal, together with disbursements fixed by this Court's Registrar.

Appeal allowed.

Coleman v Harvey

[1989] 1 NZLR 723 (CA).

Cooke P. Mr Harvey and Mr Coleman were active in the silver trade. Mr Coleman owned a company, Coleman Industrial Services Ltd, which refined silver, referred to as scrap silver, from such materials as coins, X-ray film, torpedo batteries, jewellery, candelabra. In February 1978 a contract was made orally between the two men, Mr Coleman acting on behalf of his company. It related to a quantity of coins belonging to Mr Harvey weighing about 330 kilograms and calculated to yield 166 kilograms of fine silver. In consideration of Mr Harvey's agreeing to continue to supply materials to the company, the company would refine that particular quantity of coins free of charge, for which purpose the coins would be included, with such other source materials as the company had on hand, in its processes of dissolving, furnacing and electro-refining; and out of the number of two kilogram ingots so produced the company would hold and store 166 kilograms for Mr Harvey.

The company did melt down Mr Harvey's coins together with other materials and convert the mass into ingots, but by the end of May 1978 the company in the course of its trade had disposed of all those ingots. The company never in fact set aside any of the ingots for Mr Harvey. Nevertheless on 20 June 1978 Mr Coleman supplied Mrs Harvey with a written acknowledgment that the company was holding 166 kilograms of fine silver in custody on his behalf; and on or about 12 May 1979 Mr Coleman prepared a proposed agreement, which however was unacceptable to Mr Harvey, referring to silver held by the company for Mr Harvey and providing for its "repayment" or "replacement" by instalments. In all 49 kilograms of silver were in fact delivered by the company to Mr Harvey; the damages awarded in the High Court represent the value of 117 kilograms in May 1978, together with interest.

The company was placed in receivership on 21 May 1979 and is apparently not in a position to meet its liabilities to Mr Harvey. The issue before the Court is whether Mr Coleman is personally liable to Mr Harvey on the ground that he was a joint tortfeasor with the company in converting Mr Harvey's silver in May 1978.

Davison CJ held in favour of Mr Harvey and gave judgment for him against both Mr Coleman and the company for a total of $40,994 (including interest). Mr Coleman appeals.

I have based the foregoing summary of the facts on the Chief Justice's findings of fact, which are not in dispute on the appeal. They are, however, somewhat dispersed in his judgment. When assembled they reveal that the line of legal reasoning by which he reached his conclusion appears to be unsustainable. Relying on *Makower McBeath & Co Pty Ltd v Dalgety & Co Ltd* [1921] VLR 365, 373, which concerns the creation of bailment by acknowledgment by the bailee and consent by the bailor after the bailee has originally obtained possession of the bailor's goods without the latter's knowledge or consent, the Chief Justice referred not merely to the original agreement between the parties but also to the acknowledgments of June 1978 and May 1979. Having held that the company was a bailee on that footing, he went on to say that, once the company was a bailee, wilful interference with the silver in a manner inconsistent with the bailor's rights was conversion.

That approach appears to overlook that any conversion was found to have occurred before the end of May 1978. On appeal Mr Johnson for the respondent found difficulty in supporting the reasoning in the judgment, nor was he able to make anything of the acknowledgments as giving rise to some form of estoppel capable of helping an action for conversion.

But Mr Johnson sought to support the judgment on different bases; and as a result of the thorough arguments and references to authorities that we heard from counsel on both sides and the different kind of refining process that took place during the arguments, I think that an acceptable and relatively simple answer has emerged.

For the appellant Mr Finnigan contended that the delivery of the coins to the company constituted mutuum or sale, and not bailment. He said that the coins lost their identity by chemical process and property then passed to the company. But that is to ignore or treat as irrelevant an important feature of the transaction. Some of the silver in Mr Harvey's coins was intended to be embodied in the ingots to be set aside for him; on the facts of this case, that was a necesssary consequence of the melting down together of materials from different sources. So it was not a case of mutuum, which is a loan of something not to be returned in specie but to be replaced by something similar and equivalent (*2 Halsbury's Laws of England* (4th ed) para 1534). The same feature seems to me to rule out treating the transaction as simply a sale. Though if the 166 kilograms had been duly appropriated to Mr Harvey it may be that the transaction could be described as a sale of any of the refined silver provided by him but not contained in the 166 kilograms.

In its first stage the transaction was much more like intermixture. That term and the Roman commixtio, and the distinction between these concepts and confusio, are not drawn altogether uniformly in the textbooks. I adopt the usage in *2 Halbury's Laws of England* (4th ed) para 1537:

> "1537. **Intermixture of chattels**. Where the chattels of two persons are intermixed by consent or agreement, so that the several portions can no longer be distinguished, the proprietors have an interest in common in proportion to their respective shares".

It is true that here there are two complications—the intended destruction of the identity of the coins by chemical means and the intended setting aside for Mr Harvey of ingots to the specified weight. But I do not think that either should be treated as changing the essence of the transaction. Until the company performed its contract to appropriate to Mr Harvey specific ingots, he should be treated as having a proprietary interest in any silver to which his coins contributed. Until then he had a share as a co-owner of each ingot in the proportion of his total contribution to the refined silver.

That seems to give best effect to the intention of the parties on the Chief Justice's finding as to the contract made between them. Though the contract was sui generis, or at least of a somewhat special kind, there does not appear to be any ground in principle for rejecting such a solution. It is tantamount or at least analogous to finding that there has been an implied reservation of title, which, as Professor R M Goode has remarked, is "merely an agreement between the parties as to the time when ownership is to pass" ((1984) 100 LQR 234, 238). I think that in principle support for this solution may be found in a number of authorities, among which it is sufficient to cite the following.

In *The South Australian Insurance Co v Randell* (1869) LR 3 PC 101, a case of the mixing of farmers' corn by a miller, the Privy Council, in holding that there was a sale by each farmer to the miller, attached importance to the fact that the farmer had no more than a right to claim at any time an equal quantity of corn of like quality, *without reference to any specific bulk from which it was to be taken*: see pp 108, 109, 111.

In *Sandeman & Sons v Tyzack and Branfoot Steamship Co Ltd* [1913] AC 680, 695, Lord Moulton, speaking of an accidental commixtio and the solution of ownership in common said:

> "The fact is that the conclusions of the Courts in such cases, though influenced by certain fundamental principles, have been little more than instances of cutting the Gordian Knot—reasonable adjustments of the rights of parties in cases where complete justice was impracticable of attainment."

See also *Goff and Jones on Restitution* (3rd ed, 1986) p 65.

In *Caltex Oil (Australia) Pty Ltd v The Dredge "Willemstad"* (1976) 136 CLR 529, 561, Stephen J, speaking of an agreement that the title to oil after refining should be in a supplier, said:

> "The situation as to title which the agreement created is different both from that of the wheat considered in *South Australian Insurance Co v Randell* (1869) LR 3 PC 101 and in *Chapman Bros v Verco Bros & Co Ltd* (1933) 49 CLR 306 and from that of the fruit in *Farnsworth v Federal Commissioner of Taxation* (1949) 78 CLR 504. It approaches most closely to the position referred to in Corpus Juris 2d, vol 8, pp 345-346, where a reading of the cases there cited shows that in the case of fungible goods their commingling and manufacture into other products which are to be returned to the original owner may, if the parties so intend, be consistent with a bailment, property never leaving the bailor (see generally the annotation to *Kansas Flour Mills Co v Board of Commissioners of Harper County* (1927) 54 ALR 1164 and *Commissioner of Internal Revenue v San Carlos Milling Co* (1933) 63 F (2d) 153)."

Finally I would mention the judgment of Staughton J in *Indian Oil Corporation Ltd v Greenstone Shipping SA* [1987] 3 All ER 893, a case of mixing of oil, where after an extensive review of the case law the Judge said at pp 907-908:

"Seeing that none of the authorities is binding on me, although many are certainly persuasive, I consider that I am free to apply the rule which justice requires. This is that where B wrongfully mixes the goods of A with goods of his own, which are substantially of the same nature and quality, and they cannot in practice be separated, the mixture is held in common and A is entitled to receive out of it a quantity equal to that of his goods which went into the mixture, any doubt as to that quantity being resolved in favour of A. He is also entitled to claim damages from B in respect of any loss he may have suffered, in respect of quality or otherwise, by reason of the admixture."

In my opinion the same should apply to a consensual refining such as occurred in this case, at least where the evidence does not point to an intention to part altogether with ownership from the start.

It is plain that Mr Coleman and his company disposed of the silver as trading stock in which Mr Harvey had no interest and which the company was free to sell. I did not understand Mr Finnigan to contend that the co-ownership of the company precluded this from being conversion: if he did so it was only faintly: but in any event, having had the advantage of reading the judgment in draft of Somers J, I agree with all that my brother says on this point.

Accordingly I would dismiss the appeal. The Court being unanimous, it is dismissed with costs to the respondent in the sum of $1500 together with the reasonable travelling and (if necessary) accommodation expenses of counsel, to be fixed by the Registrar.

SOMERS J:

The real issue in this case, as Mr Finnigan acknowledged, is whether Mr Harvey, in the events that happened, had a proprietary interest in 166 kilograms of silver capable of being converted by the company and hence by Mr Coleman.

The contract between the company and Mr Harvey contemplated that the latter would after refinement be the owner of 166 kilograms of silver part of which, perhaps most of which, would be the product of his coins, but part of which would previously have been the property of the company. Property in the company's silver must I think have been intended to pass Mr Harvey when the company selected or segregated 166 kilograms for Mr Harvey. At the same time that part of Mr Harvey's silver which was not included in the 166 kilograms so set aside would become the property of the company. In short no property in Mr Harvey's silver and no property in the company's silver would pass from one to the other until the company set aside 166 kilograms. As it did not ever do so neither lost any part of its property. The product of the refining process, an admixture of the silver of both was owned by both; as to 166 kilograms by Mr Harvey, as to the balance by the company. They were co-owners in common in shares proportioned to the silver each contributed.

What then happened was that the company, procured or directed by Mr Coleman, sold or disposed of the property which it and Mr Harvey owned in common. The question then is whether this was a conversion by the company and Mr Coleman.

That issue is resolved in England by s 10 of the Torts (Interference with Goods) Act 1977 which provides that co-ownership is no defence to an action founded on conversion or trespass to goods where the defendant without the authority of the other co-owner (a) destroys the goods, or disposes of the goods in a way giving a good title to the entire property in the goods, or otherwise does anything equivalent to the destruction of the other's interest in the goods, or (b) purports to dispose of the goods in a way which would give a good title to the entire property in the goods if he was acting with the authority of all co-owners. The first part of this provision is declared to be by way of restatement of the existing law so far as it relates to conversion. It is implicit, and is stated to be the case in *45 Halsbury's Laws of England* (4th ed) para 1449, that the second part alters the common law.

As there are no statutory provisions in New Zealand it is necessary to consider the common law about the sale of property by one co-owner. In *33 Halsbury's Laws of England* (2nd ed) at p 60 it is said:

> "95. A joint owner or owner in common of property is guilty of conversion as against his co-owner if he destroys the common property or excludes his co-owner from the common property, or so disposes of it as to render it impossible that the co-owner should take or use it or enjoy the proceeds, the co-owner seeking to exercise his rights and being denied their exercise. He cannot, however, be sued for conversion by his co-owner if he merely makes use of the common property in a reasonable way, or takes or keeps it, *or if he sells it*." (Emphasis added.)

38 Halsbury's Laws of England (3rd ed) at p 790 para 1313 is to the same effect but adds the words "without excluding his co-owner from the proceeds".

The difference between the two cases is clear enough. In the first the property is destroyed or disposed of by one co-owner in such a way that the other co-owner's proprietary rights are lost as in a sale in a market overt, when such was possible in New Zealand, or under s 3 of the Mercantile Law Act 1908. In the second the property still exists and the purchaser, in the case of a sale, has no lawful title to the whole. The present case raises the issue of whether there are circumstances in which a sale by one co-owner may nevertheless amount to a conversion of the interest of the other and whether in any event the distinction between destruction or loss of title on the one hand and mere sale on the other ought to be maintained.

In cases which do not involve co-ownership a wrongful sale of the plaintiff's goods by the defendant amounts to a conversion and both the seller and the buyer are liable in conversion although the buyer will not be liable if he purchases in such circumstances that he obtains a good title, as by a purchase in the market overt. One explanation of the difference in the case of co-owners was given in *Fraser v Kershaw* (1856) 2 K & J 496, 499-500, namely, that a sale by one co-owner cannot convey the other co-owner's interest; the buyer can only acquire the seller's interest and become a co-owner with the plaintiff. This is not convincing. The same may be said of a case where the defendant sells property belonging entirely to the plaintiff but the fact affords no defence. The statement by Parke B in *Morgan v Marquis* (1853) 9 Exch 145, 147 that one tenant in common may dispose of the common property is on its face in conflict with *Fraser v Kershaw*, but the case was one concerning partners one of whom had become bankrupt. In such circumstances the authority of a solvent partner to bind the firm continues so far as is necessary to wind up its affairs: see *Lindley on Partnership* (15th ed, 1984) at pp 836-839.

Conversion is the wrongful act of dealing with goods in a manner inconsistent with the owner's rights with the intention of denying the owner's rights or asserting a right inconsistent with them. One of those rights is possession or the immediate claim to it. As Professor Derham points out in his article, "Conversion by Wrongful Disposal as between Co-owners", in (1952) 68 LQR 507, 511-512 the explanation does not touch on the seller's intention to give and the buyer's to receive a right of possession excluding the non-consenting co-owner.

Nor has the distinction been universally applied. Thus in *Barnardiston v Chapman*, noted in (1715) 4 East 121, where a ship was possessed by one co-owner and sent to sea without the consent of the other and lost it was held that trover would lie. That case is referred to in *Jacobs v Seward* (1872) LR 5 HL 464, 474, and led Mason J to observe in *Kitano v The Commonwealth of Australia* (1974) 129 CLR 151 at p 172 that "Conversion may be brought at the instance of a co-owner of a chattel; in particular it will lie at the suit of a co-owner of a ship".

I think it likely that the explanation of the suggested distinction between the destruction by a co-owner of the property or title to it and a sale by him lies in the history of the actions of trespass, detinue and trover as is suggested by Professor Derham in the article mentioned.

It has to be recognised, however, that there is a respectable line of authority supporting the proposition that in the case of sale by one co-owner the remedy of the other does not lie in an action for conversion. One enactment touched on the point. Under s 27 of the Administration of Justice Act 1705 (described in the Revised Statutes and *2 Halsbury's Statutes of England* (2nd ed) as 4 & 5 Anne c 3, but frequently referred to as chapter 16) actions of account could be brought and maintained by one joint tenant or tenant in common as against the other as bailiff "for receiving more than comes to his just share or proportion". Section 27, referred to in *Jacobs v Seward* (1872) LR 5 HL 464, was repealed in England by the Law of Property (Amendment) Act 1924. It must, I think, have been in force in New Zealand by virtue of the English Laws Act 1908 and remained so, despite its repeal in England, until January 1989 when the Imperial Laws Application Act 1988 came into force. The latter statute preserves only ss 9 and 10 of the 1705 Act. In equity a co-owner has been held liable to account at the suit of others: *Strelly v Winson* (1684) 1 Vern 277.

The cases in conversion include *Mayhew v Herrick* (1849) 7 CB 229; *Morgan v Marquis* (1853) 9 Exch 145; *Heath v Hubbard* (1803) 4 East 110 and *Farrar v Beswick* (1836) 1 M & W 682, 688. But even in these the rule has not always been unequivocally stated. In the leading case of *Mayhew v Herrick* (1849) 7 CB 229 Coltman J said at pp 246-247:

"There may be such a dealing with the chattel by one of the joint owners, short of its absolute destruction, as would amount in law to a conversion. But there is nothing here to shew that the defendant has so conducted himself as to put it out of the power of the plaintiff to take his property, or to pursue his remedy against the parties who have got possession of it."

And Maule J, at pp 247-248:

"* * * that there may be dispositions of the subject-matter which will amount to a conversion if done by a stranger, that are not so if done by a tenant in common. But I do not think it therefore follows, that no dealing with the thing by one of two tenants in common, that does not amount to a total annihilation of it (if that be possible), can be a conversion as against his co-tenant. It may be that the co-tenant may, if he think fit, follow the thing, and make title to it, notwithstanding its sale and delivery to a third person. But it does not follow, that, where one tenant in common has dealt with the subject to an extent exceeding his authority, — as, where he sells out and out to a number of purchasers, who carry away the articles, — it would militate against the true understanding of the older authorities to hold that the party may treat that as a conversion."

Cresswell J, at p 250 said:

"The property may be so entirely changed by other means than destruction or sale in market overt, as to give a right of action."

The fourth Judge, V Williams J thought the true rule to be that the sale of a chattel by one of two joint tenants is not a conversion unless it operates altogether to deprive his companion of his property in it.

I am of opinion that the sale by the Coleman company was a conversion. Mr Harvey's right to possession with his co-owner was effectively taken away from him. The purchasers are unknown and whether the silver has been used or not its identification must have become quite impossible. It is not known whether it was sold in ingots or in some other form. From the point of view of the plaintiff it might just as well have been destroyed — his title to the property has effectively disappeared.

I am further of opinion that the limitation on the right of a co-owner to bring an action for conversion upon the sale of commonly owned goods by another owner save where the right of property is lost ought no longer to be sustained. It rests upon an historical basis not now consonant with the requirements of society or of justice. Population growth, increased industrialisation, the ease of transport, and the very increase in the variety of tangible goods all indicate that if the circumstances in which one co-owner may sue another in conversion are limited in the way suggested in many of the earlier cases he will, as often as not, have no remedy at all.

I would dismiss the appeal.

Appeal dismissed.

The Winkfield

[1902] P 42 (CA).

COLLINS M. R. This is an appeal from the order of Sir Francis Jeune dismissing a motion made on behalf of the Postmaster-General in the case of *The Winkfield*.

The question arises out of a collision which occurred on April 5, 1900, between the steamship *Mexican* and the steamship *Winkfield*, and which resulted in the loss of the former with a portion of the mails which she was carrying at the time.

The owners of the *Winkfield* under a decree limiting liability to 32,514*l*. 17*s*. 10*d*. paid that amount into court, and the claim in question was one by the Postmaster-General on behalf of himself and the Postmasters-General of Cape Colony and Natal to recover out of that sum the value of letters, parcels, &c., in his custody as bailee and lost on board the *Mexican*.

The case was dealt with by all parties in the Court below as a claim by a bailee who was under no liability to his bailor for the loss in question, as to which it was admitted that the authority of *Claridge* v. *South Staffordshire Tramway Co.* was conclusive, and the President accordingly, without argument and in deference to that authority, dismissed the claim. The Postmaster-General now appeals.

The question for decision, therefore, is whether *Claridge's Case* was well decided.

For the reasons which I am about to state I am of opinion that *Claridge's Case* was wrongly decided, and that the law is that in an action against a stranger for loss of goods caused by his negligence, the bailee in possession can recover the value of the goods, although he would have had a good answer to an action by the bailor for damages for the loss of the thing bailed.

It seems to me that the position, that possession is good against a wrongdoer and that the latter cannot set up the just tertii unless he claims under it, is well established in our law, and really concludes this case against the respondents. As I shall shew presently, a long series of authorities establishes this in actions of trover and trespass at the suit of a possessor. And the principle being the same, it follows that he can equally recover the whole value of the goods in an action on the case for their loss through the tortious conduct of the defendant. I think it involves this also, that the wrongdoer who is not defending under the title of the bailor is quite unconcerned with what the rights are between the bailor and bailee, and must treat the possessor as the owner of the goods for all purposes quite irrespective of the rights and obligations as between him and the bailor.

It cannot be denied that since the case of *Armory* v. *Delamirie* , not to mention earlier cases from the Year Books onward, a mere finder may recover against a wrongdoer the full value of the thing converted. That decision involves the principle that as between possessor and wrongdoer the presumption of law is, in the words of Lord Campbell in *Jeffries* v. *Great Western Ry. Co.*, "that the person who has possession has the property." In the same case he says:

> "I am of opinion that the law is that a person possessed of goods as his property has a good title as against every stranger, and that one who takes them from him, having no title in himself, is a wrongdoer, and cannot defend himself by shewing that there was title in some third person, for *against a wrongdoer possession is title*. The law is so stated by the very learned annotator in his note to *Wilbraham* v. *Snow*."

Therefore it is not open to the defendant, being a wrongdoer, to inquire into the nature or limitation of the possessor's right, and unless it is competent for him to do so the question of his relation to, or liability towards, the true owner cannot come into the discussion at all; and, therefore, as between those two parties full damages have to be paid without any further inquiry.

But, if this be the fact in the case of a finder, why should it not be equally the fact in the case of a bailee? Why, as against a wrongdoer, should the nature of the plaintiff's interest in the thing converted be any more relevant to the inquiry, and therefore admissible in evidence, than in the case of a finder? It seems to me that neither in one case nor the other ought it to be competent for the defendant to go into evidence on that matter.

But long after the decision of *Coggs* v. *Bernard*, which classified the obligations of bailees, the bailee has, nevertheless, been allowed to recover full damages against a wrongdoer, where the facts would have afforded a complete answer for him against his bailor. The cases above cited are instances of this. In each of them the bailee would have had a good answer to an action by his bailor; for in none of them was it suggested that the act of the wrongdoer was traceable to negligence on the part of the bailee.

As between bailee and stranger possession gives title—that is, not a limited interest, but absolute and complete ownership, and he is entitled to receive back a complete equivalent for the whole loss or deterioration of the thing itself. As between bailor and bailee the real interests of each must be inquired into, and, as the bailee has to account for the thing bailed, so he must account for that which has become its equivalent and now represents it. What he has received above his own interest he has received to the use of his bailor. The wrongdoer, having once paid full damages to the bailee, has an answer to any action by the bailor. See Com. Dig. Trespass B. 4, citing Roll. 551, 1. 31, 569, 1. 22, Story on Bailments, 9th ed. s. 352, and the numerous authorities there cited.

Appeal allowed.

Notes and Questions

1. For two recent District Court cases see *Brennan* v *SIMU Motor Services* [1988] DCR 34; *Sharp* v *Redan Motors* [1989] DCR 1.

2. Let us go back to the problem of A's fur coat. First assume that *she* booked the table in the restaurant, and is paying for a dinner party of eight as it is her husband's fortieth birthday. Is that relevant? What would be the result? Now assume she went to the cocktail bar for a quick drink with her boyfriend, after work. He pays for one round of drinks. They get up to leave and the theft is discovered. What would be the result?

3. A is driving from Auckland to Taupo, pulling the family caravan. The caravan breaks an axle at Taupiri. A walks to B's garage. B drives him back to the caravan to examine it, at A's request. B tells A the caravan will need to be taken to his garage for closer inspection. A asks B to arrange for this to be done and for B to phone him in Auckland with an estimate of the cost of repairs. A agrees to pay the cost of the removal and inspection. B phones A the following day with an estimate of the repair costs. A thinks it is very high, and tells B he will get a second opinion before he makes up his mind. One week later he has not been able to arrange for this to be done. Sometime during the week the caravan is stolen from B's yard. What would be the result? What if A said at the time of B's phone call, 'The quote is too high—I will collect the caravan.' A is not able to get down to Taupiri for a week and again, sometime during that week, the caravan is stolen. What would be the result? What if any other evidence would you need to address these problems?

Exclusion Clauses

Samuel Smith v Silverman

[1961] OR 648 (CA).

SCHROEDER J. A. (orally): — This is an appeal from a judgment of His Honour Judge Weaver, pronounced in the First Division Court of the County of York, on October 18, 1960, whereby he awarded the plaintiff company the sum of $174.30 and costs to compensate it for damage to its Cadillac motor car. On the evening of November 7, 1959, the vehicle was in the custody of its secretary-treasurer, one Irving Paul Sussman. The latter and his wife, accompanied by two friends, were attending a theatre and he parked the motor vehicle on the premises of the defendant parking company at 237 Victoria St. for which he paid a charge of 50c. After the theatre performance was over Sussman applied for delivery of the motor car and, finding no one on the premises he drove it away. Shortly afterwards he discovered that while it was in the custody and control of the defendant, it had been damaged to the extent indicated.

It is conceded by counsel for the appellant that this is a true case of bailment since Sussman had been requested by the parking attendant to leave the keys in the motor car in order that it could be driven as required to a suitable place on the lot. It was therefore received into the custody of the defendant and a contract of bailment for reward has been made out. At the time of the delivery of the car to the defendant's servant Sussman was given a parking ticket containing the following terms:

"WE ARE NOT RESPONSIBLE FOR THEFT OR DAMAGE OF CAR OR CONTENTS HOWEVER CAUSED."

These terms are spelled out in bold black type and in letters large enough to dispel any suggestion of an attempt on the part of the defendant to conceal the limiting conditions from the recipient. Had the defendant looked at this ticket he could not possibly have failed to see the terms quoted.

Counsel for the appellant admits that the plaintiff having proved that its motor car was damaged while in the care and custody of the defendant, it made out a *prima facie* case, subject to any special conditions in the contract, limiting or relieving the appellant from his common law liability. At the trial no attempt was made to show how or when the loss or damage in question occurred, and apart from such conditions, the plaintiff would be entitled to succeed. It is well settled that a custodian may limit or relieve himself from his common law liability by special conditions in the contract, but such conditions will be strictly construed and they will not be held to exempt the bailee from responsibility for losses due to his negligence unless the words of limitation are clear and adequate for the purpose or there is no other liability to which they can apply: *Can. Steamship Lines* v. *The King*, [1952], 2 D.L.R. 786 at p. 793, A.C. 192 at pp. 207-8.

In *Olley v. Marlborough Court Ltd.*, [1949] 1 All E.R. 127, Lord Justice Denning stated at p. 134:

People who rely on a contract to exempt themselves from their common law liability must prove that contract strictly. Not only must the terms of the contract be clearly proved but also the intention to create legal relations—the intention to be legally bound—must also be clearly proved. The best way of proving it is by a written document signed by the party to be bound. Another way is by handing him before or at the time of the contract, a written notice, specifying certain terms and making it clear to him that the contract is in those terms. A prominent public notice which is plain for him to see when he makes the contract would, no doubt, have the same effect, but nothing short of one of these three ways will suffice.

The learned trial Judge accepted the evidence of the plaintiff to the effect that he had not parked a car on this property before. He testified that he had not seen any signs erected on the premises, and that he had not read the conditions set out on the parking ticket which he had been given at the time the contract was made. There was evidence given on behalf of the defendant by the defendant's manager who stated that there were four signs erected on the defendant's lot, two of them at the front near the Victoria St. entrance, and the other two on the rear parking lot. They were at a height of approximately 8 to 10 ft. from the ground, 2½ by 3 ft. in dimension, and contained the following words:

" WE ARE NOT RESPONSIBLE FOR THEFT OR DAMAGE OF CAR OR CONTENTS HOWEVER CAUSED."

The learned Judge accepted this evidence. He found as a fact that there were signs on the lot in the four places indicated, which were lighted at the time in question, and which bore the words set out above. The point to which the Court should address itself in a case where the defendant relies upon signs of this nature is clearly stated in the judgment of Baron Alderson in the old case of *Walker et al. v. Jackson* (1842), 10 M. & W. 160, 152 E.R. 424, from which I quote at p. 173:

> The acts proved by the plaintiffs, upon which they relied to substantiate the existence of a contract, were those done with respect to persons bringing carriages. These notices were stuck up in the way for foot passengers, and it appeared that the plaintiff did not go by that way; neither was it shewn that any person with a carriage ever went by it. No reasonable probability, therefore, existed that the plaintiff, or any parties going with carriages, ever saw them.

It may well be that if the defendant were forced to rely solely upon the limiting conditions set out on the parking ticket given to the plaintiff's agent, the reasoning in *Spooner v. Starkman* and in *Appleton et al v. Ritchie Taxi* might prevail against his defence. Here, however, notice of the limiting condition was also provided in four prominently displayed signs, two of which were placed near the entrance of Victoria St., which any reasonably attentive person should have seen.

In *Brown v. Toronto Auto Parks Ltd.*, [1955] 2 D.L.R. 525, O.W.N. 456, this Court had to consider a defence based on limiting conditions contained on signs displayed on the custodian's premises. Laidlaw, J.A., delivering the judgment of the Court there stated [p. 527 D.L.R., p. 457 O.W.N.]:

In the instant case we are all satisfied that the signs displayed by the appellant were displayed with such prominence and in such a way that the respondent ought to have seen them and ought to have had knowledge of what was on the signs. We think that a person exercising reasonable care and diligence would have seen those signs and in particular he would have seen, first, that there was an attendant—the words were "Attendant in charge", and that the car and contents were left at the owner's risk. But the appellant did not satisfy the learned trial Judge, nor has it satisfied this Court, that the loss sustained by the respondent did not happen in consequence of the appellant's breach of its duty to use such care and diligence as a prudent and careful man would exercise in relation to his own property. It has not discharged the onus of proof resting in law on it as a bailee for valuable consideration.

It was held that the exculpatory signs did not assist the defendant, for while the plaintiff should reasonably have seen them, the words "car and contents at owner's risk" did not suffice clearly to relieve the defendant for liability for negligence. The Court applied the strict rule of construction to which I have referred and supported the judgment for the plaintiff on that ground alone.

The words printed on the ticket and the signs in question are not susceptible of this criticism. The clear declaration that the defendant was not to be responsible for theft or damage of car or contents *however caused*, is sufficiently broad in its terms to extend to a case where the damage occurred through the negligence either of the defendant or his servants or the negligence or carelessness of a third party whether lawfully on the premises or not.

The learned trial Judge made no finding as to whether the defendant took reasonable measures to bring to the attention of the plaintiff's agent the notice limiting its liability as custodian for hire. He considered it sufficient that the plaintiff had not seen the signs, a point as to which he had only the plaintiff's evidence. He gave no consideration to the contention that the limiting condition was binding upon the plaintiff's agent if he ought reasonably to have seen it either on the parking ticket, or on the signs, or on both. As I see it, the defendant did what was reasonable to bring the terms limiting his liability to the attention of customers and prospective customers and the plaintiff is fixed with the knowledge that its agent ought reasonably to have had. The Court is bound, in these circumstances, to give effect to the limiting conditions in the contract. The appeal is therefore allowed, the judgment at trial set aside, and the action dismissed with costs, fixed at $15 and disbursements. The defendant shall also have the costs of the appeal fixed at $25 and disbursements.

Appeal allowed.

Note

1. For a useful article see Samuels, Car Parks and Garage Mishaps (1900) 121 Sol J 364.

Statutory Modifications of Liability

There are a number of statutes in New Zealand and elsewhere which modify the common law rules in various ways.

American Express v British Airways

[1983] 1 All E R 557.

LLOYD J. In this case the plaintiffs, American Express Co and American Express International Banking Corp, sue the defendants, British Airways Board, for loss of a postal packet containing travellers cheques. The face value of the travellers cheques was $US40,000. The defendants admit the loss, but say that they are protected by s 29(3) of the Post Office Act 1969. Section 29(3) provides:

> 'No person engaged in or about the carriage of mail and no officer, servant, agent or sub-contractor of such person shall be subject except at the suit of the Post Office to any civil liability for any loss or damage in the case of which liability of the Post Office therefor is excluded by subsection (1) of this section.'

Section 29(1) provides:

> 'Save as provided by the next following section, no proceedings in tort shall lie against the Post Office in respect of any loss or damage suffered by any person by reason of—(a) anything done or omitted to be done in relation to anything in the post or omission to carry out arrangements for the collection of anything to be conveyed by post . . .'

The 'next following section' referred to in s 29(1) is s 30. Section 30 imposes a limited liability on the Post Office in respect of registered *inland* packets, and is of no relevance on the facts of this case.

Thus the sole question is whether if the Post Office had been sued in this case the proceedings would have been proceedings in tort, within the meaning of s 29(1) and, if so, whether the defendants can take advantage of the vicarious immunity provided by s 29(3).

The facts are set out in an agreed statement of fact. They are briefly as follows. On 22 February 1978 the plaintiffs handed over a postal packet containing the travellers cheques to the Post Office in Brighton. I need not distinguish between the first and second named plaintiffs. The packet was addressed to the Standard Bank in Swaziland. On 22 or 23 February the Post Office tendered the packet in a sealed airmail bag to the defendants at Heathrow for carriage to Johannesburg and onward carriage to Swaziland. The defendants employed a man called Osborne as a loader at Heathrow. In the course of loading the aircraft, Osborne stole the packet. It was never recovered. Two years later, in February 1980, Osborne pleaded guilty at the Old Bailey to theft contrary to s 1 of the Theft Act 1968. Two other men employed with Osborne as loaders at Heathrow pleaded guilty to charges of handling.

The facts are thus extremely simple. As to the law, I was told that the case raised questions of great importance and would undoubtedly be taken all the way to the House of Lords if necessary. A large number of authorities, English and American, were cited. At the end of it all, it seems to me that the law on the point is almost as simple as the facts.

The first point taken by counsel on behalf of the plaintiffs is that though the plaintiffs could undoubtedly have sued in tort for conversion, and been met by a defence under s 29(3), they are in fact suing for breach of bailment. Nothing in s 29(1) excludes liability for breach of bailment, as distinct from liability in tort. Accordingly, the defendants are not entitled to vicarious immunity under s 29(3).

Counsel for the plaintiffs referred me to a number of famous cases, including *The Winkfield* [1902] P 42, [1900-3] All ER Rep 346, in order to establish the proposition that the Post Office were bailees of the package and the defendants sub-bailees. But that proposition was conceded by counsel for the defendants at the outset. Counsel for the defendants further conceded that the defendants owed the same duty to the plaintiffs as if they were bailees for reward.

Next, counsel for the plaintiffs referred me to Professor Sir Percy Winfield's book on *The Province of the Law of Tort* (1931) and the judgment of Lord Denning MR in *Building and Civil Engineeering Holidays Scheme Management Ltd v Post Office* [1965] 1 All ER 163, [1966] 1 QB 247, in order to establish that an action in bailment is something separate and distinct from an action in tort or contract.

In the *Building and Civil Engineering Case* [1965] 1 All ER 163 at 167, [1966] 1 QB 247 at 261 Lord Denning MR said:

'An action against a bailee can often be put, not as an action in contract, nor in tort, but as an action on its own, sui generis, arising out of the possession had by the bailee of the goods.'

and then Lord Denning MR referred to *Winfield on the Province of the Law of Tort* p 100 and *Fifoot's History of the Common Law* (1949) p 24.

Again, there was not much dispute about that proposition.

The real dispute in the case is whether, granted that an action in bailment is sui generis, proceedings in bailment against the Post Office are nevertheless excluded by s 29(1) of the 1969 Act. Counsel for the plaintiffs submitted that this is still an open question and should be answered in favour of the plaintiffs. I cannot agree.

In *Triefus & Co Ltd v Post Office* [1957] 2 All ER 387, [1957] 2 QB 352 two postal packets containing diamonds were stolen by an employee of the Post Office. The plaintiffs, who were the owners of the two packets, claimed against the Post Office, inter alia, for breach of contract of carriage and breach of bailment. According to the statement of facts (see [1957] 2 QB 352 at 353), the plaintiffs alleged in their pleadings that on two dates—

'they had handed to the Post Office at Hatton Garden two postal packets containing diamonds valued at £3,380 and £17,998 respectively, for carriage and transmission to New Zealand, the packets being properly packed, secured, registered, declared, and in all respects in accordance with the appropriate Post Office regulations, all proper dues, charges and duties thereon being paid; that the Post Office had accepted the packets and thereby entered into contracts of carriage, or alternatively of bailment, with the company, the terms of which included, inter alia, that they would act reasonably in connection with the carriage and transmission, use care and diligence, employ only adequate post officers, carry and transmit the packets by an efficient and appropriate system, and not lose the packets. They alleged that the Post Office were in breach of each of those terms, whereby the packets had been mislaid or stolen, and that they had thereby suffered loss or damage.'

The Court of Appeal held on a preliminary question of law that the action must fail on the ground stated by Lord Mansfield in *Whitfield v Lord le Despencer* (1778) 2 Cowp 754, 98 ER 1344. Both Hodson and Parker LJJ referred to s 9 of the Crown Proceedings Act 1947, which is the lineal predecessor of s 29 and which, like s 29, excluded liability in tort. Parker LJ said ([1957] 2 All ER 387 at 394, [1957] 2 QB 352 at 368):

'It is true that that section is clearly dealing with tort; but, for myself, I find it inconceivable that if Parliament thought that there was any doubt as to the contractual position (or, rather, the absence of a contract) it would not clearly have been dealt with in the Act.'

Adopting the same language, it seems to me inconceivable that if Parliament thought there was any doubt as to the possible liability of the Post Office in bailment, as distinct from tort, it would not have been dealt with in the 1969 Act.

To my mind it would make nonsense of s 29 of the 1969 Act to hold that the Post Office can be liable for breach of bailment. As explained by Diplock LJ in *Morris v C W Martin & Sons Ltd* [1965] 2 All ER 725, [1966] 1 QB 716, the two most obvious duties arising out of the relationship of bailor and bailee are the duties on the part of the bailee (1) to take reasonable care of the goods and (2) not to convert them. Both negligence and conversion are, of course, typical torts. The advantage to the plaintiff in laying his action in bailment is that it shifts the burden of proof. It is for the bailee to explain how the loss occurred. In that sense the plaintiff's task is easier in bailment, the defendant's more difficult. It would be a curious result if Parliament had, by s 29(1), given the Post Office full protection in negligence and conversion where, as defendants, their task is easier, but not in bailment where, for the reaons I have just mentioned, their task is more difficult.

Furthermore, by s 30 Parliament has imposed on the Post Office, as I have already mentioned, a limited liability in respect of loss or damage of registered inland packets. It would be an even more curious result it if had left the Post Office subject to unlimited liability in the case of all other post, by allowing the plaintiff to adopt the simple expedient of suing in bailment.

In *Harold Stephen & Co Ltd v Post Office* [1978] 1 All ER 939, [1977] 1 WLR 1172 the plaintiff brought an action in detinue or bailment claiming delivery up of their mail, which had been detained by Post Office workers in pursuance of an industrial dispute. They asked the court to grant a mandatory injunction. The court refused the mandatory injunction as a matter of discretion. In the course of his judgment Lord Denning MR referred to s 9 of the Post Office Act as well as s 29, and continued ([1978] 1 All ER 939 at 942, [1977] 1 WLR 1172 at 1177):

'Counsel for the plaintiffs suggested that those exceptions were so unreasonable and so wide that it would be well if the courts could find a way round it. He hoped that we might do it by reason of an action in detinue or an action in bailment whereby these companies here could say, "You have my letters, they are addressed to me, they are mine, you are holding them up, deliver them to me". He said that the sections did not exclude an action of detinue such as that. I would like to think that that may be so, but I would not like to pronounce on it finally today. It is too difficult a subject-matter.'

However, at the very end of his judgment in the same case Lord Denning Mr said ([1978] 1 All ER 939 at 943, [1977] 1 WLR 1172 at 1179):

'Although one has the greatest sympathy with the plaintiffs (the companies) in the most injurious situation in which they have been placed, and although one would like to help them if one possibly could, it seems to me that the courts probably have no jurisdiction in view of the statute.'

Geoffrey Lane LJ started his judgment as follows ([1978] 1 All ER 939 at 944, [1977] 1 WLR 1172 at 1179-1180):

'I agree. I do not propose to consider the liability in bailment (as opposed to contract or tort) of the Post Office to any particular member of the public who may have suffered damage due to the actions of the Post Office employees, save to say that liability in bailment, if it were to exist, would seem to render largely meaningless s 29 of the Post Office Act 1969.'

I respectfully adopt what was said by Geoffrey Lane LJ in that case.

I need not explore the first submission of counsel for the plaintiffs any further, because in the end he decided not to develop the argument to its full extent, preferring to reserve the matter for a higher court.

Notes

The most important New Zealand statutes are as follows:

The Carriage of Goods Act 1979

This statute applies to 'carriers'. Under section 2 this means a person who, in the ordinary course of his business, carries or procures to be carried, goods owned by any other person, whether or not as an incident of the carriage of passengers. 'A contract of carriage' means 'a contract for the carriage of goods'. 'Goods' means 'goods, baggage, and chattels of any description; and includes animals and plants; and also includes money, documents, and all things of value . . .'.

Under section 6 of the Act, notwithstanding any rule of law to the contrary,

no carrier shall be liable as such, whether in tort or otherwise, and whether personally or vicariously, for the loss of or damage to any goods carried by him except—(a) in accordance with the terms of the contract of carriage and the provisions of the Act; or (b) where he intentionally causes the loss or damage.

This Act affects the inordinately heavy burden on carriers under the common law. A common carrier was for all effective purposes an insurer of his customer's goods. (See *Coggs v Bernard, supra*).

Section 8 of the Act provides for particular kinds of contracts of carriage: 'at owners' risk', 'at limited carriers' risk'; 'at declared value risk', 'on declared terms'. The liability of the carrier depends upon the class of contract. Under section 7 of the Act however, parties to a contract of carriage are free to make their own contract. The liability of the carrier thus depends either upon the contract of carriage itself or the provisions of the Act and the various classes of carriage described above.

Under section 12 of the Act a carrier is not liable as such, with respect to baggage that is left in his custody pending his acceptance of it for carriage, or pending its collection from him after the completion of the carriage.

Under section 16 of the Act every employee of a carrier who, in the course of his employment, intentionally causes the loss of or damage to any goods being carried by the carrier shall be liable to the owner of the goods for that loss or damage.

There are provisions in the Act relating to proceedings against carriers. Notice must be given to the carrier (see section 18) within 30 days 'after the date on which, in accordance with section 9 of the Act, the carrier's liability for the goods ceased.'

The statute is an important one, regulating as it does day to day transactions relating to the carriage of goods in New Zealand.

Securitas v *Cadbury Schweppes Hudson (CA)*

[1988] 1 NZLR 340

The judgment of the Court was delivered by

Cooke P. This is an appeal from a decision of Hardie Boys J giving judgment against a security firm (Securitas) for $53,428 and interest. The case arose out of the theft of the payroll of the plaintiff company (Cadburys) when a security guard employed by Securitas was carrying a suitcase containing banknotes amounting to the sum mentioned into the office of Cadburys in Castle Street, Dunedin. The robber was masked by a balaclava and carried a shotgun, with which he threatened the guard, and at no stage has any criticism been made of the guard's conduct in submitting and handing over the suitcase. The robber escaped in a car which he had parked at the side of the street nearby, only a short distance from the Securitas car in which the guard transported the suitcase from a bank; the Securitas car had been double-parked by the guard outside the Cadburys building; the robber's car may have been parked first.

An eye-witness of part of the episode was an employee of Cadburys who gave the following account in her evidence:

"I just stood there and watched for a minute and saw the security man get out and went to Cadburys quite fast and the door swing shut behind him. Looking at the photo, that is the door there, on the left hand side. I was just about to go and take the biscuits out and there was a movement beside me, on the left hand side. I turned around and this man was getting out of the car with a balaclava and a gun in his hand. I sort of just thought I was seeing things for a minute so I watched [what] was happening, he ran to the door and I yelled out, Hey what are you doing, he sort of looked back and kept on running and I thought how rude. I waited till he came out to see where he was going. I saw him come out. He had the bag the Securitas man had just taken in. I just stood there and said to him, hey are you for real? Then he came to where the car was and he stopped about two feet from me. I just looked at him and said, you haven't really robbed the place, have you? I asked him if it was a dummy run for security or something, as it seemed so unreal. I waited for someone to say hey, this is a hoax, but no one came. I kept on asking, are you for real? A man came down the alleyway and I thought perhaps he was in on this too. I asked if he was and he said, perhaps it is a capping stunt. He didn't get into the car till I turned my back on him. He engaged my eyes. He just stared at me, he never answered, never said a word which was quite annoying really. He didn't run, he just looked at me. This person I spoke to who came out the alleyway was a Post Office employee which I subsequently found out. Turning back to him, he was getting in the car and the other man had carried on up the stairs so I was there alone wondering what it was about. He turned the car around, I thought in case of an accident I wrote the number of the car down on my hand. I remembered about three or four bits. AA5517, something like that. Going back this, I actually took the biscuits to the staff shop and I sat down and couldn't believe this had all happened and my knees were shaking and I said, I just saw someone rob the place. I said if it was a dummy run, I thought it was a bit stupid as it would scare people so they rang up and asked what was happening and bundled upstairs and they asked me alot of questions. I saw the gun. It was quite a fine gun, like an air rifle only thicker, not a big thick gun. I am pretty sure it was a single barrel shot gun. When he came outside, he came along it with the gun by his side sort of thing. That is when I was talking to him. When he went into Cadburys—he just ran in there with the gun beside him. As to how he was, he seemed more scared than I was I think. I wondered why he stood there and stared at me and didn't do anything. It was for two, three minutes I engaged him in conversation."

The Judge held that on the occasion in question Securitas was not a common carrier but simply a bailee for reward and had failed to disprove negligence. He also rejected an argument to the effect that, even as regards negligence by Securitas, Cadburys was its own insurer. He dealt with other points also, but most of these did not arise if he was correct on those three.

The points about negligence and insurance can be disposed of quite briefly. As to negligence, the respect in which it is in issue whether Securitas fell short, and it is the only respect, is that only one man was employed in this particular operation on that day, not two. The evidence was that Securitas normally allotted one man to the Cadburys payroll collection, which was a regular weekly one, but sometimes two men. It is not certain from the evidence why there was that variation, but counsel for Securitas invited us to infer that two were used when an armoured vehicle was used, that being the normal crew for such a vehicle, whereas one only was used for the ordinary kind of car that was used normally and on this day for the Cadburys work. Be that as it may, it is clear that the contract with Cadburys left Securitas to decide how many employees to assign to the operation.

It is accepted for Securitas that, if not a common carrier, it was a bailee for reward and bore the onus of showing that it was more probable than not that the employment of two guards would have made no difference. In agreement with Hardie Boys J we cannot regard that onus as discharged. The presence of a second guard could well have deterred the robber, especially perhaps if the second man had remained in the double-parked car keeping his colleague under observation and able to move his car so as to block the robber's escape by vehicle or be able to follow. The evidence of the employee who tried to speak to the robber tends to underline this, as does the evidence that in general two guards are desirable in operation of cash conveyance through the streets.

As to insurance, the argument rests on the fact that in 1976 correspondence Securitas offered to take out "all risks" insurance covering Cadburys (and the same offer was made to their other clients), the charge for the cover being three cents per $100 carried. Cadburys replied that they did not need this cover as they were already protected under their existing policy. In agreement again with the Judge we see nothing in this that could be enough to exempt Securitas from liability for negligence. Obviously the insurers of Cadburys would be unlikely to approve of such an arrangement, and there is no indication that either Cadburys or Securitas had it in mind that the correspondence could have had that effect. The mere reference to "all risks" insurance, which would of course cover much more than losses due to negligence, does not give rise to an implication in the wording of the correspondence that exclusion of negligence liability on the part of Securitas was contemplated; and no such implication is necessary to give business efficacy to the correspondence. We mention the latter conclusion without deciding that the correspondence amounted to a contract; it would hold good whether or not the correspondence had any contractual effect.

The more substantial point is whether Securitas was acting as a common carrier, in which event it contends that its liability was limited by the Carriers Act 1948 to $40. The arrangements were that early in the working day each Thursday a Securitas vehicle would go to the Cadburys office. Inside the office a locked suitcase containing a cheque for the wages would be handed to a Securitas representative. He would have no key to the case. Securitas would then take the case by vehicle to the bank, only a few minutes away, and inside the bank a teller, who did hold a key, would unlock the case, take out the cheque and replace it with the necessary notes. He would relock the case. The vehicle would then be driven back to Castle Street and inside the Cadburys office the Securitas representative would deliver the locked case to the pay clerk, who would give Securitas a receipt. It is not in dispute that Securitas knew that the case would or could contain sums of the order of $50,000 or that occasionally the guard who saw the money being put together or produced by the teller would know the actual sum.

Whether a person is a common carrier is a mixed question of fact and law. The leading New Zealand case on the subject is the decision of this Court in *Geering v Stewart Transport Ltd* [1967] NZLR 802. References were made in the judgments there to the judgment of F B Adams J in *Drinkrow v Hammond and McIntyre Ltd* [1954] NZLR 442. Those references are of an approving character, at least as to some of the statements of law in *Drinkrow*; it was not necessary in *Geering*, nor is it necessary in this case, to approve or disapprove of the application of the law to the particular facts in *Drinkrow*. In both *Geering* and *Drinkrow* it was found that the carrier was a common carrier and so liable for loss of or damage to the goods without negligence. A convenient general statement of the law is to be found in the judgment of Turner J in *Geering* at p 810:

> "He who professes to carry goods for all indifferently, for charges in which no distinction is made between one person and another, is a common carrier of such goods, with certain privileges and exemptions from liability, and certain liabilities,

recognised by the law. A person who, as regards the generality of his transactions, is a common carrier, may, as regards any particular transaction, enter into such a special arrangement with his bailor as will remove him, as regards that particular transaction, from the class of common carriers. Whether in any case this has been done or not is a question of mixed law and fact, to be decided on the evidence in the particular case."

For the purposes of the present case it should be added that a carrier may limit his activities to goods of a certain kind without necessarily precluding his being classified as a common carrier. Mr Atkinson put it to us that the essential question is whether you deal indiscriminately with the public; we accept that approach and also his proposition that everything required to be done, and in fact done, by Securitas here can be described literally as carriage. Part of it was carriage by road, within the scope of licences held by Securitas under the Transport Act 1962. The rest, including the stages involving most security risks (taking the suitcase out of the bank to the vehicle and from the vehicle to Cadburys at the other end), was literally carriage otherwise than by road. It was a comprehensive service.

Such a service could still be common carriage, but what in our opinion is of decisive significance here is the degree of individualisation in the arrangements with customers. Mr Perkinson, the national operations manager of the company, said in evidence-in-chief, among other things:

"As to limiting our class of customers — that was more a marketing decision rather than operation decision and I would have to say there was. In the things we did carry, we carried on for special persons we had contracts with in the main."

Hardie Boys J found that individual long-term contracts were the norm; Mr Atkinson rightly commented in the course of his argument that with the kind of service provided by Securitas this was virtually inevitable. The service here was under a continuing contract evidenced by a Securitas document dated February 1977 and accurately headed Contract of Performance of Security Services. It is instructive to note the following passages in a Securitas brochure put in evidence:

"The Security Industry is very positive about its own security measures and performance standards. While the Government enforces strict regulations before granting licences, the industry itself maintains tight control through the NZSIA (Security Industry Association). All recognised security firms have membership and their services must meet very high standards for them to retain this status. Securitas, formed in 1962, is a foundation member of the N.Z. Security Industry Association (NZSIA) and is licensed in accordance with stringent Government regulations."

(The legislation referred to is the Private Investigators and Security Guards Act 1974; it is not challenged that the necessary licences were held thereunder.)

"Although there are common factors in all security situations, each individual case calls for its own combination of risk management techniques. No one solution is automatically watertight for every client. The first stage in or evaluation of your needs is an in-depth analysis of your problems. This booklet has been prepared to detail for you the scope and specifics of our security service. It is not a catalogue of ready-made protection packages, but a guide to the skills we can bring to bear on your problem. Your security solution is a job for our Security Consultant."

In the present case the evidence is not specific as to what inspections or negotiations took place before the modus operandi already described was settled on; but it is a reasonable inference that the particular circumstances and requirements of Cadburys would have been individually studied. The Securitas charge was a modest one — apparently only about $5 a week at the material time — but its modesty must have reflected an assessment by Securitas that the particular weekly operation was a relatively short and simple one. There is no evidence of any general scale of charges for security services: the presence or absence of this is relevant to the common carrier issue, though not decisive.

The evidence is virtually all one way that in respect of its security services Securitas normally and in this case acted under individualised long-term contracts or arrangements with regular clients, on terms worked out according to the individual cases. As to this kind of work we are satisfied that Hardie Boys J was at the very least entitled to find that Securitas was not a common carrier. It may even be that any other finding would not have been open on the evidence.

The transport licensing aspect calls for further reference. The licences held by Securitas certainly entitled and perhaps required the company to act as a common carrier. They are a factor to be taken into account in deciding whether it was doing so on the occasion in question. In the absence of any other evidence they might warrant an affirmative conclusion. In other words, they are relevant but not decisive. We understood Mr Atkinson in his opening argument to put the matter in that way. It is how, reading their judgments as a whole, we understand that all the Judges in *Geering* and *Drinkrow* saw it. See in *Drinkrow* [1954] NZLR Adams J at p 450 and in *Geering* [1967] NZLR Turner J at pp 810-812, McCarthy J at p 817, McGregor J at p 818. At one point in his reply Mr Atkinson sought to treat the licences as conclusive, at any rate in the context of this case, but we think that is to go too far. In such general carrying business as it may have undertaken Securitas may have been a common carrier and the term of the licences would help that conclusion; but the security services, which were undoubtedly the main ones, call for consideration on their own. As to them the terms of the licences cannot overide the distinctive features of the business as actually conducted, on which we have already dwelt.

It is as well to mention also that the provisions of the Transport Act and licences thereunder may be less important in a case such as the present where the relevant and more critical phases of the total operation do not occur during carriage by road; but this point was not argued and we have not explored it and disregard it for the purposes of this decision.

In summary the essence of our decision is that security services, not merely specialised but individualised, in many ways the very antithesis of common carriage, are at the heart of this case.

In the result we affirm the conclusion of Hardie Boys J on the three main points and no other point requires decision except one as to interest. The Judge awarded interest at 11% per annum from 20 April 1979, the date of the robbery. Having regard to the observations in the judgment of the Privy Council in *Takaro Properties Ltd v Rowling* [1987] 2 NZLR 700, 718-719, it is appropriate to amend the award to 7.5% until 31 March 1980 and 11% thereafter. There is nothing in the facts of the present case to cause us to alter the Judge's discretionary award in any other way.

Subject to that amendment, the appeal must be dismissed. In the circumstances certain points raised by a notice of cross-appeal need not be decided in this Court and Mr Marquet accepts that the proper course is to dismiss the cross-appeal as we do.

The respondent will have costs in the sum of $2000, together with the reasonable travelling and accommodation expenses of counsel, to be settled by the Registrar.

Appeal dismissed.

New Zealand Railways Corporation Act 1981

Section 18 of this statute makes the provisions of the Carriage of Goods Act 1979, so far as they are applicable, apply with respect to the receipt, custody, carriage and delivery of goods under this Act. The Act contains (in section 20) power to sell goods left by an unknown owner, and the Corporation has wide powers to act as a forwarding agent (section 21); and to retain goods for unpaid customs duty (section 22) as well as its powers to operate as a Railways Corporation.

Carriage by Air Act 1967

This statute gives effect to a Convention concerning international carriage by air known as the Warsaw Convention. Again, it creates limitations of liability (section 10) on air carriers. Part 2 of the Act relating to domestic carriage by air covers that subject matter, including such matters as the liability of the carrier for death or injury, and for delay.

The Pawnbrokers Act 1908

A pledge (or pawn) occurs when a borrower (or pledgor) delivers personal property to a bailee (the lender or pledgee) to be held as security for a loan made to the bailor. The nature of the transaction is that the property pledged is held by the lender until the debt is paid according to the terms of the contract between the parties. The whole transaction is a specialized kind of bailment, by way of security.

There is a difference between a pledge and between a real property mortgage and a lien. Only personal property which is capable of delivery can be pledged; in the case of a mortgage the mortgagee does not, under the Torrens system, normally have possession of the mortgage property. A lien on the other hand is the right of somebody who is in possession of chattels to retain possession of those chattels until some claim against the owner of them is satisfied.

The Pawnbrokers Act 1908 requires pawnbrokers to be licensed; makes provision for the recording of transactions, and regulates such a business in various ways. In particular, under section 23 of the Act no articles pledged to a pawnbroker shall be sold until the expiration of three months in the case of wearing apparel and six months in any other case from the time of the pledging of same. Under section 24 of the Act the chattels are 'forfeited, and may be sold' (section 24(1)).

For the purposes of the Act, a pawnbroker is defined as 'a person carrying on business by advancing on interest, or for or in expectation of profit, gain, or reward, any sum of money on security (whether collateral or otherwise) of any article taken by such person by way of pawn, pledge, or security' (section 2). See also the Credit Contracts Act 1981.

The Innkeepers Act 1962

This statute affects the relationship between guests and hotels or inns. These last are statutorily defined as meaning:

> any house or place whose proprietor or licencee holds out, to the extent of his available accommodation, that he will provide, without special contract, sleeping accommodation for any traveller presenting himself who appears able and willing to pay a reasonable sum for the services and facilities provided and is in a fit state to be received . . .

Under section 4 an innkeeper is liable as such for the loss of or damage to property brought to the inn by any guest whether or not the loss or damage was caused by the default or negligence of another guest or of the innkeeper or his servant or agent. However, under section 6 an innkeeper is not liable for the loss of or damage to the property of a guest if he proves that the loss or damage was caused by the default, neglect or wilful act of the guest or servant of or person accompanying the guest, or by an act of God or of the Queen's enemies. Likewise, if the guest had assumed exclusive charge and custody of the property or the room in which the property was at the time of the loss or damage so as to show an intention to relieve the innkeeper from all responsibility. Under section 7 an innkeeper is not liable for the loss of or damage to any vehicle or any property left therein or with respect to any animal. The innkeeper's liability is restricted to $300 in respect of any one article, or $1200 in the aggregate unless the guest can prove that the property was stolen lost or damaged through the default, neglect or wilful act of the innkeeper or his servant or the property was deposited for safe custody. The innkeeper, under section 9, cannot contract out of his liability under the Act. Innkeepers are given certain powers of distraint and seizure with respect to the goods of guests where debts are incurred or goods are unclaimed.

Conclusion

It will be observed that the progress of the law of bailment has mirrored that in so many other areas of property law. That is, starting from a relatively uniform and undifferentiated proposition—which made persons carrying on a number of activities affecting the property of other persons close to insurers—the common law greatly moderated that requirement, and the legislature intervened in a number of areas of human activity to further modify the liability of carriers, innkeepers and persons acting as pawnbrokers. There has also been a desire on the part of legislatures world-wide to protect unsuspecting consumers or relatively unsophisticated parties from falling foul of larger organizations utilizing standard form contracts. In this respect there has been an alliance between the courts and the legislature in an apparent desire to protect consumers from overbearing and unfair conduct. At this point bailment law shades into consumer law. However, the tension between commerce and consumer is an enduring one and achieving the 'right balance' is no easy task.

7

Alienation of Personal Property

How does personal property pass from one person to another, in law? In the case of land there is, in New Zealand, a relatively sophisticated conveyancing system which records the transaction. The transfer takes place by operation of law, and at a time prescribed by the Land Transfer Act. There are, in the common law world, some systems for recording the ownership and transfer of chattels. Torrens developed the idea for his land system from a registry system for ships in the United Kingdom. Canada is currently investigating a registration and transfer system for the thousands of private aircraft in that country. There are true title systems for motor vehicles in a number of jurisdictions in the United States. But nowhere in the common law world are there *generalized* title registry schemes for personal property.

Methods of alienation of personal property

There are, functionally, five ways in which personal property passes from one person to another:
1. under the law of succession, on death;
2. by operation of law;
3. by altering the legal capacity in which the present owner holds the property;
4. by *inter vivos* gift;
5. by sale.

Alienation under succession law

Personal propety may be left to another person by will. The formalities required are the same as for any other item of property. Likewise, if a person dies without leaving a will, that person's personal property passes to the administrator, and devolves according to the Administration Act. But as we have seen, there is some debate as to whether some of the newer kinds of property are inheritable.

Alienation by operation of law

Personal property may be taken in execution under a judgment of a court of competent jurisdiction. Or, it may pass to an Official Assignee in bankruptcy.

In such instances the personal property passes by virtue of some statutory provision, and operation of law.

Alienation by an alteration in the capacity of the holder

Sometimes the capacity in which personal property is held changes. The best example concerns the law of trusts.

Assume X owns painting Y. She may decide that she now wishes to hold that painting in trust for her favourite niece Z. She can declare herself to be the trustee of that painting for Z. X is now the legal owner. Z is the beneficial (and 'real' owner) of the painting. X holds Y for Z, and has effectively divested herself of the painting. There is more difficulty with the case where X wishes to transfer Y to A (a professional trustee company) to hold Y for Z as beneficiary. In such a case, as you will study closely in Equity, the gift to A must be 'complete' if Z is to be able to enforce the beneficial interest. (Why should this be so? See *Milroy v Lord* (1862) 4 De G F & J 264; 45 ER 1145; *Re Rose* [1952] Ch 499).

Another instance of change of capacity is where the sole owner of an item of personal property becomes a part owner. In such a case the transaction will usually involve a sale or gift of a part interest to a third party.

Alienation by way of inter vivos gift

Here we are concerned not with the passing of property on death, but whilst a person is alive. A (while alive) gratuitously transfers X to B with the intention that X shall thenceforth 'belong' to B.

There are three ways of making a gift. First, by deed or other writing. Secondly, by delivery to the recipient with the requisite intent. Thirdly, by making a declaration of trust with respect to the relevant property. (See Halsbury, *Laws of England*, Vol 20, 'Gifts', para. 1).

The first and third methods cause little difficulty in practice, and are usually carefully recorded in Deeds of Gift or Trust, by solicitors. Where difficulties arise it is normally because of poor draftsmanship; for instance, the subject matter of the gift may be ambiguous.

The second category, perhaps because it is attended with less formality, has given rise to many reported cases.

In Re Moore

(1908) 27 NZLR 261 (CA).

WILLIAMS, J.: —

 * * * In *Cochrane v. Moore* (1) the question was as to the gift of a chattel of which delivery had not been given to the donee, and it was held that, as there was no delivery, there was no completed gift. As was said by Sir F. Pollock (*Law Quarterly Review* 1890, page 450), the judgments delivered by the Court of Appeal in *Cochrane v. Moore* do not deny that a parol gift may be perfected by subsequent delivery or authorised entry into possession by the donee. In the present case the donee

had authority to collect moneys due to her father, and, according to her own account, was told by him to keep the moneys she so received as her own. If this be so, the gift of any sum would, in my opinion, be complete when she received and appropriated that sum as her own. If there is an intention to make a gift, and the subject of the gift comes into possession of the donee in the manner contemplated by and in accordance with such intention, there is a complete gift. The test is whether, looking at the nature of the property, anything remains to be done by the donor to vest the property in the donee, or, in other words, whether the donor can get back the property without the concurrence of the donee: *Milroy v. Lord; Standing v. Bowring; Re Griffin, Griffin v. Griffin; Re Smith, Bull v. Smith.* That test is satisfied with the property now in question. ✳ ✳ ✳

Williams v Williams

[1956] NZLR 970

NORTH J. The plaintiff is eighteen years of age and is the youngest of three children of the marriage of the defendant and his wife, Zelmar Iris Williams. Either before the plaintiff's birth or shortly after, the defendant purchased a "Williams" pianola which was installed in the family home. The instrument in question was originally capable of being used either as a pianola or as a piano. The plaintiff's eldest brother learnt to play the drums and the second brother the piano accordion, and their father purchased and gave them instruments for this purpose. Apparently the father could not play the piano but he enjoyed operating the pianola. When the plaintiff was about eleven years of age he received piano lessons and these continued for several years. The plaintiff says, and I accept his evidence, that his father told him shortly after he had commenced lessons that if he applied himself to his lessons he would in due course be given the pianola. The plaintiff says that later, when he had continued his tuition for some time, his father expressed satisfaction with his progress and told him that the pianola was his. The evidence of the plaintiff was corroborated by other members of the family and by an outside friend, and having heard the whole of the evidence I am satisfied that the father did tell his son that he could regard the pianola as his own property. There was the usual dispute as to the actual language used, and there were discrepancies in the evidence called for the plaintiff as to the exact words used by the father, but, as I have said, I am satisfied that the father did express a present intention to make a gift of the pianola to his son. The intention to make a gift was repeated on a number of occasions, generally when members of the family were in the kitchen. It was not claimed that on any of these occasions the defendant was in proximity to the pianola when the promise was made. About eight years ago some of the tubes in the pianola were broken and it appears from the mother's evidence that there were many discussions about having these repaired, the father always promising that he would get them repaired, but, in fact, nothing was done. Thus for the last eight years the instrument could only be used as a piano and the only person in the home capable of using it as such was the plaintiff.

The fact that there was from time to time a discussion about the repair of the pianola, however, suggests that the father still had in mind using the pianola as he had done in the past. In April, 1955, the wife left the home alleging that the defendant had been guilty of persistent cruelty to her, and it appears that on May 11, 1955, she obtained separation and maintenance orders against the defendant on this ground. The plaintiff continued to live in the house with his father for about two months, but he left the home at the time the mother brought proceedings to obtain a vesting order of the tenancy of the matrimonial home. He took this course because his sympathies lay with his mother and he proposed to give evidence on her behalf. When the son left he removed his own personal belongings but made no effort to remove the pianola, giving as his reason that he had nowhere to store it. On June 22, 1955, the mother obtained the vesting order she sought and in due course became entitled to assert her right to occupy the family home. The father then sent the furniture and the pianola to an auction mart, and the furniture has been sold but the pianola remains at the auction mart.

The cases show that in order that there should be a valid gift of a chattel inter vivos three things are necessary. First, the expression of the intention of the donor to make a gift, secondly, the assent of the donee to the gift, and thirdly, the actual or constructive delivery of the chattel to the donee. In my opinion the first two requirements have been satisfied for, while the plaintiff did not in terms say that he accepted his father's offer of the pianola, the plain inference from his evidence is that he did. In these circumstances the sole question which falls for consideration is whether there was actual or constructive delivery of the pianola by the father to the son sufficient to constitute a gift.

The leading case on the subject is *Irons* v. *Smallpiece*, (1819) 2 B. & Ald. 551; 106 E.R. 467, which decided that a gift of a chattel capable of delivery made *per verba de praesenti* by a donor to a donee whose consent is communicated to the donor does not pass the property in the chattel without delivery. The early cases are fully reviewed in *Cochrane* v. *Moore*, (1890) 25 Q.B.D. 57, and it will be sufficient to say that for a time the decision in *Irons* v. *Smallpiece*, while not overruled, had, as it has been put, "been hit hard by the subsequent cases". In 1890, however, *Cochrane* v. *Moore* came before Lord Esher M.R. and Bowen and Fry L.JJ., and the authority of *Irons* v. *Smallpiece* was re-established in clear and definite terms. In these circumstances, the only question which remains open is what constitutes delivery or constructive delivery in the special circumstances of particular cases.

There have been cases, both in England and in Canada, none of them of binding authority, where the Court has been called upon to consider, as in the present case, the legal possession of chattels purported to be given by a father to his child or by a husband to his wife where the chattels have remained in the family home. I have read these cases, and I am inclined to think with respect that in some of them at all events the observations of Lord Esher M.R. in *Cochrane* v. *Moore*, (1890) 25 Q.B.D. 57, were lost sight of. Lord Esher said:

> Upon long consideration, I have come to the conclusion that actual delivery in the case of a 'gift' is more than evidence of the existence of the proposition of law which constitutes a gift, and I have come to the conclusion that it is a part of the proposition itself. It is one of the facts which constitute the proposition that a gift has been made. It is not a piece of evidence to prove the existence of the proposition: it is a necessary

part of the proposition, and, as such, is one of the facts to be proved by evidence (*ibid.*, 75).

This essential ingredient in the constitution of a valid gift was again referred to by Lord Esher M.R. in the Court of Appeal in *Bashall* v. *Bashall*, (1894) 11 T.L.R. 152. That case concerned an action brought by a wife against her husband to recover certain articles which she said had been given to her by her husband during the marriage, the principal articles being a pony and trap, a saddle and a dog. In that case the Master of the Rolls said:

It was clear law that in order to pass property in chattels by way of gift mere words were not sufficient, but there must be a delivery. And this requirement was as essential in a case of husband and wife as in the case of two strangers. But a difficulty arose when they came to consider how a husband was to deliver a chattel to his wife so as to pass the property in it. The difficulty arose, not from the legal relation between them, but from the fact of their living together. When a husband wished to make a present of jewellery to his wife, he generally gave it into her own hands, and then it was easy to see that there was a delivery. But in the case of a horse or a carriage, that would not be so. In such a case it was true the husband might wish to make an absolute gift to his wife, but, on the other hand, he might wish to keep the horse or carriage as his own property and merely to let his wife have the use of it. In an action by the wife it was necessary for her to show that *the husband had done that which amounted* to a delivery (the italics are mine) (*ibid.*, 152-153).

In *Rawlinson* v. *Mort*, (1905) 93 L.T. 555, Bray J. was able to find a valid gift of an organ which had been loaned to a Church. The donor went to the Church with the donee (who was the organist) and put his hand on the organ using words which showed an intention to give delivery. This Bray J held was sufficient. But, of course, in that case the organ was in the physical possession of the Trustees of the Church and therefore that case on the facts is clearly distinguishable from the present case. Again, in *Kilpin* v. *Ratley*, [1892] 1 Q.B. 582, the husband Ratley had assigned all his furniture to his wife's father for valuable consideration, the furniture remaining in the dwelling occupied by Ratley and his wife. After the assignment the wife's father visited the dwelling in the husband's absence and pointing to the furniture in the room said to her: "I give you this furniture; "It will be something for you." He then left and returned to his own home. A creditor of the husband subsequently issued execution against the furniture. Hawkins J. said:

"The only objection that has been raised is that the gift was not completed by delivery of the furniture. I think that there was a sufficient delivery. The test of that is, was possession given and taken under the gift? I can see little more which Purser" [the father] "could have done to complete the gift. He seems to have come over from Nottingham to take possession of the furniture which had become his property by virtue of the assignment, and which, if it remained in Ratley's possession up to that time, remained in his hands only as being bailee for Purser. Purser's action was first to give the furniture to the claimant, and then to leave her in the room with the furniture and to go back to Nottingham" (*ibid.*, 584).

That case therefore is also clearly distinguishable for the reason that the donor was not in occupation of the premises where the chattels were, and on the facts of the case the Judge was able to hold that delivery had been made.

In the recent case of *Hislop* v. *Hislop*, [1950] W.N. 124, the Court of Appeal was concerned with the question of a gift of furniture by a husband to his wife before marriage while cohabiting with her. The case turned substantially on the question of whether the furniture remained in the apparent possession of the husband and so was available on a levy of execution on the furniture. At the conclusion of his judgment Sir Raymond Evershed M.R. (as he then was) said: "for unless delivery of the furniture to the second wife could be shown there had been no transfer of the title of the furniture to her: *Cochrane* v. *Moore*, (1890) 25 Q.B.D. 57. Here there had been no delivery". I conclude then that the line of authority still requires that even in the case of a gift to a member of the donor's family, there must be evidence of some overt act on the part of the donor which can be treated as evidence of delivery of the subject of the gift to the donee.

The present case in its essentials is very similar to the South Australian case of *Flinn* v. *White*, [1950] S.A.S.R. 195, and I agree with respect with the observations of Abbott J. in that case "that the mere circumstance that the plaintiff had exclusive use of the piano is insufficient to import custody of it" (*ibid.*, 202); and, as in that case, I find myself regretfully unable to see anything in the evidence in the present case which would provide any reasonable indication of a transfer of possession from the defendant to the plaintiff. I have carefully considered the whole of the evidence and in my view all that can be said is that the defendant declared his present intention to make a gift and from then on the pianola still remained in the possession and control of the defendant, the plaintiff in the meantime having the right as a member of the family to use the instrument as and when he pleased. If, for example, the defendant had given his son the key to the pianola (if it in fact possessed a key) that might well have been sufficient to establish constructive delivery. Again, if the defendant had gone through the ceremony of placing his hand on the pianola at the time of his declaration, then again I might have been tempted to have found this circumstance sufficient to constitute delivery. But none of these things happened and I must accordingly hold that the property in the chattel did not pass to the plaintiff.

Judgment must therefore be for the defendant, but in all the circumstances I am not prepared to allow him any costs.

Judgment for the defendant.

Rawlinson v Mort

(1904-05) 21 TLR 774 (KB)

Mr. Justice Bray read the following judgment: — This action was brought in substance to try the question as to whether an organ, then at St. Luke's mission church, Gravesend, belonged to the plaintiff; and I will consider this question before I deal with the form of the action and the parties. The facts were very little in dispute, and I find them to be as follows: — In 1897 there was in the parish of St. James's, Gravesend, a mission church or chapel at ease, known as St. Luke's Church, the freehold of which was vested in trustees upon certain trusts contained in a deed poll dated February 20, 1891, with the object of ensuring its being used subject to the direction of the incumbent of the parish for public worship under the licence of the Bishop of the diocese. Two persons were annually appointed to perform the duties of churchwardens of the church, and were called sometimes churchwardens and sometimes co-treasurers. They were not, of course, the churchwardens of the parish, and they only acted as churchwardens in reference to this church. In 1897 an organ was wanted for the church, and a Mr. Copelin, one of the then churchwardens or co-treasurers, came forward and offered to buy one and have it placed in the church; but he stated that he would only lend it, and that it was to remain his property. He accordingly bought an organ and had it erected in the church, and paid the whole cost of it, and received from Mr. Briggs, the then vicar of the parish, a letter evidencing the fact that the organ was only lent and that it remained his property. It appeared that there had been some promise that Mr. Copelin should receive £5 a year as rent, but it was not so stated in the letter and no rent was ever paid. The plaintiff became organist in 1899 and continued as such till Easter, 1902. Shortly after Easter, 1901, Mr Copelin called on the plaintiff at his rooms (not in the church), and told him that he had been thoroughly satisfied with his playing and thought he ought to have a reward, and as such he would like to offer him the organ. The plaintiff accepted the offer, and Mr. Copelin then produced and handed to him the said letter of Mr. Briggs, and the three receipts which he held for the payments he had made to the organ builder. I find that his intention was to make a present gift to the plaintiff of the organ, and that he handed him the letter and receipts as evidence or indicia of title. On a subsequent occasion, soon afterwards, the plaintiff was playing the organ at the church after service, and Mr. Copelin, in the presence of his son and the plaintiff, said to a Mr. Hedger (who had been for the previous year, but was not then, a churchwarden), putting his hand on the organ, "I have given" or "I give this to Walter" meaning the plaintiff, to which Mr. Hedger replied, "I am very glad to hear it." I find that his intention in doing this was to further complete the gift by delivery, or what he thought to be a delivery, to the plaintiff. Both before and after this the plaintiff, as organist, had the control and use of the organ, and held the key. At Easter, 1902, the plaintiff ceased to be organist, and the organ remained in the church, and was used as before for the church services. In April, 1903, the plaintiff heard that it was proposed to remove the organ from the church, and wrote to the vicar objecting and claiming the £5 rent. This led to negotiation and correspondence, which ended by the vicar repudiating the plaintiff's claim to the organ. On these facts it was contended by the plaintiff's counsel — (1) that what took place at the plaintiff's rooms constituted a complete and valid gift; and (2) that if it was not completed then, it was completed by delivery at the church. These contentions were denied by the defendants' counsel, and he took the further point that during all this time the actual possession was by virtue of the loan in the church authorities, whoever they might be, and not in the plaintiff, and that, having regard to that fact, Mr. Copelin could not give possession, and that a deed was necessary to make a valid gift. I should have felt a good deal of doubt as to this last point but for the case of "Kilpin v. Ratley" (1892, 1 Q.B., 582). In that case the owner of the goods had entrusted them to the plaintiff's husband, and they were in his possession when the owner, in the husband's absence, purported to give them to the wife, and it was held that this was a valid gift to the wife, although there was no evidence that the husband assented to or even had notice of the gift. I think this case virtually decides this point. There is nothing in "Cochrane v. Moore" (25 Q.B.D., 57) inconsistent with this, and the Court expressly declined to decide as to what was necessary where the possession at the time of the gift was in a third party. It remains to consider the points raised by the plaintiff's counsel. In "Chaplin v. Rogers" (1 East, 192), where the question was whether there had been a delivery to satisfy the Statute of Frauds, Lord Kenyon says: — "Where goods are ponderous, and incapable, as here, of being handed over from one to another, there need not be an actual delivery; but it may be done by that which is tantamount, such as the delivery of the key of a warehouse in which the goods are lodged, or by delivery of other indicia of property." I think delivery of a box can be given by handing over the key. Symbolical delivery may be actual delivery. The key was already in the plaintiff's possession, and I think the handing over of the documents evidencing the owner's title, or, as stated in "Chaplin v. Rogers," of the indicia of the property, is symbolical delivery and equivalent to actual delivery, at all events where manual delivery is practically impossible. It was not the intention of the donor or the donee that the organ should be removed from the church, and real manual delivery was impossible under these circumstances. In my opinion, there was a valid completed gift at the plaintiff's rooms. I am, however, of opinion that, if the gift was not completed then, it was completed at the church. I have found that by putting his hand on the organ and using the words (whichever they were) Mr. Copelin intended to give delivery, and I think that delivery can be made in this way when manual delivery is impossible. In "Cochrane v. Moore" the learned Judges confined their decision to cases where the article was capable of delivery. If the organ was under the circumstances capable of delivery, I think it was delivered. If it was not, I think there was symbolical delivery which was the nearest approach to delivery that could be made. I will now consider the form of the action and the parties. The action was an action of detinue to which a claim for a declaration was added, and the defendants were the vicar and the churchwardens of the parish. There was a possible difficulty in the claim for detention, because the vicar alleged that he did not detain, and no demand was made on the churchwardens: but, inasmuch as the vicar clearly repudiated the plaintiff's title, I think the action was properly brought against him for the declaration. Then, as to the churchwardens, the goods in the church were, in my opinion, technically in the possession of the vicar and churchwardens of the parish. I think, therefore, that the churchwardens were properly joined as defendants in an action where the plaintiff claimed a declaration that the organ was his. If they had appeared and merely submitted themselves to the judgment of the Court it may be that they would have been entitled to their costs, but they did not take this course; they joined with the vicar in denying the plaintiff's title. I think this disentitles them to costs, but I will not order them to pay costs. It was argued for the defendants that the trustees were the proper persons to be made defendants. In my opinion, this is not so, the organ was not affixed to the freehold, and they were not in possession of it, and it was never lent to them. My judgment must be against the defendants for a declaration that the organ is the property of the plaintiff, and the vicar must be ordered to pay the plaintiff's costs.

Pavlicic v Vogtsberger

(1957) 390 Pa 502; 136 A 2d 127

MUSMANNO, Justice.

George J. Pavlicic has sued Sara Jane Mills for the recovery of gifts which he presented to her in anticipation of a marriage which never saw the bridal veil. At the time of the engagement George Pavlicic was thrice the age of Sara Jane. In the controversy which has followed, Pavlicic says that it was Sara Jane who asked him for his hand, whereas Sara Jane maintains that Pavlicic, following immemorial custom, offered marriage to her. We are satisfied from a study of the record that it was Sara Jane who took the initiative in proposing matrimony — and, as it will develop, the proposal was more consonant with an approach to the bargaining counter than to the wedding altar.

George Pavlicic testified that when Sara Jane broached the subject of holy wedlock, he demurred on the ground that he was too old for her. She replied that the difference in their ages was inconsequential so long as he was "good to her." Furthermore, she said that she no longer was interested in "young fellows" — she had already been married to a young man and their matrimonial bark had split on the rocks of divorce. Hence, she preferred an older man. George qualified. He was 75. Sara Jane was 26.

The May-December romance began on a very practical footing in April, 1949, when Sara Jane borrowed from George the sum of $5,000 with which to buy a house, giving him a mortgage of the premises. In three and one-half years she had paid back only $449 on the mortgage. On the night of November 21, 1952, she visited George at his home and advanced the not illogical proposition that since they were to be married, there was no point in their having debts against the other and that, therefore, he should wipe out the mortgage he held on her home, George said to her: "If you marry me, I will take the mortgage off." She said: "Yes," and so he promised to satisfy the mortgage the next day. To make certain that there would be no slip between the promise and the deed, Sara Jane remained at George's home that night; and on the following morning drove him in her automobile to the office of the attorney who was to make, and did make, arrangements for the satisfaction of the mortgage.

Being enriched to the extent of $4,551 by this transaction, Sara Jane expatiated on another rational thesis, namely, that since they were going to be married and would be riding around together she should have a better car than the dilapidated Kaiser she was driving. She struck home with her argument by pointing out that in a new car he would not fall out, for it appears this was an actual possibility when he rode in her worn-out Kaiser. Thus, without any tarrying, she drove George from the Recorder of Deed's Office, where she and the mortgage had been satisfied, to several automobile marts and finally wound up at a Ford agency.

Here she selected a 1953 Ford which she said would meet her needs and keep him inside the car. George made a down payment of $70 and on the following day he gave her $800 more, the latter taken from his safety deposit box. Still later he handed her a check for $1,350, obtained from a building and loan association—and Sara Jane had her new car.

Less than a year later, Sara Jane complained that her feet got wet in the Ford and she proposed the purchase of an Oldsmobile. She explained that by trading in the Ford, which she characterized as a "lemon", she would need only $1,700 to acquire the Oldsmobile. George was not adverse to transportation which would keep his future wife's feet dry, but he said that since they were to be man and wife, and he apparently was paying for all the bills, it might be more businesslike if title to the car were placed in his name. This suggestion, according to George's testimony at the trial, made Sara Jane "mad" and he practically apologized for being so bold and inconsiderate as to ask title to an automobile which he was buying with his own money. Accordingly he withdrew his suggestion, said: "All right," and made out a check in Sara Jane's name for $1,700. And thus Sara Jane got her new Oldsmobile.

In January, 1953, in the enthusiastic spirit of an anxious swain, George presented Sara Jane with a $140 wrist watch. Sara Jane selected the watch.

In February, 1953, Sara Jane represented to George that they would both make a better appearance if she had an engagement and wedding ring. George took her to a jewelry store and she made a selection consistent with discretion. George paid $800.

Sara Jane then asked George to take care of the repairing of a ring she had received from her mother. It was a mere matter of adding a diamond. George paid the bill.

Even before George's bank book became Sara Jane's favorite literature she had prevailed upon him to advance substantial sums to her. In June, 1952, she told George she needed $800 to cover her house with insulbrick. George gave her $800 to cover her house with insulbrick.

It is not to be said, however, that Sara Jane was completely lacking in affectionate ante-nuptial reciprocity. In June, 1953, she bought George a wedding ring for him to wear. She conferred upon him at the same time a couple of woollen shirts. There is no way of learning how much the ring and shirts cost because she did not take George into her confidence or into the store where she purchased the items.

George testified that when he wore the wedding ring people laughed and asked him when he was to be married. He replied: "Pretty soon." He tried to live up to the prediction and asked Sara Jane for the wedding date. She said she could not name the month. In view of what was to develop, she could have added with truth that she could not name the year either.

In October, 1953, Sara Jane expounded to George the economic wisdom of purchasing a business which would earn for them a livelihood in his old and her young age. She suggested the saloon business. George agreed it was a good idea. She contacted a saloon-selling agent and George accompanied her to various saloons which the agent wished to sell. Georege was impressed with one saloon called the "Melody Bar", but the price was above him. Sara Jane then said that if he would give her $5,000 she would buy a cheap saloon outside of Pittsburgh. George gave her $5,000. And Sara Jane disappeared—with the $5,000.

The next time she was heard from, she was in Greensburg operating Ruby's Bar—with George's $5,000. From Ruby's Bar she proceeded to the nuptial bower where she married Edward Dale Mills. Although she had many times assured George she would marry him because she liked the idea of an old man, the man she then actually married was scarcely a contender for Methuselah's record. He was only 26—two years younger than Sara Jane.

When George emerged from the mists and fogs of his disappointment and disillusionment he brought an action in equity praying that the satisfaction of the mortgage on Sara Jane's property be stricken from the record, that she be ordered to return the gifts which had not been consumed, and pay back the moneys which she had gotten from him under a false promise to marry. Sara Jane filed an Answer and the case came on for trial before Judge Marshall of the Allegheny County Court of Common Pleas. Judge Marshall granted all the plaintiff's prayers and entered a decree from which the defendant has appealed to this Court.

The defendant urges upon us the proposition that the Act of June 22, 1935, P.L. 450, 48 P.S. §171, popularly known as the "Heart Balm Act," outlaws the plaintiff's action. This is the first time that the Act of 1935 has come before this Court for interpretation and ruling. Although the Act contains several sections, the heart of it lies in the first sentence, namely, "All causes of action for breach of contract to marry are hereby abolished."

There is nothing in that statement or in any of the provisions of the Act which touches contracts subsidiary to the actual marriage compact. The Act in no way discharges obligations based upon a fulfillment of the marriage contract. It in no way alters the law of conditional gifts. A gift given by a man to a woman on condition that she embark on the sea of matrimony with him is no different from a gift based on the condition that the donee sail on any other sea. If, after receiving the provisional gift, the donee refuses to leave the harbor,—if the anchor of contractual performance sticks in the sands of irresolution and procrastination— the gift must be restored to the donor. *A fortiori* would this be true when the donee not only refuses to sail with the donor, but, on the contrary, walks up the gangplank of another ship arm in arm with the donor's rival.

The title to the gifts which Sara Jane received, predicated on the assurance of marriage with George, never left George and could not leave him until the marital knot was tied. It would appear from all the evidence that the knot was fully formed and loosely awaiting the ultimate pull which would take title in the gifts from George to Sara Jane, but the final tug never occurred and the knot fell apart, with the gifts legally falling back into the domain of the brideless George.

The appellant in her argument before this Court would want to make of the Act of June 22, 1935, a device to perpetuate one of the very vices the Act was designed to prevent. The Act was passed to avert the perpetration of fraud by adventurers and adventuresses in the realm of heartland. To allow Sara Jane to retain the money and property which she got from George by dangling before him the grapes of matrimony which she never intended to let him pluck would be to place a premium on trickery, cunning, and duplicitous dealing. It would be to make a mockery of the law enacted by the Legislature in that very field of happy and unhappy hunting.

The Act of 1935 aimed at exaggerated and fictional claims of mortification and anguish purportedly attendant upon a breach of promise to marry. The legislation was made necessary because of the widespread abuse of the vehicle of a breach of promise suit to compel overly-apprehensive and naive defendants into making settlements in order to avoid the embarrassing and lurid notoriety which accompanied litigation of that character. The legislation was intended to ward off injustices and incongruities which often occurred when, by the mere filing of breach of promise suits innocent defendants became unregenerate scoundrels and tarnished plaintiffs became paragons of lofty sensibility and moral impeccability. It was not unusual in threatened breach of promise suits that the defendant preferred to buy his peace through a monetary settlement rather than be vindicated by a trial which might leave his good name in shreds.

There is no doubt that in the history of romance a nation could be populated with the lovers and sweethearts (young and old) who have experienced genuine pain and agony because of the defection of their opposites who promised marriage and then absconded. Perhaps there should be a way to compensate these disillusioned souls, but it had been demonstrated that the action of breach of promise had been so misemployed, had given rise to such monumental deceptions, and had encouraged blackmail on such a scale, that the Legislature of Pennsylvania, acting in behalf of all the people, concluded that the evil of abuse exceeded to such an extent the occasional legitimate benefit conferred by a breach of promise suit that good government dictated its abolition.

Thus the law of 1935 prohibited, but prohibited only the suing for damages based on contused feelings, sentimental bruises, wounded pride, untoward embarrassment, social humiliation, and all types of mental and emotional suffering presumably arising from a broken marital promise. The Act did not in any way ban actions resulting from a tangible loss due to the breach of a legal contract. It could never be supposed that the Act of 1935 intended to throw a cloak of immunity over a 26-year old woman who lays a snare for a 75-year old man and continues to bait him for four or five years so that she can obtain valuable gifts and money from him under a false promise of marriage.

George Pavlicic is not asking for damages because of a broken heart or a mortified spirit. He is asking for the return of things which he bestowed with an attached condition precedent, a condition which was never met. In demanding the return of his gifts, George cannot be charged with Indian giving. Although he has reached the Indian summer of his life and now at 80 years of age might, in the usual course of human affairs, be regarded as beyond the marrying age, everyone has the inalienable right under his own constitution as well as that of the United States to marry when he pleases, if and when he finds the woman who will marry him. George Pavlicic believed that he had found that woman in Sara Jane. He testified that he asked her at least 30 times if she would marry him and on each occasion she answered in the affirmative. There is nothing in the law which required him to ask 31 times. But even so, he probably would have continued asking her had she not taken his last $5,000 and decamped to another city. Moreover he had to accept 30 offers of marriage as the limit since she now had married someone else. Of course, mere multiplicity of proposals does not make for certainty of acceptance. The testimony, however, is to the effect that on the occasion of each proposal by George, Sara Jane accepted — accepted not only the proposal but the gift which invariably accompanied it.

The Act of 1935 in no way alters or modifies the law on ante-nuptial conditional gifts as expounded in 28 C.J. 651, and quoted by us with approval in the case of Stanger v. Epler, 382 Pa. 411, 415, 115 A.2d 197, 199, namely:

"A gift to a person to whom the donor is engaged to be married, made in contemplation of marriage, although absolute in form, is conditional; and upon breach of the marriage engagement by the donee the property may be recovered by the donor." See also 38 C.J.S. Gifts §61.

In the case of Ruehling v. Hornung, 98 Pa. Super. 535, 538, the Superior Court quoted with approval from Thornton on Gifts and Advancements as follows:

"If the intended husband makes a present after the treaty of marriage has been negotiated, to his intended wife, and the inducement for the gift is the act of her promise to marry him, if she break off the engagement he may recover from her the value of such present."

As already stated, the Act of 1935 provides that "All causes of action for breach of contract to marry are hereby abolished." This language is as clear as the noonday sun. The appellant would darken it with the eclipse of artificial reasoning. The appellant would want us to read into the statute the provision that "All causes of action *for the recovery of property* based on breach of contract to marry are abolished." The appellant would want the statute to be read: "All actions *resulting from a* breach of contract are abolished." But we cannot so read or so interpret the statute. The abolition is confined to actions *for* breach of contract to marry, that is, the actual fracture of the wedding contract.

It thus follows that a breach of any contract which is not the actual contract for marriage itself, no matter how closely associated with the proposed marriage, is actionable.

After a thorough review of the pleadings, the notes of testimony, the briefs and the lower Court's Opinion, we come to the conclusion that the final decree entered by Judge Marshall is eminently just and in accordance with established principles of law and equity.

Decree affirmed at appellant's costs.

Notes and Questions

1. What are the requirements for a valid gift *inter vivos*, not made by deed or other writing?

2. What would be the legal effect of an expressed intention to make a present gift, but without delivery? See Pollock, Gifts of Chattels Without Delivery (1890) 6 LQR 446.

3. If you say delivery *is* required for a valid gift, what precisely do you mean by that? Assume that A is bedridden, but mentally competent. He says to B: 'I want to give you my shares in Fletcher Challenge. The share certificate is in my strong-box in my study. Here is the key.' B goes and removes the certificate and hands back the key. Is there a gift? Now assume that B takes the key and

holds it, but does not remove the certificate until some weeks later. He then returns the key. What would be the result? Now assume B holds the key until after A's death, and then removes the certificate. What would be the result? Finally, assume A gives the key to C and says that the certificate is a gift for B and asks B to remove it and to give it to B. What would be the result?

4. As to the policy reasons for a delivery requirement, see Meecham, The Requirement of Delivery in Gifts of Chattels (1926) 21 Illinois LR 341, 348-49 who argues that the delivery makes 'concrete' and 'significant' the particular act; the act itself is a witness to the transaction; the fact of delivery provides prima facie evidence. See also Eisenberg, Donative Promises (1979) 47 U Chi LR 1.

5. If you say that *intention* is required, what do you mean by that? Assume that A is a bedridden, but not dying, man. He tells his daughter: 'I buried $4500 in a tin in the vegetable garden. If I die in the next year, its yours. If I don't will you give it back to me?' She says, 'Yes Daddy, I will give it back to you when you get well.' The old man then gives her some further particulars on the location of the tin. What would be the result?

6. In New Zealand, the Domestic Actions Act 1975 now addresses the problem of pre-marriage gifts where the marriage is called off. Under section 5 of the Act, actions for breach of promise to marry are abolished ('no agreement . . . to marry . . . shall be a contract'). The old actions of damages for adultery and 'enticement' of a spouse, which produced some bitter litigation, have been abolished.

Section 8 of the Act provides:

4. Property disputes arising out of agreements to marry—(1) Where the termination of an agreement to marry gives rise to any question between the parties to the agreement, or between one or both of the parties to the agreement and a third party, concerning the title to or possession or disposition of any property, any such party may, in the course of any proceedings or on application made for the purpose, apply to the Court for an order under this section.

(2) Every application under this section shall be made within 12 months of the date of termination of the agreement or within such longer period as the Court may allow.

(3) Subject to subsection (6) of this section, on any such application the Court shall make such orders as it thinks necessary to restore each party to the agreement, and any third party, as closely as practicable to the position that party would have occupied if the agreement had never been made.

(4) In determining the orders to be made on any such application, the Court shall not take into account or attempt to ascertain or apportion responsibility for the termination of the agreement.

(5) In order to give effect to subsection (3) of this section, but without limiting the general power conferred thereby, the Court may, on any such application, notwithstanding that the legal or equitable interests of all parties in any property may be defined, or that a party may have no legal or equitable interest in any property, make orders for—

(a) The sale of all or part of the property and the division or settlement of the proceeds in such shares and upon such terms as it thinks fit:

(b) The partition or division of the property;

(c) The vesting of property owned by one or two parties in two or more parties in common in such shares as it thinks fit:

(d) The conversion of joint ownership into ownership in common in such shares as it thinks fit:

(e) The payment of sums of money by any party to any other party or parties.

(6) Where any property in dispute is a gift from a third party and the Court is satisfied that the third party does not wish the gift to be returned to him, the Court may make such orders with respect to that property as appear just in all the circumstances, but without taking into account or attempting to ascertain or apportion responsibility for the termination of the agreement.

(7) An order made under this section shall be subject to appeal in the same way as an order made by a Magistrate's Court or the Supreme Court in an action in a Magistrate's Court or in the Supreme Court, respectively, would be.

(8) Nothing in this section shall limit or affect the right of any person to bring an action for money had and received.

'Property' is defined in the same terms as in the Property Law Act 1952.

Would the decision in *Pavlicic* have been any different under these provisions?

What would be the results in New Zealand on these facts? (i) A gives B an engagement ring worth $5000. B breaks off the engagement. A applies to have the engagement ring returned to him. (ii) B's sister organizes an engagement party for A and B. Gifts totalling about $5000 in value are received. The engagement is broken off. A and B are unable to agree on a division of the gifts.

7. There are a number of difficult decisions in New Zealand as to what amount to gifts for the purposes of revenue legislation. See eg. *Rossiter v CIR* [1977] 1 NZLR 195.

8. The various presumptions relating to gifts between husband and wife were abolished by the Matrimonial Property Act 1976. And see *Edgar v CIR* [1978] 1 NZLR 590.

9. In New Zealand, a gift of chattels made by Deed should be registered under the Chattels Transfer Act 1924. If it is not, it will be void against the persons mentioned in sections 18 and 19 of that Act.

10. Conditional gifts historically have given rise to difficulty, and need great care. The conditions themselves can be void for uncertainty. See *Re Lockie* [1945] NZLR 230.

11. There have been some problems with land under the Torrens system in New Zealand. Assume A has his solicitor (B) prepare a memorandum of transfer of the land in title X, from himself to C. He signs the transfer, which is in all respects in compliance with the Land Transfer Act, and hands it, but not the certificate of title, to C. Consequently, C does not register. What would be the result? Now assume A hands the memorandum of transfer and title to B, with instructions to register, and to send the title, 'when registered' to C. B has not yet registered. What would be the result? See *Scoones v Galvin* [1934] NZLR 1004; *Kennedy v Tickner* [1950] NZLR 62.

12. In general, equity will not assist a volunteer to complete an incomplete gift. There are three exceptions. First, equitable estoppel. (See *Pascoe v Turner* [1979] 1 WLR 431). Secondly, gifts *donatio mortis causa*. (see note 13, *infra*). Thirdly,

the rule in *Strong* v *Bird* (1874) LR 18 Eq 315. That is, that where the donee made an incomplete gift during his life time, the vesting of the property in the donee in his capacity as trustee or administrator completes the gift. Why should this be so? See also *Re Gonin* [1979] Ch 16, noted (1977) 93 LQR 488.

13. A gift *mortis causa* is one made in the settled expectation of death. The circumstances must show it is to take effect only in the event of death. The gift is not caught by the formalities of wills legislation. The property is recoverable by the donor if death does not occur. The subject matter of the gift must be personal property. The New Zealand commentary to Halsbury suggests that, in New Zealand, 'land cannot be conveyed simply by delivery of the certificate of title'. (C66, Gifts). For New Zealand cases on *donatio* see, *Northcott* v *Public Trustee* [1955] NZLR 694 (valid gift); *Re Huggert* (1914) 33 NZLR 1202 (CA) (invalid gift).

14. The recipient of unsolicited goods can, in some circumstances, be treated as having been given them in New Zealand, see Unsolicited Goods and Services Act 1975, section 3.

Alienation by sale

A can sell B an item of personal property. That is a transaction based on contract. A sale of goods is a specialized branch of the general law of contract. Such a transaction is different from a sale of land. In a sale of land, in New Zealand, the conveyancing (the actual transfer, through the registration mechanism) is preceded by a quite elaborate agreement for sale and purchase, and then a formal registration process. With goods there is no such split function. There is an often hazy agreement, and delivery.

Lord Mansfield was largely instrumental in the eighteenth century in integrating the law merchant and the common law. But our present system of sales law is largely nineteenth century in origin. The culmination was the enactment of the Sale of Goods Act in 1893 by the United Kingdom Parliament. (See Chalmers, Codification of Mercantile Law (1903) 19 LQR 10). Increasingly, however it has become apparent that the nineteenth century statutes do not fit the complex consumer world of the twentieth century. (See Sutton, Reform of the Law of Sales (1969) 7 Alta. L R 130; Lord Diplock, The Law of Contract in the Eighties (1981) 15 UBC LR 371). In the United States, Article Two of the Uniform Commercial Code effected a number of improvements in sales law. That article in turn built upon a Uniform Sales Act which had been prompted largely by the work of Williston. Article Two erased 'excessively refined abstractions from sales law and replaced them with functional solutions to real problems.' (Bridge, *Sale of Goods* (1988) 15. And see Honnold, American Experience under the Sales Article of the Uniform Commercial Code and Gilmore, Commercial Law in the United States; its Codification and Other Misadventures in Ziegel and Foster, *Aspects of Comparative Commercial Law* (1972).

Whatever form sales legislation takes it affects, in one way or another, the property in the goods, and hence the risks attached to those goods. If X orders Y from Z and whilst Y is still in Z's warehouse awaiting shipment it burns, who bears the loss? Questions like these are of everyday importance. Sales legislation is dealt with in detail in commercial law courses. For present purposes it is sufficient to note that the Sale of Goods Act in New Zealand contains quite specific provisions relating to the passing of property. 'Goods' for the purposes of the Act is defined, as including 'all chattels other than money or things in action . . .'. Part II of the Act provides as follows.

Sales of Goods Act 1908

Sections 18-22.

18. Goods must be ascertained — Where there is a contract for the sale of unascertained goods, no property in the goods is transferred to the buyer unless and until the goods are ascertained.

19. Property passes when intended to pass — (1) Where there is a contract for the sale of specific or ascertained goods, the property in them is transferred to the buyer at such time as the parties to the contract intend it to be transferred.

(2) For the purpose of ascertaining the intention of the parties, regard shall be had to the terms of the contract, the conduct of the parties, and the circumstances of the case.

20. Rules for ascertaining intention — Unless a different intention appears, the following are rules for ascertaining the intention of the parties as to the time at which the property in the goods is to pass to the buyer:

Rule 1. Where there is an unconditional contract for the sale of specific goods, in a deliverable state, the property in the goods passes to the buyer when the contract is made, and it is immaterial whether the time of payment or the time of delivery, or both, is postponed.

Rule 2. Where there is a contract for the sale of specific goods, and the seller is bound to do something to the goods for the purpose of putting them into a deliverable state, the property does not pass until such thing is done, and the buyer has notice thereof.

Rule 3. Where there is a contract for the sale of specific goods in a deliverable state, but the seller is bound to weigh, measure, test, or do some other act or thing with reference to the goods for the purpose of ascertaining the price, the property does not pass until such act or thing is done, and the buyer has notice thereof.

Rule 4. Where goods are delivered to the buyer on approval, or "on sale or return" or other similar terms, the property therein passes to the buyer —

(a) When he signifies his approval or acceptance to the seller, or does any other act adopting the transaction:

(b) If he does not signify his approval or acceptance to the seller, but retains the goods without giving notice of rejection then, if a time has been fixed for the return of the goods, on the expiration of such time, and if no time has been fixed, on the expiration of a reasonable time. What is a reasonable time is a question of fact.

Rule 5. (1) Where there is a contract for the sale of unascertained or future goods by description, and goods of that description and in a deliverable state are unconditionally appropriated to the contract, either by the seller with the assent of the buyer or by the buyer with the assent of the seller, the property in the goods thereupon passes to the buyer. Such assent may be expressed or implied, and may be given either before or after the appropriation is made.

(2) Where, in pursuance of the contract, the seller delivers the goods to the buyer, or to a carrier or other bailee (whether named by the buyer or not) for the purpose of transmission to the buyer, and does not reserve the right of disposal, he is deemed to have unconditionally appropriated the goods to the contract.

21. Reservation of right of disposal — (1) Where there is a contract for the sale of specific goods, or where goods are subsequently appropriated to the contract, the seller may, by the terms of the contract or appropriation, reserve the right of disposal of the goods until certain conditions are fulfilled.

(2) In such case, notwithstanding the delivery of the goods to the buyer, or to a carrier or other bailee for the purpose of transmission to the buyer, the property in the goods does not pass to the buyer until the conditions imposed by the seller are fulfilled.

(3) Where goods are shipped, and by the bill of lading the goods are deliverable to the order of the seller or his agent, the seller is prima facie deemed to reserve the right of disposal.

(4) Where the seller of goods draws on the buyer for the price, and transmits the bill of exchange and bill of lading to the buyer together to secure acceptance or payment of the bill of exchange, the buyer is bound to return the bill of lading if he does not honour the bill of exchange, and if he wrongfully retains the bill of lading the property in the goods does not pass to him.

22. Risk prima facie passes with property — (1) Unless otherwise agreed, the goods remain at the seller's risk until the property therein is transferred to the buyer; but when the property therein is transferred to the buyer the goods are at the buyer's risk, whether delivery has been made or not:

Provided that where delivery has been delayed through the fault of either buyer or seller, the goods are at the risk of the party in fault as regards any loss which might not have occurred but for such fault.

(2) Nothing in this section shall affect the duties or liabilities of either seller or buyer as a bailee of the goods of the other party.

Broadlands Finance v Shand Miller

[1976] 2 NZLR 124

QUILLIAM J. This is an appeal from a decision of the Magistrate's Court at Wellington giving judgment for the respondent upon a claim brought by the appellant for possession of certain chattels.

The facts as found by the magistrate are these. A man by the name of Horne called at the respondent's shop early in July 1973 inquiring as to the proposed purchase of some musical instruments. He discussed the question of payment and said he would go and see the appellant company in order to find out whether he could finance the whole purchase through that company. He took with him a letter from the respondent setting out details of the musical instruments concerned.

On 9 July Horne went to the appellant company and, after producing the letter to them, secured an advance of $850. He completed an instrument by way of security for that amount over the goods being purchased. The following day, 10 July, he went back to the respondent and paid them a cheque for $850 in part payment of the purchase price for the musical instruments. The total price was $2,430. He completed a conditional purchase agreement in respect of the goods which acknowledged payment of $850 and provided for payment of the balance which, including interest and other charges, amounted to $1,889. The appellant's instrument by way of security was duly registered within the prescribed time in terms of the Chattels Transfer Act 1924. The respondent's instrument, which it was acknowledged by both parties was not a customary hire purchase agreement, was not registered. The magistrate found as a fact that each party acted bona fide and the neither party was aware of the existence of the other's security.

Almost immediately Horne defaulted under the terms of both securities. Both companies got in touch with him about payment. At the respondent's suggestion Horne handed the instruments back to them to be held by them upon an informal basis until payment of the instalments owing could be arranged. When, therefore, the appellant took steps to seek repossession under its instrument the chattels were in the respondent's possession and the respondent declined to hand them over.

The question before the magistrate was which party was entitled to the chattels.

It is convenient to set out the relevant parts, for present purposes, of the two instruments. The appellant's instrument starts with the words:

"Ernest Charles William Horne . . . (hereinafter called 'the grantor') being the owner or being about to become the owner of the chattels described in the schedule hereto . . .".

Clause 26 of the instrument is as follows:

"That whenever the grantor is not at the time of the making or giving of these presents the owner of the said chattels then this loan is to be expended, in whole or in part, in the purchase of the said chattels".

Clause 2 of the respondent's security provides:

"Until total cost of the transaction and all other moneys which may become payable by the buyer to the seller under this agreement have been paid:
 (a) Property (ownership) in the goods shall not pass to the buyer.
 (b) The buyer shall not damage, alter or deface the goods but shall keep them in good order and repair, fair wear and tear excepted.
 (c) The buyer shall not part with possession of the goods except with the seller's consent.
 (d) The buyer shall notify the seller before removing the goods from the place of installation given above and shall obtain the consent of the seller before removing the goods from New Zealand.
 (e) The buyer shall notify the seller within 24 hours if the goods are seized or taken out of the buyer's possession for any reason whatever, giving full particulars and the address (if known) to which the goods have been removed".

The appellant's security related to goods which were not at the time of execution owned by Horne. The security could only be a valid one, therefore, if it was saved by a statutory provision. It was the appellant's case that it was saved by the proviso to s 24 of the Chattels Transfer Act. Section 24 is as follows:

> "Save as is otherwise expressly provided by this Act, an instrument shall be void to the extent and as against the persons mentioned in sections 18 and 19 hereof in respect of any chattels which the grantor acquires or becomes entitled to after the time of the execution of the instrument:
> "Provided that where an instrument by way of security over any chattels is therein expressed to be given as security for a loan to be expended, in whole or in part, in the purchase of those chattels, the grantor shall be deemed to have acquired the said chattels contemporaneously with the execution of the instrument".

It is necessary to determine first how wide an application the proviso to s 24 has. Read literally it might appear to have a very wide application. I am sure, however, it cannot be construed so, for example, as to apply to goods which the grantor never acquired at all but which he simply described in the instruments. The last portion of the proviso is, I think, to be construed as if it read:

> ". . . the grantor shall be deemed to have acquired the said chattels, *If he acquired them at all*, contemporaneously with the execution of the instrument".

Consideration must, therefore, be given to the effect of the conditional purchase agreement entered into between Horne and the respondent on 10 July.

The agreement itself is in common form and expressly retains to the respondent the ownership of the goods until all payments under it have been made. It was not, however, registered under the Chattels Transfer Act. It was for this reason that the appellant relied on s 19 of that Act, which is as follows:

> "Upon the expiration of the time or extended time for registration no unregistered instrument comprising any chattels whatsoever shall, without express notice, be valid and effectual as against any bona fide purchaser or mortgagee for valuable consideration, or as against any person bona fide selling or dealing with such chattels as auctioneer or dealer or agent in the ordinary course of his business".

For that section to apply the appellant had to show that it was a bona fide mortgagee for valuable consideration. It could not be said to come within any other part of that section. The appellant was certainly bona fide (as the magistrate held), and it also gave valuable consideration. Whether or not it was a mortgagee depends on whether, under the provisions of s 24, Horne is to be deemed to have acquired the goods contemporaneously with execution of the instrument. If he never acquired them at all then the proviso did not come into operation. One therefore returns to the effect upon the transaction between Horne and the respondent of the lack of registration of the conditional purchase agreement.

There is little doubt that the agreement remained perfectly effective as between the parties to it, notwithstanding it was not registered. As between those parties, therefore, Horne never acquired the goods at all. He received them into his possession but I think the word "acquired", as it appears in the proviso, must be taken to refer to ownership and not to mere possession. The argument for the appellant at this stage was that the agreement was, in terms of s 19, void and ineffectual as against the appellant, and that as possession of the goods passed the transaction must be regarded as a sale under which the property also passed. This argument was based upon the provisions of s 20 of the Sale of Goods Act 1908. That section is directly related to s 19 of that Act which provides:

> "(1) Where there is a contract for the sale of specific or ascertained goods, the property in them is transferred to the buyer at such time as the parties to the contract intend it to be transferred.
>
> "(2) For the purpose of ascertaining the intention of the parties, regard shall be had to the terms of the contract, the conduct of the parties, and the circumstances of the case".

The relevant part of s 20, for present purposes, is as follows:

> "Unless a different intention appears, the following are rules for ascertaining the intention of the parties as to the time at which the property in the goods is to pass to the buyer:
>
> "Rule 1. Where there is an unconditional contract for the sale of specific goods, in a deliverable state, the property in the goods passes to the buyer when the contract is made, and it is immaterial whether the time of payment or the time of delivery, or both, is postponed".

It was argued for the appellant that the lack of registration of the conditional purchase agreement meant that, as against the appellant, there was no agreement at all, but that as there had been delivery of the goods from the respondent to Horne then by the application of rule 1 of s 20 the property had also passed to him. In this way, therefore, he "acquired" the goods for the purposes of s 24 of the Chattels Transfer Act and the appellant's rights under its registered agreement were perfected.

I am unable to agree. Sections 19 and 20 of the Sale of Goods Act are plainly designed to govern the situation between the parties to a transaction. Nothing in either section could operate in the present case to alter the intention of the parties themselves, which was that the property in the goods should not pass. I do not consider there is any principle in equity, or by estoppel, or by statute, which would mean that in the situation which existed here the mere delivery of the goods was of itself sufficient to pass the property. I can, therefore, see no basis upon which it can be said, for the purposes of the proviso to s 24, that Horne ever "acquired" the goods at all. If that is the case then the presumption in the proviso never operated and the position is governed by the principle nemo dat quod non habet.

It is possible for the owner of chattels who has parted with possession of them, to be deprived of his title to them. This is expressly contemplated by s 18 of the Chattels Transfer Act (in the case of the assignee in bankruptcy and others), and by s 19 where that section applies. But the appellant in the present case comes into none of those categories. In the end, therefore, the appellant could obtain no better title to the goods than Horne was capable of giving.

Considerable reliance was placed, for the appellant, on the judgment of the Court of Appeal in *General Motor Acceptance Corporation v Traders' Finance Corporation Ltd* [1932] NZLR 1. That case involved two fraudulent transactions carried out by a motor dealer in which cars he had acquired on hire purchase were resold also on hire purchase. I do not propose to set out the facts of that case because I am satisfied that it has no application to the present case. The decision in that case turned almost entirely on the question of whether the instruments were customary hire purchase agreements. This is not a matter in issue in the present case. More particularly, however, the grantor of the instruments was a dealer in motor vehicles and this placed his transactions on a different footing from those of Horne in the present case. Of the two transactions in the *General Motors Acceptance Corporation* case, one was decided under the provisions of s 3(1) of the Mercantile Law Act 1908, and the other under the provisions of s 27(1) of the Sale of Goods Act. The present case does not involve any comparable situation.

I should record that the appellant, before the magistrate, sought to rely on the provisions of s 27(2) of the Sale of Goods Act. The magistrate held that this section did not apply. I was informed by counsel that as a result of the decision of O'Regan J in *NZ Securities & Finance Ltd v Wrightcars Ltd* [1976] 1 NZLR 77 there was no longer any challenge to the magistrate's decision on this point. The question of the possible application of s 27(2) was, therefore, not argued before me and I have disregarded it.

The magistrate decided this case upon the basis that the proviso to s 24 of the Chattels Transfer Act did not save the appellant's security because it did not specify with sufficient precision that the loan was to be expended in the purchase of the chattels. I do not feel able to agree with this but I think the proviso failed to save the security for the different reason that Horne never "acquired" the chattels at all. The result, however, is the same and the appeal must be dismissed.

Appeal dismissed.

Notes

1. For the passing of property under the legislation see Atiyah, *Sale of Goods* (7th ed.) 217; Lawson, The Passing of Risk and Property in the Sale of Goods — A Comparative Study (1949) 65 LQR 352.

2. Sales law has been under review for the last decade, everywhere, with mixed success. The concern tends to be at the consumer end of the transaction, rather than the 'transfer' or 'property passage' end, although there is some overlap. Post-sale consumer legislation has been discussed in New Zealand since 1977, but there has been little action. For Canada, see The Uniform Sale of Goods Act (ILRR, Report No 38, (1982)).

Reservation of Title Clauses

In the last decade the use of reservation of title clauses has become quite widespread in commercial sales contracts. The purpose of such a clause is straightforward: to protect a seller from the insolvency of a buyer in circumstances where the price is unpaid. The seller seeks to say, 'X is still mine — I *reserved* title until I was paid.'

The seller, in the event of default in payment, or insolvency, seeks priority over lenders secured and unsecured.

However, starting from that simple proposition, commercial law draftpersons have evolved quite extensive and elaborate reservation clauses. Sometimes they provide that title is reserved until all indebtedness is discharged (not just on the particular debt), or that the seller has rights in the manufactured end product.

Should reservation of title clauses be allowed at all? In their extended form? What is the effect of these clauses?

Len Vigden Ski & Leisure v *Timaru Marine Supplies*

[1986] 1 NZLR 349

BARKER J. This action was argued on an agreed statement of facts; it is thought by counsel to provide the first occasion on which this Court has had to consider a provision in a contract for the sale of goods between a supplier and a retailer whereby the vendor purports to retain ownership until payment. This type of provision has become known, in England at any rate, as a Romalpa clause.

The Romalpa clause takes its name from the decision of the English Court of Appeal in *Aluminium Industrie Vaassen BV v Romalpa Aluminium Ltd* [1976] 2 All ER 552. As is noted by the learned authors of *Benjamin's Sale of Goods* (2nd ed, 1981) §393, the existence of a Romalpa clause in a contract for sale of goods can be of serious concern to creditors of manufacturing or trading companies; in particular, to creditors who might otherwise suppose themselves secured by a floating charge over the assets of a company to which they have supplied goods; persons extending credit to such a company may have little opportunity of knowing whether goods sold to the company by trade suppliers for onsale to the public are subject to a Romalpa clause.

The first defendant is in receivership; the second defendants are its receivers appointed by a debenture holder. It is agreed in the statement of defence that, in the months of February to May 1983, the plaintiff supplied to the first defendant, at its request, certain ski apparel and equipment for retail sale by the first defendant to the public in a sports goods shop then operated in Timaru by the first defendant. No payment has been made to the plaintiff for these goods; some have been sold by the second defendants after the receivership.

At the time when the receivership commenced, all the goods were unsold; they remained unsold until after 20 June 1983. The following facts are agreed:

(a) After the commencement of the receivership, the receivers indicated that they did not intend to pay the plaintiff for the goods in the course of the receivership. The plaintiff then asked the receivers to allow it to uplift the goods. That request was in writing and was specifically based on the retention of title clause (ie the Romalpa clause).

(b) The receivers refused to allow the plaintiff to uplift the goods and expressed an intention to sell the goods.

(c) The plaintiff then told the receivers that if the goods were sold, it wished the proceeds of sale to be kept separate and placed on deposit pending the outcome of litigation.

(d) The receivers replied that they were "sure that satisfactory arrangments as to the proceeds of sale" could be made between the parties. No such arrangements were made. The goods were subsequently sold and the proceeds of sale credited to the receivers' general account.

(e) The parties traded on the basis that monthly invoices were sent showing debit balances of varying ages.

(f) The first demand for the goods was made on the receivers.

It was further agreed that, prior to supplying the goods to the first defendant, the plaintiff, on 1 February 1983, sent the following circular letter to the first defendant:

> "Prior to the commencement of deliveries we confirm for you our terms of trade as being the same as those published in our Indent Terms/Price Lists dated September 1982.
>
> "We also draw your attention to our conditions of Sale, as will now be printed on all of our invoices and packing slips. Such conditions are designed to protect this company in the event of bankruptcy or default of payment by a Debtor and are printed on the invoice and packing slip, as we here advise you below.

> *"Conditions of Sale*

> "1.   *Terms*
>
> Net Monthly Payment by 20th of month following invoice date unless within the terms of a written credit arrangement.

> "2.   *Damage Defects and Loss in Transit*
>
> Any complaints of damage, short delivery, loss in transit or defects must be made to the company within ten (10) working days of delivery to the customer. The Company shall have the right in its discretion to repair or replace the goods in respect of which any complaint as aforesaid is made and proven, or to refund or credit the portion of the purchase price applicable thereto thereby fully discharging all legal liabilities but the Company will use its best endeavours to enforce any guarantee or warranty given by the manufacturer of goods supplied and sold by the Company.

> "3.   *Warranty*
>
> The Company shall not be liable for any direct or consequential loss or damage attributable to defects in the goods nor in respect of conditions or warranties whether expressed or implied by statute or at common law or otherwise which have not been confirmed by the company in writing.

> "4.   *Ownership*
>
> Risk in any goods supplied by the Company to a Customer shall pass when such goods are delivered to the Customer or into custody on the Customer's behalf but ownership in such goods is retained by the Company until payment is made for the goods and for all other goods supplied by the Company to the Customer. If such goods are sold by the Customer prior to payment therefor and if they shall become constituents of other goods then the proceeds of sale thereof shall be the property of the Company."

It is accepted by the parties that each of the various invoices for the supply of ski equipment to the first defendant bore on the reverse the conditions of sale referred to in the circular letter.

The defendants' statement of defence admitted an allegation of the plaintiff that the only credit arrangement between the plaintiff and the first defendant was that payment for each part of the goods would not be required until the 20th day of the month following the date of the invoice relating to those goods. Despite this admission, counsel were unable to agree as to the length of the period of credit; there was at the hearing a suggestion that, in respect of some of the goods, there had been an agreement for further credit. Counsel have now advised me by memorandum that there was no other arrangement for credit.

A Romalpa clause derives its legitimacy from s 21(1) of the Sale of Goods Act 1908 which is identical to a section in the English Act.

"Where there is a contract for the sale of specific goods, or where goods are subsequently appropriated to the contract, the seller may, by the terms of the contract or appropriation, reserve the right of disposal of the goods until certain conditions are fulfilled."

In the *Romalpa* case, the plaintiff, a Dutch company, sold to the defendant, an English company, some aluminium foil which was then onsold by the defendant to subpurchasers which paid the defendant. Standard conditions of sale between the plaintiff and the defendant provided, inter alia:

(a) The ownership of the foil was to be transferred to the defendant only when it had met all that was owing to the plaintiff;
(b) Until payment, the defendant, if the plaintiff desired, was to store the foil in such a way that it was clearly the property of the plaintiff;
(c) Articles manufactured from the foil supplied were to become the property of the plaintiff as security for the full payment of the sums owing by the defendant to the plaintiff;
(d) Until such payment, the defendant was to keep the articles for the plaintiff in its capacity of fiduciary owner and was to store them in such a way as they could be recognised as such if required; and
(e) The defendant was to be entitled to sell the articles to third parties in the ordinary course of business on condition that, if the plaintiff so required, the defendant would hand over to the plaintiff any claims it might have against the third parties.

A receiver was appointed by the debenture holder in respect of the defendant's business. The plaintiff sought an order of delivery up of the foil in the possession of the receiver plus a declaration for a charge over moneys held by the receiver and a tracing order.

The Court of Appeal upheld the Romalpa clause, saying that, by virtue of the relationship of bailor/bailee expressly contemplated in the conditions of sale, the proceeds of the subsales were to be paid to the plaintiff in priority to the general body of creditors and the debenture holder.

A perusal of subsequent authority shows that each case turns on the particular wording of the contract—especially the would-be Romalpa clause.

As was noted in the most recent decision of the English Court of Appeal, *Clough Mill Ltd v Martin* [1984] 3 All ER 982, there has been a "spate of decisions" concerning Romalpa clauses in the English Courts. Robert Goff LJ said at p 985:

"But it is of great importance to bear in mind that these cases have been concerned with different clauses, very often in materially different terms, that different cases have raised different questions for decision and that the decision in any particular case may have depended on how the matter was presented to the court, and in particular may have depended on a material concession by counsel. So this is a field in which we have to be particularly careful in reading each decision in the light of the facts and issues before the court in question."

Mr Couch submitted that the clause in the present case complied with the basic requirements of s 21(1) in that it showed:

1. The ownership of the goods was retained by the plaintiff until payment had been made.
2. The nature of the ownership so retained was full legal ownership.
3. In the case of any goods sold prior to full payment, proceeds of sale were the property of the plaintiff.

Counsel submitted that there could be no problem about the first defendant selling to third persons in the normal course of trade; the second defendant had the implied right to do so, and third persons buying in good faith would receive title from the first defendant as ostensible vendor being a mercantile agent in possession (see s 27(2) of the Act; and the *Romalpa* case at p 563 per Roskill LJ).

On the question of a period of credit, Mr Couch referred to *Hendy Lennox (Industrial Engines) Ltd v Grahame Puttick Ltd* [1984] 2 All ER 152 and *Re Andrabell Ltd* [1984] 3 All ER 407. In those cases, it was held that the buyer had no duty to account to the seller for the proceeds of sale of goods sold through a period of credit because it must have been intended by the parties that the buyer be free, thoughout that period, to use the proceeds of sale as he wished. However, Staughton J, in the *Hendy Lennox* case concluded that, in respect of a sale of goods made after the credit period had expired, the company was required to account to the original supplier for the proceeds of goods.

Counsel also submitted that the present case was distinguishable from the *Hendy Lennox* and *Andrabell* cases (where Romalpa clauses failed); the clauses in those cases contained conditions which were silent as to the proceeds of sale.

Mr Moore submitted that, in line with the *Clough Mill* decision, one must look at all the terms of the contract in order to ascertain the true intendment of any particular provision. He submitted:

1. The credit arrangement was inconsistent with absolute ownership.
2. Clause 2 which requires complaints to be made within 10 days, long before the property passes, is inconsistent with a right vested in the plaintiff to retain ownership.
3. Clause 2 deals with complaints against manufacturers which term implies that a sale has taken place.

He distinguished the other cases on their facts. In the *Clough Mill* case, the clause read:

"(a) The price payable for the material shall be net and payment shall be made within the period stated overleaf ⁕ ⁕ ⁕ (c) The Seller shall be entitled to suspend or cancel further deliveries under this or any other contract between the parties hereto: (i) if any payment is overdue ⁕ ⁕ ⁕ (d) For the purpose of this condition, time of payment shall be of the essence of the contract. (e) The Buyer shall not be entitled to withhold or set-off payment for material delivered for any reason whatsoever."

Counsel submitted that the clauses in the *Clough Mill* and *Romalpa* cases were far more effective than the present. The clauses which counsel considered the most comparable to the present were those in *Re Peachdart Ltd* [1984] Ch 131, and in the *Andrabell* case.

Essentially, the plaintiff's claim rests on the provisions of cl 4 of the conditions of sale set out in its letter of 1 February 1983 to the first defendant. If "and" in the second sentence is read as meaning "or" (which is the most sensible construction), the clause refers to three classes of property:

(1) Goods supplied to the first defendant. The clause stipulated that "ownership in such goods is retained by the Company [ie the plaintiff] until payment is made for the goods and for all other goods supplied by the Company ⁕ ⁕ ⁕"

(2) The proceeds of sale of any goods in (1) which are sold by the customer "prior to payment therefor". These "shall be the property of the Company". "Therefor" may be ambiguous. It could relate back to "the goods and ⁕ ⁕ ⁕ all other goods supplied by the Company to the Customer", but probably relates back to "such goods", found earlier in the same sentence.

(3) Other goods, of which any goods in (1) "shall become constituents". Clause 4 does not expressly provide for ownership of this, but stipulates that "the proceeds of sale thereof shall be the property of the Company". "Thereof" presumably relates back to the "other goods", which may, naturally, contain material or products other than that supplied by the company, for instance material belonging to the customer or to a third party.

The plaintiff's claim is limited to the classes of property described in (1) and (2) above. None of the goods supplied by the plaintiff was altered, or mixed with or made up into other goods, by the defendants. If they were sold, they were sold in the form in which they were delivered to the first defendant. In so far as cl 4 relates to mixed or manufactured goods, or the proceeds of sale thereof, its provisions are only indirectly relevant in the circumstances of this case. This is fortunate for the plaintiff, because the cases show that retention of the title clauses which purport to preserve to a supplier of goods rights over products made by someone else from or with those goods can give rise to many problems.

The plaintiff's claim relates to (1) the proceeds from the sale of goods in the defendants' possession unsold at the date of the plaintiff's demand (in effect damages for conversion of those goods), and (2) the proceeds of sales prior to the date of the receivership.

(1) *The claim to the unsold goods*

The plaintiff claimed delivery up of the goods from the receivers by virtue of the provisions of cl 4. Any contractual terms (express or implied) limiting its right, as against the defendants, to take possession or dispose of the goods as their owner, have ceased to apply.

The agreement gives the plaintiff no express right to recover possession of goods not paid for, nor to enter onto the first defendant's premises for that purpose, nor to dispose of or sell the goods. In some, but not all, of the other cases, the contract expressly conferred on the supplier some, or all, of those rights.

In the event, the defendants refused to hand over the unsold goods to the plaintiff. If the plaintiff is to succeed, it must be entitled to the proceeds of sale of these goods. However, the criterion of determining whether it is entitled to these proceeds depends on the effectiveness of the clause permitting delivery of the goods.

Counsel for the defendants submitted that, under the agreement, it was intended that property in the goods delivered to the first defendant would pass to it at some time, unspecified, before the plaintiff was paid in full for all the goods, and that property has in fact passed accordingly. The only proprietary interest which the plaintiff would have in the goods is, it is said, an interest by way of a charge created by the first defendant. That charge being unregistered is void against the liquidator and any creditor of the first defendant, pursuant to s 103 of the Companies Act 1955.

The defendants submit that the existence of an arrangement for credit is inconsistent with an intention that the plaintiff retain absolute rights of ownership in the goods; but I do not see why this is necessarily so. That is not to say that the fact that credit is allowed to a buyer is never relevant where goods are delivered to a buyer under an effective retention of title clause; an implied term that the supplier may not recover possession of the goods until the buyer is in default in payment, the existence and length of any agreed term of credit will have a bearing on whether the supplier may claim delivery up of the goods (see *Hendy Lennox (Industrial Engines) Ltd v Grahame Puttick Ltd* [1984] 2 All ER 152, 157-161); in other words, it will affect the exercise by the supplier of the rights of ownership which he has retained.

The defendants further submitted that the provisions of cl 2 of the agreement suggest that property in the goods was not retained by the plaintiff. But the clause deals with the plaintiff's obligation to deliver, and the first defendant's to accept and pay for, goods, where the goods are damaged or defective, or have been lost in transit etc. These obligations arise and exist under the agreement quite independently of the transfer of title to the goods. It is difficult to see what bearing the provisions of cl 2 have on the question of the time at which the parties intended property in the goods to pass, or whether the plaintiff and first defendant were indeed in a fiduciary relationship.

(2) *The claim to the proceeds*

It was common ground that the agreement conferred on the first defendant an implied power to sell the goods supplied by the plaintiff, even before all the goods had been paid for and the first defendant had acquired title to them, and to receive the proceeds of sale. Clause 4 expressly refers to the proceeds of such sales.

It was also agreed that, under the subsales effected by the receivers, title to the goods sold passed to the respective subpurchasers of them, so that the plaintiff now has no proprietary interest in those goods.

The parties disagree, however, as to the terms upon which the first defendant was to receive the proceeds of sale. The plaintiff says that the first defendant was and is under an obligation to account to it for the proceeds of sale of the goods; that it must be inferred that the first defendant was to be a fiduciary in relation to goods supplied to it by the plaintiff, and not paid for; and that, therefore, the plaintiff is entitled to trace its proprietary interest in the goods into the proceeds of their sale and beyond.

The second defendants submit that the proper inference is that the first defendant, so far as the plaintiff is concerned, was to receive the proceeds for its own account; that it was and is at liberty to deal with them as it pleases and to use them for the purposes of its own business; and that no fiduciary relationship was ever created, merely one of creditor and debtor, in relation to the proceeds.

I now consider the cases as a guide to resolving these questions, but bear in mind that each Romalpa clause has to be considered "on its merits".

In *Romalpa*, the retention of title clause which the Courts had to construe fell into two parts. The opening sentence dealt with the aluminium foil which the plaintiff supplied to the defendant and provided:

(1) That "the ownership of the material . . . will only be transferred" to the defendant when it had met all that was owing to the plaintiff, and
(2) "Until the date of payment, [the defendant] is required to store this material in such a way that it is clearly the property of [the plaintiff]".

The remainder of the clause dealt in considerable detail with the situation where, after delivery, the foil was mixed with other substances or made up into a new object or objects.

The plaintiff brought an action, claiming to be entitled to (a) unmixed foil, and (b) moneys held in a separate account by the receiver, which represented the proceeds of sale of unmixed, unpaid for foil which the plaintiff had supplied to the defendant and the defendant sold to third parties, while still indebted to the plaintiff.

The foil in the possession of the receiver had not been sold, mixed with other goods, made into new objects, nor sold. So the claim of the plaintiff in *Romalpa* corresponds to the first two heads of the present plaintiff's claim.

With regard to the claim to the foil, neither Mocatta J nor the Court of Appeal was required to decide whether, under the retention of title clause, the plaintiff was entitled to the material, because the defendant conceded that, if the clause applied between it and the plaintiff (as was held to be the case at first instance and on appeal), the plaintiff was the owner of the foil and had the right to an order for its delivery up (p 555b, per Mocatta J; pp 559a-b and 561d, per Roskill LJ). In the present case, no such concession has been made.

However, the plaintiff's claim to the proceeds of sale of the goods was disputed. Unlike the present cl 4, the retention of title clause in *Romalpa* contained no reference to the proceeds of sales effected by the defendant, of unmixed foil. It was accepted in *Romalpa* (as here) that the defendant had an implied power to sell the goods supplied by the plaintiff, even before they had been paid for; and also that the plaintiff had authorised the subsales. In the present case, one could argue that, by the time the receivers sold the goods supplied by the plaintiff, the latter had effectively withdrawn the first defendant's authority to sell. This difference should not matter, because "There is no distinction * * * between a rightful and a wrongful disposition of the property, so far as regards the right of the beneficial owner to follow the proceeds" (*Re Hallett's Estate* (1880) 13 Ch D 696, 709, per Jessell MR).

The Court of Appeal, affirming Mocatta J, held that the plaintiff, on the true construction of the agreement, was entitled to trace and recover the proceeds of the subsales on the authority of *Re Hallett's Estate*, because there was a sufficient fiduciary relationship between it and the defendant, by reason of the fact that the latter was accountable to the former for the goods sold and their proceeds.

The Court rejected the defendant's submission that the power of sale to be implied into the first part of the retention of title clause should be a power to sell and to apply the proceeds for its own purposes. It concluded that the parties must have intended that the power of sale be exercisable on account of the plaintiff, in view of the following considerations:

(1) The defendant conceded that it was selling goods which the plaintiff owned at all material times (p 563g, per Roskill LJ). (A concession not made by the present defendants.)

(2) The defendant admitted it was a bailee of the foil delivered by the plaintiff (p 555c-d, per Mocatta J). (The present defendants deny that there was a bailment of the ski goods.)

(3) The defendant, it was found, as between itself and the plaintiff, sold the plaintiff's foil as agent for the plaintiff (p 563j, per Roskill LJ).

(4) An agent lawfully selling his principal's goods (like a bailee selling his bailor's) stands in a fiduciary relationship and is accountable to his principal for the goods and their proceeds (p 563j, per Roskill LJ).

If this is correct, the crucial finding in *Romalpa* was not that there was a bailment or agency, but rather that the defendant was selling the unmixed, unprocessed foil in its possession, during the period before it had been paid for, for the plaintiff's account (see *Re Bond Worth Ltd* [1980] Ch 228, 262, per Slade J). In fact, the Court of Appeal placed less emphasis than did Mocatta J on the admitted existence of a bailor/bailee relationship; it clearly saw the nature of the defendant's implied power of sale as the crucial issue on the appeal (see p 559f, per Roskill LJ; p 565d, per Goff LJ).

(5) The obvious purpose of the clause as a whole was to protect the plaintiff, should the defendant become insolvent, against the consequences of having parted with possession of, but not legal title to, the goods before payment was received. The power of sale to be implied should not be such as to defeat this purpose (p 563g, per Roskill LJ; p 566g, per Goff LJ).

The second paragraph of the present plaintiff's letter of 1 February 1983 states that cl 4 is designed to protect the plaintiff in the event of bankruptcy or default in payment by the first defendant.

(6) While not directly applicable, the provisions of the second part of the clause were relevant to the construction of the retention of title clause as a whole. The provisions referred to the defendant, pending payment of the plaintiff, keeping mixed or manufactured goods for the plaintiff as "fiduciary owner", which contemplated the creation of a fiduciary

relationship with regard to the mixed goods at least; and to the plaintiff becoming owner of these goods as security for full payment.

(7) The agreement provided that the defendant would have 75 days' credit before the price of the foil supplied became due. The defendant argued that the advantage, for it, of this provision would be destroyed if it was bound to account for the proceeds of sale of the plaintiff's goods, particularly as the passing of property in the goods was tied to the extinction of all indebtedness from it to the plaintiff, not just indebtedness in respect of goods supplied under the particular contract. If the plaintiff's argument was right, the defendant could not use the proceeds of subsales effected by it, for its own purposes, even though the period of credit allowed in respect of the goods sold had not expired when the proceeds were received, but had to pay them over to the plaintiff, unless and until it had paid the plaintiff everything it owed.

The Court recognised the force of this argument, but felt that, when the situation was viewed from the perspective of both parties, the argument was outweighed by considerations which indicated that there was an obligation to account.

The present agreement also provides for the first defendant to be given a period of credit. The defendants, like the defendant in *Romalpa*, say that this suggests that the parties to the agreement did not intend that the first defendant would be accountable for the proceeds of subsales.

One difference between *Romalpa* and the present case which may weaken the force of this submission, is the possibility, discussed earlier, that the implied obligation to account under cl 4 for the proceeds of sale of ski goods (as such) extends only to the proceeds of sale of goods for which the first defendant has not paid, and does not arise whenever, and as long as, anything is owing to the plaintiff for goods supplied. Even on this assumption, the first defendant would not have the full benefit of the agreed term of credit, but would desire some advantage from it.

In *Romalpa*, the plaintiff appears to have been awarded a sum equivalent to the gross proceeds of the subsales, with no deduction made for the defendant's expenses of sale or any profit made by the defendant on the subsales.

Romalpa was followed in time by *Re Bond Worth Ltd* [1980] Ch 228. There, Monsanto Ltd had supplied fibre to a carpet manufacturer, Bond Worth Ltd, which spun and dyed it, and wove it into carpets. A clause in the supply contract provided that "(a) . . . equitable and beneficial ownership" of the fibre would remain with Monsanto until payment in full had been received or until prior resale, in which event Monsanto's "beneficial entitlement" would "attach to the proceeds of resale or to the claim for such proceeds"; and "(b) Should the goods become constituents of or be converted into other products while subject to [Monsanto's] equitable and beneficial ownership", Monsanto would "have the equitable and beneficial ownership in such other products as if they were solely and simply the goods . . .", and subcl (a) would apply, as appropriate, to the other products.

When Bond Worth went into receivership, owing it money for fibre supplied,

Monsanto claimed to be entitled beneficially (1) as owner, to all fibre, whether raw or processed (including products made from the fibre), supplied to Bond Worth and not paid for, which remained unsold in the receiver's hands, and (2) to the respective proceeds of sale of any goods in (1) which Bond Worth had sold, on the basis that Bond Worth and the receivers were under an obligation to account for them.

As Slade J noted at the beginning of his judgment, the retention of title clause which he had to construe differed materially from that considered in *Romalpa*, which purported to reserve legal, as well as beneficial, ownership to the vendor (p 233A). In *Romalpa*, the agreement was not initially a contract of sale under which property in the foil passed to the purchaser, whereas, in *Bond Worth*, the agreements, properly construed, were absolute contracts for the sale of fibre to Bond Worth. Under each, legal title to, or property in, the fibre the subject of the contract, passed to Bond Worth on delivery.

Besides being a contract of sale, each agreement purported to reserve to Monsanto, until payment in full for the fibre, "equitable and beneficial ownership" of the fibre, the products made from it, and the respective proceeds of their sale. Monsanto had acquired charges over the raw fibre, manufactured products, and proceeds of sale. They were creating equitable charges which secured payment of the purchase prices due under the various contracts to Monsanto. As they had not been registered under the Companies Act 1948, they were void against Bond Worth's creditors.

Bond Worth is distinguishable from the present case because the retention of title clause there purported to reserve only "equitable and beneficial" ownership to the vendor, not, as in *Romalpa, Clough Mill Ltd v Martin*, and the present case, "ownership" as such. "Prima facie, in a commercial document . . . ownership means, quite simply, the property in the goods" (*Clough Mill Ltd v Martin* [1984] 3 All ER 982, 986, per Robert Goff LJ). There is nothing in the agreement made between the present plaintiff and first defendant, or in the surrounding circumstances, to suggest that the word "ownership" appearing in the first sentence of cl 4 should bear any other meaning.

Borden (UK) Ltd v Scottish Timber Products Ltd [1981] Ch 25 was another case where the plaintiff had supplied a product ie resin to the defendant, to be used in the manufacture of a composite product ie chipboard.

The issue in the Court of Appeal was whether the plaintiff was entitled to a charge over the chipboard in the defendant's possession, to the extent that it consisted of resin supplied by the plaintiff, for a sum equivalent to the outstanding balance of the purchase price of the resin; and also, to a similar charge over the proceeds of sale of chipboard made from the plaintiff's resin. The plaintiff did not make any claim to resin, as such, in the defendant's possession, which would have been worth little, if anything.

The plaintiff's claim failed because the Court held that the tracing remedy could not be invoked unless:

(1) The property to be traced could be identified at every stage of its journey through life, whereas the resin lost, irrevocably, its character and identity when it became mixed with other goods to make chipboard, an entirely different kind of product; and

(2) It was identifiable as property to which a fiduciary obligation attached in favour of the person tracing it.

Romalpa was distinguished by Bridge LJ on these grounds:

(a) The concession that there was in *Romalpa* a bailment of the aluminium foil;

(b) The plaintiff there sought to trace the foil supplied by it into the proceeds of sale of that foil, which had not been mixed with other materials, belonging for instance to the defendant or third parties, to produce a wholly new, different substance;

(c) The case turned on the construction of a particular clause; in particular on the implication which should be made as to the terms upon which the purchaser was entitled to sell the foil, whereas in *Borden* it was contemplated that the purchaser would use the resin only in the process of manufacture; and

(d) Most importantly of all, it was found in *Romalpa* that the purchaser was acting as the supplier's agent in selling the foil, in *Borden*, it could not be said that the purchaser was acting as agent for the supplier when it used up the plaintiff's resin in its own manufacturing process to make its own chipboard.

In *Re Peachdart Ltd* [1984] Ch 131, leather was supplied by one company to another for use in the manufacture of handbags, under conditions which provided that "the ownership" of the leather "shall remain with the seller". The seller reserved the right to dispose of the leather until payment in full or until the leather was sold by the buyer. If payment was overdue, the supplier could recover and resell the leather, and enter on the buyer's premises for the purpose. Payment became due as soon as there was any act or proceeding involving the buyer's solvency.

If goods were made from the leather before payment in full, the agreement provided that property in "the whole of such other goods" was to "be and remain with the seller" until payment was made, or the goods sold, when the seller's rights in the leather would "extend" to the goods. It was provided expressly that, until the seller had been paid in full for all goods supplied, the buyer would be a fiduciary with regard to the leather and goods made from or with it; and, if any of the leather or other goods was sold by the buyer, the seller would be entitled to trace the proceeds. The price of the leather became due as soon as it was delivered.

The buyer went into receivership without having paid for all the leather. Vinelott J had to decide whether the seller had a priority interest or charge in respect of the proceeds of sale of handbags made from the leather by the buyer. Some of the bags were wholly or partly manufactured when the receiver was appointed, and were sold by him. Others had been sold by the purchaser before it went into receivership, but the proceeds of sale were not received until afterwards.

Vinelott J found it unnecessary to decide whether a bailment had been created because the claim to the proceeds of sale of the handbags failed on other grounds. Under the agreement, properly construed, he held that the parties must have intended that while title to leather which had not been paid for remained initially with the supplier, as soon as any piece of the leather was appropriated by the purchaser to the manufacturing process, and work began on it, the property in that piece would pass to the purchaser (even though the parcel of leather of which it formed part had not been paid for in full), and the seller would instead acquire a charge over any handbag, finished or unfinished, made from the leather, which would move when the handbag was sold to the proceeds of sale. The charge would secure the payment of the outstanding balance of the purchase price of the parcel of leather.

It was accepted that this construction did some violence to the language of the clause, which provided that property in goods made from or with the leather would "be and remain with" the seller, but the Court was not prepared to find that the parties had intended the purchaser to be a mere bailee of the leather throughout the whole process of manufacture, until the parcel of leather was paid for in full, or to sell the handbags as agent for the supplier, so as to be accountable for the proceeds.

In *Hendy Lennox (Industrial Engines) Ltd v Grahame Puttick Ltd* [1984] 2 All ER 152, the plaintiff had supplied the defendant with diesel engines. They were used as a major component of diesel generator sets, which the defendant assembled and sold to its customers. Under the conditions of supply, "all goods [were to] be and remain the property of the [plaintiff] until the full purchase price thereof shall be paid". In the event of default in payment by the defendant, between one and two months' credit being allowed, the plaintiff had the right to retake possession of the engine. Once used in the generator sets, the engines remained easily identifiable by their respective serial numbers, and could be disconnected from the sets with relative ease.

The defendant went into receivership owing the plaintiff the purchase price of the engines delivered. At that time, most had been incorporated into generators, which had been sold to customers of the defendant. However, three others were still on the defendant's premises. Of these, two had been fully incorporated into generator sets, and the third had been incorporated in part.

The success of the plaintiff's claim to the proceeds of sale of each of the three engines depended on whether the plaintiff would have been entitled to delivery up of the engine at any time after the defendant went into receivership and before it sold the engine as part of a generator set. When the engine was sold, property in it, the plaintiff conceded, passed to the subpurchaser and the plaintiff lost its right to recover possession of the engine.

Staughton J held that, under the agreement including the retention of title clause, the plaintiff initially retained full rights of ownership in the engines, subject to any contractual terms which limited, expressly or by implication, the exercise of those rights by the plaintiff. He therefore rejected the defendant's submission that it had conferred proprietary rights over the goods on the plaintiff.

In the present case, while cl 4 purports to reserve to the plaintiff title to the ski goods in the defendant's possession, which have not been paid for, it does not expressly give the plaintiff any right to recover and sell them. In view of the purpose of the clause, a Court would be justified in implying into it a right of recovery and resale, but it would no doubt have to be a right exercisable only upon default in payment by the first defendant (and, possibly, also insolvency on the part of the first defendant). That is, by necessary implication, the plaintiff would not be entitled to recover possession of its goods while the term of credit agreed in relation to the goods was still running. In the circumstances of this case, any such restriction on the plaintiff's right to delivery up of the goods would now be of theoretical interest only, as it is clear that the term of credit allowed to the first defendant under the agreement has now expired.

In *Hendy Lennox*, the plaintiff also claimed the proceeds of the sale of other engines, supplied by it and for which it had not been paid, which the defendant had sold to third parties as components of generator sets. The proceeds had been preserved in a joint deposit account. The contract contained no reference to the proceeds of sale of either the engines or the diesel generator sets.

Leaving open the question whether the defendant purchaser was ever a bailee of the engines, Staughton J held that it was not a fiduciary in relation to the proceeds of sale; the defendant's implied power to sell engines supplied by the plaintiff as components of generator sets which it had assembled was a power to sell for its own account.

Romalpa was distinguished by the Judge in *Hendy Lennox* because:

(1) The different language used in the agreement. In particular, the retention of title clause there had dealt with mixed and manufactured goods, and had referred to the supplier as a "fiduciary owner", both of which had been "considered important by the Court of Appeal".

(2) The proceeds of sale claimed in *Romalpa* came from the selfsame goods supplied by the plaintiff, without addition or annexation by the defendant. In *Hendy Lennox*, by contrast, the implied term contended for would have had to relate to all or part of the proceeds of sale of the generator sets, which comprised more than the goods supplied by the plaintiff. The present plaintiff's claim relates to the proceeds of sale only of the actual goods supplied by it.

(3) The purchaser in *Romalpa* conceded that it was a bailee.

(4) The purchaser in *Hendy Lennox* (like the present first defendant) could not be required to store the goods so as to show clearly that they were the supplier's property.

(5) The fact that a period of credit was provided for in *Hendy Lennox* was not easy to reconcile with an obligation to keep the proceeds of subsales in a separate account, and therefore tended to negative the existence of a duty to account. Unlike *Romalpa*, other considerations did not outweigh this one.

(6) The parties in *Hendy Lennox* had concerned themselves expressly with property in the goods supplied and remedies in respect of the goods alone, which militated against the implication of a term that the proceeds of sale belong to the supplier and be kept separate.

In this case, the parties did expressly provide for property in the proceeds of sale as well as in the goods.

Staughton J held that the absence of a fiduciary relationship meant that the plaintiff could not follow its interest in the engines into the proceeds of sale of the generator sets.

In *Re Andrabell Ltd* [1984] 3 All ER 407, the plaintiff had supplied travel bags to a company under a contract providing (1) for 45 days' credit and (2) that "ownership of the [bags] shall not pass to the Company until the Company has paid to [the supplier] the total purchase price . . .". The company sold the bags in the course of its business, and paid the proceeds into its current bank account, where they were mixed with other moneys. As the parties had contemplated, the bags were sold by the purchaser in the state in which it had received them from the supplier. After selling all the bags, the purchaser went into liquidation owing the plaintiff supplier the price.

The plaintiff claimed that, under the contract, the purchaser was accountable to it for the proceeds of sale of the bags. It argued that it had effectively retained title in the bags, which had not been paid for, until they were sold to the subpurchasers; that the purchaser must have taken possession of the bags as a bailee; and was therefore under a duty to account in accordance with the normal fiduciary relationship of bailor or bailee.

While there were many similarities between the facts of *Andrabell* and those of *Romalpa*, Peter Gibson J noted also some significant dissimilarities:

(1) Differences between the wording of the respective retention of title clauses. In *Andrabell*, the passing of property in the goods was postponed until payment in full for the whole consignment; in *Romalpa*, it was postponed until the discharge of the purchaser's indebtedness to the supplier on any contract. In *Andrabell*, there was no provision in the agreement obliging the purchaser, if required, to store the plaintiff's goods in a manner manifesting the plaintiff's ownership of them, and nothing to correspond with the second part of the clause in *Romalpa*, where the existence of a fiduciary relationship was expressly acknowledged and it was provided that the seller should have the benefit of any claim against a subpurchaser of mixed or manufactured goods.

(2) The purchaser in *Andrabell* did not sell the bags as agent for the plaintiff, or for its account. Even the plaintiff submitted that the purchaser was accountable for no more of the proceeds of sale of a consignment of goods than corresponded to the amount owing in respect of the consignment. In *Romalpa*, by contrast, it was conceded that the purchaser was a bailee, and found that it sold the foil as agent for the supplier and was accountable for all the proceeds.

The present defendants do not concede that the first defendant is or was ever a bailee of the goods. The plaintiff is claiming all the proceeds of sale.

(3) The plaintiff in *Andrabell* conceded that the purchaser was under no obligation to keep the proceeds of sale of the bags separate from its own moneys. This concession (which has not been made by the present plaintiff) was important because, an indicator of an obligation to account was an obligation not to mix the moneys received by one as a fiduciary with any other moneys.

There was nothing in the express terms of the agreement to support the implication of a term that the purchaser would be bound to keep separate accounts of the proceeds of sale of the bags; and, moreover, the method of payment expressly contemplated by the parties was wholly unrelated to the actual proceeds of the subsales.

In the present case, the provision in cl 4 that the proceeds of sale "shall be the property of the Company" could be the basis for implying such a term. There is no evidence as to the method of payment contemplated in the agreement between the plaintiff and the first defendant.

(4) The provision for a fixed period of credit not determinable upon resale of the goods implied that the buyer was free to use the proceeds of subsales effected within the term of credit as it thought fit and was difficult to reconcile with the plaintiff's claim to have an interest in the proceeds.

In the present case, the parties agreed on a period of credit. The question is whether, as in *Romalpa*, the inferences to be drawn from this are outweighed by other factors tending to support the existence of a fiduciary relationship.

(5) The Court in *Andrabell* was being asked to imply a duty to account into a contract with express detailed provisions as to payment.

These considerations led the Judge to conclude that the position of the purchaser in relation to the proceeds of sale of the bags was not fiduciary, but simply that of the plaintiff's debtor.

Finally, in *Clough Mill Ltd v Martin* [1984] 3 All ER 982, the appellant had supplied yarn to a company for use in the manufacture of fabric, under a condition which provided that the "ownership" of the yarn would remain with the appellant, which reserved the right to dispose of it until it had been either paid for in full or sold by the purchaser. If payment became overdue under the contract, the appellant could enter on the purchaser's premises and recover or resell the yarn. Payment fell due immediately on the commencement of any act or proceeding involving the purchaser's solvency.

When the purchaser went into receivership, without having paid for all the yarn, the appellant tried to repossess the unsold unused yarn supplied by it and still, then, in the purchaser's possession, acting under the retention of title clause. The receiver maintained that, under the clause, property in the yarn had effectively been transferred to the purchaser, which had created a charge over the yarn, in favour of the appellant, to secure payment of the purchase price. However, the charge was void under the Companies Act 1948 because it had not been registered. He allowed the purchaser to use the yarn without paying the appellant, which claimed damages from him for wrongfully depriving it of possession of the yarn and converting it to his own use.

The issue before the Court of Appeal was whether, under the retention of title clause, the appellant had indeed retained its title to the unused yarn or whether it had, as the receiver argued, become a chargeholder.

The claim of the appellant in *Clough Mill* corresponds with the present plaintiff's first head of claim: equivalent claims arising under a differently-worded clause in *Romalpa* and *Peachdart* were not disputed by the purchasers in those cases.

The Court held that there was no reason to give the first part of the retention of title clause (which dealt with the yarn supplied, as opposed to products made from or with it) any meaning other than the natural ordinary one the words bore. The concept of a seller of goods retaining the legal property in, and a power to dispose of, them after delivery to a buyer was both legally possible and commercially familiar. By virtue of the clause, the Court held the appellant was still the owner of the yarn.

The agreement involved the appellant retaining property in the material, not the purchaser conferring any proprietary interest, for example by way of a charge, in goods it never owned and was therefore never in a position to charge. The fact that one, if not the sole, purpose of the clause was to secure to the appellant the payment of the price of the yarn did not necessarily mean that the parties had created a charge; it was open to the appellant to try to protect itself against the risk of default or insolvency on the part of the purchaser by retaining ownership of, that is, property in the yarn, as it had purported to do.

The last sentence of the retention of the title clause provided that, should the yarn be incorporated or made into other goods before it had been paid for in full, "the property in the whole of such goods" was to "be and remain with" the appellant until the yarn had been paid for or the other goods sold. If the goods were sold before the yarn was paid for, the appellant's rights in respect of the yarn were to "extend to those other goods".

Despite the wording of this part of the condition, the Court was inclined, obiter, to regard it as, in the circumstances, giving rise to a charge over the new goods in favour of the appellant. Nonetheless, there was no reason why the presence of this sentence should prevent the Court from giving effect to the earlier part of the clause, dealing with yarn as such, in accordance with its terms.

The judgments of the Court of Appeal in *Clough Mill* contain a discussion of the way in which a retention of title clause might operate where it reserves to the supplier title to material for which the buyer has paid in part. The Court thought that a seller who recovered possession of and sold goods in the exercise of his rights under the clause, during the subsistence of the contract, would be entitled to sell only the amount needed to discharge the balance of the purchase price outstanding (including the expenses of the sale), and would be accountable to the purchaser for any surplus. This was on the basis that the supplier could exercise its powers as owner only in accordance with the terms, express or implied, of the contract.

In conclusion, in relation to the present plaintiff's first basis of claim, based on its alleged entitlement to unpaid goods, the words used in the first part of cl 4 are clear. They purport to reserve to the plaintiff ownership of, that is, the property in, the goods supplied by it to the first defendant until the first defendant has paid in full for all goods supplied by the plaintiff. No payment has been made. The goods have not been sold, nor have they been mixed with or manufactured into other goods. They remain identifiable. If, by the terms of its agreement with the first defendant, the plaintiff was not entitled to retake possession of the goods until the term of credit agreed in relation to the goods had expired, that restriction on the exercise by the plaintiff of its rights of ownership no longer applies. The plaintiff now has a right to delivery up of its goods in the defendant's possession. Once that right cannot be exercised because the defendants have sold the goods, then the plaintiff is entitled to the proceeds of sale by way of damages for conversion.

The second part of the plaintiff's claim gives rise to greater difficulty. The first defendant had an implied power to use the goods supplied by the plaintiff for the purposes of manufacture and to sell them, before it had paid for them. When it sold the goods, was it bound to account for the proceeds? As in *Romalpa* and *Andrabell*, the goods were sold in the state in which the supplier delivered them to the purchaser. They had not been altered by the purchaser, nor mixed with nor added to goods or materials belonging to someone other than the supplier.

Unlike as in *Romalpa* and *Andrabell*, the retention of title clause in this case refers expressly to the proceeds of such subsales effected by the purchaser; it provides that the proceeds "shall be the property of" the plaintiff. The first part of the clause states that the goods sold by the first defendant remain the property of the plaintiff, this indicates strongly that the parties did intend that the first defendant would be accountable to the plaintiff for the proceeds, and would not receive them for its own account. It also provides a basis for implying into the agreement a duty on the part of the first defendant to keep the proceeds separate from its own moneys, consistent with the obligations of a fiduciary.

On the other hand, the provision for credit shows that the parties did not intend that the first defendant would occupy a fiduciary position with regard to the ski goods and the proceeds but merely that of a debtor. If the first defendant was under a duty to account for the proceeds of sale of goods supplied by the plaintiff, for which the latter had not been paid, as and when the proceeds were received, even if they should be received before the period of credit allowed in relation to the goods sold had expired, the first defendant would certainly be deprived of some of the benefit of the arrangement for credit, which it might have enjoyed had it not been accountable.

Nonetheless, as advised by the authorities, I look at this argument in the context of the entire agreement made between the parties. The first defendant has had the benefit of the full term of credit in relation to any goods which it did not sell during the term or which it sold, but the proceeds of which it did not receive until after the period had expired; it would have enjoyed some advantage in relation to goods which it sold and for which it received the proceeds during the term of credit, because it would not be bound to pay for them immediately on delivery, but has only after its own customers had paid it.

On balance, and after consideration of the authorities, I conclude that there was an obligation to account, while recognising that there are aspects of the agreement which tend to suggest that there was no such duty. In particular, the express provision in cl 4 relating to the proceeds of sale of the goods persuades me to reach this conclusion.

The plaintiff appears from authority to be entitled to the entire proceeds of the subsales; it is unlikely that there would be any surplus once the first defendant's indebtedness had been discharged out of the proceeds recovered from the defendants and the proceeds of sale of any goods recovered. If there is a surplus, it could well be that, under the contract, it belongs to the first defendant rather than to the plaintiff.

Accordingly, the plaintiff is entitled to appropriate declarations and is entitled to costs. I reserve liberty to apply in the event that counsel are unable to agree as to quantum or costs, or if they cannot agree as to the form of judgment.

Declarations accordingly.

Notes

1. Under Roman law, property in a chattel did not pass until there had been delivery, and the price was paid, or the seller gave credit. If a seller gave credit, it was possible to make delivery, that is the conveyance of the chattel conditional on payment of the price. And the sale could be terminated by the seller if the price was not paid by a certain date. These principles had a name: *lex commisoria*. Hence the idea of reservation to title clauses has existed for centuries in civil law, but has only recently been utilized in the British Commonwealth.

2. Analytically, is there some other way of looking at such clauses?

3. See generally, Collier, *Reservation of Title Clauses in Sale of Goods Transactions* (1989); Prior, Reservations of Title (1976) 39 MLR 585; Watts, Reservation of Title Clauses in England and New Zealand (1986) 6 Ox. J Legal Studies 456; Edwards, Reservation of Title Clauses in Theory and Practice (1983) Vol 4 #5, Bus L R 100. For the relationship between such clauses and section 2 of the Chattels Transfer Act see Scragg (1987) 2 Canterbury L R 282. See also the note on *Coleman v Harvey* in [1991] 1 LMCLQ 23 (Hudson). See also *Armour v Thyssen* [1990] 3 WLR 810 (H.L.).

Part 3

8

Registration Systems for Personal Property Interests

The fundamental concern of any person acquiring a particular piece of property is to see that they get 'good title', by which is meant that they acquire, from the seller, the full bundle of rights theretofore held by the seller. In a world in which there was not at least adequate security of title, social and commercial interaction would be very difficult and highly inefficient. Indeed it is probable that commercial and even social life as we know it today could *not* be carried on, without an adequate system of title.

Title Systems for Property Transfers

Functionally, there are four broad ways of setting up a system to deal with the transfer of individuated property rights.

First, there could be a symbolic system. That is, I could hand you a branch from a tree on my land to show that I am passing the land to you. Or I could symbolically let you into possession. Or I could deliver something to you. Other persons could witness this activity, and could later testify, if necessary, that the relevant ritual had been carried out. Systems like this have in fact existed at various times, but they are not practical in our crowded times with respect to land. We have outgrown them. Delivery, however, remains of critical importance in personal property law, at least as it currently stands.

Secondly, there could be a system of writing in which the transaction is recorded. That piece of writing itself could be the evidence of what has transpired, and could be produced before a tribunal. This category sometimes retains some of the symbolism of category one, in that the deed or other writing could also be handed over 'on settlement'.

Thirdly, it is not a long step in theory, though it involves real difficulties in practice, to a system in which these writings are recorded in some public registry. Potential purchasers, lenders or other interested parties can then examine the 'state of the title', in relation to a particular piece of property.

A fourth alternative, more sophisticated again, involves making the registration system *conclusive*. Instead of examining the deeds to which one has been alerted by the public record, the registration is itself evidence of the state of the title. One then does not have to go behind the entry on the register. And in a further bout of sophistication, the very act of registration can be made to operate to 'transfer' title. Other defined interests, such as mortgages, can also be entered on the title.

This fourth approach is in fact the central thesis of the Torrens system of title to land which has evolved in Australasia, and Canada. (See Whalen, The Origins of the Torrens System and its Introduction into New Zealand, in *The New Zealand Torrens System Centennial Essays* 1 (Hinde ed. 1971); Mapp, *Torrens' Elusive Title* (1978)); Simpson, *Land Law and Registration* (1976). It applies only to land, although Torrens developed the idea from a shipping register in the United Kingdom.

General personal property title systems have not yet evolved. The problems associated with possible registry systems are intrinsically more difficult with respect to personal property. The subject matter of personal property is diverse. It is movable, and can change hands very quickly. The value of personal property ranges from a few cents to millions of dollars. And due to the historical evolution of personal property law, little attention has been devoted to the conveyancing aspects of it. Finally, the subject has never been high on the political agenda, anywhere.

Historically, however, we appear to be moving to a period where increasing attention is being paid to the title registration problems associated with personal property. Valuable tangible chattels—ships, aeroplanes, motor vehicles—*can* quite feasibly be given their own combined, or separate, title systems. A car, for instance, could have its own certificate of title. Given that new cars routinely cost more than $20,000 in New Zealand, and evidence of frauds is quite widespread, such a system would be entirely defensible. And modern technology is quite capable of undertaking the recording and tracking process.' Increasingly, as we shall see, such systems are being put in place.

Beyond that again lurk problems associated with security interests in and transference of rights arising out of some of the new electronic technologies.

Security Interests in Personal Property

Quite apart from the question of a system of *title* registration for chattels (whether of the particular or the general variety) there is one matter which has proved consistently troublesome everywhere. That is the question of registration of *security interests* in chattels. A owns car B. It is subject to a secured loan, say a chattel mortgage to C. A sells and delivers the car to D without discharging the loan. D now 'owns' an encumbered car. The word is used advisedly—C can and will repossess the car, and D, an innocent party, will probably be the loser. Legal action against A will probably be worthless. In such cases A is usually long since gone, or is not worth powder and shot.

The most obvious solution to this kind of problem is to also have security interests of one kind or another in chattels, and perhaps in respect of other personal property, recorded somewhere. D could then search, on a *ex ante* basis, to satisfy herself that B is not encumbered. If D is armed with the relevant information, she can insist on evidence that the loan has been discharged, or will be discharged, on settlement and before the car is handed over. This is what happens with respect to a mortgage on real property. D would then have only herself to blame if she did not search the publicly available records. But as will be seen, this seemingly sensible solution has not yet been satisfactorily arrived at in New Zealand.

The remainder of this chapter is not concerned with the narrow black letter rules of personal property security law as such. That is properly the subject of intensive commercial law courses. What is of concern here is the evolving 'greater picture' of personal property registration systems and their relationship to the concept and development of personal property generally. However sufficient existing law must be dealt with so that students are not discussing pure abstractions. Moreover some students do not ever take a commercial law course as such.

Three personal property security 'systems' currently exist in New Zealand: The Chattels Transfer Act 1924; the Motor Vehicles Securities Act 1989; and in the case of the charges given by companies, the Companies Act 1955. There are also the proposals of the Law Commission for a so-called Article Nine type system in New Zealand.

The Chattels Transfer Act

This is now a venerable statute. While it is condemned by academic writers, it has worked tolerably well in practice for more than half a century. That is not to say that there are not better systems. Three aspects will be dealt with here: the kinds of property and transactions which are caught by the Act; the mechanics of registration; and the consequences of non-registration.

The Purpose and Application of the Act

The purpose of the Act is to protect the rights of persons who have property in, but not the possession of, chattels. A person in apparent possession of a chattel may pledge that chattel for credit, or even sell it, when that person is not entitled to do so. The Act endeavours to defeat such practices by requiring the registration, in a High Court Registry—on pain of certain consequences if registration is not effected—of 'instruments' over 'chattels'. The instrument, when filed, can be searched by interested parties. The apparent conceptual simplicity of the scheme is not, however, matched in practice.

The Quagmire of Chattels Security in New Zealand

Riesenfeld
Occasional Paper No 4, Legal Research Foundation (1970).

I. Some Historical and Policy Reflections

The availability of a properly functioning system of legal devices to secure credit is one of the main prerequisites of economic growth. While in days long past land was the main basis of security for lenders, modern conditions have greatly enlarged the range of assets which may and must be utilised in order to afford adequate sources of security for members of the commercial community who are willing and able to supply manufacturers or distributors with capital needed for modernisation, expansion, or steadiness of operation. The law has responded to that need but haltingly. Resort to chattels or intangibles as an object of security transactions is still replete with uncertainties, pitfalls and outmoded limitations. While that condition exists to a varying degree in practically all countries with a private enterprise system, efforts are made everywhere to remedy the situation. It would be both unrealistic and deplorable if New Zealand were content with the *status quo*. Any reform, however, must proceed on the basis of a careful assessment of the present state of the law in this area.

In New Zealand, as in many other Commonwealth countries, the law relating to security over personal property (i.e. chattels and intangibles) is artificially divided into two zones, one of which is governed by Bills of Sale legislation, while the other is controlled by Companies Acts. In New Zealand the currently operative statutes are the Chattels Transfer Act of 1924 and the Companies Act of 1955. Unfortunately the interrelation and the operation of these enactments is beset with obscurities and perplexities that can only be grasped and appreciated in the light of the legislative genealogy.

A. The English Background

At common law the principal security transaction relating to chattels was the pledge. It had, however, the unfortunate result of removing the object which served as security from the control of the borrower and placing it in the possession of the lender, thereby obviating any economic utilisation. The growth of non-possessory security interests in chattels was seriously stunted by the rule of *Twyne's Case* which exposed them to the risk of being voidable by other creditors as a fraudulent conveyance. Intangibles, such as debts, were likewise incapable of furnishing a safe basis for security. They were non-transferable at law, and equity intervened only gradually and grudgingly. Moreover, an assignment of a debt required prompt notification of the debtor. In the case of a double assignment the rule of *Dearle v. Hall* gave priority to a *bona fide* subsequent assignee who had notified the debtor of the assignment, prior to such notice by the senior assignee. Even less promising was the situation of a lender who relied for his security on after-acquired chattels or debts. Despite these formidable legal barriers, lenders persisted in groping for non-possessory security interests in chattels and the possibility of hypothecation of intangibles, and, step by step and haphazardly, Courts and Legislatures yielded to the undeniable need. The recognition in the eighteenth century of the factor's lien on the principal's goods and the proceeds from their sale was perhaps the first sign of the crumbling of the bastion.

Disregarding the development in the United States which followed an independent course of its own, the modern history of the recognition and regulation of non-possessory security interests in the common law countries commenced with the English Bills of Sale Act of 1854. This Act required that every bill of sale of personal chattels, together with an inventory or schedule of the chattels covered thereby be filed, either in the original or in a copy, with the clerk of dockets and judgments in the Court of Queen's Bench within twenty-one days after the giving or making of such bills. Non-compliance with the mandate rendered a bill of sale void against an assignee in bankruptcy or insolvency of the person whose chattels were comprised in the bill, against an assignee for the benefit of creditors of such person, and against an officer seizing the goods under process against such person as well as against the creditors in whose behalf that process was issued, provided that the chattels, after the expiration of the twenty-one days period and at the time of such bankruptcy, petition in insolvency, execution of the assignment for the benefit of creditors or seizure, were in the possession or apparent possession of the person making the bill of sale. The Act contained definitions of the terms bills of sale, personal chattels and apparent possession. The term "personal chattels" was defined to exclude, *inter alia*, choses in action, interests in the property of any incorporated or joint-stock company, and stock or produce upon any farm which by agreement or custom was not to be removed therefrom. Bills of sale did not cover transfers of goods in the ordinary course of business or documents of title. The Act did not protect persons other than creditors or creditor-representatives. An amending Act of 1866 altered the mechanics of registration and required renewal of registration after the expiration of five years.

In 1878 the two prior acts were repealed by a new Bills of Sale Act. The new legislation did not introduce any major changes in policy or scope. In the main it endeavoured to strengthen the publicity requirements, to remove a number of doubts that had arisen under the prior Acts, to curb certain abuses that had been condoned before, and to speed up the registration process. In particular the Act of 1878 required disclosure of the consideration and expanded the definition of bills of sale by specifically including "inventories of goods with receipt thereto attached, or receipts for purchase moneys of goods", as well as "any agreement, whether intended or not to be followed by the execution of any other instrument, by which a right in equity to any personal chattels, or to any charge or security thereon shall be conferred". It added "growing crops" the definition of chattels, regulating the application of the Act to transfers thereof, and redefined the subjection to the Act of trade machinery and other fixtures. It inserted a special section dealing with instruments granting powers of distress. The registration period was shortened to seven days subject to extension and a special proscription inserted against the practice of repeated execution of non-registered instruments to circumvent the limitation on registrability. The three most important changes were probably the provisions according priority in the order of registration to conflicting bills of sale, exempting transfers of registered instruments from the onus of registration and excluding chattels comprised in a registered bill of sale from the sweep of the reputed ownership clause of the Bankruptcy Act.

The Bills of Sale Act (1878) Amendment Act 1882 constituted an important change in legislative policy. While the prior legislation had the purpose of protecting creditors against latent, *i.e.*, non-possessory, interests in chattels created by debtors in possession, the aim of the new statute was to protect needy debtors from being entrapped into signing complicated documents which they might often be unable to comprehend and so being subjected by their creditors to the enforcement of harsh and unreasonable provisions. The amending Act does not apply to bills of sale other that "bills of sale by way of security for the payment of money". For them the old regime continues to be in force. Bills of sale by way of security for the payment of money, however, are subject to the new scheme. In the first place they must be made in accordance with a prescribed form; otherwise the transaction embodied therein is wholly void both as to the indebtedness beyond money had and received and the security over the chattels. In the second place the bills of sale covered by the amending Act must be attested as specified therein and must be registered within seven days after their execution. Non-compliance renders the security granted thereby void, even *inter partes*. Finally, every such bill must contain or have annexed thereto an inventory specifically describing the chattels comprised therein. Otherwise the security over such chattels is void, except against the grantor.

The statute introduced a number of important limitations on the permissible content of bills of sale. It outlawed powers of repossession by the grantee except for specified causes. Most of all it curbed the effect of after-acquired property clauses, rendering them void except against the grantor. To that extent it brought an important reversal of a trend which had found important judicial support. Prior to 1882 English draftsmanship had developed three types of instruments giving creditors rights over after-acquired chattels, *viz.*, (a) instruments containing a covenant to hypothecate future chattels; (b) instruments granting a power or license to seize future chattels; (c) instruments expressly charging future chattels. Frequently all three types were combined. After some initial reluctance the Courts tended to uphold instruments of these types. Grantees of powers to seize future goods prevailed over assignees for the benefit of creditors, assignees in bankruptcy or insolvency, and execution creditors, if they had exercised their power prior to the assignment, bankruptcy or levy, though they failed if bankruptcy or a levy intervened prior to seizure. Grantees to whom an interest in future chattels had been assigned prevailed even without seizure.

The Act of 1882 outlawed bills of sale, by way of security, in the form of a power to seize after-acquired chattels completely and permitted bills of sale of after-acquired chattels in the prescribed form only with respect to currently growing crops and with respect to fixtures, plant or trade machinery brought upon the respective premises in substitution of such items specifically described in the schedule. Curiously enough, violation of the interdict against after-acquired property clauses benefited only third parties and not the grantor himself. Of course, since the Act did not apply to choses in action, the assignment of future book debts was not prohibited or affected by the Act.

Another significant change in policy was the partial repeal of section 20 of the Act of 1878 which exempted chattels covered by a registered bill of sale from the operation of the "reputed ownership clause" of the Bankruptcy Act. As a result with respect to bills of sale by way of security for the payment of money, the pre-1878 law was restored and registration does not prevent chattels to be in the reputed ownership of the grantor, the matter depending solely on the circumstances of the possession and the consent of the owner to the reputation of ownership in the possessor.

The Act of 1882 concludes with the provision that "nothing in this Act shall apply to any debentures issued by any * * * incorporated company and secured upon the * * * goods, chattels, and effects of such company". The meaning of this section as well as of the provision in the Act of 1878 which excluded "interests in the property of incorporated or joint stock companies" from the definition of personal chattels caused many conflicting views in the adjudicated cases until the opinion of the Court of Appeal in *In re Standard Manufacturing Company*. Bowen L.J., writing for a unanimous Court, held:

> "Without going so far as to decide that no corporation can be under any circumstances within the Bills of Sale Act 1878 * * * we think * * * that the mortgages and charges of any incorporated company for the registration of which other provisions have been made by the Companies Causes Act 1845 or the Companies Act 1862 are not within the Bills of Sale Act of 1878."

Of course, this left the door open for the applicability of the Act of 1878 to bills of sale other than mortgages and charges. A case of that type arose in *In re Roundwood Colliery Company; Lee* v. *Roundwood Colliery Company*. In that case the need for registration under the Act of 1878 of a power to distrain for rent reserved in a lease made by the Earl of Effingham to an incorporated mining company with respect to company assets was in issue. The court did not even allude to the question whether the Act of 1878 might be inapplicable because the power was granted by an incorporated company but it disposed of the question on the sole ground that the grant of the power of distress for rent in a mining lease was not within the purview of the Act.

In re Standard Manufacturing Company resulted in a need for better publicity of corporate mortgages and charges than that afforded by s. 43 of the Companies Act 1862. This step was taken in the Companies Acts Amendment Act of 1900. Section 14 of that Act provided for registration with the Registrar of Joint Stock Companies of

(a) a mortgage or charge for the purpose of securing any issue of debentures; or

(b) a mortgage or charge on uncalled capital of the company; or

(c) a mortgage or charge created or evidenced by an instrument which, if executed by an individual, would require registration of a bill of sale; or

(d) a floating charge on the undertaking or property of the company.

Failure to file for registration within twenty-one days after their creation resulted in the invalidity of such charge or mortgage against a liquidator or any creditor of the company.

Subsequent Companies Acts retained this pattern of publicity for mortgages or charges on company assets, but expanded the catalogue of the mortgages and charges covered by the registration requirements and added other details governing the operation of this scheme. Thus the Companies Acts Amendment Act of 1907 added mortgages or charges on any land or any interest therein and mortgages or charges on book debts. The latter extension was necessitated by the fact that the English Bills of Sales Acts did not cover book debts and contained no registration requirements with respect thereto. The Companies Act 1929 added charges on calls made but not paid, charges on a ship or any share in a ship, and charges on goodwill, patents, trademarks, copyrights and licences under patents or copyrights.

It should be noted that the statutory effects of non-registration under the Companies Acts vary in many respects from that under the Bills of Sales Acts of 1878 and 1882. The protection is accorded to the liquidator and any creditor without need for resort to any execution process or possession by the debtor at that time. As a result it was held in *In re Monolithic Building Co.* that failure to register a land mortgage under the Companies (Consolidation) Act 1908 resulted in priority of a subsequent registered incumbrancer with notice.

B. *Chattels Securities Legislation in New Zealand*

New Zealand quickly followed the English model and in 1856 enacted a statute providing for the recording of bills of sale of personal chattels which, with minor alterations and deletions, was an exact copy of the English Act of 1854. The registration provisions of the Act were amended by the Bills of Sale Registration Amendment Act 1862 which re-defined the official with whom a bill of sale had to be filed and extended the time for filing with respect to bills of sale made in a province other than that where the personal chattels were situate. In 1867 the two prior Acts were replaced by the Bills of Sale Act 1867 which included the prior provisions in a new arrangement, with the modification that the registration period was shortened by ten days. In the next year the period was again lengthened to twenty-one days. The quinquennial renewal requirement was imported from England in 1875.

The bills of sale legislation discussed heretofore was supplemented by Acts requiring registration of security transactions or bailments relating to particular chattels such as the future produce of wool, whale oil and whale bone, stock and crops. Registration of bailments of stock or other chattels was provided for to achieve exemption from the reputed ownership clause of the Bankruptcy Act. Undoubtedly the Mortgage of Stock Registration Act 1868 was the most elaborate and carefully drafted Act among the various enactments listed. It expressly exempted mortgages registered thereunder from the application of the Bills of Sale Act. It required registration within twenty-one days and specified that an unregistered mortgage was invalid against purchases for valuable consideration even though they had knowledge of such mortgage and accorded priority to junior mortgagees who registered within twenty-one days and prior to the registration of the prior mortgage. A mortgage executed sixty days prior to an adjudication and properly registered protected the mortgagee against the reputed ownership clause, provided that the mortgage secured a contemporaneous loan or purchase money for a station or stock acquired within twenty-one days. The mortgage extended to increase and progeny as well as to other stock with the same brand at the premises described in the mortgage.

In 1880 New Zealand consolidated the various statutes relating to securities over personal chattels in the Chattels Securities Act 1880. This statute left the prior law virtually untouched and consisted mainly in a more systematic arrangement of the operative provisions and a slight rephrasing of the text of the prior legislation. It extended the quinquennial renewal requirement to mortgages and leases of live stock and leases of other chattels. Otherwise it retained different filing periods for different classes of instruments and the divergent rules relating to the effects of non-registration in these cases. Non-registration of a bailment of chattels, accordingly, resulted only in subjection to the reputed ownership clauses, but not in the protection of creditors as in the case of bills of sale.

The Chattels Securities Act remained on the books for nine years. Most of the innovations introduced by the English Bills of Sale Act 1882 were with astounding dispatch engrafted upon the New Zealand Act by the Chattels Securities Act Amendment Act 1883, curiously without also incorporating the changes made by the English Bills of Sale Act 1878, and thus leaving to that extent the law in the form of the English Act of 1854. Thus the New Zealand statute of 1883 followed the English model in requiring a full, true and clear statement of the consideration, and specifying that non-fulfilment of the requirement rendered the bill of sale void. It required further the annexation or incorporation of a schedule containing an inventory of the chattels comprised in a bill of sale; otherwise the bill was void so far as it regarded the property in, or the right to the possession of, any personal chattel not comprised in such schedule. It provided for the registration of instruments constituting both a bill of sale and a stock mortgage and clarified the provisions relating to affidavits.

Most of all, the Act of 1883 outlawed bills of sale of after-acquired property by providing: "No bill of sale shall be valid, or have any effect as regards any goods or chattels acquired by the grantor after execution of such bill of sale." This provision, as its English counterpart, eliminated the availability of future stock-in-trade as security which prior to that time had been recognised in a number of New Zealand decisions. The section was, moreover, ambiguous with respect to the extent of such invalidity, leaving it uncertain whether only the chattel security or the whole instrument was rendered void.

It is, however, important to note that the amending Act of 1883 did not incorporate all the features of the English Act of 1882 in the law of New Zealand. Most of all it did not prescribe a mandatory form of bills of sale and did not attach invalidity to such instruments because of failure to comply with formal requirements.

In 1889 the law relating to chattels securities was subjected to a recodification by the Chattels Transfer Act of that year. The Act made a vast number of substantial changes. Perhaps the most significant features of the reform were the following two:

(a) Adoption in New Zealand of many of the modifications brought about in England by the Bills of Sale Act 1878, as discussed before;

(b) Consolidation of the law governing instruments of bailment of chattels (which originated in New Zealand with the Act of 1869) with the law governing bills of sale.

The impact of the English Act of 1878 can be seen in the catalogue of instruments which were specifically excluded from the definition of instruments, the provisions relating to securities over trade machinery and other fixtures, the provisions against multiple instruments, the provisions governing priority between conflicting instruments comprising the same chattels, the clarification of the attestation requirements and the exemption from registration of transfers of instruments.

The consolidation of the law relating to the registration of bills of sale and the law relating to the registration of instruments of bailment (which had no counterpart in England) resulted in a broadening of the definition of the term "instrument" and a consequential expansion of the protection of creditors against unregistered instruments of bailment.

The new Act retained the special treatment of mortgages and leases of livestock, securities over crops and securities over wool.

Even where the Act of 1889 showed the imprint of the English model, significant modifications were made in a number of instances. This was the case in particular with respect to the details of the attestation requirements, the consequences of an absence of a proper schedule, the regulation of the priority between several instruments and the effect of an optional registration of transfers of instruments by way of security. An important and perhaps unfortunate change was made in the effect of an omission from the instrument of any defeasance, condition or declaration of trust to which it is subject at the time of registration. While heretofore, as under the English Acts of 1854 and 1878, non-compliance defeated only the effects of registration, the Act of 1889 deprived such instrument of all effect as regards the property in or right to possession of the chattels affected thereby.

With the exception of the special provision relating to the protection of *bona fide* purchasers for valuable consideration against unregistered instruments comprising stock, wool and crops and of the new proviso governing the priority of subsequent grantees without notice of a prior unrecorded instrument under an instrument which is registered first and within the proper time, the law retained its limitation to creditors and creditor representatives of its protection against unregistered instruments.

The consolidation of the provisions relating to instruments of bailment with the provisions relating to other instruments was also reflected in the extension of the exemption from the reputed ownership clause of the Bankruptcy Act to instruments other than instruments by way of bailment. Similar provisions were contained in the Bankruptcy Acts since 1883. The bankruptcy provisions, however, exempted only chattels covered by registered instruments, while the Chattels Transfer Act extended the exemption during the period allowed for registration. Last, but not least, the Act of 1889 deleted the troublesome requirement of a full, true and clear statement of the consideration for the instrument which the amending Act of 1883 had imported from the English Act of 1882 and which had caused a good deal of litigation.

In 1895 the Chattels Transfer Act was extended to book and other debts. The definition of chattels which before that had excluded choses-in-action was modified so as to include "book and other debts", except debts secured or charged on land. Each debt was to be deemed a separate chattel, to be described in the schedule "by setting forth the name of the debtor . . . and the amount of the debt, so far as may be reasonably necessary to show by whom the debts are owing". In the following year the periods allowed for registration were re-defined.

In 1908 the whole law relating to chattel securities was recodified. The statute made a number of changes in arrangement and phraseology but did not aim at any revision. It may be noted, however, that in the section relating to the order of priority among several conflicting instruments the drafters of the recodification deleted the former requirement that the registration affording priority must be made within the time allowed by the Act for registration.

The Chattels Transfer Act 1908 remained on the books until 1924 but was, during that period, subjected to three amending Acts; the Chattels Transfer Amendment Act 1919, the Chattels Transfer Amendment Act 1922, and the Chattels Transfer Amendment Act 1923. The amendment of 1919 repealed the provision of the 1908 Act avoiding instruments by way of security given to secure an antecedent debt within four months prior to the filing of a petition in bankruptcy because it conflicted with an analogous section of the Bankruptcy Act. In addition it expanded the catalogue of exceptions from the term "instrument" by adding a new subsection listing "mortgages or charges granted or created under the Companies Act, if entered in the register of mortgages of that company and registered with the Registrar of Companies pursuant to the provisions of the said Act . . ."

Prompted by two recent cases, the amendments of 1922 accorded an increased protection of *bona fide* purchasers and mortgagees. As has been stated before, traditionally the Bills of Sales Acts protected only creditors against latent security interests. As an exception New Zealand had introduced a protection of *bona fide* purchasers against unregistered instruments in the case of mortgages of stock by the Mortgages of Stock Registration Act 1868, and had later extended it to wool and crops by the Chattels Transfer Act of 1889. The new protection was also accorded to auctioneers and dealers in the ordinary course of trade. In addition the amending Acts of 1922 and 1923 expanded the scope of the instruments comprising stock with respect to the natural increase or other additions and modified the provisions pertaining to security over wool.

In 1924 it was felt that a major overhaul of the law relating to chattels transfers was in order. The revision was enacted as the Chattels Transfer Act 1924. The principal substantive innovations related to a new regime for customary hire purchase agreements, notice effect ascribed to registration, and invalidation of instruments comprising after-acquired property (except stock, wool and crops or fixtures, plant or trade machinery) only in regard to creditors and *bona fide* purchasers rather than absolute invalidity. Other changes related to the effects of the omission from the instruments of a defeasance, condition or declaration of trust to which it is subject at the time it is made or given, special provisions for the description of stock not properly the subject of distinctive marking, a re-definition of the exclusion from the definition of instrument of mortgages or charges granted or created by a company incorporated or registered under the Companies Act and a special provision listing the sections of the Act that also govern mortgages, charges and debentures registered with the Registrar of Companies. The two last changes were prompted by the decision in *Carnross* v. *Wilson's Motor Supplies Ltd*. The Act retained the provisions of the prior law relating to the assignment of book debts, adding an exemption relating to floating charges covering book debts provided that such charge is registered under the Companies Act. It failed, however, to retain the reference to book debts in the definition of chattels.

Unfortunately the revision of 1924 did not prove to be as successful as was hoped, and a series of amendments were called for in the course of time. The first was made in the year following the passage of the principal Act. It restricted the notice effect of registration and immunised grantees of any prior registered instruments relating to the same chattels. The regime governing customary hire purchase agreements which was the great innovation of the Act of 1924 proved troublesome and the problems presented by *Traders' Finance Corporation Ltd.* v. *General Motors Acceptance Corporation* necessitated a revamping of the applicable law. Section 57 as originally enacted defined customary hire purchase agreements as a deed or agreement in writing made between the owner of or a dealer in certain privileged categories of chattels and a conditional purchaser of those chattels, whether in form of a conditional sale or a bailment with an option to buy. A customary hire purchase agreement of the privileged type was exempt from the onus of registration, and the vendor or bailor in such agreement was protected against illegal disposition by the conditional purchaser or bailee, against the effects of the reputed ownership clause in the bankruptcy of the conditional purchaser or bailee, and against the effects of affixation to realty.

The Chattels Transfer Amendment Act 1931 was primarily designed to clarify the position of finance corporations engaged in the financing of customary hire purchase agreements. The statute provided that a finance corporation engaged in the financing of hire purchase agreements of "customary chattels" (a term introduced by the Act of 1931) was to be in the position of a dealer in such chattels; with the result that hire purchase agreements of customary chattels between a finance corporation and a conditional purchaser were to be treated as customary hire purchase agreements with the legal effects attached thereto. The statute extended the exemption from the onus of registration under the Chattels Transfer Act to assignments of customary hire purchase agreement, whether absolute or by way of mortgage, and accorded to such assignments a similar privilege with respect to registration under the Companies Act. It made the limitation on the power of disposition of the bailee or buyer under a customary hire purchase agreement subject to s. 3 of the Mercantile Law Act. It granted, subject to specified conditions, the assignee in bankruptcy and the assignee for the benefit of creditors of the conditional purchaser the power of acquiring the chattels in his possession upon payment of the outstanding balance. The statute denied the benefits of the privileged status of customary hire purchase agreements to arrangements between manufacturers, wholesale dealers or finance corporations and retail dealers by which the retailer is given possession of the chattel, but it exempted customary chattels, owned by a wholesale dealer and in the possession of a retail dealer, from the application of the reputed ownership rule.

In addition the amending Act of 1931 exempted instruments executed to secure loans of purchase money on chattels to be acquired therewith from the proscription against instruments covering after-acquired property and extended the exemption from the rules on after-acquired property, extraneous conditions or defeasances and itemised description in the schedule to tractors, engines and farming equipment used upon or in connection with premises specified in the instrument.

In 1936 it was provided that the exemption from the onus of registration was not to extend to the inventory requirement and that customary hire purchase agreements were instruments for that purpose.

The next important amendment occurred in 1939 and consisted of a revision of the provisions on book debts. The inclusion in the Act of sections relating to instruments comprising book debts, without extending the definition of chattels to book debts, had caused conflicting judicial decisions. The faulty draftsmanship was remedied and at the same time a definition of "book debts" was inserted in s. 31 of the principal Act, coupled with a deletion of subs. (4) of former s. 31 which excluded the application of that section to floating charges registered with the Registrar of Companies.

Subsequent amendments were mostly of a technical nature. Special mention need only be made of the revision of the provisions governing the renewal of registration and of the extension of the exemption from registration of any assignment of chattels subject to customary hire purchase agreements. The first of these two amendments codified the result reached in *In re an Instrument, Perry to Bank of Australia*, while the second one was designed to alleviate doubts stemming from language contained in the opinion of Smith J., in *Dempsey and another and the National Bank of New Zealand Ltd.* v. *The Traders' Finance Corporation Ltd.*

Similar to the impact of the English legislation on bills of sale on the Chattels Transfer Acts and their predecessors was the effect of the English statutes on the

New Zealand statutes relating to the registration of debentures and charges created by registered companies. As has been stated before, the Chattels Transfer Act 1889 was the first New Zealand Act relating to the registration of bills of sale which expressly excluded "debentures . . . issued by any company or other corporate body . . . and secured upon the capital stock or chattels of such company or other corporate body" from the definition of "instrument". The Companies Act 1882 which was in force at the time provided, like its English counterpart, that limited companies under this Act should keep a register of all mortgages and charges specifically affecting property of the company and that such register should be open to inspection by any creditor or member of the company. The scope of the exemption of company charges puzzled the New Zealand Courts. In *Bank of New Zealand* v. *Walter Guthrie and Co. Ltd.* the Court held that there was no general exemption of instruments given by registered companies from the coverage of the Act of 1889 and that the exception applied strictly to instruments of debenture. Accordingly, it was held that mortgages in the form of floating charges given by affiliated companies over all their assets of every description for the purpose of securing debentures of the principal company were void becuase of the violation of the prescription against securities over after-acquired property. Williams J. based his holding on the ground that the exception of interests in the property of any corporate body from the definition of chattels (an exception which dated back to the first English Bills of Sale Act of 1854 and was copied into each of its progeny) meant only interest of shareholders or members and not any type of interest in corporate assets. He rejected the policy reasons of the famous *Standard Manufacturing Company's* case as inapplicable to the New Zealand Act since the latter, in contrast to the English Act of 1878, contained also provisions dealing with matters other than publicity in the interest of creditors. Conversely in *Geoghegan* v. *Greymouth-Point Elizabeth Railway & Coal Company* the Court of Appeal held that debentures and a trust deed given to secure the debentures and referred to in the body of such debentures were outside the provisions of the Chattels Transfer Act of 1889 although the company kept no register of mortgages and charges in New Zealand. The Court relied at length upon the policy reasons adduced in the *Standard Manufacturing Company's* case.

In 1900 the perplexity of the profession was alleviated by the enactment of the Companies Act Amendment Act 1900. This statute provided for registration with the Registrar of Companies of instruments creating mortgages of three types:

(1) Mortgages of uncalled or unpaid capital of the company;
(2) Mortgages for the purpose of securing any issue of debentures;
(3) Floating mortgages on the undertaking or property of the company, not being a lien by law or a mortgage created in the ordinary course of business.

Failure to register within twenty-one days after the execution of the instrument (accompanied by an affidavit) rendered the morgage without effect either at law or in equity. The statute was implemented the following year by provisions detailing additional particulars. The Companies Act 1903 modified the existing system in important respects, following (nearly verbatim) the provisions of the English Act to amend the Companies Acts 1900 discussed before. It extended the duty of registration with the Registrar of Companies to four classes of mortgages, *viz.*:

(1) A mortgage or charge for the purpose of securing any issue of debentures,
(2) A mortgage or charge on uncalled capital of the company,
(3) A mortgage or charge created or evidenced by an instrument which, if executed by an individual, would require registration as a bill of sale,
(4) A floating charge on the undertaking or assets of the company.

Failure to register within twenty-one days after the execution of the instrument creating such mortgage resulted in invalidity of the security against the liquidator or any creditor of the company. The law has remained in this form through successive Companies Acts until the present day, although the catalogue of mortgages or charges to be registered with the Registrar of Companies was expanded in the course of time. The Companies Act 1933, following the example of the English Companies Act of 1929, listed nine classes of charges subject to registration, adding charges on book debts, land, calls made but not paid, ships or any share therein and goodwill, patents, trademarks or copyrights or licences under patents or copyrights to the four categories previously specified. The special inclusion of book debts needs comment. Under the English Bills of Sales Acts book debts were not considered as chattels and consequently not covered thereby. Accordingly, they were not caught by the clause requiring the registration of instruments "which if executed by an individual would require registration as a bill of sale". Registration of instruments assigning book debts was required in England only under the Bankruptcy and Deed of Arrangement Act 1913, if made by a person engaged in any trade or business and covering existing or future book debts other than book debts due at the date of assignment from specified debtors or becoming due under specified contracts. The registration was to be made under the Act of 1878 "as if the assignment were a bill of sale given otherwise than by way of security for the payment of a sum of money", regardless of whether the assignment actually was by way of security or created merely a charge. Non-compliance rendered the assignment void as against the trustee in bankruptcy but not against execution creditors or other creditor representatives. As a result the separate listing of charges on book debts as registrable charges under the English Companies Acts was called for. In New Zealand, however, the situation was quite different, as the Chattels Transfer Acts since 1895 extended to book debts. Certainly, since the Statutes Amendment Act 1939, book debts would fall squarely under the clause relating to instruments "which, if executed by an individual, would require registration under the Chattels Transfer Act", and therefore the listing of charges on book debts as a separate registrable item in the Companies Act is redundant, if not misleading.

Conclusions

The foregoing discussion is designed to highlight some of the inconsistencies and uncertainties of the present New Zealand law governing secured transactions. In the current discussions about a reform of the commercial law of New Zealand they should be particularly pertinent.

One of the major policy questions to be resolved should focus on the wisdom and expediency of the two-track system: one for companies and one for individual traders. Is it really advisable to have two different registers and two sets of rules governing the permissible scope of the security on after-acquired property and the protection of third parties? Would it not be preferable to have unified or uniform rules governing chattel transactions, regardless whether the grantor is unincorporated or a company? Special consumer protection ought to be the subject of separate legislation.

On the other hand, care should be taken not to lean too heavily on Article 9 of the Uniform Commercial Code of the United States. It has now become abundantly clear that this legislation, although based on some excellent basic ideas, is replete with over-refined distinctions and plagued by gaps and uncertainties, especially in regard to its regulation of priorities. Most of all, the concept of the floating charge is not used in the United States. Should it be retained and extended to non-corporate businesses or should it be buried? Does it make sense to allow both: floating charges on future assets and specific charges on after-acquired property? Without careful attention to such fundamental issues little could be gained from a reform.

Chattels Transfer Act 1924

Section 2

Instruments

"Instrument" means and includes any bill of sale, mortgage, lien, or any other document that transfers or purports to transfer the property in or right to the possession of chattels, whether permanently or temporarily, whether absolutely or conditionally, and whether by way of sale, security, pledge, gift, settlement, bailment, or lease, and also the following:

    (a) Inventories of chattels, with receipt thereto attached:

    (b) Receipts for purchase money of chattels:

    (c) Other assurances of chattels:

    (d) Declarations of trust without transfer:

    (e) Powers of attorney, authorities, or licences to take possession of chattels as security for any debt:

    (f) Any agreement, whether intended to be followed by the execution of any other instrument or not, by which a right in equity to any chattels, or to any charge or security thereon or thereover, is conferred:

"Instrument" does not include the following:

    (a) Securities over, or bailments or leases of, fixtures (except "trade machinery" as hereinafter defined), when mortgaged or leased in any mortgage or lease of any freehold or leasehold interest in any land or building to which they are affixed, and whether or not such fixtures are separately mortgaged or leased by mention thereof in separate words, and whether or not power is given by such mortgage or lease to sever such fixtures from the land or building to which they are affixed without otherwise taking possession of or dealing with such land or building:

    (b) Assignments for the benefit of the creditors of the person making the same:

    (c) Transfers of or agreements to transfer instruments by way of security:

    [(d) Transfers or assignments of any ship or vessel or any share thereof if executed before the 1st day of October 1940, or if at the time of execution the ship or vessel is registered or required to be registered under the provisions of [[Part XII of the Shipping and Seamen Act 1952]]:]

(e) Transfers of chattels in the ordinary course of business of any trade or calling:

(f) Debentures and interest coupons issued by any Government or local authority:

(g) Bills of sale of chattels in any foreign parts, or at sea:

(h) Bills of lading, warehouse keepers' certificates, warrants, or orders for the delivery of chattels, entries in auctioneers' books, or any other document used in the ordinary course of business as proof of the possession or control of chattels, or authorising or purporting to authorise, either by endorsement or delivery, the possessor of such document to transfer or receive the chattels thereby represented.

(i) Debentures and interest coupons issued by any company or other corporate body and secured upon the capital stock or chattels of such company or other corporate body:

(j) Mortgages or charges granted or created by a company incorporated or registered under [the Companies Act 1955]:

(k) Customary hire purchase agreements as defined in this Act:

[(l) Mortgages or charges granted or created by a society registered under the Industrial and Provident Societies Act 1908:]

"Instrument by way of bailment" means an instrument whereby chattels are leased or bailed:

"Instrument by way of security" means an instrument given to secure the payment of money or the performance of some obligation:

Chattels

"Chattels" means any personal property that can be completely transferred by delivery, and includes machinery, stock and the natural increase of stock as hereinafter mentioned, crops, and wool [and also includes book debts], but does not include—

(a) Chattel interests in real estate, title deeds, choses in action [(not being book debts)], negotiable instruments; or

(b) Shares and interests in the stock, funds, or securities of any Government or local authority; or

(c) Shares and interests in the capital or property of any company or other corporate body; or

(d) Debentures and interest coupons issued by any Government, or local authority, or company, or other corporate body:

Williams & Kettle v O A Harding

(1908) 27 NZLR 871

WILLIAMS, J.:—

The appellants are stock and station agents and auctioneers. The bankrupt, Harding, was a stock-dealer. The appellants had had dealings with him. He bought stock from them either by auction or privately, and sold stock through them in the same way. Mr. Kettle, the appellants' managing director, says that the usual conditions were cash, although they did not always get cash; but in the ordinary course of business sales were cleared within fourteen days or a month, and that special arrangements might be made in respect of any particular sale, as, for instance, that he might arrange to send in stock for the next sale to cover the amount, the appellants delivering the stock on the faith of his promise. In the beginning of August, 1907, Harding was indebted to the appellants in the sum of £1,171 14s. 11d., and on the 9th of August Mr. Monteith, an agent of the appellants, intimated to him that the appellants wanted his account settled or reduced. Harding said, "Oh! it's all right. You've still got those bullocks. I have still got them on hand." Afterwards on the same day Harding wrote the following letter: —

"Kiritaki, 9th August, 1907. — MESSRS. WILLIAMS & KETTLE, — On looking over my account I find I owe you a considerable amount, and, as I have 200 cattle grazing at Ongaonga which were bought through you, I am giving you sole right to them. The amount the cattle cost is between £1,000 and £1,100. I only ask that I be allowed to jockey the cattle off through your firm. *Re* 700 wethers advertised of mine, will not come forward, but will replace with 900 good hoggets. I think I can get them through in time. — Yours faithfully, GEORGE HARDING."

Afterwards, on the 13th, Monteith had again a conversation with Harding. Monteith told Harding that Mr. Bunny, the appellants' manager at Dannevirke, had asked Monteith to speak to Harding with reference to getting his account squared, and that if he did not do so they would sell him no more stock. Harding replied that he had posted a letter to the firm giving them the sole right to the bullocks, and asked whether that would satisfy the firm. The letter of the 9th of August and the above conversations are all that passed between Harding and the appellants as to giving security over these cattle. On the 9th of August the 200 head of cattle were grazing on the land of one Chamberlain. They were taken possession of by the appellants on the 20th of August, and removed on the 21st. Harding had absconded on the 15th of August, and on the 5th of September he was adjudged bankrupt on that ground. The bankruptcy thus dated back to the 15th of August. The appellants retained possession of the cattle, and sold them on the 15th of October. The Assignee now seeks to recover their value.

I agree with Mr. Justice Cooper in the Court below that the true construction of the letter is that it gives, and was intended to give, to the appellants the right to take the cattle into possession, to sell them, and to place the proceeds to the credit of Harding's debt. The sale authorised would be a sale in the usual way, either by auction or privately. The request that Harding should be allowed to jockey them off through the appellants' firm means simply that he should be allowed, as agent for the firm, to dispose of them to the best advantage. The 79th section of "The Bankruptcy Act, 1892" subsection 2, enacts

that every instrument by way of security under 'The Chattels Transfer Act, 1889,' or any Act repealed thereby, over any property of a bankrupt shall be null and void as against the Assignee of the bankrupt's estate if it has been executed within four months prior to the adjudication, except as to money actually advanced or paid, or the actual price or value of goods or chattels sold or supplied by the grantee of the security to the grantor contemporaneously with or at any time after the execution thereof.

Section 82 of the Bankruptcy Act, which protects certain transactions, does not protect such instruments, as that section is expressly made subject to the provisions of the Act with respect to the avoidance on bankruptcy of the conveyances and dispositions mentioned in the Act. It was held also by this Court in *In re Marsh* that the 3rd subsection of section 79 does not apply to protect the grantees under the instruments avoided by the 2nd subsection. If, therefore, the letter of the 9th of August is an instrument by way of security under "The Chattels Transfer Act, 1899," it is void as against the Assignee in bankruptcy. If the interpretation of the letter of the 9th of August be correct, it is undoubtedly a document which purports to transfer the right to the possession of chattels by way of security. It is therefore an instrument as defined by section 2 of the Chattels Transfer Act, unless it is a document which comes within one of the exceptions mentioned in that section. If it is an instrument it is certainly an instrument by way of security as defined by the Act, as it was given to secure the payment of money. It was contended, however, that it was not an instrument under the Act, as it came within the exceptions (*e*) and (*h*) in section 2: (*e*) excepts transfers of chattels in the ordinary course of business of any trade or calling; (*h*) excepts bills of lading, warehouse-keeper's certificates, warrants, or orders for the delivery of chattels, or any other document used in the ordinary course of business as proof of the possession or control of goods, or authorising or purporting to authorise, either by indorsement or delivery, the possessor of such document to transfer or receive the goods thereby represented. The construction of two exceptions, couched practically in the same language, was discussed by the Privy Council in the case of *Tennant v. Howatson*. This case was not cited at the hearing, but Mr. Justice Edwards has kindly called my attention to it. The case shows, at any rate, that if a document appears *prima facie* to be within the operation of the Act it lies upon those who assert it is excluded to adduce clear proof that it is one of the special transactions which is excluded. Apart from any authority, it is perfectly clear that the document is not within exception (*h*). The letter here bears no resemblance at all to the class of documents referred to in that exception. As to exception (*e*), there is no evidence at all that the letter was a transfer of the stock in the ordinary course of business. As was said of the document in question in *Tennant v. Howatson*, the execution of such a document may be of frequent occurrence, but it is not shown to be the common practice, and it must be shown to be the common practice before it can be said to be a transfer in the ordinary course of business. Even if it were shown to be the common practice it does not follow that it is in the ordinary course of business. The judgment in the above case goes on to say,

> "Moreover, though it is not easy to say with any precision at all what is meant by the expression 'the ordinary course of business,' their Lordships are of opinion that it does not point to the borrowing of money on mortgage or special agreement, though such a thing may be frequent among certain classes of persons."

If the letter here is within exception (*e*) because it was given in the ordinary course of business, it is difficult to see why any letter from a customer to his banker or from a retail to a wholesale dealer undertaking to give security over goods to secure a debt due should not be within the exception. In the present case the letter was not a mere memorandum accompanying a parol agreement. Any rights the appellants have over the cattle rest on the document and on the document alone. That being so, the cattle were in the possession of the appellants and were unsold at the time of the adjudication. The adjudication makes the instrument void. If before the adjudication the cattle had been sold and the money received by the appellants, the appellants would have been entitled to retain the money. The instrument would have ceased to exist before the adjudication. The adjudication cannot avoid an instrument which at the time of adjudication has ceased to have any existence. That was decided in *In re McCandlish*. See also *Cookson* v. *Swire*. The Court will not revive an extinct instrument for the purpose of avoiding it. Here, however, the cattle were not sold. The only authority the appellants had from Harding to retain possession of and deal with the cattle was by virtue of letter. But the letter becomes a void instrument when the order of adjudication is made. The result is that the appellants at the time of the adjudication have property in their hands belonging to the bankrupt, over which they have no right either of possession or disposition. In such a case, if they sell it the Assignee is entitled to recover the proceeds.

A point, however, was raised in this Court which was not raised in the Court below. It appears from the judgment of Mr. Justice Cooper that the sum of £514 12s., part of the total indebtedness of Harding to the appellants, was for sheep purchased from the appellants on the 23rd of July. It was contended that, as this was less than twenty-one days before the 9th of August, the letter was a valid security over the cattle, at any rate for this sum, by virtue of the concluding part of subsection 2 of section 79 of the Bankruptcy Act. I have already quoted the first part of the subsection. It goes on to enact as follows:

> "Any unpaid purchase-money for any property shall be deemed to be money actually advanced at the time of execution: Provided that the instrument for securing the same be executed within twenty-one days after the sale of the property."

I have had the opportunity of reading the judgment of Mr. Justice Edwards, where this question is fully discussed, and for the reasons he has given I agree that the term "any property" refers to the like term in the earlier part of the section—that is, that it means property over which the instrument by way of security is given, and is limited to such property. The sheep in question were not part of the property over which the security was given. I think, therefore, that the appeal should be dismissed. It becomes unnecessary, therefore, to consider the cross-appeal. As we intimated at the hearing, we agreed with Mr. Justice Cooper that there was no fraudulent preference, and the minor point on the cross-appeal was abandoned by the respondent.

ANZ Banking Group v John Jones

[1984] 2 NZLR 29

PRICHARD J. The plaintiff in this action ("the bank") is the grantee of an instrument by way of security executed by a Mr and Mrs Trow. The instrument purports to create a charge over 105 dairy cattle owned by Mr and Mrs Trow and to secure payment of the amount from time to time owing by Mr and Mrs Trow to the bank. A copy of the instrument was filed in the office of the Registrar of the High Court, Hamilton, on 12 July 1979.

The defendant company is an auctioneer. For convenience, I will refer to the defendant company by that description.

It is common ground that on 10 March 1980, the auctioneer sold stock belonging to Mr and Mrs Trow for a total amount of $19,555.27. Out of the proceeds of the sale, the auctioneer paid a sum of $9134.08 to a first charge holder—the Rural Banking & Finance Corporation. The balance was paid by the auctioneer to its principals, Mr and Mrs Trow. The Trows then left for parts unknown, owing the bank about $8600.

There is no evidence that the auctioneer had actual notice of the instrument by way of security. The question is whether it had constructive notice by virtue of the registration of the instrument. Section 19 of the Chattels Transfer Act 1924 reads:

> "Upon the expiration of the time or extended time for registration no unregistered instrument comprising any chattels whatsoever shall, without express notice, be valid and effectual as against any bona fide purchaser or mortgagee for valuable consideration, or as against any person bona fide selling or dealing with such chattels as auctioneer or dealer or agent in the ordinary course of his business."

This provision was first enacted by the Chattels Transfer Amendment Act 1922 as an amendment to the Chattels Transfer Act 1908. It may be inferred that the protection thus afforded to auctioneers, dealers and agents acting in the ordinary course of business was in consequence of the judgment of Herdman J in *R v Buckland & Sons Ltd* [1922] NZLR 683. In that case, Herdman J was constrained to hold that an auctioneer who had in good faith sold a number of pigs which were imperfectly described in an instrument by way of security was liable to account to the grantee of the instrument for the proceeds. Herdman J said at pp 688-689 of the report:

> "As s 25 of the Chattels Transfer Act, 1908, provides that imperfectly described stock are not secured to the grantee of an instrument as against the persons mentioned in s 16 of the statute, it would seem to follow that a *bona fide* purchaser for value without notice (being a person mentioned in subs 3 of s 16) who buys stock which are not reasonably capable of identification by reference to brands, or marks, or by reference to the other means of identification referred to in s 25, is protected. If, then, the buyer of such stock is secure from attack, why should an auctioneer, who sells the same stock *bona fide* and without any knowledge of the existence of a security, be held liable for wrongful conversion?"

It is the defendant's case in this action that the stock sold were not sufficiently described in the instrument and that, even if they were, the instrument was not duly registered.

The description in the schedule to the instrument reads as follows:

> "*Stock*
> 70 mixed age Friesian Dairy Cattle
> 35 Jersey mixed age Dairy Cattle."

In the body of the instrument appears the following covenant:

(j) That the Grantor "will brand earmark and mark" all the said stock as follows:

Males   Females

However, in the purported copy filed on 12 July 1979, the covenant is as follows:

(j) That the Grantor "will brand earmark and mark" all the said stock as follows:

Males   Females

Here I observe that the covenant as it appears in the original of the instrument applies to male — not to female — animals. I think I am able to draw on my judicial knowledge of the sex of dairy cattle in order to hold that the convenant does not therefore apply in terms to the animals described in the schedule. However, the point taken by Mr Houston for the defendant is simply that the document filed in the office of the Registrar is not, as it purports to be, a true copy of the instrument. In my view the point is well taken. The discrepancy is not a minor one: in the absence of any other adequate description the earmarking of the animals is of crucial significance.

The purported copy of the instrument filed in the office of the Registrar is a carbon copy, signed by the grantors, and is authenticated as a true copy of the instrument by a document signed by the solicitor who witnessed their signatures. Although not sworn as an affidavit, the authenticating document is in the form which was prescribed prior to the enactment of the Chattels Transfer Amendment Act 1970 by s 5 and set out in the first schedule to the Act. Since 1 January 1971, the statutory requirement is that in lieu of the affidavit formerly prescribed there be annexed to a true copy of the instrument a certificate in the form set out in the first schedule to the amending Act "or to the like effect". The form used in the present case was therefore about nine years out of date. Section 5(1) is mandatory in its terms:

"Registration of an instrument shall be effected by filing the same and all schedules endorsed thereon, or referred to therein, or a true copy of such instrument and the schedules, and certificate in the form numbered (1) in the First Schedule hereto or to the like effect ＊ ＊ ＊."

Mr Houston submits that the affidavit is not "to the like effect" of the certificate, in particular because the certificate includes an acknowledgement by the signatory that he is aware that he is guilty of an offence if he gives the certificate negligently. The offence referred to is a statutory offence created by s 2(3) of the Chattels Transfer Amendment Act 1973, rendering the negligent signatory of a certificate which is false in any material respect liable on conviction to a fine not exceeding $100.

The penalty for giving a false certificate is substantially less than that prescribed by s 110 of the Crimes Act 1961 for making a false oath—but under the Chattels Transfer Act, negligence is sufficient to constitute the offence, intention to mislead is not an ingredient.

Here, again, I am of the view that Mr Houston's point is well taken.

Section 28 of the Act requires not only that the stock comprised in the instrument be described or referred to, either by brand or mark or by sex, age, name, colour or other mode of description as to be reasonably capable of identification but also that "the land or premises on which the stock are or are intended to be depastured or kept shall be described or mentioned". In the present case, the land in question is described as follows: "Farmland containing 54 hectares situated at Waikare Road, RD 1, Te Kauwhata." This description is about as informative as the description of the stock contained in the schedule.

Whether this is a sufficient description of the land is at least questionable. The question is one of fact; at least one witness who is familiar with the district said that from the description given, he would not be able to identify the property.

Finally, as regards earmarks, there is a term in the body of the instrument reading as follows:

" 'The said stock' means the whole of the stock and classes of stock of the Grantor at any time during the continuance of this security on the lands and premises as hereinafter defined including (but not limited to) the stock and classes of stock described or referred to in the Schedule hereto and also all stock which by the terms of the said Act are included and all other stock of the Grantor at any time during the continuance of this security on the lands and premises as hereinafter defined. And also all the brands earmarks and marks now or hereafter to be registered in the name of the Grantor or otherwise having relation to the said stock."

What is meant by the reference in this clause to "the brands earmarks and marks now or hereafter to be registered in the name of the Grantor or otherwise having relation to the said stock" is not evident, unless it means that the grantee is to have security over such brands marks and earmarks—which hardly makes sense. I do not think this provision in the instrument assists in the identification of the stock.

Section 28 provides that an instrument which fails to describe the stock in such a way that they are reasonably capable of identification shall be void to the extent and as against the persons mentioned in s 18. Those persons are the Official Assignee, an assignee or trustee for the benefit of creditors, and a sheriff, bailiff or other person acting in execution of the process of any Court.

Section 16 of the Chattels Transfer Act 1908 was in the same terms as s 18 of the present Act but with an additional subsection:

"(3) No instrument comprising stock, or made or executed in respect of wool or crops, shall be valid or effectual against any *bona fide* purchaser for valuable consideration without express notice, unless such instrument is duly registered under this Act."

By the Chattels Transfer Act 1922, s 16(3) of the Act of 1908 was amended to provide that the avoidance of instruments comprising inadequately described stock as against bona fide purchasers for value was extended to cover auctioneers and dealers. Thus, when s 25 of the Act of 1908 provided that an instrument in which stock are inadequately described was void as against the persons mentioned in s 16 of the 1908 Act, this referred, inter alia, to bona fide purchasers, dealers and auctioneers. The provision in favour of bona fide purchasers, dealers and auctioneers is now the subject of s 19 of the Chattels Transfer Act 1924. That section relates to unregistered instruments but not expressly to instruments comprising insufficiently described stock. Thus, with the enactment of the Chattels Transfer Act 1924, the provision in favour of bona fide purchasers, dealers and auctioneers is taken out of s 18, the effect being that by s 19, unregistered instruments are expressly declared by s 19 to be void as against bona fide purchasers (etc) but instruments comprising inadequately described stock are not so declared by s 28.

In my view, this makes no real difference because an instrument which does not comply with the requirements of s 28 is incapable of registration under the Act, or if so registered does not give the grantee the benefit of such registration; (per Denniston, J in *Lee v Official Assignee* (1903) 22 NZLR 747, 750) at least as regards any stock which are insufficiently described (*Re Fairbrother, Official Assignee v Baddeley* (1905) 25 NZLR 546, 548).

In my view the instrument by way of security on which the plaintiff relies is not validly registered. "Registration" is defined by s 2 of the Act (as amended by the Chattels Transfer Amendment Act 1973) as follows: " 'Registration' means the filing of an instrument with schedule of inventories, or a true copy thereof, with the certificate hereinafter mentioned."

Section 5, as amended by the Chattels Transfer Amendment Act 1973 reads as follows:

"(1) Registration of an instrument shall be effected by filing the same and all schedules endorsed thereon, or referred to therein, or a true copy of such instrument and the schedules, and a certificate in the form numbered (1) in the First Schedule hereto or to the like effect, in the High Court Office of any Registrar in the provincial district within which the chattels comprised in the instrument are situated * * *"

The purported copy filed differed in a material respect from the original and the certificate was not in the form prescribed by the Act or "to the like effect". The "copy" is, however, signed by the grantors, Mr and Mrs Trow, so that the document may be regarded as an original (or executed couterpart) complying with the first limb of ss 2 and 5, and the defective certificate treated as surplusage. Even so, the inadequate description of the stock in the document so registered renders the registration ineffective: it does not attach the defendant with constructive notice that the animals sold at auction were the subject of an instrument by way of security in favour of the plaintiff.

There will be judgment for the defendant with costs accordingly to scale as on a claim for $8663.46 with disbursements and witnesses expenses as fixed by the Registrar.

Judgment for defendant

The Mechanics of Registration

This is dealt with in sections 4 to 13 of the Act, which should be read, *carefully*. Their essence is that registration of the instrument, or a true copy, must be made in the High Court Registry within which the chattels are situated at the time of giving or making thereof (section 5), within 21 days from the date of execution of the instrument (section 8). The Registry is a public registry, and registration is public notice (section 4).

The Consequences of Non Registration

Consider the following sections and cases. What *is* the effect of not registering an instrument within the meaning of the Act?

Chattels Transfer Act 1924

18. Unregistered instruments to be void in certain cases — (1) Every instrument, unless registered in the manner hereinbefore provided, shall, upon the expiration of the time for registration, or if the time for registration is extended by a Judge of the [High Court], then upon the expiration of such extended time, be deemed fraudulent and void as against —

(a) The Assignee in Bankruptcy of the estate of the person whose chattels or any of them are comprised in any such instrument:

(b) The assignee or trustee acting under assignment for the benefit of the creditors of such person:

(c) Any sheriff, bailiff, and other person seizing the chattels or any part thereof comprised in any such instrument, in execution of the process of any Court authorising the seizure of the chattels of the person by whom or concerning whose chattels such instrument was made, and against every person on whose behalf such process was issued —

so far as regards the property in or right to the possession of any chattels comprised in or affected by the instrument which, at or after the time of such bankruptcy, or of the execution by the grantor of such assignment for the benefit of his creditors, or of the execution of such process (as the case may be), and after the expiration of the period within which the instrument is required to be registered, are in the possession or apparent possession of the person making or giving the instrument, or of any person against whom the process was issued under or in the execution of which the instrument was made or given, as the case may be.

19. Unregistered instrument not to affect bona fide purchaser for value — Upon the expiration of the time or extended time for registration no unregistered instrument comprising any chattels whatsoever shall, without express notice, be valid and effectual as against any bona fide purchaser or mortgagee for valuable consideration, or as against any person bona fide selling or dealing with such chattels as auctioneer or dealer or agent in the ordinary course of his business.

OA v *Colonial Bank*

(1887) NZLR 5 SC 456

Action by the plaintiff as Official Assignee in Bankruptcy of the property of one
Samuel Stanford, a storekeeper, at "The Elbow", a country township, claiming
the value of goods wrongfully converted by the defendant. The statement of claim
alleged that the plaintiff was, on the 16th day of September, 1886, in possession
of certain horses, cattle, implements and stock in trade, and other chattels, and
that the defendant bank on that day converted said goods and chattels to its own
use, and wrongfully deprived the plaintiff of the possession of the same, and the
plaintiff claimed their value. The statement of defence denied the plaintiff's
possession, admitted seizing and selling the goods and chattels, and claimed and
justified such seizure and sale under a bill of sale dated the 9th September, 1882,
from Stanford to Messrs. Buchanan and Irvine, and an assignment dated the 18th
August, 1886, by them of the debt secured by the bill of sale, and the benefit
of the bill of sale and all covenants and conditions thereunder.

The action was heard before Williams, J., without a jury. It was admitted that
on the 9th September, 1882, a bill of sale of the goods and chattels seized had
been duly executed by Stanford to Messrs. Buchanan and Irvine, and that on the
18th August, 1886, the same had been duly assigned by Messrs. Buchanan and
Irvine to the bank; that three days before the bankruptcy of Stanford a bailiff from
the bank had gone to his store at "The Elbow," had taken an inventory of the
stock in trade with Stanford's assistance, that on the first two days after such seizure
the bailiff had sold some goods, retaining the money, and that on the third day
Stanford went to Invercargill to file a bankruptcy petition, and that on the day
preceding such filing the bailiff had locked up the store and also the inside door
communicating with the dwelling house, but he had since the seizure lived at
an hotel some hundred yards from the store. He had not done anything towards
taking possession of the stock, horses, cattle, or implements, beyond counting
them, and they remained in the paddocks and about the house as usual until some
days after the bankruptcy, when Stanford resumed possession as the bank's agent.

The covenant for payment in the bill of sale was as follows:—

"Now this deed witnesseth that in pursuance of the said agreement and in
consideration of the premises he, the mortgagor, doth hereby for himself, his heirs,
executors and administrators, covenant with the mortgagees and each of them, their
and each of their executors, administrators and assigns, *that he the mortgagor, his executors,
administrators or assigns, shall and will on demand in writing being made by the mortgagees,
or either of them, their or either of their executors, administrators or assigns,* or by the said
firm, pay to the mortgagees, their executors, administrators or assigns, or the said
firm, all sums of money which now are and shall from time to time hereafter become
due or payable from the mortgagor to the mortgagees or to the said firm on any
account whatsoever."

The words in italics had been, by an error of the copying clerk, omitted from
the copy filed under the "Chattels Securities Act 1880."

The bill of sale contained several references to "such demand as aforesaid" and toward the end of it the following words "and" [it is agreed]

"also that the demand of payment hereinbefore mentioned shall be in writing and signed by the mortgagees or either of them their or his executors administrators or assigns or by the said firm, and may be delivered to the mortgagor or his executors, administrators, or assigns, either personally or by letter addressed to him or them and left at the said store."

WILLIAMS, J.: —

The object of the provision in the Bills of Sale Act that a true copy of the bill of sale should be registered, was to give information to any member of the public that chose to seek for it as to the precise transaction that any person entered into with respect to his chattel property. It seems to me that the Legislature in providing for registration, contemplated that the copies which were to be registered would be read not only by members of the legal profession, but by the general public. In order that the copy to be filed may be a true copy it is not necessary, as has been held several times, that it should be an absolutely correct copy. It is sufficient, as was said by Chief Judge Bacon, "that it shall be so true that nobody reading it can by any possibility misunderstand it." Now, as I have said, the filed copy is intended to be read and to be understood, not only by lawyers, but by the general public, some of whom would in any case have difficulty in making out what the terms of a legal document really were, and it is in my opinion, from that point of view that we should consider the expression of Chief Judge Bacon—that the copy is so true that nobody reading it can by any possibility misunderstand it. The copy of the bill of sale in this case omits certain words which appear in the covenant for payment of the money secured by the bill of sale, and without these words the covenant for payment standing by itself is unintelligible. It does not say when or under what conditions payment is to be made. It is true there are a number of references later on in the document from which it can be inferred that payment was to be on a demand of some kind. The bill of sale, however, is a document of considerable length, and there is nothing in the copy from which one could infer the exact mode in which the demand was to be made until we come nearly to the end of it. Then there is a provision which says that the "demand of payment hereinbefore mentioned" etc. Now, no doubt a professional man reading this document, and reading it right through, would come to the conclusion that what had probably been omitted in the covenant for payment was the provision that payment was to be on demand in writing. These filed copies are intended, however, as I have said, to be read by the general public as well as by lawyers, and it seems to me it is impossible to say this omission is not one by which a layman might by some possibility be deceived. The omission is that of a very material part of what is itself perhaps the most material part of the document, viz., the convenant for payment. It is only by careful perusal of the document from beginning to end that even a professional man would be able to draw an inference as to what the omission was. If I were to hold that this is a true copy, I should be going really further than any of the cases which have been cited. Looking at the particular nature of this bill of sale, I think it is all the more important that there should be no doubt about the covenant. It covers not only present property, but all future property, and in a bill of sale of that kind it is all the more important for creditors to know beyond the shadow of a doubt what the terms of it are. I think, therefore, though I am sorry to upset the document because of what is a palpable slip, that this is not a true copy, either within the letter or the spirit of the Act, which requires a true copy to be filed.

Then comes the question as to whether the goods were, at the time of Stanford's bankruptcy, in his apparent possession. So far as the goods in the shop go, I believe the authorities justify me in holding that from the evidence before me they were not in his apparent possession. They were taken possession of by the bailiff of the Colonial Bank on the Monday. On the Tuesday goods were sold by the bailiff with Stanford at his elbow giving the prices, while the bailiff took the money. Then Stanford comes to town and the bailiff locks up the shop and takes the key and keeps the shop locked until after the bankruptcy. He goes about the place with the key in his pocket, and he also locks the door leading from the shop into the private part of the house. Stanford goes away; none of his family, or anybody representing him, have access to the shop, or deal at all with the goods in it. The bailiff puts up at a public house. This took place, as I understand, at Lumsden. Now, I have no judicial knowledge of Lumsden, but I believe it is a small country place, and of course, everything happening in a place of its size is known perfectly well to all the people in it. Probably they knew a great deal more about Hutton's business than he did himself. I should say therefore that the taking possession of the goods was sufficient and notorious; that Hutton got possession of the shop and what it contained, and that Stanford did not have apparent possession of them at the time of his bankruptcy. As to the rest of the goods, they were of course not taken possession of. They belonged to Stanford, and no true copy of the bill of sale having been filed, they pass to the Assignee in his estate. Judgment will therefore be for plaintiff, with costs on the lowest scale.

Judgment accordingly.

OA v Bartosh

[1955] NZLR 287

Action brought by the Official Assignee of the bankrupt estates of Jack Barrington Casey and his wife against the defendant, asking for a declaration that an unregistered instrument by way of security was, under s. 18 of the Chattels Transfer Act, 1924, fraudulent and void as against him.

On August 6, 1953, Mr. and Mrs. Casey were carrying on in Taihape, a restaurant and delicatessen business; and on that date they executed in favour of defendant an instrument by way of security over certain chattels situated in the premises in which the Casey's business was being carried on. The instrument was to secure repayment of a loan of £2,000. It was never registered under the Chattels Transfer Act, 1924.

In December, 1953, the Caseys were in financial difficulties and Mr. Casey consulted the Official Assignee in Taihape. He had a "general discussion on the effects of bankruptcy"; and, in particular, he sought information as to what would happen to his house and furniture. No final decision was made at that time or at a further interview in December with the Official Assignee; but it seemed to be understood that if Mr. Casey were to file his petition he would do it in January after the Official Assignee had returned from a period of leave, which was to be taken in January.

During December, the bankrupts were being pressed by some of their creditors. Judgments had been obtained against them, and distress warrants were issued. By paying off their most active creditors, they managed to avoid the execution of any of these warrants; but the fact that they were in financial difficulties must have been known in certain quarters in Taihape. At all events it came to the knowledge of Mr. R. C. Ongley, who was the defendant's solicitor. Shortly before Christmas, Mr. Ongley saw Casey at his shop. Mr. Ongley had heard that Mr. Casey was going to file in bankruptcy and, though Mr. Ongley did not say so in his evidence, Mr. Casey said that Mr. Ongley asked him it that was true, and Mr. Casey replied that "we hadn't decided". Again, according to Mr. Casey (for Mr. Ongley said nothing on this point), Mr. Ongley advised that nothing should be done till he returned from Auckland early in January.

Mr. Ongley returned to Taihape on January 5. He said that "about the first thing he heard was that Casey had closed down". The next morning, January 6, Mr. Ongley went to the bankrupt's premises. He took the instrument by way of security with him, and told Mr. Casey he was going to "seize the stuff in the bill of sale". (Not all the chattels in the shop were included in the bill of sale.) The shop was not open for business. It had been closed on the night of December 24, and remained closed right up to January 21, when the Caseys were adjudged bankrupt on their own petitions.

On January 6, with Mr. Casey's assistance, Mr. Ongley checked over the items in the bill of sale, and marked thereon which of them were still on the premises. Some were missing, though whether as a result of breakages or not was not disclosed in the evidence. At the completion of the check, Mr. Ongley distinctly told Mr. Casey that he had taken possession on behalf of the grantee of the instrument of such of the chattels comprised in the bill of sale as had then and there been found. There was no dispute as to that; and it was also common ground that Mr. Ongley was then handed the keys to the premises and that he retained them in his own custody right down to the date of the bankruptcy.

The Official Assignee of the estates of Mr. and Mrs. Casey claimed first a declaration that in the circumstances just described, and by virtue of s 18 of the Chattels Transfer Act, 1924, the instrument was fraudulent and void as against him.

BARROWCLOUGH, C. J. [After summarizing the facts, as above:] As the instrument was unregistered it would clearly be fraudulent and void as against the Official Assignee, in terms of s 18 of the Chattels Transfer Act, 1924,

> so far as regards the property in or right to the possession of any chattels comprised in . . . the instrument which, at or after the time of such bankruptcy, are in the possession or apparent possession of the person making or giving the instrument . . . .

Mr *Gilliand*, for the Official Assignee, submits that the goods seized by Mr.

Ongley were at the date of bankruptcy, and notwithstanding the seizure, in the apparent possession of the bankrupts.

Before examining the evidence on this topic, it is necessary to consider what is meant by "apparent possession". The phrase is not defined in our Chattels Transfer Act, 1924; but in s. 4 of the Bills of Sale Act, 1878 (41 & 42 Vict., c. 31) (*3 Halsbury's Statutes of England*, 2nd Ed. 557, 558)—it is defined as follows:

> Personal chattels shall be deemed to be in the "apparent possession" of the person making or giving a bill of sale, so long as they remain or are in or upon any house, mill, warehouse, building, works, yard, land, or other premises occupied by him, or are used and enjoyed by him in any place whatsoever, notwithstanding that formal possession thereof may have been taken by or given to any other person.

The definition in the Bills of Sale Act, 1854 (Eng.) was in almost identical terms and is to the same effect as the definition just quoted from the Bills of Sale Act, 1878 (Eng.). *Williams*, J., adopted it in this country in *Official Assignee of Slattery v. Slattery* (1895) 16 N.Z.L.R. 332, 334). The definition must be read, however, in the light of various cases which have been decided in England and New Zealand. The giving up to the grantee of the keys of the premises in which the chattels were placed has, in certain circumstances, been held to put an end to the occupation of the grantor and so to take the chattels out of the apparent possession of the grantor: *Robinson* v. *Briggs* (1870) L.R. 6 Exch. 1) and *Official Assignee* v. *Colonial Bank of New Zealand* (1887) N.Z.L.R. 5 S.C. 456). But it is clear, from *3 Halsbury's Laws of England*, 3rd Ed., p. 309, para 378 that the mere handing over of keys with nothing more is not enough:

> To terminate the grantor's apparent possession there must be more than formal possession on the part of another. Something must be done which in the eyes of everybody who sees the goods, or who is concerned in the matter, plainly takes them out of the possession, or apparent possession of the grantor.

The mischief which s. 18 of the Chattels Transfer Act, 1924, seeks to avoid is similar to the mischief which is aimed at by s. 61 (*c*) of the Bankruptcy Act, 1908. Judicial comments that have been made on "reputed ownership" both in England and New Zealand are of assistance, therefore, in understanding what is meant by "apparent possession". This similarity between the doctrine of reputed ownership under the Bankruptcy Act, 1908, and the doctrine of apparent possession under the Chattels Transfer Act, 1924, was adverted to by *Fair*, J., in *Auckland Milk Co., Ltd.* v. *Levy* [1934] G.L.R. 798, 801). He pointed out that *Edwards*, J., in *In re Alloway* ([1916] N.Z.L.R. 433; [1916] G.L.R. 327), treated the two phrases as interchangeable.

The following extracts from the speech of *Lord Selborne*, L.C., in *In re Couston, Ex parte Watkins* ((1873) L.R. 8 Ch. 520) are therefore both helpful and authoritative:

> "The doctrine of reputed ownership does not require any investigation into the actual state of knowledge or belief, either of all creditors, or of particular creditors, and still less of the outside world, who are no creditors at all, as to the position of particular

goods. It is enough for the doctrine if those goods are in such a situation as to convey to the minds of those who know their situation the reputation of ownership, that reputation arising by the legitimate exercise of reason and judgment on the knowledge of those facts which are capable of being generally known to those who choose to make inquiry on the subject. It is not at all necessary to examine into the degree of actual knowledge which is possessed, but the Court must judge from the situation of the goods what inference as to the ownership might be legitimately drawn by those who knew the facts. I do not mean the facts that are only known to the parties dealing with the goods, but such facts as are capable of being, and naturally would be, the subject of general knowledge to those who take any means to inform themselves on the subject. So, on the other hand, it is not at all necessary, in order to exclude the doctrine of reputed ownership, to show that every creditor, or any particular creditor, or the outside world who are not creditors, knew anything whatever about particular goods, one way or the other" (*ibid.*, 528). "It was accordingly laid down by *Sir James Mansfield*, in *Thackthwaite* v. *Cock* (3 Taunt. 487) that if the facts are such that those who deal with the bankrupts may see and know that the goods may not be the property of the bankrupts, that is enough to exclude the doctrine of the reputation of ownership" (*ibid.*, 530).

In the present case, the chattels comprised in the bill of sale were clearly in the possession of the bankrupts down to the date of their seizure by Mr. Ongley on January 6, 1954. After that date, they were in Mr. Ongley's possession; but they would remain in apparent possession of the bankrupts because they were "in or upon the premises of the persons making or giving the bill of sale" and they would so remain until "something was done which, in the eyes of everybody who sees the goods, or who is concerned in the matter, plainly takes them out of the apparent possession of the grantor." What then was done, and was it enough to put an end to the apparent possession? In examining that question, let us bear in mind what was said by *Lord Selborne* in regard to the allied doctrine of reputed ownership.

All that was done was this: Mr. Ongley and Mr. Casey entered the shop by going through an alleyway to the back door. It was not proved that anyone saw them enter, or saw them in the shop. Mr. Ongley then took possession and retained the keys. The shop, which had been closed down before, remained closed down. So far as the evidence went, there was no obvious change that could have been apparent to anyone but these two. The facts in the present case are very different from those which were proved in *Official Assignee* v. *Colonial Bank of New Zealand* (1887) N.Z.L.R. 5 S.C. 456). In that case, the bailiff who effected a seizure of the goods in a shop seized them openly. The shop was open, and for two days customers who came in saw the shopkeeper selling the goods with the bailiff at his elbow collecting the money that was paid for them. *Williams*, J., said he had no judicial knowledge of Lumsden, but he believed it to be a small country place. I have no judicial knowledge of Taihape; but I know it well, and I knew Lumsden fifty years ago; and, if I am permitted to say what I believe, it would be that the Lumsden to which *Williams*, J., referred was but a hamlet compared with the town of Taihape to-day. There is no comparison between the two places.

There was evidence—though not much—from which I could possibly infer that it was commonly known in Taihape by January 6, at all events that the Caseys were "closing down". This is an entirely irrelevant fact. There was no evidence at all that anybody knew the really important fact that Mr. Ongley had seized some of the goods in the Casey's shop. Mr. Auld, the owner of a shop adjoining the Casey's shop, said that before April, 1954, he "had no knowledge of the seizure of the bankrupts' goods". Mr. Ackroyd was the owner of the shop on the other side of the Casey establishment. He said that he was interviewed by the Official Assignee in April, 1954, and that "at the time he saw me I didn't know a seizure of Caseys' goods had been effected". There is here no proof that those who dealt with the bankrupts "might see and know that the goods might not be the property of the bankrupts so as to exclude the doctrine of reputation of ownership". There was no proof that those who might "take any means to inform themselves on the subject" knew of the seizure. All they were likely to know was that the premises were closed down; but they could have been closed down and were in fact for a time closed down without any seizure having been made. Upon the evidence, I can come to one conclusion only—namely, that at the date of the bankruptcy the goods, though formally seized, were still in the apparent possession of the bankrupts. The plaintiff is therefore entitled to a declaration that the instrument in question is fraudulent, and void as against him.

The plaintiff set up three alternative causes of action; but, as he has succeeded on his first cause of action, it is unnecessary to consider the others. The plaintiff should have his costs according to scale with disbursements for fees of Court and witnesses' expenses, to be fixed by the Registrar if necessary.

Judgment for the plaintiff.

Notes and Questions

1. The system of registration in the High Court applies only to natural persons: see Companies Act 1955, section 102(2)(c) and *Re Manuera Transport Ltd* [1971] NZLR 909. What therefore should you do in practice?

2. What are the practical consequences of requiring filing in the nearest High Court Registry?

3. What difficulties can you identify in the existing 'system'?

4. For commentary on this Act, see Riesenfeld, *supra* who criticizes trenchantly its less satisfactory features. See also the *Report of the Contracts and Commercial Law Reform Committee* (1973) and D V McLauchlan (1978) NZLJ 137. For general commentary on the provisions of the Act, see Farrar, *Butterworths Commercial Law in New Zealand* (1985) 435 *et seq.*

The Motor Vehicles Securities Act

In 1989 the New Zealand Parliament enacted this statute in response to what it (on both sides of the House) viewed as a serious problem. Purchasers had discovered that their cars were quite often encumbered by a hire purchase agreement. The vehicle was subsequently repossessed by a finance company.

Hon. G R Palmer (as Minister of Justice)

Hansard, 3 May 1989, 3860.

Rt. Hon. Geoffrey Palmer (Minister of Justice): I move, *That the Motor Vehicle Securities Bill be introduced*. The Bill deals with a problem familiar to many members of Parliament, both past and present. It is the problem of a person who buys a motor vehicle and then finds that a finance company has the right to repossess it because the seller owed money to the finance company under a hire purchase agreement, a chattel mortgage, or some other form of security.

The problem arises for two main reasons: the first is that hire purchase agreements over motor vehicles are not required to be registered anywhere. They are valid against subsequent purchases, even when a purchaser did not know that the agreements existed. The second reason is that, whilst security interests such as mortgages are required to be registered, they are not required to be registered in a central place. Instead, an agreement is registered in the High Court nearest to the place where the motor vehicle is when the agreement is entered into — and motor vehicles are notoriously mobile. That means that a purchaser may have to check the chattels registry in the High Court registries in at least the 11 main centres.

A solution to the problem has been sought for a considerable time. A scheme suggested by the New Zealand Law Society as long ago as 1953 involved annotating the motor vehicle registration papers. In 1975 an interdepartmental working party proposed restrictions on those who could hold the registration papers. There were various objections to that and similar suggestions, including the practical point that duplicate registration papers are easily obtainable.

The advent of computerisation, and its use in Australian schemes, suggested a path for New Zealand to follow. In 1984 a computerised central register of securities over motor vehicles came into operation in the state of Victoria, and other Australian states soon adapted the same approach. The finance industry, the motor trade, and the consumer organisations in New Zealand all favoured the establishment of a central register in this country. The Bill is the result of that concern. It provides the legal framework for the establishment of a computerised central register of securities over motor vehicles.

The Bill defines security interests very widely. The intention is to bring into the ambit of the Bill the circumstances in which one person has an interest in a vehicle but another person has possession of it. In such cases a third party dealing with the possessor can be misled into thinking that the possessor has an unfettered right to dispose of the motor vehicle. Thus the definition of security interests specifically includes hire purchase agreements, mortgages, and leases. A fixed charge creted by a company over a motor vehicle may be registered. A floating charge that has become fixed is not registrable. However, like other security interests, it is extinguished in relation to the motor vehicle in the absence of actual knowledge that it had become fixed. The secured party is defined as the person who holds the security interests, and the debtor as the person who created the security interest.

Part I of the Bill provides for secured parties to register their security interests on the centralised register, which will be run by the Department of Justice. The rules on the effect of registration or non-registration of a security interest are found in Part II. Once a security interest is registered, potential purchasers are deemed to have notice of it; thus, a purchaser buying a motor vehicle from a debtor in a private sale should check the register before completing the transaction.

I reiterate that very important point—when the Bill becomes law, the purchaser of a motor vehicle from a debtor in a private sale should check the register before completing the transaction. If that is done, many of the difficulties that have arisen in the past will evaporate. If a secured party does not register its interest on the register, and if the purchaser does not have actual notice of the security interests, the security interest is extinguished in respect of the purchaser. Secured parties, of course, retain their rights of recovery against debtors, but the important point relates to the eternal triangle that has so much characterised that part of the law— whereby the innocent party often bore all the loss. Those innocent parties will be in a much better position than they have been in the past. Indeed, many generations of law students and lawyers will find to their great relief that some of the case law will be rendered unnecessary.

A purchaser may check the register by applying, under clause 10, for a certificate showing the state of the register in relation to that motor vehicle. In addition, before finalising the sale, the purchaser may make an oral inquiry under clause 9 about the state of the register. In the interests of privacy, the name of the debtor and the amount of the debt will not be disclosed to a general inquirer, but may be made available to secured parties wanting to settle questions of priority.

The security interest is extinguished when a purchase is made from a licensed motor vehicle dealer. However, if the licensed motor vehicle dealer was aware of the security interest, either because it was registered or because he or she had actual knowledge, the secured party is entitled to recover from the dealer the outstanding amount owed under the security interest. If the dealer defaults on that obligation, the secured party may claim from the Motor Vehicle Dealers Fidelity Guarantee fund.

A check of the register is, of course, a facility open to motor vehicle dealers before they buy or sell vehicles. The Bill also deals with persons who, rather than buying a motor vehicle outright from the debtor, buy it on hire purchase or lease it. In a private transaction of that kind, the secured party may step in to the shoes of the debtor and claim the payments due. When a person buys an encumbered vehicle on hire purchase from a dealer, or leases the vehicle, the security interest is extinguished. However, if a motor vehicle dealer had notice of the security interest, the dealer—or, in default, the fund—is liable to reimburse the secured party.

In line with the approach adopted in New South Wales, the Bill provides in clause 8 for the entry into the register of the theft of a motor vehicle, as such vehicles are often later sold. Information about stolen vehicles will be furnished by the Commissioner of Police at his or her discretion. Such entries do not, of course, create security interests. Provision is made for them purely as an information service for persons buying or otherwise dealing with motor vehicles. Compensation is payable under clauses 47 to 50 for loss caused because the register is inaccurately kept or because inaccurate information is given. Jurisdiction to determine claims for compensation is vested in the small claims tribunal, which, for that purpose, is not subject to any jurisdictional limit.

Part III deals with the priorities of registered and unregistered security interests. The rule that registered interests have priority over unregistered interests is an important one, and registered interests have priority according to the time of registration. Unregistered interests have priority according to the time of creation, and the common law rules on priority of company charges are unaffected. The law on the enforcement by secured parties of their secured interests in unchanged by the Bill, and clause 53 preserves the general provisions of the Chattels Transfer Act 1924.

It is my devout wish that the Chattels Transfer Act 1924 be removed from the statute book as soon as possible. However, that task is a bigger one than that involved in the Motor Vehicle Securities Bill. Indeed, the Bill is restricted to motor vehicles. The Department of Justice is working on a revision of the Act, and it is hoped that one day soon New Zealand will have a less eccentric law relating to chattel security than it has had for all these years. The Act is something of a museum piece that attracts interest from many overseas experts, who come to see the strange chattel security law that exists in New Zealand.

The approach of the Bill has been taken because the subject of remedies for creditors as they apply to all security interests in all goods is being studied by a consultant employed by the Department of Justice, and a report from that consultant is expected in August. Depending on the recommendations contained in that report, the select committee may be able to improve clause 53 before the Bill is reported back.

Part V provides for a 6-month transitional period during which existing security interests may be either newly entered on the register or transferred from the High Court chattels registry.

The Bill deals with major difficulties created by the present law on personal property security. It will be greatly welcomed by consumer groups. I know that the Minister of Consumer Affairs has taken an active and positive role in promoting the measure, because consumer groups that have been in touch with her have a great interest in it. The Bill's provisions will finally get rid of the difficulties that have bedevilled New Zealand law for many years—really since the time motor vehicles became common.

The Bill will be welcomed by the motor trade, the finance industry, and the consumer groups that have pressed for such protection for a long time. Indeed, the only people who will be adversely affected by the Bill are the dishonest people who try to sell motor vehicles to which they are not entitled or that they have mortgaged to others without disclosing the nature of the security to the purchaser. I commend the Bill to the House.

Mr. Graham (Remuera): I listened carefully to the speech made by the Minister. The Opposition applauds the introduction of the Bill, and will welcome its consideration by the select committee. As the Minister said, the problems that arise when innocent people purchase vehicles only to find a repossession agent at the door a month or two later are legion in New Zealand. That problem has occurred for decades. The Minister said that one way to counteract it was to adopt the English system of a log-book, which, in effect, is another certificate of title similar to a land transfer title. Any charges or hire purchase agreements that the owner has entered into would be registered on that title. However, I agree that that is a clumsy way of dealing with the problem. It is better to have a central register to record the transactions. If the person with the security does not bother to register the security, then be it on his own head.

The system should work well provided the central register operates efficiently and provided there is an instant answer when oral inquiries are made under clause 9. The central register is to commence in October 1989. That should provide sufficient time for people to reregister their securities, and to give notice to people of the proposed change to the law. However, it will be essential to ensure that the registrar of motor vehicles has the equipment and the computer technology to enable him or her to record register applications immediately and to provide that information immediately to an inquirer. I am a little concerned that oral inquiry is sufficient, because there could often be a lack of proof of what was said by the registrar to the inquirer.

Rt. Hon. Geoffrey Palmer: People can't rely on oral inquiries.

Mr Graham: I am obliged to the Minister. It is obvious that the person making the inquiry will want a certificate subsequently, as provided in the Bill. However, that seems to be the most efficient way of handling what has clearly been a major problem for some time. The only other matter that requires comment after an initial examination of the Bill is clause 7, which relates to the registration of the security. The particulars that are registered are the details of the motor vehicle involved, the name and address of the secured party—the lender of the money— the type and term of the security interest, the date on which it was registered, and the debt. Clause 7 does not mention the person who grants the security or the person who is pledging the vehicle. I am not very sure why that is so— perhaps the Minister in reply could explain that. It seems to me that the purchaser of the vehicle would want to know first whether there was a charge against the car registered at the central registry office, and, if there was a charge against the vehicle, who registered it. The person with whom he or she is dealing may or may not be the person who gave the security in the first place. Therefore I am not sure why the person granting the security has been left out of clause 7.

Another matter that is worthy of comment at this stage is the position of the debenture holder. Under clause 34 the debenture holder under a floating charge runs the risk that what he or she considers to be part of his or her security— namely, a motor vehicle—could be removed from the security of the debenture if it is not registered in accordance with the Bill. Indeed, those people who customarily issue debentures—banks, other finance companies, and trading companies—will henceforth have to ensure, if motor vehicles are involved, that they specifically register them with the central registry office to obtain the security that they require.

The Bill is long and detailed. However, it seems to be well set out and reasonably easy to follow. People granting securities over motor vehicles, people to whom the security is granted, and people purchasing vehicles will obviously be dramatically affected by the BIll. I am sure that the Bill will attracts many submissions at the select committee hearings. I look forward to the consideration of the Bill by the select committee, and the reporting back of the Bill to the House.

Hon Margaret Shields (as Minister of Consumer Affairs)

Hansard, 3 May 1989, 3863.

*   *   *

Every person who buys a used car runs [a] risk. It could happen to anyone at any time—it could happen to a member tomorrow. The Motor Vehicle Securities

Bill is designed to stamp out such insecurity. The Motor Vehicle Dealers Institute surveyed it members in 1986 and found that, during the previous 12 months, 95 encumbered vehicles had been sold and the dealer had paid off the finance companies. A further 28 purchasers have been paid off by the Motor Vehicle Dealers Fidelity Guarantee Fund when the dealers had failed in the obligations. Those numbers do not include vehicles that were sold privately, when it is more difficult for consumers to obtain redress. The problem is not theoretical—it is an everyday happening in New Zealand.

The Motor Vehicle Securities Bill sets out to solve that problem by establishing a central registry for all debts registered against vehicles. A central registry does not exist at present; securities are registered in the 11 chief High Court offices. In theory it is possible to check personally whether any outstanding debts are registered against a vehicle. However, it is not easy to check on such matters quickly. Most important, most people do not even know that the check should be made, because they do not realise that the ownership of their vehicle might be at risk. Not many car buyers would be willing to check personally with each of the 11 offices about used cars that they are considering purchasing. The few people who do go through the process receive no guarantee that the absence of a registered security necessarily means that the vehicle is free of debt because the Chattels Transfer Act—rather extraordinary legislation—does not require that hire purchase agreements be registered for those agreements to be valid and effectual.

It is apparent that a central body of information relating to vehicles will not only enable consumers to investigate potential purchases for themselves but will also encourage them to do so. The present system is not fair to consumers, and that is why the Ministry of Consumer Affairs is very pleased to support the introduction of the Motor Vehicle Securities Bill. The ministry has been aware for some time of the need for new legislation to deal with securities for motor vehicles, and it has been consulted throughout the drafting process of the Bill. The current legal position is highly unsatisfactory for consumers. Under the present law consumers have some redress, but the method is time-consuming, and can be expensive. If the vehicle is purchased from a registered dealer the consumer can claim from the Motor Vehicle Dealers Fidelity Guarantee Fund. However, if the vehicle is purchased privately the consumer has to sue the previous owner—if he or she can be found—for the loss of both the vehicle and the money. The consumer purchases the vehicle in good faith, and does nothing wrong. Why should she or he have to suffer through a long song and dance to receive what was paid for? That procedure should not be necessary, and it will not be necessary after the Bill is passed.

The aim of the Motor Vehicle Securities Bill is to provide consumers who purchase vehicles with more protection than they receive from the Chattels Transfer Act at present. Many people use a hire purchase scheme to purchase vehicles. Hire purchase schemes allow consumers to have the immediate use of vehicles, and they are paid for over a period; the payments are fixed to suit the purchaser's budget. The system is useful, and it is used successfully by many companies and consumers. However, the system can be abused. As the law stands at present, a vehicle can be repossessed if a previous owner still owes money on it, or if a previous owner has used the vehicle as security and subsequently defaulted on loan payments. Under financial pressure a consumer may default on one monthly payment, another monthly payment, and another, until the final solution is to sell the vehicle. The money from the sale of the vehicle may or may not be used to pay off the outstanding debt. The new owner will not know anything about the previous arrangement until the vehicle collector comes to call. As more people use the hire purchase system to purchase vehicles it becomes more important that those agreements be registered in order to protect both vehicle dealers and buyers.

The Bill protects consumers in several ways. It establishes a central registry from which consumers who are interested in purchasing vehicles can find out for themselves whether the vehicle is subject to a debt. If the system shows that no debts are outstanding on a vehicle and the consumer purchases it, the consumer owns the vehicle irrespective of any claims that are made later. The member for Remuera raised the matter of whether oral advice was sufficient. It is obvious that oral advice would need to be followed by written evidence, and certificates will be provided for that purpose. In that way the information that is provided on the register will be guaranteed.

An additional asset in relation to the register is that if the certified information contained on the register is later found to be inaccurate, and the consumer suffers a loss as a result of such information, he or she will be entitled to seek compensation from the registrar of motor vehicle securities. That back-up procedure is designed to ensure that consumers can trust the information provided by the system, and it will encourage consumers to use it.

The registry will also be important for motor vehicle dealers, because dealers can use the information to protect themselves against buying vehicles that are encumbered by debt. Dealers will have to check the register before they sell the vehicle. In that way, consumers will not have to worry about debts owing on vehicles they have been sold by a motor vehicle dealer. In relation to private sales, consumers will be advised to check the register themselves. The details for operating the system have yet to be finalised, although certain criteria have already been established. The service must be provided quickly, simply, and cheaply. The registry will be self-funding, and it is important that financial barriers are not placed in the way of consumers who want to secure their interest when purchasing such expensive items.

The registry will give consumers peace of mind. The information provided will need to be accurate. It will need to enable purchasers to buy a vehicle and receive immediate good title. In addition to registering debts owing against vehicles the system will also notify a potential purchaser of whether the vehicle has been stolen. That information will help the police to claim vehicles that are offered for sale by thieves. It is doubtful whether thieves will find the legislation pleasing. A quick check through the register by motor vehicle dealers or purchasers should alert them to the police notification of stolen vehicles.

Motor vehicles are an integral part of modern living. They provide people with independence and mobility, and are essential for many people in the course of their work, or in their access to work. More important, most motor vehicles are a major financial commitment. It is high time for consumers to be protected against the loss of one of their most valuable possessions. That protection is the aim of the measure. I welcome the Bill's introduction, and I hope that by October 1989 nobody will need to fear the loss of such a commodity.

Notes

1. The Bill was not preceded by any published or unpublished report. It looked to recent Australian reforms. See Motor Vehicle Securities Act 1986 – Queensland, Banking Law Bulletin, Vol 2, Number 3, 31.

2. The Act has been forcefully criticized by Professor McLauchlan in Motor Vehicles Securities: The Quagmire Deepens (1989) NZLJ 211.

Article Nine Type Systems

This system was evolved as part of the development of the United States Commercial Code. It has been adopted in most States and several Canadian jurisdictions. It has been recommended by the Law Commission for New Zealand.

Reform of Personal Property Security Law

Law Commission, Preliminary Paper Number 6, (1988)
(By Professor Farrar and Mark O'Regan).

* * *

A Summary of the Defects of the Present System

Under the present system there is a multiplicity of forms each with their own regime which are not fully integrated by the statutory schemes. This creates law which is complex and almost as confusing to the profession as it is to lay people. There is a core of good sense in the New Zealand Chattels Transfer Act. This is largely the result of indigenous reforms – the assimilation of bailment and hire purchase, the recognition to some extent of purchase money security interests, flexible agricultural securities, facilitation of stock in trade financing, the protection of the bona fide purchaser for value without notice and the coverage of book debts. All these anticipate an Article 9 system but the reduction of them to statutory form is studiously repulsive and in some respects resembles an archeological digging of an early colonial site where each generation has left its own deposit with resulting complexity. This complexity and confusion leads to an increase in transaction costs, unnecessary risk in routine transactions and the possibility of real injustice.

Another substantial defect of the present system is the lack of a central computerised register for all chattel securities. The existence of two separate regimes is also intrinsically problematic. The Chattels Transfer system operates by a localised system of registration in the High Court. There are sometimes difficulties in determining the office at which to register an instrument under the Chattels Transfer Act and problems of taking security over goods which have yet to be brought into the jurisdiction. The Companies Act registration is based on the Commercial Affairs Division of the Justice Department. There is no co-ordination of the two systems. Both are manual systems with all the problems which arise from that and both require registration of a copy of the security document, causing enormous problems of storage for the registries. It would be interesting to know how many identical copies of the standard form of debenture of the major New Zealand banks are stored in expensive premises of the Commercial Affairs Division in Wellington and Auckland. Because both are manual systems, it is possible for the records to go astray or be destroyed or mutilated. Only one person can search the Companies register at a time. The existence of defined registration periods and the need for a registration out of time to be the subject of an application to the High Court is unnecessarily complicated and expensive.

The effects of registration under the two systems is not clear. Registration under the Chattels Transfer Act seems to be a priority point and yet this is eroded by some later provisions, one of which retains a concept of knowledge. The Companies Act system is an incomplete security system. Registration is not a priority point. Priority is determined by the date of the instrument. Non registration merely gives rise to invalidity of a charge as against the liquidator and creditors and it is difficult at times to determine priorities. To do so involves considering the fact of registration and non-registration and the common law and equitable priority rules.

In the case of corporate chattels securities there are difficulties which arise from the cross-referencing to the Chattels Transfer Act and there seems to be duplicated provision for book debts. There are problems of drafting with the attempt to incorporate hire purchase into the Chattels Transfer Act and then exclude customary hire purchase from the registration requirements. These provisions do not mesh with the companies provisions. There are subtle distinctions which arise with the two types of hire purchase and arbitrary category questions in determining what are customary hire purchase agreements. There are problems under both systems with determining the rights attaching to competing securities and there is no clear priority given to a purchase money security interest.

Neither system provides for the possibility of priority or subordination agreements although this problem is to some extent mitigated by the practice of some assistant registrars of companies of allowing documents to be filed which are technically outside the scope of the Companies Act. Neither system provides for variation of instrument. Neither system provides adequately for stock in trade financing. The 1974 amendments to the Chattels Transfer Act have not generally proved popular in practice. There are problems in creating a fixed charge over stock in trade. There are instrinsic problems with the floating charge which recent case law has highlighted—what interest is conferred before crystallisation, what constitutes crystallisation and what are the priority rules. Increasingly the protection afforded by a floating charge is being reduced by the inroads of reservation of property clauses and legislation giving priority to taxes and other preferred debts.

Reservation of property clauses are an area of continuing confusion and complexity. The registration requirements are far from clear under either system. There are problems under both systems with an attempt to take security over part of a chattel.

The list of registrable charges in the Companies Act needs up-dating and there needs to be some integration with the Chattels Transfer Act. Instead of a system based on constructive notice there should be a system of perfection based on the time of registration. There needs to be a statutory statement of priorities as in the Australian Companies Code or under Article 9 of the U.S. Uniform Commercial Code.

Lastly, there is a need for an integrated computerised system with terminals in all of the main centres. This should be coupled with the possibility of telephone searches.

*   *   *

The Basis of a Fair and Rational System

General Principles

Before getting embroiled in detail it is necessary to consider what are the essentials of a rational and fair system. In an article in the Law Quarterly Review, "The Modernisation of Personal Property Security Law" (1984) 100 LQR 234 at p. 237, Professor Roy Goode, a distinguished English Commercial Lawyer with extensive experience in practice as well as a teacher of law, identified these as the five features.

1. That all transactions intended as security should be regulated as secured transactions, regardless of the technical legal form in which they are cast.

2. That in any transaction thus characterised as a secured transaction the creditor's interest should be limited to a security interest, that is, to what is necessary to give him the amount he is owed, together with interest or charges.

3. That a person who in good faith acquires an interest in an asset of the debtor company should not be subordinated to a prior security interest of which he had neither knowledge nor the means of discovery.

4. As a corollary of (3), that a secured creditor who wishes to leave the debtor in possession of the security should be furnished with simple, efficient and inexpensive legal machinery by which he may give public notice of the existence of his security interest.

5. The priority rules should be so designed as to avoid unjust enrichment of one creditor at the expense of others.

In *"Credit and Security in Australia — the Legal Problems of Development Finance"* pp. 20-23, Professor David Allan and his co-authors gave more detailed criteria. These included the following:

Identification of the Collateral

The general body of property law regulates the type of collateral. It should enable the lender to verify the borrower's interest quickly and certainly. Formalities for the creation of this security should be as simple and as cheap as possible but should provide a permanent record of the transaction.

Registration of the Security

Registration should be essential as a form of public notification for the protection of the security except where this is adequately provided by means e.g. possession. Any system of registration should be simple and inexpensive. What should be registered is not documents but the fact of the security interest. The consequences of failure to register should be prescribed. This should be the invalidity of an unregistered security interest against third parties.

Priority of Security Interests

This should depend entirely on the time of perfection.

* * *

An Outline of the Main Features of Article 9 of the UCC

Article 9 looks to the *substance* of the transaction, not the form. It catches all transactions intended as security, regardless of form. The parties can use whatever form they wish. Article 9 does not stipulate the particular form of security which must be used. Under the code the agreement is known as a *security agreement* and the interest it creates a *security interest*.

Article 9 applies to security over all types of personal property, tangible or intangible. Its approach is *functional*. There are special rules inter alia for inventory financing, equipment and consumer goods.

The person in whom the security interest is vested is called "the secured party" and the person who owes the obligation for which the security interest is security is called the "debtor". The subject matter of the security is called the "collateral". "Collateral" covers any kind of personal property but Article 9 creates a classification into different types of collateral: goods, documents of title, instruments, securities, chattel paper and intangibles.

Goods are divided into four sub-categories: inventory; consumer goods; farm products; and equipment.

Inventory is goods which are held by a person who holds them for sale or lease or to be furnished under contracts of service or if he has so furnished them, or if they are raw materials, work in process or materials used or consumed in a business. Inventory of a person is not to be classified as his equipment.

Consumer goods are goods used or brought for use primarily for personal, family or household purposes.

Farm products which is a category not adopted by the Canadians are goods which are crops or livestock or supplies used or produced in farming operations or if they are products of crops or livestock in their manufactured states and if they are in possession of a debtor engaged in farming operations.

Equipment covers goods if they are used or bought for use primarily in business or by a debtor who is a non-profit organisation or government agency or if the goods are not included in the other categories. Thus equipment is a residual catch-all category.

Document of title includes bill of lading, dock warrant, dock receipt, warehouse receipt or order for the delivery of goods, and also any other document which in the regular course of business or financing is treated as adequately evidencing that the person in possession of it is entitled to receive, hold and dispose of the document and the goods it covers.

Instrument means a negotiable instrument or any other writing which evidences a right to the payment of money and is not itself a security agreement or lease and is of a type which is in the ordinary course of business transferred by delivery with any necessary indorsement or assignment.

Chattel paper means a writing or writings which evidence both a monetary obligation and a security interest in or a lease of specific goods, but a charter or other contract involving the use or hire of a vessel is not chattel paper. When a transaction is evidenced both by such a security agreement or a lease and by an instrument or a series of instruments, the group of writings taken together constitutes chattel paper. An example of a chattel paper in the New Zealand context would be a retail conditional sale agreement.

Two concepts are central to the scheme of Article 9. These are "attachment" and "perfection".

Attachment: Under Article 9-203(1) attachment takes place when (a) the collateral is in the possession of the secured party pursuant to the agreement or the debtor has signed a security agreement which contains a description of the collateral and where necessary a description of the land concerned (b) value has been given and (c) the debtor has rights in the collateral. Paragraph (a) reflects the fact that Article 9 is concerned with consensual transactions. Value is defined in Article 1-201(44). It normally means consideration for the purposes of the law of contract but includes past consideration. Requirement (c) may be satisfied by something less than title but more than mere possession of the goods (see *Cain* v *Country Club Delicatessan of Saybrook Inc* (1964) 203 A 2d 441; *Euroclean Canada Inc* v *Forest Glade Investments Ltd* (1985) 4 PPSAC 271 (Ont. CA)).

Perfection means taking the steps necessary to give the secured interest the greatest bundle of rights available under the legislation vis-a-vis other parties claiming an interest in the collateral. In other words perfection is about priority and does not necessarily refer to an absolute validity against third parties (Gilmore, "*Security Interests in Personal Property*", Vol. II, p. 653). Perfection is achieved in one of two ways:
(1) registration of the interest against the name of the debtor or
(2) taking possession of the collateral.

In the case of some types of collateral such as goods and chattel paper the security interest can be perfected in either manner. In other cases, which are usually self-explanatory, perfection can only take place by one of these methods. The underlying logic is that for collateral which has some of the attributes of negotiability the only sufficient method is by taking possession. In the case of collateral with no physical or documentary existence the security interest may only be perfected by registration. Thus intangibles need perfection by registration. The prevalent Canadian philosophy is that *all* security interests should be capable of perfection by registration. The closest thing to invulnerability under Article 9 is a purchase money loan on the security of goods over which the debtor is given no power of disposition but even this case can be subjected to a *non consensual* lien such as a common law lien (see Gilmore ibid).

One of the accomplishments of Article 9 was to facilitate a fixed security in stock in trade. Previously this had not been possible under U.S. laws because of the decision of the United States Supreme Court in *Benedict* v *Ratner* 268 U.S. 353. Technically that decision only applied to New York law although it was often cited in other jurisdictions. U.S. laws did not recognise the floating charge. The result of Article 9 is that *Benedict* v *Ratner* is overturned and it is now possible under Article 9 to create a fixed charge over fluctuating assets. In Canada where the floating charge was recognised the status of the floating charge under the Article 9 system has been the matter of some controversy. Eventually this debate will wither away as people see the wisdom of opting for a fixed charge over fluctuating assets. If it is possible to create a fixed charge over fluctuating assets in the case of a company then there will be the immediate advantage under the law as it now stands of the secured creditor having priority over the revenue.

Article 9 provides a simple system of filing based on the concept of "*notice filing*". The idea is to confine the particulars to a minimum.

Article 9 adopts *a set of priority rules* based not on the traditional legal or on equitable rules but on sound commercial conceptions of what is *a fair result* in the typical case. The essence of the system is that filing is a priority point. A perfected security interest in an inventory carries through to proceeds subject to some qualifications requiring reperfection in some cases.

The main priority rules are that amongst unperfected creditors the first to attach has priority. Where one creditor has perfected his or her secured interest he or she has priority. Amongst perfected creditors the general rule is priority is given to the interest filed first. There are, however, special rules for purchase money security interests which are given a measure of super priority. In addition there are detailed sub-systems which apply to different types of collateral.

Article 9 also contains a code of remedies applicable on default by the debtor. Upon the debtor's default the secured party can take possession of the collateral, he or she may also dispose of the collateral and apply the proceeds towards expenses and the amount of the indebtedness. In limited circumstances the defaulting debtor has the right to redeem the collateral or reinstate the security agreement.

A Personal Property Securities Act for New Zealand

Law Commission, Report Number 8 (1989)
Report of Advisory Committee (pps 6-14).

*   *   *

The Case for Reform

The need for reform of the law relating to security over chattels and intangibles in New Zealand was outlined in Preliminary Paper No 6, and was accepted by the Commission in the foreword to that report. The view of Professor Farrar and Mr O'Regan that there was an urgent need for the famous 'quagmire' of chattel security in New Zealand to be drained was universally accepted by the members of the Committee and by all parties who accepted the Commission's invitation to comment on Preliminary Paper No 6. In summary (full details may be found in Preliminary Paper No 6), the law in New Zealand is currently characterised by a complete lack of coherence which means that the legal requirements for the granting of a security interest in personal property will depend on a number of features, including:

- the nature of the debtor — whether it is a company, incorporated society, or non-corporate body;
- the form of the documentation — whether it is expressed as being a charge, hire purchase agreement, lease, conditional sale, *Romalpa* provision or other legal form of security interest;
- the nature of the personal property over which security is given — this will be accentuated if the Motor Vehicle Securities Bill becomes law and a new regime peculiar to security interests in motor vehicles is superimposed on the existing complications.

The Nature of Reform

The committee strongly believes that the best models for personal property security law reform in New Zealand are provided by Article 9 of the Uniform Commercial Code (which has been adopted in all 50 states of the United States) and the legislative regimes based on Article 9 which have been adopted in a number of Canadian provincial jurisdictions. In particular, the Committee believes that:

(1) the existence of Article 9 regimes in Canadian provinces and territories which have similar legal traditions to those of New Zealand, and which, prior to the adoption of an Article 9 regime, had similar laws relating to personal property security as those which now apply in New Zealand, makes the Article 9 model more accessible to New Zealand;

(2) the Article 9 system provides for a regime which is comprehensive and, for the great bulk of transactions, simple, and one which has been successful in reducing the complexity of financing transactions and facilitating the provision of credit in the jurisdictions in which it has been introduced;

(3) the availability of the necessary computer technology from a number of Canadian provincial jurisdictions in which Article 9 regimes have been adopted means that the introduction of the system in New Zealand should be able to be achieved with a minimum of cost and delay;

(4) the introduction of a Personal Property Securities Act would meet the needs of innocent purchasers of personal property who, under the current law, can be deprived of title to the property which they have purchased because of the existence of a security interest of which they were unaware and of which they were unable to become aware. This problem, as it relates to motor vehicles, is the major policy reason for the Motor Vehicle Securities Bill, but that Bill is restricted in its application to motor vehicles only, and it does not therefore address the problem in relation to other consumer items, nor does it overcome the acknowledged inadequacies of the current requirements of Part IV of the Companies Act, and the Chattels Transfer Act.

Some members of the Committee have seen Article 9 systems in operation, and spoken to lawyers acting for financiers, borrowers, and insolvency practitioners, bankers, consumer advocates, registry officials and law reform bodies in a number of jurisdictions where Article 9 regimes have been introduced. The experience gathered from those jurisdictions is that the system works extremely well in practice.

United Kingdom Developments

Since Preliminary Paper No 6 was published the United Kingdom Department of Trade and Industry has published the report of its consultant, Professor Aubrey Diamond. The Diamond Report recommends the adoption of a Personal Property Securities Act based on the North American models, echoing an earlier recommendation by the Crowther Committee on Consumer Credit in 1971. Because of local problems involving Scots law there will however be a delay and in the meantime certain immediate reforms to company charges are recommended. The longer term goal of a Personal Property Securities Act is nevertheless clear. No other EEC country has such a system and it is envisaged that the United Kingdom would take the lead in this respect, earlier attempts to harmonise *Romalpa* clauses having failed to make progress.

Harmonisation

The introduction of an Article 9 regime in New Zealand should provide a model for harmonisation of the various regimes which now apply in New Zealand and the Australian jurisdictions in a way which would enhance the standardisation of business laws and practices in New Zealand and Australia. At the moment, most Australian states have attempted limited reforms to their legislative equivalents of the Chattels Transfer Act 1924, but have retained the distinction between corporate and non-corporate security interests. There is, however, still a lack of consistency between the Australian states, and the adoption of the Motor Vehicle Securities Bill in New Zealand may increase the lack of harmonisation between New Zealand and Australia in this area of the law. Significantly, correspondence which the Committee has had with Australian commentators in this area indicates that there is an enthusiasm in Australia for the adoption of an Article 9 system amongst leading experts in the subject (see Appendix B).

The Committee believes that the introduction of a Personal Property Securities Act in New Zealand, based on the Canadian and United States models, and consistent with major reforms now being recommended in the United Kingdom by Professor Diamond, will mean that New Zealand will not only provide a lead in the adoption of standardised procedures between Australia and New Zealand but also play a significant role in harmonisation between the Australasian jurisdictions and their major trading partners in Canada, the United States and the United Kingdom.

Overview of System

The system proposed in the draft Personal Property Securities Act, which to a large extent follows the Personal Property Security Bill introduced into the Parliament of British Columbia early in 1988, has the following general features:

(1) *Uniform Rules:* The Bill creates a set of uniform rules for all forms of security interests, disregarding the distinctions which are drawn under current law between various types of security interests, such as chattel mortgages, leases, conditional sale agreements, '*Romalpa*' provisions, fixed and floating charges, floor plan agreements and so on. The fundamental concept is the concept of security interest which includes all of the above legal relationships.

(2) *Perfection:* The Bill provides to a creditor with a security interest in personal property the means of perfecting that security interest. Thus, once a security interest has attached to personal property (which occurs when a debtor having rights in personal property grants a security interest in that property to a creditor, and the creditor gives value) the creditor may perfect the security interest either by registration of a financing statement on a personal property security registry, or by taking possession of the property.

(3) *Registration:* While perfection by possession will be common where the collateral is, for example, a negotiable instrument, most secured transactions will now involve the registration of a financing statement giving details of the security interest claimed by the creditor in the collateral. This will involve the establishment of a computerised national register, on which details of all security interests in personal property will need to be entered. The current practice of registering copies of security agreements will be discontinued, but the register will give to a party conducting a search

the necessary details of the security arrangement and the Bill will give rights to certain parties to obtain copies of security agreements from creditors in appropriate circumstances.

(4) *Priorities:* The Bill provides a comprehensive set of rules to resolve the priority conflicts between competing security interests. In most cases, priority will be determined by the first-to-file rule under which the earlier registration affords the secured party priority in respect of after-acquired property and future advances without regard to knowledge of intervening interests. However, the Bill entitles purchase money creditors to obtain a super-priority over earlier registered floating security interests.

(5) *Transaction costs:* Because the system envisaged by the Bill provides for a much greater degree of certainty than that provided by the current law, and because the registration system will allow for the registration to be completed easily (without the involvement of lawyers in most cases) and for searches to be undertaken by telephone, the introduction of the system should see a considerable improvement in the efficiency of the provision of credit by financiers and a reduction in the transaction costs involved.

Practical Impact

The Committee believes that the introduction of a system along the lines of the draft Bill in New Zealand would lead to a simplification of the practical steps required by financiers, as well as ensuring that different providers of finance are treated equally. Two important examples are:

Banking facilities: Under the current regime, many banks require sole traders to incorporate, so that the debtor is able to give the bank a debenture creating fixed and floating charges, which unnecessarily increases the number of companies on the register. Under an Article 9 system, sole traders can give security to a financier over their personal property, both present and future, in the same way as companies can. Further, the floating security anticipated by the statute is fixed from the outset in the sense that no additional act (such as 'crystallisation') is needed to render it effective against third parties; and

Romalpa provisions: Many suppliers of goods reserve title to the goods until they receive payment in full. This type of arrangement does not require the formalities which a mortgage or charge requires—in particular an agreement signed by the debtor and registration of particulars of the arrangement on a public register. An Article 9 regime would treat such arrangements in the same way as other security arrangements. A supplier wishing to protect its position would therefore need to have the purchaser sign an agreement setting out the terms of future supplies and register a financing statement on the personal property security register. One registration is all that is required—it would not be necessary to register a new financing statement for each supply.

The Committee stresses that the draft Bill will not disrupt present security arrangements. The most significant change is that a floating security interest will become effective against third parties without the necessity of crystallisation. If it is enacted, creditors will need to make few if any changes in existing security documents such as finance leases, hire purchase contracts, chattel mortgages and debentures. However, as explained above, a supplier of goods on the basis of reservation of title until payment will have to obtain the signature of its customer on a document. For many creditors the only consequence for contracting practice will be the necessity of registering a financing statement.

Scope of the Report

The draft Bill does not include provisions relating to the rights and remedies available to secured creditors holding security interests when a default occurs, as is done in both the United States and Canadian models. The omission of these provisions was due to some extent to the tight deadline facing the Committee, but was also based on a reluctance of some members of the Committee to adopt provisions similar to those appearing in, for example, the British Columbia Bill, given that some elements of those provisions were intended as consumer protection measures, and that comprehensive consumer protection legislation is already under consideration in New Zealand by the Ministry of Consumer Affairs. It is to be hoped that this legislation will govern the rights of secured creditors not only in respect of security interests in personal property, but also in respect of security interests over real property. In the view of the Committee, adoption of the draft Personal Property Securities Bill need not await completion of this further work as the questions of priority and remedies are distinct from each other and need not (perhaps should not) appear in the same Act. However, it was acknowledged that, if no legislation relating to rights of secured creditors on default is enacted, then one of the objectives of the United States and Canadian models, the standardisation of creditor rights and remedies, will not be met by the draft Bill. Accordingly, the Committee intends to continue its work after the publication of this report with a view to formulating a comprehensive set of secured creditor remedies in conjunction with the work currently being undertaken by the Ministry of Consumer Affairs.

Special Features

A number of special features of the draft Bill need to be highlighted. These are:

(1) *Consumer protection:* The draft Bill does not include specific consumer protection measures. The Committee believed that these should be incorporated in general consumer protection legislation. However, one of the objects of the legislation is the protection of innocent purchasers of personal property which is subject to a security interest, and the Bill achieves the objective of providing such purchasers with a means of ensuring that they are able to take good title when goods are purchased;

(2) *The effect of non-perfection:* The effect of clause 15 as it appears in the draft Bill is that a failure to perfect a security interest would not make it void against the Official Assignee or liquidator. In this respect the draft Bill follows the policy adopted by the Department of Justice in relation to the Motor Vehicle Securities Bill. Under the American and Canadian models, a security interest which has not been perfected is subordinated

to the interest of a judgment creditor as well as the equivalent of the Official Assignee or company liquidator of the debtor. This part of the equivalent section in the draft Bill (clause 15) has been deleted in the draft. The Committee was almost evenly divided on this issue and the commentary to section 15 therefore sets out in details the alternative arguments;

(3) *Motor Vehicle Securities Bill:* The draft Bill proceeds on the assumption that the adoption of a Personal Property Securities Act in New Zealand would render the Motor Vehicle Securities Bill unnecessary, and that this legislation would therefore not proceed or if passed be repealed. The Motor Vehicle Securities Bill does, however, contain specific consumer protection measures relating to consumers purchasing motor vehicles from motor vehicle dealers, and these provisions could be incorporated into the draft Bill if it was considered necessary to do so. The Committee has prepared draft provisions for this purpose, and these are included in Appendix C to this report;

(4) *Securities over wool:* One of the features of the Chattels Transfer Act is the special provisions which it provides for the taking of securities over both crops and wool. Although the provisions relating to crops have been largely retained in the draft Bill (clause 30), no provisions have been added for securities over wool. This is partly due to the apparent inconsistency in the Chattels Transfer Act which provides for securities over sheep's wool but not similar fibre products from other animals, and the fact that the lack of restrictions in the Bill on the taking of security over future acquired property would mean that a secured party holding a security interest which is expressed as covering both the sheep and the wool from the sheep could claim an interest in wool from those sheep, even after the wool had been shorn. This largely obviates the need for a special regime for securities over wool;

(5) *Receiverships:* The absence of provisions relating to remedies also means that the provisions in the British Columbia model relating to receiverships do not appeal in the Bill. The Committee has been informed by the Commission that provisions relating to the reform of the law of receivership will be included in the report on company law which is to be published by the Commission soon, and that it is likely that the Commission will recommend the adoption of a comprehensive regime for receiverships, whether or not the debtor is a corporate or non-corporate entity.

(6) *Statutory charges:* The draft Bill is intended to relate to security interests created by agreement and does not therefore apply to charges imposed by statute. However, the Committee would support any moves to require statutory authorities claiming security interests in personal property to register those interests under the Personal Property Securities Act as a protection to other creditors and third party purchasers.

Comprehensive Reform

The Committee endorses the Commission's desire to see the adoption of a Personal

Property Securities Act as part of a comprehensive reform of the Companies Act and the law of insolvency. The Committee believes that consistency between these reform initiatives is essential and that they should proceed together.

Urgency

The Committee believes that the time for reform in this area of law is long overdue, that the merits of the draft Bill are clear, and that the draft Bill should be introduced to the House as part of, and at the same time as, the company law reform measures which are to be proposed by the Commission.

*   *   *

Notes

1. The literature on Article 9 is vast. The leading US texts are Grant Gilmore, *Security Interests in Personal Property* (1965, 2 vols.); Coogan, Hogan and Vagts, *Secured Transactions Under the Uniform Commercial Code* (1963, 4 vols, looseleaf). For Canada, see McLaren and De Jong, *Secured Transactions in Personal Property in Canada* (1979), and Ziegel, Geva and Cuming, *Commercial and Consumer Transactions* (2nd ed. 1987), chap. 21.

2. For journal literature see Goode, The Modernisation of Personal Property Security Law (1984) 100 LQR 234; Ziegel and Cuming, The Modernisation of Canadian Personal Property Security Law (1981) 31 UTLJ 249.

A Motor Vehicle Title System for New Zealand?

The question of personal property title and security registration systems can be tested in one final way. Would New Zealand have been better advised to enact a *formal* system of title to motor vehicles? It would also be feasible to include security interests under such a system — in effect there would then be a Torrens system for vehicles. Consider the following extract. What are the arguments for and against such an approach in New Zealand?

Motor Vehicle Title Systems in the USA and Canada

Law Commission, Preliminary Paper No 6, (1988) 88.

*   *   *

In most states of the U.S.A. motor vehicles are subject to title systems and are excluded from the operation of Article 9 (see Article 9-103). That is not to say, however, that inventory financing operations with regard to the sale of motor vehicles will necessarily be excluded from Article 9. This is often not the case under particular state title systems. These transactions are then included within Article 9. Where the collateral is a motor vehicle or other goods covered by Certificate of Title issued by any state the security interests are often required to be perfected by notation of the Certificate of Title. In some systems such as Wyoming filing of a financing statement and concurrent notation of the security interest on the certificate of title are required to perfect the security interest (see *Slates* v *Commercial Credit Corp* 412 P 2d 444, 445-6).

Except in cases of state where there is no title system or where there are concurrent systems such as Wyoming the perfection of a security interest must be accomplished in the manner provided by the motor vehicle title law. Corpus Juris Secundum Vol. 79 Secured Transactions para. 33 describes the practice in various states as follows:

"Many certificate of title laws provide that a security interest is perfected when an application for a certificate of title which notes the security interest is delivered to a specified officer or agency. Under some certificate of title laws, a security interest is perfected as of the time it was created or attached if the certificate is delivered to the designated officer within a specified number of days, but otherwise as of the date of delivery to the officer. Other statutes make it necessary that the designated officer or agency actually issue a certificate on which the security interest has been noted before the interest is perfected.

Provisions for perfection of a security interest in a vehicle by notation on the certificate of title require only substantial compliance. So the perfection of a security interest is not prevented by a failure to declare the date of the security interest on the application form where other information on the application indicated the date; and the failure of the certificate of title to show the date of the security agreement is not fatal where it is not shown that the omission was prejudicial to any person.

Where a prior certificate of title delivered by the debtor to the secured party to be presented with an application for a certificate showing the security interest shows no title in the debtor no security interest can be perfected.

Where the statute requires a dealer who sells a new automobile to prepare the application for a certificate of title indicating the existence of a security interest, it is his duty to note the interest of a bank which financed the purchase, and he will be liable to the bank for any unpaid balance due if it fails to do so.

A statutory requirement that a financing statement be filed with a state officer to perfect a security interest in a motor vehicle not created in connection with a sale of the vehicle requires a secured party who held a perfected purchase money interest in vehicles to file again with respect to subsequent advances."

We give as an example of a Certificate of Title jurisdiction, Illinois. In Illinois which has had such a system since the 1920s the motor vehicle title system is a substantial operation with a large computer entry and checking staff. This seemed to be bigger than the registry staff for the whole Personal Property Security Registry in Toronto. The volume of new titles was approximately three million per year and on the day of our visit twenty-seven thousand new titles were issued. Many of these were updates of old titles where a transfer of ownership or change in a security interest had occurred. We were informed that the registry had 65 to 70 people working in two shifts and at present was not able to produce a title until about 3-4 weeks after a request was made. During that time the vehicle was driven under a temporary permit. The motor vehicle certificate of title was printed on bank note paper which was difficult to counterfeit with a specially prepared engraved border which was hard to reproduce and a lamination strip which protects the vehicle information from being altered, allows changes to be detected under retro-reflective light and is of such a form that the removal of the lamination will destroy the information. Before these security features were introduced several hundred counterfeit or altered titles were discovered each year in Illinois. Since June 1978 when the security features were introduced there has been a continual decrease in counterfeit and altered titles. In addition to Certificates of Title there are separate certificates for junking and salvage.

Vehicle information is processed through the National Crime Information Center and LEADS Hot Check to determine whether a vehicle has been reported stolen. This is not entered on the register itself. Thousands of stolen vehicles have been identified since the implementation of a computerised title system. Illinois has had a title system for motor vehicles since the 1920s.

In the Canadian provinces there are no title systems for motor vehicles. We understand that such a system was considered in Ontario in the 1950s but was rejected as a result of pressure from motor vehicle dealers who were worried about being unable to confer title in a sale effected at the weekend. We did not find this a very convincing reason for the rejection of a title system. The result of not having such a system means that all motor vehicle transactions come under the Ontario Act. In Ontario over 90% of all transactions recorded under the Ontario Act are concerned with motor vehicles or the financing of motor vehicles or dealers. We understand that a similar proportion would apply in the other provinces.

Compared with this a title system takes the pressure off the Article 9 system. In the Article 9 registry in Illinois 600-700 financing statements were filed daily. There were two people working fulltime entering particulars on the computer and dealing with searches. The system had been computerised in 1972.

There was little doubt to us that the title system seemed to work well in practice and ease the pressure off the Article 9 system, as well as providing prospective purchasers of motor vehicles with notice of security interests without the need to undertake a search. This was due to the degree of specialisation involved and in keeping the bulk of motor vehicles transactions off the Article 9 registry. The Canadian provinces have to contend with motor vehicles and a variety of other transactions. There is at the same time also a greater degree of uncertainty regarding the title to motor vehicles in Canadian provinces. While the problems concerned with title are cut down by a Personal Property Security Act they are not eliminated, because, though security interests can be ascertained from the register, the identity of the owner is not itself recorded. However, the ability to obtain searches of motor vehicles by reference either to the debtor or the identification number of the vehicle reduces this shortcoming somewhat.

The optimal system seems to us to be to have a title system for motor vehicles separate from an Article 9 system. We set out in Appendix H the Illinois Motor Vehicles Code which deals inter alia with the issue of title certificates, transfer and security interests. However, with a country the size of New Zealand this would probably make a separate Article 9 system impractical. The number of transactions which were non-motor vehicle transactions would probably not justify the economics of running a separate computerised system. On the other hand it would be possible to have an integrated system whereby there was a title system for motor vehicles with the security arrangements perfected by endorsement on the title certificate or by concurrent filing of a financing statement but in other respects the security to be governed by an Article 9 system. It is interesting to note that the state motor vehicle title systems which were looked at used conceptual terminology which was compatible with an Article 9 system. The reason why they are not fully integrated is the existence of a Title Register before Article 9 was introduced.

Question

You are a senior policy adviser to the Minister of Justice. You are asked to recommend what steps New Zealand should now take, taking into account the existence of CER with Australia, with respect to security and title systems for chattels in New Zealand. What advice would you give, and why?

Appendix A

Moore v Regents Of University of California

California Court of Appeal (Second District).
(1988) 202 Cal. Rptr. 494

[M had hairy-cell leukemia. He had his spleen removed at UCLA Medical Centre. G, his Doctor, and Q, a UCLA employee, determined that his cells were unique. Using genetic engineering techniques they produced a cell-line from M's cells which are capable of producing enormous therapeutic and commercial value. The University, G and Q patented the cell-line along with methods of producing products therefrom. The market value of these products was estimated to be three billion dollars by 1990. Without informing M, G and UCLA continued to monitor him and take tissue samples for almost seven years following the removal of his spleen. M survived his cancer and sued, alleging, *inter alia*, conversion and interference with prospective advantageous economic relationships. The latter is actionable under California law.] ROTHMAN J.

*   *   *

[2] The complaint alleges that plaintiff's tissues, including his spleen, blood, and the cell-line derived from his cells "are his tangible personal property." This is the crux of plaintiff's case for conversion.

As the ensuing analysis will establish, we have concluded that plaintiff's allegation of a property right in his own tissue is sufficient as a matter of law. We have been sited to no legal authority, public policy, nor universally known facts of biological science concerning the particular tissues referred to in this pleading (Evid. Code, §451) which compel a conclusion that this plaintiff cannot have a sufficient legal interest in his own bodily tissues amounting to personal property. Absent plaintiff's consent to defendants' disposition of the tissues, or lawful justification, such as abandonment, the complaint adequately pleads all the elements of a cause of action for conversion.

We have approached this tissue with caution. The evolution of civilization from slavery to freedom, from regarding people as chattels to recognition of the individual dignity of each person, necessitates prudence in attributing the qualities of property to human tissue. There is, however, a dramatic difference between having property rights in one's own body and being the property of another. To our knowledge, no public policy has ever been articulated, nor is there any statutory authority, against a property interest in one's own body. We are not called on to determine whether use of human tissue or body parts ought to be "gift based" or subject to a "free market." That question of policy must be determined by the Legislature. In the instant case, the cell-line has already been commercialized by defendants.

We are presented a *fait accompli*, leaving only the question of who shares in the proceeds.

Until recently, the physical human body, as distinguished from the mental and spiritual, was believed to have little value, other than as a source of labor. In recent history, we have seen the human body assume astonishing aspects of value. Taking the facts of this case, for instance, we are told that John Moore's mere cells could become the foundation of a multi-billion dollar industry from which patent holders could reap fortunes. For better or worse, we have irretrievably entered an age that requires examination of our understanding of the legal rights and relationships in the human body and the human cell.

> Genetic engineering promises a revolution more far-reaching than that wrought by the computer, one that may bring to a close the industrial revolution that has been the major shaper of our society for three hundred years . . . . [I]t is impossible to exaggerate the potential of genetic engineering for good and, if misused, for evil. (Sylvester and Klotz, *The Gene Age* (1983) pp. 1-2.)

Since it is not possible to foresee all of the implications of our decision, judicial determinations will be necessary on a case-by-case basis. A scientific revolution of this magnitude may also compel legislative intervention.

In our evaluation of the law of property, we consider the definition of the word "property" and cases and statutes involving such issues as the right of dominion over one's own body; disposition of bodies after death; cornea transplants from deceased persons; and medical experimentation on live human subjects. We find nothing which negates, and much which supports, the conclusion that plaintiff had a property interest in his genetic material.

> As a matter of legal definition, 'property' refers not to a particular material object but to the right and interest or domination rightfully obtained over such object, with the unrestricted right to its use, enjoyment and disposition. In other words, [in] its strict legal sense 'property' signifies that dominion or indefinite right of user, control, and disposition which one may lawfully exercise over particular things or objects; thus 'property' is nothing more than a collection of rights. (63A Am.Jur.2d, Property, §1, p. 228; fns. omitted.)

The definitions of property are not restrictive and exclusive. "In legal usage, the word 'property' is a term of broad and extensive application, and it is also a term of large import, with the very broadest and most extensive signification." (73 C.J.S. Property, §4, pp. 163-164.)

Civil Code section 654 defines property as follows: "The ownership of a thing is the right of one or more persons to possess and use it to the exclusion of others. In this Code, the thing of which there may be ownership is called property." Civil Code section 14, subdivision (3) provides: "The words 'personal property' include money, goods, chattels, things in action, and evidences of debt. . . ." Although the definition of section 14 seems narrower than section 654, use of the word "include" indicates that the section is plainly not intended to be an exhaustive list. These sections have been interpreted to mean that "the word 'property' is a generic term which includes anything subject to ownership [citation] . . ." (*Canfield v. Security First Nat. Bk.* (1935) 8 Cal.App.2d 277, 284, 48 P.2d 133.)

Property is " 'every species of right and interest capable of being enjoyed as such upon which it is practicable to place a money value.' " (*Yuba River Power Co. v. Nevada Irr. Dist.* (1929) 207 Cal. 521, 523, 279 P. 128, quoting 22 R.C.L., p. 43, sec. 10.)

Plaintiff's spleen, which contained certain cells, was something over which plaintiff enjoyed the unrestricted right to use, control and disposition.

The rights of dominion over one's own body, and the interests one has therein, are recognized in many cases. These rights and interests are so akin to property interests that it would be a subterfuge to call them something else.

Venner v. State (1976) 30 Md. App. 599, 354 A.2d 483, involved determination of whether police illegally seized narcotics filled balloons found with defendant's feces in a hospital bedpan. The court dealt with the question of whether the balloons were abandoned. In discussing this point, the court noted: "It could not be said that a person has no property right in wastes or other materials which were once a part of or contained within his body, but which normally are discarded after their separation from the body. It is not unknown for a person to assert a continuing right of ownership, dominion, or control, for good reason or for no reason, over such things as excrement, fluid waste, secretions, hair, fingernails, toenails, blood, and organs or other parts of the body, whether their separation from the body is intentional, accidental, or merely the result of normal body functions." (*Id.*, 354 A.2d at p. 498, fn. omitted.)

Although the subject matter here does not equate with or have the dignity of the human cell, the legal significance of this reference is the court's statement that it *cannot* be said that a person has no property right in materials which were once part of his body.

In *Bouvia v. Superior Court* (1986) 179 Cal.App.3d 1127, 225 Cal.Rptr. 297, the court confirmed the long established rule that: " '[A] person of adult years and in sound mind has the right, in the exercise of control over his own body, to determine whether or not to submit to lawful medical treatment.' [Citation.] It follows that such a patient has the right to refuse *any* medical treatment, even that which may save or prolong her life. [Citations.]" (*Id.*, at p. 1137, 225 Cal.Rptr. 297; emphasis in original.) The court reiterated Judge Cardozo's statement in *Schloendorff v. Society of New York Hospital* (1914) 211 N.Y. 125, 105 N.E. 92, 93, that: " 'Every human being of adult years and sound mind has a right to determine what shall be done with his own body. . . .' " (*Bouvia v. Superior Court, supra*, 179 Cal.App.3d at p. 1139, 225 Cal.Rptr. 297.) This control of one's own body is certainly an incident of interest in property.

Some of the briefs suggest that the law which has developed with respect to dead bodies is analogous to the instant case. We do not completely agree. The "care of dead human bodies and the disposition of them by burial or otherwise have such a relation to the public health that they may well be regulated by law. [Citation.]" (22 Am.Jur.2d, Dead Bodies, §1, p. 9, fn. 2.) Significant limitations imposed by law on the disposition of a body after death reflect public health concerns, rather than a legislative policy against a property interest in a living body. We see no inconsistency between the cases dealing with dead bodies and our conclusion.

In *O'Donnell v. Slack* (1899) 123 Cal. 285, 55 P. 906, the court summarized existing authorities by saying that although a decedent's next of kin might not have full proprietary ownership of the body, there exist some *"property rights* in the body which will be protected, and for a violation of which [the next of kin] are entitled to indemnification." (*Id.*, at p. 289, 55 P. 906; emphasis added.)

In *Enos v. Snyder* (1900) 131 Cal. 68, 63 P. 170, a decedent's surviving estranged wife and daughter demanded possession of decedent's body, for the purpose of burial, from the person with whom the decedent had been living at the time of his death. The decedent had expressed in his will the desire that he be buried in accordance with the wishes of the person with whom he had lived. The issue before the court was whether the next of kin had a right to the possession of decedent's body notwithstanding his wishes. The court held that, absent statute, "there is no property in a dead body, that it is not part of the estate of the deceased person, and that a man cannot by will dispose of that which after his death will be his corpse." (*Id.*, at p. 69, 63 P. 170.)

Over the years, the legal position set forth by *Enos* has been clarified. The present state of the law regarding a dead body is reflected in *Cohen v. Groman Mortuary, Inc.* (1964) 231 Cal.App.2d 1, 41 Cal.Rptr. 481. In *Cohen*, the court noted that there is "a *quasi* property right to its possession . . . for the limited purpose of determining who shall have its custody for burial. [Citations.]" (*Id.*, at p. 4, 41 Cal.Rptr. 481.) The court pointed to the duty to bury the corpse and preserve the remains as a legal right the courts have recognized. (*Cohen v. Groman Mortuary, Inc., supra*, 281 Cal.App.2d at pp. 4-5, 41 Cal.Rptr. 481.) Thus, even though full property rights are not recognized in a dead body, a limited property interest has been found. (See Health & Saf. Code, §7100, concerning the right to control disposition of remains, and §7150, et seq., the Uniform Anatomical Gift Act.)

This property interest is also reflected in statutes and cases concerning the use of the corneas of a deceased person and statutes regarding medical experimentation on human subjects.

The law that has emerged in the area of cornea transplants recognizes that body parts are not free for the taking, but are subject to the heir's right to dispose of them. (See *Tillman v. Detroit Receiving Hosp.* (1984) 138 Mich.App. 683, 360 N.W. 2d 275, 277; *Georgia Lions Eye Bank, Inc. v. Lavant* (1985) 255 Ga. 60, 335 S.E.2d 127.)

The Protection of Human Subjects in Medical Experimentation Act, adopted in 1978, expresses a strong public policy that medical experimentation on human subjects "shall be undertaken with due respect to the preciousness of human life and *the right of individuals to determine what is done to their own bodies.*" (Health & Saf. Code, §24171; emphasis added.) The statutory scheme is designed "to provide *minimum* statutory protection for the citizens of this state with regard to human experimentation . . . ." (Health & Saf. Code, §24171; emphasis added.) The principal device for this protection is the adoption of an "experimental subject's bill of rights," which includes full advisement of the experiment and informed consent. (See Health & Saf. Code, §§24172 to 24175.)

The essence of a property interest—the ultimate right of control—therefore exists with regard to one's own human body.

[3] Even though the rights and interests one has over one's own body may

be subject to important limitations because of public health concerns, the absence of unlimited or unrestricted dominion and control does not negate the existence of a property right for the purpose of a conversion action. (See *Corey v. Struve* (1915) 170 Cal. 170, 173, 149 P. 48) (disapproved on another point *Maben v. Rankin* (1961) 55 Cal.2d 139, 144, 10 Cal.Rptr. 353, 358 P.2d 681.)

Defendants' position that plaintiff cannot own his tissue, but that they can, is fraught with irony. Apparently, defendants see nothing abnormal in their exclusive control of plaintiff's excised spleen, nor in their patenting of a living organism derived therefrom. We cannot reconcile defendant's assertion of what appears to be their property interest in removed tissue and the resulting cell-line with their contention that the source of the material has no rights therein.

[4] Defendants also claim that plaintiff cannot have an interest in the cell-line derived from his tissues since he is only the source of the thing studied. "Thus, the cells involved have no inherent value until a cell line is derived and created to produce useful products. Plaintiff tries to obscure this unassailable fact by creating the impression his cells *themselves* have miraculous curative powers . . . ." (Emphasis in original.)

Defendants contend that plaintiff has no property right in the knowledge gained or the new things made in the course of the study of his cells. This is an inaccurate characterization of this case. Plaintiff's complaint does not allege a conversion of ideas gained from study of his cells, but conversion of the cells, and their progeny, themselves. Plaintiff was not simply the object of study to increase knowledge. His spleen and cells were taken by defendants to their laboratory, where they extracted his genetic material, placed it in a growth medium, and, by cell division, created an "immortal" cell-line—one that could forever produce products of enormous commercial value to defendants. Human cells were essential to the creation of the cell-line. (See sources cited in Note, *Toward the Right of Commerciality: Recognizing Property Rights in the Commercial Value of Human Tissue* (1986) 34 UCLA L.Rev. 207, 209, fns. 6-9 (hereinafter *Toward the Right of Commerciality*.)) The complaint alleges that defendants exploited plaintiff's cells, not just the knowledge gained from them. Without these small indispensable pieces of plaintiff, there could have been no three billion dollar cell-line.

The fact that defendants' skill and efforts modified the tissue and enhanced its value does not negate the existence of a conversion. Any questions as to defendants' alteration of plaintiff's tissue go to what damages, if any, he might be entitled if successful at trial.

[5] Defendants further contend that plaintiff's spleen could not be converted because, being diseased, it was a thing of no value. The allegations in the complaint, however, indicate the opposite is true. While removal of plaintiff's spleen may have been necessary to the treatment of his disease, the cells it contained became the foundation of a multi-billion dollar industry. The extraordinary lengths to which defendants went to obtain a specimen for their works shows their belief in its value. This belief has proven correct. The fact the spleen was at one time of little utility to plaintiff does not mean its value was so minimal it could not be converted.

[6] Defendants' argument that the DNA from plaintiff's cells is not a part of him over which he has the ultimate power of disposition during his life is also untenable.

In *Motschenbacher v. R. J. Reynolds Tobacco Company* (9th Cir. 1974) 498 F.2d 821, the court found that, although California courts had not yet spoken on the subject, they would "afford legal protection to an individual's proprietary interest in his own identity." (*Id.*, at p. 825.) The court went on: "We need not decide whether they would do so under the rubric of 'privacy', 'property', or 'publicity'; we only determine that they would recognize such an interest and protect it." (*Id.*, at pp. 825-826, fns. omitted; see also *Midler v. Ford Motor Co.* (9th Cir. 1988) 849 F.2d 460.)

In *Lugosi v. Universal Pictures* (1979) 25 Cal.3d 813, 160 Cal.Rptr. 323, 603 P.2d 425, the Supreme Court avoided determining whether the interest of Bela Lugosi in his name, face, likeness and Count Dracula persona, in connection with any kind of business was "property". Turning to Prosser, the court found the dispute "pointless." " 'Once protected by the law, [the right of a person to the use of his name and likeness] . . . is a right of value upon which plaintiff can capitalize by selling licences.' " (*Id.*, at p. 819, 160 Cal.Rptr. 323, 603 P.2d 425, emphasis omitted, quoting Prosser, Law of Torts (4th ed. 1971) p. 807.) The court found the right was personal to Lugosi and did not survive him.

Plaintiff's cells and genes are a part of his person. Putting aside the effect of environment, "[a]n individual's genotype contains all of the genetic instructions essential for human development, growth, and reproduction . . . [¶] All human traits, including weight, strength, height, sex, skin color, hair texture, fingerprint pattern, blood type, intelligence and aspects of personality (for example, temperament), are ultimately determined by the information encoded in the DNA." (Gordon Edlin, *Genetic Principles — Human and Social Consequences* (1984) pp. 406-407.) If the courts have found a sufficient proprietary interest in one's persona, how could one not have a right in one's own genetic material, something far more profoundly the essence of one's human uniqueness than a name or a face?

A patient must have the ultimate power to control what becomes of his or her tissues. To hold otherwise would open the door to a massive invasion of human privacy and dignity in the name of medical progress.

In oral argument, the Regents expressed concern over the implication of our decision on medical research. They contended that *unencumbered* access to human tissue for research is essential to progress and public health. They argued that these sources must remain unencumbered, and medical researchers be free to both combine these materials with tissue taken from others, and dispose of the tissues, without answering to the person from whom the tissue was taken.

The Regents cite no statutory or case law which authorizes such an invasion of fundamental rights. We have no reason to believe that medical research will suffer by requiring the consent of a donor of the tissue before it can be appropriated. Absent lawful authority, medical researchers are no more free to impose their priorities over the unconsented use of cells than any intruder on any other property.

We are told that if plaintiff is permitted to have decision making authority and a financial interest in the cell-line, he would then have the unlimited power to inhibit medical rersearch that could potentially benefit humanity. He could conceivably go from institution to institution seeking the highest bid, and if dissatisfied, "would claim the right simply to prohibit the research entirely."

[7,8] We concede that, if informed, a patient might refuse to participate in

a research program. We would give the patient that right. As to defendants' concern that a patient might seek the greatest economic gain for his participation, this argument is unpersuasive because it fails to explain why defendants, who patented plaintiff's cell-line and are benefiting financially from it, are any more to be trusted with these momentous decisions than the person whose cells are being used. It has been suggested by writers that biotechnology is no longer a purely research oriented field in which the primary incentives are academic or for the betterment of humanity. Biological materials no longer pass freely to all scientists. As here, the rush to patent for exclusive use is rampant. The links being established between academics and industry to profitize biological specimens are a subject of great concern. If this science has become science for profit, then we fail to see any justification for excluding the patient from participation in those profits.

It is also argued that by giving patients a financial interest in their tissues, donations could be inhibited, costs increased and people of modest means driven out of the health care market. To the extent that unacceptable consequences, which can now only be the subject of speculation, do follow, legislative solutions are possible and likely. The court's role in this instance is not to provide solutions to all possible social concerns, but to resolve the dispute presented as to individual rights and interests.

C. ISSUE OF ABANDONMENT OF TISSUE IN SURGERY

Defendants argue that even if plaintiff's spleen is personal property, its surgical removal was an abandonment by him of a diseased organ. They assert that he cannot, therefore, bring an action for conversion.

[9] The essential element of abandonment is the intent to abandon. The owner of the property abandoned must be " 'entirely indifferent as to what may become of it or as to who may thereafter possess it.' " (*Martin v. Cassidy* (1957) 149 Cal.App.2d 106, 110, 307 P.2d 981, quoting 1 Cal.Jur.2d, Abandonment, §2, p. 2.)

> It may be said that abandonment is made up of two elements, act and intent, and the intent must be gathered from all the facts and circumstances of the case. [Citations.] (*Peal v. Gulf Red Cedar Co.* (1936) 15 Cal.App.2d 196, 199, 59 P.2d 183.)

[10-13] The question whether the plaintiff abandoned his spleen, or any of the other tissues taken by the defendants, is plainly a question of fact as to what his intent was at the time. A demurrer does not reach such questions. A consent to removal of a diseased organ, or the taking of blood or other bodily tissues, does not necessarily imply an intent to abandon such organ, blood or tissue. The only facts alleged in the complaint on the subject is that the spleen was surgically removed, and that, had plaintiff known of defendants' intentions regarding the spleen, he would not have consented to its removal at UCLA. While it may be true that many people under such circumstance would be entirely indifferent to the disposition of removed tissue, we cannot assume plaintiff shared this state of mind. Nothing in the complaint indicates that plaintiff had an intent to abandon his spleen, and we do not find that, as a matter of law, anyone who consents to surgery abandons all removed tissue to the first person to claim it. Certainly, in the example of an unconscious patient, the concept of abandonment becomes ridiculous.

[14] In California, absent evidence of a contrary intent or agreement, the reasonable expectation of a patient regarding tissue removed in the course of surgery would be that it may be examined by medical personnel for treatment purposes, and then promptly and permanently disposed of by internment or incineration in compliance with Health and Safety Code section 7054.4. Simply consenting to surgery under such circumstances hardly shows indifference to what may become of a removed organ or who may assert possession of it. Any use to which there was no consent, or which is not within the accepted understanding of the patient, is a conversion. It cannot be seriously asserted that a patient abandons a severed organ to the first person who takes it, nor can it be presumed that the patient is indifferent to whatever use might be made of it.

An inference of abandonment is particularly inappropriate when it comes to the use undertaken by defendants involving recombinant DNA technology. Almost from the beginning, this technology has incited intense moral, religious and ethical concerns. There are many patients whose religious beliefs would be deeply violated by use of their cells in recombinant DNA experiments without their consent, and who, on being informed, would hardly be disinterested in the fate of their removed tissue.

* * *

GEORGE J (Dissenting).

* * *

I part company with the majority in its conclusion that "plaintiff's allegation of a property right in his own tissue is sufficient as a matter of law" (majority opn., *ante*, p.504), and that "the law of property" contains "nothing which negates . . . the conclusion" that tissue of living persons constitutes tangible personal property, the wrongful disposition of which can constitute conversion. (Majority opn., *ante*, pp. 504-505.)

It is the plaintiff's burden to establish that his bodily substances constituted "personal property" at the time they allegedly were converted by defendants. "The elements of conversion are: (1) plaintiff's ownership or right to possession in the *property at the time of the conversion*; (2) defendant's conversion by a wrongful act or disposition of plaintiff's *property* rights; and (3) damages. [Citation.] In this action [*plaintiff*] *had the burden of proving the existence of each of the above elements.*" *(Chartered Bank of London v. Chrysler Corp.* (1981) 115 Cal.App.3d 755, 759-760, 171 Cal.Rptr. 748, emphasis added.)

In order to determine what constitutes "property" in the context of a suit for conversion, resort must be had to the provisions in the Civil Code setting forth a definition of that concept. The Legislature, in enacting the Code in its original form, still in effect today, provided in nineteenth-century prose that "the thing of which there may be ownership is called property," stating further that "[t]he ownership of a thing is the right of one or more persons to possess and use it to the exclusion of others." (Civ.Code, §654.) "Property is either: 1. Real or immovable; or, 2. Personal or movable." (§657.) "Every kind of property that is not real is personal." (§663.) "The words 'personal property' include money, goods, chattels, things in action, and evidences of debt." (§14, subd. 3.)

"Goods" comprise " 'moveables; household furniture; personal or movable estate; wares; merchandise; commodities bought and sold by merchants and traders.' " (*In re Holmes* (1921) 187 Cal. 640, 643, 203 P. 398. See also §1802.1; Com. Code. §2105.) "Chattels" comprise personal and movable property, as opposed to real property, and "may refer to animate as well as inanimate property." (Black's Law Dict. (5th ed. 1979) p. 215, col. 1.) "Conversion has been defined as 'an act of wilful interference with a *chattel*, done without lawful justification, by which any person entitled thereto is deprived of use and possession.' [Citations.]" (*de Vries v. Brumback* (1960) 53 Cal.2d 643, 647, 2 Cal.Rptr. 764, 349 P.2d 532, emphasis added.)

Unlike the gizzards of domestic poultry (§655), the spleens of human beings do not come within the definition of "goods" or "chattels" any more than they fit the remaining definitions of personal property ("money," "things in action," and "evidences of debt"). (§14.)

The majority, seeking to avoid the constraints of the statutory definition of personal property, asserts that section 14 "is plainly not intended to be an exhaustive list" and that the provisions of the Civil Code "have been interpreted to mean that 'the word "property" is a generic term which includes anything subject to ownership,' " citing *Canfield v. Security First Nat. Bk.* (1935) 8 Cal.App.2d 277, 284, 48 P.2d 133. (Majority opn., *ante*, p. 23.) Specific provisions such as section 14, however, qualify a general provision such as section 654. (See §§3509, 3534; *Neumarkei v. Allard* (1985) 163 Cal.App.3d 457, 463, 209 Cal.Rptr. 616.)

The majority also finds in the "rights of dominion over one's own body, and the interests one has therein," something "so akin to property interests that it would be a subterfuge to call them something else." (Majority opn., *ante*, p. 505.)

I find the foregoing assertions by the majority unpersuasive, as I do its reliance on case authority dealing with the harvesting of a beet crop, the right of a deceased motion picture actor during his lifetime to exploit his own name and likeness as Count Dracula, and the right of surviving family members to control the burial of a dead body.

A spleen is not "personal property" which the patient, to avoid sale by the hospital as unclaimed property, must claim within "a period of 180 days following the departure of the owner from the hospital." (§1862.5.) It is instead the type of "recognizable anatomical part [ ]" or "human tissue [ ]" which is subject to "scientific use." (Health & Saf. Code, §7054.4.)

Treatment of plaintiff's spleen, body tissue, and blood as "property" is incompatible with other statutory provisions dealing with the acquisition and disposition of property. As provided by section 1000, "Property is acquired by: 1. Occupancy; 2. Accession; 3. Transfer; 4. Will; or, 5. Succession." "Property of any kind may be transferred, except as otherwise provided . . . ." (§1044.) "A will may dispose of . . . property" (Prob. Code, §6101), which term is defined in the Probate Code as "anything that may be the subject of ownership and includes both real and personal property and any interest therein." (Prob. Code, §62.)

An interest labelled 'property' normally may possess certain characteristics: it can be transferred to others; it can be devised and inherited; it can descend to heirs at law; it can be levied upon to satisfy a judgment; it comes under the jurisdiction of a bankruptcy court in a brankruptcy proceeding; [fn. omitted] it will be protected against invasion by the courts; it cannot be taken away without due process of law. [Fn. omitted.]" (*First Victoria Nat. Bank v. United States* (5th Cir. 1980) 620 F.2d 1096, 1103-1104.)

The only direct support in the law cited by the majority opinion, reflecting its expansive definition of personal property encompassing human parts and human refuse, is *Venner v. State* (1976) 30 Md.App. 599, 354 A.2d 483, a case dealing with a seizure of human feces from a hospital bedpan by police officers in quest of contraband narcotics. Although the Maryland Court of Special Appeals observed that "[i]t is not unknown for a person to assert a continuing right of ownership, dominion, or control . . . over such things as excrement, [fn. omitted] fluid waste, secretions, hair, fingernails, toenails, blood, and organs or other parts of the body" (*id.* at p. 498), this dictum is a weak foundation upon which to construct a property right in a patient's surgically-removed body tissue and fluid. In any event, I am not prepared to extend the constitutionally sanctified right of property (U.S. Const., 5th & 14th Amends.; Cal.Const., art. I, §§1, 7) to the refuse found on the floor of the barbershop or nail salon, in the hospital bedpan, or in the operating room receptacle.

* * *

Even if one accepts the majority's premise that the diseased spleen and other bodily tissue and fluids removed from plaintiff constituted "property", the allegations in the third amended complaint necessitate consideration of the issue whether plaintiff abandoned any property interest he possessed in such substances.

Plaintiff alleges, "Prior to surgical removal of his spleen, . . . plaintiff signed a written consent form authorizing . . . surgeons at the UCLA [University of California at Los Angeles] Medical Center, to perform a splenectomy upon plaintiff." On several subsequent occasions he voluntarily agreed to the removal of blood samples.

The only suggestion that no abandonment took place is the allegation plaintiff's consent to the surgery and the taking of blood samples was not an *unconditional* relinquishment of whatever interest he possessed in such bodily tissue and fluids, because he did not assent expressly to research and commercial use of those substances, a matter considered in the following section of this dissenting opinion.

Aside from the alleged economic interest in their use asserted by plaintiff, a patient who consents to surgical removal of his bodily substances has no reasonable expectation as to their subsequent use other than an understanding that the licensed medical personnel involved in the removal and use of these substances will comply with applicable medical standards and legal constraints, such as the mandate that substances removed from his body "*following conclusion of scientific use* . . . be disposed of by interment, incineration, or any other method determined by the state department to protect the public health and safety." (Health & Saf. Code, §7054.4, emphasis added.)

Control of Excised Tissues Pending Implantation

B Dickens
(1990) Vol 7 No 1 Transplantation/Implantation Today 36

Introduction

After tissues for transplantation are removed from bodies, whether of living donors or after death, they will be prepared for implantation into a recipient and perhaps be transported to a different location. The issue to be addressed here concerns legal control over the management and disposition of such tissues between the times of their removal from their original sources and their transplantation into human recipients or their other employment, wastage or deliberate destruction such as by incineration.

Living donors tend not to donate solid organs to the world at large, but dedicate them to designated recipients, who are often family members of others for whose welfare the donors care and are willing to make sacrifices. Donation for payment of a commercial nature is not unknown, but comes under heavy moral and legal condemnation. Most living donation is primarily of an altruistic character, although donors' out-of-pocket expenses may be repaid. When materials removed from a living patient for reasons of that person's own therapeutic or related care are of value for transplantation, the donor may consider that use of minor concern and have no interest in who a recipient is. A distinction may therefore exist between the former donors, who intend specific cherished recipients to be the beneficiaries of their altruism, and the latter, who become donors incidentally, and have no interest in which recipient benefits, or whether any may benefit.

Family members who consent to the removal of tissues after death from the bodies of recently deceased (or soon to die and currently legally incompetent) relatives tend to have no interest in who specific recipients may be, but are concerned that the dedication of tissues from a loved one that they make not be wasted by incompetency. They may also cater their agreement to donate to an identified institution or purpose, so that any alternate use will be objectionable to them. Similarly, living people who complete some legal process of making their tissues available after their deaths tend to have no specific persons or types of persons in mind as intended recipients, but may refine the terms of their *post mortem* donation to favour, or to exclude, particular institutions, types of people, or purposes. Any deliberate or negligent departure from the terms of their gifts will be a posthumous betrayal.

A special case of donation may arise when women are willing to manage induction of abortion to maximize utility of fetal tissues for the benefit of others, principally children, who are in need of them. Although women's abortions should not be unduly delayed for this purpose and the proposed techniques of the procedure should not be affected by concerns such as to preserve tissues like organs intact for transplantation, women are free to request management that satisfies their own goals. The woman's interest may be even more compelling when she forgoes abortion of an anencephalic fetus and continues her pregnancy to term in the hope that at death soon after its live birth, or at stillbirth, its tissues may be harvested for transplantation. Such women, although donating to unspecified recipients, have a special claim that the intentions that have governed their well-meaning behaviours be afforded particular protection.

The Role of Property Law

The concept of "property" is used in law to protect a legitimate interest. The word is often applied to the solid objects and lands themselves in which legal interest arise, but it can also be applied in law to refer to objects that do not yet exist, so that an interest in next year's harvest will be an interest in a property "future", and to such interests as can arise from an agreement, such as the ability to oblige another person to fulfil a contract. For instance, professional sports players make agreements to play for particular clubs and, subject to the terms of an agreement, a club may then sell the right to a player's services to another club. The player is not property, but the legitimate interest that the club has acquired in the player's exclusive services is a property interest that can be traded.

A property interest protects the value of a legal right to use an object or to prevent its use by another, or legally to be able to compel another person to behave in a certain way, such as by being able to recover financial compensation if the person behaves wrongfully. The value that property law protects can be symbolic, such as when related to self-esteem, spiritual, such as in the value of objects of religious faith, or decorative. Before modern industrial techniques found a use for gold, for instance, its mechanical properties made it valuable only for shaping into decorations such as could be worn on the body or in it, like in teeth. Usually, however, value arises from a combination of utility and scarcity. Items that are commonly available and have no use, such as dead leaves falling from trees, are not considered to be property because they have neither use nor value. A leaf from a specially cultivated or genetically prepared rare tree or a mass of leaves that may become horticulturally valuable compost may, however, constitute property.

Historically, dead bodies had no use, and it is accepted in law that they can not be property. Accordingly, they are not part of the deceased person's estate, and cannot be bequeathed by will. The so-called "no property" rule has survived into present times, so that the dead body of a particularly celebrated person, such as a movie star, or a notorious person, that might be preserved and exhibited for a fee would probably not be considered property, although an Australian court has held that a two-headed stillborn fetus exhibited in a public display was saleable property. Misuse of a dead body is generally not a property offence, but the crime of causing indignity to a human corpse. At most, family members have a "quasi-property" interest in the reasonable recovery of a body for dignified and sanitary disposal.

Derived from the "no property" principle, although not necessarily flowing from it logically, has been the idea that organs and other body tissues, from deceased or living people, are not capable of constituting property. This idea has been progressively refined, however, and today it may be at or beyond the point of rejection and reversal. As long ago as 1905 an Oklahoma court found that a corpse lawfully appropriated for the benefit of science may be property, and in 1974 a Kentucky court found that an amputee could have directed the disposition of his severed limb, if he had taken the initiative to give directions in time. The court in that case asked "Is it the duty of the surgeon to take a dismembered part of a human body into his care and custody — for the amputee? We think not", but this may be different following the recent development of microsurgical techniques for the reattachment of severed undiseased limbs. Indeed in less sympathetic circumstances in 1976 a court observed that "It could not be said that a person has no property rights in wastes or other materials which were once a part of or contained within his body, which normally are discarded after their separation from the body". The value of a property right possessed by the source of discharged body wastes lies not in the fact that they are usable, but in that others may be prevented from taking them, unless they are voluntarily given or available by independent authority of law, for testing for drugs or other substances.

In a decision that may have far-reaching implications for individuals' control of their removed body materials, the California Court of Appeal held in 1988, in *Moore* v. *Regents of the University of California*, that a living person's body tissues, including in this case the plaintiff's cells, spleen, blood and genetic material, could be the subject of misappropriation or "conversion", which in civil or non-criminal law is the name of the wrong of unlawful taking of property. The criminal law equivalent is theft or larceny. The Court adopted the definition that conversion is "a distinct act of dominion wrongfully exerted over another's personal property in denial of or inconsistent with his title or rights therein . . . without the owner's consent and without lawful justification."

The case arose from the therapeutic removal of the plaintiff's spleen and its subsequent use for development of cell-lines that were potentially of immense commercial value. After surgery, the plaintiff gave the researchers additional tissues including blood, blood serum, skin, bone-marrow aspirate, and sperm for their purposes, of which he was unaware at the time. The trial court accepted the defendants' claim that Moore could have no property interest in his removed body materials but that, because of the special skills and resources they had applied to the materials, the defendants had created their own property interest. The Court of Appeal, in a majority decision, reversed this legal ruling on the ground that Moore could have a property interest in his removed body materials and that the defendants' dealings with them that were incompatible with his wishes and interests could be unlawful conversion.

Commerce and Property Interests

In classical law, determination of property interests is a preliminary step to facilitation of commerce. A property owner enjoys the legal right to sell the property, to lease it and otherwise to translate powers of legal control of a scarce, useful asset into means of personal enrichment. The legal fields of intellectual, industrial and artistic property, expressed in such laws as those governing patents, copyrights, trade marks and trade secrets, have been created to regulate how types of property can be used for commercial advantage and monetary gain. It may therefore be asked whether an individual's control of human tissues, whether removed from the individual's own body or from another over which he or she has control, such as the body of a deceased relative, can be exercised for personal profit. In the *Moore* case, for instance, the plaintiff claimed the right to recover the economic benefits of use of his tissues that he would have sought had he been made aware, as he claimed he should have been, of their potential to arise, amounting to billions of dollars.

There is strong resistance in many official, academic and professional quarters to the emergence of markets involving human tissues. The perception is that if the poor were to regard their bodily tissues as saleable assets they would be induced to take the risks of donation in exchange for monetary reward, and be exposed to exploitation and abuse. Some have concluded that recognition of property rights in human tissues would lead to such objectional commerce, and that denial of property rights would present a valuable defence against unconscionable trade. The dissenting judge in the *Moore* case, for instance, endorsed this view as well as public policy reasons to oppose the restrictions on access to transplantable tissues claimed to be liable to arise with recognition of donors' proprietary interests. He cited with approval an academic authority who has observed that:

"Although compelling arguments support recognizing property rights in human tissue, arguments against recognition may also be raised. These arguments include: the potential for adverse effects on organ donation for transplantation usage; the moral aversion to treating the body as a commodity; the effect of patient hold-outs and higher transaction costs on research and tissue availability; and the threat of improper motivation in the area of tissue acquisition . . . Several potentially persuasive arguments against property rights arise in the context of organ transplantation. Opponents of organ sales predict a variety of adverse effects should a market in human organs arise: decreases in the number of organs charitably donated; increases in the number of inferior organs; competitive bidding between patients for limited resources; financial pressure on the poor to sell their organs; and unacceptable risks of death for a pecuniary profit. Without question, any adverse effects of property rights on the organ donation system are of critical importance to the health of the populace."

Two distinctions need to be made. First, payments may legitimately be made for services that are separate from proprietary acquisitions, even though the services make usable human tissues available. Second, and more important, recognition of property rights need not lead inevitably to acceptance of commercial rights. That is, property rights can be recognized in law when the right to trade in such rights for commercial purposes, particularly for financial gain, is legally excluded. The majority and minority judges in the *Moore* case disagreed about the interaction of courts and legislatures. The majority found a property right and observed that if that was dysfunctional or otherwise disfavoured, legislatures could intervene, noting that *"To the extent that unacceptable consequences, which can now only be the subject of speculation, do follow, legislative solutions are possible and likely."* The dissenting judge found it proper not to recognize a property right, however, and to leave it to legislatures to constitute such a right if they considered it desirable.

The feasibility of a non-commercial property right has recently been urged regarding fetal tissues, in order to preclude abortions for profit while leaving tissues appropriately available for transplantation. Tendencies to engage in commercial transactions concerning any human tissues are already curbed by substantial legislation in most if not all Western and Westernized jurisdictions, of varying but usually wide scope. In Canada, all provinces have legislation that prohibits monetary dealings in tissues for transplantation, except blood and blood constituents. Similarly, most if not all U.S. jurisdictions prohibit such sales, and the National Organ Transplant Act prohibits interstate commerce of organs for transplantation. Accordingly, property rights of control can be accommodated without leading to objectionable commerce. Property rights may indeed increase altruistic donation of a variety of different transplantable tissues, by affording donors of their own or deceased relatives' tissues legal means to ensure that their donations are used for the purposes for which they were made, or for sufficiently analogous purposes, and are not misdirected nor squandered after donation but before implantation in a designated or otherwise approved recipient.

Abandonment

The *Moore* case resulted in the California Court of Appeal reversing the lower court's finding that the plaintiff could in law have no proprietary interest in his separated tissues, and sending the case back for trial on its merits. The case may deal separately with therapeutic removal of the plaintiff's spleen, and his donation of tissues after the splenectomy. His continuing property interest in the latter may be accepted, but the question remains of whether he necessarily retained a property interest in his spleen following its removal in therapeutic surgery, or whether he may have abandoned any interest that he had. The issue is significant in that people who donate tissues such as organs expressly in order that they may be implanted in others, particularly designated others, will have an interest in the tissues reaching their intended destination, whereas patients who yield tissues in therapeutic surgical or other care may have no expectations about their subsequent disposition, except perhaps that they will be incinerated.

The historic understanding has been that patients abandon any legal interest they may have in tangible body products resulting from surgery or other bodily function, such as labour or miscarriage, unless they indicate a contrary intention at an appropriate time. Large fetuses might be sent to a hospital mortuary, but damages were denied a mother when a hospital negligently lost the body of her prematurely born baby. The general presumption of abandonment appears in the judicial finding that "By the force of social custom, we hold that when a person does nothing and says nothing to indicate an intent to assert his right of ownership, possession, or control over such material [as comes from his body by intent, accident or the result of normal bodily functions], the only rational inference is that he intends to abandon the material".

The *Moore* Court, however, did not accept the defendants' claim that the plaintiff had abandoned his therapeutically removed spleen. The majority judges observed that, under the general law, the essential element of abandonment is the intent to abandon, amounting to entire indifference as to what may become of the separate body material or as to who may thereafter possess it. They added that whether or not that intent existed was a matter of fact, to be determined following a proper trial of the evidence of fact, but that "*A consent to removal of a diseased organ, or the taking of blood or other bodily tissues, does not necessarily imply an intent to abandon such organ, blood or tissue . . . we do not find that, as a matter of law, anyone who consents to surgery abandons all removed tissue to the first person to claim it. Certainly, in the example of an unconscious patient, the concept of abandonment becomes ridiculous*".

The judges accordingly rejected earlier inferences that a patient who does nothing and says nothing to indicate an intent to assert a property right to control separated bodily materials abandons them. On the contrary, they found that, while patients may be content that their expectation of pathological examination followed by prompt and permanent disposal of such materials such as by incineration be met, they are not indifferent to any alternative use or disposal nor consenting to anyone's possession. In particular, they found it inappropriate to infer abandonment when the defendants proposed to use the spleen in such procedures as recombinant DNA experimentation, which would be a source of concern and discomfort to many patients, and hardly a source of disinterest.

The dissenting judge did not expressly find abandonment of a proprietary interest, but denied original existence of any such interest. He reinforced his point, however, by observing that damages for conversion of any property interest were to be set as at the time of the conversion. The inference was that the diseased spleen itself was close to worthless, in contrast to the commercial value of the cell line subsequently produced by the application of refined laboratory skills and advanced biotechnology. Modest commercial value does not in itself indicate an intention to abandon, however, since a property right may be retained for the purpose of preventing unwanted disposition, testing or use of bodily materials, or of compelling their use for a particular non-commercial purpose, such as implantation.

Bailment of Property

A classical description of the circumstances by which a bailment of goods arises is that *"in general any person is to be considered as a bailee who otherwise than as a servant either receives possession of a thing from another or consents to receive or hold possession of a thing for another upon an undertaking with the other person either to keep and return or deliver to him the specific thing or to (convey and) apply the specific thing according to the directions antecedent or future of the other person."* By this test, a recipient of bodily tissues who has not unlawfully converted them to his or her own use, such as by employing them contrary to the owner's directions or destroying them, holds them as a bailee. Bailment distinguishes ownership (in the bailor) from possession (in the bailee), indicating that the bailee is subject to the bailor's direction on disposition, and may be liable for misuse in an action for conversion or breach of the bailment agreement if (as may or may not be the case) it is in the nature of a legal contract. A bailee also owes the bailor a duty of care to retain or use the property as undertaken, breach of which may be actionable as legal negligence when legal damage is proven to have been caused by such breach.

The law of bailment is ancient, traceable to elements of historic Roman law, and complex. It appears, however, that an unpaid (or gratuitous) bailee owes only *"that degree of diligence which men of common prudence generally exercise about their own affairs. In order, therefore, that an action may be maintained, in the case of a gratuitous deposit, the defendant must have been guilty of either a breach of orders, gross negligence or fraud."* Modern practice holds a bailee to more strict account, however, in that the concept of "gross" negligence is now held to be no more than *"ordinary negligence with the addition of a vituperative epithet."* Accordingly, a physician or other health professional, or an officer of a hospital in which a patient has given tissues (whether through surgical or other therapeutic or natural means or as a specific donation of a person's own tissues or of those from a body over which the person has dispositional authority by law) who is in legal possession of such tissues but receives no specific payment for their management, may be held to legal account for misappropriation or for negligent use of them that defeats the donor's intention in permitting or making the bailment of the tissues.

There is some academic disagreement on whether a bailee's innocent misdelivery of goods held on bailment constitutes conversion, but even if not, a misdelivery such as by applying designated tissues to the wrong patient or using tissues for a purpose other than that for which they were donated might constitute breach of contract or the tort of negligence. A further uncertainty is whether an involuntary bailee, such as a doctor or hospital coming into possession of bodily materials of a person in emergency care whom the hospital declined to admit as a patient, can give the source appropriate notice and opportunity to repossess them, and consider them abandoned if the source refuses or fails to do so in a reasonable time, when the bailee may treat them as his, her or its own and, for instance, discard them.

When the bailment of tissues is to rest on a contract, a health professional or hospital considered the bailee may propose terms during negotiation, such as exemption terms or temination conditions that will eliminate or end legal liability to the bailor if certain contingencies occur. Hospitals that admit patients to scheduled surgery, for instance, may undertake to meet their reasonable requirements as to disposition of acquired tissues, but reserve their freedom of action if events occur that prevent, obstruct or raise hospital costs of meeting patients' wishes.

Gifts Inter Vivos

When one person makes a tissue gift to another, called an *inter vivos* gift (between living persons) as opposed to a gift that takes effect *post mortem* (after death), the intended or designated recipient acquires a legal interest in the tissue only when it has been delivered to him or her, and accepted as a gift, and the donor's donative intent is adequately evidenced. In most *inter vivos* donations intent is not in issue, but questions may arise about whether and when the intended recipient for implantation has in law taken delivery of the tissue, and whether a given health professional such as the implant surgeon is the intended recipient's agent so that delivery to the surgeon constitutes in law delivery to the intended recipient. Until delivery that completes the donation, the physicians and other personnel and institutions involved in the exchange will be bailees of the donor's, and have no legal duties to the intended recipient arising from the management of any property the law considers to have become his or hers. Independent duties may arise before delivery of the tissue to the intended recipient, however, such a duty of care an intermediary owes in negligence law to such recipient because he or she is a person in a special relationship with the intermediary so likely to be affected by the intermediary's negligent act or omission that the intermediary ought reasonably to have him or her in mind.

A special case of a gift made by one living person to another is a gift made in contemplation of death, called a *donatio mortis causa*. Although lacking the form of a testamentary gift (that is, a bequest by will), such a gift may be given legal effect when made by a person *in extremis* who apprehends his or her death from an imminently presented cause and, in the event that death should occur from that cause, wants a designated person legally to acquire an item of property. The acquisition is given legal effect only if the apprehended sudden cause does in fact result in death, so that the gift is finalized *post mortem*. In that the law requires actual delivery of the property to the recipient at the time of intended donation, however, this gift can have little application to tissue implants from a living donor, since such a donation would not be made conditional on death, returnable should the donor's death not result. In practice if such a gift were to be made it would operate as a regular *inter vivos* gift.

The problem of *inter vivos* gifts intended to take effect in the future is whether a purely gratuitous gift (that is, one not part of a contractual exchange) is legally binding, and whether it can be revoked as unilaterally as it is made. Usually, gratuitous gifts can be recalled before actual delivery occurs, but this may not be so when the prospective recipient has been induced to rely on the promise of the gift to his or her detriment. The doctrine of injurious reliance (or *estoppel*) may entitle a designated future recipient of tissues to claim them when, for instance, he or she declined to receive alternative adequately suitable tissues when they became available in reliance on the promise made, that may have been of tissues more genetically compatible than those declined.

A gift of property intended to take effect on death must normally be in the legal form of a will. It has been seen that bodies themselves are not considered property governed by wills. The *Moore* case raises the question, however, of whether tissues that are considered property transferable *inter vivos* can be bequeathed by will. The question is probably theoretical regarding tissues for transplantation since, although a will takes effect at the moment of death, transplantable tissues are more effectively managed under the almost invariably applicable terms of legislation on individuals' donations of their tissues intended to take effect *post mortem*.

Post Mortem Gifts and Trusts

Because gifts operative on death are obviously beyond the donors' legal compulsion but may not have legally vested in intended recipients, they tend to be governed in law through the concept of the trust. A trust is in principle a legally imposed and enforceable conscientious obligation to act in accordance with a moral commitment. Trust can arise by express creation, but also by operation of law to constitute a person in possession of an asset not its owner but only its trustee, bound to act in the interests and perhaps at the direction of the legally identified beneficiary or beneficiaries. Others may also have legal standing to enforce the trust, including almost invariably the senior law officer of the jurisdiction, who is residual guardian of the integrity of the law and of the public interest, the Attorney General.

Completion of a tissue donation to operate *post mortem* in favour of a designated recipient may constitute that recipient the beneficiary of a trust arising at the donor's death governing the tissues donated, and a person or institution aware of the donation while in lawful possession of such tissues, whether in the body of the deceased or separate from the other remains, the trustee. Accordingly, the beneficiary and, in default, the Attorney General, can take action to direct their due preservation and delivery for their intended purpose. When a beneficiary has not been identified as recipient of the property, but tissues have been donated as a general *post mortem* gift, they may be deemed to be subject to a general charitable trust that may be enforced even against the deceased's family's opposition, by a person or officer with legal standing. A person who can show an interest exceeding that of general members of society, such as a prospective or potential tissue recipient or such a recipient's spouse or family member, may be accorded legal standing. That this does not occur in practice, and that a deceased person's family member's veto is usually permitted to prevail, shows a lack of initiatives to enforce the law rather than a failing of the law itself.

When, however, a donor makes a general gift for *post mortem* effect to a particular hospital, university or comparable institution, the gift probably operates as a gift to the named recipient itself for its general purposes, so that no potential transplantation patient may claim to be a beneficiary with rights of enforcement. If, however, a purpose is specified, such as medical education or research, different employment of the tissues may be restrained by or on behalf of a person with an interest in that use.

When a gift is made by a family member of tissues from the body of a deceased relative, by authority of legislation, that donor or another family member with the same legal status as the donor may enforce the gift directly, as outlined above, but may also be legally entitled to enforce a trust in favour of designated or non-designated but potential beneficiaries. That is, in addition to whoever else may be entitled to enforce the trust, the donating relative of a deceased person may be held to have a special interest in upholding the terms on which he or she donated the tissues, in accordance with the legislation that permits the donor so to dedicate the deceased person's tissues. An almost invariable term of human tissue gift legislation is that no person can knowingly make a gift that violates the deceased person's wishes formed when living.

When for some reason the terms of a charitable trust cannot be discharged exactly, or become impracticable, the trustee has the duty to apply the terms as closely as possible (*cy près*) to another charitable purpose. A gift made for *post mortem* effect to a designated prospective recipient may not rank as a charitable trust because it fails to meet the test of general charitable intent, in which case impossibility to perform it, for instance by the designated recipient's death or unfitness for surgical implantation, may result in the gift simply failing and the tissue, or the deceased's general remains becoming governed by the general law. When a gift is for such a benefit as to be charitable, however, which a gift for a general health, educational or scientific purpose may be, a trustee's inability to complete its precise purpose leaves the trustee obliged to seek to satisfy the spirit of the gift as closely as can reasonably be done. In principle, a court will be able to guide a trustee by determining whether a prospective use satisfies this obligation, but if reasonable use of an asset is incompatible with the time or resources required for a court application and hearing, a trustee who can show good faith in attempting to serve the general goals of the trust will be exonerated from liability for breach.

Conclusion

The accumulation and interaction of the provisions of property law outlined above may afford tissue donors the reasonable prospect of their intentions being legally enforceable. A gift for *inter vivos* donation to a designated recipient remains under the donor's legal control until delivery to the recipient, by virtue of legal provisions such as on bailment and conversion. Similarly, a person who donates tissues taken from a deceased body over which the person has acquired a legal power of disposition can use the same provisions to ensure that the purpose of donation will be achieved, for instance to offer availability to potential recipient patients or institutions. Intermediaries in possession of such tissues can be legally required to respect the donor's intention. When a living source of potentially transplantable tissues has yielded them through therapeutic surgery or they have otherwise become available from the source's body to his or her benefit or relief, the source may have no interest in their use, and abandon them to whoever possesses them or first wishes to, provided that they not be employed against the wishes of the source, such as for incrimination or identification.

Greater complexities affect enforcement of a tissue gift a donor makes to operate after his or her death. A general gift by a person now deceased may be enforced as a trust, which may be a charitable trust, by a person with standing to enforce it, and always by an Attorney General of the relevant jurisdiction. Legislation may also afford a surviving relative the power to donate tissues from a deceased person and to enforce the gift as if made regarding tissues from his or her own body, but an alternative may exist to enforce the donation through a trust such as a charitable trust. In practice, such gifts are often non-specific as to use and recipient institution, so that whichever eligible institution has possession, such as that in which a deceased person died, can claim that delivery has been completed and that the gift has lawfully passed under its full control.

Note

1. For further reading see Field, Evolving Conceptualisations of Property: A Proposal to De-Commercialise the Value of Fetal Tissue (1989) 99 Yale L J 169; Dickens, Morals and Markets in Transplantable Organs (1989) Vol 6(4) Transplantation/Implantation Today 23.

Moore v *Regents of the University of California*

Supreme Court of California
(1990) 793 P.2(d) 479.

[*Moore*, page 306, above, was appealed to the Supreme Court. The Supreme Court held that in soliciting a patient's consent to medical treatment, a physician has a fiduciary duty to disclose all information material to a patient's decision. The Court held that in this case Mr Moore had stated a cause of action for breach of fiduciary duty or lack of informed consent based upon allegations that the physician had concealed his economic interest in the post splenectomy takings of blood and other samples for use in research, and that the physician had failed to disclose that he had begun to investigate and initiate procedures for obtaining a patent on a cell line developed from the patient's cells. The Supreme Court held, however, that Moore did not retain an ownership interest in the cells following their removal. What follows are extracts from the judgment of Justice Panelli (for the majority); and Justice Mosk, who delivered a powerful dissent. (Footnotes are omitted.)]

* * *

PANELLI J.

We first consider whether the tort of conversion clearly gives Moore a cause of action under existing law. We do not believe it does. Because of the novelty of

Moore's claim to own the biological materials at issue, to apply the theory of conversion in this context would frankly have to be recognized as an extension of the theory. Therefore, we consider next whether it is advisable to extend the tort to this context.

1. Moore's Claim Under Existing Law

[5] "To establish a conversion, plaintiff must establish an actual interference with his *ownership or right of possession* . . . .. Where plaintiff neither has title to the property alleged to have been converted, nor possession thereof, he cannot maintain an action for conversion." (*Del E. Webb Corp.* v *Structural Materials Co.* (1981) 123 Cal.App.3d 593, 610-611, 176 Cal.Rptr. 824, emphasis added. See also *General Motors A. Corp.* v *Dallas* (1926) 198 Cal. 365, 370, 245 P. 184.)

Since Moore clearly did not expect to retain possession of his cells following their removal, to sue for their conversion he must have retained an ownership interest in them. But there are several reasons to doubt that he did retain any such interest. First, no reported judicial decision supports Moore's claim, either directly or by close analogy. Second, California statutory law drastically limits any continuing interest of a patient in excised cells. Third, the subject matters of the Regents' patent — the patented cell line and the products derived from it — cannot be Moore's property.

Neither the Court of Appeal's opinion, the parties' briefs, nor our research discloses a case holding that a person retains a sufficient interest in excised cells to support a cause of action for conversion. We do not find this surprising, since the laws governing such things as human tissues, transplantable organs, blood, fetuses, pituitary glands, corneal tissue, and dead bodies deal with human biological materials as objects sui generis, regulating their disposition to achieve policy goals rather than abandoning them to the general law of personal property. It is these specialized statutes, not the law of conversion, to which courts ordinarily should and do look for guidance on the disposition of human biological materials.

Lacking direct authority for importing the law of conversion into this context, Moore relies, as did the Court of Appeal, primarily on decisions addressing privacy rights. One line of cases involves unwanted publicity. (*Lugosi* v *Universal Pictures* (1979) 25 Cal.3d 813, 160 Cal.Rptr. 323, 603 P.2d 425; *Motschenbacher* v *R. J. Reynolds Tobacco Company* (9th Cir.1974) 498 F.2d 821 [interpreting Cal. law].) These opinions hold that every person has a proprietary interest in his own likeness and that unauthorized, business use of a likeness is redressable as a tort. But in neither opinion did the authoring court expressly base its holding on property law. (*Lugosi* v *Universal Pictures*, supra, 25 Cal.3d at pp 819, 823-826, 160 Cal.Rptr. 323, 603 P.2d 425; *Motschenbacher* v *R. J. Reynolds Tobacco Company*, supra, 498 F.2d at pp. 825-826). Each court stated, following Prosser, that it was "pointless" to debate the proper characterization of the proprietary interest in a likeness. (*Motschenbacher* v *R. J. Reynolds Tobacco Company*, supra, 498 F.2d at p. 825, quoting Prosser, Law of Torts (4th ed. 1971) at p. 807; *Lugosi* v Universal Pictures, supra, 25 Cal.3d at pp. 819, 824, 160 Cal.Rptr. 323, 603 P.2d 425.) For purposes of determining whether the tort of conversion lies, however, the characterization of the right in question is far from pointless. Only property can be converted.

Not only are the wrongful-publicity cases irrelevant to the issue of conversion, but the analogy to them seriously misconceives the nature of the genetic materials and research involved in this case. Moore, adopting the analogy originally advanced by the Court of Appeal argues that "[i]f the courts have found a sufficient proprietary interest in one's persona, how could one not have a right in one's own genetic material, something far more profoundly the essence of one's human uniqueness than a name or a face?" However, as the defendants' patent makes clear—and the complaint, too, if read with an understanding of the scientific terms which it has borrowed from the patent—the goal and result of defendants' efforts has been to manufacture lymphokines. Lymphokines, unlike a name or a face, have the same molecular structure in every human being and the same, important functions in every human being's immune system. Moreover, the particular genetic material which is responsible for the natural production of lymphokines, and which defendants use to manufacture lymphokines in the laboratory, is also the same in every person; it is no more unique to Moore than the number of vertebrae in the spine or the chemical formula of hemoglobin.

Another privacy case offered by analogy to support Moore's claim establishes only that patients have a right to refuse medical treatment. (*Bouvia* v *Superior Court* (1986) 179 Cal.App.3d 1127, 225 Cal.Rptr. 297.) In this context the court in *Bouvia* wrote that "'[e]very human being of adult years and sound mind has a right to determine what shall be done with his own body . . ..'" (Id., at p. 1139, 225 Cal.Rptr. 297, quoting from *Schloendorff* v *Society of New York Hospital*, supra, 211 N.Y. 125, 105 N.E. at p. 93.) Relying on this language to support the proposition that a patient has a continuing right to control the use of excised cells, the Court of Appeal in this case concluded that "[a] patient must have the ultimate power to control what becomes of his or her tissues. To hold otherwise would open the door to a massive invasion of human privacy and dignity in the name of medical progress." Yet one may earnestly wish to protect privacy and dignity without accepting the extremely problematic conclusion that interference with those interests amounts to a conversion of personal property. Nor is it necessary to force the round pegs of "privacy" and "dignity" into the square hole of "property" in order to protect the patient, since the fiduciary-duty and informed-consent theories protect these interests directly by requiring full disclosure.

The next consideration that makes Moore's claim of ownership problematic is California statutory law, which drastically limits a patient's control over excised cells. Pursuant to Health and Safety Code section 7054.4, "[n]otwithstanding any other provision of law, recognizable anatomical parts, human tissues, anatomical human remains, or infectious waste following conclusion of scientific use shall be disposed of by interment, incineration, or any other method determined by the state department [of health services] to protect the public health and safety." Clearly the Legislature did not specifically intend this statute to resolve the question of whether a patient is entitled to compensation for the nonconsensual use of excised cells. A primary object of the statute is to ensure the safe handling of potentially hazardous biological waste materials. Yet one cannot escape the conclusion that the statute's practical effect is to limit, drastically, a patient's control over excised cells. By restricting how excised cells may be used and requiring their eventual destruction, the statute eliminates so many of the rights ordinarily attached to property that one cannot simply assume that what is left amounts to "property" or "ownership" for purposes of conversion law.

It may be that some limited right to control the use of excised cells does survive the operation of this statute. There is, for example, no need to read the statute to permit "scientific use" contrary to the patient's expressed wish. A fully informed patient may always withhold consent to treatment by a physician whose research plans the patient does not approve. That right, however, as already discussed, is protected by the fiduciary-duty and informed-consent theories.

Finally, the subject matter of the Regents' patent—the patented cell line and the products derived from it—cannot be Moore's property. This is because the patented cell line is both factually and legally distinct from the cells taken from Moore's body. Federal law permits the patenting of organisms that represent the product of "human ingenuity," but not naturally occurring organisms. (*Diamond v Chakrabarty* (1980) 447 U.S. 303, 309-310, 100 S.Ct. 2204, 2208, 65 L.Ed.2d 144.) Human cell lines are patentable because "[l]ong-term adaptation and growth of human tissues and cells in culture is difficult—often considered an art . . .." and the probability of success is low. (OTA Rep., supra, at p. 33; see fn. 2, ante.) It is this *inventive effort* that patent law rewards, not the discovery of naturally occurring raw materials. Thus, Moore's allegations that he owns the cell line and the products derived from it are inconsistent with the patent, which constitutes an authoritative determination that the cell line is the product of invention. Since such allegations are nothing more than arguments or conclusions of law, they of course do not bind us. (*Daar* v *Yellow Cab Co.*, supra, 67 Cal.2d at p. 713, 63 Cal.Rptr. 724, 433 P.2d 732.)

2. Should Conversion Liability Be Extended?

[6] As we have discussed, Moore's novel claim to own the biological materials at issue in this case is problematic, at best. Accordingly, his attempt to apply the theory of conversion within this context must frankly be recognized as a request to extend that theory. While we do not purport to hold that excised cells can never be property for any purpose whatsoever, the novelty of Moore's claim demands express consideration of the policies to be served by extending liability (cf. *Nally v Grace Community Church*, supra, 47 Cal.3d at pp. 291-300, 253 Cal.Rptr. 97, 763 P.2d 948; *Foley* v *Interactive Data Corp.*, supra, 47 Cal.3d at pp. 694-700, 254 Cal.Rptr. 211, 765 P.2d 373; *Brown* v *Superior Court*, supra, 44 Cal.3d at pp. 1061-1066, 245 Cal.Rptr. 412, 751 P.2d 470) rather than blind deference to a complaint alleging as a legal conclusion the existence of a cause of action.

There are three reasons why it is inappropriate to impose liability for conversion based upon the allegations of Moore's complaint. First, a fair balancing of the relevant policy considerations counsels against extending the tort. Second, problems in this area are better suited to legislative resolution. Third, the tort of conversion is not necessary to protect patients' rights. For these reasons, we conclude that the use of excised human cells in medical research does not amount to a conversion.

Of the relevant policy considerations, two are of overriding importance. The first is protection of a competent patient's right to make autonomous medical decisions. That right, as already discussed is grounded in well-recognized and longstanding principles of fiduciary duty and informed consent. (See, e.g., *Cobbs* v *Grant*, supra, 8 Cal.3d at pp. 242-246, 104 Cal.Rptr. 505, 502 P.2d 1; *Bowman* v *McPheeters*, supra, 77 Cal.App.2d at p. 800, 176 P.2d 745.) This policy weighs in favor of providing a remedy to patients when physicians act with undisclosed motives that may affect their professional judgment. The second important policy consideration is that we not threaten with disabling civil liability innocent parties who are engaged in socially useful activities, such as researchers who have no reason to believe that their use of a particular cell sample is, or may be, against a donor's wishes.

To reach an appropriate balance of these policy considerations is extremely important. In its report to Congress the Office of Technology Assessment emphasized that "[u]ncertainty about how courts will resolve disputes between specimen sources and specimen users could be detrimental to both academic researchers and the infant biotechnology industry, particularly when the rights are asserted long after the specimen was obtained. The assertion of rights by sources would affect not only the researcher who obtained the original specimen, but perhaps other researchers as well.

"Biological materials are routinely distributed to other researchers for experimental purposes, and scientists who obtain cell lines or other specimen-derived products, such as gene clones, from the original researcher could also be sued under certain legal theories [such as conversion]. Furthermore, the uncertainty could affect product developments as well as research. Since inventions containing human tissues and cells may be patented and licensed for commercial use, companies are unlikely to invest heavily in developing, manufacturing, or marketing a product when uncertainty about clear title exists." (OTA Rep., *supra*, at p. 27.)

Indeed, so significant is the potential obstacle to research stemming from uncertainty about legal title to biological materials that the Office of Technology Assessment reached this striking conclusion: "[R]egardless of the merit of claims by the different interested parties, resolving the current uncertainty may be more important to the future of biotechnology than resolving it in any particular way." (OTA Rep., *supra*, at p. 27.)

We need not, however, make an arbitrary choice between liability and nonliability. Instead, an examination of the relevant policy considerations suggests an appropriate balance: Liability based upon existing disclosure obligations, rather than an unprecedented extension of the conversion theory, protects patients' rights of privacy and autonomy without unnecessarily hindering research.

To be sure, the threat of liability for conversion might help to enforce patients' rights indirectly. This is because physicians might be able to avoid liability by obtaining patients' consent, in the broadest possible terms, to any conceivable subsequent research use of excised cells. Unfortunately, to extend the conversion theory would utterly sacrifice the other goal of protecting innocent parties. Since conversion is a strict liability tort, it would impose liability on all those into whose hands the cells come, whether or not the particular defendant participated in, or knew of, the inadequate disclosures that violated the patient's right to make an informed decision. In contrast to the conversion theory, the fiduciary-duty and informed-consent theories protect the patient directly, without punishing innocent parties or creating disincentives to the conduct of socially beneficial research.

Research on human cells plays a critical role in the medical research. This is so because researchers are increasingly able to isolate naturally occurring, medically useful biological substances and to produce useful quantities of such substances through genetic engineering. These efforts are beginning to bear fruit. Products developed through biotechnology that have already been approved for marketing in this country include treatments and tests for leukemia, cancer, diabetes, dwarfism, hepatitis-B, kidney transplant rejection, emphysema, osteoporosis, ulcers, anemia, infertility, and gynecological tumors, to name but a few. (Note, *Source Compensation for Tissues and Cells Used in Biotechnical Research: Why a Source Shouldn't Share in the Profits* (1989) 64 Notre Dame L.Rev. 628 & fn. 1 (hereafter Note, Source Compensation); see also OTA Rep., supra, at pp. 58-59.)

The extension of conversion law into this area will hinder research by restricting access to the necessary raw materials. Thousands of human cell lines already exist in tissue repositories, such as the American Type Culture Collection and those operated by the National Institutes of Health and the American Cancer Society. These repositories respond to tens of thousands of requests for samples annually. Since the patent office requires the holders of patents on cell lines to make samples available to anyone, many patent holders place their cell lines in repositories to avoid the administrative burden of responding to requests. (OTA Rep., supra, at p. 53.) At present, human cell lines are routinely copied and distributed to other researchers for experimental purposes, usually free of charge. This exchange of scientific materials, which still is relatively free and efficient, will surely be compromised if each cell sample becomes the potential subject matter of a lawsuit. (OTA Rep., supra, at p. 52.)

To expand liability by extending conversion law into this area would have a broad impact. The House Committee on Science and Technology of the United States Congress found that "49 percent of the researchers at medical institutions surveyed used human tissues or cells in their research." Many receive grants from the National Institute of Health for this work. (OTA Rep., supra, at p. 52.) In addition, "there are nearly 350 commercial biotechnology firms in the United States actively engaged in biotechnology research and commercial product development and approximately 25 to 30 percent appear to be engaged in research to develop a human therapeutic or diagnostic reagent . . .. Most, but not all, of the human therapeutic products are derived from human tissues and cells, or human cell lines or cloned genes." (Id., at p. 56.)

In deciding whether to create new tort duties we have in the past considered the impact that expanded liability would have on activities that are important to society, such as research. For example, in *Brown v Superior Court*, supra, 44 Cal.3d 1049, 245 Cal.Rptr. 412, 751 P.2d 470, the fear that strict product liability would frustrate pharmaceutical research led us to hold that a drug manufacturer's liability should not be measured by those standards. We wrote that, "[i]f drug manufacturers were subject to strict liability, they might be reluctant to undertake research programs to develop some pharmaceuticals that would prove beneficial or to distribute others that are available to be marketed, because of the fear of large adverse monetary judgments." (Id., at p. 1063, 245 Cal.Rptr. 412, 751 P.2d 470.)

As in *Brown*, the theory of liability that Moore urges us to endorse threatens to destroy the economic incentive to conduct important medical research. If the use of cells in research is a conversion, then with every cell sample a researcher purchases a ticket in a litigation lottery. Because liability for conversion is predicated on a continuing ownership interest, "companies are unlikely to invest heavily in developing, manufacturing, or marketing a product when uncertainty about clear title exists." (OTA Rep., supra, at p. 27.) In our view, borrowing again from *Brown*, "[i]t is not unreasonable to conclude in these circumstances that the imposition of a harsher test for liability would not further the public interest in the development and availability of these important products." (*Brown* v *Superior Court*, supra, 44 Cal.3d at p. 1065, 245 Cal.Rptr. 412, 751 P.2d 470.)

Indeed, this is a far more compelling case for limiting the expansion of tort liability than *Brown*. In *Brown*, eliminating strict liability made it more difficult for plaintiffs to recover actual damages for serious physical injuries resulting from their mothers' prenatal use of the drug diethylstilbestrol (DES). (*Brown* v *Superior Court*, supra, 44 Cal.3d at pp. 1054-1055, 245 Cal.Rptr. 412, 751 P.2d 470.) In this case, by comparison, limiting the expansion of liability under a conversion theory will only make it more difficult for Moore to recover a highly theoretical windfall. Any injury to his right to make an informed decision remains actionable through the fiduciary-duty and informed-consent theories.

If the scientific users of human cells are to be held liable for failing to investigate the consensual pedigree of their raw materials, we believe the Legislature should make that decision. Complex policy choices affecting all society are involved, and "[l]egislatures, in making such policy decisions, have the ability to gather empirical evidence, solicit the advice of experts, and hold hearings at which all interested parties present evidence and express their views . . .." (*Foley* v *Interactive Data Corp.*, supra, 47 Cal.3d at p. 694, fn. 31, 254 Cal.Rptr. 211, 765 P.2d 373.) Legislative competence to act in this area is demonstrated by the existing statutes governing the use and disposition of human biological materials. Legislative interest is demonstrated by the extensive study recently commissioned by the United States Congress. (OTA Rep., supra.) Commentators are also recommending legislative solutions. (See Danforth, *Cells, Sales, and Royalties: The Patient's Right to a Portion of the Profits* (1988) 6 Yale L. & Pol'y Rev. 179, 198-201; Note, Source Compensation, supra, 64 Notre Dame L.Rev. at pp. 643-645.)

Finally, there is no pressing need to impose a judicially created rule of strict liability, since enforcement of physicians' disclosure obligations will protect patients against the very type of harm with which Moore was threatened. So long as a physician discloses research and economic interests that may affect his judgment, the patient is protected from conflicts of interest. Aware of any conflicts, the patient can make an informed decision to consent to treatment, or to withhold consent and look elsewhere for medical assistance. As already discussed, enforcement of physicians' disclosure obligations protects patients directly, without hindering the socially useful activities of innocent researchers.

For these reasons, we hold that the allegations of Moore's third amended complaint state a cause of action for breach of fiduciary duty or lack of informed consent, but not conversion.

* * *

MOSK J.

I dissent.

Contrary to the principal holding the Court of Appeal, the majority conclude that the complaint does not—in fact cannot—state a cause of action for conversion. I disagree with this conclusion for all the reasons stated by the Court of Appeal, and for additional reasons that I shall explain. For convenience I shall discuss the six premises of the majority's conclusion in the order in which they appear.

1.

The majority first take the position that Moore has no cause of action for conversion under existing law because he retained no "ownership interest" in his cells after they were removed from his body. (Maj. opn., *ante,* p. 156 of 271 Cal.Rptr., p. 489 of 793 P.2d.) To state a conversion cause of action a plaintiff must allege his "ownership or right to possession of the property at the time of the conversion" (*Baldwin* v *Marina City Properties, Inc.* (1978) 79 Cal. App.3d 393, 410, 145 Cal.Rptr. 406). Here the complaint defines Moore's "Blood and Bodily Substances" to include inter alia his blood, his bodily tissues, his cells, and the cell lines derived therefrom. Moore thereafter alleges that "he is the owner of his Blood and Bodily Substances and of the by-products produced therefrom . . .." And he further alleges that such blood and bodily substances "are his tangible personal property, and the activities of the defendants as set forth herein constitute a substantial interference with plaintiff's possession or right thereto, as well as defendants' wrongful exercise of dominion over plaintiff's personal property rights in his Blood and Bodily Substances."

The majority impliedly hold these allegations insufficient as a matter of law, finding three "reasons to doubt" that Moore retained a sufficient ownership interest in his cells, after their excision, to support a conversion cause of action (Maj. opn., *ante,* p. 156 of 271 Cal.Rptr., p. 489 of 793 P.2d.) In my view the majority's three reasons, taken singly or together, are inadequate to the task.

The majority's first reason is that "no reported judicial decision supports Moore's claim, either directly or by close analogy." (Maj. opn., *ante,* p. 156 of 271 Cal.Rptr., p. 489 of 793 P.2d.) Neither, however, is there any reported decision rejecting such a claim. The issue is as new as its source—the recent explosive growth in the commercialization of biotechnology.

The majority next cite several statutes regulating aspects of the commerce in or disposition of certain parts of the human body, and conclude in effect that in the present case we should also "look for guidance" to the Legislature rather than to the law of conversion. (*Id.* at p. 156 of 271 Cal.Rptr., at p. 489 of 793 P.2d.) Surely this argument is out of place in an opinion of the highest court of this state. As the majority acknowledge, the law of conversion is a creature of the common law. "'The inherent capacity of the common law for growth and change is its most significant feature. Its development has been determined by the social needs of the community which it serves. It is constantly expanding and developing in keeping with advancing civilization and the new conditions and progress of society, and adapting itself to the gradual change of trade, commerce, arts, inventions, and the needs of the country.' [Citation.] [¶] In short, as the United States Supreme Court has aptly said, 'This flexibility and capacity for growth and adaptation is the peculiar boast and excellence of the common law.' [Citation.] . . . Although the Legislature may of course speak to the subject, in the common law system the primary instruments of this evolution are the courts, adjudicating on a regular basis the rich variety of individual cases brought before them." (*Rodriguez* v *Bethlehem Steel Corp.* (1974) 12 Cal.3d 382, 394, 115 Cal.Rptr. 765, 525 P.2d 669.)

Especially is this true in the field of torts. I need not review the many instances in which this court has broken fresh ground by announcing new rules of tort law: time and again when a new rule was needed we did not stay our hand merely because the matter was one of first impression. For example, in *Sindell v Abbott Laboratories* (1980) 26 Cal.3d 588, 163 Cal.Rptr. 132, 607 P.2d 924, we adopted a "market share" theory of liability for injury resulting from administration of a prescription drug and suffered by a plaintiff who without fault cannot trace the particular manufacturer of the drug that caused the harm. Like the opinion in the case at bar, the dissent in *Sindell* objected that market share liability was "a wholly new theory" and an "unprecedented extension of liability" (*id.* at pp. 614, 615, 163 Cal.Rptr. 132, 607 P.2d 924), and urged that in view of the economic, social, and medical effects of this new rule the decision to adopt it should rest with the Legislature (*id.* at p. 621, 163 Cal.Rptr. 132, 607 P.2d 924). We nevertheless declared the new rule for sound policy reasons, explaining that "In our contemporary complex industrialized society, advances in science and technology create fungible goods which may harm consumers and which cannot be traced to any specific producer. The response of the courts can be either to adhere rigidly to prior doctrine, denying recovery to those injured by such products, or to fashion remedies to meet these changing needs." (*Id.* at p. 610, 163 Cal.Rptr. 132, 607 P.2d 924.) We took the latter course.

The case at bar, of course, does not involve a drug-induced injury. Yet it does present a claim arising, like Sindell's, from "advances in science and technology" that could not have been foreseen when traditional tort doctrine—here, the law of conversion—was formulated. My point is that if the cause of action for conversion is otherwise an appropriate remedy on these facts, we should not refrain from fashioning it simply because another court has not yet so held or because the Legislature has not yet addressed the question. We need not wait on either event, because neither is a precondition to an exercise of our longstanding "power to insure the just and rational development of the common law in our state" (*Rodriguez* v *Bethlehem Steel Corp., supra,* 12 Cal.3d 382, 394, 115 Cal.Rptr. 765, 525 P.2d 669).

2.

The majority's second reason for doubting that Moore retained an ownership interest in his cells after their excision is that "California statutory law . . . drastically limits a patient's control over excised cells." (Maj. opn., *ante*, p. 158 of 271 Cal.Rptr., p. 491 of 793 P.2d.) For this proposition the majority rely on Health and Safety Code section 7054.4 (hereafter section 7054.4), set forth in the margin.

The majority concede that the statute was not meant to directly resolve the question whether a person in Moore's position has a cause of action for conversion, but reason that it indirectly resolves the question by limiting the patient's control over the fate of his excised cells: "By restricting how excised cells may be used and requiring their eventual destruction, the statute eliminates so many of the rights ordinarily attached to property that one cannot simply assume that what is left amounts to 'property' or 'ownership' for purposes of conversion law." (Maj. opn., *ante*, pp. 158-159 of 271 Cal.Rptr., pp. 491-492 of 793 P.2d.) As will appear, I do not believe section 7054.4 supports the just quoted conclusion of the majority.

First, in my view the statute does not authorize the principal use that defendants claim the right to make of Moore's tissue, i.e., its commercial exploitation. In construing section 7054.4, of course, "we look first to the words of the statute themselves" (*Long Beach Police Officers Assn. v City of Long Beach* (1988) 46 Cal.3d 736, 741, 250 Cal.Rptr. 869, 759 P.2d 504), and give those words their usual and ordinary meaning (*California Teachers Assn. v San Diego Community College Dist.* (1981) 28 Cal.3d 692, 698, 170 Cal.Rptr. 817, 621 P.2d 856).

By its terms, section 7054.4 permits only "scientific use" of excised body parts and tissue before they must be destroyed. We must therefore determine the usual and ordinary meaning of that phrase. I would agree that "scientific use" at least includes routine postoperative examination of excised tissue conducted by a pathologist for diagnostic or prognostic reasons (e.g., to verify preoperative diagnosis or to assist in determining postoperative treatment). I might further agree that "scientific use" could be extended to include purely scientific study of the tissue by a disinterested researcher for the purpose of advancing medical knowledge— provided of course that the patient gave timely and informed consent to that use. It would stretch the English language beyond recognition, however, to say that commercial exploitation of the kind and degree alleged here is also a usual and ordinary meaning of the phrase "scientific use."

The majority dismiss this difficulty by asserting that I read the statute to define "scientific use" as "not-for-profit scientific use," and by finding "no reason to believe that the Legislature intended to make such a distinction." (Maj. opn., *ante*, p. 159, fn. 34 of 271 Cal.Rptr., p. 492, fn. 34 of 793 P.2d.) The objection misses my point. I do not stress the concept of profit, but the concept of *science:* the distinction I draw is not between nonprofit scientific use and scientific use that happens to lead to a marketable by-product; it is between a truly *scientific* use and the blatant *commercial* exploitation of Moore's tissue that the present complaint alleges. Under those allegations, defendants Dr. David W. Globe and Shirley G. Quan were not only scientists, they were also full-fledged enterpreneurs: the complaint repeatedly declares that they appropriated Moore's tissue in order "to further defendants' independent research and commercial activities and promote their economic, financial and competitive interests." The complaint also alleges that defendant Regents of the University of California (hereafter Regents) actively assisted the individual defendants in applying for patent rights and in negotiating with bioengineering and pharmaceutical companies to exploit the commercial potential of Moore's tissue. Finally, the complaint alleges in detail the contractual arrangements between the foregoing defendants and defendants Genetics Institute, Inc., and Sandoz Pharmaceuticals Corporation, giving the latter companies exclusive rights to exploit that commercial potential while providing substantial financial benefits to the individual defendants in the form of cash, stock options, consulting fees, and fringe benefits. To exclude such traditionally commercial activities from the phrase "scientific use," as I do here, does not give it a restrictive definition; rather, it gives the phrase its usual and ordinary meaning, as settled law requires.

Secondly, even if section 7054.4 does permit defendants' commercial exploitation of Moore's tissue under the guise of "scientific use," it does not follow that—as the majority conclude—the statute "eliminates so many of the rights ordinarily attached to property" that what remains does not amount to "property" or "ownership" for purposes of the law of conversion. (Maj. opn., *ante,* p. 159 of 271 Cal.Rptr., p. 492 of 793 P.2d.)

The concepts of property and ownership in our law are extremely broad. (See Civ. Code, §§ 654, 655.) A leading decision of this court approved the following definition: "'The term "property" is sufficiently comprehensive to include every species of estate, real and personal, and everthing which one person can own and transfer to another. It extends to every species of right and interest capable of being enjoyed as such upon which it is practicable to place a money value.'" (*Yuba River Power Co.* v *Nevada Irr. Dist.* (1929) 207 Cal. 521, 523, 279 P. 128.)

Being broad, the concept of property is also abstract: rather than referring directly to a material object such as a parcel of land or the tractor that cultivates it, the concept of property is often said to refer to a "bundle of rights" that may be exercised with respect to that object—principally the rights to possess the property, to use the property, to exclude others from the property, and to dispose of the property by sale or by gift. "Ownership is not a single concrete entity but a bundle of rights and privileges as well as of obligations." (*Union Oil Co.* v *State Bd. of Equal.* (1963) 60 Cal.2d 441, 447, 34 Cal.Rptr. 872, 386 P.2d 496.) But the same bundle of rights does not attach to all forms of property. For a variety of policy reasons, the law limits or even forbids the exercise of certain rights over certain forms of property. For example, both law and contract may limit the right of an owner of real property to use his parcel as he sees fit. Owners of various forms of personal property may likewise be subject to restrictions on the time, place, and manner of their use. Limitations on the disposition of real property, while less common, may also be imposed. Finally, some types of personal property may be sold but not given away, while others may be given away but not sold, and still others may neither be given away nor sold.

In each of the foregoing instances, the limitation or prohibition diminishes the bundle of rights that would otherwise attach to the property, yet what remains is still deemed in law to be a protectible property interest. "Since property or title is a complex bundle of rights, duties, powers and immunities, the pruning away of some or a great many of these elements does not entirely destroy the title . . . ." (*People* v *Walker* (1939) 33 Cal.App.2d 18, 20, 90 P.2d 854 [even the possessor of contraband has certain property rights in it against anyone other than the state].) The same rule applies to Moore's interest in his own body tissue: even if we assume that section 7054.4 limited the use and disposition of his excised tissue in the manner claimed by the majority, Moore nevertheless retained valuable rights in that tissue. Above all, at the time of its excision he at least had *the right to do with his own tissue whatever the defendants did with it:* i.e., he could have contracted with researchers and pharmaceutical companies to develop and exploit the vast commercial potential of his tissue and its products. Defendants certainly believe that *their* right to do the foregoing is not barred by section 7054.4 and is a significant property right, as they have demonstrated by their deliberate concealment from Moore of the true value of his tissue, their efforts to obtain a patent on the Mo cell line, their contractual agreements to exploit this material, their exclusion of Moore from any participation in the profits, and their vigorous defense of this lawsuit. The Court of Appeal summed up the point by observing that "Defendants' position that plaintiff cannot own his tissue, but that they can, is fraught with irony." It is also legally untenable. As noted above, the majority cite no case holding that an individual's right to develop and exploit the commercial potential of his own tissue is *not* a right of sufficient worth or dignity to be deemed a protectible property interest. In the absence of such authority—or of legislation to the same effect—the right falls within the traditionally broad concept of property in our law.

3.

The majority's third and last reason for their conclusion that Moore has no cause of action for conversion under existing law is that "the subject matter of the Regents' patent—the patented cell line and the products derived from it—cannot be Moore's property." (Maj. opn., *ante*, p. 159 of 271 Cal.Rptr., p. 492 of 793 P.2d.) The majority then offer a dual explanation: "This is because the patented cell line is *factually* and *legally* distinct from the cells taken from Moore's body." (*Ibid.*, italics added.) Neither branch of the explanation withstands analysis.

*   *   *

4.

Having concluded—mistakenly, in my view—that Moore has no cause of action for conversion under existing law, the majority next consider whether to "extend" the conversion cause of action to this context. Again the majority find three reasons not to do so, and again I respectfully disagree with each.

The majority's first reason is that a balancing of the "relevant policy considerations" counsels against recognizing a conversion cause of action in these circumstances. (Maj. opn., *ante*, p. 160 and 271 Cal.Rptr., p. 493 of 793 P.2d.) The memo identifies two such policies, but concedes that one of them—"protection of a competent patient's right to make autonomous medical decisions" (*id.* at p. 160 of 271 Cal.Rptr., p. 493 of 793 (P.2d)—would in fact be promoted, even though "indirectly," by recognizing a conversion cause of action. (*Id.* at p. 160 of 271 Cal.Rptr.,at p. 493 of 793 P.2d.)

The majority focus instead on a second policy consideration, i.e., their concern "that we not threaten with disabling civil liability innocent parties who are engaged in socially useful activities, such as researchers who have no reason to believe that their use of a particular cell sample is, or may be, against a doctor's wishes." (Maj. opn., *ante*, p. 160 of 271 Cal.Rptr., p. 493 of 793 P.2d.) As will appear, in my view this concern is both overstated and outweighed by contrary considerations.

The majority begin their analysis by stressing the obvious facts that research on human cells plays an increasingly important role in the progress of medicine, and that the manipulation of those cells by the methods of biotechnology has resulted in numerous beneficial products and treatments. Yet it does not necessarily follow that, as the majority claim, application of the law of conversion to this area "will hinder research by restricting access to the necessary raw materials," i.e., to cells, cell cultures, and cell lines. (Maj. opn., *ante*, p. 161 of 271 Cal.Rptr., p. 494 of 793 P.2d.) The majority observe that many researchers obtain their tissue samples, routinely and at little or no cost, from cell-culture repositories. The majority then speculate that "This exchange of scientific materials, which still is relatively free and efficient, will surely be compromised if each cell sample becomes the potential subject matter of a lawsuit." (Maj. opn., *ante*, p. 162 of 271 Cal.Rptr., p. 495 of 793 P.2d.) There are two grounds to doubt that this prophecy will be fulfilled.

To begin with, if the relevant exchange of scientific materials was ever "free and efficient," it is much less so today. Since biological products of genetic engineering became patentable in 1980 (*Diamond* v *Chakrabarty* (1980) 447 U.S. 393, 100 S.Ct. 2204, 65 L.Ed.2d 144), human cell lines have been amendable to patent protection and, as the Court of Appeal observed in its opinion below, "The rush to patent for exclusive use has been rampant." Among those who have taken advantage of this development, of course, are the defendants herein: as we have seen, defendants Golde and Quan obtained a patent on the Mo cell line in 1984 and assigned it to defendant Regents. With such patentability has come a drastic reduction in the formerly free access of researchers to new cell lines and their products: the "novelty" requirement for patentability prohibits public disclosure of the invention at all times up to one year before the filing of the patent application. (35 U.S.C. §102(b).) Thus defendants herein recited in their patent specification, "At no time has the Mo cell line been available to other than the investigators involved with its initial discovery and only the conditioned medium from the cell line has been made available to a limited number of investigators for collaborative work with the original discoverers of the Mo cell line."

An even greater force for restricting the free exchange of new cell lines and their products has been the rise of the biotechnology industry and the increasing involvement of academic researchers in that industry. When scientists became entrepreneurs and negotiated with biotechnological and pharmaceutical companies to develop and exploit the commercial potential of their discoveries—as did defendants in the case at bar—layers of contractual restrictions were added to the protections of the patent law.

In their turn, the biotechnological and pharmaceutical companies demanded and received exclusive rights in the scientists' discoveries, and frequently placed those discoveries under trade secret protection. Trade secret protection is popular among biotechnology companies because, among other reasons, the invention need not meet the strict standards of patentability and the protection is both quickly acquired and unlimited in duration (Note, *Patent and Trade Secret Protection in University—Industry Research Relationships in Biotechnology* (1987) 24 Harv.J. on Legis. 191, 218-219.) Secrecy as a normal business practice is also taking hold in university research laboratories, often because of industry pressure (*id.* at pp. 204-208): "One of the most serious fears associated with university-industry cooperative research concerns keeping work private and not disclosing it to the researcher's peers. [Citation.] . . . Economic arrangements between industry and universities inhibit open communication between researchers, especially for those who are financially tied to smaller biotechnology firms." (Howard, *supra*, 44 Food Drug Cosm.L.J. at p. 339, fn. 72.)

Secondly, to the extent that cell cultures and cell lines may still be "freely exchanged," e.g., for purely research purposes, it does not follow that the researcher who obtains such material must necessarily remain ignorant of any limitations on its use: by means of appropriate record-keeping, the researcher can be assured that the source of the material has consented to his proposed use of it, and hence that such use is not a conversion. To achieve this end the originator of the tissue sample first determines the extent of the source's informed consent to its use—e.g., for research only, or for public but academic use, or for specific or general commercial purposes; he then enters this information in the record of the tissue sample into the hands of any researcher who thereafter undertakes to work with it. "Record keeping would not be overly burdensome because researchers generally keep accurate records of tissue sources for other reasons: to trace anomalies to the medical history of the patient, to maintain title for other researchers and for themselves, and to insure reproducibility of the experiment." (*Toward the Right of Commerciality, supra,* 34 UCLA L.Rev. at p. 241.) As the Court of Appeal correctly observed, any claim to the contrary "is dubious in light of the meticulous care and planning necessary in serious modern medical research."

The majority rely on *Brown v Superior Court, supra,* 44 Cal.3d 1049, 245 Cal.Rptr. 412, 751 P.2d 470 (hereafter *Brown*), but the case is plainly distinguishable. In a unanimous opinion that I authored for the court, we considered inter alia whether pharmaceutical manufacturers should be held strictly liable for injuries caused by "defectively designed" prescription drugs. We declined to so hold for several policy reasons. (*Id.* at pp. 1063-1065, 245 Cal.Rptr. 412, 751 P.2d 470.) One of those reasons was our concern that "the fear of large adverse monetary judgments" might dissuade such manufacturers from developing or distributing potentially beneficial new drugs. (*Id.* at p. 1063, 245 Cal.Rptr. 412, 751 P.2d 470.) The majority now seek to draw an analogy between *Brown* and the case at bar, but the analogy fails because liability exposure in the *Brown* context is qualitatively far greater. As we acknowledged in *Brown*, "unlike other important medical products . . . harm to some users from prescription drugs is *unavoidable*." (*Ibid.*, italics added.) On an industry-wide basis, therefore the imposition of strict liability for defective prescription drugs would inevitably result in hundreds, if not thousands, of meritorious claims by often seriously harmed plaintiffs, most of them likely to be seeking exemplary as well as compensatory damages. Given the innocence and vulnerability of the typical plaintiff in such cases, sympathetic juries might well return substantial verdicts again and again, and the industry's total liability could reach intimidating proportions. Indeed, in *Brown* we chronicled actual instances in which the mere threat of such liability did cause the industry to refuse to supply new prescription drugs. (*Id.* at p. 1064, 245 Cal.Rptr. 412, 751 P.2d 470.)

None of the foregoing is true in the case at bar. The majority claim that a conversion cause of action threatens to "destroy the economic incentive" to conduct the type of research here in issue (maj. opn., *ante,* p. 162 of 271 Cal.Rptr., p. 495

of 793 P.2d), but it is difficult to take this hyperbole seriously. First, the majority reason that with every cell sample a researcher "purchases a ticket in a litigation lottery." (*Id.* at p. 162-163 of 271 Cal.Rptr., at p. 495-496 of 793 P.2d.) This is a colourful image, but it does not necessarily reflect reality: as explained above, with proper record-keeping the researcher acquires not a litigation-lottery ticket but the information he needs precisely in order to avoid litigation. In contrast to *Brown*, therefore, here the harm is by no means "unavoidable." Second, the risk at hand is not of a multiplicity of actions: in *Brown* the harm would be suffered by many members of the public—the users of the end product of the process of developing the new drug—while here it can be suffered by only one person—the original source of the research material that began that process. Third, the harm to the latter will be primarily economic rather than the potentially grave physical injuries at issue in *Brown*.

In any event, in my view whatever merit the majority's single policy consideration may have is outweighed by two contrary considerations, i.e., policies that are promoted by recognizing that every individual has a legally protectible property interest in his own body and its products. First, our society acknowledges a profound ethical imperative to respect the human body as the physical and temporal expression of the unique human persona. One manifestation of that respect is our prohibition against direct abuse of the body by torture or other forms of cruel or unusual punishment. Another is our prohibition against indirect abuse of the body by its economic exploitation for the sole benefit of another person. The most abhorrent form of such exploitation, of course, was the institution of slavery. Lesser forms, such as indentured servitude or even debtor's prison, have also disappeared. Yet their specter haunts the laboratories and boardrooms of today's biotechnological research-industrial complex. It arises wherever scientists or industrialists claim, as defendants claim here, the right to appropriate and exploit a patient's tissue for their sole economic benefit—the right, in other words, to freely mine or harvest valuable physical properties of the patient's body: "Research with human cells that results in significant economic gain for the researcher and no gain for the patient offends the traditional mores of our society in a manner impossible to quantify. Such research tends to treat the human body as a commodity—a means to a profitable end. The dignity and sanctity with which we regard the human whole, body as well as mind and soul, are absent when we allow researchers to further their own interests without the patient's participation by using a patient's cells as the basis for a marketable product." (Danforth, *supra*, 6 Yale L. & Pol'y Rev. at p. 190, fn. omitted.)

A second policy consideration adds notions of equity to those of ethics. Our society values fundamental fairness in dealings between its members, and condemns the unjust enrichment of any member at the expense of another. This is particularly true when, as here, the parties are not in equal bargaining positions. We are repeatedly told that the commercial products of the biotechnological revolution "hold the promise of tremendous profit." (*Toward the Right of Commerciality, supra*, 34 UCLA L.Rev. at p. 211.) In the case at bar, for example, the complaint alleges that the market for the kinds of proteins produced by the Mo cell line was predicted to exceed $3 billion by 1990. These profits are currently shared exclusively between the biotechnology industry and the universities that support that industry. The profits are shared in a wide variety of ways, including "direct entrepreneurial ties to genetic-engineering firms" and "an equity interest in fledgling biotechnology firms" (Howard, *supra*, 44 Food Drug Cosm.L.J. at p. 338). Thus the complaint alleges that because of his development of the Mo cell line defendant Golde became a paid consultant of defendant Genetics Institute and acquired the rights to 75,000 shares of that firm's stock at a cost of 1 cent each; that Genetics Institute further contracted to pay Golde and the Regents at least $330,000 over 3 years, including a pro rata share of Golde's salary and fringe benefits; and that defendant Sandoz Pharmaceuticals Corporation subsequently contracted to increase that compensation by a further $110,000.

There is, however, a third party to the biotechnology enterprise — the patient who is the source of the blood or tissue from which all these profits are derived. While he may be a silent partner, his contribution to the venture is absolutely crucial: as pointed out above (pt. 3, *ante*), but for the cells of Moore's body taken by defendants there would have been no Mo cell line at all. Yet defendants deny that Moore is entitled to any share whatever in the proceeds of this cell line. This is both inequitable and immoral. As Dr. Thomas H. Murray a respected professor of ethics and public policy, testified before Congress, "the person [who furnishes the tissue] should be justly compensated . . . . If biotechnologists fail to make provision for a just sharing of profits with the person whose gift made it possible, the public's sense of justice will be offended and no one will be the winner." (Murray, *Who Owns the Body? On the Ethics of Using Human Tissue for Commercial Purposes* (Jan.-Feb. 1986) IRB: A Review of Human Subjects Research, at p. 5.)

There will be such equitable sharing if the courts recognize that the patient has a legally protected property interest in his own body and its products: "property rights in one's own tissue would provide a morally acceptable result by giving effect to notions of fairness and preventing unjust enrichment . . . . [¶] Societal notions of equity and fairness demand recognition of property rights. There are bountiful benefits, monetary and otherwise, to be derived from human biologics. To deny the person contributing the raw material a fair share of these ample benefits is both unfair and morally wrong." (*Toward the Right of Commerciality, supra,* 34 UCLA L.Rev. at p. 229.) "Recognizing a donor's property rights would prevent unjust enrichment by giving monetary rewards to the donor and researcher proportionate to the value of their respective contributions. Biotechnology depends upon the contributions of both patients and researchers. If not for the patient's contribution of cells with unique attributes, the medical value of the bioengineered cells would be negligible. But for the physician's contribution of knowledge and skill in developing the cell product, the commercial value of the patient's cells would also be negligible. Failing to compensate the patient unjustly enriches the researcher because only the researcher's contribution is recognized." (*Id.* at p. 230.) In short, as the Court of Appeal succinctly put it, "If this science has become science for profit, then we fail to see any justification for excluding the patient from participation in those profits."

5.

The majority's second reason for declining to extend the conversion cause of action to the present context is that "the Legislature should make that decision." (Maj. opn., *ante*, p. 163 of 271 Cal.Rptr., p. 496 of 793 P.2d.) I do not doubt that the Legislature is competent to act on this topic. The fact that the Legislature may intervene if and when it chooses, however, does not in the meanwhile relieve the courts of their duty of enforcing—or if need be, fashioning—an effective judicial remedy for the wrong here alleged. As I observed above (pt. 1, *ante*), if a conversion cause of action is otherwise an appropriate remedy on these facts we should not refrain from recognizing it merely because the Legislature has not yet addressed the question. To do so would be to abdicate pro tanto our responsibility over a body of law—torts—that is particularly a creature of the common law. And such reluctance to act would be especially unfortunate at the present time, when the rapid expansion of biotechnological science and industry makes resolution of these issues an increasingly pressing need.

The inference I draw from the current statutory regulation of human biological materials, moreover, is the opposite of that drawn by the majority. By selective quotation of the statutes (maj. opn., *ante*, p. 156, fns. 22 & 23 of 271 Cal. Rptr., p. 489, fns 22 & 23 of 793 P.2d) the majority seem to suggest that human organs and blood cannot legally be sold on the open market—thereby implying that if the Legislature were to act here it would impose a similar ban on monetary compensation for the use of human tissue in biotechnological research and development. But if that is the argument, the premise is unsound: contrary to popular misconception, it is not true that human organs and blood cannot legally be sold.

As to organs, the majority rely on the Uniform Anatomical Gift Act (Health & Saf.Code, §7150 et seq., hereafter the UAGA) for the proposition that a competent adult may make a post mortem gift of any part of his body but may not receive "valuable consideration" for the transfer. But the prohibition of the UAGA against the sale of a body part is much more limited than the majority recognize: by its terms (Health & Saf.Code, §7155, subd. (a)) the prohibition applies only to sales for "transplantation" or "therapy." Yet a different section of the UAGA authorizes the transfer and receipt of body parts for such additional purposes as "medical or dental education, research, or advancement of medical or dental science." (Health & Saf.Code, §7153, subd. (a)(1).) No section of the UAGA prohibits anyone from selling body parts for any of those additional purposes; by clear implication, therefore, such sales are legal. Indeed, the fact that the UAGA prohibits *no* sales of organs other than sales for "transplantation" or "therapy" raises a further implication that it is also legal for anyone to sell human tissue to a biotechnology company for research and development purposes.

With respect to the sale of human blood the matter is much simpler: there is in fact no prohibition against such sales. The majority rely (maj. opn., *ante*, p. 156, fn. 23 of 271 Cal.Rptr., p. 489, fn. 23 of 793 P.2d) on Health and Safety Code section 1606, which provides in relevant part that the procurement and use of blood for transfusion "shall be construed to be, and is declared to be . . . the rendition of a service . . . and shall not be construed to be, and is declared not to be, a sale . . . ." There is less here, however, than meets the eye: the statute does *not* mean that a person cannot sell his blood or, by implication, that his blood is not his property. "While many jurisdictions have classified the transfer of blood *or other human tissue as a service rather than a sale, this position does not conflict with the notion that human tissue is property." (Columbia Note, supra,* 90 Colum.L.Rev. at p. 544, fn. 76.) The reason is plain: "No State or Federal statute prohibits the sale of blood, plasma, semen, or other replenishing tissues if taken in nonvital amounts. Nevertheless, State laws usually characterize these paid transfers as the provision of services rather than the sale of a commodity . . . [¶] The primary legal reason for characterizing these transactions as involving services rather than goods is to avoid liability for contaminated blood products under either general product liability principles or the [Uniform Commercial Code's] implied warranty provisions." (OTA Rep., *supra,* at p. 76 fn. omitted.) The courts have repeatedly recognized that the foregoing is the real purpose of this harmless legal fiction. (See, e.g., *Hyland Therapeutics* v *Superior Court* (1985) 175 Cal.App.3d 509, 220 Cal.Rptr. 590; *Cramer* v *Queen of Angels Hosp.* (1976) 62 Cal.App.3d 812, 133 Cal.Rptr. 339; *Shepard* v *Alexian Brothers Hosp.* (1973) 33 Cal.App.3d 606, 109 Cal.Rptr. 132.) Thus despite the statute relied on by the majority, it is perfectly legal in this state for a person to sell his blood for transfusion or for any other purpose—indeed, such sales are commonplace, particularly in the market for plasma. (See OTA Rep., *supra,* at p. 121.)

It follows that the statutes regulating the transfers of human organs and blood do not support the majority's refusal to recognize a conversion cause of action for commercial exploitation of human blood cells with consent. On the contrary, because such statutes treat both organs and blood as property that can legally be sold in a variety of circumstances, they impliedly support Moore's contention that his blood cells are likewise property for which he can and should receive compensation, and hence are protected by the law of conversion.

6.

The majority's final reason for refusing to recognize a conversion cause of action on these facts is that "there is no pressing need" to do so because the complaint also states another cause of action that is assertedly adequate to the task (maj. opn., *ante,* p. 163 of 271 Cal.Rptr., p. 496 of 793 P.2d); that cause of action is "the breach of a fiduciary duty to disclose facts material to the patient's consent or, alternatively, . . . the performance of medical procedures without first having obtained the patient's informed consent" (*id,* at p. 150 of 271 Cal.Rptr., at p. 483 of 793 P.2d). Although last, this reason is not the majority's least; in fact, it underlies much of the opinion's discussion of the conversion cause of action, recurring like a leitmotiv throughout that discussion.

The majority hold that a physician who intends to treat a patient in whom he has either a research interest or an economic interest is under a fiduciary duty to disclose such interest to the patient before treatment; that his failure to do so may give rise to a nondisclosure cause of action; and that the complaint herein states such a cause of action at least against defendant Golde. I agree with that holding as far as it goes.

I disagree, however, with the majority's further conclusion that in the present context a nondisclosure cause of action is an adequate—in fact, a superior—substitute for a conversion cause of action. In my view the nondisclosure cause of action falls short on at least three grounds.

First, the majority reason that "enforcement of physicians' disclosure obligations" will ensure patients' freedom of choice. (Maj. opn., *ante*, p. 164 of 271 Cal.Rptr., p. 497 of 793 P.2d.) The majority do not spell out how those obligations will be "enforced"; but because they arise from judicial decision (the majority opinion herein) rather than from legislative or administrative enactment, we may infer that the obligations will primarily be enforced by the traditional judicial remedy of an action for damages for their breach. Thus the majority's theory apparently is that the threat of such an action will have a prophylactic effect: it will give physician-researchers incentive to disclose any conflicts of interest before treatment, and will thereby protect their patients' right to make an informed decision about what may be done with their body parts.

The remedy is largely illusory. "[A]n action based on the physician's failure to disclose material information sounds in negligence. As a practical matter, however, it may be difficult to recover on this kind of negligence theory because the patient must prove a *causal* connection between his or her injury and the physician's failure to inform." (Martin & Lagod, *Biotechnology and the Commercial Use of Human Cells: Toward an Organic View of Life and Technology* (1989) 5 Santa Clara Computer & High Tech L.J. 211, 222, fn. omitted, italics added.) There are two barriers to recovery. First, "the patient must show that if he or she had been informed of all pertinent information, he or she would have declined to consent to the procedure in question." (*Ibid.*) As we explained in the seminal case of *Cobbs* v *Grant* (1972) 8 Cal.3d 229, 245, 104 Cal.Rptr. 505, 502 P.2d 1, "There must be a causal relationship between the physician's failure to inform and the injury to the plaintiff. Such a causal connection arises only if it is established that had revelation been made consent to treatment would not have been given."

The second barrier to recovery is still higher, and is erected on the first: it is not even enough for the plaintiff to prove that he personally would have refused consent to the proposed treatment if he had been fully informed; he must also prove that in the same circumstances *no reasonably prudent person* would have given such consent. The purpose of this "objective" standard is evident: "Since at the time of trial the uncommunicated hazard has materialized, it would be surprising if the patient-plaintiff did not claim that had he been informed of the dangers he would have declined treatment. Subjectively he may believe so, with the 20/20 vision of hindsight, but we doubt that justice will be served by placing the physician in jeopardy of the patient's bitterness and disillusionment. Thus an objective test is preferable: i.e., what would a prudent person in the patient's position have decided if adequately informed of all significant perils." (*Cobbs* v *Grant, supra*, 8 Cal.3d 229, 245, 104 Cal.Rptr. 505, 502 P.2d 1.)

Even in an ordinary *Cobbs*-type action it may be difficult for a plaintiff to prove that no reasonably prudent person would have consented to the proposed treatment if the doctor had disclosed the particular risk of physical harm that ultimately caused the injury. (See, e.g., *Morgenroth* v *Pacific Medical Center, Inc.* (1976) 54 Cal.App.3d 521, 534, 126 Cal.Rptr. 681 [affirming nonsuit in *Cobbs*-type action on ground, inter alia, of lack of proof that plaintiff would have refused coronary arteriogram if he had been told of risk of stroke].) This is because in many cases the potential benefits of the treatment to the plaintiff clearly outweigh the undisclosed risk of harm. But that imbalance will be even greater in the kind of nondisclosure action that the majority now contemplate: here we deal not with a risk of physical injuries such as a stroke, but with the possibility that the doctor might later use some of the patient's cast-off tissue for scientific research or the development of commercial products. Few if any judges or juries are likely to believe that disclosure of such a possibility of research or development would dissuade a reasonably prudent person from consenting to the treatment. For example, in the case at bar no trier of fact is likely to believe that if defendants had disclosed their plans for using Moore's cells, no reasonably prudent person in Moore's position—i.e., a leukemia patient suffering from a grossly enlarged spleen—would have consented to the routine operation that saved or at least prolonged his life. Here, as in *Morgenroth (ibid.)*, a motion for nonsuit for failure to prove proximate cause will end the matter. In this context, accordingly, the threat of suit on a nondisclosure cause of action is largely a paper tiger.

The second reason why the nondisclosure cause of action is inadequate for the task that the majority assign to it is that it fails to solve half the problem before us: it gives the patient only the right to *refuse* consent, i.e., the right to prohibit the commercialization of his tissue; it does not give him the right to *grant* consent to that commercialization on the condition that he share in its proceeds. "Even though good reasons exist to support informed consent with tissue commercialization, a disclosure requirement is only the first step toward full recognition of a patient's right to participate fully. Informed consent to commercialization, absent a right to share in the profits from such commercial development, would only give patients a veto over their own exploitation. But recognition that the patient[s] [have] an ownership interest in their own tissues would give patients an affirmative right of participation. Then patients would be able to assume the role of equal partners with their physicians in commercial biotechnology research." (Howard, *surpa*, 44 Food Drug Cosm. L.J. at p. 344.)

Reversing the words of the old song, the nondisclosure cause of action thus accentuates the negative and eliminates the positive: the patient can say no, but he cannot say yes and expect to share in the proceeds of his contribution. Yet as explained above (pt. 4, *ante*), there are sound reasons of ethics and equity to recognize the patient's right to participate in such benefits. The nondisclosure cause of action does not protect that right; to that extent, it is therefore not an adequate substitute for the conversion remedy, which does protect the right.

Third, the nondisclosure cause of action fails to reach a major class of potential defendants: all those who are outside the strict physician-patient relationship with the plaintiff. Thus the majority concede that here only defendant Golde, the treating physician, can be directly liable to Moore on a nondisclosure cause of action: "The Regents, Quan, Genetics Institute, and Sandoz are not physicians. In contrast to Golde, none of these defendants stood in a fiduciary relationship with Moore or had the duty to obtain Moore's informed consent to medical procedures." (Maj. opn., *ante*, p. 153 of 271 Cal.Rptr., p. 486 of 793 P.2d.) As to these defendants, the majority can offer Moore only a slim hope of recovery: if they are to be liable on a nondisclosure cause of action, say the majority, "it can only be on account of Golde's acts and on the basis of a recognized theory of secondary liability, such as respondeat superior." (*Ibid.*) Although the majority decline to decide the question whether the secondary-liability allegations of the complaint are sufficient, they strongly imply disapproval of those allegations. And the majority further note that the trial court has already ruled insufficient the allegations of agency as to the corporate defendants. (Maj. opn., *ante*, p. 154 of 271 Cal.Rptr., p. 487 of 793 P.2d.)

To the extent that a plaintiff such as Moore is unable to plead or prove a satisfactory theory of secondary liability, the nondisclosure cause of action will thus be inadequate to reach a number of parties to the commercial exploitation of his tissue. Such parties include, for example, any physician-researcher who is not personally treating the patient, any other researcher who is not a physician, any employer of the foregoing (or even of the treating physician), and any person or corporation thereafter participating in the commercial exploitation of the tissue. Yet some or all of those parties may well have participated more in, and profited more from, such exploitation than the particular physician with whom the plaintiff happened to have a formal doctor-patient relationship at the time.

In sum, the nondisclosure cause of action (1) is unlikely to be successful in most cases, (2) fails to protect patients' rights to share in the proceeds of the commercial exploitation of their tissue, and (3) may allow the true exploiters to escape liability. It is thus not an adequate substitute, in my view, for the conversion cause of action.

7.

My respect for this court as an institution compels me to make one last point: I dissociate myself completely from the amateur biology lecture that the majority impose on us throughout their opinion. (Maj. opn., *ante*, fns. 2, 29, 30, 33 and 35, and text at pp. 157-158 of 271 Cal.Rptr., at pp. 490-491 of 793 P.2d.) For several reasons, the inclusion of most of that material in an opinion of this court is improper.

First, with the exception of defendants' patent none of the material in question is part of the record on appeal as defined by the California Rules of Court. Because this appeal is taken from a judgment of dismissal entered after the sustaining of general and special demurrers, there is virtually no record other than the pleadings. The case has never been tried, and hence there is no evidence whatever on the obscure medical topics on which the majority presume to instruct us. Instead, all the documents that the majority rely on for their medical explanations appear in an appendix to defendant Golde's opening brief on the merits. Such an appendix, however, is no more a part of the *record* than the brief itself, because the record comprises only the materials before the trial court when it made its ruling. (See Cal.Rules of Couurt, rules 4 through 5.2.) Nor could Golde have moved to augment the record to include any of these documents, because none was "part of the original superior court file," a prerequisite to such augmentation. (Cal.Rules of Court, rule 12(a).) "As a general rule, documents not before the trial court cannot be included as a part of the record on appeal." (*Doers v Golden Gate Bridge etc. Dist.* (1979) 23 Cal.3d 180, 184, fn. 1, 151 Cal.Rptr. 837, 588 P.2d 1261.)

Second, most of these documents bear solely or primarily on the majority's discussion of whether Moore's "genetic material" was or was not "unique" (see maj. opn., *ante*, pp. 157-158 of 271 Cal.Rptr., pp. 490-491 of 793 P.2d), but that entire discussion is legally irrelevant to the present appeal. As Justice Broussard correctly observes in his separate opinion, "the question of uniqueness has no proper bearing on plaintiff's basic right to maintain a conversion action; ordinary property, as well as unique property, is, of course, protected against conversion." (Conc. and dis. opn. of Broussard, J., *ante*, p. 170 of 271 Cal.Rptr., p. 503 of 793 P.2d.)

Third, this nonissue is also a noncontention. The majority claim that "Moore relies . . . primarily" on an analogy to certain right-of-privacy decisions (maj. opn., *ante*, p. 156 of 271 Cal.Rptr., p. 489 of 793 P.2d), but this is not accurate. Under our rules as in appellate practice generally, the parties to an appeal are confined to the contentions raised in their briefs (see Cal.Rules of Court, rule 29.3). In his brief on the merits in this court Moore does not even cite, less still "rely primarily," on the right-of-privacy decisions discussed by the majority, nor does he draw any analogy to the rule of those decisions. It is true that in the course of oral argument before this court, counsel for Moore briefly paraphrased the analogy argument that the majority now attribute to him; but a party may not, of course, raise a new contention for the first time in oral argument.

Fourth, much of the material that the majority rely on in this regard is written in highly technical scientific jargon by and for specialists in the field of contemporary molecular biology. (See, e.g., articles cited in maj. opn., *ante*, fn. 30, 2d par., & fn. 35, 2d par.) As far as I know, no member of this court is trained as a molecular biologist, or even as a physician; without expert testimony in the record, therefore, the majority are not competent to explain these arcane points of medical science any more than a doctor would be competent to explain esoteric questions of the law of negotiable instruments or federal income taxation, or the rule against perpetuities. In attempting to expound this science the majority run two serious risks. First, because they have no background in molecular biology the majority may simply misunderstand what they are reading, much as a layman might misunderstand a highly technical article in a professional legal journal. Indeed, I suggest the majority have already fallen into this very trap, since some of their explanations appear either mistaken, confused, or incomplete (e.g., maj. opn., *ante*, fn. 29).

The second risk is that of omission. The majority have access to most of the legal literature published in this country; but even if the majority could understand the medical literature, as a practical matter they have access to virtually none of it. This is demonstrated by the fact that every one of the medical articles now relied on by the majority came into their possession as reprints furnished to this court by one of the parties to this lawsuit—obviously not an unbiased source. Because the majority are thus not equipped to independently research the medical points they seek to make, they risk presenting only one side of the story; it may well be that other researchers have reached different or even contrary results, reported in publications that defendants, acting in self-interest, have not furnished to the court. I leave it to professionals in molecular biology to say whether the majority's explanations on this topic are both correct and balanced. Because I fear they may be neither, I cannot subscribe to any of them.

I would affirm the decision of the Court of Appeal to direct the trial court to overrule the demurrers to the cause of action for conversion.

Appendix B

Pākehā and Māori conceptions of Property

Difficulties have continued to arise in a number of contexts between Māori and Pākehā concepts of property and ownership. Two recent examples, which merit considerable reflection and debate, are suggested hereafter.

Police v Mareikura [1990] DCR 1.

In this case a Māori Defendant was charged with offences under the Wildlife Act 1953 and the Arms Act 1983, as a result of shooting four wood pigeon (kererū). The Defendant invoked Article 2 of the Treaty of Waitangi 1840, and sought to show that at the time of the incident he was exercising a traditional or customary right to hunt kererū. Evidence was given that such a right was only exercised on significant occasions, or for particular reasons, by members of the Defendant's tribe, the Ngati Rangi; that the kererū was regarded as a sacred bird; that there were certain customs which attended the hunt, and that the hunt had to have (by customary Māori law) the tacit approval of the elders of the particular tribe. It was argued that this old established cultural custom justified the breaches of the statutory law. In the result, the District Court held that the Treaty of Waitangi might have preserved the rights of Māori tribes to hunt kererū, but the Wildlife Act 1953 and its predecessors had extinguished such rights.

The judgment contains a description of Māori custom which reveals a quite different way of thinking and perceiving events to a pattern of European thought. The sophistication of the ideas and philosophy surrounding the taking of kererū are part of ngā tikanga Māori (Māori culture). Do European conceptions of property deliberately narrow the range of interests which can be attached to any 'thing' as opposed to the views of indigenous peoples, which imbue such matters with many more layers of practice, custom, and 'rights'? And, is it the case that Europeans have attached to land the degree of sophistication that pre-European societies attached to personal property?

The death of Billy T James

In August of 1991 the death of New Zealand's best known comedian, Billy T James (a Māori) gave rise to an extensive national debate. Mr James died at Auckland. He was married to a European woman. He left no will. Billy T had had a heart transplant in November 1989. In New Zealand, the families of donors are not supposed to know to whom a heart has been donated. But, by means which are not here relevant, the donor family had come to know (prior to Billy T's death), to whom his heart had been donated.

Shortly after his death, members of Billy T's tribe (Tainui) arrived at his family home, and, against the wishes of his widow, took his body to another town. There his body was to lie, in accordance with Māori custom, on a marae, before being taken for burial to Taupiri Mountain, the sacred mountain of his tribe. It was said that the body could only be buried on Taupiri Mountain, in accordance with Māori custom, if it had first lain at the marae. It seems to have been the case that Billy T had wished to have a European funeral service in Auckland, New Zealand and then to be buried on Taupiri Mountain, thereby recognizing both sides of his lifestyle. (This account is taken from the New Zealand Herald for Friday August 9, 10 and 12, 1991).

It became apparent, in the case of the public debate which followed, that arguments over burial rights are not uncommon in Maoridom.

Writing in the New Zealand Herald (August 10, 1991, Section 1, page 9), Paul Benseman noted:

> The argument over Billy T James' funeral arrangements has, perhaps for the first time, widely publicised common features of Maori funeral protocol.
>
> Many Pakeha have regarded the matter as little more than body snatching, and it seems that the actions of Billy T's Maori relatives may have been against the law, at least against "Pakeha" law.
>
> If Billy T had requested, as has been reported, that his funeral should be in Auckland, that he should have a woman officiate over the service and that his body should stay at his house beforehand, then the central question is simply one of whether his dying wishes are binding in law.
>
> The Public Trust Office says that the executor of a will has the power to determine funeral arrangements, and that person is bound to follow the deceased's requests unless it is impossible to do so.

*   *   *

> However, that law, which follows rulings in Britain, does not take account of Maori custom. Often if a popular or highborn Maori elder has cross-tribal connections, for example one parent from each tribe, there is bitter debate about which area and marae should host his or her tangihanga. Usually, the matter is settled by a compromise—a night on one marae and one on another, for example. If the husband or wife of the deceased is from a different tribal area, a similar compromise is usually reached. In every case all relatives are given a chance to join in, and mourn.

*   *   *

> Canon Hone Kaa, said that under Maori custom it was the tribe that determined funeral arrangements, not the grieving family. "According to our protocol when you die you belong to your people from whom you come," he said. "Though you have wishes yourself, in the end it's your family who bid you farewell."
>
> The Professor of Maori at Waikato University, Professor Timoti Karetu, said Billy T's funeral had raised for general debate, at last, an underlying difference between the cultures. While there might be a wish in the case of many Pakeha funerals to avoid any conflict and to restrict participation, the opposite was the case in tangihanga, especially those for well-known people. Professor Karetu said he could not recall an

instance such as Billy T's, where a national identity had been taken by his tribal group against the wishes of the wider society. Conflict at tangihanga was common, but usually was kept within Maoridom. There had been cases of bodies being sneaked away in the night from one marae to another, but in most cases the argument was restricted to passionate debate on the marae, and this usually result in compromise.

* * *

Professor Karetu said national figures such as Sir Apirana Ngata and the Maori Battalion leader Colonel Peta Awatere were the subject of the conflict between tribes and maraes after their deaths. "I believe the debate and conflict over the deceased is a marvellous custom which should not be prevented or feared," Professor Karetu said. The tangihanga brought families together, including long-separated relatives. It provided an opportunity for old wounds to be aired sincerely and honestly, and to be healed.

* * *

Questions

As a matter of existing law, what, if any, rights did Mr James' widow have? How could she have acquired rights? What, if any, rights did the heart-donor family have? Did those Māori persons who removed Mr James body to the marae run the risk of any criminal or civil proceedings? What form would those proceedings take?

Now, assume that you are a lawyer in the Department of Justice. Assume that the Minister of Justice has, in a broad way, come to the conclusion that there must be legislation to prevent these unfortunate events, or events like them, occuring again. Would you endeavour to persuade the Minister not to enact legislation? Why? If you thought legislation would be a 'good thing', why would you make such a recommendation? What form do you think the legislation should take? What legal problems would need to be addressed in such an exercise?

Appendix C

The Chattels Transfer Act

Elders Pastoral v BNZ

[1991] 1 NZLR 386 (P.C.)

The judgment of their Lordships was delivered by

LORD TEMPLEMAN. By a stock security dated 11 June 1987 and made between the respondent Bank of New Zealand (the bank) of the one part and

William Neville Gunn (the grantor) of the other part, the grantor assigned and transferred to the bank the flocks of sheep and cattle and other stock enumerated in the first schedule, including the natural increase of stock depastured upon the farm of the grantor described in the second schedule. The assignment and transfer were declared to be by way of mortgage for securing the payment by the grantor to the bank upon demand of all moneys then or thereafter owing by the grantor to the bank. The Chattels Transfer Act 1924, as amended, (the Act of 1924) provided for registration of the stock security being an instrument transferring the property in chattels by way of mortgage and the stock security was duly registered.

By s 50 of the Act of 1924 and cl 9 of the Fourth Schedule, there is implied in every instrument by way of security over stock a covenant by the grantor that he will not sell mortgaged stock except in the ordinary course of business. Section 54 provides that the implied covenants may be negatived, modified, or altered, or others may be added to them, by express words in the instrument. The provisions of cl 9 of the Fourth Schedule were added to by cl 15 of the stock security which, so far as relevant, provided that:

> ". . . (in the absence of any direction to the contrary by the Bank) all moneys payable in respect of the sale of any of the said stock . . . shall be paid to the Bank whose receipt therefor shall be a sufficient discharge for or on account of the Grantor/s and the Grantor/s shall direct every purchaser . . . accordingly."

By s 4(1) of the Act of 1924:

> ". . . all persons shall be deemed to have notice of an instrument and of the contents thereof when and so soon as such instrument has been registered as provided by this Act:"

On 13 January 1988 the appellants Elders Pastoral Ltd ("Elders") as agents for the grantor sold some of the mortgaged stock and received the purchase price from the purchaser. The bank claim the net proceeds of sale from Elders and seek summary judgment on the grounds inter alia that cl 15 of the stock security created an equitable assignment to the bank by way of charge of the purchase price payable by the purchaser and that by virtue of s 4(1) of the Act of 1924 Elders had notice of that assignment. Elders deny that cl 15 created an equitable assignment and deny that s 4(1) gave notice to Elders of the provisions of cl 15 relating to the proceeds of sale of mortgaged stock. Elders claim to have appropriated the net proceeds of sale of the stock sold by Elders in satisfaction of an outstanding debt owed by the grantor to Elders.

The first question is whether cl 15 of the stock security created an equitable assignment by way of charge on a future chose in action, namely the right of the grantor to receive and recover from a purchaser the sale price of stock mortgaged to the bank. The requirements of an equitable assignment of a debt were reaffirmed in *William Brandt's Sons & Co v Dunlop Rubber Company* [1905] AC 454. The document creating the assignment need not purport to be an assignment nor use the language of an assignment. Lord Macnaghten said at p 462:

> "An equitable assignment does not always take that form. It may be addressed to the debtor. It may be couched in the language of command. It may be a courteous

request. It may assume the form of mere permission. The language is immaterial if the meaning is plain. All that is necessary is that the debtor should be given to understand that the debt has been made over by the creditor to some third person. If the debtor ignores such a notice, he does so at his peril. If the assignment be for valuable consideration and communciated to the third person, it cannot be revoked by the creditor or safely disregarded by the debtor."

In the present case cl 15 gives to understand that the future proceeds of sale of mortgaged stock shall be made over by the grantor to some third party, the bank. A promise by a debtor to a creditor that a sum owed or which will or may become due to the debtor from a third party shall be paid to the creditor by the third party is a clear form of equitable assignment, particularly when the promise is given for valuable consideration, in this case the grant of loan facilities to the grantor by the bank, and particularly where the debt assigned arises out of a disposition of property mortgaged to the creditor. Clause 15 contains an equitable assignment by way of charge of a future chose in action, namely the right of the grantor to receive from the purchaser the proceeds of sale of mortgaged stock sold to the purchaser. Clause 15 shows an intention that as the stock sold ceases to be charged to the bank, so the charge attaches to the proceeds of sale of that stock.

On behalf of Elders it was submitted that the fact that cl 15 permitted the bank to direct that the purchase price should not be paid to the bank and the fact that the grantor agreed to direct the purchaser to pay the bank in some way prevented the purchaser and Elders from understanding that the purchase price had been assigned to the bank and that they must comply with the provisions of cl 15 whether the grantor so directed or not. But these provisions only served to emphasise that the purchase price was charged to the bank (which might of course release the charge before or after the sale) and that the grantor had no right to receive the purchase price. The purchaser and Elders were not entitled to assume that the bank has issued a "direction to the contrary". The purchaser and Elders were entitled and bound to insist on paying the bank unless the grantor produced the requisite direction to the contrary from the bank.

It was not argued that the fact that the debt in respect of the purchase price was not in existence when the stock security was executed and could not come into existence until the mortgage stock was sold in some way prevented the debt being charged in equity in favour of the bank pursuant to cl 15. In *Tailby v Official Receiver* (1888) 13 App Cas 523 an assignment of future book debts was held to be effective and Lord Macnaghten said at p 543:

"It has long been settled that future property, possibilities and expectancies are assignable in equity for value. The mode or form of assignment is absolutely immaterial provided the intention of the parties is clear. To effectuate the intention an assignment for value, in terms present and immediate, has always been regarded in equity as a contract binding on the conscience of the assignor and so binding the subject-matter of the contract when it comes into existence, if it is of such a nature and so described as to be capable of being ascertained and identified."

In the present case the assignment of the future right to the proceeds of sale of mortgaged stock was made for value, namely the making of advances by the bank to the grantor. The intention was clear that these proceeds of sale should be paid to the bank as mortgagee. The subject-matter of the contract namely the proceeds of sale when the mortgaged stock was sold was ascertainable and identified.

The construction and effect of cl 15 of the stock security did not figure largely in the Courts below. Cooke P said at [1989] 2 NZLR 180, 185 that:

> "I do not think that cl 15 goes as far as to amount to a contract by the farmer to assign a future chose in action; there is a contrast with certain express provisions of cl 19 about dairy factory moneys."

But cl 15 contains an express provision that the purchase price of mortgaged stock shall be paid to the bank and imposes a positive obligation on the grantor to direct the purchaser to pay the bank. Somers J said at p 191:

> "I am of opinion that the provisions of cl 15 are not sufficiently clear to amount to a contract to assign future property. The clause contains a requirement that the purchase moneys be paid to the Bank and a promise by Mr Gunn so to direct purchasers. Had an assignment been intended it is to be expected that his obligation would be to give notice of the Bank's right. The security is a running and continuing security, it is to apply whether or not Mr Gunn is in credit with the Bank. The possibility of such a circumstance also suggests assignment was not intended. The distinction between a contractual obligation short of assignment and assignment itself is apparent from cl 19 of the security with which the present clause may be compared."

The Board consider that the express provisions of cl 15 that the purchase moneys must be paid to the bank and that the grantor must give notice to the purchaser that the moneys must be paid to the bank, sufficiently clearly assigned to the bank the right to receive the purchase money as mortgagee and in the place of the mortgaged stock sold to the purchaser. The grantor, Mr Gunn was placed under an obligation to give notice of the bank's right to receive the purchase moneys. The fact that the security was running and continuing and the possibility that Mr Gunn might be in credit with the bank cannot affect the construction of cl 15. The grantor could always draw cheques on the bank to the extent of his credit balance and up to the agreed limit of any overdraft facility. The cl 15 assignment of the proceeds of sale of mortgaged stock to the bank however protected the bank by putting them in control of the proceeds of sale so that they could insist that any obligation of the grantor to the bank be reduced by the amount of the proceeds of sale.

Clause 19 of the stock security upon which Cooke P and Somers J relied consists of a covenant by the grantor to:

> ". . . deliver all milk cream butterfat cheese and other milk products the produce of the cows for the time being and from time to time subject to this security . . . to such company firm or person as the Bank shall appoint and will assign to the Bank the moneys payable by such company firm or person therefor and will from time to time if and when the Bank shall so stipulate sign and deliver to the Bank such deed or deeds of assignment or irrevocable order or orders to ensure the payment to the bank of the said moneys or such part thereof as the Bank shall require."

Milk products were not mortgaged chattels and no reasonable purchaser of milk products from a farmer would search under the Act of 1924 or pay the bank instead of the farmer unless the bank produced a written assignment or order of the farmer. Hence the provisions of cl 19 which are presumably only enforced by the bank when the financial position of the farmer causes the bank to interfere with the day to day running and financing of the farm. Clause 15 on the other hand dealt with mortgaged chattels and applied to every purchaser of every sale of mortgaged chattels comprised in the registered security. The obligation of such a purchaser to pay the bank is clearly set forth in cl 15 and needs no supplementary assignment or order. Their Lordships do not consider that cl 19 affects the construction of cl 15 whereby the proceeds of sale or mortgage stock are mortgaged to the bank.

When the grantor agreed that all moneys payable in respect of the sale of mortgaged stock should be paid to the bank he thereby conferred on the bank the right to receive those moneys. The simplest form of an equitable assignment of a debt is an agreement by a debtor with a creditor that a debt due or to become due to the debtor from a third party shall be paid by the third party to the creditor. Of course the third party is only bound by that assignment if he receives notice of the agreement by registration or actual notice. The obligation imposed by the stock security on the grantor to direct the purchaser to pay the bank ensured, so far as possible, that the purchaser would receive actual notice of the rights of the bank as well as the statutory implied notice arising from registration of the security under the Act of 1924. Accordingly, their Lordships take the view that cl 15 effected the equitable assignment of the proceeds of sale of the mortgaged stock.

The second question is whether the purchaser and Elders had notice of the equitable assignment created by cl 15 of the stock security.

Section 4(1) of the Act of 1924 provides that:

> ". . . all persons shall be deemed to have notice of an instrument and of the contents thereof when and so soon as such instrument has been registered as provided by this Act:"

A registrable instrument, defined by s 2 of the Act includes:

> ". . . any . . . mortgage . . . or any other document that transfers . . . the property in . . . chattels . . ."

Chattels, as defined by s 2 include:

> ". . . stock and the natural increase of stock . . ."

Stock is defined to include any sheep, cattle and horses and embraces the stock mortgaged by the stock security.

Thus the stock security was a registrable instrument and s 4(1) gave notice to the world of its contents. On behalf of Elders it was submitted that the legislature cannot have intended that the registration should give notice of every provision contained in a registrable instrument whether or not that provision relates to chattels. Proceeds of sale of chattels are not themselves chattels and so, it was argued, registration under the Act does not give notice of any provision dealing with proceeds of sale. Reliance was placed on s 4(2) which provides that:

> ". . . all persons shall be deemed to have notice of a security granted wholly or partly upon chattels by a company registered under the Companies Act . . .

and of the contents of such security, so far as it relates to chattels, immediately upon the registration of such security in the manner provided by the . . . Companies Act . . ."

A registered instrument which contained a positive prohibition against a sale of mortgaged chattels by the grantor or provided that such a sale required the prior consent of the mortgagee would plainly relate to chattels and would be binding on purchasers and auctioneers. It would be strange if a registered instrument gave notice of a prohibition against a sale of mortgaged chattels but did not give notice of a provision which required the purchase price of mortgaged chattels to be paid to the mortgagee. Clause 15 relates to chattels and deals with the sale of chattels. Clause 15 gave notice that the stock security had not modified the provisions of the Act of 1924 which enabled the purchaser to purchase mortgaged chattels free from the mortgage and at the same time gave a purchaser notice that on any such purchase he must pay the purchase price to the mortgagee.

Counsel for Elders relied on the decision of the Court of Appeal in *Dempsey v Traders' Finance Corporation Ltd* [1933] NZLR 1258. In that case a company registered, under the Companies Act 1908, a debenture which created a floating charge, prohibited the company from creating any mortgage or charge in priority to the debenture and prohibited the sale and disposal of any property except merchandise and that only in the ordinary course of business. The company later mortgaged its interests under hire purchase agreements relating to motor vehicles. The majority of the Court of Appeal held that registration of a floating charge was only notice of the existence of the charge and not of its contents because, per Smith J at p 1290:

". . . a floating charge belongs to a class of documents which may or may not, but does not necessarily, affect the title to property and the Court will not, in respect of such documents which affect commercial transactions, apply the doctrine of constructive notice though it is sought to found it on the public registration of such documents."

In the present case the fixed charge on the stock comprised in the stock security and on the proceeds of sale of such mortgaged stock affects the title to the mortgaged stock and the title to the proceeds of sale. The majority also held that the hire purchase agreements constituted a mode of disposal permitted by the debenture and that the mortgagee of the benefit of the hire purchase agreements had no notice under s 4(2) of the Act of 1924 or otherwise that the acquisition of such rights which were choses in action and not chattels constituted on infringement of the restrictive qualifications of the debenture. In the present case the mode of disposal of the mortgaged stock permitted by the Act of 1924 and the stock security imposes on the purchaser an obligation to pay the proceeds of disposal to the bank. The purchaser has notice that his right to acquire the mortgaged chattels involved him in an obligation to pay the purchase price to the bank.

In the opinion of the Board, the contents of the stock security of which all persons are deemed to have notice include those contents which are relevant to any dealing with chattels comprised in the instrument. The purchaser who asserts that, under and by virtue of the Act of 1924 and the stock security, the grantor was entitled to sell and the purchaser was entitled to purchase mortgage chattels freed and discharged from the mortgage without the concurrence of the mortgagee cannot at the same time deny that he had notice under and by virtue of s 4(1) of the Act of 1924 of the contents of the stock security which require him to pay the purchase price to the mortgagee. The auctioneer who sells the mortgaged chattels and receives the purchase price is in no different position.

It was submitted that the result would produce some inconvenience. If there is any inconvenience it is due to the legislature, for good reason, enacting that registration of a stock security shall be notice of the contents of the instrument and due to the stock security which, for good reason, assigned to the bank the proceeds of sale of mortgaged chattels. It is not clear that great inconvenience will be caused. A purchaser of chattels may either trust his vendor or trust the auctioneer or carry out a search against the vendor. An auctioneer may either know or inquire from the vendor or search against the vendor to ascertain if there is any stock security which either forbids a sale without the prior consent of the mortgagee or requires the proceeds of sale to be paid to the mortgagee. It is likely that an auctioneer will be aware of the terms of the standard form of the stock security issued by the bank. It is likely that any prudent lender on the security of stock will also require the proceeds of sale of mortgaged stock to be paid to the lender. The purchaser need not pay and the auctioneer need not transmit the purchase moneys to the vendor until it is clear that no registered instrument requires payment to some other person. The protection afforded by a registered instrument under the Act of 1924 would be much weakened if a mortgagee of mortgaged chattels was unable to secure the proceeds of sale of the mortgaged chattels.

Their Lordships conclude that the proceeds of sale of stock comprised in the stock security were charged to the bank and that Elders had notice of that charge as a result of the registration of that stock security under the Act of 1924.

The Court of Appeal considered that the stock security drafted by the bank did not charge the proceeds of sale of the mortgaged stock. The Court decided that even if there was no charge, Elders held the proceeds of sale as constructive trustees for the bank. Having decided that cl 15 of the stock security did create a charge, their Lordships do not find it necessary to consider whether the judgment of the Court of Appeal should be affirmed on other grounds. Their Lordships will humbly advise Her Majesty that this appeal should be dismissed. Elders must pay the costs of the bank before the Board.

Appeal dismissed.